THE POPULAR
BIBLE
PROPHECY
COMMENTARY

TIM LAHAYE
ED HINDSON

WAYNE A. BRINDLE
Managing Editor

HARVEST HOUSE PUBLISHERS

EUGENE, OREGON

Cover by Terry Dugan Design, Bloomington, Minnesota

Cover photos © Steve Allen/Brand X Pictures/Alamy; Mark Duffy/Alamy

THE POPULAR BIBLE PROPHECY COMMENTARY
Copyright © 2006 by Pre-Trib Research Center, Tim LaHaye, and Ed Hindson
Published by Harvest House Publishers
Eugene, Oregon 97402
www.harvesthousepublishers.com

Library of Congress Cataloging-in-Publication Data
LaHaye, Tim F.
The popular Bible prophecy commentary / Tim LaHaye and Ed Hindson.
p. cm.—(Tim LaHaye prophecy library)
ISBN-13: 978-0-7369-1690-5 (hardcover)
ISBN-10: 0-7369-1690-3
1. Bible—Prophecies. 2. Bible—Commentaries. I. Hindson, Edward E. II. Title. III. Series: LaHaye, Tim LaHaye prophecy library series.
BS647.3.L35 2006
220.1'5—dc22

2006010921

Printed in the United States of America

07 08 09 10 11 12 13 14 / LB-CF / 12 11 10 9 8 7 6 5 4 3 2 1

To David Jeremiah—
a master expositor
of the prophetic Word.

EDITORS AND CONTRIBUTORS

GENERAL EDITORS

Tim LaHaye, Litt.D., D.Min.
    President, Tim LaHaye Ministries
    Cofounder, Pre-Trib Research Center
    El Cajon, CA
Ed Hindson, M.A., Th.M., Th.D., D.Min., Ph.D.
    Assistant Chancellor, Dean of the Institute of Biblical Studies
    and Distinguished Professor of Religion
    Liberty University
    Lynchburg, VA

ASSOCIATE EDITOR

Wayne A. Brindle, Th.M., Th.D.
    Chairman and Professor of Biblical Studies
    Liberty University
    Lynchburg, VA

CONTRIBUTING AUTHORS

Mal Couch, Th.M., Th.D., Ph.D.
    New Testament
    Founder of Tyndale Theological Seminary
    Fort Worth, TX
Arnold Fruchtenbaum, Th.M., Ph.D.
    Isaiah, Jeremiah, Minor Prophets
    Founder and Director, Ariel Ministries
    San Antonio, TX
Steven Ger, Th.M.
    Law, History, Poetry
    Founder and Director, Sojourner Ministries
    Garland, TX
Randall Price, Th.M., Ph.D.
    Ezekiel, Daniel
    President, World of the Bible Ministries
    San Marcos, TX

Acknowledgment

Our sincere appreciation to Amanda Stanley, who typed most of the
original manuscript and assisted in managing the electronic files.

CONTENTS

INTRODUCTION

Bɪʙʟᴇ ᴘʀᴏᴘʜᴇᴄʏ ᴍᴀᴋᴇꜱ ᴜᴘ ᴏɴᴇ-ꜰᴏᴜʀᴛʜ of the written Word of God. Thus, it is imperative that any serious study of the scriptures must include a proper understanding of this important area of inspired truth. From Genesis to Revelation, the Bible is filled with over one thousand predictive prophecies. Half of these have already been literally fulfilled, indicating that the other half will yet be literally fulfilled as well. It is these yet-to-be-fulfilled future prophecies that are the subject of this book.

We have assembled a team of biblical scholars who are experts in the area of Bible prophecy. They know the original languages of Scripture. They are committed to the grammatical, historical principles of biblical interpretation. Most of all they have a deep personal love of Christ and sincere respect for the inerrant Word of God as our only sure guide to understanding the future. While they may differ slightly on minor points of discussion, they are all in agreement with the major issues of biblical eschatology, particularly in relation to the pre-tribulational and premillennial view of eschatology.

The present volume is a key resource in the LaHaye Prophecy Library, which was launched in conjunction with Harvest House Publishers several years ago. As a comparison volume to *The Popular Encyclopedia of Bible Prophecy, The Popular Bible Prophecy Commentary* covers every major biblical passage that deals with a prediction of future events. The scope is comprehensive, while the focus is eschatological. We have endeavored to comment in detail on the biblical prophecies that await their final fulfillment in the future.

The uniqueness of this study is that it provides pastors, teachers, scholars, and laymen alike with an eschatological commentary on every predictive passage of Scripture. While there is certainly much discussion within Christian circles over how these prophecies are to be interpreted, we believe you will find the research in this present volume of the highest quality of careful, insightful, and intense biblical exegesis and exposition. It is our sincere prayer that God will inform your mind, ignite your soul, and motivate your heart with these great prophecies of the future.

In the meantime, may we continue "looking for the blessed hope, and the glorious appearing of the great God and our Savior Jesus Christ" (Titus 2:13).

Tim LaHaye
Ed Hindson

OLD TESTAMENT
PROPHECIES

THE
LAW

GENESIS

GENESIS IS THE BOOK OF BEGINNINGS. It tells the story of the beginnings of the human race and the Hebrew nation. It also lays the foundation for the beginning of biblical prophecy. Genesis offers a rich tapestry of prophetic promise, predominantly messianic prophecy. The first book of the Bible fires an attention-seizing opening salvo of messianic prophecy of both the figure of the Messiah Himself as well as the magnificent messianic age to come. Indeed, Genesis establishes the template from which all other prophetic expectations spring. Specific, temporal prophecies are assuredly found within the pages of this foundational volume, but the majority of prophetic action in this text concerns vast, enduring themes that span protracted timetables, such as the Abrahamic Covenant, Israel's future hope, and, of course, the aforementioned promised Messiah.

THE WARNING ABOUT THE TREE
Genesis 2:16-17

THE LORD, AFTER CREATING ADAM as the pinnacle of His creation, executes His initial command. The instruction contains both divine consent and prohibition, blessing and warning, stretching the limits of Adam's yet untapped moral capacities. Adam would be allowed unlimited access to the fruit of every tree within the Garden of Eden, with the sole exception of "the tree of the knowledge of good and evil." The command concludes with the conditional warning that death would result from violation of the prohibition (2:16-17).

Eventually, both Adam and Eve succumb to the serpent's temptation. They willingly disobey the Lord's command by eating the forbidden fruit of the tree of the knowledge of good and evil. Although Adam and Eve thought the fruit would give them the satanically promised divine ability to comprehend good and evil, as Walvoord points out, neither of them realized that eating the fruit would result in their "knowing the good without being able to do it and knowing the evil without being able to avoid it" (Walvoord, *Prophecy Knowledge Handbook,* p. 20). Instead of the anticipated instant wisdom, they experience immediate shame, guilt, and alienation from one another and God (3:6-13). As God had promised, from that moment onward, death would plague Adam and his progeny (3:19; 5:5).

THE PROPHECY ABOUT THE MESSIAH
Genesis 3:15

GENESIS 3:15 FORESEES a coming Messiah, born of a woman, who will defeat Satan. This earliest and foundational messianic prophecy is found a mere three chapters into the Bible.

Following the moral failure of Adam and Eve and in conjunction with the explanation of the harsh and enduring consequences wrought by their disobedience (3:6-13,16-19), this *proto-evangelium* ("first gospel") provides hope for the redemption of the fallen human race. It proclaims the coming of a Savior who will enter the human race and defeat the power of Satan.

The Lord declares war on the motivating cause of Edenic sin, the serpent (Satan), who is identified by the apostle John as "the serpent of old" (Revelation 20:2). In the Lord's curse on the serpent, we see an initial glimpse of the divine plan for humanity's redemption. This passage contains far more than the mere origin of the antagonistic relationship between mankind and snakes. It is the theological explanation for the conflict between good and evil. A descendant of Eve would be born who would successfully wage holy war against Satan and his offspring. Although both holy warrior and evil adversary will sustain punishing injury (to heel and head, respectively) in the conflict, the damage dealt to Satan will prove fatal. The bruising of the Savior's heel is especially insightful in relation to the bruised heels and torn flesh of crucifixion victims. Although the identity of God's chosen warrior is shrouded in mystery, this individual will be the offspring of a woman—a prophetic reference to the virgin birth of Christ.

The New Testament clearly teaches that the Messiah's resurrection will most assuredly signal the final victory over Satan (Revelation 20:10). Indeed, the apostle Paul encourages the believers in Rome that God would shortly crush Satan underneath their feet (Romans 16:20).

EVE'S EXPECTATION OF THE MESSIAH
Genesis 4:1

IN LIGHT OF the aforementioned prophecy concerning the promise of an ultimate deliv-

erer for humanity, Eve's reaction to the birth of her firstborn son, Cain, is not surprising. Most versions of Scripture add additional words to this text ("with the help of," NIV, NASB, RSV or "from," NKJV) in an attempt to make the translation clearer. While this is certainly an interpretively and grammatically valid decision, such an addition is not grammatically necessary and actually detracts from the messianic implication of the Hebrew text. The simplest reading of the text sees the Hebrew particle *et* as the accusative indication of object. The text of Genesis 4:1 would then have Eve stating, "I have obtained a man, the Lord" (Hebrew, *et-YHWH*).

This grammatical understanding, while not held by the Septuagint (Greek translation of the original Hebrew text), is shared by the other ancient Jewish sources. For example, both the ancient Aramaic *Jerusalem Targum* and *Targum Jonathan* paraphrase this text to read, "I have gotten a man, the angel of YHWH." Fruchtenbaum (*Messianic Christology*, p. 16) notes that the discussion of this verse within the Midrash on Genesis reveals ancient rabbinic interpretive discomfort with accepting the plain, unembellished grammatical construction of the text. He argues that "Eve has clearly understood from God's words in Gen. 3:15 that the serpent will be defeated by a God-man. She obviously thinks that Cain *is* Jehovah. Her basic theology is correct: Messiah would be both man and God....She has assumed that Cain, her first child, was the promised God-man."

THE "RAPTURE" OF ENOCH
Genesis 5:24

THE NARRATIVE OF GENESIS briefly introduces the reader to Enoch, a man whose lifestyle is characterized by a deeply intimate relationship with the Lord ("Enoch walked with God"). Without warning, the text abruptly records that Enoch "was not, for God took him" (5:24). In contrast with the text's matter-of-fact citation of the death of a plethora of Enoch's ancestors (5:1-20), the Lord uniquely allows Enoch to avoid the experience of death, taking him directly into the divine presence, no doubt, to better enjoy their advanced level of fellowship.

The absence of the specific term "rapture" in the English Bible in no way invalidates the presence of the concept within both Testaments. Genesis 5:24 is a small gem tucked away in the midst of a sea of genealogy that should be treasured as a potent preview of the church's "blessed hope" (Titus 2:13), the experience the New Testament promises for one unique generation of believers—those who are alive when Messiah returns (1 Corinthians 15:51-55; 1 Thessalonians 4:13-18).

MESSIAH TO REVERSE THE CURSE
Genesis 5:21-29

EARLY HUMANITY'S continued messianic expectation is again evident with the birth of Noah. Lamech, Noah's father, has great yet incorrect expectations of his son, mistakenly identifying Noah as the divinely promised yet shadowy messianic figure (3:15). While not meeting Lamech's hope of providing mankind "rest from our work...from the ground which the LORD has cursed" (5:29), Noah would, nonetheless, prove a savior of sorts, representing humanity's last, best hope within his generation (Genesis 6:8-22).

JUDGMENT THROUGH A GLOBAL FLOOD
Genesis 6:7-18; 7:4

THE GENESIS NARRATIVE RECORDS that eventually humanity had become so morally self-corrupted (6:11-12) that the Lord determines to destroy His creation with a flood and start

anew (6:7,17). However, Noah, a "righteous" and "blameless" individual who, like Enoch before him (5:24), experiences an intimate relationship with God, has "found favor" with the Lord (6:8-9). The Lord graciously determines to preserve a faithful remnant of humanity and to establish a covenant with Noah (6:18). He instructs Noah to build an ark as a vessel of preservation for Noah and his family, along with representative pairs of every animal (6:14-18). One week prior to the flood, God specifies to Noah that it will continue to rain for "forty days and forty nights," again reiterating His plan to destroy all life outside the safety of the ark (7:4). The narrative records the fulfillment of this prophecy in Genesis 7:10-23.

THE NOAHIC COVENANT
Genesis 8:21-22; 9:15-16

SOME 371 DAYS AFTER first entering the ark (7:11; 8:13-14), Noah, his family, and the animals emerge. Noah's first recorded action on dry land is to erect "an altar to the LORD," on which he makes a sacrifice (8:20). This prompts the Lord's articulation of the central promise of the newly established Noahic Covenant to never again "curse the ground" or "destroy every living thing" through means of flood (8:21-22; see also 9:15). The "everlasting covenant" is made by God without condition, not only with Noah, but also universally, with "every living creature." The sign of the covenant is, of course, the rainbow (9:16). The promises of this covenant are still in effect today.

NOAH'S PROPHECY ABOUT HIS DESCENDANTS
Genesis 9:25-27

SOME TIME LATER, Noah's son, Ham, exhibits vulgar disrespect to his father (9:20-24). This prompts Noah to a harsh reprisal of prophetic judgment against Ham's future descendants, the Canaanites. The Canaanites would be subservient to the descendants of both Shem and Japheth. This subjugation of the Canaanites is, indeed, seen throughout Old Testament history (one such example of this is found in Joshua 8:27). In contrast to the cursing of Ham's descendants, Noah subsequently blesses the descendants of his other two sons, Shem and Japheth, who would remain in close geographic proximity and maintain friendly relations (Genesis 9:25-27). The initial descendants of Noah's three sons and their geographic dispersal is recorded in Genesis 10:1-32.

THE ABRAHAMIC COVENANT
Genesis 12:1-3,7; 13:14-17; 15:1-21; 17:1-21; 22:15-18

THE GENESIS NARRATIVE reveals that the Abrahamic Covenant is a complex of unconditional promises that are stated and reiterated over a period of years within a series of six recorded encounters between God and Abraham. Each successive restatement expands upon and enlarges the promised provisions of the primary, central core of the covenant.

The first passage, Genesis 12:1-3, records God's initial encounter with Abraham, in which He communicates His commission and His initial promised blessings to Abraham. The narrative records the divine instruction for Abraham to leave his home in Mesopotamia and go "to the land which I will show you." Although the promises contained within the Abrahamic Covenant are unconditional (see below), the establishment of the covenant itself is conditioned upon Abraham's initial act of obedience to this command. Every provision and promise is contingent upon Abraham's voluntary abandonment of his home and relocation to the land that God promises to reveal. Without this initial act of obedience on Abraham's part, the covenant would not have been established, and the Genesis nar-

rative (and world history) would have taken a different turn. However, Abraham is obedient (12:4-6).

This initial iteration of the covenant contains promises of personal blessing ("I will bless you") in specific relation to numerous offspring ("make you a great nation"), reputation ("make your name great") and universal influence ("you shall be a blessing" and "in you all the families of the earth will be blessed") (12:2-3). This universal influence would extend to divine, retributive justice in regard to how Abraham (and by implication, his offspring) is treated by others ("I will bless those who bless you, and the one who curses you I will curse").

The *first expansion* of the Abrahamic Covenant's promises is revealed in Genesis 12:7. Following Abraham's arrival in the land of Canaan, the Lord promises that Abraham's descendants would inherit the land as a gift ("to your descendants I will give this land"). Abraham later identifies this promise as a divine oath, a solemn, unconditional guarantee (24:7).

The *second expansion* of the Abrahamic Covenant's promises is contained in Genesis 13:14-17. After Lot departs for richer pastures, the Lord again appears to Abraham and reconfirms His intention to give the entirety of Canaan to Abraham's descendants. While not providing specifics concerning borders, the Lord commands Abraham that the land, in every direction, belongs to him and to his descendants. Abraham is divinely encouraged to expand his depth of view by walking the length and breadth of the land. One expansion of the covenant promises relayed here is the revelation of Abraham's personal possession of the land, which had previously only been promised to his descendants. Another expansion is the eternal duration of his offspring's ownership of the land ("I will give it to you and to your descendants forever"). The Lord also defines the parameters of what He had previously meant by the promise of a "great nation" in 12:2 ("I will make your descendants as the dust of the earth"—13:16).

The *third expansion* of the Abrahamic

Covenant's promises is contained in Genesis 15:1-21. Abraham, frustrated by his continued childlessness, is divinely reassured that he will indeed have a physical heir (15:1-4). This is followed by another mention of numerous offspring, like the stars (15:5). In response to a second divine verbal reassurance, this time concerning the gift to Abraham of the land, Abraham requests additional, more tangible assurance (15:7-8).

God then leads Abraham through a solemn covenant ritual designed to remove all doubt. The ritual, described in 15:9-17, corresponds to the ancient Near Eastern covenant practice of blood covenant (Pentecost, *Thy Kingdom Come*, p. 57), with one similarity being the cutting of the animals and placing of the severed sections in two parallel rows. However, both parties to the covenant would normally walk between the rendered animal pieces, indicating the mandatory nature of the covenant and the severe penalty for future infraction. In this unique instance, Abraham is rendered impotent, completely passive, and unable to move (15:12). God alone binds Himself to the covenant by passing as "a flaming torch" through the animal pieces (15:17), graphically demonstrating the unconditional nature of the covenant. As Pentecost notes, Abraham is not a *participant in* the covenant but a *recipient of* the covenant (*Thy Kingdom Come*, p. 58).

Chisholm sees this ritual as a land grant, marking "the actual transfer of the land to Abraham's offspring" as well as (by implication) the ratification of the promise of offspring (Chisholm, "Evidence from Genesis," pp. 41-42). The actual geographic borders of the Promised Land are specified at this time, extending from "the river of Egypt" in the south to "the great river," the Euphrates, in the north (15:18). In addition, the current inhabitants of the land are enumerated, in prophetic preparation for their displacement (15:19-21).

During this covenant ritual, the Lord prophetically reveals to Abraham that while he would die peacefully at an advanced age, his descendants would be "strangers in a land that is not theirs," where they would be enslaved and oppressed for 400 years. The oppressor nation would experience divine judgment, however, and Abraham's descendants would not depart empty-handed. They would return to the Promised Land when the iniquity of Canaan's current inhabitants had sufficiently ripened (15:13-16). This prophecy would be fulfilled with the nation of Israel's Egyptian sojourn, enslavement, and exodus, as well as their conquest of the land (recorded in the books of Exodus through Joshua).

The *fourth expansion* of the Abrahamic Covenant's promises is contained in Genesis 17:1-21. God again appears to Abraham, identifying Himself as God Almighty (Hebrew, *el shaddai*), "the one who grants fertility and life" (Chisholm, "Evidence from Genesis," p. 42). This encounter adds the requirement of circumcision, a physical sign of the covenant, on the eighth day for Abraham and his male descendants (17:10-14). This is to serve as a vivid reminder, in blood, to every descendant of Abraham of God's "everlasting covenant" (17:7).

At this time, in conjunction with the reiteration of the promise of innumerable descendants, the Lord changes Abraham's name from *Abram* ("exalted father") to *Abraham* ("father of multitudes"). The covenant blessing is expanded to incorporate not just a single nation to issue forth from Abraham, but "nations," as well as kings. Reiterated, as well, is the promise of Abraham's and his descendants' eternal possession of the land (17:1-8). And another promise is added to the covenant complex—that of a personal relationship with Israel ("I will be their God"—17:8).

The *fifth and climactic expansion* of the Abrahamic Covenant is found in Genesis 22:15-18, in conjunction with the famous narrative of the binding of Isaac, the ultimate test of the faith of Abraham, the father of multitudes (22:1-13). Having been prepared to obediently sacrifice his only son, the son of promise, Abraham is divinely recognized as the worthy recipient of the covenant promises (22:16).

Using the most intensive form of divine oath ("by Myself I have sworn"—22:16), the Lord restates and ratifies four separate components of the covenant. First, hearkening back to the initial promise of 12:2, the Lord restates His intention of divine blessing. Second, echoing the promises of Genesis 13:16, 15:5, and 17:2-6, God restates His promise of innumerable descendants. Third, summarizing the promises of possession of the land in Genesis 12:7, 13:15, 15:18, 17:8, and with veiled reference to the nations mentioned in 15:19-21, the Lord promises Abraham's descendants possession of enemy cities. Fourth, hearkening back to the initial set of promises concerning universal influence in 12:3, the Lord reaffirms that all nations would be blessed through the seed of Abraham (22:15-18).

The influence of the Abrahamic Covenant is woven throughout the tapestry of Scripture, from the twelfth chapter of Genesis through the final chapter of Revelation. It forms the foundational basis for every subsequent covenant in the Bible. Absent this covenant (or through the neutering of the covenant through the spiritualization of its promises), Israel's right to the land is incomprehensible, the messianic age could never be anticipated, and the bringing together of Jews and Gentiles in spiritual union would be unthinkable. Echoes of the Abrahamic Covenant's celebrated themes of blessing resound from the exodus through conquest, from kingdom to exile, from incarnation to resurrection, and from the nation of Israel to the universal dominion of the Messiah.

GOD'S PROMISES CONCERNING ISHMAEL
Genesis 16:7-13; 17:20; 21:18

THE GENESIS NARRATIVE RECORDS three divine prophetic promises concerning the destiny of Ishmael. The *first promise* is found in 16:7-13. Abraham's firstborn son is Ishmael, a product of "the man of faith" prematurely taking genealogical matters into his own hands with Sarah's maid, Hagar. Pregnant and des-perate to flee Sarah's harsh treatment, Hagar encounters the angel of the Lord. This is the first reference within the Old Testament to a physical manifestation of God Himself—that is, a preincarnate appearance of the second person of the Trinity (Genesis 18:1-2; 19:1; 22:11-12; 31:11-13; Exodus 3:1-4; Numbers 22:22; Judges 2:1-4; 5:23; 6:11,16,22; 13:22-23; Zechariah 3:1-2; 12:8).

Hagar is instructed to return to Sarah and to her work, for she would be divinely blessed with innumerable descendants, beginning with the son currently in her womb. His name is to be *Ishmael,* meaning "God hears" (to which Hagar enthusiastically responds by christening the Lord with a name that means "a God who sees"). Ishmael would live as "a wild donkey," a roaming, free spirit, hostile by nature and at odds with most of society, experiencing continuous conflict. He would dwell "to the east of all his brothers" (16:7-12). Twenty-one chapters later in the narrative, Ishmaelites are the means by which Joseph, Abraham and Sarah's great-grandson, is carried off to Egypt (37:28).

The *second promise* concerning Ishmael is found in 17:20. While Abraham receives divine instruction regarding circumcision, the sign of the covenant, along with an encouraging reminder of his wife's prophesied pregnancy with Isaac, Abraham expresses concern that Ishmael not be divinely neglected. God responds that He has heard Abraham's concern that "God hears" (Ishmael) not be overlooked. As Abraham's son, Ishmael would also experience divine blessing and would become "the father of twelve princes," who together would flourish into "a great nation" of innumerable descendants (17:20).

The *third promise* concerning Ishmael is found in 21:18. It is a reconfirmation to Hagar, discouraged after having been sent away, of God's promise, previously made to Abraham, that Ishmael would flourish into "a great nation" (21:18). Indeed, Ishmael's 12 sons are listed in 1 Chronicles 1:28-31.

The apostle Paul later uses Genesis' account of Ishmael's birth as typological of the Torah, in contrast to the typological use of Isaac, the son of promise, in reference to the believer's freedom in the Messiah (Galatians 4:21-31).

ISAAC AS A TYPE OF MESSIAH
Genesis 22:1-13

Regarding Abraham's divinely initiated and subsequently aborted sacrifice of his son, commonly known in Jewish tradition as the *Akedah,* "the binding of Isaac," the rabbinic teaching has always viewed the willing sacrifice of Abraham, and especially Isaac's willingness to offer himself, as an act of vicarious atonement throughout the future history of their descendants, the nation of Israel. The righteousness of the patriarchs could be vicariously applied to their descendants in time of spiritual need.

The rabbis were not completely off base when they saw a picture of atonement in Isaac. The events of Genesis 22 are a prime example of what Scripture calls "a mere shadow of what is to come" (Colossians 2:17). Isaac was a prophetic type, a picture, of the Messiah. Jesus was not only the ultimate Israel, the ultimate David, and the ultimate Moses, but also the ultimate Isaac. Both Isaac and Jesus were the sons of promise. Both men had miraculous births. Both were obedient and willing sons who were prepared and ready to lay down their lives at their Father's behest. Both sons even carried the wood for their own sacrifice.

Both Isaac and Jesus had fathers who were prepared to slay them to fulfill a larger purpose. As Abraham was willing to sacrifice his son, so too was God willing to sacrifice His only Son. Yet God did not demand of Abraham what He demanded of Himself. The Lord provided a substitute sacrifice for the son of Abraham, a ram caught in the thicket. However, there was no alternative sacrifice for the Son of God. Jesus became the Lamb of God, slain for the sin of the world (John 1:29). If indeed Christ Himself was the angel of the Lord who called to Abraham, then He was not willing that Abraham slay his son. Yet He was willing to let the Father sacrifice Him on our behalf.

THE ABRAHAMIC COVENANT AND ISAAC
Genesis 26:2-5

Following the death of Abraham, the Lord appears to Isaac to reaffirm the Abrahamic Covenant with Abraham's heir, saying, "I will establish the oath which I swore to your father Abraham." Instructing Isaac to remain in the land of his inheritance, the Lord reaffirms the covenant blessings of His personal presence, numerous descendants ("as the stars of heaven"), universal blessing ("by your descendants all the nations of the earth shall be blessed"), and permanent ownership of the land ("to you and to your descendants I will give all these lands") (26:2-5). The appearance concludes with a reminder of the unconditionality of the Abrahamic Covenant, which was based upon Abraham's initial act of obedience to God (Genesis 12:4).

ISAAC'S BLESSING OF JACOB
Genesis 27:27-29

Having earlier obtained Esau's birthright through a trade (25:27-34), Jacob now steals his older brother's rightful blessing through duplicity and deception (27:1-26). Taking advantage of his father Isaac's blindness by disguising himself as Esau, Jacob comes before his father. He then receives the prophetic blessing meant for Isaac's firstborn son, Esau (27:27-29). Isaac's blessing of Jacob is fourfold: First, blessing is granted in the area of agricultural and economic prosperity. Second, blessing is granted in the area of intercultural relations with other nations and clans. Third, Jacob is granted his father's patriarchal authority over

Esau and his descendants. And fourth, Isaac transfers the inheritance of the Abrahamic Covenant upon his son by quoting God's foundational promise of reciprocal blessing and cursing (originally made to Abraham in Genesis 12:3).

THE ABRAHAMIC COVENANT AND JACOB
Genesis 28:3-4,13-15; 35:9-13

JACOB, PRIOR TO FLEEING the retributive wrath of his brother Esau for the theft of their father's blessing, is summoned into Isaac's presence for an additional, final blessing. Whereas earlier Isaac had unknowingly transferred the inheritance of the Abrahamic covenant upon Jacob (27:29), here he grants a blessing to Jacob with purpose and intention. The patriarch petitions the Lord for Jacob and his progeny to receive the "blessing of Abraham," summarized as the multiplication of Jacob's seed and possession of the land "which God gave to Abraham" (28:3-4).

Shortly thereafter, Isaac's blessing is confirmed to Jacob by the Lord through a divine reaffirmation of the Abrahamic Covenant. After Jacob departs the land of promise and while he is resting on his journey toward Haran, the Lord appears to him and identifies Himself as "the God of your father Abraham and the God of Isaac." At this time, Jacob is unconditionally promised inheritance of the land, the multiplication of his descendants ("like the dust of the earth"), universal blessing ("in your descendants shall all the families of the earth be blessed"), and the continued presence and protection of the Lord (28:13-15).

Many years later, in the same location (which Jacob had commemoratively called Bethel, "house of God"—28:19), the Lord appears again to bless Jacob and to reconfirm both the Abrahamic Covenant as well as Jacob's name change to Israel. Identifying Himself to Jacob as "God Almighty" (Hebrew, el shaddai), the Lord reiterates His unconditional promise of numerous (and royal) descendants ("a nation and a company of nations shall come forth from you, and kings shall come forth from you"). In addition, He reiterates His unconditional promise, made previously with both Abraham and Isaac, of Jacob's and his progeny's possession of the land (35:9-13).

This passage, the final patriarchal reconfirmation of the Abrahamic Covenant in the Genesis narrative, is designed to recall God's specific, confirming appearance to Jacob's grandfather, Abraham, in Genesis 17:1-8. Chisholm points out striking parallels between the two texts (Chisholm, "Evidence from Genesis," p. 52). These similarities include the Lord's identification of Himself as "God Almighty" (35:11; 17:1); the changing of the patriarch's name (from Jacob to Israel in 35:10 and Abram to Abraham in 17:5); the promise of numerous descendants, including kings (35:11; 17:2,6); and the promise of land inheritance (35:12; 17:8).

JACOB WRESTLES WITH GOD
Genesis 32:9-31

THIS FAMOUS PASSAGE describes an unforgettable turning point in Jacob's life, centered within a moment of crisis. Having been long absent from his homeland, the land of promise, and now on its outskirts, Jacob prays, on the basis of the Abrahamic Covenant (Genesis 12:1-3; 12:7; 13:14-17; 15:1-21; 17:1-21; 22:15-18; 28:13-15), for divine deliverance from the vengeance of his long-estranged brother, Esau (32:9-11). Having sent the entirety of his travel party on ahead, "Jacob was left alone" (32:24).

Sometime that evening, Jacob has an unexpected visitor. Rather than spending the night in fearful contemplation of Esau's potentially hostile reaction to his return, Jacob finds himself preoccupied in a wrestling match with this visitor. The match lasted through the night until daybreak (32:24). With dawn approaching and the contest between the two wrestlers ongoing, the mysterious figure dislocates the socket of Jacob's thigh, severely disabling Jacob. He then demands that Jacob break off the contest. Jacob, however, continues to cling furiously, unwilling to allow the mysterious figure to depart without giving Jacob a blessing (32:25-26). At some point during the wrestling match, perhaps at the moment of his crippling injury, Jacob realizes that his opponent is no mere man, but the angel of the Lord, a physical manifestation of God Himself—that is, a preincarnate appearance of the second person of the Trinity (Genesis 18:1-2; 19:1; 22:11-12; 31:11-13; Exodus 3:1-4; Numbers 22:22; Judges 2:1-4; 5:23; 6:11,16,22; 13:22-23; Zechariah 3:1-2; 12:8).

The angel of the Lord renames Jacob *Israel* ("God fights," or "he who fights [wrestles] with God"), for Jacob, now Israel, had "striven with God and with men and [had] prevailed" (32:28). Israel then receives the divine blessing (32:29). He names the location *Peniel* ("face of God"), saying, "I have seen God face to face, yet my life has been preserved" (32:30). This was an unforgettable encounter with the divine in which not only Jacob's name was changed, but his lifestyle as well.

The name *Israel* is a double-sided prophetic portrait. On one side is the history of the stubborn, stiff-necked nation of God's chosen people, "he who fights with God"—a nation that has wrestled with the Lord from their national inception at Sinai. On the other side are the promises of that nation's God, a deity whose fierce passion and covenant commitment to His people knows no limitation and whose ardor for His chosen people guarantees their eventual restoration. He is "the God who fights" tirelessly and unceasingly on Israel's behalf.

JOSEPH'S PROPHECY ABOUT HIS BROTHERS
Genesis 37:5-11

JOSEPH WAS JACOB'S ELEVENTH SON, but as the firstborn of Jacob's beloved wife, Rachel, Joseph was clearly his father's favorite. Joseph's multicolored coat was an indication that Jacob sought to elevate Joseph to firstborn status (37:3). Certainly the matter of a younger son supplanting elder siblings had durable family precedent with Isaac and Ishmael and with Jacob and Esau.

At the age of 17, Joseph is given two prophetic dreams. In the first dream, the harvested sheaves belonging to Joseph's brothers bow down before his own sheaf. In the second dream, the sun, moon, and eleven stars bow before Joseph. Joseph's brothers react to the dreams with hatred and jealousy, for they realize both dreams indicated that Joseph's whole family would one day prostrate themselves before him in submission (37:5-11).

The brothers' jealousy and contempt for Joseph leads to his being sold into slavery (37:18-36). The Genesis narrative records how Joseph, over the next 20 years, rose in Egypt from his roles as both slave and convict to eventual ruler of the nation, second only to Pharaoh (39–41). Joseph's prophetic dreams later found fulfillment when his brothers traveled to Egypt during a famine and, not yet recognizing him, bowed before Joseph to beg for food (42:6).

In the book of Acts, Stephen presents Joseph as a prophetic type of the Messiah (7:9-16). Although Joseph had been rejected by his own family, he had been accepted by foreigners in a foreign land, Egypt, and exalted by God's hand. Moreover, Stephen argues that Joseph, who eventually had progressed from rejection to exaltation, became the savior of those who had rejected him. Joseph's brothers did not recognize Joseph the first time they saw him. It was not until their second visit that they recognized their brother (Genesis 42–45). In other words, the sons of Israel did not perceive that their own brother was their savior until their second appearance before him.

Stephen's parallel is clear: The first time the descendants of the sons of Israel saw Jesus, they likewise did not recognize Him. It will take a second viewing for perception to dawn. Unfortunately, the vast majority of the Jewish people will not perceive that Jesus is their

Messiah until His glory is eminently manifest upon His return.

of plenty followed by seven years of famine, just as Joseph predicted (41:47-57).

JOSEPH, THE CUPBEARER, AND THE BAKER
Genesis 40:12-13,18-19

WHILE JOSEPH IS IN PRISON, two fellow prisoners approach him and ask him to interpret their recent dreams. After the first man, Pharaoh's former cupbearer, relays the details of his dream, Joseph interprets it as predicting the cupbearer's restoration to royal favor in three days' time (40:12-13). Indeed, the cupbearer is later restored to his former position (verse 21).

When the second man, Pharaoh's former chief baker, relays the details of his dream, Joseph interprets it as predicting the baker's execution in three days' time (verses 18-19). As Joseph predicted, the baker is later executed (verse 22).

JOSEPH'S PROPHECY ABOUT EGYPT
Genesis 41:1-32

TWO YEARS AFTER JOSEPH'S successful interpretation of the cupbearer's and baker's dreams, he is summoned from prison to appear before Pharaoh to interpret two dreams that puzzled Pharaoh. The cupbearer, who until this time had forgotten about Joseph, had suggested that Pharaoh allow Joseph the opportunity to interpret these dreams. Joseph correctly interprets the dreams to indicate that Egypt will experience seven years of agricultural plenty, which will be followed by seven years of famine. Joseph then makes recommendations as to how the nation could prepare for the next 14 years. Pharaoh responds by elevating Joseph to ruler of the nation, second only to Pharaoh. The text records the occurrence of seven years

JACOB PROMISED BLESSING IN EGYPT
Genesis 46:1-6

HAVING JOYOUSLY DISCOVERED that his son Joseph, whom he had believed to be dead for two decades, is alive, Jacob, along with the entire family, emigrates to Egypt to live under Joseph's munificence. On the way to Egypt, Jacob offers sacrifices to God at Beersheba (46:1). That evening the Lord reassures Jacob of His divine blessing. Jacob is not to be afraid of an Egyptian sojourn, for while Jacob's family is in Egypt, God would forge them into "a great nation" (46:3). The Israelites' time in Egypt would be temporary, was for their benefit, and would be divinely superintended (46:2-4). That Jacob understood God's reassurance concerning the temporary nature of his family's time in Egypt is evidenced by Joseph's deathbed request that his bones accompany the Hebrews upon their eventual exodus from Egypt back into the land of promise (Genesis 50:24-25).

A special reassurance is that Jacob is about to see his son, Joseph, and that the two would not part again before Jacob's death (46:4). The narrative of Genesis 46:29 relays how Joseph, riding to meet his beloved father in his royal chariot, is emotionally reunited with his Father.

JACOB BLESSES HIS 12 SONS
Genesis 49:1-28

ON HIS DEATHBED, Jacob delivers his final blessing to his 12 sons. Just as Isaac's blessing of Jacob took the form of a prophetic oracle, so did Jacob's blessing of his sons. Jacob's words are fraught with prophetic significance; indeed, the patriarch himself emphasizes the prophetic content of his remarks by identifying them as revealing what the future holds for his family "in the days to come" (Hebrew, *b'acharit hayyamim,* "the end of days"—49:1-2).

Reuben, Jacob's firstborn and heir, was disinherited from the position of family pre-eminence (49:3-4) because of his affair with Bilhah, his father's concubine (35:22). The tribe of Reuben would never reassert preeminence throughout Israel's history.

Simeon and Levi, the next eldest brothers, are treated together (49:5-7). Correctly char-acterized by their father as violent and angry (34:25-29), they too are passed over for the mantle of family preeminence. Both tribes are predicted to be scattered in the land. Simeon would eventually be subsumed within the larger tribe of Judah, while Levi, as the eventual priestly tribe, would never possess a geographic tribal inheritance. Rather, the Levites would live throughout Israel's territory.

Judah, the fourth son, is dealt with next (49:8-12). It is Judah, the "lion," to whom the mantle of tribal leadership is passed. Judah is recognized as being worthy to receive the privileges of the firstborn. (For more on this, see the commentary for 49:10-12.)

The tribe of Zebulun would be "a haven for ships," enriched by maritime trade (49:13). Although the tribe of Issachar was naturally equipped for hard work, they would not live up to their potential (49:14-15). Dan would provide leadership to Israel (49:16-17). Gad would both be attacked and counterattack (49:19). Asher's tribal territory would prove abundantly fertile (49:20). Naphtali would be a speedy doe, roaming free (49:21).

Joseph receives a superior, double blessing. The tribe of Joseph would be characterized by prosperity and military capability, broadly blessed in every way. Joseph is "the one distin-guished among his brothers" (49:22-26).

Finally, Benjamin is characterized as a tribe of violent warriors (49:27).

The section concludes with the affirmation that every son/tribe was blessed "with the blessing appropriate to him" (49:28).

THE MESSIAH FROM THE TRIBE OF JUDAH
Genesis 49:10-12

WITHIN JACOB'S PROPHETIC blessings of his 12 sons is the promise that Judah's tribe will rightfully rule (possess the "scepter," the symbol of royalty—49:10) over the rest of the tribes until a particular moment in history, the coming of "Shiloh" (49:10). The mysterious term *Shiloh* can be translated as "to whom it belongs" (as it is usually translated in Ezekiel 21:27 concerning the royal crown of Israel's prince).

Shiloh has traditionally been understood as a messianic title, a pseudonym for *Messiah.* The first-century Aramaic paraphrases of the Scripture, the Targums, consistently treat this as a messianic prophecy. Targum Onkelos reads, "Kings shall not cease from the house of Judah...until Messiah come, whose is the kingdom" (quoted in Kac 19). The Palestinian Targum likewise reads, "Kings shall not cease from the house of Judah...until the time that is King Messiah shall come, whose is the kingdom" (as quoted in Kac 19-20). Targum Jonathan holds this interpretation of the verse as well, reading much the same as the other Targums, yet adding the expectation that "because of him [Messiah] nations shall melt away."

In addition, the Midrash, a vast corpus of homiletical commentary, holds this interpreta-tion of the passage (Midrash Rabbah, Genesis XCVII, new version; XCVIII, 8, 9; Midrash on Proverbs, chapter 19, 21, as quoted in Huckel, *The Rabbinic Messiah,* elec. ed.; see also Santala, *Messiah in the Old Testament,* pp. 50-53). Fur-thermore, the Talmud (Babylonian Talmud, *Sanhedrin* 98b), the Jewish oral law, and Rashi, the eleventh-century rabbinic "goliath," all take *Shiloh* with reference to "King Messiah" (Kac 20).

The point is patently emphasized through the genealogies recorded within the Gospels—whether through Jesus' adopted father (Mat-thew 1:1-17) or his mother (Luke 3:23-38)—that

Jesus belongs to the tribe of Judah. Interestingly, if Jesus had not come prior to the destruction of the temple and the accompanying loss of all its stored genealogical records that would occur a mere 75 years hence, any claims that He had to tribal descent from Judah would have been hopelessly unverifiable. God's timing for the appearance of *Shiloh,* the one "to whom it belongs," was impeccable.

EXODUS

The book of Exodus tells the dramatic story of the call of Moses to lead the Israelites out of Egypt to the Promised Land. It includes numerous specific prophecies about Israel's destiny as well as the prophetic typology of the Passover meal and the tabernacle. In this book we find the biblical foundations of Judeo-Christian ethics and religion.

THE ANNOUNCEMENT OF MOSES' APPOINTMENT
Exodus 3:10

At the age of 80, Moses encounters the visible manifestation of God's presence, the Shekinah glory, in a flaming bush. The Lord reveals Himself to Moses as the God of Israel's fathers, Abraham, Isaac, and Jacob. The mention of the patriarchs would have served as an electrifying reminder that God had not forgotten the ancient promises He had made in the Abrahamic Covenant. God reassures Moses that He has seen and heard the affliction and sorrows of His people and that His compassion toward them is now leading Him to decisive action on their behalf. God indicates His direct involvement in the rescue operation that will not only free the people of Israel from slavery but also bring them out of Egypt and into their inheritance, the land of promise (3:1-8).

In Exodus 3:9-10, God reiterates His identity as the One who sees and hears His people and feels compassion for them. He then reveals that the method by which He will decisively intervene is through His chosen instrument of redemption, Moses. Moses is told to return to Egypt to deliver the Hebrews. In a bit of literary foreshadowing, although there are two components to God's plan, deliverance from Egypt and entrance into Canaan, Moses specifies that his divine commission extended only to the Israelites' deliverance from Egypt and not to their deposition into the Promised Land. Indeed, Moses later delivers God's people from Egyptian bondage (Exodus 12:37-50), but he was not the one to lead them into Canaan (Deuteronomy 32:48-52).

THE CONFIRMATION OF MOSES' APPOINTMENT
Exodus 3:12–4:9

Moses objects to his role in God's exodus plan. He is all too aware that he is not the same man he was 40 years ago. No longer an Egyptian prince and now an obscure shepherd, he no longer possesses his former sense of divine destiny. His first of several objections to God is that he is personally unable to accomplish a task of this magnitude.

God responds to Moses' first objection with the assurance of His abiding personal presence, which will empower Moses. Moses' ability to deliver Israel will be confirmed when he leads the Hebrews back to this very same mountain for the purpose of worship. The Israelites would not go directly from Egypt to the land of promise, but would first enjoy a roughly 150-mile detour to Mount Sinai (3:12).

In response, Moses then raises his second objection. He reasons that arriving at Mount Sinai would indeed prove confirmation of his commission after the fact. But until that point, what would motivate the Hebrews to trust that Moses could actually deliver them? While he himself might be aware of God's personal abiding presence, how would the people be certain of Moses' divine commission (verse 13)?

To this objection God responds with the revelation of the essence and substance behind His personal name. He identifies Himself as "I AM WHO I AM" (verse 14). The personal name of the Lord is YHWH, often presumed to be pronounced Yahweh, Yahveh, or Jehovah. (The actual pronunciation of the Lord's personal name is today a matter of uncertainty; the ancient Hebrew priesthood so guarded the ineffable name of God that with the passage of time following the destruction of the temple in A.D. 70, knowledge of its correct articulation was lost. The uncertainty stems from the lack of vowels in the basic construction of Hebrew words.) Moses is to remind the people that this is the name by which God has always wished to be known and worshipped, the name that expresses His character as the God who both remembers His covenant and keeps His promises (verses 14-15).

Moses is instructed to go to Pharaoh, together with the Hebrew leaders, and request of the king not their wholesale freedom from slavery, but rather, a brief departure. They are to petition Pharaoh for three days' vacation from their tasks that they may worship the Lord outside the borders of Egypt. God then says Pharaoh will not grant even this minimal request (verses 16-19).

After a demonstration of God's wonders (at this point unspecified), the Hebrews will be free. And the Egyptians will be so favorably disposed toward them that they will not allow the Israelites to leave empty-handed. The Hebrews will receive from their taskmasters the recompense due for their labors (3:20-22), thus fulfilling God's promise to Abraham that Israel would leave Egypt possessing great wealth (Genesis 15:14).

Despite the divine assurance of such a wondrous outcome, Moses raises a third objection to his role in God's plan. He is still uncertain that the Hebrews will believe him or that he can inspire their confidence so they will grant him authority to lead them (4:1).

To answer this objection, God enables Moses to perform three authenticating supernatural signs that establish his credentials as the Lord's spokesman (4:2-9). First, Moses is empowered to change his shepherd's staff into a snake and back again. Second (just in case the first sign is insufficient to generate the people's trust), Moses is empowered to make the flesh of his hand leprous and then normal again. And third (in case the first two signs prove insufficient), Moses is empowered to turn the water of the Nile River into blood. Interestingly, unlike the first two signs, this one is not immediately reversible. This sign, however, serves as a warm-up for the first plague (7:17-21).

The subsequent narrative in Exodus provides a series of substantial confirmations of Moses' divine appointment. Moses' messages are confirmed through mighty and numerous signs and wonders. However, neither the message nor the authenticating signs make a sufficient impression upon Pharaoh. This provokes the Lord to exercise great judgments of destruction upon Egypt.

THE FIRSTBORN OF EGYPT TO DIE
Exodus 4:22-23

FROM THE OUTSET OF Moses' mission, the Lord makes clear His divine intention to exercise powerful leverage with Pharaoh. The highest of stakes would be in play—the future of the firstborn sons of Egypt (Exodus 11:5;

12:12). This is appropriate because, in relation to God, Israel is His "son...my firstborn." This powerful term, used elsewhere in Scripture (Jeremiah 31:9-20; Hosea 11:1), illustrates the Hebrews' uniquely intimate relationship to God (4:22-23).

The fulfillment of this expressed intention is relayed in 12:29-30 with the unleashing of the tenth plague. At midnight the plague suddenly begins to roil the nation. Not one home is left unaffected by the abrupt loss of all the firstborn males, from the royal court of Pharaoh to the prison house. Each family loses at least one member as firstborn sons, fathers, and grandfathers are struck down. Even the firstborn of the cattle are killed.

THE REASSURANCE TO MOSES
Exodus 6:1-8

BECAUSE THE HEBREWS' situation had deteriorated so rapidly since Moses' arrival on the scene, Moses questions God as to his call and purpose as their deliverer, reminding the Lord that contrary to his expectation, the people had not yet been delivered from bondage in any way (5:22-23).

The Lord replies to Moses with immediate reassurance. Moses will now see what God will do. Because Pharaoh rejected the Lord's initial request, the Lord will now make the king an offer he cannot refuse. This would result in Pharaoh not just passively letting the Hebrews go, but forcefully driving them out. Moses is reminded of the Lord's identity as the covenant God and of His powerful, timeless commitment to the Israelites. The Lord will neither forget His promises nor ignore His covenantal obligations (6:1-2).

The patriarchs, Abraham, Isaac, and Jacob, knew the Lord as the architect of the Abrahamic Covenant and guarantor of its promises. However, they had not lived long enough to witness the fulfillment of those promises, as Moses' generation soon would. God was about to reveal much more of Himself and His power

to the patriarchs' descendants than they themselves had ever experienced. Moses was reassured of God's compassion toward His people and once again reminded that God had not abandoned His covenantal promise to bring the Hebrews back into Canaan (6:3-5).

God continues with a sevenfold declaration of purpose, pledging Himself to seven related promises:

1. I will separate you from the burdens of Egypt.

2. I will deliver you from slavery.

3. I will redeem you with a magnificent display of power.

4. I will make you My people.

5. I will be your God—that is, the relationship between the Lord and His people will be formalized and take on a new and deeper dimension.

6. I will bring you into the Promised Land.

7. I will give you that land as an inheritance (6:6-8).

The divine promises found in this passage form the basis for the names of the four cups that are consumed during the contemporary Passover seder meal. Each cup is named after one particular promise or set of promises: the cup of sanctification, the cup of deliverance, the cup of redemption, and the cup of consummation. Each promise that God made to Moses found fulfillment in Israel's history as expressed through the narrative of exodus, wandering, and conquest (Exodus through Joshua).

THE TEN PLAGUES UNLEASHED ON EGYPT
Exodus 7:1–12:36

WHEN MOSES AND AARON ask Pharaoh to let the people of Israel go, Pharaoh challenges the brothers to work a miracle. Throughout the narrative, the Lord repeatedly mentions the impact His actions and reactions will have on the Egyptians' minds (Exodus 7:5,17; 8:10,22; 14:18). He is not unconcerned with establishing and maintaining His reputation among the Egyptians, and He freely demonstrates His power to make a lasting impression.

As Moses had done with his staff at Sinai, so now Aaron does with his own staff. He casts it down before Pharaoh, and it becomes a serpent. Pharaoh summons his wise men (sacred scribes educated in both human wisdom and supernatural secrets) and sorcerers (the priests of the Egyptian religious cults) who served as the magicians of Egypt. Through the exercise of demonic power, they are able to duplicate God's sign and transform their rods into serpents as well. Jewish tradition records the names of two of the magicians who opposed Moses, Jannes and Jambres (2 Timothy 3:8). However, in this initial supernatural power encounter between God and the Egyptian deities, the superiority of the Lord is demonstrated when Aaron's rod swallows the rods belonging to the magicians and sorcerers (7:11-12).

The Lord could have delivered the Hebrews from Egypt with one powerful and dramatic act, but He chose to prolong the process through a series of ten plagues delivered over an approximate period of six to nine months, spanning the late summer or early fall of 1446 B.C. through the spring of 1445 B.C. With each plague the intensity of God's judgment on Egypt escalates and there is a marked increase in the people's suffering and the land's devastation.

The ten Egyptian plagues serve *four divine purposes*. The *first* and most obvious purpose for the plagues is to compel Pharaoh to release the Hebrews from bondage. The *second* is to punish the Egyptians for their harsh treatment of the Hebrews. This purpose references the reciprocal conduct clause of the Abrahamic Covenant, which states that God will curse those who curse Israel (Genesis 12:3). The *third* is to demonstrate God's sovereign power and absolute authority to both the Hebrews and the Egyptians (Exodus 9:14,16; 10:2).

The *fourth* reason is to demonstrate the Lord's superiority over Egypt's many false gods (Exodus 12:12; 18:11; Numbers 33:4). There were some 80 ancient Egyptian gods, each one the personification of some animal or object. In addition, Pharaoh himself was considered to be the incarnation of the god Horus, with the court magicians serving as his priests. Each of the ten plagues was designed to challenge a specific god or several gods within the Egyptian pantheon and ultimately, topple the credibility of Pharaoh's own divinity as well.

THE TYPOLOGICAL SIGNIFICANCE OF THE PASSOVER
Exodus 12:1-36,39,46-47

INTERRUPTING THE TENTH PLAGUE narrative are instructions for the observance of the Feast of Passover, the most frequently mentioned holiday in the Old and New Testaments (for example, Numbers 9:1-5; Joshua 5:10; 2 Kings 23:21-23; 2 Chronicles 30:1-27; 35:1-19; Ezra 6:19-22; Luke 2:41-43; John 2:13,23; 6:4; 11:55–12:1). This is the initial festival in Israel's annual cycle of seven festivals (see Leviticus 23). The holiday serves as the catalyst for the inauguration of a new religious calendar system for the Hebrews. The Passover is observed in the first month of the new year. This month is called *Aviv* (Exodus 13:41; 23:15; 34:18; Deuteronomy 16:1), but following the Babylonian captivity, it became known as *Nisan* (Nehemiah 2:1; Esther 3:7). Passover is the annual celebration of new beginnings and a yearly reminder of the Hebrews' new identity as a people and nation (12:1-2).

In the next section of narrative, Moses relays the divine instructions for Israel's selection and slaying of the original Passover lambs. On the tenth day of Aviv, each family is to select and set aside a lamb for their household. In the event that a family is too small to consume an entire lamb, they are to join a neighboring family. Jewish tradition determined that ten people comprise the minimum number required to constitute a household large enough to consume a Passover lamb. The reason for this minimum is that the entire lamb had to be eaten the evening of the holiday.

The qualifying requirements for selecting a lamb were that it be either a sheep or a goat, that it be without blemish or physical imperfection of any sort, and that it be one year old. Each household's lamb was to be set aside for four days of observation and maintenance of its perfect condition. It was then to be killed in the evening on the fourteenth day of Aviv. The text in 12:6 literally reads "between the evenings" and has been understood in Jewish tradition to mean either the time between sunset and full darkness (that is, twilight), or between three o'clock in the afternoon and sunset. The second rendering was accepted and applied to the Passover sacrifices during the temple era, with the lambs being slaughtered on the afternoon of the fourteenth of Nisan. The blood of the sacrificed lamb was to be stained onto the two side posts and lintel of the home in which the lamb would be eaten that evening. At the corner where the side posts met the lintel, the bloody stain would have formed a cross (12:3-7).

On the evening that the Lord came to destroy the firstborn males of all Egypt, both human and animal, He passed over the houses belonging to the Hebrews on account of the blood on the doorposts. The origin of the term *Passover* is a stark reminder that the Hebrews were not automatically exempt from the Lord's judgment simply because of their racial status. Although the Lord had chosen to discriminate between the Egyptians and Hebrews from plagues four through nine, He changed that pattern here. From this point on in the collective life of Israel, Passover would serve as an annual object lesson and a lasting reminder of the necessity of blood to avert God's wrath. And it was to be celebrated in perpetuity— that is, as long as the Torah was still in effect (12:13-14).

According to 12:22, hyssop, a small plant indigenous to the Middle East mentioned elsewhere in the Torah in relation to purifica-

tion for sin (Leviticus 14:4,6,49,51-52; Numbers 19:6,18; Psalm 51:7; Hebrews 9:19), was to serve as the "paintbrush" for applying the lambs' blood on the Hebrews' doorposts and lintels. (In most Passover seders today, a sprig of parsley is used to symbolize the hyssop.) This application of blood created a zone of safety from God's judgment, and no one was to leave the safe house that evening until God's wrath had passed them over. God moved throughout Egypt that evening in the company of the angel of death, and He restrained the angel from entering any home covered by the blood of a Passover lamb (12:22-23).

Next God gives specific instructions for the eating of this sacred meal. Additional liturgical elements have accrued to the Passover seder throughout the centuries, but three indivisible elements are divinely commanded and non-negotiable, regardless of individual or regional tradition. The meal is to center on the eating of the lamb and be accompanied by both matzah (unleavened bread, Exodus 12:34,39) and some variety of bitter herb (such as horseradish or endive) symbolizing the bitterness of the slavery experience. The animal is to be roasted with fire, not eaten raw or cooked by boiling, and must be roasted whole with its head, legs, and inner parts intact. And the lamb is to be eaten that same evening; there are to be no leftovers. Anything left over must be disposed of by fire by the following morning (12:8-10).

This meal is to be eaten with the Hebrews' "loins girded" (that is, garment folds tucked away into the belt), sandals on, and staff in hand (verse 11). It is also to be eaten "in haste." This is not a divine command for the Hebrews to rapidly "wolf down their food." "In haste" simply means with "an attitude of trembling expectancy or trepidation."

The term *Passover* is used in the Scripture to describe not only the festival but also the sacrificed lamb itself. In 12:11 it is also used to describe the actual event itself, the redemptive moment in history when the Lord executed judgment against all the gods of Egypt (12:12).

A second holiday was established in conjunction with Passover, the Feast of Unleavened Bread, which is celebrated immediately following Passover for the duration of another seven days, commencing on Aviv (or Nisan) 15. Together, the combined observance of Passover and the Feast of Unleavened Bread lasts eight days. Although technically two separate holidays, the Bible usually links them together and often treats them as a single unit (for example, Mark 14:12; Acts 21:3-4).

The observance of this holiday is characterized by the strict removal of leaven out from the home. In the Bible, leaven (yeast) is frequently used as a powerful symbol of sin (see Luke 12:1; 1 Corinthians 5:8). With the removal of all leaven from the home and diet for the duration of the holiday, the home is symbolically purified and becomes a sin-free zone. This potent custom is still practiced today in the homes of observant Jewish families. In the event that anyone eats food containing leaven during the holiday, the penalty is quite severe—excommunication or even execution ("shall be cut off from Israel"—Exodus 12:15).

Both the first and seventh days of the Feast of Unleavened Bread are days of rest. No work is to be done. This seven-day holiday, like the one-day holiday of Passover, is to be observed by Israel in perpetuity as an enduring memorial of the day of Hebrew liberation from Egyptian bondage (12:15-20).

Both Passover and the Feast of Unleavened Bread are to be observed annually, upon the Hebrews' entrance into the land of covenant promise (12:24-25). Emphasis is placed on the older generations passing down the significance of the observances to the younger generations. For some 3500 years now, the events of Passover have been relayed, generation after generation, from Jewish parents to their children. The meal is an object lesson, a teaching tool for the purpose of recalling God's mercy, and children have always played a central role in its implementation (12:26-28).

The historical explanation is provided (beginning in 12:34 and continuing in 12:39) for both the centrality of unleavened bread in the Passover ritual and the ensuing seven-day feast. Armies move on their stomachs, and the Hebrews, in their haste to leave (on what was the first day of the seven-day festival) were to grab only the food they had on hand, their as-yet unleavened bread dough. They were to form the dough into cakes and hoist the pans up onto their shoulders. The sun would then bake the cakes into matzos, or unleavened bread.

Exodus 12:46-47 provides two more general rules of observance. The Passover meal is to be eaten by each household within the confines of each house; there are to be no progressive Passover seders from home to home, and there is to be no eating of the ritual meal out on the porch or in the backyard. In addition, God prohibited the breaking of any of the lamb's bones.

Passover was one of three annual pilgrimage festivals (along with Pentecost and the Feast of Tabernacles) when every Israelite family was commanded to congregate at the central location of worship, initially the tabernacle and later, the temple (Exodus 23:14-17; 34:22-24; Deuteronomy 16:16).

Passover finds prophetic fulfillment in the death of the Messiah. The rich typological significance of Passover is highlighted in several places in the New Testament. John uses the imagery of the unblemished, sacrificed lamb to refer to Jesus ("Behold, the Lamb of God who takes away the sin of the world"—John 1:29, and "worthy is the Lamb"—Revelation 5:12), as do both Peter ("a lamb unblemished and spotless" 1 Peter 1:19) and Paul ("Christ our Passover also has been sacrificed"—1 Corinthians 5:7). Paul also applies unleavened bread imagery to the believers' lifestyle goal of holiness (1 Corinthians 5:8). In addition, John explicitly alludes to the Passover by pointing out that none of Jesus' bones were broken during His crucifixion (John 19:36, see also Psalm 34:20).

Jesus Himself referenced His typological fulfillment of both the Passover and the Feast of Unleavened Bread during the Last Supper. Christ's reinterpretation of the Passover meal instituted the celebration of communion and announced a new era in human history (Luke 22:14-23). Indeed, implicit in the Last Supper teaching is the promise of future celebrations of Passover and the Feast of Unleavened Bread within the messianic kingdom (Luke 22:16). This future observance is confirmed by the prophet Ezekiel (Ezekiel 45:21).

THE ESCAPE AT THE RED SEA
Exodus 14:13-21

AFTER THE PEOPLE OF ISRAEL are freed from Egyptian bondage, Moses leads them to camp between the wilderness and the Red Sea. One last time, Pharaoh hardens his heart and changes his mind, and he decides to send his army to chase after the Israelites. With Egypt's slave labor force set free and departed from their midst, the question arises as to just who would set about the task of rebuilding Egypt's cities from the monumental devastation wrought by the ten plagues sent by YHWH. Pharaoh's change of heart and mobilization of Egypt's great military machine would afford YHWH a final opportunity to impress His glory upon the Egyptian people. Pharaoh mobilizes a vast military force, which is led by 600 of his select charioteers. The king and his army, traveling much faster by chariot than the unwieldy two million Hebrews on foot, quickly approach their former slaves as they camp by the seaside (14:1-9).

In terror and surprise, the people of Israel, noticing the dramatic approach of Pharaoh's army in all its strength, cry out to the Lord. Their prayer, however, is not one of supplication but of protest. They complain to Moses that they would have been better off as Egyptian property. They remind Moses that they had initially rejected his leadership and had asked him not to upset the status quo. They may have been slaves, but it was better to be a living slave than a dead freeman. Typical Jewish ironic humor even becomes apparent when the rhetorical question is asked of Moses

as to the need for the Hebrews to be buried in the desert for want of available graves in Egypt, a nation that prided itself on studding its landscape with the most extravagant and elaborate graves in the world, the pyramids (14:10-12).

Moses responds with a twofold command: "Do not fear! Stand by" (verse 13). He then said the Hebrews would never see the Egyptians again, and the Lord Himself would fight this battle on their behalf. That day they would witness the salvation of the Lord and see the mighty and unprecedented deliverance of His people (verses 13-14).

Apparently Moses then began to intercede before the Lord, but he was interrupted by YHWH. He directs Moses to stop praying and start instructing the Hebrews to press toward the sea. The Lord commands Moses to take his staff and stretch it out over the sea. This would cause the waters to divide and create a pathway of dry ground on which the Hebrews may cross through the midst of the sea and escape. The Lord then hardened not only Pharaoh's heart but also the hearts of his charioteers and military men so that they would be emboldened to follow the Hebrews into the midst of the sea. In this defeat, God's sovereignty over the Egyptians would be clear (14:15-18).

At this time the Shekinah glory, the pillar of dark cloud, moved from its normative position before Israel to behind them, placing itself directly between the camp of the Egyptians and the camp of Israel. The side of the cloud that faced the Egyptian army brought darkness, but the opposite side—facing the rear of the Hebrew camp—shone brightly, enabling the Hebrews to keep traveling all through the night. This allowed the Hebrews—two million men, women, children, and their animals—enough time to cross the pathway through the Red Sea (14:19-20).

The narrative's description of how God parts the Red Sea is surprisingly terse. Rather than cultivating the high spectacle and drama of a climactic cinema scene, the narrative proceeds with matter-of-fact yet athletic prose.

God's salvific activity betrays no hint of divine exertion or strain. When Moses raises his staff over the water, the Lord causes a strong east wind to blow throughout the evening. This gale results in the division of the sea down the center. This miracle has two components: First, there is the separation of the waters themselves. And second, the pathway through the sea is not comprised of the thick mud normally associated with the bottom of a seabed. The Hebrews would never have gotten very far in such muck. Instead, the people cross on dry land, which is quite conducive to rapid travel. The Egyptians are not so fortunate.

THE DESTRUCTION OF THE AMALEKITES
Exodus 17:8-16

THE ORIGIN OF ISRAEL'S four-century-long antagonistic relationship with the nation of Amalek is presented in Exodus 17:8-16. The Amalekites were distantly related to the Hebrews through their common patriarch, Isaac (descended through Esau's son Eliphaz—Genesis 36:12). Although they shared a familial bond as cousins of a sort, the Amalekites "came and fought with Israel in Rephidim" (Exodus 17:8). This is Israel's first military engagement. For details of Amalek's ignominious attack on Israel's vulnerable rear, see Deuteronomy 25:17-19.

Moses, Aaron, and Hur ascend a hilltop to observe the battle. This is no ordinary military campaign. Rather, it is a supernatural expression of Israel's complete dependence on God's provision, the first of many divinely ordained wars to come. As Moses holds up the rod of God, Israel prevails in battle. Conversely, as he lets down his hand, Amalek prevails. The conflict would not be determined by military prowess but by the power of God. A problem arises when Moses' arms become tired and he has difficulty holding them up. He is, after all, 80 years old. Aaron and Hur solve this disability first by providing Moses with a stone on

which to sit, and second by taking a position on either side of him in order to hold up his arms for the remainder of the battle, which continued until nightfall (17:8-12).

With Israel's forces victorious, the Lord instructs Moses to record this event in a book so it would serve as a memorial. This book would have been a scroll, a long strip of leather or papyrus on which scribes wrote in columns (Jeremiah 36:23) with pen (Isaiah 8:1) and ink (Jeremiah 36:18), sometimes on both sides (Ezekiel 2:10; Revelation 5:1). It is essential that Joshua, as military commander and Moses' successor, sustain his awareness of the perpetual enmity between Israel and Amalek. From this point on, the Lord "has it in" for the Amalekites: "I will utterly blot out the memory of Amalek" (Exodus 17:14). The divine curse against the Amalekites is reiterated in Numbers 24:20 and Deuteronomy 25:19.

Enmity between Israel and Amalek continued for approximately four centuries and was acted upon in various conflicts until the might of the Amalekites was definitively broken by kings Saul (1 Samuel 14:48; 15:1-8,32-33) and David (1 Samuel 27:8; 30:1-20; 2 Samuel 8:12). The Lord effectively erased them from the world stage.

THE GIVING OF THE MOSAIC COVENANT
Exodus 19:1–20:21

MOSES HAS NOW DISCHARGED his divine commission to return to Sinai with the liberated Hebrews. This was to be a confirmation to Moses of the Lord's presence (Exodus 3:12). All that now remained was for the people to worship YHWH in this locale, and this chapter focuses on the preparations for corporate worship.

On Mount Sinai, the Lord gives Moses the first message he is to convey to the nation. In passionate language reminiscent of a groom charming his bride, the Lord reminds the Hebrews how He had rescued them and brought them to Himself. The Hebrews are described as the Lord's personal property, His private possession, His treasure. The Lord had specifically chosen this particular group of people with whom to maintain a covenant relationship, and the reason they are so valuable to God relates back to His initial sovereign choice of Abraham and the establishment of His covenant promises, which were made to both the patriarch and his descendants, the nation of Israel.

The Mosaic Covenant is an unconditional gift to His people, but the multiple covenant blessings are completely conditional, dependent upon the peoples' obedience and response. Israel is divinely identified as both a kingdom of priests and a holy nation, and is to remain distinct and separate from all other nations and, at the same time, engage those nations on behalf of YHWH. Possessing a special relationship to YHWH and enjoying singular access to Him, they are to be His holy representatives on the international stage. Just as an individual priest's function is to act as an intermediary between God and man and to make intercession on behalf of others, this corporate nation of priests is commissioned to intercede on behalf of entire nations (19:1-6).

Moses descends the mountain and communicates the Lord's message to Israel's leadership, who then broadcast the message to the people. The nation responds to the Lord's invitation with resounding optimism, saying, "All that the LORD has spoken we will do!" Moses then ascends the mountain to relay the people's response to the Lord (19:7-8).

The Lord then prepares Moses for a public demonstration of His establishment of him as Israel's mediator and intercessor. It is crucial that the entire nation understand Moses and YHWH's unique relationship and accept Moses' divinely sanctioned authority. The Shekinah glory would publicly appear before Moses and converse with him, firmly establishing Moses' credentials in the eyes of the people through what would be an audiovisual object lesson (19:9).

In preparation for the divine manifestation of the Shekinah glory on Mount Sinai, the people would have to go through a purification process. First, they would have two days to prepare, for on the third day the Lord would be manifest upon Sinai. Second, they had to wash themselves and their clothing. Third, they were to abstain from sexual relations to avoid the possibility of finding themselves ritually unclean (Leviticus 15:18; 1 Samuel 21:4-5). Fourth, Sinai was off limits; a boundary line was set around the mountain. Sinai would become holy during the time that the Lord's presence was manifest on it—His manifest holiness instantly transforms any location into holy ground. The penalty for any person or animal making even minimal contact with the mountain would be death by stoning or arrows. Having profaned God's holiness, the violator himself would be off-limits; hence the prescribed forms of noncontact capital punishment. There would be only one period of time when the nation could even approach the mountain—on the third day, when a trumpet (the shofar, a ram's horn) sounded the signal (19:10-13).

On the morning of the third day, the people awaken to a frightening theophany on Mount Sinai. The Shekinah glory appears with thunder and lightning, a thick cloud, the piercing blast of the shofar, and smoke and fire. Indeed, the whole mountain is quaking violently. The author of Hebrews characterized this dramatic scene as one of absolute terror (Hebrews 12:18-21). No wonder the narrative relates that all the people "trembled" with fear (the same Hebrew word used to describe the mountain's violent quaking is used to describe the people's trembling). Moses leads the terrified people out of the camp to meet with God, and they all stand at the foot of the mountain (19:16-18).

As the volume of the shofar continues to increase, Moses speaks, and God answers him audibly, giving Israel the Ten Commandments, or the "ten words" (Hebrew) or the Decalogue (Greek)—the preamble to the total of 613 positive ("thou shalt") and negative ("thou shalt not") commandments that comprise the

Mosaic legislation. These commandments would become the foundation and core of God's Torah, the heart of the Mosaic Covenant. It is not clear how God spoke; He may have answered Moses as thunder or with the trumpet, yet contextually it seems best to conclude that the Lord spoke in an actual intelligible voice. This voice would have been one of inestimable force to have been understood over the violent storm (19:19–20:17).

After this majestic transaction, the Hebrews remain terrified by God's pyrotechnic display of supernatural thunder, lightning, trumpet blowing, and smoke. There is no danger that they will approach the mountain; in fact, they run in the opposite direction because they have had enough of this direct access to YHWH. Fearing for their lives, the Hebrews were ready to return to having Moses serve as their divine intercessor and intermediary. The author of Hebrews mentions Israel's fear of God's voice and the mountain (Hebrews 12:19-20).

Moses tells the people not to fear, and explains that God had given them a healthy dose of holy "shock and awe" that would serve as a corporate deterrent to sin. While the nation maintains its distance from Sinai, Moses draws near to the thick darkness and into God's presence (20:18-21). The additional 603 commandments are studded throughout the remainder of Exodus, as well as within Leviticus, Numbers, and Deuteronomy.

In the New Testament, Paul reveals Israel's need for the Torah, the Mosaic law. The Mosaic Covenant, often misrepresented as a means of salvation, serves rather as a complement to the Abrahamic Covenant to reveal God's standards of obedience for the Israelites to enjoy the promised blessings of the Abrahamic Covenant (Galatians 3:17-21). As Pentecost states, "the Law of Moses was given to *a redeemed people,* not to *redeem a people*" (Pentecost, *Thy Kingdom Come,* p. 87, emphasis in original). And while the Hebrews had been removed from Egypt, it would take time for Egypt to be removed from the Hebrews. The nation's spiritual immaturity necessitated a spiritual primer.

Pentecost summarizes *ten purposes of the law* (Pentecost, *Thy Kingdom Come,* pp. 88–93). First, the law was given to reveal the holiness of God, which was the underlying foundation for the Torah's every requirement. Second, the law was given to provide a basis of comparison between God's holy standards and Israel's behavior. It helped expose Israel's sin as the nation chose to conform or not to conform to God's ethical requirements.

Third, the law was given to reveal God's high ethical standards for those who would enjoy fellowship with Him. Fourth, as Paul said, the law was to serve as Israel's tutor, bringing the people to a sufficient level of spiritual maturity to receive their Messiah through faith (Galatians 3:24). Fifth, the law was given as Israel's national constitution. Sixth, the law was given to maintain Israel's separateness from the corrupting forces of surrounding, idolatrous nations and to provide the basis for Israel's mediation as priests (Exodus 19:5-6) on behalf of those other nations.

Seventh, the law was given to provide a way in which the people could be restored to fellowship after committing sins against God and the community. Individual Israelites "received forgiveness for specific sins through the various offerings that God provided" (Pentecost, *Thy Kingdom Come,* p. 91). Eighth, the law was given to provide instructions to guide Israel's worship. The minutiae of the laws concerning the Levitical priesthood, the tabernacle's structure and service, the weekly Sabbath, the monthly new moons, and the annual cycle of festivals were all given to ensure Israel's regulation of acceptable worship practice.

Ninth, the law was given as a standard to reveal whether an individual Israelite was properly related to the Lord. And tenth, the law was given as a means to prophetically reveal the Messiah to Israel. As this volume reveals, the Torah is studded with messianic prophecy. After all, Jesus is the incarnate Word, the indwelling Torah, to all those who believe (John 1:1).

Although the Torah is "holy and righteous

and good" (Romans 7:12), it was only a temporary provision for Israel that served a purpose and ran a course. Its areas of deficiency, such as its inability to justify an individual (Hebrews 10:4), let alone transform the human heart (Hebrews 10:2), led to its being replaced by the superior New Covenant (Jeremiah 31:31-34; Luke 22:20; Hebrews 7:11-19,22-24,28; 8:6-7).

There are 12 reasons the *New Covenant* is a superior and final replacement for the Mosaic Covenant. Paul provides the first seven reasons:

1. The Messiah is the goal and completion of the Torah (Romans 10:4).

2. Believers are now under grace, not the Torah (Romans 6:14).

3. Believers no longer need a tutor to reveal our innate, terminal sinful condition. That tutor (the law) prescribed that the only antidote and cure to our terminal state is the Messiah (Galatians 3:19–4:7).

4. We who are alive in Christ are necessarily released from the Torah (Romans 7:1-6; 8:2). We were once married, but after a spouse dies, we are free to remarry. We are released from the law and alive in Messiah.

5. The law of Christ (our freedom within the New Covenant) provides liberty in lifestyle for the purpose of winning others (1 Corinthians 9:19-21).

6. The Mosaic law has been nailed to the cross (Colossians 2:14-17). In comparison to the New Covenant, Paul labeled the Torah the ministry of death (2 Corinthians 3:2-11). The New Covenant is a ministry of life!

7. The Mosaic law was abolished for the purpose of uniting Jewish and Gentile believers together in Messiah (Ephesians 2:11-16).

8. Implicit in the very fact of the New Covenant's being promised to Israel is the inferiority of the Old Covenant

it is designed to replace, as well as the fact that the Old Covenant's days are numbered and limited. The deficiencies of the Mosaic Covenant are addressed within the very fabric of the New Covenant (Jeremiah 31:31-34).

9. Jesus came to fulfill the Torah through His perfect obedience, even to the point of death (Matthew 5:17-19).

10. Peter labels the Mosaic law a yoke that Jews cannot bear (Acts 15:9-11).

11. The key argument of the author of Hebrews is that with a new and improved permanent priesthood necessarily comes a new and improved permanent law, yielding a new and improved permanent hope by which to relate to God, who provides a permanent guarantee of a new and improved permanent covenant based upon new and improved promises (7:11-19,22-24,28; 8:6-7).

12. Two millennia ago, the author of Hebrews wrote that the Mosaic Covenant was obsolete, old, and disappearing (8:13). That which was on the verge of disappearing two millennia ago is now completely replaced by a superior covenant.

THE PROMISE OF SUPERNATURAL ASSISTANCE
Exodus 23:20-31

THIS PASSAGE REVEALS THAT the angel of the Lord, a preincarnate manifestation of the second person of the Trinity, will both protect the Israelites and deliver them into their land. This angel must be diligently obeyed. Defiance of Him will result in His refusal to forgive sin. This angel acts with an authority that belongs to God alone—He forgives sins and possesses the divine covenant name; He is a manifestation of YHWH. The reward for obedience to this angel is that He would be the adversary of

Israel's enemies and would personally ensure their defeat (23:20-23).

Once in the land, Israel must never worship idols. Rather, the false gods of Canaan must be utterly destroyed. The five rewards promised for the Hebrews' unwavering allegiance to the true God are the provision of food, the removal of sickness, the avoidance of miscarriages, the absence of barrenness, and personal longevity (23:24-26).

In a breathtaking crescendo of "I wills," God promises that He Himself will be responsible for the expulsion of the Canaanites from the Promised Land. He will be like a swarm of hornets from which the Canaanites would eventually flee. God would not drive out the land's inhabitants all at once or even within the year, but in gradual stages, little by little, to prevent a sudden desolation that would make it possible for the land to become overrun by wild animals. As the Israelites' presence in the land increased, the Canaanites would proportionately decrease until the Hebrews enjoyed their entire geographic inheritance. The seven-year-long campaign of Joshua (1406–1399 B.C.) would wipe out most, but not all, of the land's tenants. The ultimate boundaries of the Promised Land are provided here as the Red Sea on the south, the Mediterranean on the west, the desert (likely present-day Jordan) on the east, and the Euphrates River on the north (23:27-31). These borders, corresponding to the geographic boundaries expressed within the Abrahamic Covenant, will finally be enjoyed by Israel in the messianic kingdom.

Hebrews from Egypt. He reminds God that, despite His current fierce wrath, the Hebrews were still His people. God would not have exerted all the power and effort of freeing the people from Egypt if He did not love them and have a unique relationship with them.

Second, Moses raises the matter of God's reputation among the surrounding Gentile nations, Egypt in particular. If God were to destroy the Hebrews so quickly after the exodus, the Egyptians might well conclude that He removed them from Egypt merely to destroy them. The Egyptians would not respect a god who behaved in that sort of cruel and arbitrary fashion.

Third, Moses brought up God's solemn covenant oaths to the patriarchs concerning both seed (Genesis 15:5; 22:17; 26:4; 28:14; 32:13) and land (Genesis 15:18-21; 22:17; 26:4; 28:13; 32:13). Throughout their relationship, from the burning bush onward, YHWH had always taken great pains to emphasize His identity as the promise-keeping God who remembers the Abrahamic Covenant, not a promise breaker and capricious adjuster of covenants.

YHWH responds favorably to Moses' petition and adjusts His course of action accordingly. This passage is an excellent reminder that while the Lord's character is unchanging, He does respond and may alter the course of future events to suit His plan.

THE NATURE OF THE ABRAHAMIC COVENANT
Exodus 32:11-14

ISRAEL'S GROSS REBELLION at Sinai with the golden calf places Moses in the position of intercessor. Moses immediately appeals to God for mercy, interceding on Israel's behalf by using three lines of argument. First, Moses points to God's recent deliverance of the

LEVITICUS

LEVITICUS IS SATURATED WITH affirmations of God's holiness and directives as to the development and maintenance of Israel's holiness. And amid the book's plethora of regulatory prescriptions relating to holiness are three weighty passages of notable prophetic consequence.

TYPOLOGY AND THE DAY OF ATONEMENT
Leviticus 16

LEVITICUS 16:1-34, WHICH PROVIDES a description of the high priest's activities on the Day of Atonement, coupled with the broad congregational duties for the holy day outlined in Leviticus 23:26-32, imparts a complex portrait of the most sacred day on Israel's liturgical calendar. This holy day falls on Tishri 10, ten days after the Feast of Trumpets. The purpose of this day is to make atonement for the sanctuary, the tabernacle, the congregation, the altar, the priests, and the people of Israel. It is a time for a national confession for sins not confessed and forgiven throughout the year, a reminder that the normal everyday sacrifices were insufficient to atone for sin (Leviticus 16:29-34).

As to congregational responsibilities (Leviticus 23:26-32), on this day absolutely no labor of any kind is to be performed. In fact, the performance of any work is an infraction of capital consequence. This day is to function like a Sabbath of Sabbaths (Hebrew, *shabbat shabbaton*), a super-Sabbath. The Israelites are to humble their souls (verses 29,31), or practice self-denial, primarily through a fast, a complete avoidance of food and water for a 25-hour period (an additional hour is added to the day at the front end according to Leviticus 23:32).

The Day of Atonement (Hebrew, *Yom Kippurim*), commonly called Yom Kippur, is more accurately translated as the "Day of Coverings." The term *kippurim* conveys a slightly different nuance than what is normally understood as the meaning of the theological term *atonement*. *Kippurim* does not denote the removal of sins as much as the covering over of them. *Yom Kippurim* refers to the great "holy carpet" under which God swept Israel's sins during His annual fall cleaning. However, regardless of how meticulously dirt is swept under a rug, the dirt is still there, merely having been covered over.

This is an illustration of how the Day of Atonement worked. The covering for the sin of God's people was blood, the symbol of life, for "it is the blood...that makes atonement" (Leviticus 17:11). A basic yet vital concept of Scripture is that without blood there can be no atonement. Blood is the only means of covering, or atonement, that the Bible recognizes.

God established a relationship with His chosen people, Israel. Yet the Jewish people, being human, were prone to sin. This propensity to sin put a crimp in their relationship with God. God, in His grace, gave Israel the sacrificial system in order to restore their relationship, to cover over their sin on an annual basis. Each year the Israelites received a clean slate, a fresh start before God, a re-covering.

Of course, Israel's annual atonement lasted only as long as individuals remained free from committing sinful acts. After dirt is swept under a carpet, the carpet remains clean only until it inevitably becomes resoiled. The day after all the elaborate and meticulous rituals on the Day of Atonement, the daily and weekly Levitical sacrifices immediately recommenced.

The central chapter within Leviticus, chapter 16, is devoted almost entirely to enumerating the high priest's holy day rituals and practices. The chapter commences with the clear affirmation that only one man, Israel's high priest, could approach God. And while the high priest is the only individual authorized to approach the divine presence, he is not free to do so anytime he wants or any way he desires. The high priest could only enter God's presence on the day and in the manner that God had approved. Any deviation would mean certain death (16:1-2). The high priest represented the people of Israel before God, and the portentous responsibility of their atonement rested squarely upon his priestly shoulders. On the Day of Atonement, Israel's most sacred figure could enter into the nation's most sacred place to perform its most sacred rituals on its most sacred day.

After performing the standard morning sacrifice in beautiful, golden robes, the high priest sets the robes aside and, after the first of several ritual washings throughout the day, exchanges them for a simple white linen garment similar to that of an ordinary priest.

The high priest would then sacrifice a male bull for himself, his family, and his fellow priests. Prior to making atonement for the people, he first had to take care of his own sin. Placing two hands upon the bull's head, he made confession for himself and his family (16:3-6). Following the bull's sacrifice, the blood would be collected in a bowl and carried by an assistant priest into the temple, being stirred all the while so that it did not coagulate. Concurrently, the high priest filled an incense censer with burning coals from the altar of sacrifice and carried the censer into the temple, solemnly approaching the Holy of Holies.

Then came time for a special lottery, in which two fairly identical goats were brought before the high priest. The priest would put his hands into a box where there were two lots, small tablets on which were written the Hebrew words *l'YHWH* ("to the Lord"), and *l'azazel* ("removal"). The high priest would pull out the lots to determine the fates of the goats. The lot on the right was assigned to the goat on the right, the one on the left to the goat on the left. The one designated as "to the Lord" was destined for sacrifice, and the one designated to *l'azazel*, commonly referred to as the scapegoat, would be driven out into the wilderness (16:7-10).

After the high priest sacrificed the goat designated "to the Lord" on behalf of the nation, he reentered the Holy of Holies for a third time and sprinkled the blood of the goat in the Holy of Holies. Then he picked up the bowl containing the bull's blood and sprinkled the veil outside the Holy of Holies. He would then purify the altar of sacrifice by mixing together the blood from the sacrificed bull and goat. These rituals served to "reboot" the altar, the tabernacle or temple, and the congregation of Israel for a fresh year (16:15-19).

The high priest would then turn his attention to the second goat. By placing his hands on the goat's head and making public confession on behalf of all Israel, the high priest transferred the sins, transgressions, and iniquities of the nation onto the scapegoat. The goat now served as a substitute for the Jewish people.

The scapegoat was then escorted by another priest outside of the camp and far into the wilderness, where it was to be set free (16:20-22). By New Testament times, however, this changed. The scapegoat was escorted outside of Jerusalem and into the Judean desert. To assuage the nations' nagging fear of the possibility that the scapegoat, having had Israel's sins transferred upon it, might somehow find his way back into the midst of Israel, an innovation had been added so as to remove all doubt. The goat was led to a high cliff and driven off to remove all possibility of return.

Of all Israel's holy days, only the Passover demonstrates a close connection between Jesus and one of the feasts. The main thrust of the New Testament letter to the Hebrews is to portray Jesus as the fulfillment of the Day of Atonement. In chapters 2, 7, 9, and 10, two facets of this connection are explored.

The initial way that the Day of Atonement has been fulfilled is through Jesus serving as God's perfect High Priest. Hebrews tells us that Jesus became "a merciful and faithful high priest…to make propitiation for the sins of the people" (Hebrews 2:17). In Israel's history, high priests came and went as they died or were replaced for political purposes. Jesus, as a resurrected High Priest, will minister permanently. There is not one moment of any day when Christ is not serving as High Priest. Therefore, our salvation is secured eternally (Hebrews 7:23).

The author of Hebrews continues this theme, arguing that Jesus is the perfect High Priest. He had no need to first make a sacrifice for Himself before He could minister on our behalf because He Himself was a perfect, sinless sacrifice. Furthermore, unlike animal sacrifices, His sacrifice did not need to be continually offered on a daily, weekly, or annual basis, but was a perfect offering for the total and complete eradication of sin once and for all (Hebrews 7:26; 9:25-26).

In addition, Jesus does not serve as High Priest within a sanctuary "made with [human] hands, a mere copy of the true one" (Hebrews 9:24). Jesus' high priesthood functions within the Holy Place in heaven itself. The Holy of Holies in which He enters is the heavenly presence of God. The atoning blood that this High Priest bears is not the inferior blood of animals but His own blood, the blood of the Messiah (Hebrews 9:11,24).

The connection between Jesus and the high priest on the Day of Atonement runs still deeper. Just as the high priest exchanged his normative, glorious garments for humble robes, so too did Jesus exchange His glory for humble human flesh (Philippians 2:5-8). Furthermore, no weeklong, all-night study sessions were necessary for this High Priest, nor was an understudy waiting in the wings. He had no need to memorize the Word of God; He is the incarnate Word of God.

The second facet of Jesus' typological fulfillment of the Day of Atonement, according to Hebrews, is as God's perfect sacrifice. Not only is Jesus the perfect High Priest, He also offered up blood superior to that possessed by bulls and goats. Animal blood could only cover up sin and never completely remove it. The Messiah's sacrifice, by contrast, thoroughly sanctifies us in the sight of God. This perfect sacrifice, indeed, makes us holy. No Levitical high priest could possibly pretend that his sins were definitively dealt with on the Day of Atonement. He only cleansed the external, the flesh. The fact that the Day of Atonement sacrifices had to be repeated annually proved that they were insufficient. If they had truly cleansed sin, they would not have needed to be done again and again. The rituals contained an abbreviated expiration date. However, Jesus, offering the perfect sacrifice, cleansed the heart as well (Hebrews 10:1-10).

The author of Hebrews also sees a typological connection between Jesus and the disposing of the bodies of the slain bull and goat. Just as it was necessary for their bodies to be burned outside the camp (or city), so too, Jesus, bearing Israel's (and the world's) sin, suffered and was executed outside the walls of Jerusalem (Hebrews 13:10-14). Interestingly, in a stunning foreshadowing of the circumstances surrounding Jesus' sacrifice (Isaiah 50:6), the Mishnah records the Jewish population's usual abusive hitting and plucking out of the second goat's (scapegoat) hair as the doomed animal departed the city (Mishnah, *Yoma* 6:4).

A final typological fulfillment of the Day of Atonement will occur during the Tribulation, "the time of Jacob's distress" (Jeremiah 30:7), when the nation of Israel will experience an unprecedented affliction of both body and soul. However, the Tribulation will powerfully conclude with Israel's repentance and salvation at the very moment of miraculous rescue by its Messiah at His second coming (Zechariah 12:1–13:1).

TYPOLOGY AND THE FEASTS OF ISRAEL
Leviticus 23

ISRAEL'S SEVEN HOLY FEASTS listed together in Leviticus 23:1-44 and in the parallel passage Numbers 28:16–29:40 (which contains further sacrificial details), are often called "the feasts of Israel." They are better thought of by using the terminology employed throughout this passage (23:2,4,37,44): "the LORD's appointed times" or "the appointed times of the LORD." These dates were to be "holy convocations" (Hebrew, *miqra*), solemn occasions in which the Levitical worship system of priests and sacrifices, based within the tabernacle (and later the temple), would play the significant role. Usually, some degree of congregational participation was also required.

The seven holy feasts can be subdivided into a *spring cycle* comprising the initial four holy days, and a *fall cycle* comprising the remaining three feasts, with a three-and-a-half month break between the two cycles. It is essential to note that the Lord specifically refers to these feasts as "*His* appointed times" (23:1-2,4); these festivals are correctly viewed as belonging to the Lord just as they belong to Israel.

Prior to enumerating the seven holy feasts, the Lord summarizes the specific appointed time that Israel is to observe throughout the entirety of the annual cycle, the weekly Sabbath, which still had to be observed regardless of whether it fell, as it often did, in direct conjunction with one of the seven holy feasts.

The *Sabbath* (Hebrew, *shabbat*, which means "to cease, desist, rest") is mentioned 111 times within the Old Testament, and an additional 67 times within the New Testament. On this day, the priests were to double the quantity of the normal tabernacle sacrifices (Numbers 28:9-10). Most critically, however, the people of Israel were to remain in their dwellings and enjoy a complete rest (Hebrew, *shabbat shabbaton*) and cessation of all labor (23:3). The only Israelites who were exempt from this mandatory cessation of labor within the confines of their own neighborhood were the priests functioning within the tabernacle.

The first two of the seven main appointed times, *Passover* and the *Feast of Unleavened Bread,* occur together in the spring (23:5-8). (For more on this, see commentary on Exodus 12:1-36,39,46-47.)

The observance of the holy day of *Firstfruits,* the third of the seven main appointed times, was agricultural in nature. This feast was not to be observed during the wilderness wanderings, but was to commence only after Israel had settled into the land of promise. On this holy day, a sheaf of barley, the firstfruits of the barley harvest, was given to the priest to wave before the altar. The priest would then retain the sheaf for his personal enjoyment. In addition to the waving of the sheaf, a year-old, unblemished lamb was sacrificed for a burnt offering, and offerings were made of both grain and wine. The instructions for this day conclude with the prohibition on consumption of any produce of the barley harvest until the firstfruits sheaf had been presented before the Lord within the sanctuary (23:9-14).

There is a typological connection between Jesus and the day of Firstfruits that was fulfilled by Jesus' resurrection. During the events of the gospels and Acts, the Jewish religious leaders known as the Sadducees were in control of temple worship. This means that their system of determining the Feast of Weeks date was probably in place at the time, meaning that both Jesus' resurrection and the Pentecost events described in Acts 2 fell on Sundays, 50 days apart. Later, following the destruction of the temple in A.D. 70, the Jewish leaders known as Pharisees determined the Feast of

Weeks date, using a methodology that differed from the one used by the Sadducees.

Specifically, if the Sadducees' reckoning was the accepted practice in the year of Jesus' crucifixion (universally accepted as falling between A.D. 29–33), then Jesus' resurrection on Sunday, Nisan 17, would have corresponded with Israel's observance of Firstfruits. If, however, the Pharisees' reckoning held sway (and Josephus indicates that it did, *Antiquities* III, x 5; 250, 96), then Jesus' resurrection would have occurred on the day following Firstfruits. Since the initial day of the Feast of Unleavened Bread fell on Friday, Nisan 15, then, according to the Pharisees' methodology, the offering of Firstfruits would have occurred on Saturday, Nisan 16, while Jesus was yet in His tomb.

But whether Firstfruits was recognized in that particular year as occurring on Saturday, Nisan 16, or Sunday, Nisan 17, Jesus' resurrection still prophetically fulfilled the holy occasion. On this subject the teaching of Paul possesses indisputable clarity:

> Now Christ has been raised from the dead, the first fruits of those who are asleep. For since by a man came death, by a man also came the resurrection of the dead. For as in Adam all die, so also in Christ all will be made alive. But each in his own order: Christ the first fruits, after that those who are Christ's at His coming (1 Corinthians 15:20-23).

Firstfruits is also used typologically within the New Testament in reference to the believers' possession of the Holy Spirit (Romans 8:23) and to Jewish believers in Jesus, both contemporary (James 1:18) and future (Revelation 14:4).

The fourth of Israel's holy feasts, and the last holy day of the spring cycle, is the *Feast of Weeks* (23:15-21). This was one of the "big three" pilgrimage festivals when, as during Passover and Tabernacles, every Jewish male was commanded to worship at the tabernacle or temple (Deuteronomy 16:16). In Deuteronomy 16:9-10, the holiday is designated as *Hag Hashavuot*, "the Festival of Weeks." This

name *Shavuot* was so designated because seven weeks, or 50 days, are counted down from the determinative day falling within the week of Passover and the Feast of Unleavened Bread (see earlier discussion concerning the date of Firstfruits) until the arrival of this holiday. The name *Pentecost* (Greek, *pentekoste*, "fifty"), was used interchangeably with the Hebrew *Shavuot*. The holiday is referenced as *Pentecost* three times within the New Testament.

The Feast of Weeks is also called *Hag Hakatzir*, "the Feast of Harvest" (Exodus 23:16). This day marks the end of the barley harvest, which began at Passover, and the initial ripening of the wheat harvest. Yet another designation is *Yom Habikkurim*, "the Day of the Firstfruits" (Numbers 28:26). Again, this is the firstfruits of the wheat harvest of summer, not the Passover Feast of Unleavened Bread week's firstfruits offering of the barley harvest, as previously discussed. Similar to its companion holiday, Firstfruits, the date of the Feast of Weeks may only be determined in relation to the date of Firstfruits.

At the conclusion of this 50-day countdown, each family brought an offering of two leavened loaves of wheat bread to the Temple. These loaves were baked from the firstfruits of the wheat harvest. These leavened loaves were to be waved before the altar of the Lord. It is important to note that these loaves, being leavened, were neither burnt nor offered on the altar; this would have violated the staunch prohibition against the offering of leaven, which represents sin. In fact, some say that these leavened loaves were representative of the worshippers' sinfulness.

The New Testament boldly records the prophetic fulfillment of this holy day in Acts 2. In Acts 2:1, Luke purposely chose the term *sumpleroo*, which means "to completely fulfill," to indicate that what he related was the prophetic consummation of this biblical feast.

The events of Pentecost, as described by Luke in Acts 2 some 1500 years after Israel's Sinai experience, are the God-directed sequel to the foundational events related by Moses. Luke's description of the Holy Spirit's supernatural manifestation among the apostles within the temple resembles Moses' description of God's Shekinah glory manifest on Mount Sinai (Exodus 19:18). The Holy Spirit, so long absent from the temple, was once again gloriously manifesting Himself in the midst of Israel.

This was a direct fulfillment of John the Baptist's prophecy that the Messiah would baptize with the Holy Spirit as well as with fire (Matthew 3:11). This also fulfilled Jesus' promise, given some seven weeks earlier on Passover at the Last Supper, that He would send the Comforter, the Teacher (John 14:26; 16:7-15). Additionally, this was the empowering event that Jesus had told His apostles to anticipate (Acts 1:4-8).

The pouring out of God's Holy Spirit on Pentecost would have been profoundly appreciated by Jewish recipients. The anniversary of the divine gift of the Torah was the most eloquent of moments for the revelation of the divine Spirit. This was indeed the logical sequel to the Sinai experience. The God who came near on Sinai had now come near as He indwelled believers with His Spirit.

The Spirit's presence in the temple at Pentecost was marked by three signs similarly experienced at Sinai: violent wind, fire, and supernatural sounds. In Acts 2:1-3 Luke described the wind and the fire, and in 2:4 he mentioned the supernatural sounds. The result of this outpouring of the Spirit was the apostles' newly acquired supernatural ability to communicate "with other tongues" (2:4), or in known, intelligible spoken languages. From this point on, the apostles would be empowered as witnesses whom Christ had commissioned.

On this Pentecost, there was indeed something new under the sun—the birth of the church, the beginning of a new era. From this point on, all believers would be permanently indwelled by the Spirit, forever united with Christ and each other.

Pentecost reminds us that God has personally engraved His righteous standards on our hearts by His Spirit (Jeremiah 31:31-33). He has given His Spirit to indwell us permanently, enabling immediate and direct access to the Father. He has provided the perfect Intercessor: the great High Priest, Jesus, the incarnation of the Torah (John 1:1). Unlike Moses or the Levitical priests, this intermediary is no mere middleman; He is God Himself in human flesh. We now have the eternal, abiding presence of Immanuel, God with us.

Finally, the two leavened loaves which were customarily presented on Pentecost prophetically prefigured the church, a church that is composed of two groups, Jews and Gentiles, both of whom are leavened, sinful, and desperately in need of the indwelling Holy Spirit.

Fruchtenbaum sees Leviticus 23:22 as referencing a prophetic interval between Israel's spring and fall cycles (*Leviticus,* cassette tape lectures, cassette 11). This interval is currently being fulfilled in the present church age, which is characterized by labor in a harvest of "the needy and the alien" (Gentiles).

The *Feast of Trumpets* (23:23-25) is the initial holy day of the three festivals of Israel's fall cycle. Each of the three festivals occurs successively within the seventh month, Tishri. The Feast of Trumpets is the seventh and most solemn new moon observance of the year (seven being the biblical number of perfection).

Moses reveals very little about this day, with neither Leviticus nor Numbers providing even a complete name or motivating reason for this day. Unlike most of the Jewish festivals, the Feast of Trumpets is not biblically linked to any historical deliverance or agricultural occasion. It was a one-day celebration, to be observed as a Sabbath, on which tabernacle offerings were presented by the priests and no labor was to be carried out among the people. The word *trumpets* itself must be supplied by the context, as it does not even appear within the original Hebrew text, which merely has a phrase that translates to "a memorial of blowing" (Hebrew, *zikhron teru'ah*).

As to what the memorial was to commemorate, the text is similarly silent. God's silence in this matter, however, proved motivational to the ancient rabbis, who wasted no time before assigning various meanings to this biblical mystery. They called this holiday *Yom Ha-Din,* "the Day of Judgment," and *Yom Ha-Zikhraron,* "the Day of Remembrance," creatively recognizing the day as the anniversary of the world's creation, on which God annually judges His people for their sin and inscribes their fate for the impending year (see further discussion in commentary on Psalm 69:28).

Annually, at the outset of the ten-day period of divine judgment bracketed by the two holy days, the Feast of Trumpets and the Day of Atonement, known collectively as the "Days of Awe," three scrolls (or books) are opened in the heavenly courts. One scroll is designated for the completely righteous, who are inscribed in the "book of life." Another scroll is designated for the thoroughly reprobate, who are immediately recorded in the "book of death." And a third scroll is designated for the temporary inscription of the names of the vast majority of Jews, those somewhere in between the states of thoroughly righteous and reprobate.

As to the trumpet itself, the shofar (ram's horn) retains great significance within Jewish theology and practice. The shofar is the only biblical musical instrument still utilized within the Jewish synagogue worship service. Today the shofar is blown every day for 30 days in preparation for the Feast of Trumpets. On the day itself, a total of 100 blasts are blown on the shofar. The final, dramatic series of blasts blown during the service, urgently calling the congregation, one final time, to repentance, is called the *tekiah gedolah,* the "great trumpet." The theme of the festival could be summarized as "repent, for the kingdom of God is at hand."

The Feast of Trumpets is typologically prophetic of two messianic events, one related to the church and the other related to Israel. Both events are connected to the supernatural blowing of the shofar. For the church, Paul taught that a supernatural blowing of the shofar would occur with the rapture:

The Lord Himself will descend from heaven with a shout, with the voice of the archangel and with the trumpet of God, and the dead in Christ will rise first. Then we who are alive and remain will be caught up together with them in the clouds to meet the Lord in the air (1 Thessalonians 4:13-18).

We will not all sleep, but we will all be changed, in a moment, in the twinkling of an eye, at the last trumpet; for the trumpet will sound, and the dead will be raised imperishable, and we will be changed (1 Corinthians 15:51-55).

Both the resurrection of dead believers and the drawing up into the air of living believers to meet Christ are precipitated by the supernatural blowing of God's shofar.

For Israel, the supernatural blast of the shofar announces the nation's final regathering in the land. Isaiah wrote that "it will come about also in that day that a great trumpet will be blown, and those who were perishing in the land of Assyria and who were scattered in the land of Egypt will come and worship the LORD in the holy mountain at Jerusalem" (Isaiah 27:13). Jesus affirmed the prophet's teaching, promising the disciples that God "will send forth His angels with a great trumpet and they will gather together His elect from the four winds, from one end of the sky to the other" (Matthew 24:31). This event will follow Israel's mass repentance and belief in the Messiah when they see Him return (Zechariah 9:14; 12:10).

Today, this holy day is observed as the Jewish New Year, and is most commonly referred to as *Rosh Hashanah,* "the head of the year."

The Feast of Trumpets is followed ten days later by Israel's sixth holy festival, the *Day of Atonement* (23:26-32). (For more on this, see commentary on Leviticus 16:1-34.)

The final festival in Israel's fall cycle is the *Feast of Booths* (Hebrew, *sukkot*). Its popular name, Tabernacles, is derived from Latin. This festival begins on Tishri 15, five days after the Day of Atonement. This is a seven-day feast, with one extra day tacked on at the end for spiritual punctuation. It is the seventh feast and it occurs in the seventh month. As seven is the biblical number of perfection and completion, the Feast of Booths serves as the culmination of every one of God's appointed times for the year (23:33-44). There are a tremendous number of sacrifices necessary for this eight-day feast, which is exceeded only by the number of sacrifices necessary for celebrating the Passover (Numbers 29:12-38). Confirming the importance of the number seven in relation to this holiday, the quantity of sacrifices for the Feast of Booths is divisible by seven.

Every Israelite family was commanded to construct a *sukkah* (singular of *sukkot*), a booth or hut, to commemorate perpetually how God led the nation for 40 years in the desert. Although the biblical command is to live in these homemade backyard kiosks for seven days, today most Jewish people fulfill the command by eating at least one meal a day inside the *sukkah*. The particularly observant will sleep in them as well.

The Feast of Booths is also known as the *Feast of Ingathering* (Exodus 23:16). It is the last of the agricultural feasts and celebrates the third harvest of the year, the grain harvest (the other two biblical harvest festivals being Firstfruits and Weeks). The Israelites were commanded to assemble and bring their crops to the central location of worship, the tabernacle (and later, the temple). They were to bring a tenth of their produce, or the monetary equivalent. This was one of the three mandatory pilgrimages feasts, along with Passover/the Feast of Unleavened Bread and Pentecost.

The Feast of Booths, in New Testament times, was characterized by tremendous expectation for the Messiah as well as the *Ruach Hakodesh,* the Holy Spirit. A theological connection was made between the experience of religious joy and possession of the Holy Spirit. This connection took ritual form within the holy festival's ceremony of water drawing, the *Simchat Beit Hashoavah*. Although this tradition is not found in Scripture, by the time of Jesus, the ceremony had become the highlight of *Sukkot* and perhaps the most important element of the temple festivities.

The ceremony was accentuated by dancing, singing, and music. The worshippers were considered, by their very acts of worship, to be inspired by the Holy Spirit. The Spirit, according to the ancient rabbis, could only be received by those whose hearts were full of religious joy. Throughout the seven days of the festival, a procession of priests, flute players, and crowds of people brought water in a golden pitcher from the pool of Siloam, at the foot of Jerusalem and carried it to a basin at the altar in the temple. The high priest would take the pitcher, ascend a ramp to reach the top of the altar, and pour out the water, which symbolized the outpouring of the Holy Spirit on the people of Israel.

In the midst of this water pouring, trumpet blasting, palm waving, psalm chanting, and joy on the last day, Jesus entered the temple courts. Interrupting the festivities, He invited the whole assembly of Israel (Pharisees, Sadducees, the Sanhedrin, all 24 divisions of priests and Levites, and the high priest, Caiaphas himself) to come to Him and thereby drink of the living water, the Holy Spirit, which only He (and pointedly, not the Jewish leadership) could provide. It is unmistakable that Jesus was boldly declaring His messianic identity to all present (John 7:37-39). The various reactions to his proclamation clearly show that they got the message (John 7:40-52). Jesus chose this particular feast to reveal publicly that He was Messiah and boldly taught in the temple that this celebration was fulfilled in Him.

Many see the fulfillment of these two seasonal cycles in the first and second advents of the Messiah. Regarding the *four-feast spring cycle,* Jesus has fulfilled Passover by becoming our Passover. He fulfilled the Feast of Unleavened Bread through His sinless offering, and the Feast of Firstfruits through His resurrection. Pentecost was fulfilled through the church's receipt of the eternal, indwelling Holy Spirit.

Regarding the *three-feast fall cycle,* the Feast of Trumpets is typological of Christ's returning for His church at the rapture and the regathering of Israel at the advent of the messianic age. *Yom Kippur,* the Day of Atonement, is typological of Christ's atoning work on the cross and His victorious second coming, when all Israel will be saved by placing their faith in their Messiah. Finally, the Feast of Booths is typological of the Messiah's incarnation and gift of His Spirit, and will find complete fulfillment in the establishment of His great millennial kingdom. The Festival of Ingathering points to an era when God gathers in His harvest, all those who believe, both Jews and Gentiles together.

COVENANT BLESSINGS AND CURSES
Leviticus 26:3-45

LEVITICUS 26:3-45 CONTAINS a catalog of the Mosaic Covenant's blessings and curses, parallel to and overlapping the similar passage of Deuteronomy 28:1-68 (see also the commentary on Deuteronomy 29:1–30:20). In line with Deuteronomy 28, as well as other contemporary suzerain-vassal treaties, the curses here consume proportionately three times more literary real estate than do the blessings. However, contrary to custom, as in Deuteronomy, the blessings are listed prior to the curses, an indication of God's love for Israel and desire to bless them.

Ross (*Holiness to the Lord,* p. 467) provides a useful definition of blessing as "some gift, some enrichment of life, or some enablement for prosperity that comes from God." Unlike the nature of the blessings attached to the unconditional Abrahamic Covenant, the blessings of the conditional Mosaic Covenant were each dependent for realization on Israel's obedience to the stipulations of the Mosaic Covenant ("if you walk [Hebrew, *halak*] in My statutes and keep [Hebrew, *shamar*] My commandments"—26:3). The Lord's goal was to elevate Israel above all other nations, but He would not bless them indiscriminately or without their cooperation. The people of Israel would reap what they had sown, for better or worse, blessing or curse. The enjoyment of every blessing depended on Israel's obedience to the covenant through which those blessings emanated.

The introduction to the covenant blessings and curses contain three of the Torah's foundational requirements for maintaining Israel's holiness. First is a prohibition against idolatry (Exodus 20:4-6), second is the observance of the Sabbath, and third is ample reverence of Levitical tabernacle worship (26:1-2).

At verse 14 the passage segues from blessings to curses. Every curse is conditioned upon Israel's covenantal disobedience. Disobedience and infidelity to the Mosaic Covenant will yield the exact opposite of the previously enumerated blessings (26:14-15). YHWH will not be snubbed by His people. The terms used here, "reject" (Hebrew, *ma'as*) and "abhor" (Hebrew, *ga'al*), convey the strongest level of faithlessness and contempt. In meting out these curses upon Israel, the blessings the nation had previously experienced would reverse, unraveling one by one. Indeed, the curses seem to be simply a removal of the blessings, the realistic outworking of the absence of divine intervention in the daily life of Israel.

Although Israel was to experience a limited measure of these curses during the Assyrian and Babylonian oppressions, the nation did not experience the totality of these curses until their two revolts against Rome in A.D. 70 and A.D. 135. Sadly, the prediction concerning Israel's perpetually tenuous situation in their dispersion has unquestionably proven accurate for the past two millennia.

The passage describing the curses closes with a curious explanation for the continuance of Israel's suffering. The text states that the Jewish people will continue to suffer not merely for the sins of their distant ancestors, whose behavior triggered Israel's dispersion from the land, but also for their own sin committed while in exile (26:39). Because the

Jewish people were exiled from their land by the Romans in A.D. 70 and A.D. 135, the only specific sin that could sufficiently satisfy the text's double criteria for both ancient Israelites to have committed in the land and for their subsequent descendants to continue to have committed outside the land would be the sin of rejecting their Messiah, Jesus.

The identification of the rejection of Jesus as Israel's critical and ultimate act of covenant infidelity is confirmed in the next passage, which mentions Israel's eventual restoration (26:40-45). Leviticus 26:40 provides the transition, expressing the prophetic certainty that a particular generation of Israel will confess (Hebrew, *v'hitvadu*) their iniquities as well as one particular iniquity (Hebrew, *avon,* singular) of their ancestors. The one specific sin that must be confessed that was committed by both their ancestors and continued by the current generation was the rejection of the Messiah.

Sometimes the interpretation of an entire passage comes down to the translation of one ostensibly trifling preposition, or lack thereof, within a single verse. So it is in the instance of Leviticus 26:40. What is at stake here is whether Israel's restoration ultimately rests on the condition of their obedience, or rather, on the Lord's sovereign initiative. Specifically, there is no grammatical or contextual reason to go beyond the actual Hebrew text and insert a conditional particle in order to translate the text with the reading "but if they confess" as do the KJV, NASB, and NIV translations.

Israel's future international movement of *repentance* and subsequent *restoration* are not mere possibilities. Rather, the unadorned, plain Hebrew text affirms that Israel's resto-

ration is a prophetic certainty. It will occur during the Tribulation, just prior to the establishment of the Messiah's reign and the millennial kingdom. Therefore, the translation of 26:40 should commence as "*when* they confess" (see NET) or "*and* they shall confess" (see ASV, Tanakh, JPS [Jewish Publication Society Bible]). At long last, with newly "circumcised hearts" the people of Israel will recognize that their long suffering was a result of faithlessness to the Lord.

This repentance will prove all that is necessary for the Lord to restore His chosen people to the place of blessing that is promised in the Abrahamic Covenant. The Lord's unconditional commitment to the patriarchs will, at last, trump the Mosaic Covenant's conditioned judgments. In fact, this passage contains a final set of "I wills" (26:42,45), plus one resounding, forceful "I will not" (reject or destroy Israel) in 26:44. Israel will never be completely rejected by the Lord or totally annihilated. The Abrahamic Covenant is inviolate and therefore, regardless of how dire the nation's straits become, a remnant of Israel will always be divinely preserved upon whom the Lord may lavish His restorative blessings. Therefore, the Jewish nation will be restored to the land, which had been desolate in their absence. The passage concludes with a reminder that just as Israel's original redemption in the exodus from Egypt had as its basis the Abrahamic Covenant, so too will their final restoration.

See also the commentary on the parallel and overlapping expanded text of Deuteronomy 29:1–30:20 for further comments on the prophetic fulfillment of God's promised restoration of His chosen people.

NUMBERS

The book of Numbers contains the census of the exodus population and tells the story of Israel's 40-year wilderness journey through the Sinai desert. Included are several prophecies regarding Moses, Aaron, and the future of Israel. These include the amazing prophetic oracles of Balaam, who blesses Israel and predicts the rise of the star of Jacob against his own will (24:17).

TYPOLOGY AND THE PASSOVER
Numbers 9:1-4

See the commentary on Exodus 12:1-36, 39,46-47.

A WARNING TO THE EXODUS GENERATION
Numbers 14:20-34

When the people of Israel finished their journey from Egypt to the Promised Land, 12 spies are sent into the land to scout it out. When the spies return, ten of them said, "We are not able to go up against the people, for they are too strong for us" (Numbers 13:31). This negative report resulted in Israel's wholesale rebellion against the Lord (Numbers 14:1-10). The nation's wanton disbelief in the Lord's ability to fulfill His promise to give them possession of the Promised Land, coupled with its unashamed rejection of Moses' leadership, yielded bitter fruit. Although the Lord expressed a desire to exterminate the entire nation (Numbers 14:12), Moses' subsequent intercession on their behalf produced divine pardon, sparing the nation (14:20).

Nonetheless, divine forgiveness did not mitigate the nation's need for divine punishment. Indeed, their rebellion could not be ignored or forgotten. Israel's grievous sin still necessitated the suffering of grave consequences. The exodus generation, having been eyewitness to the Lord's power and participant in His miracles, was completely without excuse. The Lord's intention of national destruction was replaced with His double-edged judgment of generational loss of both land and life.

The Lord charges His people with both disobedience ("have not listened to My voice") and having "put Me to the test these ten times" (14:22). In addition to this rebellion at Kadesh-Barnea (Numbers 13–14), Jewish tradition (Babylonian Talmud, *Arakin* 15b) delineates these nine additional rebellious incidents: the testing of the Lord at the Red Sea (Exodus 14:10-12), at Marah (Exodus 15:23-24), in the Wilderness of Sin (Exodus 16:2), twice regarding the handling of manna (Exodus 16:20,27-28), at the waters of Rephidim (Exodus 17:1-7), at Sinai in the golden calf incident (Exodus 32:1-35), at Taberah (Numbers 11:1-3), and at Kibroth-hattaavah (Numbers 11:4-34). Although the Talmud's list of rebellions is not completely exhaustive, it does serve well as a summary of divine indictment.

As a result of the nation's blatant faithlessness, none of the exodus generation, the adult population divinely liberated from Egyptian slavery (all those aged 20 or older, numbered in the census described in 1:1-46), would be allowed possession or even entry into the land of promise. Instead, they would wander in the wilderness for the next 38 years (Deuteronomy 2:14) until the entirety of their generation died, with the exceptions of "Caleb the son of Jephunneh and Joshua the son of Nun" (Numbers 14:30). These two faithful men, alone of their generation, would possess the land (Joshua 14:6-15; 24:29-30; Judges 1:11-15).

Unavoidably, the wilderness generation, the children of the exodus generation, would likewise share in their parents' punishment as they wandered outside the land alongside their parents. Eventually, however, at the appointed time, the children would possess their inheritance. The divine judge is not remiss in highlighting that the children, whom their faithless parents feared would become a prey to be swallowed up in the land, would with divine surety become Canaan's conquerors (14:31-33). Reckoning from Israel's exodus to their eventual conquest of Canaan, the nation was to spend a total of 40 years in the wilderness, one year for each day of the spies' ill-fated mission (Numbers 14:34). The Lord's judgment was carried out just as the text relates (Numbers 26:63-65).

MOSES AND AARON'S AUTHORITY VINDICATED
Numbers 16:1–17:11

DURING THE NATION OF ISRAEL'S desert sojourn, Korah, a member of the tribe of Levi, along with confederates Dathan and Abiram, both Reubenites, challenge Moses and Aaron for Israel's religious and political leadership. Rebels from Levi, the priestly tribe, and Reuben, Israel's firstborn tribe, prove a potent and apparently persuasive combination. Recruiting 250 additional malcontents to their cause, this movement develops into a vigorous rebellion. However, because it is God who put Moses and Aaron in positions of power, Korah

and his followers are engaging in a rebellion against the Lord Himself (16:1-3).

Moses sends word that the matter would be publicly settled the following morning. Korah and his gang, not content with being mere Levites and seeking to usurp the priesthood, are to approach the tabernacle with censors of fire and incense. Aaron would do likewise. As both the legitimate leaders of Israel and the usurpers stood together in the tabernacle's entryway, the Shekinah glory of God would appear and choose between the two. When this occurs, Moses and Aaron are commanded to place a distance between themselves and the rest of Israel so that the Lord could destroy them (16:4-19).

Moses made immediate intercession for his people, asking that God not punish everyone for one man's sin (verse 22). The Lord then presents new instructions, this time for the congregation to separate themselves from the doomed rebels Korah, Dathan, and Abiram and their families (16:20-27). Moses then says,

> By this you shall know that the LORD has sent me to do all these deeds; for this is not my doing. If these men die the death of all men or if they suffer the fate of all men, then the LORD has not sent me. But if the LORD brings about an entirely new thing and the ground opens its mouth and swallows them up with all that is theirs, and they descend alive into Sheol, then you will understand that these men have spurned the LORD (16:28-30). Immediately the ground split open and swallowed the three men, their families, and their possessions, closing up again over their heads (16:31-33).

Next, God sends an outbreak of fire that annihilates the 250 confederate rebels offering fire before the tabernacle (16:35). The 250 fallen censors are gathered up by the priests and hammered into bronze plating for the altar to serve as a perpetual reminder to Israel that only Aaron's sons were God's authorized priests (16:36-40).

Unbelievably, yet perhaps quite in character for the congregation of Israel, this demonstration does not curb the grumbling of the people against Moses and Aaron. Again the Shekinah glory of God appears at the tabernacle, and again Moses and Aaron are commanded to place distance between themselves and the rest of Israel so that the Lord could destroy the ungrateful, faithless nation. As a plague begins to break out against the people, Moses instructs Aaron to make an atoning offering on the people's behalf. Aaron swiftly places himself at the crux between the 14,700 dead and the living, checking the plague before any more Israelites fall (16:41-50).

So as to quell all further challenges to Aaron's high priestly authority, Moses commands that all 12 tribal leaders carve their names onto their staffs and submit them to Moses for deposit in front of the tabernacle. On the following day it is discovered that Aaron's staff alone had sprouted buds, blossoms, and even almonds, thus publicly and finally vindicating the divine choice of Aaron as a leader over Israel (17:1-11).

serpent could simply look with faith at the elevated bronze replica and receive healing (Numbers 21:8-9).

In John's Gospel, Jesus referenced the account of the bronze serpent as a prophetic type of His mission. Just as Israel could look at the bronze serpent and receive salvation from physical, temporal death, so could men look at the Son of Man—the crucified Messiah, elevated upon a cross—and receive eternal life (John 3:14-15; 12:32-33).

McFall points out *three elements of typological correlation* between the bronze serpent and Jesus. First, as the replica had the form of the deadly serpent yet was without poisonous venom, so the Messiah possessed the "likeness of sinful flesh" yet was without sin (Romans 8:3; see also 2 Corinthians 5:21). Second, just as the replica serpent seemed a counterintuitive solution for the Israelites' dilemma, so did a crucified Messiah seem an unlikely cure for the sin of mankind. Third, just as looking with faith at God's provision for Israel (the bronze serpent) resulted in physical healing, looking with faith at God's provision for mankind (the Messiah) results in spiritual salvation (McFall, "Serpents," in Alexander and Rosner, *New Dictionary of Biblical Theology,* elec. ed.).

THE BRONZE SERPENT
Numbers 21:8-9

DURING THE NATION OF ISRAEL'S continuing desert sojourn, their combination of forceful impatience and gross ingratitude results, yet again, in divine punishment. In Numbers 21:8-9, the Israelites are plagued with a plethora of deadly, venomous snakes. Only after several Israelites have been struck down does the nation finally repent from its sin and seek Moses' intercession for the Lord to mercifully conclude this latest debacle (Numbers 21:1-7).

Moses is told to fashion a bronze (or copper) replica of one of the serpents and mount it on a pole in a central location in the camp. From that moment on, whoever was bitten by a

THE ORACLES OF BALAAM
Numbers 22–24

BALAAM IS NOT A JEWISH prophet but a syncretistic Gentile seer, or soothsayer, from the region of Mesopotamia (Numbers 22:5; 23:7). Balak, the king of Moab, commissioned Balaam to supernaturally curse Israel. So renowned was Balaam's reputation as an effective diviner that, according to Numbers 22:6, it was believed that whomever he blessed would indeed be blessed, and whomever he cursed would likewise be cursed (in a twisted echo of the Abrahamic Covenant's promise that whoever blessed or cursed Abraham's progeny would be reciprocally blessed or cursed—Genesis 12:3). Apparently more than a little nervous at the prospect of Israel's arrival at his nation's border, Balak designs an offensive strategy built upon his expectation of Balaam's powerful sorcery and magic (Numbers 22:1-6).

Prior to Balaam's journey to Moab, the soothsayer has three consultations with the Lord (Numbers 22:7-35). In the ancient world, it was believed that the particular gods worshipped by specific nations wielded the greatest power over those nations, so naturally, Balaam consulted Israel's God (probably one of many deities to whom Balaam gave homage). In these encounters, Balaam is repeatedly told to speak only the word of the Lord and, specifically, not to curse Israel, whom God has blessed. In fact, once Balaam arrives in Moab, not one of his efforts to curse Israel will come to fruition. Rather, they will result in the blessing of God's chosen people.

The first three of Balaam's four prophetic oracles (Hebrew, *mashal*) to Balak are each preceded with the setting up of seven altars and the sacrifice of one bull and one ram on each altar. The discovery in the 1930s of thousands of cuneiform Mari tablets dating from circa 1700 B.C. revealed the existence of a school of Mesopotamian seers whose recorded divination activities strongly resemble Balaam's practices as described in this narrative (Merrill, "Numbers," p. 241).

The *initial oracle* (22:41–23:12) expresses two reasons Balaam is unable to fulfill his commissioned mandate to curse Israel. First, as God's covenant nation, Israel was to be different, distinct, and separated from all other nations (23:8-9). Second, Israel was blessed by God (23:8,10). The nation's numerical strength at this time confirms God's covenantal promise to Abraham of incalculable numbers of descendants (Genesis 13:16). The oracle concludes with Balaam's expressed wish that his final destiny would be like Israel's (23:10). Understandably, Balaam's blessing does not sit well with his patron, Balak.

Balaam's enigmatic *second prophetic oracle* (23:13-26) has engendered various interpretive opinions among students of the Scriptures. It is best to understand it as applying to Israel's future, alluding to both a messianic kingdom and a messianic king. Numbers 23:21 relates that God has not observed sin within Israel. Of course, on the surface, this would seemingly contradict an enormous portion of Israel's exodus narrative, from the crossing of the Red Sea (Exodus 14:10-12) to the present point in the Numbers narrative. Some hold that this statement merely expresses the fact that God does not hold Israel's many sins against the nation. Others believe it expresses the blamelessness, in God's eyes, of the new wilderness generation, innocent of their parents' transgressions.

While both above interpretive positions possess some merit, neither position is entirely convincing. In light of the clear messianic prophecy contained in Balaam's fourth oracle (see 24:17 especially), the second oracle probably likewise refers to an ideal, future moment in Israel's history when Israel is at peace with God. This peace will be effected through the rule of the messianic king within their midst (23:21). This is the traditional Jewish view of this passage as expressed within Targum Jonathan (Edersheim, *Life and Times of Jesus the Messiah*, 2:714).

The oracle concludes with Balaam's recognition that neither divination nor magic can reverse the Lord's divine blessing on Israel. No nation will prevail over them (23:23-24). Balak's response is that if the seer cannot say anything subversive, then it is better to say nothing at all. At any rate, these blessings must cease (23:25).

The circumstances surrounding Balaam's *third prophetic oracle* (23:27–24:13) differ slightly, in four areas, from the circumstances surrounding his initial statements. First, rather than going off alone and seeking to commune with the Lord in solitude, Balaam stays with Balak. Second, rather than seeking a locale that affords a visual overview of Israel's encampment, Balaam's view is simply of the desert. Third, since, as Balaam expresses, "There is no omen against Jacob, nor is there any divination against Israel" (23:23), the seer dispenses with his usual rituals. Finally, the narrative relays that with this oracle, the "Spirit of God came upon him" (24:2).

The third oracle contains a litany of blessings for Israel. Balaam expresses how his eyes are now opened, allowing him to perceive God's attitude toward and relationship with Israel (24:3-4). The superlative blessings accumulate until, in 24:7-9, there is a prophecy of a coming messianic king ruling over an exalted messianic kingdom that exercises dominion over the nations. This messianic figure will be superior to the royal dynasty of the Amalekites, Israel's archetypal enemies (Exodus 17:14-16). The Septuagint endorses the ancient Jewish messianic interpretation. "There shall come a man out of his seed, and he shall rule over many nations; and the kingdom of God shall be exalted, and his kingdom shall be increased." The oracle concludes with a quotation from the Abrahamic Covenant, "Blessed is everyone who blesses you, and cursed is everyone who curses you" (24:9; see also Genesis 12:3; 27:29). At this, Balaam's third blessing over Israel, Balak loses his temper and demands Balaam's immediate departure (24:10-11).

Before Balaam departs, the soothsayer leaves his former patron with a *fourth prophecy* (24:14-25), which also expresses blessing over Israel. This time, Balaam dispenses with his usual initial procedure of sacrificing seven rams and bulls upon seven altars. In a fashion similar to that of the third oracle's commencement (24:3-4), Balaam's fourth oracle begins with the mention of the uncovering of the seer's eyes. The topic is the prophetic future, specifically, the messianic age. Balaam speaks of an extraordinary individual in Israel's far future, a star coming from Jacob and a scepter rising from Israel (24:17). This prophecy, coupled with the prophecy contained in Jacob's blessing of Judah (Genesis 49:10), solidifies the Messiah's identity as the Jewish king whose coming would be heralded by the astronomical sign of a star.

Allen cogently notes that

> this keenly debated verse (24:17) has been debased by some, devalued by others, and allegorized by still others.…this text speaks unmistakably of the coming of

the Messiah. That this prophecy should come from one who was unworthy makes the prophecy all the more dramatic and startling.…The words of Balaam the pagan mantic, *when he was speaking under the control of the Holy Spirit of God,* were as sure as the words of the Savior Jesus in a red-letter edition of the NT ("Numbers," p. 909, emphasis added).

This verse has traditionally been seen by the Jewish people as a messianic prophecy. The ancient Targum Onkelos reads, "A king shall arise out of Jacob and be anointed the Messiah out of Israel" (Craig A. Evans, "Messianism," elec. ed.). Maimonides saw here two "anointed ones"—in the first part of this passage a foretelling of King David, and in the second half, a foretelling of the future Messiah.

> "I see him but not now"—this is David; "I behold him but not near"—this is the Anointed King. "A star has shot forth from Jacob"—this is David; "And a brand will rise up from Israel"—this is the Anointed King (Maimonides, *Mishnah Torah,* Hilkhot Melakhim Umilchamoteihem, chapter 11).

This prophecy was infamously ascribed in the second century A.D. to the disastrously failed messiah Bar Kokhba by Rabbi Akiva. The revered rabbi set alight the hopes of millions as well as the second Jewish rebellion against Rome when he renamed Simon Bar Kosiba with the messianic designation Bar Kokhba, the "son of a star." Unfortunately the great rabbi recognized only the victorious, royal half of Scripture's prophetic messianic portrait and consequently gave an endorsement of a mere man, resulting in his own death, the death and enslavement of countless fellow Jews, and the dispossession of Jerusalem and the land of Israel.

This prophecy should be indelibly inscribed in each believer's heart in association with the familiar story, told and retold annually, of wise men from the east (likely, Mesopotamia) who followed the star to find the one "born King of the Jews" (Matthew 2:1-2). The imagery of Balaam's prophecy is also evoked with John's description of Jesus as the "bright morning star" (Revelation 22:16).

Balaam's prophecy concludes with an assertion that Israel's dominion would eventually encompass Balak's hegemony. The Messiah would defeat the nation of Moab, and Edom would become Israel's possession (24:17-19). In addition, Amalek, which was the first nation to attack Israel (Exodus 17:8-16), would be destroyed (24:20). This destruction was successively carried out in history by kings Saul (1 Samuel 14:48; 15:1-8,32-33) and David (1 Samuel 27:8; 30:1-20; 2 Samuel 8:12), although one ancient Jewish interpretation, as expressed within Targum Jonathan, views this as a description of the final messianic conquest (Edersheim, *Life and Times of Jesus the Messiah,* 2:714, also Huckel, "Numbers," elec. ed.). The Kenites, who were a friendly subgroup of Midianites who lived in secure kinship among the Israelites (Judges 1:16), would eventually face destruction as well. The Assyrians ("Asshur" in 24:22) would eventually carry this out in the eighth century B.C. when they destroyed the northern kingdom of Israel.

Finally, in 24:23-24, brief mention is made of ships from a western power (perhaps Rome) called "Kittim" (Jeremiah 2:10; Daniel 11:30), coming to destroy Asshur (Assyria) and Eber (understood by some, including the Septuagint, to be the original name for the Hebrews—Merrill, "Numbers," p. 245). If this interpretation holds, then this prophecy was fulfilled with the Roman conquest of both the remnants of the Assyrian/Persian empire and the Hasmonean kingdom of Israel in the first century B.C.

THE CANAANITES WILL ENSNARE THE ISRAELITES
Numbers 33:51-56

Addressing the children of Israel on the plains of Moab, across from Jericho, just prior to the apportionment of the Promised Land, Moses presents the Lord's rules concerning the expulsion of the inhabitants of Canaan. Israel is to thoroughly cleanse the land of its inhabitants ("drive out all the inhabitants of the land from before you"), as well as totally demolish all the idols and pagan places of worship (33:52). Israel is to "take possession of the land and live in it," for it is given as a divine gift (verse 53). And the land allotments are to be determined by lot and tribal size (verse 54).

An incomplete expulsion of the Canaanites from the land will result in the remaining inhabitants becoming both splinters in Israel's eyes and thorns in the side—small irritants that can create powerful disturbances for the nation. This ultimately will result in the Lord doing to Israel what He had planned for the Canaanites—that is, expulsion from the land of promise (33:55-56). Unfortunately, Israel fails to completely carry out God's command to expel the Canaanites, and the people are indeed ensnared by the idolatrous ways of the land's inhabitants. This results in Israel's expulsion from the land, just as predicted in this passage (see also 2 Kings 17:7-20). It must be remembered that while Israel's ownership of the land is an unconditional component of the Abrahamic Covenant, still, each generation's enjoyment of the land is strictly conditioned on obedience to the Mosaic Covenant.

DEUTERONOMY

DEUTERONOMY MEANS "THE SECOND LAW." This book comprises Moses' restatement of the law to the nation of Israel, which took place at the end of their wilderness journey. Thus, it closes the period of the exodus and sets the stage for the periods of conquest and settlement of the Promised Land. Included in this final book of the Penteteuch (Hebrew, *torah*) are several unique prophecies about the future of Israel and its Messiah.

A WARNING AND A PROMISE
Deuteronomy 4:25-31

MOSES PREDICTS THAT, centuries hence, future generations of Israelites will neglect the covenant and allow themselves to be corrupted by idolatry. This will inevitably result in the provocation of the Lord to anger. With heaven and earth as his witnesses (Deuteronomy 30:19; 31:28; 32:1), Moses declares that the product of Israel's future idolatry will be two stages of divine judgment. The initial stage will be characterized by the destruction of a great percentage of the people, dispossession of their land, and dispersion among the nations. Violation of the Torah will result in Israel's reduction to a small remnant. The second stage of judgment will be a giving over of Israel's remnant to the serving of the local idols of their host nations.

However, in this dark hour of national distress, Israel will repent of her sin. She will remember their former passion for her covenant God and once again will fervently seek to obey Him with all her heart and soul. While Israel's repentance is predicated on the stipulations of the Mosaic Covenant, the Lord's forgiveness is predicated on the timeless Abrahamic Covenant (Genesis 15:18-21; 17:7-8; 26:3-5; 28:13-15; 35:12). The Lord is a merciful God who will not abandon His people forever but will remember the covenant He made to the patriarchs.

Moses specifies for Israel the time of this future national repentance. First, it will occur during a time of tribulation, a moment in history when all the judgments of Deuteronomy befall Israel. These judgments will occur within a period of time referred to in Scripture as the latter days, the period immediately preceding and leading into the millennial kingdom and reign of the Messiah. Israel's future national repentance will occur outside of the land, while the people are still dispersed among the nations. Then they will return to the land in conjunction with the inauguration of the millennium.

A PROPHET LIKE MOSES
Deuteronomy 18:15-19

THIS SIGNIFICANT PROPHECY of the prophet like Moses (Deuteronomy 18:15) explains that the Messiah will also be the greatest of the Jewish prophets. YHWH's alternatives to pagan diviners and necromancers for Israel are prophets—men and women through whom He reveals Himself and His will to His people. In Deuteronomy 18:15-19, Moses prepares the people not merely for a series of coming Israelite prophets, but for his ultimate successor, the Messiah. The need for this ultimate prophet was based upon the Israelites, at the Sinai revelation, having deferred any further direct communication with God (Exodus 20:18-19). Moses promises that the Lord will elevate a prophet like himself from among the people of Israel.

The quality that made Moses distinct from all other Jewish prophets was his intimate relationship with the Lord, speaking together with Him "face to face" (Deuteronomy 34:10) and "mouth to mouth" (Numbers 12:8). Moses' relationship with the Jewish people was also unique for a prophet. He was both their deliverer (Exodus 3:10) and an intercessor between them and God (Exodus 20:19).

In Deuteronomy 18:15 Moses stresses that obedience to the prophet like him would be so crucial, of such utmost importance to God, that those who neither recognize this prophet nor obey him will suffer the severest penalty. God's harshest judgment will fall on those who willingly disregard this singular prophet.

The two common contemporary Jewish interpretations of these verses are that the prophet like Moses is either Joshua or a collective reference to the successive line of prophets in Israel who followed Moses. Yet the conclusion of Deuteronomy itself plainly rejects Moses' own prophetic successor, Joshua, as having fulfilled this prophecy (Deuteronomy 34:10). Furthermore, in even a surface reading of the passage there is no reason to assume that the grammatically singular term "prophet" (Hebrew, *navi*) should be read as a collective singular. A surface reading of the passage indicates that the concept of a collective singular prophet is not what the passage teaches, nor was that the common interpretation in New Testament times, a mere 14 centuries later, the

era of the second temple (Philo, The Special Laws, I, 65).

The nascent church viewed the Messiah's identification with Moses as a key messianic element. Indeed, Jesus' fulfillment of this prophecy was an association that had been made by Jewish people throughout Jesus' ministry (John 1:21,25,45; 5:46; 6:14; 7:40) and was powerfully contended for by both Peter and Stephen in the early days of the church (Acts 3:22-26; 7:37).

Jesus' ministry shared certain unique features with Moses.' Jesus exhibited similar intimacy with the One He called "My Father." Jesus also represented God to the people of Israel with an authority unmatched since Moses cradled the two stone tablets in his arms. Jesus is the embodiment, the fulfillment, the essence, and the application of every regulation, statute, and commandment recorded by Moses. Jesus is the living, breathing, resurrected embodiment of God's Word (John 1:1). To reject the prophetic messianic implications of Deuteronomy 18:15 is to fail to recognize that no other man or woman in the history of Israel other than Jesus functioned with either God or the people of Israel in a fashion similar to Moses.

A PROPHETIC MESSIANIC ILLUSTRATION
Deuteronomy 21:23

FOLLOWING THE EXECUTION of a criminal for a capital crime, his corpse was often hung on a tree (or perhaps impaled by a pole) to serve as a graphic deterrent to the community. However, the body was not to be left on the tree overnight, but be buried that same day to prevent the land's defilement by the exposed, decomposing corpse (Leviticus 18:24-27; Numbers 35:33-34). Moses does not say that the criminal was cursed by being impaled, but rather, that he was impaled because he was cursed through committing his crime. Paul quotes from Deuteronomy 21:23—"he who is hanged is accursed of God"—to illustrate by way of analogy how Jesus came under God's curse to redeem believers "from the curse of the Law" (Galatians 3:13).

COVENANT BLESSINGS AND CURSES
Deuteronomy 28

DEUTERONOMY 28 IS A CATALOG of the Mosaic Covenant's blessings and curses. In line with other contemporary suzerain-vassal treaties, the curses comprise about four times more literary real estate than do the blessings. However, contrary to custom, the blessings are listed prior to the curses, which reveals God's love for Israel and His desire to bless them. These blessings differ from those attached to the unconditional Abrahamic Covenant in the sense that the *blessings* of the *conditional Mosaic Covenant* depended on Israel's obedience to God.

Through Moses the Lord offered a totality of blessing in every area of life: Israel is to experience the blessing of military superiority. They are to experience material prosperity. YHWH will establish Israel as His holy people, a blessing of unprecedented relational intimacy. Israel will be blessed with the reputation of belonging to the Lord, causing fear in the surrounding nations. The Hebrews will be blessed by both the agricultural productivity of their land and the biological fertility of their families. Israel is to experience unparalleled economic blessings and political capital in relation to other nations. However, the enjoyment of every blessing is dependent upon Israel's obedience to the covenant through which those blessings emanate (28:1-14). Covenantal disobedience would yield the exact opposite of these blessings.

Beginning with verse 15, Moses elaborates on the *curses*. Every act of disobedience is a de facto declaration of God's inconsequentiality to the covenant violator. Again, Moses included approximately four times more curses

than blessings. He begins by mentioning curses related to disease and drought. The rain would be incapable of penetrating the sky, which would magnify the sun's heat. The land would be completely unproductive, and sandstorms would plague the land (28:20-24).

Disobedience would also bring about military defeat in battle, dispersion from the land, and the disgrace of corpses being eaten by animals instead of being properly buried. Israel would be inflicted with a plethora of horrible diseases, such as the boils the Egyptians experienced in the sixth plague, hemorrhoids, the scab, the itch, madness, blindness, and bewilderment of heart. Israel would be so afflicted by both physical and mental disease that they would lose all effectiveness in every area (28:25-29).

Outsiders would enjoy Israel's possessions and the fruit of their labors. Israel's women would be raped, families displaced, and property destroyed or stolen. Ultimately, the people of Israel would be exiled from the land and deported to foreign nations as spoils of war. There they would be oppressed and forced to serve gods of wood and stone. So dizzying would be Israel's fall from power that the nation would become an astonishment, a proverb, and a byword among all nations (28:30-37). Sadly, this prediction concerning Israel's worldwide reputation has unquestionably proven accurate for the past two millennia.

Israel's economy would be wrecked by locust invasions, worms, and crop failures. Worse, the people's children would be taken from the land into captivity. Israel would also experience a total loss of economic power. In this upside-down scenario, the stranger, the resident alien, normally one of society's more vulnerable members, would become more prosperous than the Israelites around him (28:38-44).

Israel eventually proved sufficiently disobedient that these curses were fulfilled. And their fulfillment would serve, as did the plagues to Pharaoh, as confirmation of YHWH's power and covenant commitment. Because Israel neglected to serve the Lord joyfully in times of abundance, He would ensure that they would serve their enemies in hunger, thirst, nakedness, and want. There would be a complete reversal of fortune, with Israel again enslaved (28:45-48).

Moses went on to warn that disobedience would bring about an invasion by a foreign nation distant enough that their language would be unknown to Israel (verses 49-50). Neither the Assyrians nor Babylonians could be in view here, as they spoke Semitic cognate languages related to Hebrew. The Latin-speaking Romans, however, were a different story. Indeed, Rome also fulfills the text's description of geographic distance ("from afar"—verse 49) and a reputation for brutal efficiency. The foreign military force would successfully besiege Israel's fortifications. Ultimately the reason Israel's city defenses would fail is that their trust was not exclusively in YHWH to protect them, but in their fortifications.

So lengthy would be the foreign military's siege that city food supplies would be exhausted. This would eventually lead to the horrors of cannibalism. Because the invading army will have devoured the fruit of the land, Israelite parents would be forced to consume their children—the fruit of their womb, the greatest of YHWH's many gifts—to survive. Even a man normally considered to be gentle and refined will be stingy in sharing the flesh of his children with the rest of his family. Indeed, tender and delicate women, so refined they would normally never consider going barefoot, will eat their newborn secretly to avoid sharing (28:56-57). Examples of this curse being fulfilled in biblical history are found in 2 Kings 6:24-29, Jeremiah 19:9, Lamentations 2:20, and 4:10, and during the postbiblical Roman siege of Jerusalem.

As God metes out these curses upon Israel, the blessings the nation had formerly experienced will unravel one by one, until their status reverts to that of Egyptian slaves (in a reversal of the exodus). Israel will be devastated by interminable plagues and sicknesses, and the population, formerly numerous as the stars of heaven (Deuteronomy 1:10; see also Genesis 13:16; 15:5; 22:17; 26:4), will be decimated. Israel will be exiled, divinely dispersed throughout all nations, where they will serve other gods and find no rest or comfort. Rather, Israel will experience distress and anguish. Persecution will be the norm. Israel will enjoy none of the safety or security she had previously enjoyed within her own borders (28:58-68). Although a measure of these curses were experienced by Israel following the Assyrian and Babylonian exiles (2 Kings 17:6; 25:21), it was not until Rome's final series of victories in A.D. 70 and A.D. 135 that Hebrew masses returned via ship to Egypt as slaves (Deuteronomy 28:68).

THE LAND COVENANT
Deuteronomy 29–30

DEUTERONOMY 29:1 RELAYS the introduction to an additional, parallel mini-covenant between YHWH and Israel. Moses clearly differentiates between the Mosaic Covenant made at Sinai and this additional, contrasting covenant ("the covenant…besides the Covenant which He had made with them at Horeb"—verse 1). What follows is not a recapitulation of what has already been set forth in detail, but a description of Israel's national restoration following the devastation that results from violation of the Mosaic Covenant.

Some have traditionally called this the *Palestinian Covenant* based on academia's unfortunate and nonbiblical label for the Promised Land. (Following the failure of the second Jewish revolt against Rome in A.D. 135, Emperor Hadrian, attempting to repress the Jewish connection to the land, and with spiteful reference to Israel's traditional enemies, renamed the land *Palestina*.) However, a more appropriate and accurate designation is the Land Covenant, which addresses the covenant's main theme.

The *Land Covenant* finds its basis in the unconditional promises contained within the Abrahamic Covenant and functions in a fashion parallel with the Mosaic Covenant. The Land Covenant illustrates the principle that eternal ownership of the land is unconditional but temporal possession of the land is conditioned upon obedience to God through the law. The Land Covenant reaffirms Israel's right to the land solely on the basis of the Abrahamic Covenant, regardless of the nation's unfaithfulness to God and the Mosaic Covenant.

The Land Covenant contains *five restorative blessings* Israel will experience following her expulsion from the land and subsequent worldwide dispersion. First, Israel will repent (30:1-2). Second, the people will be regathered and returned to their land to once again possess their inheritance (30:3-5). Third, the nation will experience regeneration (30:6). Fourth, Israel's oppressors will experience divine judgment (30:7). And fifth, Israel will experience the divine blessings of productivity and fertility (30:8-10).

Moses then explains to his people that although they had been personal witnesses to the redemptive exodus event and accompanying miracles, they still retained an ignorant perspective. He reminds them of all the Lord had done for them "in order that He may establish you…as His people and that He may be your God" (verse 13).

The nation's Egyptian experience and wilderness wanderings had exposed the people to the bitter poison of *idolatry.* And when the Mosaic Covenant was violated in secret by one person, that individual's actions corrupted the entire holy community. Therefore, such a person is to be dealt with accordingly. Any participation in idolatry by future generations of Israel would likewise cause the people to experience God's judgment. This would lead to the people's banishment from the land, which would become a barren, agriculturally unproductive region. This, in turn, would cause the Gentile nations to wonder why God had dealt angrily with Israel. Moses then pauses at this point to affirm that the voluminous content of prophetic revelation that God had

chosen to divulge was given to encourage the people's continued obedience to the Mosaic Covenant (29:16-29).

Moses is well aware that, in due time, *future generations* of his people will indeed experience both the blessing of enjoying their land and the curse of exile. Israel's accelerated tumble into ruin inevitably causes the nation to reflect on the texts within Deuteronomy that prophetically foretold their situation. These texts mention both the root cause of their punishment, national idolatry, and its antidote, national repentance. Israel's international movement of repentance is prophetically certain. It will occur during the Tribulation, just prior to the beginning of the Messiah's reign and the establishment of His millennial kingdom (30:1-2).

Israel's repentance is the trigger that will spur God's intervention toward reversing the curses of the Mosaic Covenant. Just as God will be the instrumental cause of Israel's dispersion, so will He orchestrate the people's return to their land from the ends of the earth (Zephaniah 3:20). When Israel returns to God, He will likewise compassionately return to them. God's return to His people in conjunction with their return to their land will literally be fulfilled by the Messiah's second coming (Isaiah 59:20–62:12; Matthew 24:31; Mark 13:27). Once the people return to the land, they will finally possess all the territory that God had promised to their ancestors, the patriarchs.

Indeed, the *restored nation* will experience greater blessings than those experienced by any of Israel's previous generations. At this time the Lord will circumcise the people's hearts, personally ensuring the spiritual sensitivity of that generation and all future generations. Through divine regeneration, God will sovereignly accomplish for Israel the level of internally motivated righteousness that the people had previously been incapable of realizing (30:3-6).

Accompanying Israel's restoration will be *judgment on their enemies.* This is in fulfillment of the Abrahamic Covenant's promise of reciprocal blessing for blessing and cursing for cursing (Genesis 12:3). Conversely, the time of Israel's restoration—that is, the millennial kingdom reign of the Messiah—will be characterized by a surfeit of divine blessings on Israel. In addition, at that time the Lord and Israel will share a degree of relational intimacy unmatched since the time of the patriarchs (30:7-9).

Sometimes the interpretation of an entire passage comes down to the careful translation of a preposition within a single verse. So it is in the instance of Deuteronomy 30:10. What is at stake here is whether Israel's restoration ultimately rests on the condition of her obedience, or rather, on the Lord's sovereign initiative. Specifically, there is no grammatical or contextual reason to translate, as do the KJV and NASB, the Hebrew preposition *ki* with the conditional "if." The use of *ki* generally indicates a degree of unconditional certainty and is typically translated as "for," "when," "then," "because," "indeed," "since," and the like. This is how the KJV and NASB translate the same preposition a mere nine verses earlier, in 30:1. Therefore, the translation of 30:10 should commence as "*when* you will" or "*for* you will."

The events spoken of within the Land Covenant are assured and unconditional, as are its promises of restoration, blessing, forgiveness, and spiritual circumcision. Just as certain as Israel's violation of the Mosaic Covenant and experience of that covenant's curses is the divine promise to mercifully restore the nation from the profound depths of its misery. This passage depicts divine initiative awash with consummate grace, not human responsibility drenched in moral rectitude. Israel's ultimate restoration to their land and to YHWH's favor could never be initiated through the nation pulling itself up by its own moral bootstraps. That is why the Land Covenant exists. It is a formal expression of the Abrahamic Covenant's foundational truth that while Israel's enjoyment of the land may be conditioned on its adherence to the Mosaic Covenant, the nation's perpetual ownership of the land is as unmitigated and unconditional as every other divine promise made to Abraham, Isaac, and Jacob.

The Land Covenant concludes with Moses making it clear that what was at stake for Israel was nothing less than a communal choice of life or death, blessing or cursing. Adherence to YHWH's holy standards would yield communal blessing in the land and a protracted presence there. Spiritual infidelity, by contrast, would yield both divine denunciation and a truncated enjoyment of the land. In view of the projected consequences to both the contemporary generation and their posterity, Moses urges the people to choose life. Obedience to YHWH's law is synonymous with life, personal longevity, and the privilege of national longevity in the land of promise (30:11-20).

The entirety of Israel's subsequent history, both biblical and postbiblical, can be seen as the outworking of the predictions and provisions of the Land Covenant. The basis of the call to repentance of every biblical prophet was the stipulations of this covenant. The ministry of Jesus Himself commenced with the call for Israel to repent (Matthew 4:17). Israel's infidelity to the Mosaic Covenant resulted in both the northern kingdom's destruction (2 Kings 17:7-41) and the southern kingdom's captivity in Babylon (2 Kings 25:1-21). The termination of seven decades of exile came with the nation's concurrent repentance (Daniel 9:16-19).

Israel was exiled yet again and dispersed by Rome as a result of its leadership's official rejection of their Messiah (Acts 2:23; 3:14-15; 4:10). That exile, although excruciatingly lengthy in duration, has today begun the process of conclusion in preparation for the final repentance that will occur in conjunction with the return of the Messiah.

In the book of Acts, Peter, resting his argument on the basis of the Land Covenant, speaks to this very situation (3:17-21). Peter explains that the crowd's guilt, and that of the leaders of Israel, in rejecting and condemning the Messiah as well as their abject failure to recognize God's holy and righteous servant, the Prince of life, was the result of ignorance. However, ignorance was no excuse.

They were still collectively and individually responsible.

Peter then repeats the solution to Israel's problem, which he initially proclaimed in his earlier sermon at Pentecost (Acts 2:38). The Jewish people must exhibit repentance. They must change their mind about Jesus. Not only must Israel's mind and perception about Jesus change, their allegiance must also be changed. Israel must demonstrate a return to God by joining the messianic movement, the church. They must turn around and march again in cadence with God's drumbeat. Peter insisted that Israel's faith was askew; something was desperately wrong. Their Messiah, Israel's centerpiece, their foundation, was missing.

Peter promises *three formidable results* of this repentance and return. *First,* the immediate fruit of repentance would be forgiveness. Any Jewish person could have his sins wiped away, blotted out, rubbed out, erased, simply by accepting God's provision of the Messiah. *Second,* when the Jewish people have been forgiven as a result of their corporate repentance, "times of refreshing" would be granted by God (Acts 3:19). The phrase "times of refreshing" does not refer to various periods of spiritual revival within the church age. Rather, these "times of refreshing" are specifically described as being the result of corporate Jewish repentance. Therefore, the "times of refreshing" must refer to the establishment of the messianic kingdom (Ezekiel 37:21-28; Hosea 11:9-11; 14:4-7; Amos 9:11-15; Zechariah 12:10-14).

The *third* result of corporate Jewish repentance is the return of Jesus, which firmly establishes the identity of "times of refreshing" with the messianic kingdom. The "times of refreshing" and the return of the Messiah are simultaneous events. Therefore, the cumulative fruit of individual Jewish repentance would be the messianic King's return to establish the era of His sovereign rule, the "times of refreshing."

Peter goes on to relate these two events to the "restoration of all things"—things that had been prophesied in the Old Testament. The "all things" are not limited just to spiritual bless-ings. "All things" means *all* things. This is the long-anticipated "age to come" (Isaiah 11:1-12), the messianic kingdom, in which the Jewish people will experience all the promises God had made to them through the prophets, beginning with Moses (Deuteronomy 3:1-10).

Jesus Himself referred to this restoration in the Gospel of Matthew as the time of the coming physical kingdom, in which He will rule from Jerusalem on the throne of His father David, with the 12 apostles seated at His side on thrones of their own (Matthew 19:28). This kingdom is the ultimate fulfillment of the Land Covenant.

THE COMMISSIONING OF JOSHUA
Deuteronomy 31:23

GOD REVEALED THAT sometime following Moses' death, Israel would egregiously violate the covenant. Israel's idolatry would cause YHWH to hide His face from them. Moses was to compose a song for the Hebrews to memorize as a deterrent against future apostasy and to provide an antidote for them when their behavior provoked divine retribution and judgment (verse 22). Publicly commissioning Joshua as Israel's next leader and God's chosen instrument to lead Israel's successful conquest of the Promised Land, Moses charged his successor to "be strong and courageous," for the Lord would be with him (verse 23). The narrative of the book of Joshua confirms the success of this commission.

A PROPHECY ABOUT ISRAEL'S FUTURE
Deuteronomy 31:28–32:44

IN HIS FINAL DAYS as Israel's leader, Moses delivered a covenant-renewal song. The song prophetically portrays Israel's future as being characterized by apostasy and the resulting divine judgment. The song is Hebrew poetry and, while rehearsing themes common to the entire book of Deuteronomy, adds a unique hue to the composition. The song begins with a call to two witnesses, the heavens and the earth (Deuteronomy 31:28). Based on the nation's previous track record of rebellious uprisings under his leadership, Moses knew that Israel's apostasy was only a matter of time (31:28–32:2).

In the first section, God's faithfulness is contrasted with Israel's infidelity. YHWH possesses both stability of character and constancy of personality. Moses will use this metaphor again within the song (32:15,18,20-31). By way of contrast, Israel was "a perverse and crooked generation" (32:5).

Moses calls upon the nation's collective memory of their history. He refers to God as "the Most High" (Hebrew, *Elyon*—the only occurrence of this name for God in Deuteronomy), emphasizing YHWH's sovereignty over all creation (verse 8). An interesting fact is revealed in verse 8: Because Israel was God's special inheritance, He set the territory of every nation according to the number of the children of Israel. This verse can be understood as teaching that God established every international boundary according to his geographic plan for Israel (Genesis 10:1–11:9). Alternatively, it may indicate that the actual quantity of nations is based on the number of Israelites at some point in Israel's history—most likely the number 70 at the Jewish people's initial entrance into Egypt.

YHWH's provision and care for Israel throughout its history has been unimpeachable. Israel is called "the pupil of His eye," a metaphor indicating that YHWH protects His people just as a person automatically and diligently protects the pupils of his eyes (verse 10). It indicates that when Israel is attacked or treated abusively, it is as if the attacker poked YHWH in the eye, and such hostility will automatically provoke a commensurate divine reaction.

Israel is referred to as *Jeshurun,* a poetic and idealistic name meaning "upright one" (32:15). Yet this Jeshurun, in the midst of prosperity, would rebel against God through idolatry. Israel's worship was not merely confined to "strange gods," but also to demons (Hebrew, *shadim*—winged cherubesque supposed guardians of health, mentioned elsewhere only in Psalm 106:37). Israel would tire of the worship of YHWH alone and instead follow every latest religious fashion, worshipping trendy new gods to their own ruin (32:15-18).

This will cause YHWH to hide His face from Israel. Their actions will move Him to jealousy and anger. The Lord will then punish Israel commensurately by moving them to jealousy with "those which are not a people" and provoking them to anger with a "foolish nation" (32:19-22). Judgment will come upon Israel through a Gentile nation. This passage was quoted by Paul to illustrate Israel's failure to grasp the gospel (Romans 10:19). The apostle also alludes to its language of provocation to jealousy, albeit of a far more irenic variety, concerning the example believers in Messiah are to set before unbelieving Israel (Romans 11:11).

Israel's egregious violation of the Mosaic Covenant will be answered by a variety of punishments which Moses sets forth in poetic detail. Furthermore, Israel will be scattered throughout the earth and its memory almost blotted out. YHWH admits, however, that He is restrained from the most severe venting of His wrath by His fear that the Gentile nations would attempt to take credit for Israel's destruction.

When YHWH perceives that Israel, having undergone divine judgment, is finally in a state of complete helplessness, He will then taunt His people concerning their misplaced trust in false gods in order to make them realize that YHWH is their only hope for salvation and restoration (32:19-38).

The song climaxes with words about the divine restoration Israel will experience following judgment. Israel will be forced through extreme circumstance to realize that Jehovah is not just another god in a regional pantheon;

He is the only God. There is no more foundational biblical truth than Jehovah's claim of divine singularity. In verse 43 YHWH calls upon the Gentile nations to join Israel in rejoicing at His people's restoration to His favor and to their land (32:39-44).

THE FINAL BLESSING OVER ISRAEL
Deuteronomy 33

In accord with ancient biblical custom, Moses, in his role as *pater familias,* pronounces blessing upon the nation, just as Jacob had done prior to his death in Egypt (Genesis 49). While not considered as prophecy per se, the family patriarch's blessing is accepted as somewhat revelatory concerning the offspring's destiny. In a historical review of covenant history rife with vivid imagery, Moses recounts YHWH's majestic sweeping in from the wilderness to give Israel the law at Sinai (33:1-5).

The blessing mentions every tribe by name with the exception, for reasons unknown, of Simeon. Moses begins with three sons of Leah (Reuben, Judah, and Levi), moves to Rachel's two sons (Benjamin and Joseph) shifts back to two more of Leah's sons (Zebulon and Issachar), and concludes with the four sons of Jacob's two concubines (Gad, Dan, Naphtali, and Asher).

The blessing of Reuben was an expressed desire that the tribe continue in posterity. The blessing of Judah concerned that tribe's future military success. The blessing of Levi concerned the Levites' function as Israel's tribe of priests, teachers of the law, and worship leaders at the central sanctuary. The blessing of Benjamin concerned that tribe's safety and security. The blessing of Joseph (including individual mention of its composition of the two subtribes of Ephraim and Manasseh) concerned that tribe's economic prosperity, agricultural fertility, and military success. The blessings of Zebulon and Issachar are linked together, likely based upon the precedent set by Jacob's blessing (Genesis 49:13-15; see also Judges 5:14-15), and concern future economic prosperity from both land and sea. The blessing of Gad probably concerns the tribe's military prowess and courage. The blessing of Dan portrays that tribe as vigorously relocating their territory to Israel's northern borders. The blessing of Naphtali mentions the tribe's possession of their territorial allotment. The blessing of Asher spoke of the tribe's abundant posterity and financial prosperity, economic extravagance, and military security (33:6-25).

The blessings conclude with Moses' final praise of YHWH's sovereign majesty and His eternal rule over all creation. The prophet left Israel a reminder that the success of their coming military campaigns in Canaan rested securely on YHWH's power, provision, and promises. These are most likely the final words of Deuteronomy personally authored by Moses himself.

A FINAL WORD FROM GOD
Deuteronomy 34:4

God's final words to Moses serve to re-emphasize that the Abrahamic Covenant is the underlying basis for Israel to, at long last, finally enter the land of its inheritance.

THE
HISTORY

JOSHUA

The historical books of the Old Testament trace the story of Israel in the Promised Land. Beginning with the conquest under Joshua and moving on to the era of the judges and the kings, these books provide a detailed account of the theocratic kingdom from the conquest of the Promised Land to the return from the Babylonian captivity. They cover a period of time from 1400 b.c. to 400 b.c. During these 1000 years, we see Israel at its best and at its worst. Throughout, the promises and prophecies of God remain the hope of the faithful, who long for the coming of the Messiah and the establishment of His kingdom on earth.

PREDICTION OF THE PROMISED LAND
Joshua 1:1-9

With Joshua's ascension to leadership following the death of Moses (1:1), the Lord made Joshua a promise of His personal divine presence throughout Israel's conquest of Canaan. Included within that promise were explicit, measurable territorial dimensions that correspond with the boundaries mentioned in the initial promises of land in the Abrahamic Covenant (Genesis 13:14-17; 15:18-21; 17:7-8; 22:16-18; 26:3-5; 28:13; 35:12) and reiterated to Moses (Exodus 3:15-17; 6:8; 23:23; Deuteronomy 1:7; 11:24-25).

Israel successfully conquered vast amounts of territory under Joshua, but the narratives of both Joshua and the opening chapters of Judges are quite clear that the nation in no way came close to possessing all the land God had promised. Indeed, Hess takes this opening text as a broad outline of the conquest and a summary of the book of Joshua itself (Hess, *Joshua*, p. 68). While the nation always held a divinely bestowed title to the entirety of the Promised Land as their divine inheritance (Hebrew, *nachala*), Israel's complete possession and enjoyment of that land depended on its national obedience to the Mosaic Covenant. As Woudstra (*The Book of Joshua*, p. 60) points out, "Only during the period of Israel's greatest territorial expansion, under David and Solomon, were these boundaries approximated."

Even under the monarchy's greatest territorial hegemony, however, the scriptural account makes clear that much of the Gentile regions were mere tributary nations, under Israel's military control only, not yet incorporated into Israel proper (1 Kings 4:21). The balance of scriptural revelation discloses that Israel's possession of the land, settled by Jews from promised border to promised border, awaits future fulfillment within the context of the messianic kingdom (for example, Amos 9:14-15).

PROMISED CONQUEST OF JERICHO
Joshua 6:1-5

The first great Canaanite city on Joshua's itinerary of conquest was Jericho, an oasis in the midst of a difficult, dry, and rugged region. Control of Jericho's water sources would prove crucial to a successful start of Israel's military campaign. In accord with the divine promise of 1:1-9, the Lord assured Joshua that Jericho would fall to Israel in a very anomalous, unorthodox, and site-specific fashion. The use of the perfect tense (that is, the "prophetic perfect") for the Hebrew *nethan,* "I have given," indicates that while the action of giving Jericho into Joshua's hand is still future, it is nonetheless divinely viewed as completely certain and assured. Israel followed this directive, and indeed, at the appropriate juncture, the imposing walls of Jericho collapsed, in sensational fashion, precisely as was divinely promised.

CURSE FOR THE REBUILDING OF JERICHO
Joshua 6:26

FOLLOWING JERICHO'S successful conquest, Joshua pronounced a solemn curse upon any members of future generations who undertake the rebuilding of Jericho's fortifications: "Then Joshua made *them* take an oath at that time, saying, 'Cursed before the LORD is the man who rises up and builds this city Jericho; with the loss of his firstborn he shall lay its foundation, and with the loss of his youngest he shall set up its gates'" (6:26).

Woudstra (*The Book of Joshua,* p. 116) offers the following insight: "This curse is not meant for those who…used the site of Jericho for habitation. Only he who will use Jericho as a city with a 'foundation' and 'gates' will be affected by the curse." This prophecy was literally fulfilled roughly six centuries later when, during the reign of King Ahab, Hiel of Bethel lost two sons after rebuilding Jericho's fortifications: "In his days Hiel the Bethelite built Jericho; He laid its foundation with the loss of Abiram his firstborn, and set up its gates with the loss of his youngest son Segub, according to the word of the LORD, which He spoke by Joshua the son of Nun" (1 Kings 16:34).

PROMISED CONQUEST OF AI
Joshua 8:1-29

THE LORD INSTRUCTED JOSHUA to lead Israel in conquest of the city of Ai: "Now the LORD said to Joshua: 'Do not fear or be dismayed. Take all the people of war with you and arise, go up to Ai; see, I have given into your hand the king of Ai, his people, his city, and his land.'…Then the LORD said to Joshua, 'Stretch out the javelin that is in your hand toward Ai, for I will give it into your hand'" (8:1,18).

The victory of the chosen nation is described in the subsequent text as the promise is fulfilled: "Joshua did not draw back his hand, with which he stretched out the spear, until he had utterly destroyed all the inhabitants of Ai" (8:24-26).

DEFEAT OF THE FIVE AMORITE KINGS
Joshua 10:1-28

JOSHUA IS NEXT DIVINELY encouraged to lead his people to preordained victory against the five Amorite kings that have come against Israel's ally, Gibeon: "The LORD said to Joshua, 'Do not fear them, for I have given them into your hands; not one of them shall stand before you'" (10:8). The remainder of the passage describes how the Lord accomplished Israel's smashing victory through means of supernatural, meteorological phenomena (10:9-28).

DEFEAT OF THE NORTHERN KINGS
Joshua 11:1-15

IN THE SAME FASHION, Joshua is divinely encouraged to lead his people to preordained victory against the seemingly overwhelming forces of the kings of the north: "The LORD said to Joshua, 'Do not be afraid because of them, for tomorrow at this time I will deliver all of them slain before Israel; you shall hamstring their horses and burn their chariots with fire'" (11:6). Joshua 11:7-15 then goes on to describe the details of Israel's comprehensive victory.

ISRAEL'S POSSESSION OF THE PROMISED LAND
Joshua 11:23; 21:43-45

THESE TWO PORTIONS OF JOSHUA, 11:23 and 21:43-45, have engendered a great deal of misunderstanding among interpreters. When these verses are taken by themselves and read outside the larger context of the book's entire narrative account, it is not surprising that some, specifically interpreters of a Covenant theological persuasion, have mistakenly interpreted them as teaching the fulfillment of the land promises contained within the Abrahamic Covenant (Genesis 13:14-17; 15:18-21; 17:7-8; 22:16-18; 26:3-5; 28:13; 35:12).

Understood within the book's context, however, and read in light of other sections such as 13:1-6; 15:63, and 16:10, it becomes quite clear to the careful reader that huge chunks of Canaan failed to be conquered or controlled by Israel under Joshua.

Upon comparison with other passages, it becomes clear interpretively that the author of Joshua is making use of the well-known Hebrew idiom of a part standing for the whole. Accordingly, although Joshua only conquered key regional centers throughout the entirety of Canaan, as an idealized concluding statement it can be summarized as if he had taken the whole of the land (Madvig, "Joshua," p. 311; Woudstra, *The Book of Joshua*, p. 194; Hess, *Joshua*, pp. 284-86). Indeed, as Campbell ("Joshua," p. 364) notes, basing his observation on Deuteronomy 7:22, "This did not mean that every corner of the land was in Israel's possession, for God Himself had told Israel they would conquer the land gradually."

Even under the monarchy's greatest territorial hegemony, under kings David and Solomon, the scriptural account makes clear that much of the Gentile regions were mere tributary nations, under Israel's military control only, not incorporated into Israel proper (1 Kings 4:21). The balance of the revelation of Israel's history, beginning immediately following Joshua in the subsequent book of Judges (1:19,21,27,29-36; 2:1-3,20-23), discloses that Israel's possession of the land, settled by Jews from promised border to promised border, awaits future fulfillment within the context of the messianic kingdom (see, for example, Amos 9:14-15).

JUDGES

THE BOOK OF JUDGES RECORDS THE 300 YEARS of Israel's turbulent settlement of the Promised Land. During these years Israel suffered numerous defeats and reversals, but God remained faithful to His promises. Recorded within the book of Judges' narrative are several instances of divine prophecy that were fulfilled relatively quickly within the immediate (or nearly immediate) context of the specific historical account.

JUDAH PROMISED VICTORY OVER THE CANAANITES
Judges 1:1-4

AS THE CONQUEST OF CANAAN began under Joshua and continued following his death, the Lord provided divine guidance and promised victory to the tribe of Judah, which was to be the first to advance against the enemy. The narrative relays immediate fulfillment: "Now it came about after the death of Joshua that the sons of Israel inquired of the LORD, saying, 'Who shall go up first for us against the Canaanites, to fight against them?' The LORD said, 'Judah shall go up; behold, I have given the land into his hand.'...Judah went up, and the LORD gave the Canaanites and the Perizzites into their hands" (1:1-4).

THE PREDICTION OF THE INCOMPLETE CONQUEST
Judges 2:1-3

DUE TO ISRAEL'S DISOBEDIENCE to the Mosaic Covenant, the Lord carried through on the covenant's provision for such disobedience and promised Israel an incomplete conquest of the Promised Land.

The angel of the LORD came up from Gilgal to Bochim. And he said, "I brought you up out of Egypt and led you into the land which I have sworn to your fathers; and I said, 'I will never break My covenant with you, and...you shall make no covenant with the inhabitants of this land; you shall tear down their altars.' But you have not obeyed Me; what is this you have done? Therefore I also said, 'I will not drive them out before you; but they will become as thorns in your sides and their gods will be a snare to you' " (2:1-3).

THE PREDICTION OF ISRAEL'S INCONSISTENCY
Judges 2:11-23

THE FOLLOWING RELATED PASSAGE describes a cycle that is repeated by Israel several times throughout the book of Judges—a cycle of transgression and disobedience followed by eventual repentance. Israel's continued disobedience gave further impetus to the Lord's resolution not to grant the nation complete victory over the inhabitants of Canaan.

> The anger of the LORD burned against Israel, and He said, "Because this nation has transgressed My covenant which I commanded their fathers and has not listened to My voice, I also will no longer drive out before them any of the nations which Joshua left when he died, in order to test Israel by them, whether they will keep the way of the LORD to walk in it as their fathers did, or not." So the LORD allowed those nations to remain, not driving them out quickly; and He did not give them into the hand of Joshua (2:20-23).

THE PROMISE OF VICTORY OVER SISERA
Judges 4:1-11

AFTER SUFFERING 20 YEARS of oppression, one of Israel's judges, Deborah the prophet, and her commander, Barak, were divinely promised victory over Sisera, a Canaanite commander. Owing to Barak's unsatisfactory reaction to Deborah's conveyance of divine military instructions, Deborah prophesied that the ultimate victory over Sisera would be by means of a woman.

This prophecy was immediately fulfilled both literally and viscerally, as revealed in the ensuing narrative of 4:15-21.

THE PROMISE OF VICTORY OVER THE MIDIANITES
Judges 6:11-24

TO GIDEON, A SUBSEQUENT JUDGE, the Lord promised victory over the Midianites: "The LORD said to him, 'Surely I will be with you, and you shall defeat Midian as one man'" (6:16).

This prophecy found immediate fulfillment (7:1-25). The defeat of the Midianites is unambiguously miraculous in nature, as Gideon's army had been whittled down to a mere 300 fighting men. Furthermore, as additional divine encouragement for Gideon, God allowed Israel's judge to overhear a prophetic dream and interpretation that foretold of Midian's impending doom at the hands of the Israelites.

DELIVERANCE AFTER ISRAEL'S CHANGE OF HEART
Judges 10:13-14

WHEN THE AMMONITES CAME against Israel, the people of Israel became distressed and cried out to God for help. At first God promised a lack of personal action on Israel's behalf (10:13-14), but because of the nation's repentant heart, He intervenes yet again on behalf of His covenant people through Jephthah's decisive military victory over the Ammonites (10:15–11:40).

DELIVERANCE FROM THE PHILISTINES
Judges 13:5

THE ANGEL OF THE LORD, that is, God Himself (Cundall, *Judges*, p. 63), announced to an Israelite couple that they would give birth to a unique judge, Samson (13:5). Samson, through divinely bestowed supernatural strength, would commence Israel's deliverance from the oppression of the Philistines.

Although Samson's career as a judge was flawed and erratic, still, God worked through him to bring about a series of victories over the Philistines (15:14-17; 16:25-30). At least 4000 Philistines died at his hands (14:19; 15:8,15; 16:27).

The deliverance begun through Samson would reach its conclusion when King David won final, lasting victory over the Philistines (2 Samuel 5:25).

RUTH

The book of Ruth, falling within the genre of historic Hebrew narrative, is devoid of specific prophetic content. Yet, the story as a whole has great eschatological value because it contains the history of the royal messianic lineage of King David through the tribe of Judah. Israel's Messiah was to be a descendant of David, so Ruth has long been interpreted in Jewish tradition as possessing great typological messianic significance (Midrash Rabbah *Ruth,* V, 6; VII, 2, 15; Babylonian Talmud, *Sanhedrin* 93a-b as quoted in Huckel, "Ruth," electronic edition; see also Santala, *Messiah,* pp. 41, 132, 203).

Furthermore, the single most important Hebrew word within the book, *goʾel,* which means "kinsman-redeemer" and appears within the text in reference to the "family savior," is typological of Jesus. As was Boaz in 2:20 and 3:9 and his son in 4:14, Jesus is our *goʾel.* He is our blood relative (John 1:14, and with particular reference to Israel, Hebrews 2:14-17) who was willing and able to pay the necessary redemption cost for us—in this instance, His life (Matthew 20:28; Mark 10:45).

Though the book of Ruth is not eschatological, it does provide a *type* or *prophetic picture* of Christ as our Redeemer. He, like Boaz, comes from Bethlehem to redeem a Gentile bride and bring her into the family of God by a marriage covenant.

1 SAMUEL

The books of I and 2 Samuel begin the history of the united monarchy of Israel. First Samuel traces the life of the prophet Samuel as the transitional figure from the period of the Judges to that of the Kings. Samuel himself uniquely served in three major offices—prophet, priest, and judge.

After Samuel's death, the narrative of I Samuel focuses on the unsuccessful reign of King Saul and ends with his demise. Second Samuel is an account of King David's reign as a "man after God's own heart." These two books contain specific prophecies about the failure of Saul's kingdom and the success of David's royal line—the messianic line.

THE PROMISE OF HANNAH'S SON
1 Samuel 1:10-17

Hannah, distressed and shamed at her barrenness, prayed before the Lord at the tabernacle at Shiloh. In her prayer she vowed that if the Lord granted her a son, she would dedicate him to the Lord's service at the tabernacle for his entire lifetime. In addition, she made a commitment that he would live the life of a Nazirite (Numbers 6:5). The high priest and Israel's judge, Eli, mistaking Hannah's passionate and emotional plea before the Lord for public drunkenness, rebuked her. Realizing his error following correction by Hannah, the priest benevolently responded, "May the God of Israel grant your petition that you have asked of Him" (1:17). Hannah understood Eli's words as the Lord's response to her prayer. The fulfillment of this "promise" was recorded in verse 20: "It came about in due time, after Hannah had conceived, that she gave birth to a son; and she named him Samuel, saying, 'Because I have asked him of the LORD'" (1:20).

Three years later, in fulfillment of her commitment, Hannah delivered her son, Samuel, to the tabernacle and into the care of Eli the priest (1 Samuel 1:24-28).

THE PROPHECY OF A FUTURE ISRAELITE KING
1 Samuel 2:10

Within the concluding verse of Hannah's beautiful song of praise to the Lord (2:1-10) is the introduction of one of the Hebrew Bible's central theological terms and concepts. First Samuel 2:10 contains Scripture's initial use of the word *Messiah* (or "anointed," Hebrew, *mashiach*). The biblical concept of the messianic king finds its origin in this passage:

Those who contend with the LORD will be shattered; against them He will thunder in the heavens, the LORD will judge the ends of the earth; and He will give strength to His king, and will exalt the horn of His anointed.

From this preliminary reference and through both books of Samuel and the remainder of the historical writings and the Hebrew prophets, the complex of Jewish messianic thought, hope, and expectation develops, culminating in the revelation of the Messiah Himself within the Gospel narratives. Undoubtedly, Mary's familiarity with Hannah's song and its messianic content prompted her, following her angelic visitation and announcement, to use this ancient poem as a prototype for her own song of praise to the Lord, often referred to as the *Magnificat* (Luke 1:46-55). This passage has long been interpreted in Jewish tradition as a messianic text (Midrash Rabbah *Lamentations,* II, 6 as quoted in Huckel, "1 Samuel," *Rabbinic Messiah,* electronic edition).

ELI'S PROPHETIC BLESSING
1 Samuel 2:20-21

ELI WOULD HAVE OCCASION to see Samuel's parents, Elkanah and Hannah, as they came annually to the tabernacle at Shiloh to worship God and visit their son. Just as he had pronounced blessing on Hannah following their unique introduction, "Eli would bless Elkanah and his wife and say, 'May the LORD give you children from this woman in place of the one she dedicated to the LORD'" (2:20). Hannah, once barren and distraught, eventually gave birth to three more sons and two daughters (2:21).

THE LINE OF ELI DIVINELY CURSED
1 Samuel 2:27-34,36; 3:11-14

IN CONTRAST TO HANNAH'S SON, who was dedicated to the Lord, Eli's sons, Hophni and Phinehas, were "worthless men" who habitually sinned grievously against the Lord through abuse of their priestly office (2:12-17), including ritual fornication and adultery with the women serving within the tabernacle (2:22). An unnamed "man of God" (a prophet) addressed Eli with a message of divine condemnation (2:27-36). As a result of the priesthood's corruption under Eli's adminis-

tration, the hereditary priesthood would no longer advance from the house, or dynasty, of Eli. His family line would be disastrously cut off, and it would become normative for the family's men to die young, "in the prime of life" (verse 33). From this time onward, the continuation of the priesthood would proceed through the lineage of another of Aaron's direct descendants.

The divine sign of confirmation would be the death of Eli's two sons on the same day (2:27-34). As if to add insult to injury, the Lord predicts that Eli's descendants will be impoverished and will beg to serve as priests in order just to eat (2:36). The Lord's judgment is reconfirmed when He repeats His message directly to Samuel (3:11-14).

The prophecy was fulfilled and divine judgment carried out when the two sons of Eli, Hophni and Phinehas, fell in battle against the Philistines. The Philistine victory over Israel resulted in the capture of the Ark of the Covenant, which Eli's sons had unadvisedly carried out into battle (4:11). The news of this catastrophe was brought to Eli, who, when he heard it, "fell off the seat backward beside the gate, and his neck was broken and he died, for he was old and heavy" (4:18).

Eli's priestly dynasty continued for three more generations over the next 13 decades until it was replaced by the dynasty of Zadok (1 Kings 2:26-27,35).

A NEW PRIESTHOOD TO BE ESTABLISHED
1 Samuel 2:35-36

WITH ELI'S PRIESTLY LINE soon to be deposed, the Lord promises an enduring replacement dynasty whose actions would be more in keeping with the holy office: "I will raise up for Myself a faithful priest who will do according to what is in My heart and in My soul; and I will build him an enduring house, and he will walk before My anointed always" (2:35).

This is eventually fulfilled at the ascension

of Solomon to Israel's throne. The final priest of Eli's line, Abiathar, after having been the sole survivor of Saul's slaughter of the priests at Nob, served as David's high priest (1 Samuel 22:20-25; 1 Chronicles 24:1-6). At the end of David's reign, Abiathar made the colossal misjudgment of siding with the faction supporting Adonijah's succession to David's throne against Solomon. Solomon had Abiathar, a descendant of Aaron's son Ithamar, deposed as high priest and replaced with Zadok, a descendant of Aaron's son Eleazar (1 Kings 2:26-27,35). From this point forward, Zadok's dynasty would control the priesthood.

The prophecy includes a referent to "My anointed" (Hebrew, *mashiach,* or the Messiah). While in the prophecy's immediate context the term most certainly references Zadok's service to the dynasty of King Solomon, it also has an eschatological, future fulfillment within the messianic kingdom. The prophet Ezekiel envisioned an era when the priests of Zadok's dynasty would serve the messianic king within the millennial temple (Ezekiel 40:46; 43:19; 44:15-31; 48:9-11).

THE ARK SENT TO BETH-SHEMESH
1 Samuel 6:8-9

THE FIVE RULERS OF the Philistines, having experienced national devastation from their possession of Israel's Ark of the Covenant, resolved to placate Israel's gods with an offering of gold (6:1-7). They placed the ark on a newly constructed cart along with a container holding their offering and hitched two cows to the cart, which would not have a human driver.

The conclusion of this matter is described in 6:13–7:1. The cows pulled the cart holding the ark directly to the town of Beth-Shemesh, which confirmed the power of God to the watching Philistines. But this did not work out so well for the citizens of Beth-Shemesh,

where the Lord struck down 70 men for presumptuously peering into the ark.

THE PROMISE OF DELIVERANCE
1 Samuel 7:3-13

TAKING FIRM GRASP of the reins of his judgeship, Samuel issued a call for the Israelites to abandon their idolatrous practices and return to the Lord. This would be the only means by which Israel would be delivered from the Philistine oppression. The nation's repentant response to Samuel's challenge was immediate (7:1-9). The subsequent passage describes the great military victory that Israel won over the Philistines through the Lord's meteorological intervention (7:10-13).

THE PREDICTION OF OPPRESSION
1 Samuel 8:11-18

FOLLOWING IN THE UNFORTUNATE parental footsteps of his mentor, Eli, Samuel failed to raise godly sons who could carry on as Israel's leaders after Samuel's death. Therefore, the tribal leaders of Israel approached Samuel, rejecting the model of local, transitory judgeship and demanding that a more permanent leader, a king, be appointed over them (8:1-5). The Lord revealed to Samuel that it was not his leadership that Israel was rejecting, but the leadership of the Lord Himself. Although Moses had anticipated a monarchy in Israel (Deuteronomy 7:14-15; 28:36), God recognized that Israel was making the request with a wrong motive. They were requesting a king based on their fear of the surrounding nations and their failure to trust the Lord. God directed Samuel to proceed with a stern warning as to the future results of being a nation ruled by a king (8:6-10).

The people of Israel were granted their

request. And all the predictions Samuel made were fulfilled over the course of Israel's rule by kings (1 Samuel 14:52; 2 Samuel 15:1; 1 Kings 12:2-15; 21:6-7).

SAUL CHOSEN AS ISRAEL'S FIRST KING
1 Samuel 9:15–10:1

WHILE ON A FAMILY MISSION to locate some missing donkeys, Saul and his servant determined to consult the local prophet, Samuel (9:5-14). The Lord had already told Samuel to expect the young man and said that Saul was the divine choice for Israel's king (9:15-16). Upon meeting, Samuel revealed the Lord's decision to Saul (9:17-27). Samuel then privately anointed Saul, consecrating him as Israel's king (10:1).

With this action, Saul became what would soon be labeled "the LORD's anointed," the original prototype of a messiah (24:6,10; 26:9,11). Saul was publicly proclaimed king in 1 Samuel 10:17-27; his anointing was renewed and confirmed in 1 Samuel 11:14-15.

THREE SIGNS FOR SAUL
1 Samuel 10:2-13

SAMUEL TOLD SAUL THAT on his way home that day, he would receive three signs that would authenticate his anointing as Israel's king. First, he would meet two men with a specific message at Rachel's tomb. Second, he would meet three men at the oak of Tabor heading to Bethel for worship, each carrying specific items. And third, in his hometown, he would encounter a band of prophets carrying specific musical instruments and engaged in prophetic activity (10:2-5). At this point, "the Spirit of the LORD will come upon you mightily, and you shall prophesy with them and be changed into another man" (10:6). The narrative relates in 10:9-13 that these con-

firming signs occurred just as anticipated: "Then it happened when he turned his back to leave Samuel, God changed his heart; and all those signs came about on that day" (10:9).

PROMISE OF BLESSING AND JUDGMENT
1 Samuel 12:13-15,24-25

IN SAMUEL'S FAREWELL ADDRESS, as he passes the reins of leadership to Israel's new king, he addressed the nation with a promise of corporate blessing for obedience and judgment for disobedience. Samuel's words were then confirmed by a stunning meteorological display (12:17-18).

With the conclusion of this address, Israel's era of judges came to an end, and the period of monarchy officially inaugurated. Samuel's prophesied blessings and judgment plays out throughout Israel's checkered history as recorded in the biblical record.

SAUL'S DYNASTY TO BE TEMPORARY
1 Samuel 13:13-14

ON THE THRESHOLD OF BATTLE, desperate in the face of mass desertion and anxiously impatient for Samuel's arrival, Saul presumptuously bowed to the pressure of the moment and offered a sacrifice. This was in direct disobedience to the prophet's previous instruction to wait for his arrival (10:8). More egregiously, for Saul, a Benjaminite, to offer a Levitical sacrifice was in flagrant violation of Mosaic legislation (Leviticus 6:8-13). As if on ruinous cue, Samuel immediately arrived on the scene to condemn the king for his act of audacious imprudence (13:8-12). As he did so, he prophesied the end of Saul's dynasty (verses 13-14).

Saul was not divinely rejected as king, but his dynasty was rejected. Even now God was already in the process of raising up a successor king who would be "a man after His own heart"—as much a preparatory statement to the reader regarding the author's imminent introduction of David to the narrative as a stinging indictment to Saul. This prophecy was fulfilled some decades later when the united tribal elders of Israel anointed David as their king (2 Samuel 5:1-4).

DIVINE INSTRUCTION AGAINST THE AMALEKITES
1 Samuel 15:1-3

Saul RECEIVED EXPLICIT instructions from Samuel to offer no quarter to the Amalekites. The Amalekites were Israel's ancient enemies, dating back 400 years to the early days of the exodus. After this initial confrontation, the Lord marked the entire Amalekite nation for complete and merciless extermination (Exodus 17:14-16). That's because Amalek had fallen afoul of one of the stipulations of the unconditional Abrahamic Covenant: "The one who curses you I will curse" (Genesis 12:3).

Samuel's orders were carried out by Saul, but imperfectly. Saul not only spared the life of Amalek's king, Agag, but he also allowed the Israelites to cull from destruction all the Amalekites' finest animals and possessions. This resulted in the Israelites' destruction only of that which no one wanted to take for himself as spoil. Against God's clear command, a remnant of the Amalekites survived this confrontation, and the nation would not be conclusively eradicated by Israel until the events described within 1 Chronicles 4:43.

SAUL REJECTED AS KING
1 Samuel 15:22-35

WHEN SAMUEL HEARD the bleating of sheep and the lowing of oxen (15:14), he confronted Saul about his disobedience. Saul ineffectually attempted to justify his actions to the prophet (see 13:13-21). Samuel responded to Saul's pitiful excuses with a message of severe and irrevocable divine rejection (15:22-26).

Saul, though divinely rejected, would still remain king of Israel for at least another decade. However, from this point onward, the narrative relates the unavoidable decline of Saul and the inevitable rise of God's chosen successor, the future King David (2 Samuel 5:1-4).

DAVID ANOINTED KING
1 Samuel 16:12-23

FOLLOWING GOD'S ANNOUNCEMENT of His rejection of Saul as king, Samuel was commissioned to discreetly meet and anoint Saul's successor at the home of Jesse of Bethlehem (16:1-11). After Samuel viewed a parade of Jesse's sons, the youngest, David, a teenager, was finally invited into the gathering and identified as the Lord's choice (16:12). Even then, more than a decade would go by before David was publicly recognized as king, first over Judah (2 Samuel 2:4), and finally, over all Israel (2 Samuel 5:1-4).

Concurrent with David's rise and his being filled with the Spirit of the Lord was the departure of God's Spirit from Saul and his being terrorized by a divinely authorized evil spirit (1 Samuel 16:14). A summons was issued for a skillful musician to play the lyre within the royal court in order to soothe the king. God providentially arranged for the summons to be answered by David, who now would gain entry into Saul's world. Becoming Saul's personal attendant, David successfully forged a trusting relationship with the acutely troubled king, the man whom David was ordained to replace (16:15-23).

DAVID'S VICTORY OVER GOLIATH
1 Samuel 17:45-47

IN THE RENOWNED STORY of David's confrontation with Goliath, David issued a confident prediction of victory to his oversized foe (1 Samuel 17:45-47). The subsequent passage describes how David's prediction was immediately vindicated and how his actions fueled a major Israelite victory over the Philistines (17:48-54).

ISRAEL'S VICTORY OVER THE PHILISTINES
1 Samuel 23:1-5

ISRAEL'S VICTORY OVER THE PHILISTINES
1 Samuel 23:1-5

IN 1 SAMUEL 23:1, the people of Judah came to their popular champion, David, with concerns over the Philistine raids on the town of Keilah's harvest. Abiathar the priest possessed the ephod of the high priest (23:6), so David inquired of the Lord, through the ancient means of the Urim and Thummim, as to whether he should lead his men in an assault on the Philistine raiders.

Although the Lord responded in the affirmative, David's men balked at the mission. They reasoned that as they had concerns over facing Saul's forces, they should be that much more concerned over facing the forces of the Philistines (23:2-3). David inquired of the Lord yet again, seeking and receiving a measure of additional divine confirmation that their assault on the Philistines would be successful (23:4). David's victory at Keilah is described in the subsequent verse (23:5).

A WARNING OF BETRAYAL
1 Samuel 23:10-13

WHEN SAUL HAD RECEIVED intelligence that David and his men were at Keilah, he summoned an army for the purpose of trapping his rival within the confines of a walled city. David, learning of the mobilization of Saul's forces, inquired yet again of the Lord through the Urim and Thummim as to whether he would be betrayed to Saul by the Keilahites. When he received an affirmative divine response that served to verify the duplicitous intentions of the Keilahites, David marshaled his 600 men and escaped (23:10-13).

A PREDICTION OF SAUL'S DEATH
1 Samuel 28:16-19

ON THE EVE OF BATTLE against the Philistines, a desperate Saul summoned Samuel from Sheol, the realm of the dead. The prophet delivered an ominous message from beyond the grave and made four devastating points.

First, he informed Saul that the Lord had not only departed from the king's life, but, due to Saul's disobedience in the Amalek affair, had actually become his adversary. Second, since Samuel and Saul's heated confrontation over the Amalek matter a decade and a half earlier (1 Samuel 15:22-35), God had been in the corner of Saul's rival, David, to whom the kingdom of Israel had been divinely conferred. Third, Israel's army would suffer a crushing defeat on the following day at the hands of the Philistines. And finally, Saul and his three sons would fall in course of battle, joining Samuel in the realm of the dead (28:16-19).

The ignominious deaths of Saul and his sons, as well as Israel's defeat, are described in 31:1-8 and 1 Chronicles 10.

VICTORY OVER THE AMALEKITES
1 Samuel 30:7-8

DURING THE ABSENCE of David and his men from Ziklag, the Amalekites again enter the narrative by torching the town and kidnapping the families of David and his men (30:1-6). David sent for Abiathar the priest and inquired of the Lord through means of the Urim and Thummim as to whether he could successfully overtake the Amalekite raiders. He received an encouraging prediction of victory, and his forces pursued their enemies (30:7-9). The subsequent defeat of the Amalekites and the liberation of the kidnapped families are recorded in 30:9-20.

2 SAMUEL

FOR INTRODUCTORY REMARKS, see the introduction to 1 Samuel on page 71.

DAVID RECOGNIZED AS ISRAEL'S KING
2 Samuel 5:1-2

AT LONG LAST, some 15 years after the private anointing by Samuel (1 Samuel 16:13), representatives of Israel's 12 tribes came together to publicly declare their allegiance to David as king of Israel's united monarchy. Their commitment is based on their pragmatic choice of nationalism over tribalism, David's military prowess, and the Lord's personal choice of David as Israel's shepherd and ruler (2 Samuel 5:1-2; 1 Chronicles 11:1-3).

THE DAVIDIC COVENANT
2 Samuel 7:8-16; 1 Chronicles 17:7-14

IN 2 SAMUEL 7:8-16 and 1 Chronicles 17:7-14 (which are parallel passages) we find the establishment of the Davidic Covenant, the unconditional set of promises that God made to David of a perpetual dynasty, an unshakable kingdom, and an eternal throne. God established an indissoluble covenant in which David was promised that one of his descendants would forever rule over Israel (2 Samuel 7:12-13; Psalm 89:3-4; 132:11). Although these promises are not actually labeled as a covenant per se within the text of these two passages, they were later recognized as a covenant

(2 Samuel 23:5; 1 Kings 8:23; 2 Chronicles 13:5; Psalm 89:3,28,34,39; Isaiah 55:3).

The importance of these two parallel passages cannot be overstated, although it is not for want of trying on the part of commentators. For example, Brueggemann (*First and Second Samuel*, p. 259) most effusively pronounces his judgment that "this oracle with its unconditional promise to David [is] the most crucial theological statement in the Old Testament." Pentecost (*Thy Kingdom Come*, p. 148) adds that "the covenant God made with David became the foundation of Israel's hope.... The basis for Israel's expectation that a king would arise from the house of David who would...bring them into the blessings of the covenants." Bergin (*1, 2 Samuel*, pp. 336-37) concurs, pointing out that "the Lord's words recorded here constitute the longest recorded monologue attributed to him since the days of Moses.... The covenant that the Lord established with the House of David became the nucleus around which messages of hope proclaimed by Hebrew prophets of later generations were built."

The Davidic Covenant consists of *seven related components:*

First, while the immediate introductory context of 2 Samuel 7 concerns David's desire to build a temple for the Lord, the Lord makes a clever reversal. Rather than David building the Lord a house (in the sense of a temple), God Himself pronounced that He will build a house (in the sense of a royal dynasty) for David (2 Samuel 7:11).

Second, upon David's death, the son, who at this time has yet to be born, will serve as his successor and heir and reign securely (2 Samuel 7:12-16). As Scripture unfolds, it is revealed that this is fulfilled through the rule of David's son Solomon (1 Chronicles 22:8-10).

Third, this immediate heir of David would be the one permitted to build a temple for the Lord (2 Samuel 7:13). Indeed, Solomon did build the temple, fulfilling this prophecy (1 Kings 6; 2 Chronicles 3–5) and fulfilling Moses' expressed prophetic expectation of a central, permanent location of Israelite worship (Deuteronomy 12:11-12,21; 14:23-24; 16:2,6,11; 26:2).

Fourth, the throne of this son's kingdom will be established forever. Only the Davidic dynasty would possess the exclusive, divinely authorized authority to rule over the nation of Israel. This theme of the eternality of the Davidic throne, mentioned in 2 Samuel 7:13,16 is further developed within the parallel 1 Chronicles passage.

Fifth, as God had long ago promised to make His servant Abraham's name great (Genesis 12:2), He likewise promised that He would make His servant David's name great (2 Samuel 7:9). This was already being accomplished within David's lifetime, and even now, some three millennia afterward, he is still both beloved and revered by the Jewish people.

Sixth, God pronounced that at some unspecified future time, Israel, planted securely within her land, would experience an unprecedented era of permanent tranquility, peace, security, and justice (Amos 9:11-15) that had, as its basis, the Davidic Covenant (2 Samuel 7:10). This coming millennial kingdom is the oft-mentioned, fervently anticipated hope of the Hebrew prophets who wrote in the wake of this covenant.

Seventh, there is an unconditional divine commitment to this covenant, expressed in the promise never to remove the Lord's covenant love/mercy (Hebrew, *chesed*) from the dynasty as it had been removed from Saul, whose dynasty was subsequently cut off. Although divine discipline would be meted out for individual kings' sins, David's dynasty would never

be abolished and would continue in perpetuity (2 Samuel 7:15). Certainly Solomon, who did indeed sin according to the biblical record, required and received the Lord's discipline (1 Kings 11:14,24-26). Yet the Davidic dynasty continued, although Solomon's kingdom split almost immediately subsequent to his death (1 Kings 11:31-38).

Interestingly, the 1 Chronicles passage, which so closely parallels much of the 2 Samuel passage, omits any mention of the possibility of the future Davidic heir sinning. That is because 1 Chronicles looks beyond David's immediate and imperfect successor, Solomon, and looks ahead to a future, perfect, ultimate Son of David.

THE MESSIAH, THE SON OF DAVID
2 Samuel 7:11-16;
1 Chronicles 17:10-14

FROM THE MOMENT OF its initial publication in 2 Samuel and its reiteration and amplification in 1 Chronicles, the Davidic Covenant has been perhaps the main fount of biblical messianic expectation. Indeed, "this enduring promise to David has placed messianism at the heart of both Judaism and Christianity" (Brueggemann, *First and Second Samuel,* p. 258). Baldwin (*1 and 2 Samuel,* p. 213) is in agreement, writing that "this chapter was to become the source of the messianic hope as it developed in the message of prophets and psalmists." Bergin (*1, 2 Samuel,* p. 337) explains:

> The significance of the eternal covenant between the Lord and David for the New Testament writers cannot be overemphasized....The hopes that were raised by the Lord's words—that God would place a seed of David on an eternal throne and establish a kingdom that would never perish—were ones that no Israelite or Judahite monarch satisfied, or even could have satisfied. But they were ones that the first-century

Christians understood Jesus to fulfill. The Lord's words recorded here arguably play the single most significant role of any Scripture found in the Old Testament in shaping the Christian understanding of Jesus.

Indeed, it is impossible to comprehend the basis of the Hebrew Scripture's numerous messianic prophecies (Isaiah 9:6-7; 11:1-16; Jeremiah 23:5-8; 30:1-11; 33:14-17; Ezekiel 34:23-27; Hosea 3:5; Amos 9:11-12) without the foundational expectations relayed within the Davidic Covenant.

An additional yet vital component of the Davidic Covenant enumerated solely in the 1 Chronicles 17 account is the promise of a unique future descendant, an undying son "established forever" (verse 14) to permanently guarantee the previous promises. While the 2 Samuel passage emphasizes the Davidic dynasty, kingdom, and throne, 1 Chronicles emphasizes an eternal king. As Fruchtenbaum (*Messianic Christology*, p. 79) summarizes, "David's line will eventually culminate in the birth of an eternal Person whose eternality will guarantee David's dynasty, kingdom and throne forever."

The New Testament contains multiple references to *Jesus being the royal fulfillment and living embodiment of the Davidic Covenant,* beginning with the opening statement of Matthew's Gospel that identifies Jesus as "son of David" (Matthew 1:1) and continuing with Luke's record of the angelic announcement made to inform Mary, David's direct descendant through his son Nathan (Luke 3:23-31), that she would soon give birth to the Messiah, the long-anticipated Davidic heir. The annunciation refers to the Davidic Covenant in the angel's very specific, unmistakable, and unambiguous regal and covenantal terminology:

> He will be great and will be called the Son of the Most High; and the Lord God will give Him the throne of His father David. And He will reign over the house of Jacob forever, and His kingdom will have no end (Luke 1:32-33).

In first-century Israel, the title Son of David carried a potent political punch. It was widely understood to refer to an idealized political revolutionary who would cast off the shackles of Roman oppression, judge the wicked, and purge evil from the midst of Israel. Israel enthusiastically anticipated that the dynasty of David would be restored and the kingdom of Israel made glorious. This expectation, based on the Hebrew prophets (Isaiah 11:1-16; Jeremiah 23:5-8), is widely espoused throughout first-century Jewish literature, including the Dead Sea Scrolls.

Jesus conducted His ministry amid this whirlwind of amplified Davidic anticipation. In fact, one of the foremost messianic titles ascribed to Jesus in the New Testament is Son of David. This designates Jesus as the recipient of all the promises God had made to David concerning the future and eternal government of one of his descendants. It specifies Jesus to be a royal, majestic Messiah who is entitled by birthright to rule over all Israel.

While Jesus carried out His earthly ministry, He accepted Son of David as a title applicable to Himself (Matthew 9:27-28; 20:31-32; Mark 10:48-49), but He abjectly refused to be drawn into either political intrigue or revolutionary activity. While Herod the Great feared the one who was born "King of the Jews" (Matthew 2:2), and though Jesus was crucified as "king of the Jews" (Luke 23:38), He forcefully proclaimed that His kingdom, at least for the present time, was "not of this world" (John 18:36).

According to the teaching of the apostles, the Son of David concept is primarily applicable to Jesus' future function as king of the earth, when He reigns from His father David's throne in Jerusalem. The Son of David concept is specifically linked to Jesus by both Peter (Acts 2:30-31) and Paul (Acts 13:23) and was an important theological component within the presentations of both apostles when they addressed a Jewish audience.

In Acts 2:30-31, Peter argued that the Holy

Spirit enabled David to look ahead into the future and understand precisely how God's Davidic Covenant promise of an eternal throne was to be fulfilled. God showed David that an eternal throne and an unending dynasty required an immortal descendant. David had been allowed to see the future Anointed One, the Messiah, the One who would neither decompose nor be abandoned to the abode of the dead (Greek, *Hades;* Hebrew, *Sheol*). After resting in the grave and abiding in Hades, the Messiah, paradoxically, would still live forever (Psalm 16:9-11). To fulfill the Davidic Covenant, this Son of David would of necessity need to be resurrected.

In Acts 13:23, Paul argued that Jesus, the promised Son of David, is the ultimate Davidic king, the prophesied Branch and Root of Jesse (Isaiah 11:1,10). God's promise to David had entailed an eternal throne, and this eternal Davidic dynasty required an eternal Davidic descendant. Through the establishment of the Davidic Covenant, God had prepared Israel for the Messiah's coming. In fact, the fifteenth of the 18 benedictions contained in the *Amidah* (a Jewish prayer), corporately recited by Jewish congregations during worship, explicitly prays for the coming of this Messiah, reading, "Speedily cause the Branch of your servant David to flourish. Exalt his horn by your salvation, because we hope for your salvation all the day. Blessed are you, O Lord, who causes the horn of salvation to flourish."

Furthermore, in Acts 1:6-7, following Jesus' resurrection and glorification and just prior to His ascension, the apostles specifically asked Jesus a question that squarely rested on his identity as the eternal Davidic king who would reign over the eternal Davidic kingdom prophesied in 1 Chronicles 17:10-14. Jesus had primarily been teaching the apostles about the coming kingdom of God over the 40 days following His resurrection (Acts 1:3) and, in fact, during His three years with the apostles, Jesus' preaching was continually characterized by such kingdom-oriented instruction.

For example, during the last Passover meal

Jesus had with the 12, on the evening of His betrayal, Jesus made *two specific promises* concerning the coming kingdom. *First,* He promised He would not eat another Passover meal until the festival was fulfilled in the kingdom (Luke 22:16-18). *Second,* He promised that in the kingdom, the apostles would sit upon 12 thrones and judge the 12 tribes of Israel (Luke 22:30). In fact, what had immediately precipitated this promise was the disciples' argument over which of them was to be the most respected leader in the future kingdom (Luke 22:24)!

Jesus' answer to the apostles indicates that He accepted their question about the kingdom (Acts 1:6) as a logical one. But He refused to provide specifics, treating their question with a serious, yet mysterious, answer. He indicated His agreement with His students that the issue was *when* and not *if* the kingdom is restored to Israel. It was simply a matter of divine timing, which happened to be none of the apostles' business. The kingdom would assuredly come, but at an unknown future time. That knowledge was reserved only for the Father (Matthew 24:36).

There are some, however, who mistakenly hold that the apostles were off base to have asked Jesus about the establishment of Israel's national theocracy. These people do not accept the validity of such a conception of the kingdom. For them, the kingdom that Jesus brings is for the church and not for Israel—a spiritual kingdom and not a literal, national one. In fact, they say, this spiritual kingdom is already here, among the church, as Jesus reigns within our hearts and lives. Because His "eternal Davidic throne" is merely spiritual in nature, what the church is currently experiencing is the entire and only kingdom that we can hope to expect until the day when Jesus returns and takes us back with Him to heaven.

However, the apostles would have wondered what other sort of kingdom could be in view if not the physical kingdom promised to Israel throughout the Old Testament. The apostles would have had no conception of the church being a "spiritual" kingdom or any sort of kingdom at all. The concept of a "spiritual Davidic kingdom" is an ingenious notion born in European ivory spires a great distance removed in both chronologic time and geographic space from first-century Jerusalem or the apostolic witness.

The *apostles' literal understanding of the Davidic Covenant* is further, and decisively, confirmed in Acts 15:15-18 through James's (Jesus' brother's) quotation of Amos 9:11-12, a passage that speaks of God's restoration of the fallen ruins of the tabernacle of David—that is, the house of David, the Davidic dynasty—during the future messianic kingdom. The dynasty metaphorically fell into ruin when the final Davidic king was deposed from power by Babylon (2 Kings 25:7), and Amos promised that, in fulfillment of the Davidic Covenant, the dynasty of David would be restored to its former glory within the context of the messianic kingdom.

Some misinterpret both James and Amos here, believing that James was arguing that Amos's prophecy was fulfilled by first-century contemporary circumstances. They erroneously suppose that the ruined tabernacle of David is the church. It is difficult to determine how they could hold this broadly spiritualized view, as David's tabernacle is described as fallen and in ruins, in need of restoration. The first 15 chapters of Acts show that this description is not true of the victorious first-century church! Amos was prophesying about Israel, not the church, which was an undisclosed mystery within the Hebrew Scriptures (Ephesians 3:4-5; Colossians 1:26-27).

There is no question that both Testaments of the Scriptures together present and confirm the reality of the future restoration of Israel as a nation and the reestablishment of an actual, physical, political Davidic kingdom. The coming messianic age will be characterized by the physical, actual reign of the Messiah, Jesus. His throne will be that of His ancestor, King David, and as the kings of Israel did in ancient days, Jesus will rule from Jerusalem. Although he may not have known his greatest

descendant's name, this literal interpretation was most assuredly David's understanding, as he himself marveled in his response to the covenant:

> You have spoken also of the house of Your servant concerning the distant future.... For You have established for Yourself Your people Israel as Your own people forever, and You, O LORD, have become their God. Now therefore, O LORD God, the word that You have spoken concerning Your servant and his house, confirm it forever, and do as You have spoken, that Your name may be magnified forever, by saying, "The LORD of hosts is God over Israel"; and may the house of Your servant David be established before You.... Now therefore, may it please You to bless the house of Your servant, that it may continue forever before You. For You, O Lord GOD, have spoken; and with Your blessing may the house of Your servant be blessed forever (2 Samuel 7:19-29).

Finally, in the closing verses of the entire Bible, in what is the next-to-last recorded statement by the risen Lord Jesus, the Messiah Himself reveals His literal understanding of the Davidic Covenant: "I, Jesus, have sent My angel to testify to you these things for the churches. I am the root and the descendant of David, the bright morning star" (Revelation 22:16).

A PROMISE OF DIVINE JUDGMENT
2 Samuel 12:10-12

AS A RESULT OF DAVID'S ABUSE of his royal power in having Uriah the Hittite killed and taking Uriah's wife Bathsheba for himself (12:9), Nathan pronounces divine retribution against David:

The remainder of David's life would be

characterized by warfare, even within his own family. The fulfillment of this prophecy occurs through the calamitous interactions of David's children Amnon, Tamar, and Absalom (2 Samuel 13), which eventually resulted in Absalom's full-scale rebellion against his father (2 Samuel 14:25–18:18). In the same way that David had taken another man's wife in secret, David's wives would be taken from him publicly. This prophecy was fulfilled through the agency of David's son Absalom when, during the rebellion, he took David's concubines for himself (2 Samuel 16:22).

Although David's sins were serious enough to be punishable by death (Exodus 21:12; Leviticus 20:10), the Lord forgave David his sin and mercifully spared his life. However, because David's actions had given the Lord's enemies occasion to blaspheme, the baby born as a result of David's union with Bathsheba would not survive. The subsequent passage relates the fulfillment of the prophecy concerning the baby's death (2 Samuel 12:15-23).

A PUNISHMENT FOR TAKING A CENSUS
2 Samuel 24; 1 Chronicles 21:1-13

THIS STORY, IN MUCH abbreviated form, is also found in the parallel passage of 1 Chronicles 21:1-13. For reasons not provided within the narrative, the Lord's wrath was provoked by David having undertaken a census (24:1-9). Upon receiving the compiled census data, David realized his sin and repented (24:10). The prophet Gad presented *three calamities* from which to choose for God to unleash judgment upon Israel: three years of famine, three months of enemy pursuit, or three days of plague—the intensity of each calamity rising in proportion to its brevity (24:13-14). The outcome of David's choice of pestilence is documented in 2 Samuel 24:15-25.

The entire account reminds us of the seriousness of impetuous acts of pride which may result in dire consequences. It also serves to emphasize the importance of doing all things to God's glory and not our own.

1 KINGS

THE TWO BOOKS OF KINGS RECOUNT EVENTS in the golden era of the biblical prophets, when not only well-known men such as Elijah and Elisha roamed the land of promise, but also a number of less familiar, even unnamed prophets spoke the Lord's word. Consequently, the prophecies within the books of Kings feel both qualitatively and quantitatively distinct from those in the other Old Testament historical books. Qualitatively, the character of the prophecies are, in general, less timelessly "covenantal" in nature, usually restricted to immediate circumstances wherein fulfillment can meet prediction within a limited time. Quantitatively, the Kings narrative is studded with predictive prophecies addressed to both small and great, as well as groundbreaking prophecies often alongside offbeat, diminutive, digestible prophetic nuggets scattershot throughout the text.

SOLOMON GRANTED DIVINE BLESSINGS
1 Kings 3:10-14; 2 Chronicles 1:10-12

THE LORD APPEARS TO SOLOMON in a dream and asks the newly installed king what request he would have the Lord grant. Solomon requests sufficient wisdom and discernment with which to effectively judge his subjects (3:5-9). Solomon's specific request so pleases the Lord (3:10) that He grants the king not only the wisdom for which he had asked, but also the wealth and renown that he had not requested (3:11-14; cf. 2 Chronicles 1:10-12).

The newly bestowed wisdom of Solomon is famously on display in the immediately subsequent passage relaying the story of the two mothers (3:16-28), and both 1 Kings and 2 Chronicles lavishly attest to the king's greatness (1 Kings 10:14-29; 2 Chronicles 9:13-28).

SOLOMON PROMPTED TO REMAIN OBEDIENT
1 Kings 6:11-13

DURING THE CONSTRUCTION of the temple, the Lord addresses Solomon with both encouragement and exhortation. God's blessing on Israel and personal presence within the temple would be dependent upon the king's obedience to the Torah.

Now the word of the LORD came to Solomon saying, "Concerning this house which you are building, if you will walk in My statutes and execute My ordinances and keep all My commandments by walking in them, then I will carry out My word with you which I spoke to David your father. I will dwell among the sons of Israel, and will not forsake My people Israel" (6:11-13).

SOLOMON ASSURED OF GOD'S BLESSINGS
1 Kings 9:1-9; 2 Chronicles 7:12-22

SECOND CHRONICLES 7:12-22 IS a parallel to 1 Kings 6:11-13, but with one major addition. Following the construction of the temple, the Lord again appears to Solomon. He addresses the king in light of the stipulations of the Davidic Covenant (2 Samuel 7:8-16; 1 Chronicles 17:10-14) and in answer to his celebratory prayer delivered at the temple's dedication (1 Kings 8:22-53; 2 Chronicles 6:12-42).

The Lord assures Solomon that his prayer has been heard and the temple consecrated with the personal presence of God. However, the Lord's permanent presence in the temple is conditioned upon the obedience of the Davidic king (see 1 Kings 6:11-13; Deuteronomy 17:14-17). If the king or any of his descendants lead his nation into habitual violation of the Mosaic Covenant, the glorious temple would be reduced to rubble and the people cast out of their land (Deuteronomy 28:37; 29:22-28).

While the Davidic Covenant was unconditional, any Davidic descendant's enjoyment of the covenant was completely conditional, based on his faithfulness to God's law. The perpetuity of the Davidic dynasty was both sure and certain; however, a particular descendant's participation and longevity within the dynasty depended on his commitment to the Lord. In this address, this truth was particularly pointed toward Solomon, who was gently reminded that he was, as would be every future royal descendant of David, only one cog in an extremely prolific dynastic machine and, therefore, ultimately replaceable (1 Kings 9:1-9). The national consequences for Davidic disloyalty warned of here were finally carried out in the Babylonian captivity (2 Chronicles 36:14-21).

SOLOMON TO RECEIVE DIVINE JUDGMENT
1 Kings 11:9-13,31-39

THE FINAL PORTION OF Solomon's reign is characterized by exactly the manner of disobedience and covenantal disloyalty he had been divinely warned to avoid (9:1-9). Guilty of violating Deuteronomy 17:14-17, Solomon is admonished by the Lord that his behavior warrants the removal of the kingdom of Israel from his progeny's rule. This punishment would not affect Solomon's rule but would begin with the rule of Solomon's heir. To maintain divine fidelity to the unconditional Davidic Covenant (2 Samuel 7:8-16; 2 Chronicles 17:10-14), the king's son would not lose the kingdom in its entirety, but would retain control over the people of his own tribe, Judah (the diminutive tribe of Benjamin was thought of as a subset of the substantial Judah), and their territory, including the holy city of Jerusalem.

This judgment is confirmed in the subsequent passage, which details the message to Jeroboam of his imminent ascendancy (1 Kings 11:31-39). There is one telling detail in the final verse of this recapitulation of Davidic punishment that must not be overlooked. "Thus I will afflict the descendants of David for this, but not always" (11:39). This gloomy message of judgment ends with a lustrous phrase of grace and hope—"but not always." There will come a future era when the Lord will restore a united Israel to the perfect reign of the ultimate Son of David, Jesus the Messiah, within His millennial kingdom (2 Chronicles 17:10-14).

JEROBOAM TO RULE OVER THE NORTHERN KINGDOM
1 Kings 11:31-39

ABIJAH THE PROPHET CONFRONTS Jeroboam with the divine message that the Lord had selected him to replace Solomon's dynasty and succeed Solomon in ruling over Israel's ten northern tribes, offering him the promise of his own enduring royal dynasty (11:31-35).

When Solomon's son Rehoboam becomes king, the united kingdom of Israel splits in half, and Jeroboam is made king over the northern kingdom of Israel, in fulfillment of Abijah's prophecy (12:20).

BODIES OF THE FALSE PRIESTS TO BE BURNED
1 Kings 13:1-3

DURING JEROBOAM'S REIGN, a prophet declares that a future Davidic king, Josiah, would one day burn on an altar the bones of the priests who officiated at the idolatrous high places in Israel. This prophecy is immediately confirmed through a miraculous sign when, as the prophet had predicted, the altar splits (13:5). Some three centuries later, the prophecy was fulfilled by King Josiah (2 Kings 23:15-17).

A DISOBEDIENT PROPHET TO DIE
1 Kings 13:20-26

THE PROPHET WHO HAD proclaimed the Josiah prophecy (13:1-3) had been divinely instructed not to eat. However, another prophet meets him and falsely relays instruction for the first prophet to eat. The first prophet mistakenly believes the second prophet's message, learning too late, after having eaten, that the second prophet has misrepresented himself as having received the Lord's instruction (13:14-19). Strangely, the second prophet, who had purposely misrepresented himself, now receives a divine message directed to the first prophet. This message, one of judgment, reveals that the first prophet would die because he had taken the unconfirmed word of the second prophet, contrary to the previous instruction he had personally received from the Lord (13:20-22). A lion kills the first prophet later that same evening (13:23-26).

JEROBOAM WARNED OF IMPENDING DISASTER
1 Kings 14:1-16

IN 1 KINGS 14:1-16, AHIJAH, the prophet who had revealed to Jeroboam that he would be king (11:31-39), delivers a harsh message of divine judgment to Jeroboam. As recompense for Jeroboam's unprecedented extravagance of idolatry, the royal dynasty of Jeroboam would be cut off—not only from the rule of Israel, but from life itself, beginning with the immediate death of Jeroboam's own son. This judgment would not be limited to Jeroboam's dynasty, but would eventually extend to the entire northern kingdom of Israel, who would be dispossessed from the land of promise (14:15-16).

The death of Jeroboam's son is recounted in the subsequent passage (14:17-20), and the annihilation of Jeroboam's dynasty in 15:29-30.

DYNASTY OF BAASHA TO BE TERMINATED
1 Kings 16:1-4

HERE, JEHU THE PROPHET prophesies the termination of Baasha's dynasty. Although Baasha is the instrument God uses to cut off Jeroboam's dynasty, Baasha is guilty of the same sins of idolatry for which Jeroboam was judged. The dynasty of Baasha is shattered by Zimri, fulfilling this prophecy (16:11-13).

DROUGHT TO COME AT ELIJAH'S COMMAND
1 Kings 17:1

THE PROPHET ELIJAH PROCLAIMS to King Ahab that Israel will experience a period of unrelenting drought, with rain to come solely at the discretion of Elijah himself (17:1). The narrative records the ensuing drought (17:7) and the rain that finally comes at Elijah's request (18:41-45).

WIDOW TO BE CONTINUOUSLY RESUPPLIED
1 Kings 17:7-16

WHILE STAYING AT THE HOME of the impoverished widow of Zarephath, Elijah predicts that her meager supply of flour and oil will be continuously resupplied so that their needs are met. The narrative recounts this miracle within the immediate text (17:15-16).

ARAMEANS TO BE DEFEATED BY AHAB
1 Kings 20:13-14

A PROPHET APPROACHES King Ahab with the encouraging news that he will be victorious over Ben-Hadad's Aramean forces (20:13-14). Ahab's subsequent victory is recounted in verses 19-21.

ARAMEANS TO ATTACK AHAB AGAIN
1 Kings 20:22

THE SAME PROPHET DELIVERS a preparatory warning to Ahab that the Arameans will attack again at the time of the new year. When the Aramean forces were arrayed against Israel, another prophet assured Ahab of victory (20:26-30).

ANOTHER DISOBEDIENT PROPHET TO DIE
1 Kings 20:35-36

IN A BIZARRE EPISODE, one member of the prophetic guild (Hebrew, *b'nay ha'navi'im*), the "sons of the prophets," having received divine instruction, asks a fellow guild member to strike him. The second prophet flatly refuses to hurt the first prophet (20:35). Consequently, the Lord's judgment is exercised against the disobedient prophet and the Lord reveals that he would soon be killed by a lion. The narrative then records the fulfillment of this prophecy (20:36).

BEN-HADAD TO BRING DISASTER
1 Kings 20:42

HAVING FINALLY FOUND a fellow prophet to strike him in obedience to the Lord's directives (see commentary on 20:35-36), the wounded prophet prophesies to Ahab that disaster will befall Ahab on account of his sparing of Ben-Hadad's life. This prophecy is fulfilled shortly thereafter when Ahab is killed in battle (22:34-35).

AHAB TO DIE
1 Kings 21:17-20

AHAB HAS AN INNOCENT MAN, Naboth, murdered in order to confiscate Naboth's vineyard. The prophet Elijah, confronting Ahab over his sin, relays a message of God's judgment: "In the place where the dogs licked up the blood of Naboth the dogs will lick up your blood, even yours" (21:19).

Elijah's message of condemnation and humiliation continues, predicting that not only would Ahab's life soon be forfeited for his crimes against God and men, but that his royal dynasty would be replaced, as Jeroboam's and Baasha's dynasties previously had been (21:21-22). The dogs did indeed lap up the blood of Ahab's corpse, just as Elijah had predicted (22:37-38). Ahab's 70 sons are later assassinated, cutting off the dynasty (2 Kings 10:7-11). This message of divine condemnation against Ahab's dynasty is echoed by Elisha in 2 Kings 9:7-9.

DOGS TO EAT JEZEBEL
1 Kings 21:23; 2 Kings 9:10

AFTER ELIJAH CONDEMNS AHAB, the prophet also predicts that Jezebel, Ahab's queen and the chief motivating force behind his wicked activity, would be eaten by dogs in Jezreel. Later, Elisha's prophetic associate recapitulates this prophecy, adding the detail that her corpse would not be buried (2 Kings 9:10). This wicked queen's grisly end is recorded in 2 Kings 9:30-37.

MICAIAH PREDICTS AHAB'S DEFEAT
1 Kings 22:13-28; 2 Chronicles 18:12-27

CONTEMPLATING AN ALLIANCE of war, kings Ahab and Jehoshaphat consult Israel's prophetic guild for divine direction. After receiving a suspiciously positive report from Ahab's local prophets, Jehoshaphat requests one more opinion, that of the prophet Micaiah. At first Micaiah gives the two kings a similarly positive answer, but when the prophet is pressed for a truthful answer that found its source in divine revelation, Micaiah conveys a negative report of forthcoming military failure that would result in Ahab's death.

A notable and peculiar inclusion in the narrative is Micaiah's vision of an executive brainstorming session within the heavenly court, in which the Lord solicits plans from spiritual beings to entice Ahab to charge to his doom. A volunteer comes forward to serve as a "lying spirit" to deceive Ahab's prophetic advisors (1 Kings 22:19-23; 2 Chronicles 18:18-22).

Disregarding the true word of the Lord, Ahab goes out to war and is killed in battle (1 Kings 22:34-38; 2 Chronicles 18:33-34). This account, like so many in the annals of the Kings, reminds us of the importance of our obedience to God's Word.

2 KINGS

For introductory remarks, see the introduction to 1 Kings on page 83.

ELIJAH PROPHESIES AHAZIAH'S DEATH
2 Kings 1:1-4

The prophet Elijah opens 2 Kings with a prophecy that King Ahaziah, as a result of attempting consultation with the prophet of a foreign god instead of the Lord Himself, would not recover from an injury (1:1-4). This prophecy is recapitulated in 1:16 and fulfilled in 1:17.

ELISHA PROMISED A DOUBLE PORTION
2 Kings 2:1-14

The second chapter of 2 Kings contains a mini-complex of prophecies relating to the transport of Elijah to heaven and the consequent transfer of prophetic authority from Elijah to Elisha. First, Bethel's prophetic guild (Hebrew, *b'nay ha-navi'im*, "sons of the prophets") informs Elisha that the Lord will take Elijah that day (2:3). Second, Jericho's prophetic guild offers the same information (2:5). Third, after a miraculous crossing of the Jordan, Elisha asks Elijah if he could receive a "double portion" of Elijah's spirit after his mentor has been taken (2:9). Elijah replies, "You have asked a hard thing. Nevertheless, if you see me when I am taken from you, it shall be so for you; but if not, it shall not be so" (2:10).

Elisha witnesses Elijah being taken up in a chariot of fire and so receives his request, taking up the mantle of Elijah and following in his prophetic footsteps (2:11-14).

ELISHA PREDICTS THE DEFEAT OF MOAB
2 Kings 3:15-20

Unless this passage describes an anomalous situation, some insight may be gleaned here into the ancient prophetic process. Either to set an inspirational mood or to help provide the correct frame of mind, Elisha requests that a musician play prior to his prophesying. It is while the music plays that "the hand of the Lord came upon him" (3:15). Elisha proclaims that Jehoram and Jehoshaphat, the respective kings of Israel and Judah, will have military success against the Moabites. They are instructed to have ditches dug to contain the water the Lord would suddenly and spectacularly provide, without rain, for the refreshment of their forces and animals (3:16-20).

This prophecy is fulfilled when the Moabite forces mistake the water-filled trenches glistening in the sunlight for a blood-soaked battlefield. Expecting an easy victory, they come against Israel and instead, experience a grueling defeat (3:21-27).

WIDOW'S JARS TO BE FILLED
2 Kings 4:3-4

In 2 Kings 4 Elisha encounters the desperate, debt-encumbered widow of one of his fellow prophets. Learning that all she had to her name was a meager supply of oil, Elisha instructs her to borrow from her neighbors as many jars as are available, prophesying that God would miraculously multiply her oil (4:3-4). The multiplied amount of oil fills every vessel in the home, providing a sufficient amount for her to sell and live off the profit (4:5-7).

PREDICTION OF THE POT OF STEW
2 Kings 4:38-41

During a time of famine, Gilgal's prophetic guild, in the company of Elisha, begins to eat a dish of stew. Unfortunately, poisonous gourds were among the ingredients in this stew. In the midst of their meal, the prophets realize that there is "death in the pot" and the stew could not be eaten, regardless of the intensity of their hunger (4:40). Elisha, introducing a quantity of flour into the stew, prophetically declares it is now edible, and it is eaten with no adverse effects (4:41).

ELISHA PROPHESIES THE PROVISION OF FOOD
2 Kings 4:42-44

A man brings a firstfruits offering of bread and grain to Elisha and his prophetic guild associates (4:42-44). Although it is an insufficient quantity to adequately feed 100 prophets, Elisha prophesies that not only do they have a sufficient amount to feed everyone, but there would be leftovers as well. This prophesy is fulfilled as expected (verse 44).

NAAMAN PROMISED HEALING OF HIS LEPROSY
2 Kings 5:10

Naaman, the leprous commander of the Aramean army, seeks healing at the hand of Elisha (5:1-9). Elisha instructs Naaman that after he washes himself seven times in the Jordan, he will be healed (5:10). At first Naaman balks, expecting a more dramatic encounter and set of instructions. However, upon following Elisha's prophetic instruction, the Aramean commander is healed exactly as the prophet had predicted (5:11-14).

PREDICTION OF GEHAZI'S LEPROSY
2 Kings 5:20-27

When Naaman offers Elisha a reward for the healing of his leprosy, Elisha refuses. But Elisha's servant, Gehazi, was not as altruistic. Behind Elisha's back, Gehazi, claiming to speak on Elisha's behalf, requests and receives a reward. When Elisha confronts Gehazi, the latter lies, denying his unauthorized encounter with Naaman. In response, Elisha predicts that Naaman's leprosy would now terminally afflict Gehazi and his descendents in perpetuity. Thus afflicted, Gehazi takes his leave from Elisha (verse 27).

THE LORD'S PROTECTION OF ELISHA
2 Kings 6:8-23

Elisha prophetically warns Israel's king to avoid a series of ambushes planned by the Aramean army (6:8-10). Enraged at the unexpected foiling of his plans, Aram's king demands of his men the identity of the traitor in their midst who had obviously passed along classified information to the enemy camp (verse 11). He was informed that it was not a spy, but Elisha, who had so frustrated his goal (6:12).

Enraged, the king of Aram sends an impressive army to capture the prophet. In the morning, when Elisha's servant sees they are surrounded by the Aramean army, he panics. Elisha answers, "Do not fear, for those who are with us are more than those who are with them" (6:16). The servant then sees the supernatural forces the Lord had arrayed to protect them. The prophet then prays that the Aramean army would be struck with blindness. Elisha then leads the blinded foreign army into the heart of Samaria. There, the Lord restores the Arameans' vision, and they realize that Elisha has led them into the presence of Israel's king. Instead of execution, Elisha counsels mercy, instructing the king of Israel to feed the now-humbled army and send them home. Apparently a sufficient impression had been made, for these particular Aramean marauders troubled Israel no more (verse 23).

ELISHA PREDICTS FAMINE RELIEF
2 Kings 6:24–7:2

DURING A TIME of severe famine, Elisha predicts famine relief within the next 24 hours. The officer of Israel's king, one of the men to whom this prophecy is addressed, scoffs at Elisha's prophecy. Elisha responds with a prophetic addition to the message: The disdaining unbeliever would be dead within 24 hours and would completely miss experiencing the famine relief. The famine miraculously concludes the following day when the people of Israel realize that the Aramean army had left food in their camp. In their frantic hunger-fueled haste, the mob stampedes through the city gate, in the process fatally trampling the cynical officer of the king, who, as Elisha had predicted, failed to enjoy the respite from famine (7:16-20).

PREDICTION OF SEVEN-YEAR FAMINE
2 Kings 8:1

IN 2 KINGS CHAPTER 8, Elisha successfully predicts a seven-year period of famine over Israel (verse 1).

BEN-HADAD'S DEATH PREDICTED
2 Kings 8:7-10

IN DAMASCUS, the king of Aram, Ben-Hadad, inquires of Elisha through Hazael whether he will recover from his present illness. Elisha reveals to Hazael that Ben-Hadad would in fact recover from his sickbed, but that he would still die anyway, only not from sickness (8:7-10). Hazael returns to his king, reports to the king that his illness is not fatal, and then himself assassinates the king (8:14-15).

PREDICTION OF HAZAEL'S MASSACRE
2 Kings 8:12-13

DURING ELISHA'S conversation with Hazael, the prophet foresees a brutal massacre of Israelites at the hand of Hazael. When pressed by Hazael as to how this could be, Elisha further reveals that Hazael will become Aram's king (8:12-13). After Hazael assassinates Ben-Hadad, he does indeed become the king of Aram (8:15). Hazael's destructive path through Israel is described in 2 Kings 10:32; 12:17-18; 13:3,22.

JEHU TO RULE ISRAEL
2 Kings 9:1-9

IN 2 KINGS 9:1 ELISHA SENDS one of his associates in the prophetic guild on a mission to the military garrison at Ramoth-gilead. The prophet is to search out one of Israel's military commanders, Jehu, anoint him as the future king of Israel, charge him with the destruction of Ahab's dynasty, and then effect a hasty escape. The prophetic proclamation and anointing of Jehu is fulfilled as Jehu and his men carry out a coup against the king of Israel (9:14-28). The condemnation of Ahab's dynasty echoes Elijah's previous prophecy of divine condemnation against Ahab's dynasty (1 Kings 21:21-22). Ahab's 70 sons are later assassinated by Jehu, and the entire royal dynasty is cut down (2 Kings 10:7-17).

DOGS TO EAT JEZEBEL
1 Kings 21:23; 2 Kings 9:10

THIS IS ELISHA'S recapitulation of a prophecy Elijah gave earlier (1 Kings 21:23). Along with the prophet's anointing of Jehu and prediction of ruin for Ahab's dynasty, the prophet also includes the prediction that Jezebel, Ahab's wicked queen, would be eaten by dogs in Jezreel, adding the detail that her corpse would not be buried. Jezebel's grisly end is recorded in 2 Kings 9:30-37.

THE PROPHECY OF JEHU'S DYNASTY
2 Kings 10:30-31

THE LORD REVEALS to Jehu that his dynasty will continue for four generations (10:30-31). This is fulfilled in 2 Kings 15:8,12.

THE PROPHECY OF JOASH'S VICTORIES
2 Kings 13:14-19

ON HIS DEATHBED, Elisha prophesies to King Joash that Israel will achieve three military victories over the Arameans. This is fulfilled in 2 Kings 13:25.

KING OF ASSYRIA TO BE ASSASSINATED
2 Kings 19:5-7

ISAIAH PROPHESIES to Hezekiah that he should not fear Assyria, for their king, Sennacherib, would soon abandon his siege of Jerusalem and be assassinated in his homeland. Indeed, the king meets his fate while at worship within an Assyrian temple (19:36-37; 2 Chronicles 32:21).

JERUSALEM TO BE SAVED
2 Kings 19:20-34

ISAIAH DELIVERS an extensive prophecy to Hezekiah and predicts that the Assyrian siege of Jerusalem will prove futile. The Lord guarantees the security of Jerusalem for a period of three years (19:20-33), saying, "I will defend this city to save it for My own sake and for My servant David's sake" (19:34). That very evening the Lord annihilates 185,000 of the Assyrians encamped around Jerusalem, terminating the Assyrian threat and fulfilling the prophecy (19:35-36; 2 Chronicles 32:21).

HEZEKIAH GIVEN AN EXTENSION OF LIFE
2 Kings 20:1-11; 2 Chronicles 32:24

ISAIAH INFORMS the gravely ill King Hezekiah of the Lord's directive to set his affairs in order, for the king would not recover from his illness (20:1). In response, Hezekiah cries out to the Lord for an extension of mercy (20:2-3). Before Isaiah departs from the palace, the Lord, referencing the Davidic Covenant, tells his prophet that Hezekiah would indeed receive divine mercy, and would be healed from his disease. Indeed, an extension of 15 years is granted to Hezekiah (20:4-6). God grants the king miraculous confirmation by reversing a shadow that is cast along a palace stairway (20:8-11). Second Chronicles 32:24 briefly summarizes these events.

BABYLONIAN CAPTIVITY TO COME
2 Kings 20:16-19

THE LORD, FURIOUS WITH King Hezekiah for exhibiting Jerusalem's treasure to a Babylonian prince, sends Isaiah to the king to proclaim a devastating message. In a period following Hezekiah's death, both Judah's treasure and citizens, including members of Hezekiah's own dynasty, would be carried away into Babylonian captivity (20:16-19). The Babylonian conquest and activity is depicted in 2 Kings 24:10–25:21 and 2 Chronicles 36:1-21.

PREDICTION OF MANASSEH'S DOWNFALL
2 Kings 21:10-15

So SEVERE IS the Lord's judgment against the wicked king Manasseh that it takes multiple prophets to deliver the warning. The Lord condemns the king's unparalleled idolatry and promises unprecedented judgment upon both king and citizenry (21:10-15). Choosing to ignore the prophecy, Manasseh is captured by the Assyrian army and led off in chains to Babylon (2 Chronicles 33:10-11).

JOSIAH NOT TO WITNESS GOD'S JUDGMENT
2 Kings 22:15-20; 2 Chronicles 34:14-28

FOLLOWING THE REDISCOVERY of the book of Deuteronomy during Josiah's renovation of the temple, consultation is made with the prophetess Huldah (2 Kings 22:1-14; 2 Chronicles 34:1-22). Huldah prophesies to Josiah that Judah's habitual idolatry would cause the divine retribution promised for covenant disloyalty, as described in Deuteronomy 28:15-68, to be unleashed upon the nation (2 Kings 22:15-17; 2 Chronicles 34:23-25). This will not occur, however, until after Josiah's death, due to his fidelity to the Mosaic Covenant (2 Kings 22:18-20; 2 Chronicles 34:26-28).

JUDAH'S JUDGMENT IMPENDING
2 Kings 23:26-27

ALTHOUGH JOSIAH HAS renovated the temple, rediscovered the book of Deuteronomy, reinstituted Passover observance, and brought about numerous other reforms, the Lord's previous prophecies of Judah's judgment are still reiterated.

The Babylonian conquest and captivity is depicted in 2 Kings 24:10–25:21 and 2 Chronicles 36:1-21.

1 CHRONICLES

Much of the narrative of 1 Chronicles recapitulates events and statements that appear in 1 and 2 Samuel. The Chronicles were written by the priests of Israel as a parallel account to the narrative of the prophets as recorded in the books of Samuel and Kings. Second Chronicles parallels much of 1 and 2 Kings. Together, the books of Kings and Chronicles provide a thorough picture of the kings of Israel and Judah and the spiritual life of the people.

THE DAVIDIC COVENANT
1 Chronicles 17:7-14

See commentary at 2 Samuel 7:8-16.

THE PUNISHMENT OF ISRAEL
1 Chronicles 21:1-13

The fulfillment of the prophecy in 1 Chronicles 21:1-13 is described in the subsequent passage, 1 Chronicles 21:14-17. This is a parallel account of the sin, prediction, and punishment relayed within the narrative of 2 Samuel 24.

THE PROPHECY REGARDING SOLOMON
1 Chronicles 22:8-10

Much of 1 Chronicles 22:8-10 is a confirmation, recapitulation, and expansion of central aspects of the Davidic Covenant (see 2 Samuel 7:8-16). David, toward the conclusion of his life, charged his son and chosen heir, Solomon, to construct the Lord's temple (1 Chronicles 22:6-7). It was the Lord's expressed desire and purpose for His temple to be built through Solomon. Unlike his father's blood-spattered career, Solomon's reign would be characterized by peace.

2 CHRONICLES

For introductory remarks, see the introduction to 1 Chronicles on page 93.

SOLOMON GRANTED DIVINE BLESSINGS
2 Chronicles 1:10-12

For commentary, see the parallel passage of 1 Kings 3:10-14.

SOLOMON IN LIGHT OF THE DAVIDIC COVENANT
2 Chronicles 7:12-22

Second Chronicles 7:12-22 is parallel to 1 Kings 9:1-9. There is only one significant difference between the two passages, the noteworthy addition in 2 Chronicles, placed there for specific theological emphasis, of God's promises in 7:12-15. These pledges supply the answer to the content of Solomon's preceding prayer, especially within 6:22-39, that the Lord "would hear the prayers offered in or directed toward the temple" (Williamson, *1 and 2 Chronicles*, p. 225).

The Lord appeared to Solomon at night and said to him, "I have heard your prayer and have chosen this place for Myself as a house of sacrifice. If I shut up the heavens so that there is no rain, or if I command the locust to devour the land, or if I send pestilence among My people, and My people who are called by My name humble themselves and pray and seek My face and turn from their wicked ways, then I will hear from heaven, will forgive their sin and will heal their land. Now My eyes will be open and My ears attentive to the prayer offered in this place" (7:12-15).

The context of this passage is the people's worship in the temple, the "house of sacrifice" (7:12) of the nation of Israel. The Lord promises His covenant nation that He will be "attentive to the prayer offered in this place" (7:15) and that the land He is committed to healing is "their" (Israel's) land (7:14).

MICAIAH PREDICTS AHAB'S DEFEAT
2 Chronicles 18:12-27

For commentary, see parallel passage of 1 Kings 22:13-28.

JAHAZIEL PROPHESIES JUDAH'S VICTORY
2 Chronicles 20:15-17,20-25

Jahaziel the Levite prophesies to Judah, Jerusalem, and King Jehoshaphat the encouraging news that the Lord would provide them victory without any actual military conflict. They were merely to march down to the enemy position in the wilderness of Tekoa—the Lord would do the rest! This was literally fulfilled the following day as the Ammonites and Moabites destroyed one another (20:20-25).

ELIEZER PROPHESIES JEHOSHAPHAT'S FAILURE
2 Chronicles 20:37

Due to King Jehoshaphat's alliance with Israel's King Ahaziah, Eliezer prophesies that Jehoshaphat's shipbuilding endeavor would come to naught. This was immediately fulfilled, as "the ships were broken and could not go to Tarshish" (20:37).

ELIJAH PROPHESIES JUDGMENT
2 Chronicles 21:12-20

FOLLOWING JEHOSHAPHAT'S death, his son, the ultraviolent and morally bankrupt Jehoram, begins his reign over Judah (21:1-11). When Jehoram's multiple sins against the Lord and the nation finally reach the tipping point of divine wrath, Elijah the prophet sends a letter of denunciation to the king, prophesying calamity against both Jehoram and his entire family.

Interestingly, the Lord's judgment was directed specifically toward Jehoram and his family, and not the Davidic line as a whole, for according to 2 Chronicles 21:7, God had an unconditional commitment to the nation and the Davidic line as previously expressed within the Davidic Covenant (2 Samuel 7:8-16; 1 Chronicles 17:10-14).

Elijah's prophecy against Jehoram was fulfilled when Judah's enemies invaded the land, pillaged the king's possessions, and took captive his wives and all but one son. Jehoram then succumbed to a terminal intestinal disease that proved both painful and, within two years, fatal (21:16-19). Jehoram was buried with ceremonial minimalism, having "departed with no one's regret, and they buried him in the city of David, but not in the tombs of the kings" (21:20).

ZECHARIAH PROPHESIES BAD TIDINGS
2 Chronicles 24:20-25

A SERIES OF PROPHETS are sent to warn King Joash and his administration that they are falling afoul of the Lord. Finally, the Lord raises up Zechariah, the son (possibly the grandson—see Matthew 23:35) of the late Jehoiada, a priest who had a tremendous reforming influence over King Joash, to proclaim a warning of divine displeasure (24:20). This warning so infuriates the king and his officials that the mob immediately stones Zechariah in the temple courts (24:21). The prophet's final words are, "May the LORD see and avenge!" (24:22).

Within the year, both divine judgment and Zechariah's vindication come. The Arameans invade Judah and Jerusalem and, although they are a modest force, they leave great damage in their wake (24:23-24). Joash's own servants "conspired against him because of the blood of the son of Jehoiada the priest, and murdered him on his bed" (24:25).

AN UNNAMED PROPHET DENOUNCES KING AMAZIAH
2 Chronicles 25:15-16,27

JOASH IS SUCCEEDED BY his son, Amaziah. An unnamed prophet is sent to denounce him for the grave sin of idolatry. Instead of repenting of his sin, Amaziah offers the prophet a haughty, unremorseful attitude coupled with a threat. In parting, the prophet promises Amaziah that "God has planned to destroy you, because you have done this and have not listened to my counsel" (25:16). Eleven verses later, Amaziah is exiled and soon after, assassinated (25:27).

GOD PROMISES HEZEKIAH MORE YEARS
2 Chronicles 32:24

FOR COMMENTARY, SEE the extended parallel passage in 2 Kings 20:1-11.

EZRA

THE FINAL THREE BOOKS OF HISTORY IN THE OLD TESTAMENT were written after the Babylonian captivity and record the events of Israel's return to the Promised Land. Ezra, falling within the genre of historic Hebrew narrative, is devoid of eschatological content, with the exception of one general statement of prophetic praise.

GOD'S ETERNAL LOVE FOR ISRAEL
Ezra 3:11

ON THE FESTIVE OCCASION of laying the foundation for the rebuilt temple in Jerusalem, the assembled priests and Levites sing public songs of praise, "praising and giving thanks to the LORD, saying, 'For He is good, for His lovingkindness is upon Israel forever'" (3:11).

Most likely the words recorded within the text are merely a brief marker quotation, signaling the praise song's expanded content, which could be Psalm 100, 106, 136, or a combination of these historic exaltations of worship. The proclamation of God's mercy (Hebrew, *chesed,* or His undying covenant loving loyalty) is based upon the unconditional promises contained within the Abrahamic Covenant, which was established with Abraham and his progeny (Genesis 12:1-3,7; 13:14-17; 15:1-21; 17:1-21; 22:15-18).

NEHEMIAH

NEHEMIAH FOCUSES ON THE CHALLENGES OF REBUILDING the walls of Jerusalem during the era of the Persian occupation. Falling within the genre of historic Hebrew narrative, Nehemiah contains only two eschatological passages.

GOD'S LAND COVENANT WITH ISRAEL
Nehemiah 1:8-9

HAVING HEARD DEVASTATING news about Jerusalem's current state of disrepair, Nehemiah couples a representative confession of Israel's sins with a fervent plea for the Lord's aid in restoring the status of both His people and His holy city. Nehemiah bases his appeal on prophetic content contained within Israel's Land Covenant with God, recorded by Moses (Deuteronomy 28:64; 30:1-5).

Although the prophecy did not receive ultimate fulfillment within the narrative of Nehemiah, his inclusion of prophetic content within his prayer serves as both a helpful reminder of God's faithfulness to His covenants and a personal prompt concerning the potential content of each believer's own personal prayers.

NEHEMIAH'S ASSURANCE OF GOD'S HELP
Nehemiah 2:20

FACING HARSH OPPOSITION in his restoration efforts (2:19), Nehemiah, speaking prophetically, solemnly affirms his unreserved confidence that his community's endeavor would result in unqualified success. He bases this confidence not on his plans, his people, or their perseverance, but on the merciful aid of God Himself.

This prophecy found fulfillment upon the completion of the restoration project a mere 52 days later, much to the consternation of the Jewish people's opposition. "The wall was completed on the twenty-fifth of the month Elul, in fifty-two days. When all our enemies heard of it, and all the nations surrounding us saw it, they lost their confidence; for they recognized that this work had been accomplished with the help of our God" (6:15-16).

ESTHER

WHILE THE BOOK OF ESTHER NEITHER MENTIONS GOD'S eschatological program nor contains even an overt reference to God Himself, the narrative itself is a prophetic document that is undergirded throughout by God's providential hand. Esther is an explicit testament to God's faithfulness in preserving His chosen people, Israel, through every historic time and circumstance (Jeremiah 30:8-11; 31:23-40). This preservation is based on His unflagging commitment to the unconditional covenant established with Abraham and his progeny some 15 centuries earlier (Genesis 12:1-3,7; 13:14-17; 15:1-21).

The absence of the divine name in Esther is countered by the divine action of God on behalf of His people, preserving both them and the messianic line of Christ. This can be seen especially in Esther's decision to fast in preparation for her petition to King Xerxes. Jewish fasting is typically accompanied by sincere and serious praying to the Lord, the God of Israel.

Indeed, what unfolds within the narrative of Esther is the Abrahamic Covenant's earliest promises of divine reciprocal blessings and curses in regard to man's treatment of Israel. The plot of Esther is driven by Haman's attempt to exterminate the Jewish people. However, as the narrative nears conclusion, the tables are turned and Haman himself is executed, in realization of God's promise: "I will bless those who bless you, and the one who curses you I will curse. And in you all the families of the earth will be blessed" (Genesis 12:3).

THE POETRY

JOB

The book of Job falls within the literary genre of Hebrew poetry. As such, there is little overt prophetic content within the pages of this familiar story. Although some have interpreted as prophecy certain statements contained within the extended speeches of Job's friends, it seems better to identify these statements as theological truisms devoid of prophetic application. Nonetheless, eschatological content, although sparse within Job, may be found in two specific passages: 19:25-27 and 23:10-11.

JOB'S REDEEMER TO STAND ON THE EARTH
Job 19:25

In Job 19:25, Job makes this powerful statement about God: "I know that my Redeemer lives, and at the last He will take His stand on the earth." In the midst of his multiple afflictions, Job faithfully proclaimed his confidence that God was his redeemer, vindicator, and protector. The Hebrew word *go'el* is the same term used elsewhere to indicate God Himself as champion of His people Israel (Exodus 6:6) as well as the "kinsman-redeemer" of Ruth (2:20). Regardless of the fate that would befall Job in the near future, he possessed confidence that God remained alive and well and in perfect control of all creation. Ultimately, this statement would be fulfilled when man's ultimate *go'el*—the Redeemer, Vindicator, and Messiah—walked the earth in His first advent.

JOB, IN A RESURRECTED BODY, WOULD SEE GOD
Job 19:26-27

Immediately after Job confesses confi-

dence in his future, he confesses this about the eternal state:

> After my skin is destroyed, yet from my flesh I shall see God, whom I myself shall behold, and whom my eyes will see and not another. My heart faints within me! (Job 19:26-27).

Realizing that the current deterioration of his body would eventually lead to his death, Job is certain that his life would nonetheless continue on through bodily resurrection. In this resurrected body, He would behold (Hebrew, *chazah*, "see") God in person. The Hebrew construction of this passage is notoriously difficult. As Anderson (*Job*, p. 193) states, "There is no need for the loud note of Job's certainty of ultimate vindication to be drowned by the static of textual difficulties."

While some fail to see actual physical, bodily resurrection in Job's plea to physically see God following his body's deterioration, there are two reasons to affirm that the concept of resurrection is contextually intended. First, as Anderson (*Job*, p. 193) points out, "The references *to skin, flesh* and *eyes* make it clear that Job expects to have this experience as a man, not just as a disembodied shade, or in his mind's eye." Second, Job had made earlier reference to his confident resurrection hope: "Oh, that You would hide me in Sheol, that

You would conceal me until Your wrath returns to You, that You would set a limit for me, and remember me!" (Job 14:13).

It is clear, then, that the doctrine of bodily resurrection was not a relatively late, intertestamental development within Jewish theology, but rather, an expectation and hope that dates to the period of the very earliest of biblical manuscripts.

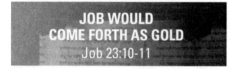

JOB WOULD COME FORTH AS GOLD
Job 23:10-11

JOB IS CONFIDENT about the ultimate outcome of His sufferings and proclaims His future vindication and eventual elevation in this way: "He knows the way I take; when He has tried me, I shall come forth as gold" (Job 23:10). Commentators state,

> The analogy here is that of the process of the purification of gold. Gold is refined or purified by means of a process called cupellation. The gold is placed in a crucible with lead and melted. As air is blown across the surface of the molten mixture, the impurities are absorbed as dross and the purified metal remains. Like the gold that comes forth from the purifying process, Job will have his honor restored after his own "purifying process" (Matthews, Chavalas, Walton, "Job," elec. ed.).

This restoration of divine favor was fulfilled at the climax of the narrative: "The LORD blessed the latter days of Job more than his beginning....And Job died, an old man and full of days" (42:12,17).

PSALMS

THE BOOK OF PSALMS CONTAINS A DIVERSE ASSORTMENT of Hebrew poetry composed for both public and private worship. The collection embraces a thematic variety extending from praise to prayer to prophecy. The psalms' assorted eschatological material contains rehearsals of both the Abrahamic and Davidic Covenants as well as both implicit and explicit expressions of fervent messianic expectation.

On the surface, the book of Psalms is not classified as one of the Old Testament's eschatological volumes. However, it is unquestionable that the poetic nuances of the vast majority of the psalms reveals their composers' confident, foundational hope in Israel's God and their ardent anticipation of Israel's glorious future. Jesus Himself indicated the psalms' weighty quantity of messianic prophecies to His disciples, saying, "All things which are written about Me in the Law of Moses and the Prophets and the Psalms must be fulfilled" (Luke 24:44). Indeed, the New Testament includes over 200 quotations from or allusions to passages, titles, and ideas contained within the book of Psalms.

WORDS OF JUDGMENT AND REWARD
Psalm 1:1-6

THE FIRST PSALM PULLS NO prophetic punches in its pessimistic portrayal of the eternal destiny of those "sinners" whose ungodly and self-destructive actions cause them to be identified as "the wicked" (verse 1). In the end, these individuals "will not stand in the judgment" (verse 5), but will be wafted away "like chaff" (verse 4). By contrast, the passage relates that both present and future blessings are in store for those whose "delight is in the law of the LORD" (verse 2). These godly individuals know the Lord and their ways are known to Him.

THE MESSIAH IS THE SON OF GOD
Psalm 2:1-12

THIS IS THE FIRST OF several messianic psalms written by David, who is both a king and a prophet. The psalm opens with a description of an impudent and conspiratorial worldwide opposition ("the kings of the earth take their stand and the rulers take counsel together") to both God and to "His Anointed" (Hebrew, *mashiach*), the Messiah (2:1-3). This is followed by a depiction of the Lord's wrath being unleashed on all those who contest the Jewish King whom He has personally installed ("My King") to rule Israel from Jerusalem, "upon Zion, My holy mountain" (2:4-6).

David's poetry shifts from third-person narrative to the first-person voice of the Messiah (2:7-9). The text affirms that the Messiah is the Lord's Son, endowed with the very authority of God Almighty Himself ("You are My Son, today I have begotten You"). This authority extends not only over Israel, but over all nations of the earth ("Ask of Me, and I will surely give the nations as Your inheritance, and the very ends of the earth as Your possession"). The phrase "son of God" appears in the Old Testament to denote the unique qualities of the relationship between God and Israel (Hosea 11:1) and God and the Davidic king of Israel within the context of the Davidic Covenant (2 Samuel 7:11-16; 1 Chronicles 17:10-14). Within this psalm, the phrase "My Son" denotes the relationship between God and the promised Messiah (Psalm 2:7).

This psalm's descriptions and imagery force the reader into making a crucial interpretive choice. Historically, neither David nor his royal descendants ever possessed the worldwide authority attributed to this psalm's king (2:8). As Kidner argues, the second psalm "presents him in terms which leave the limitations of local kingship far behind" (Kidner, *Psalms 1–72*, p. 18). Unless one attributes to David a vast hyperbolic perpetration, one must undoubtedly conclude that the scope of what David described here extends far beyond the immediate prospects of any contemporary Old Testament Israelite king and into the far reaches of an eschatological future.

The passage then shifts back to the third person with a warning of the unqualified severity of the Son of God's judgment and wrath ("that He not become angry, and you perish in the way, for His wrath may soon be kindled") to be directed toward all those who do not worship the Lord by showing due reverence toward His Son ("Worship the LORD with reverence and rejoice with trembling. Do homage to the Son"). A person's rapport with the Lord is determined through his stance regarding His Son, the messianic King ("How blessed are all who take refuge in Him!") (2:10-12).

Without question, this passage traditionally has been recognized as messianic. As the revered eleventh-century rabbi Rashi (who always stood ready with an alternative interpretation to various pesky messianic prophecies that did not fit his theological grid) acknowledges, "Our rabbis relate it as relating to King Messiah" (Fruchtenbaum, *Messianic Christology*, p. 80). Additional ancient Jewish sources have endowed Psalm 2 with messianic import. Edersheim begins his discussion by noting that the psalm, "as might be expected, is treated as full of Messianic references" (Edersheim, *Life and Times of Jesus the Messiah*, 2:716). For example, commenting on 2:7-8, the Talmud records this messianic scenario based upon the two-messiah theory then in vogue:

> Our Rabbis taught, The Holy One, blessed be He, will say to the Messiah, the son of David (May he reveal himself speedily in our days!), "Ask of me anything, and I will give it to thee," as it is said, *I will tell of the decree* etc. *this day have I begotten thee, ask of me and I will give the nations for thy inheritance.* But when he will see that the Messiah the son of Joseph is slain, he will say to Him, "Lord of the Universe, I ask of Thee only the gift of life." "As to life," He would answer him, "Your father David has already prophesied this concerning you," as it is said, *He asked life of thee, thou gavest it him* [*even length of days for ever and ever*] (Babylonian Talmud, *Sukkah 52a*, as quoted in Huckel, "Psalms," elec. ed).

Huckel likewise supplies a veritable laundry list of supporting quotations from ancient Jewish sources (Babylonian Talmud, *Berakoth 10a; 'Abodah Zarah 3b*; Midrash on Psalms, *Book One*, Psalm 2,2; 2,3; 2,8; 2,10; *Book Four*, Psalm 92,10; Midrash Rabbah, *Genesis* XLIV, 8; XCVII, New Version; Pesiqta de-Reb Kahana, *Piska* 9, 11, as quoted in Huckel, "Psalms," elec. ed).

The entirety of the New Testament and the Gospel of John in particular rest comfortably on the foundation of the prophetic truths contained in this psalm. Peter applied this psalm to the hostile Jewish leaders in Jerusalem (Acts 4:25-26), and Paul quoted from this psalm in order to demonstrate that Jesus is the resurrected Messiah (Acts 13:22-30; Romans 1:4). Likewise, Hebrews emphasizes God's exaltation of Jesus through His first advent resurrection, proclaiming His divine sonship through the prophetic declaration in Psalm 2:7: "You are My Son, today I have begotten You" (Hebrews 1:5). The complete prophetic fulfillment of this psalm, however, extends beyond Jesus' first coming and into His second advent and the establishment of the messianic kingdom.

THE MESSIAH WILL RULE THE EARTH
Psalm 8:4-5

This psalm, interpreted in its original context, concerns the exalted role of man with God's creation. However, the author of Hebrews related the application of this passage to Jesus, the ultimate messianic ruler over all creation (Hebrews 2:6-8), who was "man *par excellence*" (Kidner, *Psalms 1–72*, p. 22).

THE LORD WILL JUDGE ALL
Psalm 9:7-8; 11:6-7

Within the context of a Davidic hymn of praise is revealed this prophetic truth: God will sit in judgment over both righteous and wicked, having "established His throne for judgment, and He will judge the world in righteousness" (9:7-8). This prophetic fact will ultimately find fulfillment at the judgment seat of Christ (Romans 14:12; 2 Corinthians 5:10) and at the final judgment of the wicked (Revelation 20:11-15). In the midst of a paean to God's sheltering protection, David proclaims the prophetic truth that God hates the wicked,

and their final judgment will result in "fire and brimstone and burning wind." Alternately, the righteous are beloved of God and "will behold His face" (11:6-7).

THE FUTURE RESTORATION OF ISRAEL
Psalm 14:7

David writes of the joyful reaction the people of Israel will have when they are restored from a future captivity through the salvation (Hebrew, *yeshua*) of the messianic king ruling from Jerusalem ("that the salvation of Israel would come out of Zion"). While some interpret this verse to refer to the restoration of the Jewish people to their land following the Babylonian exile, the absence of either a contemporaneous Jewish king coupled with the lack of any manner of salvation emanating from Jerusalem indicates that this more probably relates to Israel's corporate return to both the Lord and to their land during the events relating to the establishment of the messianic rule of Jesus (Hebrew, *Yeshua*) in the kingdom (Isaiah 59:20; Romans 11:26-27).

THE RESURRECTION OF THE MESSIAH
Psalm 16

This is another messianic psalm of David, written in the first-person voice of the Messiah, his descendant. The specific circumstances attending David's composition of this psalm are unknown. However, it begins with David's plea for God's preservation of his life (16:1). It continues with praise for God's mercy (16:2) and goodness (16:3,5-7) and comments on the hopelessness of others foolish enough to worship other gods instead of the one true God (16:4). David concludes the psalm with a confirmation of confidence in the Lord's sustenance of his flesh and soul, both in the present and beyond death (16:8-11). He rejoices that his "flesh also will dwell securely," for "You will not abandon my soul to Sheol; nor will You allow Your Holy One to undergo decay."

Some understand this psalm, in context, as the *poetic expression* of David's immediate experience of divine deliverance from death. Many psalms appear only in New Testament hindsight to reveal a larger prophetic truth than their initial historical contexts originally suggested. Ross cogently expresses this view:

> The same ambiguity applies to the messianic psalms. With the knowledge of full revelation in Jesus Christ, one can look back to the Psalms…and see that they often speak of Christ.…Yet to Old Testament believers, the full meanings of these passages were not often evident. On the one hand a psalmist described his own suffering or triumph, and on the other hand those expressions, which may have seemed extravagant for the psalmist's actual experience, later became true of Jesus Christ (Ross, "Psalms," p. 789).

This psalm, however, does not fit into that somewhat nebulous category. The unambiguous apostolic teaching is that this psalm contains direct prophecy. In the book of Acts, Peter manifestly affirmed the prophetic aspect of David's writing, interpreting this passage to argue the point that David, writing 1000 years earlier, was consciously aware that his subject was the Messiah's resurrection (Acts 2:25-32). Without mincing words, Peter reminded his audience of David's prophetic capacity (Acts 2:30) and argued that David, both king and prophet, actually had written the psalm in the first-person voice of the Messiah, his descendant. Peter boldly and confidently argued that David could not possibly have been writing about himself, for David died, was buried, and most assuredly had not been resurrected.

However, God had established an indissoluble covenant with David in which David was promised that one of his descendants would forever rule over Israel (2 Samuel 7:12-13; 1 Chronicles 17:10-14; Psalm 89:3-4; 132:11). The Holy Spirit enabled David to look ahead into the future and understand precisely how God's Davidic Covenant promise of an eternal throne was to be fulfilled. God showed David that an eternal throne and an unending dynasty required an immortal descendant. David had been allowed to see the future Anointed One, the Messiah, the One who would neither decompose nor be abandoned to the abode of the dead (Greek, *Hades;* Hebrew, *Sheol*). After resting in the grave and abiding in Hades, the Messiah, paradoxically, would still live forever. In order to fulfill the Davidic Covenant, this Son of David would of necessity need to be resurrected.

Peter's point in quoting this particular prophetic psalm to his audience was that since *Jesus' messianic identity* had been clearly demonstrated through His resurrection, ascension, and exaltation to the right hand of God, it was only a matter of time before He returned to claim His birthright, the throne of David, and finally establish the messianic kingdom (Acts 2:30-36; 3:19-21).

Peter's citation of Psalm 16:8-11 in Acts 2:25-31 is one of the clearest examples in the New Testament of the *specific fulfillment of messianic prophecy.* There is no other way to interpret Peter's affirmation. Empowered and infused with the Holy Spirit (Acts 2:1-4), Peter could not have been mistaken in his interpretation, neither could he have been creatively or imaginatively appropriating the psalm to fit his theological purpose. With vibrant confidence he preached to thousands of people that one of the most exalted and revered figures in their history, David, in one of the most sacred portions of the Hebrew Scripture, the Psalms, had prophesied that the Messiah would be resurrected.

Likewise, Paul quoted this psalm in Acts 13:35-37, masterfully demonstrating the necessity of Jesus' resurrection and exaltation. The "holy and sure blessings of David" (verse 34) were the promises contained in the Davidic

Covenant. In order for the everlasting covenant to be fulfilled, the Davidic king had to be immortal. Using the same argument that Peter had made at Pentecost (Acts 2:29-32), Paul reasoned that since David had died and subsequently decomposed in his tomb, his prophecy in Psalm 16:10 could not possibly apply to David, but could only apply to a resurrected Messiah.

Therefore, the Messiah's resurrection and immortality have established the groundwork for the eventual fulfillment of the Davidic Covenant, when the kingdom of God is established. It probably would not be inappropriate to understand Paul as affirming that Jesus' glorification had launched an initial and preliminary fulfillment of the Davidic Covenant, a down payment on the day when Jesus takes His seat on David's throne in Jerusalem.

For discussion on the Son of David, see 2 Samuel 7:11-16; 1 Chronicles 17:10-14.

A TYPOLOGICAL HINT OF RESURRECTION
Psalm 17:15

THE SURFACE CONTEXT of this psalm is similar to that of the preceding psalm's surface context—a prayer from David for protection from his enemies. As discussed in the commentary on Psalm 16, the prophetic context of Psalm 16 concerned the Messiah's resurrection. Indeed, the placement of Psalms 16 and 17 together in such close proximity within the Psalter warrants a closer look at the final statement in Psalm 17: "As for me, I shall behold Your face in righteousness; I will be satisfied with Your likeness when I awake" (verse 15).

While it is possible to attribute the hopeful anticipation expressed here to poetic hyperbole, it is not necessary to do so. In Israel's history to that time, only Moses had known God "face to face" (Deuteronomy 34:10), and it therefore seems an unlikely expression to use. Furthermore, the word "sleep" has long been a recognized Jewish metaphor for death

(1 Corinthians 11:30; 15:51). Ross states that while "nowhere in the Psalms is there a clear, unambiguous expression of hope in the resurrection...some passages in the Psalms do seem to break through to express a hope of continued fellowship with God after this life" (Ross, "Psalms," p. 789).

A REFERENCE TO GENTILE SALVATION
Psalm 18:49

PSALM 18:49, IN CONTEXT an affirmation of the Davidic king's commitment to proclaim the Lord's greatness to the surrounding Gentile nations, is applied by Paul to the Gentile salvation that has commenced as the result of the Messiah's accomplishment (Romans 15:9).

A REAFFIRMATION OF THE COVENANT
Psalm 18:50

IN THE CONCLUSION of this victorious paean of praise, the psalm reaffirms the Lord's commitment to the Davidic Covenant through expressing loving covenant loyalty "to His anointed, to David and his descendants forever" (18:50). (For more on the Davidic Covenant, see the commentary for 2 Samuel 7:11-16; 1 Chronicles 17:10-14).

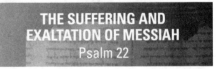

THE SUFFERING AND EXALTATION OF MESSIAH
Psalm 22

AS IS THE CASE WITH many messianic psalms (see commentary on Psalm 16), there is an interpretive difference of opinion as to exactly how much, if any, of the psalm can be classified as actual predictive prophecy. As noted elsewhere, many psalms appear, only in New

Testament hindsight, to reveal a larger prophetic truth than their initial historical contexts originally suggested.

> To Old Testament believers, the full meanings of these passages were not often evident. On the one hand a psalmist described his own suffering or triumph, and on the other hand those expressions, which may have seemed extravagant for the psalmist's actual experience, later became true of Jesus Christ (Ross, "Psalms," p. 789).

However, one would search the Scriptures in vain for an event in the life of David that corresponds to this psalm's imagery. The New Testament authors understood the ultimate referent of the psalm to be Jesus Himself. As Ross himself forthrightly says,

> No known incident in the life of David fits the details of this psalm. The expressions describe an execution, not an illness; yet that execution is more appropriate to Jesus' crucifixion than David's experience.... Thus the church has understood this psalm to be typological of the death of Jesus Christ. This means that David used many poetic expressions to portray his immense sufferings, but these poetic words became literally true of the suffering of Jesus Christ at His enemies' hands. The interesting feature of this psalm is that it does not include one word of confession of sin, and no imprecation against enemies. It is primarily the account of a righteous man who was being put to death by wicked men (Ross, "Psalms," p. 809).

The psalm opens with David's anguished cry over his perceived abandonment by the Lord. "My God, my God, why have You forsaken me? Far from my deliverance are the words of my groaning. O my God, I cry by day, but You do not answer; and by night, but I have no rest" (verses 1-2). Jesus Himself would quote the psalm's opening verse while hanging on the cross, having taken on Himself

the sin of mankind and consequently reaping the full intensity of divine wrath (Matthew 27:46; Mark 15:34).

The psalm continues with David's remembrance of prior instances of God's deliverance in Israel's history (verses 3-5). David then portrays himself as "a worm and not a man, a reproach of men and despised by the people." He describes the sneering insults, taunting, and ridicule of contemptuous passersby who view the Lord's failure to vindicate or rescue as an indication of divine rejection (verses 6-8). This corresponds with the description of the crowd's mocking of Jesus' faith and the absence of divine rescue (Matthew 27:39,42-44).

Despite the humiliation, David expresses the confident trust he has had in God from birth (Psalm 22:9-10). This also corresponds to the experience of Jesus. It is interesting to note, as does Fruchtenbaum, that "there are references here to the mother of Messiah but, as in all other messianic prophecies, there is never any mention of a human father" (Fruchtenbaum, *Messianic Christology*, p. 84).

This is followed by a detailed description of David's suffering. He calls on the Lord for deliverance from his overwhelming, all-surrounding enemies (verses 11-13,16). Notably, the physical agony David describes next (verses 14-17) goes far beyond that of any sickness or situation that can be imagined, other than the symptoms endured by one undergoing the torturous procedure of crucifixion. Indeed, the following passage is remarkably faithful, point by point, to the experience of Jesus as described in the Gospels:

> I am poured out like water, and all my bones are out of joint; my heart is like wax; it is melted within me. My strength is dried up like a potsherd, and my tongue cleaves to my jaws; and You lay me in the dust of death. For dogs have surrounded me; a band of evildoers has encompassed me; they pierced my hands and my feet. I can count all my bones (verses 14-17).

The psalm describes its victim as experiencing severe physical impairment, acute perspiration leading to dehydration, odd skeletal dislocation and protrusion, heart failure, and, most revealing, his enemies' perforation of both his hands and feet (the older rendering of the Septuagint, "pierced," is to be preferred over the later, likely corrupted, Masoretic text's "like a lion," which makes little contextual sense). The suffering continues with the victim's clothing being divided among the ill-intentioned onlookers through the casting of lots (verses 17-18).

This bears striking correspondence to what Jesus experienced on the cross (Matthew 27:35; Mark 15:24; Luke 23:34; John 19:23-24). In fact, it is hard to imagine David actually experiencing anything close to what is described here, even making allowance for poetic hyperbole, and it is, therefore, quite difficult to avoid concluding that what David has written is actual, unambiguous, predictive prophecy. The description of physical suffering is followed by a cry for divine assistance (verses 19-21).

The next section contains a remarkable change from the preceding verses. Unexpectedly the one who just described the multiplicity of agonies is present in the midst of the congregation of the Israelite faithful, enthusiastically and energetically extolling the Lord's virtues. Somehow, unrecorded within the text, between couplets, the victim's cry has been miraculously answered, and he has been rescued from his dire straits (verses 22-31). The juxtaposition of this passage of praise with the passage on physical suffering is not only jarring but challenging to interpret without the clarifying illumination that results by reading this psalm through the grid of Jesus' suffering, resurrection, and glorious reign within the messianic kingdom. The author of Hebrews, likewise understanding this psalm in a messianic sense, attributes the king's praise of 22:22 to the Messiah, Jesus (Hebrews 2:12).

Edersheim mentions early Jewish sources that apply this psalm to the Messiah (*Life and Times of Jesus the Messiah,* 2:718).

A MESSIANIC QUOTATION
Psalm 31:5

THE GOSPEL OF LUKE records that among Jesus' final words while on the cross were these words from Psalm 31:5: "Into Your hand I commit my spirit." Jesus quoted from this psalm of confident trust to apply a familiar psalmic expression to His personal experience in a typological fashion (Ross, "Psalms," p. 790). The ancient rabbis invested this psalm with messianic import (Midrash Rabbah, *Exodus* L, 5 *Deuteronomy* I, 19 Pesiqta deRab Kahana, Supplement 5, 3; Supplement 6, as quoted in Huckel, "Psalms," elec. ed.).

THE SUFFERING OF THE MESSIAH
Psalm 34:20

THE CONTEXT OF PSALM 34 speaks of God's goodness to His people, Israel. However, one verse, "He keeps all his bones, not one of them is broken" (34:20), when placed in conjunction with Exodus 12:46, which concerns the preparation of the Passover lamb, is used typologically in the Gospel of John in reference to Jesus' crucifixion. Contrary to standard practice, Jesus, having died relatively rapidly, did not need death hastened by having His legs broken while on the cross. John found great significance in this fact and highlighted it (John 19:36). Ross provides a helpful explanation of this method of biblical association:

The New Testament writers drew heavily on the Psalms to express many aspects of the person and work of Jesus, the Messiah. As the anointed Davidic King par excellence, Jesus is the great Antitype of the messianic psalms, those psalms that have the king in the foreground. Expositors must exercise caution, however; they must recognize that not *all* the contents of messianic psalms apply to Christ (i.e., not all the parts are typological). Therefore one must remember that these psalms had a primary meaning in the experience of the authors. The analysis of the historical, contextual, and grammatical meaning of the text should precede the analysis of the New Testament application to Jesus (Ross, "Psalms," p. 789).

THE DEVOTION OF THE MESSIAH
Psalm 40:7-8

THE CONTEXT OF PSALM 40 contains David's self-disclosure of sacrificial devotion to the ways of the Lord and to following His law. However, much of the psalm extends beyond any probable personal experience of David and into the prophetic realm of the future Messiah to come. Indeed, the author of Hebrews typologically singles out 40:7-8, "Behold, I come; in the scroll of the book it is written of me. I delight to do Your will, O my God; Your Law is within my heart," applying it to the Messiah's perfect obedience to the law and to His definitive sacrificial devotion to the Lord through His death (Hebrews 10:5-7). Of particular note is the deeper significance of 40:7-8 in light of Jesus' incarnation as the living embodiment of God's law (John 1:1).

THE BETRAYAL OF THE MESSIAH
Psalm 41:9

PSALM 41, IN CONTEXT, describes David's experience of mercy following his confession of sin and his plea for vindication following betrayal. Yet Jesus Himself, recognizing a typological correspondence between David's experience and His own, quoted verse 9—"even my close friend in whom I trusted, who ate my bread, has lifted up his heel against me"—in reference to Judas' betrayal, applying a familiar psalmic expression to a current event. John's Gospel records the typological fulfillment of this psalm (John 13:18).

THE DIVINE BRIDEGROOM
Psalm 45

CONTEXTUALLY, PSALM 45 IS a royal wedding song, its public recitation likely designed to be incorporated within the festivities. However, nestled snuggly within the psalm is an audacious assertion concerning the divine nature of the king, startling in its very matter-of-factness. The king himself is recognized as God (Hebrew, *elohim*): "Your throne, O God, is forever and ever" (verse 6). Furthermore, in verse 7, the divine king ("O God") of 45:6 is clearly distinguished from God Himself ("Therefore God, Your God, has anointed You with the oil of joy above Your fellows").

Although many have interpreted this passage as hyperbolic, it is important to realize that, as with many messianic prophecies (for example, Isaiah 9:6), the author has interwoven a measure of tense ambiguity in his designation of divinity to the king that can only be fully relieved in the light of the New Testament's revelation of the messianic incarnation. As Spurgeon so effectively wrote,

> Some see here Solomon and Pharaoh's daughter only—they are short-sighted; others see both Solomon and Christ— they are cross-eyed; well-focused spiritual eyes see here Jesus only, or if Solomon be present at all, it must be like those hazy shadows of passersby which cross the face of the camera, and therefore are dimly traceable upon a photographic landscape (Spurgeon, *Treasury of David*, 1:315).

Kidner calls Psalm 45 "perhaps the boldest Messianic oracle in the Psalter" (*Psalms 1–72*, p. 21).

The author of Hebrews applied this passage in reference to the intrinsic superiority of the Messiah over angels (Hebrews 1:8-9).

Furthermore, John appropriated the psalm's royal wedding imagery and typologically applied it to the Messiah's eternal marriage to His bride, the church, in the eschaton (Revelation 19:6-21).

It is indisputable that Psalm 45 was interpreted through a messianic lens by the ancient Jewish rabbis. The Targum to the Hagiographa paraphrased 45:2 as follows: "Your beauty, O King Messiah, surpasses that of ordinary men. The spirit of prophecy has been bestowed upon your lips; therefore the Lord has blessed you forever." The Midrash likewise connects this psalm with the prophecy in Genesis 49:10 of the scepter not departing from Judah (Midrash Rabbah, Genesis XCIX, 8; see also Babylonian Talmud, *Shabbath* 63a as quoted in Huckel, "Psalms," elec. ed.).

THE COMING FINAL PEACE
Psalm 46:8-10

Psalm 46 presents the Lord as Israel's certain defense and concludes with an image of a divinely (and violently) wrought peace on earth that results in God's universal exaltation. This will be fulfilled at the Messiah's second coming and establishment of the millennial kingdom (Zechariah 12:1-3; 14:2) or perhaps at its conclusion (Revelation 20:7-9).

JERUSALEM IN THE MESSIANIC KINGDOM
Psalm 48

This is a psalm of praise extolling Jerusalem, "the city of the great King" (verse 2). While this psalm may be understood as a hyperbolic ode to the Jerusalem of the Davidic era, it is better to read it as a description of the royal city during the messianic era. Certainly, from the moment Jerusalem became David's capital up through today, few would extol this storied and controversial city as "the joy of the whole earth" (verse 2). That, realistically, awaits the age of the Messiah, when the King will reign from His capital, enthroned in glory.

A PROPHETIC HINT OF RESURRECTION
Psalm 49:15

In sharp contrast to the eternal fate awaiting the wicked, the author provides a prophetic hint, an allusion, to his hopeful expectation of future resurrection from Sheol, the abode of the dead: "God will redeem my soul from the power of Sheol, for He will receive me" (49:15). As Ross states, while "nowhere in the Psalms is there a clear, unambiguous expression of hope in the resurrection...some passages in the Psalms do seem to break through to express a hope of continued fellowship with God after this life" (Ross, "Psalms," p. 789).

THE DESTRUCTION OF DAVID'S ENEMIES
Psalm 63:9-11

In Psalm 63, David expresses his complete trust in God's protection and his faith that those who sought to kill him would not only meet with failure, but lose their own lives (verses 9-11). This prophetic expectation was fulfilled multiple times within David's lifetime (1 Samuel 31:4; 2 Samuel 4:7; 18:14-15).

A PROPHECY OF THE MESSIANIC ERA
Psalm 67:3-7

In the messianic kingdom, all nations will know the Lord's ways and His salvation, for they will be ruled with unparalleled equity and justice by the messianic King. At that future moment, the Gentile nations will join with Israel in praising the Lord for His abundant blessings.

CHRIST'S MESSIANIC VICTORY
Psalm 68:18-19

THE APOSTLE PAUL, by way of analogy, applied the poetic imagery of God's majestic rule over the geographic region of Jerusalem to Christ's conquest over death and victorious distribution of spiritual gifts (Ephesians 4:8). The ancient Jewish interpretation held this psalm as possessing messianic reference (Edersheim, *Life and Times of Jesus the Messiah,* 2:19; Babylonian Talmud, *Pesahim* 118*b;* Midrash Rabbah, *Exodus* XXXV, 5; Midrash Rabbah, *Esther* I, 4, as quoted in Huckel, "Psalms," elec. ed.).

PROPHECIES OF MESSIAH'S SUFFERING
Psalm 69:4,8-9,19-21,25

PSALM 69 HOLDS A UNIQUELY prominent position among the Old Testament typological messianic passages cited by the New Testament authors. In context, the psalm transparently relates the persecution of either David or a Davidic figure and includes his vigorous imprecatory prayers for God to visit visceral punishment upon his enemies (69:22-28). The apostles extracted from this psalm six different examples of either messianic typology or analogical messianic experience. Furthermore, David's imprecatory section stands in sharp antithesis to the ultimate Son of David's singular prayer of forgiveness in the face of extraordinary persecution (Luke 23:34).

First, "Those who hate me without a cause are more than the hairs of my head" (69:4).

Jesus applied this image to Himself, perceiving a corresponding experience regarding His relationship to unbelieving Israel (John 15:25).

Second, "I have become estranged from my brothers and an alien to my mother's sons" (69:8). This was analogically true of Jesus' relationship to His brothers prior to His resurrection (John 7:5).

Third, "Zeal for Your house has consumed me" (69:9). John typologically applied this to Jesus in connection with His cleansing of the temple (John 2:17).

Fourth, "The reproaches of those who reproach You have fallen on me" (69:9). Paul analogically applied this to Jesus regarding Christian self-denial on behalf of others (Romans 15:3).

Fifth, "They also gave me gall for my food and for my thirst they gave me vinegar to drink" (69:21). This passage was typologically applied in the gospels in connection with the vinegar given to Jesus on the cross (Matthew 27:48; Mark 15:36; Luke 23:36; John 19:29).

A sixth and final passage, 69:25, combined with 109:8, was used in the broadest analogical sense by Peter in regard to selecting Judas' replacement (Acts 1:20). Peter did not argue that these passages were prophecies fulfilled by Judas; rather, he was pointing out the applicability of these two imprecatory psalms to their current situation, linking Scripture to contemporary circumstances through one point of similarity. These psalms, written by David about the king's adversaries, could certainly be applied to the adversary of the Son of David. The psalms' original point about the unrighteous in an abstract sense could certainly be applied to one specific, reprehensible individual.

The state of biblical literacy was so high in first-century Jewish culture that it was common practice for a speaker (or author) to quote just one verse, or even one portion of a verse, and assume that the audience, their educated minds functioning as biblical mini-concordances, would know the context from which that quote came.

THE BOOK OF LIFE
Psalm 69:28

Psalm 69:28 makes reference to being blotted out of God's "book of life," a concept that intermittently appears a few times in Scripture (Exodus 32:32; Daniel 7:10; 12:1; Revelation 20:15). The Book of Life (here paralleled with being "recorded with the righteous") refers to a heavenly scroll, or ledger, that contains the names of all who are destined for life. In postbiblical Jewish history, this concept was further developed within Judaism and attained pride of place within the theology of Judaism's two most solemn holy days, *Rosh Hashanah* (the Feast of Trumpets/Jewish New Year) and *Yom Kippur* (the Day of Atonement).

Every year, at the outset of the ten-day period of time of divine judgment bracketed by these two holy days, known as the "Days of Awe," three scrolls (or books) are said to be opened in the heavenly courts. One scroll is designated for the completely righteous, who are immediately inscribed in the Book of Life. Another scroll is designated for the thoroughly reprobate, who are immediately recorded in the book of death, and a third scroll is designated for the temporary inscription of the names of the vast majority of Jews, those somewhere in between.

Everyone's fate for the coming year is divinely inscribed on *Rosh Hashanah* and finally sealed ten days later on *Yom Kippur.* Their destiny is written "in pencil" until the Day of Atonement, when it will finally be sealed in indelible ink. During the ten days of repentance between *Rosh Hashanah* and *Yom Kippur,* the Jewish people's fate hangs in the balance. This refers not to eternal salvation, but actual life and death for the coming year. During that time, God decides who will live and who will die. The job of the observant Jewish person at *Rosh Hashanah* is to attempt to influence God's decision through prayer, repentance, and righteous deeds.

THE MESSIAH'S KINGDOM REIGN
Psalm 72:5-11,15-20

Psalm 72 is one of two in the Psalter (72; 127) that are attributed to Solomon. The psalm begins with the familiar prophetic and psalmic themes of royal righteousness, justice, and prosperity (72:1-4), but then abruptly transitions from the poetic to the prophetic for much of the rest of the psalm.

> The New Testament nowhere quotes it as Messianic, but this picture of the king and his realm is so close to the prophecies of Isaiah 11:1-5 and Isaiah 60–62 that if those passages are Messianic, so is this…. It exalted this [the reigning king's high calling] so far beyond the humanly attainable (*e.g.* in speaking of his reign as endless) as to suggest for its fulfillment no less a person than the Messiah (Kidner, *Psalms 1–72*, p. 254).

There is a textual discrepancy in 72:5 between the Hebrew Masoretic text, which reads, "They shall fear you," and the Greek Septuagint, which reads, "May he endure." Nonetheless, whether the text is to be understood as positing a king who is feared in perpetuity or who reigns in perpetuity ("while the sun endures, and as long as the moon…"), the messianic intent underlying either text must be acknowledged by the interpreter.

The geographic extent of the messianic king's domain is spelled out in the following section, "from sea to sea and from the River to the ends of the earth" (verse 8). The universal extent of His reign is specified in verse 11: "Let all kings bow down before him, all nations serve him." Solomon's borders, while expansive, and his reign, while extensive, do not correspond to this description. The Messiah must be in view here.

Using highly recognizable covenant terminology, the messianic king's connection to the Abrahamic Covenant (Genesis 12:1-3) is climactically highlighted in Psalm 72:17, which reads, "May his name endure forever; may his name increase as long as the sun shines; and let men bless themselves by him; let all nations call him blessed." This will be fulfilled in the millennial reign of Christ.

Among the ancient Jewish sources, this psalm was almost universally understood as depicting the messianic era. The Targum to the Hagiographa renders 72:1 (in Aramaic paraphrase) as "Give the sentence of Thy judgment to the King Messiah, and Thy justice to the Son of David the King" (Edersheim, *Life and Times of Jesus the Messiah,* 2:719). Likewise, the Midrash on Psalms, Book Two, *Psalm 72, 3, 4, 5, 6;* Book Four, *Psalm 90, 1, Psalm 93, 3;* Midrash Rabbah, *Genesis* I, 4; XLVIII, 10; Midrash Rabbah, *Numbers* XIII, 14; Midrash Rabbah, *Esther* I, 4; Midrash Rabbah, *Lamentations* I, 16-17; Midrash on Proverbs, *Chapter 8, 19, 21;* Sifre on Deuteronomy, *Piska* 310; Pesiqta deRab Kahana, *Piska* 18; and the Babylonian Talmud, *Nedarim* 39*b; Pesahim* 54 (as quoted in Huckel, "Psalms," elec. ed.; also Edersheim, *Life and Times of Jesus the Messiah,* 2:719) all hold a messianic interpretation of this psalm.

A PROPHETIC HINT ABOUT ETERNITY
Psalm 73:24

Psalm 73:24, which says, "With Your counsel You will guide me, and afterward receive me to glory," contains a hint of Asaph's expectation of spending eternity in the presence of God.

THE MESSIAH TO TEACH IN PARABLES
Psalm 78:2

From the introduction of this psalmic rehearsal of Israel's history Matthew plucked a familiar verse—"I will open my mouth in a parable; I will utter dark sayings of old" (Psalm 78:2)—that he applied typologically to Jesus' teaching method (Matthew 13:34-35).

THE MESSIAH TO BE AT GOD'S RIGHT HAND
Psalm 80:17

Although it is fashionable in certain circles to understand this psalm as being an interpretively uncomplicated prayer to God, it has long been understood as an appeal for the coming of Messiah. Edersheim reveals just how long it has been so understood in reference to the Targum of the Hagiographa's Aramaic paraphrase of 80:17, "the son of man," with "King Messiah" (Edersheim, *Life and Times of Jesus the Messiah,* 2:719). The understanding that the "Shepherd of Israel" (verse 1) is indeed Israel's messianic Savior (80:1-7) has a lengthy Jewish (and Christian) pedigree. The "man of [God's] right hand" (verse 17) corresponds to the exalted One who sits at the right hand of God (Psalm 110:1; Matthew 22:44-45; Mark 12:35-37; Luke 20:42; Acts 2:34-35).

THE REITERATION OF THE DAVIDIC COVENANT
Psalm 89

Psalm 89 is attributed to Ethan the Ezrahite and may be described both as an artistic reiteration of the Davidic Covenant (see 2 Samuel 7:8-16; 1 Chronicles 17:10-14) and a prayer for God to maintain divine fidelity to His covenant promises. This psalm is rich in messianic imagery and reaffirms through the strongest language the eternal throne of the eventual, ultimate Davidic king: "I have made a covenant with My chosen; I have sworn to David My servant, I will establish your seed forever and build up your throne to all generations" (89:3-4).

The psalm moves to a rehearsal of the Lord's

choice and exaltation of David in 89:19-29. David was divinely "anointed," "established," and "strengthen[ed]" (verse 21) with God's loving covenant loyalty (Hebrew, *chesed*) and faithfulness (89:24). He will be called God's royal "firstborn," possessing the right to call God, "my Father" (verses 26-27). In comparison with the original text of the Davidic Covenant (2 Samuel 7:8-16; 1 Chronicles 17:10-14), it is clear that the Davidic line was to produce a king who would be as much a Son of God as a Son of David. David's dynasty will be established in perpetuity (89:26-27), and God had blessed David and will curse his enemies (89:21-23).

If certain of David's descendants were to break faith with the Lord through disobedience, they would be divinely disciplined, yet the Lord would remain faithful to His covenant promises (89:30-37). The Lord's loving covenant loyalty is inviolate and unalterable, as fixed as the astrological bodies. The Lord had solemnly sworn by His holiness that David's "descendants shall endure forever and his throne as the sun before Me. It shall be established forever like the moon, and the witness in the sky is faithful" (89:36-37). At least one traditional Jewish source understands Psalm 89:37 to refer to the Messiah (Midrash Rabbah, *Genesis XCVII,* new version, as quoted in Huckel, "Psalms," elect. ed.).

The remainder of the psalm looks longingly toward the unknown future era of the reign of the ultimate scion of David, the goal of the royal Davidic dynasty, the Messiah (89:38-52). A variety of ancient rabbis likewise interpreted this psalm with the most vivid of messianic coloring, in particular the final verse, "with which Your enemies have reproached, O Lord, with which they have reproached the footsteps of Your anointed" (89:51), which was understood to refer to the morally dark days surrounding the coming of Messiah, who would be reviled by His generation (Midrash Rabbah, *The Song of Songs* II, 13, 4; Midrash on Psalms, Book One, Psalm 18, 5; Targum to the Hagiographa; Pesiqta deRab Kahana, *Piska* 5, 9 as quoted in Huckel, elect. ed., also

Edersheim, *Life and Times of Jesus the Messiah,* 2:720). A clear example is found in the Talmud (Babylonian Talmud, *Sanhedrin 97a,* as quoted in Santala 141): "The Messiah, the Son of David, will not come until the whole world is filled with apostates" (or heretics, Hebrew, *minim,* incidentally often understood as a reference to Christians!). In addition, the psalm's final punctuation of praise, "Blessed be the LORD forever! Amen and Amen" (89:52), was likewise interpreted with reference to the messianic era (Midrash Rabbah, *The Song of Songs* II, 13, 4 as quoted in Huckel, "Psalms," elect. ed.).

THE MESSIANIC KING IS COMING
Psalm 96:10-13

PSALM 96 IS AN enthronement psalm, which describes "the coming of the Lord and the consummation of His kingdom"(Ross, "Psalms," p. 789)—that is, the events surrounding the second coming and the establishment of the millennium. There is in this passage a typological hint that the author's expectation extends beyond poetic hyperbole, extolling God's majesty over the prospect of an actual visitation of the Lord for the purpose of distributing justice throughout His creation. Certainly this psalm's imagery ignites the hope expressed by the apostles Peter (Acts 10:42) and Paul (Acts 17:31) of the judgment associated with Jesus' return. The Messiah is coming; "He is coming to judge the earth. He will judge the world in righteousness and the peoples in His faithfulness" (96:12-13).

THE DAWNING OF THE MESSIANIC ERA
Psalm 98:1-9

PSALM 98, WHICH IS SIMILAR TO Psalm 96 from a prophetic standpoint, is also classified as an "enthronement psalm" and exuberantly looks forward to the era of the messianic kingdom and the rule of the messianic king in language even more explicit than that found in Psalm 96.

The author begins with a proclamation of divine victory and the successful universal broadcast of the Lord's righteous "salvation" (Hebrew, *yeshua*) to the nations. This proclamation is particularly fraught with meaning when one is reminded that *Yeshua* is Jesus' Hebrew name. This opening stanza is laden with praise for both the extension of God's salvation to the nations and His unflagging covenant fidelity (Hebrew, *chesed,* "covenantal loyal love") to His people, Israel. This faithfulness hearkens back to the ancient promises contained within the Abrahamic Covenant (Genesis 13:14-17; 15:18-21; 17:7-8; 22:16-18; 26:3-5; 28:13; 35:12).

The psalm concludes with an appeal for the entire creation to extol the virtues of the individual who is identified as "the King, the LORD," who is "coming to…judge the earth; He will judge the world with righteousness and the peoples with equity" (98:6,9). The New Testament authors' expectation of Jesus' return was undoubtedly both informed and colored through this psalm's imagery (for example, Acts 10:42; 17:31; Revelation 19:11).

A PROPHECY OF THE MESSIANIC KINGDOM
Psalm 102:12-28

THIS PSALM BEGINS as a lament (102:1-11), but concludes with a section of prophetic praise that describes conditions during the messianic kingdom (102:12-28). At that time, the Lord will "have compassion on Zion," for "the appointed time has come" (102:13). Zion will be "built up" and the Lord will appear "in His glory" (102:16). The nations and their kings will join Israel in worship of the Lord (102:15,22). Ancient Jewish interpreters also see this psalm as referring to the messianic age (Midrash Rabbah, *Genesis* LVI, 10, as quoted in Huckel, "Psalms," elec. ed).

In fact, the psalm identifies itself as a prophetic message to a future "generation to come, that a people yet to be created may praise the LORD" (102:18). The author of Hebrews treats this psalm as prophetic, quoting 102:25-27 in Hebrews 1:10-12 to indicate that the Messiah, Jesus, was the divine, eternal instrument of all creation: "Of old You founded the earth, and the heavens are the work of Your hands. Even they will perish, but You endure; and all of them will wear out like a garment; like clothing You will change them and they will be changed. But You are the same, and Your years will not come to an end" (102:25-27).

A PREDICTION OF RESURRECTION HOPE
Psalm 103:4

WITHIN THIS PSALM OF PRAISE is a reference to redemption of life from "the pit" (Hebrews, *shachat*) that, when taken together with Psalm 16, reveals a level of expectation, however undeveloped, of resurrection hope and impending life beyond the grave, or *Sheol,* the abode of the dead.

THE ABRAHAMIC COVENANT REMEMBERED
Psalm 105:7-12,42

THE HEART OF PSALM 105 IS an extended reiteration of the unconditional promises that God made to Abraham and his progeny (Genesis 12:1-3,7; 13:14-17; 15:1-21; 17:1-21; 22:15-18).

THE LOVE OF GOD FOR ISRAEL
Psalm 106:1

IN POTENT CORRELATION with the previous psalm (see commentary above), the proclamation of God's mercy (Hebrew, *chesed,* His undying covenantal loyal love) is based upon the unconditional promises contained within the Abrahamic Covenant (Genesis 12:1-3,7; 13:14-17; 15:1-21; 17:1-21; 22:15-18).

AN ANALOGICAL REFERENCE TO JUDAS
Psalm 109:8

PSALM 109:8, IN combination with 69:25, was used in the broadest analogical sense by Peter in regard to selecting Judas' replacement (Acts 1:20). Peter did not argue that these passages were prophecies fulfilled by Judas; rather, he was pointing out the applicability of these two imprecatory psalms to their current situation, linking Scripture to contemporary circumstances through one point of similarity. These psalms, written by David about the king's adversaries, could certainly be applied to the adversary of the Son of David. The psalms' original point about the unrighteous could certainly be applied to one specific individual.

First-century Jews were so biblically literate that when a speaker or author quoted just one verse, or even one part of a verse, the speaker or author could count on most of the audience being able to figure out the context of the quote.

THE ORDER OF MELCHIZEDEK
Psalm 110:1-7

THERE ARE THREE INDIVIDUALS designated within the first verse of this psalm from David: "The LORD says to my Lord: 'Sit at My right hand until I make Your enemies a footstool for Your feet.' The LORD will stretch forth Your strong scepter from Zion, saying, 'Rule in the midst of Your enemies'" (verses 1-2). The initial pair of individuals are both called "Lord," and there is the author, David. In the English translation it is more difficult to perceive the

messianic dynamic of the psalm than in the original Hebrew, primarily because David, in reference to these two individuals, used two different words, both of which are translated as "Lord" in English. The first "LORD" is the name YHWH and refers to the covenant-making God of Abraham, Isaac, and Jacob. The second "Lord" is the Hebrew *Adonai.* This second "Lord," *Adonai,* is the individual whom David called "my Lord."

If the first Lord refers to God and the second Lord is David's Lord, then, obviously, neither of these "lordly" individuals could have been David. Indeed, it was universally accepted that David had neither been resurrected nor had he ascended into heaven. This raises a question: If God is the first Lord, and David is the "my" of "my Lord," then just who is David's Lord? Jesus Himself had vexed the Pharisees by posing this perplexing question (Matthew 22:44-45). Certainly, while he lived, David had no mortal lord. As the undisputed sovereign of all Israel, his only Lord was God Himself.

Of course, the answer to this prophetic riddle is Jesus, as Peter revealed in the book of Acts (Acts 2:34-35). He announced that through God's exaltation of Jesus, Israel could be supremely confident that Jesus had been exalted by God and was both Lord and Christ. Jesus applied this psalm to Himself (Matthew 22:44; Mark 12:35-37; Luke 20:42). Hebrews also uses this psalm in reference to Jesus (1:13). Indeed, Psalm 110:1 is the most frequently cited messianic prophecy in the New Testament.

This passage has a long pedigree—within both Jewish tradition and rabbinic literature—of being interpreted in reference to the Messiah (albeit, never with reference to Jesus). For example, the Midrash on Psalms, Book One, *Psalm 18, 29* interprets 110:1 as follows: "R. Yudan said in the name of R. Hama: In the time-to-come, when the Holy One, blessed be He, seats the lord Messiah at His right hand..." (as quoted in Huckel, "Psalms," elec. ed.).

Edersheim adds that in this particular interpretation, while Messiah is on the Lord's right, Abraham is pictured as sitting on His left (Edersheim, *Life and Times of Jesus the Messiah*, 2:721).

In addition, both Midrash Rabbah, *Genesis* LXXXV, 9 and Midrash Rabbah, *Numbers* XVIII, 23 (as quoted in Huckel, elec. ed.) interpret Psalm 110:2 messianically: "...And thy staff alludes to the royal Messiah, as in the verse *The staff of thy strength the Lord will send out of Zion....*" And, "...that same staff also is destined to be held in the hand of the King Messiah (may it be speedily in our days!); as it says, *The staff of thy strength the Lord will send out of Zion: Rule thou in the midst of thine enemies.*"

The New Testament teaches that Jesus' exaltation fulfilled this prophecy. Our Messiah is currently sitting as an equal to God at His right hand, until such time as Jesus' enemies are made His "footstool."

> We know from I Kings 2:19 that anyone who sits at a king's right hand must be equal with the king. When one king made a visit of state to another king, he would sit at his host's right hand. Since Messiah is invited to sit at God's right hand, it follows that Messiah must be equal with God (Fruchtenbaum, *Messianic Christology*, p. 88).

Psalm 110:4 builds upon the identification of a glorified Messiah with an additional extraordinary declaration. The Messiah would not only be a king but also a priest. However, He would not be a Levitical priest because he was David's Son, descended not from Levi, but Judah. His priesthood, by divine design, would necessarily need to circumvent the law of Moses and find its basis, instead, in that of the inscrutable figure of Genesis 14:18, the righteous king, Melchizedek, priest of the Most High. Furthermore, His priesthood possesses an eternal nature. The psalm affirms that "You are a priest forever" (110:4). The book of Hebrews affirms in great detail that Jesus is, indeed, both eternal priest and king (Hebrews 5:6; 6:20). The psalm concludes with a description of the divine wrath and judgment to come

upon the nations when the Messiah comes to inaugurate His kingdom (110:5-7).

THE MESSIAH'S REJECTION AND EXALTATION
Psalm 118

PSALM 118 IS PART OF a collection that was called the "Psalms of Hallel," which consisted of Psalms 113–118. *Hallel* is the Hebrew word for *praise,* and this collection of psalms was sung on every Jewish holy day, especially the three major pilgrim festivals of Passover, Pentecost, and Tabernacles. Needless to say, this psalm was firmly embedded in the memory of every Jewish family member who had ever participated in congregational worship.

The psalm devotes the first four verses and the concluding verse to the proclamation of God's mercy (Hebrew, *chesed,* His loving, undying covenantal loyal love). As discussed in the commentary on Psalm 106:1, this mercy is based on the unconditional promises contained within the Abrahamic Covenant (Genesis 12:1-3,7; 13:14-17; 15:1-21; 17:1-21; 22:15-18).

The next section (118:5-21) segues from corporate worship to the description of a beleaguered individual in "distress" (verse 5) and surrounded by "nations" (verse 10). Yet triumph would be attained through the intervention of the Lord, who, according to verse 14, becomes the individual's "salvation" (Hebrew, *yeshua*). Therefore, the individual can confidently declare that "I will not die, but live, and tell of the works of the LORD" (118:17).

The *messianic implications* of the psalm become even clearer through the New Testament's forceful employment of the psalm's section dealing with the "rejected stone" of 118:22-23: "The stone which the builders rejected has become the chief corner stone. This is the LORD's doing; it is marvelous in our eyes." Peter quoted this passage, identifying Jesus as the stone that was rejected by the builders yet became the chief cornerstone

(Acts 4:11; 1 Peter 2:7). Peter also associated the Sanhedrin, the Jewish leadership, with the passage's foolish builders. Of course Jesus quoted this familiar passage as well, with pointed reference to Himself (Matthew 21:42; Luke 20:17).

Psalm 118 also is the textual source of the crowd's shouts of "hosanna" ("do save, we beseech You") and "blessed is He who comes in the name of the Lord" when Jesus made His triumphal entry into Jerusalem (Mark 11:9; John 12:13). These words were part of a refrain that was familiar to the Jewish crowd of Jesus' day: "This is the day which the LORD has made; let us rejoice and be glad in it. O LORD, do save, we beseech You; O LORD, we beseech You, do send prosperity! Blessed is the one who comes in the name of the LORD; we have blessed you from the house of the LORD" (118:24-26).

That the crowd in Jesus' day understood and accepted this psalm as messianic is undeniable. The worshippers in Jerusalem publicly demonstrated their messianic expectations of the individual whom they believed was fulfilling the passage before their eyes. However, when Jesus didn't do what people expected, they became disillusioned, which may explain their failure to apply verse 27 to Jesus: "The LORD is God, and He has given us light; bind the festival sacrifice with cords to the horns of the altar." Not only had God provided Jesus as Israel's (and the world's) messianic light (John 9:5), but He had also provided the Messiah to serve as the perfect sacrifice (Hebrews 9:26).

ISRAEL'S FUTURE REDEMPTION
Psalm 130:7-8

PSALM 130 EXTENDS BEYOND teaching Israel of God's merciful forgiveness to a future redemptive era that is to be waited and hoped for by Israel, when the Lord would "redeem Israel from all his iniquities" (130:7-8). Although this era has dawned through the death and resurrection of Messiah, the psalm's ultimate fulfillment awaits the Messiah's second advent, when "all Israel will be saved" (Romans 11:26).

REITERATION OF THE DAVIDIC COVENANT
Psalm 132:10-18

THE SECOND HALF OF Psalm 132 is firmly rooted in the promises contained within the Davidic Covenant (2 Samuel 7:8-16; 1 Chronicles 17:10-14). The ultimate, future Son of David is designated as God's "anointed" (132:10,17) and the "horn of David" (132:17). Ancient rabbinic sources affirm a messianic interpretation of 132:11, 14, and 17 (Midrash on Psalms, Book Two, *Psalms 42, 43;* Midrash Rabbah, *The Song of Songs* VII, 5, Pesqita deRab Kahana, *Piska* 20, 7; Midrash Rabbah, *Leviticus* XXXI, 11; Targum to the Hagiographa as quoted in Huckel, "Psalms," elec. ed.).

GOD'S ETERNAL LOVE FOR ISRAEL
Psalm 136

THE PROCLAMATION OF God's mercy (Hebrew, *chesed,* His covenantal loyal love) is based upon the unconditional promises contained within the Abrahamic Covenant (Genesis 12:1-3,7; 13:14-17; 15:1-21; 17:1-21; 22:15-18).

PROVERBS

PROVERBS IS A COLLECTION OF WISE SAYINGS AND APHORISMS that offer guidance for everyday living. Though this poetic Hebrew wisdom literature includes no overt prophetic or eschatological content, nonetheless, one proverb does indeed offer a tantalizing prophetic glimpse of Israel's coming Messiah.

THE NAME OF GOD'S SON
Proverbs 30:4

Who has ascended into heaven and descended? Who has gathered the wind in His fists? Who has wrapped up the waters in His garment? Who has established all the ends of the earth? What is His name or His son's name? Surely you know! (30:4).

THE AUTHOR OF PROVERBS 30 is King Agur. Within 30:4, Agur asks *four rhetorical questions,* each of which possesses an identical answer. No human individual is capable of performing such majestic feats of creative spectacle (Ross, "Proverbs," p. 1119). Therefore, to even the least educated student of Proverbs, the obvious answer to the four questions is God Himself. The fifth question, while not

rhetorical, is equally obvious; God's covenant name, YHWH, was revealed to Israel centuries prior to the time of Agur or his readers (Exodus 3:14-15).

The answer to the sixth and final question, however, unlike its companions, is less readily apparent: What is...His son's name? The answer to that question would remain shrouded in mystery for God's people until the first century and Messiah's first advent. As Fruchtenbaum (*Messianic Christology,* p. 90) writes, "At this stage of progressive revelation, no one *could* know His name. It is only in the New Testament that His name is revealed as Jesus."

It is encouraging to note that nestled snugly within myriad nuggets of truth designed to direct the reader toward godly wisdom is one proverb that provides a prophetic glimpse of the greatest truth of all—God's Son.

ECCLESIASTES

Ecclesiastes is an example of the Hebrew wisdom literature genre, and therefore includes no overt prophetic or eschatological content. Nonetheless, while not prophecy per se, the final two verses in the book do reveal a prophetic truth concerning God's final judgment of human activity:

> The conclusion, when all has been heard, is: fear God and keep His commandments, because this applies to every person. For God will bring every act to judgment, everything which is hidden, whether it is good or evil (12:13-14).

While this proclamation is true in a general, universal sense, this prophetic fact will ultimately find fulfillment at the judgment seat of Christ (Romans 14:12; 2 Corinthians 5:10) and at the final judgment of the wicked (Revelation 20:11-15). As Kaiser (*Ecclesiastes,* p. 125) concludes, "Men are responsible beings...who are destined to live to confront the past with the God that they either feared or flouted."

SONG OF SOLOMON

Many faithful individuals through the ages, within both Judaism and Christianity, have interpreted Song of Solomon as a prophetic allegory expressing either God's love for His people or Christ's love for His church. When the book is interpreted *literally*, historically, and grammatically, it consists purely of love-themed Hebrew poetry and includes no prophetic or eschatological content. When viewed *typologically*, however, the story of the love of a shepherd boy for an outcast girl and his return for her after he has become a king may picture the relationship of Christ to His bride, the church.

THE
MAJOR
PROPHETS

ISAIAH

Of all the Old Testament prophets, Isaiah spoke the most about the Messiah. Other prophets wrote much about the messianic kingdom, but Isaiah had the most to say about the person of the Messiah Himself. Isaiah contains more prophecies about the Messiah's first coming than does any other book of the Old Testament.

LET US REASON TOGETHER
Isaiah 1:24-31

The book of Isaiah begins with five sermons of prophetic confrontation, calling Israel to repent before God's judgment falls upon them. After spelling out Israel's sins and the judgments, the Lord calls the people to come and reason with Him (1:18). The first chapter closes with a positive message of Israel being judged and then redeemed. The nation's condition is so hopeless that God Himself must take things in hand. Therefore, the leaders who led the nation astray will be destroyed (verse 24), and all Israel's other impurities will also be purged (verse 25). God will provide righteous leaders for Israel just as He had provided men such as Joshua and Samuel. Zion will again become the center of righteousness (verse 26). In fact, Zion will be redeemed for justice and righteousness (verse 27). The Hebrew word for "redeem" speaks of a redemption that requires the payment of a price. In Isaiah 53:1-9, the prophet reveals that the price will be Messiah's own blood.

Chapter 1 concludes with the prophecy of a coming destruction of the wicked (verses 28-31), which includes the facts that the wicked will be consumed (verse 28) and that their idolatry will be eliminated (verses 29-31).

This prophecy calls upon all people, Jews and Gentiles alike, to be accountable to the God of heaven.

JERUSALEM PURGED AND BLESSED
Isaiah 2:1–4:6

In 2:2-4, Isaiah begins by describing the messianic kingdom. The earthquakes in connection with the second coming will bring some major geographical changes within the land of Israel, one of which will include the "mountain of the Lord's house" becoming the highest of all the mountains in the world. Ezekiel 40–48 describes the details of this mountain, but Isaiah provides some small hints of what it will be like. Isaiah clearly states that the mountain upon which the Lord's house will stand in the messianic kingdom will be the highest of the mountains and by far the most exalted. All the nations will move toward this mountain to worship the God of Israel (verse 2). The messianic kingdom law will emanate from this mountain, and for this reason Gentiles will migrate to Israel to this mountain to learn of God's ways so that they can walk in His paths (verse 3). The old Mosaic law has given way to the present law of the Messiah, but in the future the kingdom law will emanate from Mount Zion.

The nations will migrate toward this mountain not only to worship but also to have their differences settled. In the messianic kingdom, differences will still arise among the nations, but the differences will not be settled by war but by the Word of God coming from this mountain (verse 4). The peaceful arbitration from Jerusalem will lead to three results: First, all weapons of war will be turned into farm equipment; second, any military conflicts among the nations will cease; and third, people will not learn about war anymore, and military forces will be abolished.

All this is now contrasted with Zion's pathetic present condition and impending judgment (2:5–4:1). The passage begins with a call to Israel to return to the Lord (2:5). Since Gentiles will be coming to the Lord in the future, Israel should be coming to the Lord even now. Isaiah then lists the various sins of Israel (2:6-8), which leads to the announcement of coming judgment (2:9-11). In 2:12-21 Isaiah finally reveals the timing of this judgment that he describes as being in "the day of the LORD" (verse 12 NKJV). This explains what Isaiah meant by the phrase "that day" in verse 11. That day of judgment will be during the day of the Lord, which is the most common biblical term for the seven-year Tribulation period. In describing the day of the Lord, Isaiah uses the phrase "that day" seven times in this passage (2:11,17,20; 3:7,18; 4:1,2). God has a special day of judgment reserved for rendering out His vengeance.

In verses 12-16 Isaiah enumerates the various things that God will judge, including pride, trees, mountains and hills, defensive towers and walls, and foreign wealth. Israel was trusting in these things, but the Lord would destroy them. In verses 17-21 Isaiah spells out the results of the day of the Lord, which include Israel's repudiation of all the things it has been trusting in instead of trusting the Lord.

Because Israel's leaders bore responsibility for leading the nation astray, they could expect specific judgment (2:22–3:15). God will judge all men, but God will especially hold leaders accountable for their actions.

There is also a special indictment against the women of Israel (3:16–4:1) because of their focus on luxurious and materialistic living while the poor have suffered. A list mentions 21 luxury items that will be removed, and the women will go from ornate refinement to sackcloth. The judgment on the women includes a sharp decrease in the male population, leaving a ratio of seven Jewish women to one Jewish man. Such a curse would be viewed as a state of reproach in that society.

Isaiah then comes back to where he began— the messianic kingdom (4:2-6). Referring to the Messiah as "the Branch of the LORD," he points out this is a shoot of the Lord Himself and points to Messiah's divine nature—a point he will develop more fully in 11:1-10. As for the messianic people (verses 3-4), they will be characterized by holiness and these are among those whose names have been written in the Book of Life. God will have washed away their sins, and the blood of Jerusalem will be purged. The Holy Spirit, referred to here as "the spirit of judgment" and "the spirit of burning," will bring them to the Lord.

Isaiah concludes by describing one of the facets of the Shekinah glory in that day (verses 4-5). The Shekinah glory is the visible manifestation of God's presence. Whenever the invisible God became visible and whenever His omnipresence was localized, this visible localized presence was the Shekinah glory. Throughout the Old Testament it was manifest either as a light, fire, or cloud. In the New Testament, the glory came in the person of Jesus (John 1:14).

The messianic kingdom will include five different contemporaneous manifestations of the Shekinah glory and the one Isaiah describes here is the glory that will overshadow the whole of the new Mount Zion described earlier (Isaiah 4:2-4). Here the Shekinah glory is described as a cloud and as smoke by day and the shining and flaming fire by night. This reflects previous manifestations of the

Shekinah glory of Israel in the wilderness, where it appeared as a pillar of cloud by day and a pillar of fire by night. Over all the glory is a covering that provides protection from the heat, storms, and rain.

As Ezekiel points out, the new and exceedingly high mountain that will be overshadowed in this glory has a 50-square-mile plateau on top, with the millennial Jerusalem sitting on the south side of the mountain and the millennial temple located on the north side. Over this mountain will be the visible manifestation of the Shekinah glory in a cloud, smoke, and flaming fire—just like the manifestation over Mount Sinai and in the tabernacle during the wilderness wanderings. This will be a sign of God's protection over the nation for the whole messianic kingdom.

ISAIAH'S CALL
Isaiah 6

THE FIVE SERMONS OF chapters 1–5 are followed by an account of Isaiah's call to the ministry. While chapter 6 deals primarily with Isaiah's call to be the prophet of his day, verse 13 is eschatological. There he describes a return of the Jewish people from dispersion, but even then they will experience divine judgment. This judgment is described within the book as the judgment of the Tribulation. However, the remnant will be like a felled oak tree that still has life and can spring to life again. The holy seed will spring to life and grow into a large tree, which the prophet represents as the establishment of the messianic kingdom—a kingdom in which Israel once again will believe in the Lord and serve Him.

THE BOOK OF IMMANUEL
Isaiah 7–12

THIS SECTION OF ISAIAH is sometimes called the Book of Immanuel because the name *Immanuel* appears twice (7:14; 8:8). In parts of

this segment of Isaiah the prophet deals with prophecy that has already been fulfilled, and in other parts he speaks of prophecies yet to be fulfilled.

Isaiah 7:14 contains the prophet's famous prediction of the virgin birth of Christ, who is given the prophetically symbolic name *Immanuel,* meaning "God with us." Much has been written about this amazing prophecy. The apostles, the early church fathers, the medieval theologians, and Protestant reformers were unanimously confident that this messianic prophecy was fulfilled in the virgin birth of Christ. In fact, the prophecy so clearly predicts the miraculous virginal conception that medieval Jewish scholars attempted to explain it away in order to defend their rejection of Christ as the promised Messiah. Despite this, one is hard-pressed to find any Christian writers who objected to this interpretation prior to the eighteenth century.

Isaiah carefully selected the Hebrew word *almah* to denote "a young woman" of marriageable age, a virgin. The definite article *ha* specifies her as "the virgin." Thus she is a specific virgin, not just any woman who might get pregnant and bear just any son. The child Immanuel is connected with the divine child in 6:9, where He is called the *el gibbor* ("mighty God"). The entire prophecy (chapters 7–12) points to the miraculous birth of a divine Messiah who is coming in the future.

Isaiah 9:6-7 describes for us a child who is born into the Jewish world and destined to rule. The passage focuses on both His humanity and His royalty. In the second part of the verse He is given four names, three of which clearly imply deity: Wonderful Counselor, Mighty God, and Eternal Father. The exception is the Prince of Peace. However, the two parts of verse 6 clearly emphasize the Messiah as being the God-Man. Verse 7 describes His future reign upon the throne of David in fulfillment of the Davidic Covenant. He will rule in the messianic kingdom, and peace will be established and upheld everywhere. This will be accomplished by means of justice and righteousness, and it will last forever. The fact that this will indeed come to pass is given as a pledge and guarantee in that "the zeal of the LORD of hosts will accomplish this" (9:7).

FUTURE REGENERATION OF ISRAEL
Isaiah 10:20-23

Isaiah 10:20-23, focuses on the regeneration of Israel (verse 20). The phrase "in that day" puts the prophecy into the prophetic future. Just as Israel once leaned upon the Assyrians, in the future they will lean upon the Antichrist, who eventually will smite them, as pointed out in 28:14-22. The remnant of Israel, who are referred to as the "escaped" of the house of Jacob, will one day no longer lean upon the Antichrist, but rather, upon the Lord, "the Holy One of Israel" (verse 20). This points to a future national regeneration of Israel. According to verse 21, the remnant of Israel will return to the Mighty God, which is one of Messiah's names in 9:6. Finally, Isaiah points out that even though God will issue a decree of destruction against the whole earth, a remnant of Israel will survive, and though God will make a "determined end in the midst of all the land," a remnant of Israel will always survive to carry the line of Israel into the future.

The Messianic Person

The final segment, 11:1–12:6, is also eschatological and deals with the three lines of messianism. The first line of messianism introduces the messianic person, Immanuel, who will someday rule on this earth as King (11:1-5). In verse 1, Isaiah makes key statements concerning His origin. The picture is that the house of David will be reduced to what it was in Jesse's day—poor and without any power or glory whatsoever. The Messiah would grow up in such an environment. He would come in a state of humility and live in poverty, low to the ground. But that state of humiliation would eventually lead to exaltation and perfection because the twig would become a tree. The twig, when it first came, resembled Jesse; but ultimately, it will resemble David.

Isaiah then lists seven of Immanuel's attributes (verse 2). Verses 3-4 go on to list five results of the Messiah's receiving of this sevenfold fullness of the Holy Spirit. First, "His delight is in the fear of the LORD"; the Messiah will have a power of perception with the implication that He receives pleasure from it. Second, "He shall not judge by the sight of his eyes, nor decide by the hearing of his ears." He will not judge by outward appearances. Third, the standard of His judgment will be absolute righteousness; the standard will not be outward appearances but inward righteousness. Fourth, He will judge the earth, which is His prerogative as the King. And fifth, He will "slay the wicked" (verse 4), also a prerogative of kingship. Immanuel will be righteous and faithful (verse 5). This is the messianic person, the One who will be King. When He comes as King, He will no longer appear as a Jesse, but as a David.

The Messianic Kingdom

In dealing with the second line of messianism (11:6-10), Isaiah divides the messianic program into two units: the animal kingdom and the Gentile nations. First, as for the animal kingdom (verses 6-9), the wolf and the lamb, the leopard and the kid, the calf and the young lion will stay together peacefully. The whole animal kingdom will be safe for a little child to lead. In the messianic kingdom, all presently carnivorous animals will become vegetarian. What's more, mankind and snakes, the two oldest enemies, will be able to dwell together because all snakes that are presently poisonous will no longer be dangerous in the kingdom.

Peace will flourish within the animal kingdom, and animals will no longer kill each other (the same point is made in Isaiah 65:25). Isaiah then gives the reason: The reign of Immanuel will ensure that all the animals will live at peace, and God's holy mountain will extend over the entire earth. In Scripture, "mountain" often symbolizes a king, kingdom, or throne. In this context, it is a reference to the messianic kingdom. Furthermore, the "knowledge of the LORD" will permeate the entire earth, "as the waters cover the sea" (verse 9).

Second, in verse 10, Isaiah describes how the messianic program deals with the peoples, the Gentile nations. The timing is "in that day." In what day? In *that day* when the kingdom is established; in "that day" when the members of the animal kingdom are living in peace with each other, in "that day" when the "Root of Jesse" will have a different meaning, in "that day" when the "Root of Jesse" shall stand for a signal or standard. In those days, a signal with waving banners was erected on a high pole at the top of a lofty hill as a sign for the people to assemble. In a highly visible place, the waving banners could be easily seen and would attract attention. The people saw the raising of the standard as a signal for them to start gathering at this place for one reason or another. When the kingdom is established, the Root of Jesse will no longer be insignificant. Instead, the Messiah will become the signal. The Root of Jesse that once grew on the ground will now become a mighty tree lifted high upon a mountain. The purpose of the Messiah's being a signal is for the gathering of the Gentiles in obedience. When this happens, it will be a fulfillment of the prophecy in Genesis 49:10, which states, "To Him shall be the obedience of the peoples." Furthermore, Isaiah 11:10 states that "His resting place shall be glorious," or more correctly, "His resting place shall be glory." The point is that the Messiah is going to be characterized by being the Shekinah glory. The very brightness of the Shekinah glory is what will start attracting Gentiles toward Him, a point Isaiah makes several times throughout the latter part of his book.

The Messianic People

The third line of messianism is the messianic people (11:11–12:6). Isaiah makes two main points: their regathering and their song of praise.

In verses 11-16 Isaiah makes four points about the regathering. First, this will be a second and final worldwide regathering for the messianic kingdom (verses 11-12). Verse 11 states that this is the second time He recovers His people. If this is a second worldwide

regathering, when was the first one? It could not be the return from Babylon because that was hardly a worldwide regathering. Rather, it was a return of a remnant of Jews from one country, Babylon, to another country, Israel. Here, Isaiah speaks of a *second* worldwide regathering, emphasizing that the first one was also worldwide. The first worldwide regathering must be that of the present Jewish state of Israel. This will someday be followed by a second worldwide regathering, which will be for the kingdom.

The Old Testament prophets spoke of two worldwide regatherings of the Jewish people. The first is a worldwide regathering in unbelief in preparation for judgment—the judgment of the Great Tribulation. This worldwide regathering has been fulfilled with the present state of Israel. But this present state will collapse at the middle of the Tribulation, and one more dispersion out of the land will require a second worldwide regathering. This second regathering will be in faith in preparation for the blessing of the messianic kingdom. Isaiah is speaking of the second worldwide regathering in these verses—the regathering in faith in preparation for blessing.

This is why the Gentiles are gathered in verse 10. The signal will be placed on a high mountain so that the Gentiles can aid in conducting the Jewish people back to their land. The second worldwide regathering in preparation for the blessings of the messianic kingdom will be accomplished with Gentile help. That is the reason the word "standard" is used in verse 12: "he will lift up a standard for the nations"—something he already mentioned in verse 10. These nations "will assemble the banished ones of Israel" and will "gather the dispersed of Judah from the four corners of the earth" (verse 12).

The second point concerning the regathering of the messianic people is the restoration of the unity between Judah and Israel (verses 13-14). First, there will be a restoration of peace between the two kingdoms (verse 13). After the death of Solomon, the kingdom of Israel split in two: Israel became the northern kingdom, and Judah became the southern kingdom. They have never reunited into a single kingdom since then. What was this "jealousy of Ephraim" about (verse 13)? The reason for the jealousy is found in Psalm 78:9-11, where we read that Ephraim turned away from righteousness. Because of this, God chose Judah over Ephraim (see Psalm 78:67-68). As a result, the temple remained in Jerusalem and was not moved to Ephraim in the northern kingdom. The Shekinah glory remained in the Holy of Holies of the temple in Jerusalem, and this created an envy on the part of Ephraim toward Judah. But this envy will be removed, and there will be a restoration of peace between the two kingdoms (Jeremiah 3:18; Ezekiel 37:15-23).

Second, Israel and Judah will become united in battle against their opponents (verse 14). In the past they fought against each other, but now they will fight together against their opponents—the Philistines to the west, and Edom, Moab, and Ammon to the east.

Third, Isaiah mentions two nations from which the regathering will occur: Egypt and Assyria. Concerning Egypt, "the tongue of the Sea of Egypt," or the Gulf of Suez, will dry up. Concerning Assyria, Isaiah states that the Euphrates River will be smitten and broken into seven smaller streams to make crossing that much easier. That will benefit the Jews who are now regathering back to the land. Isaiah 27:12-13 also emphasizes that much of the regathering will be from Egypt and Assyria.

Fourth, in that final regathering, there will be a highway from Assyria as there once was a highway from Egypt at the time of Exodus (verse 16). Indeed, the final worldwide regathering is often pictured as a new exodus (Jeremiah 16:14-15; 23:7-8). The concept of a highway to accomplish the work of God is common in Isaiah (19:23; 35:8; 40:3; 49:11). Here the highway aids in the return of the Jewish people from the land of Assyria.

In keeping with the exodus motif introduced in verses 15-16, Isaiah 12 is a song of praise. After the exodus under Moses, the Jewish people sang a hymn (Exodus 15:1-18). After this second and final exodus, they will also sing a song of praise. This song has two stanzas, each beginning with the expression, "And in that day." The first stanza is in verses 1-3. In verse 1, the people thank God for turning away His anger. Verse 2 points out that Jehovah is their salvation, and in verse 3, they sing of the waters of salvation, a common picture of the Holy Spirit (John 7:37-39). God is their salvation because they have trusted in Immanuel, the messianic person of Isaiah 11:1-5.

The second stanza is in verses 4-6. In verse 4, they ask the nations to "call on His name," for anyone who calls upon the name of the Lord will be saved. In verse 5 the people sing to Jehovah about the great things He has done on their behalf. They want His work to "be known throughout the earth." The picture here is one of spreading the good news. And finally, in verse 6 the Jews are exhorted to cry out and shout the good news to the Gentile nations—the news that "the Holy One of Israel" is great.

ORACLES AGAINST THE NATIONS
Isaiah 13–23

In Isaiah 13–23, the prophet focuses on a number of different Gentile nations, primarily the ones surrounding Israel. He gives some definite and specific prophecies about these nations.

THE FALL OF BABYLON
Isaiah 13:1–14:23

In Isaiah 13:1 Isaiah identifies his topic, which is "the oracle concerning Babylon." Some prophecy teachers view this prophecy as already having been fulfilled, but if the normal literal hermeneutic is followed, it has not been fulfilled in the manner Isaiah requires. Furthermore, in 13:6,9, Isaiah clearly puts the prophetic fulfillment of this in "the day of the Lord," which is the most common biblical term for the Tribulation. Isaiah is not describing any destruction of Babylon that has ever happened in history but one that is yet to take place at a future time. In 14:1-2, Isaiah connects this with Israel's final restoration, which is a future event and in fact will be a key result of Babylon's destruction.

Isaiah then focuses on the fall of the city of Babylon (13:2-22). He describes the gathering of the anti-Babylon forces (verses 2-5), pointing out that they come from different parts of the world and the surrounding territories. The ones destroying Babylon are referred to as God's "consecrated ones" (verse 3), which may mean they are sanctified and set apart to be the ones to destroy Babylon, or it may just as easily mean that God will use the Gentile believers of the Tribulation to destroy the city of Babylon. The answer to God's call is a gathering of many nations, and God is the One who musters all these nations together for the battle. The goal is to destroy the whole land of Babylon (verses 4-5).

In verses 6-16, Isaiah spells out the timing of the destruction. It will happen during "the day of the LORD," a phrase he uses three times (verses 6,9,13). It will be a time of terror (verses 6-8) that results in the mass destruction of humanity throughout the land of Babylon (verses 9-12). In fact, the destruction will be so great that people will become rarer than even the fine gold of Ophir (verse 12). Verses 13-16 describe the devastation of Babylon within the day of the Lord, which will include the flight of Jews and other foreigners and the violent deaths of the nationals.

Verses 17-22 go on to spell out the results of the destruction. Verse 17 identifies the leaders of the confederacy as the Medes, though many nations from all directions will take part. The Medes are located north of Babylon in what is now southern Turkey and northern Iraq. (It's possible that the modern-day Kurds are descendants of the ancient Medes.) The Medes will lead these armies to destroy both the population (verse 18) and the city of Babylon (verse 19). Isaiah says the human population will be replaced by desert animals (verses 21-22). However, these are not literal animals.

The Hebrew word used here is *seirim,* a word that refers to demons in goat form (Leviticus 17:7), and the fact that Babylon will become a residence of demons is verified by Revelation 18:2. The passage closes with the fact that once the appointed time comes, there will be no delay in the execution of this prophecy.

Babylon's fall will coincide with Israel's final restoration (14:1-2). In contrast to the eternal destruction of Babylon, Israel will be restored. God intends to get the people of Israel back into the land, and He will use Gentiles to help gather them. Furthermore, Gentiles will become servants to the Jewish people in the messianic kingdom.

Isaiah then returns to prophesying about the fall of Babylon—more specifically, the king of Babylon (14:3-23). Verses 3-8 describe the breaking of the king of Babylon's staff, and verses 9-11 tell of the arrival of the king's soul into hell. The souls that preceded the king to hell rise up in astonishment at the discovery that he, too, has suffered the same demise as they. Elsewhere in Scripture we are told the final ruler over Israel will be the Antichrist, so this is most likely a prophecy of the Antichrist described as "the king of Babylon," for Babylon will be his world capital during the Tribulation.

There are two possible ways to understand verses 12-15. Some believe Isaiah is still describing the king of Babylon as well as some of his various boisterous remarks. A second option is that after describing the Antichrist's descent into hell, Isaiah now refers to that personage that will control the Antichrist, who also once fell from a higher state because of the claims he made. Isaiah thus turns to the controller of the Antichrist, Satan, before dealing with the body of the Antichrist on earth. The outline would then be as follows: verses 9-11 describe the soul of the Antichrist in hell; verses 12-15 describe the fall of Satan from heaven to earth into the Abyss; and verses 16-20 describe the body of the Antichrist on earth.

If this passage is about the fall of Satan, then verse 12 summarizes his fall, calling him *heileil* in Hebrew, which means "daystar." It is not unusual for a star to be used symbolically to represent angels—good or bad—and with perhaps one exception, this is always the case. Thus Isaiah describes Satan as the daystar that has fallen from heaven, and it is a fall that will continue all the way down to Sheol. Verses 13-14 give the reason for Satan's fall—a self-declaration of the five "I wills." Isaiah's point is that Satan fell because of his pride and boastful remarks, and the Antichrist will fall for the same reasons.

Isaiah then returns to what happens to the body of the Antichrist on earth (verses 16-20). He describes the body as lying on the ground, and people are astonished that this one could so easily die (verses 16-17). The prophet adds that the body of the Antichrist will never see burial but will instead be trampled by his own soldiers (verses 18-20). While Isaiah does not give the reason for this, Revelation 19:20 says that the Antichrist will be cast alive into the lake of fire and will be resurrected for that purpose. Verses 21-23 conclude with the results, including a total destruction of the city from which the Antichrist ruled.

JUDGMENT ON EGYPT
Isaiah 19

Isaiah 19:1-10 describes the punishment of Egypt, which will be characterized by civil war, desolation, and famine. Isaiah adds in verses 11-15 that the root cause of Egypt's devastation is the fact that its leaders have led the nation astray. In fact, in recent history, Egypt has gone to war with Israel on two occasions. Both times, the Egyptian army suffered heavy losses and the Egyptian economy was affected.

Isaiah then describes the future national salvation of Egypt, which will come in three stages. Each stage is introduced with the prophetic phrase "in that day." The first stage is that Egypt will develop a fear of Israel. Never in ancient history has this been true. Egyptian forces passed through the land of Israel freely even in the days of Solomon. Only since 1948, especially following the Six-Day War, has Egypt developed such a fear.

Having lost three wars against Israel, with heavy casualties all three times, Egypt now has a deeply rooted fear. In the second stage (verse 18), Isaiah prophesies that five cities in Egypt will someday speak the "language of Canaan." In Isaiah's day, this would have been the Hebrew language. Just how this will come to fulfillment is yet to be seen, but he clearly prophesies that five Egyptian cities will be speaking Hebrew rather than Arabic. Then will come the third stage (verses 19-22), or Egypt's national salvation. Egypt, as a result of being under a cruel dictator, will turn away from its national religion—presumably Islam—and turn to the God of Israel. The Egyptians will come to know the Lord and worship the God of Israel with sacrifices and vows. The same God who brought judgment upon Egypt will bring about the nation's regeneration. Just as there will someday be a national salvation of Israel, there will also be a national salvation of Egypt.

Verses 23-25 add that there will also be a national salvation of Assyria, which is presently northern Iraq. Verse 23 describes an economic unit that will encompass Egypt, Israel, and Assyria. The highway mentioned is the ancient Via Maris that ceased to function in 1948 when Israel became a state and Egypt and Syria closed their borders. In the messianic kingdom, when Israel, Egypt, and Assyria are all worshipping the same God, peace will be restored and the borders will once again be opened. Once again traffic will flow from Egypt and Assyria through the land of Israel. The means by which this will occur is conversion. The three former enemies will have a spiritual unity as well as an economic and political unity. Thus, God declares, "Blessed is Egypt my people, and Assyria the work of my hand, and Israel My inheritance" (verse 25).

JUDGMENT ON EDOM
Isaiah 21:11-12

The next prophetic segment focuses on the future of Edom, which today comprises southern Jordan. Isaiah refers to Edom as *Duma,* which is a word play. The meaning of *Edom* is "red," and the meaning of *Duma* is "silence." The change of names becomes a symbol of Edom's future fate. *Duma* does not merely mean silence here, but rather, it speaks of the silence of death, so Edom is the land of the dead (Psalm 31:17; 94:17; 115:17). It is a silence of death-like stillness, death-like sleep, and death-like darkness. Isaiah the watchman hears an anonymous voice from Mount Seir (the main mountain range in the land of Edom) asking the question, "Watchman, how far gone is the night? Watchman, how far gone is the night?" In the Hebrew text, the first "night" is the long form *lailah,* and the second "night" is the short form *leil,* which conveys a heightened anxiety and sense of urgency and haste. In other words, "What part of the night is it? How much of the night has passed? How much more must we endure before the light of the morning comes?" Isaiah answers in Aramaic and says, "The morning comes and also the night"—meaning that morning is coming, but it, too, will be night. That is, there will be no relief or consolation for Edom. While there is a call to repentance, Edom does not respond to the call. This short prophecy predicts the rather total destruction of Edom, which will be explained in greater detail later by Isaiah (34:1-17; 63:1-6).

LITTLE APOCALYPSE OF ISAIAH
Isaiah 24–27

The Greek word *apocalypsis* translates to the English word *revelation* and has the meaning of "unfolding" or "unveiling." The basic outline of this portion of Isaiah is very similar to that of the apocalypse, or the book of Revelation—hence the title of this section. Also, the cataclysmic judgments of these chapters are similar to the apocalyptic judgments found in Revelation.

THE GREAT TRIBULATION
Isaiah 24

Isaiah 24 describes the Great Tribulation,

the great worldwide judgment upon the earth, and includes four points.

The first point is the worldwide judgment of God (verses 1-13). Verses 1-4 spell out this massive, universal judgment, which will affect all social and economic classes. The source of this judgment is God, and by the time it has run its course, the results on the earth will be fourfold: He will make the earth empty, He will make it waste, He will turn it upside down (almost picturing the South Pole becoming the North Pole), and He will "scatter its inhabitants" (verse 1). The reason for this judgment is the violation of "the everlasting covenant" (verses 5-6). Which covenant is he speaking of in this passage? The covenant that was made with the world in general, or the Noachin Covenant in Genesis 9:1-17. By violating the statutes of this covenant, man has polluted the earth.

The Noachin Covenant contains several statutes: First, man was to, "be fruitful and multiply, and fill the earth" (verse 1); second, man was to subject the earth for proper use (verse 2); third, man was allowed to eat both vegetables and animals (verse 3); fourth, the drinking of blood was forbidden (verse 4); and, fifth, capital punishment was instituted (verses 5-6). Whereas man has been faithful in keeping a minority of the provisions of the Noachin Covenant, he is far from keeping the majority of them. By means of disobedience to this covenant the earth has been polluted.

The Noachin Covenant gave man authority over the earth, but it was authority to subject the earth for proper use, not improper use. So when man violated this covenant, he also polluted the earth. Consequently, God is going to send a tremendous judgment or curse upon the entire earth—specifically, the judgment of the Great Tribulation.

In the Great Tribulation, a massive proportion of humanity will be destroyed by fire; therefore, "the inhabitants of the earth are burned" (Isaiah 24:6). Indeed, many of the judgments in the book of Revelation are judgments by fire. Fire will be the major means God will use to destroy people in the Great Tribulation (2 Peter 3:10-12), and Isaiah sees that "few men are left" (Isaiah 24:6). Furthermore, all sources of joy and gladness will be cut off as stated in verses 7-9, and the city will be stricken desolate (verses 10-12). Isaiah uses the definite article *the* to point to a specific stricken city, which, based on this description, will be the city of Babylon. The city of Babylon, however one interprets it, will become the world capital under the Antichrist. And as a result of divine judgment, the capital of the world will become a city of desolation.

According to verse 13, what is true of Babylon individually will also be true of the world in general—God's judgment is going to be worldwide. There will be massive destruction of the world's human population until only a remnant of people are left. One of God's key purposes for the Tribulation is to bring an end to wickedness and wicked ones (Isaiah 13:9), and Isaiah 24:1-13 emphasizes this purpose.

The second point deals with the worldwide glorification of God's name, which comes suddenly from all directions (24:14-16). It comes from the west, the east, and the uttermost parts of the earth. Even in the midst of the massive judgment that falls upon the earth during the Great Tribulation, there will still be worldwide glorification of God's name. The song these people sing is "Glory to the Righteous One!" (verse 16). Who are these people? Jewish and Gentile believers who are on earth during the Great Tribulation.

Isaiah does not provide the details, but interestingly, Revelation 6–7 follows the same outline as Isaiah 24. For example, Revelation 6 describes the seal judgments, in which there is massive destruction of the earth's surface and population. Isaiah 24:1-13 spells out judgments corresponding to those described in Revelation 6. In Revelation 7:1-8 we read of 144,000 Jews who are glorifying God. Revelation 7:9-17 records that myriad of Gentiles are saved by the preaching of these 144,000 Jews, and they too are glorifying God's name. Isaiah 24:14-16 describes a scene that corresponds to Revelation 7. In Revelation 8–9 John lists the trumpet judgments, which correspond to the devastation described in Isaiah 24:16-20.

The third point returns to the theme of judgment—the devastation of the earth (24:16-20). Isaiah is caught up in this vision and becomes a participant in verse 16: "I said, 'Woe to me! Woe to me! Alas for me! The treacherous deal treacherously, and the treacherous deal very treacherously.'"

The point of this verse is that although there are many who are praising God's name, there is judgment nonetheless. Isaiah then emphasizes the inescapableness of the judgments. In verse 17 he states that people are unable to escape terror, the pit, and the snare. In verse 18, those who may escape terror shall fall into the pit; those who escape the pit end up by falling into the snare. Indeed, the judgments of the Great Tribulation will fall upon all. In verse 18 there is also an allusion to the Noachin flood: "For the windows above are opened, and the foundations of the earth shake." These statements are similar to those made of the universal flood in Genesis 7:11 and 8:2. Just as the flood was a judgment upon the whole earth, destroying masses of humanity and leaving only a small remnant, similarly, the Tribulation will be a judgment that falls upon the whole earth, leaving only a remnant alive.

We know from the book of Revelation that by the time the Tribulation runs its course, between two-thirds and three-quarters of the earth's surface and population will have been destroyed. Verses 19-20 again emphasize one of the purposes of the Tribulation: to make an end of wickedness. In verse 19, the Hebrew text is emphatic and literally reads, "Broken down, there is a breaking down of the earth; cracked through, there is a cracking through of the earth; shaken, there is a shaking of the earth." Verse 20 tells us the earth will be shaken so violently by these judgments that it will stagger like a drunken man. Verse 20 concludes by saying that the earth's transgression will indeed "fall, never to rise again."

The fourth point marks the end of the Tribulation (24:21-23). Verse 21 reveals that when the Tribulation ends, two groups of beings will be judged. First, God will punish the "host of heaven on high," which refers to the fallen angelic beings. Second, He will punish the "kings of the earth on earth," which refers to people. After this judgment, both the fallen angels and men will be confined (verse 22). There are two different places assigned for their confinement: "the dungeon" and "the prison." The "dungeon" refers to hell, where fallen, unregenerated, unsaved humanity will be condemned. This is the judgment described in Matthew 25:31-46 and Joel 3:1-3. The other place of confinement, "the prison," is for fallen angels and refers to the abyss, that section of Sheol or Hades that is a temporary holding place for fallen angels. Satan will be confined to the abyss in Revelation 20:1-3. Isaiah then states, "and after many days they will be punished." Once they are confined to these places, they will not be a concern again until after "many days," which refers to the 1000 years of the millennial kingdom. They will be dealt with after the millennial kingdom, at which point they will be summoned to the Great White Throne Judgment. In the meantime, during the millennial kingdom, the Shekinah glory will outshine both the moon and the sun.

THE SONG OF PRAISE
Isaiah 25

The second unit of the Little Apocalypse of Isaiah is a song of praise that the nation of Israel will sing during the millennial kingdom. In this song, the Jewish people in the kingdom will praise God for three things: deliverance, millennial blessings, and the judgment of Israel's enemies.

Verses 1-5 give praise to God for His deliverance. *Three reasons* are given for this praise, the first being, "You have done wonderful things." In Isaiah 9:6 one of the messianic names ascribed to the Lord is Wonderful Counselor. Here the people praise God for the wonders He has done and His plans (KJV, counsels) of old. What will be happening in the kingdom was conceived long ago in the plan of God.

The second reason for this praise is that God has destroyed Babylon (verses 2-3). During the Great Tribulation the imperial city of the Antichrist will be the city of Babylon, which is destined to become the capital of the world. However, this city will be destroyed at the end of the Tribulation and will never be rebuilt.

The third reason for this praise is God's deliverance of the faithful remnant (verses 4-5). The Old Testament prophets, especially Isaiah, used the terms "the poor" and "the needy" to speak of the faithful Jewish remnant of the Great Tribulation. God has delivered them from "the storm" and "the heat"—references both to literal storms and heat and to the persecution that the faithful remnant had undergone.

Second, the people praise God for two key millennial blessings: the wedding feast and the removal of "the covering" (verses 6-8). Verse 6 states the kingdom will begin with the wedding banquet, in which Israel will be remarried to God. The wedding banquet will include "choice pieces with marrow," a symbol of goodness and abundance, and "refined, aged wine." This refers to mature wine at rest, or good-tasting wine that is smooth. These will be served at the wedding feast.

The second millennial blessing is the removal of "the covering" (verse 7). The Hebrew word for "covering" emphasizes the completeness of the covering, and the word for "veil" emphasizes the thickness of the covering. The picture is that of Israel covered by a complete, thick cover. This covering is not the "partial hardening [that] has happened to Israel" that is mentioned in Romans 11:25. In the context of the Old Testament, a thick covering such as this was a symbol of sorrow (2 Samuel 15:30; 19:4; Jeremiah 14:3-4). The removal of the covering, then, means a removal of sorrow.

The reasons for the removal of the covering are given in verse 8. First, there will be no more death for believers in the kingdom. According to Isaiah 65:20, unbelievers will die at 100 years of age, but believers will not face death. Second, God "will wipe tears away from all faces." And third, the reproach of Israel will be removed. The assurance of this is "for the

LORD has spoken." That which God has spoken will surely come to pass.

The third thing the people praise God for is the judgment of Israel's enemies (verses 9-12). While Israel has received both spiritual and physical salvation from the Lord (verse 9), Israel's enemies have been trodden down (verses 10-11). In verse 10 Isaiah names Moab, a key representative of Israel's enemies. The judgment of Moab is typical of the judgment God will pour out upon other Gentile nations that have turned against the Jews. By the time God's judgment has run its course, the enemy nation will have become like a watery cesspool. Verse 11 goes on to say the Lord's hands will be placed upon Zion for protection, and will be placed against Moab or other enemies to destroy them. The picture is that of Israel's enemies trying to swim through a cesspool, but the struggle of swimming results in their sinking farther into it. Someone sinking into a cesspool has lost any sense of pride or dignity, and those who exercise pride over Israel will experience this kind of demotion. And finally, God will destroy every enemy fortress (verse 12).

THE SONG OF SALVATION
Isaiah 26:1-19

The third unit of the Little Apocalypse of Isaiah contains a second song: the song of salvation. This unit has five parts.

Part 1 (26:1-6)

The first section is the tale of two cities: Jerusalem and Babylon (verses 1-6). The first city is Jerusalem (verses 1-4). The land of Judah will sing a new song about the joys of a strong city (verse 1). Verse 2 reveals this city is empty. Having just been built, the gates are suddenly commanded to be opened so the people of Israel can enter. The nation that inhabits the Jerusalem of the messianic kingdom will have two attributes: first, it is a righteous nation; and second, it is a nation that has kept its faith. The means by which it has kept its faith is stated in verse 3: It is the faithful remnant or one-third of the Jewish nation of the Great Tribulation that

did not trust the covenant with the Antichrist, but instead trusted God.

Because these people trusted in God, their mind was kept by God. And because of this state of mind, God has kept them in perfect peace. Verse 4 exhorts these people to continue in this state of mind, trusting in Jehovah forever because He is an everlasting Rock.

The second city here is Babylon (verses 5-6), which will serve as the world capital during the Great Tribulation. Whereas God, as a Rock, is a sure foundation for the building up of Jerusalem, as far as Babylon is concerned, God, as a Rock, is going to have a crushing influence. Verse 5 tells of how God will bring down Babylon. Isaiah has mentioned Babylon twice before in the Little Apocalypse (24:10-12; 25:2-3), and here he describes the destruction of the city. The city will be trodden down by the faithful remnant of Israel—the very ones whom the Babylonians sought to destroy will be the ones who trample them down.

Part 2 (26:7-10)

The second part of the song of salvation deals with the learning of righteousness by means of judgment. The characteristics of the righteous are described in verse 7. The "way of the righteous" is directed by an upright God. Isaiah reiterates a theme mentioned earlier in 24:14-16, where he described a group of people who praise and worship God in the midst of judgment. We see similar praise here in verses 8-9. Throughout the judgments of the Tribulation the righteous have waited for the Lord, and now they desire His name and the remembrance of Him. They want to have an intimate knowledge of God that encompasses the whole man: "My soul longs for You, indeed, my spirit...seeks You diligently."

The judgments of the Great Tribulation have two purposes: to bring an end to wickedness and wicked ones, and to bring people to their senses. Indeed, many will learn righteousness "when the earth experiences Your judgments" (verse 9). The many who become believers during the Great Tribulation will become so because of God's judgments. In the end, those who will not learn righteousness will suffer in hell, and those who learn righteousness will have the privilege of entering into the messianic kingdom.

Interestingly, the very same judgments poured out by God will receive two very different reactions. And according to verse 10, even if God shows mercy to the unrighteous, "he does not learn righteousness." Even if they live in the "land of uprightness" they will still refuse to submit to the "majesty of the LORD." During the Tribulation, some will interpret God's judgments as meaning that He is unjust and therefore turn away from Him. Others will see the righteousness of God in the judgments and turn to Him. The same thing will be true during the millennium. Whereas the Tribulation will be characterized by judgment, the Millennium will be characterized by favor or grace. Indeed, many will respond to God's favor in faith. And yet, after 1000 years of living in the most perfect environment and having all their needs provided for, many others will revolt against God's authority. That is why sin and death will continue even in the kingdom.

Part 3 (26:11-15)

The third part of the song of salvation praises God for the deliverance of Israel. Isaiah describes God's zeal for Israel in verse 11 by saying that God's "hand is lifted up" in judgment against Israel's enemies. Those who come against Israel will be devoured by the fire of God's judgments. And according to verse 12, there will be peace for Israel.

Isaiah then describes Israel's previous lords in verses 13-14, explaining that *many* lords have held sway over Israel throughout Jewish history. Israel's past failures have caused her to be dominated by other lords, but not in the kingdom. Those past lords will now be dead, but Israel will be alive and her new Lord, Jehovah, will live forever. Verse 14 states that as for Israel's other lords, "the departed will not rise" again. The Hebrew word for "departed" refers to the "shades" of Sheol. All those previous lords merely had a shade-like

existence; there is no longer any remembrance of them.

According to verse 15, Israel will be blessed by new growth. Two things will be involved in this new growth: First, there will be no more anti-Semites to reduce Israel's population. And second, the borders of the land will be expanded. Israel will possess *all* of the Promised Land for the first time in its history.

Part 4 (26:16-18)

The fourth part of this song of salvation describes Israel's travail. According to verse 16, Israel has repented in that they looked to God in troubled times; "they could only whisper a prayer" while being chastened (Psalm 79–80; Isaiah 64). During the campaign of Armageddon at the end of the Tribulation, Israel will turn to God and pray the prayer that will result in Israel's national salvation. Israel's previous failure to produce is now removed, according to verses 17-18. The nation has been in birth pain after birth pain, but there has never been a delivery. But now, there is a change.

Part 5 (26:19-21)

The fifth and last part of this song of salvation is one of the few Old Testament passages dealing with the resurrection of the Old Testament saints:

> Your dead will live; their corpses will rise. You who lie in the dust, awake and shout for joy, for your dew is as the dew of the dawn, and the earth will give birth to the departed spirits (Isaiah 26:19).

This is a statement of resurrection—specifically, the resurrection of the Old Testament saints. They will not be resurrected at the rapture along with the church saints; rather, their resurrection comes after the Tribulation, in preparation for the kingdom. This resurrection is also found in Daniel 12:2 and Hosea 13:14. When they are resurrected, they will be as the dew of the morning.

THE COMING RESTORATION
Isaiah 26:20—27:13

The fourth unit of the Little Apocalypse

of Isaiah describes the restoration of Israel (26:20–27:13). It begins with a summary of Israel's refuge during the Great Tribulation (25:20-21), introduced with a summons to Israel in verse 20. The call is to go into hiding "until indignation runs its course." The term "indignation" is one of the many Old Testament names for the Tribulation. The believing Jewish remnant is told to hide until this indignation is past. This is also seen in Matthew 24:15-16, where the Jewish people flee to the mountains, and in Revelation 12:6,12-13, where the Jewish people flee to the wilderness. Micah 2:12 (KJV) states that the Jewish remnant will flee to the city of Bozrah, which is better known by its modern name, Petra.

The purpose of the indignation is "to punish the inhabitants of the earth for their iniquity; and the earth will reveal her bloodshed" (verse 21). The blood will serve as continuous, visible evidence of the wickedness of humanity, and it is for their wickedness that the indignation will punish them. Israel is to go into hiding until the indignation, or the Tribulation, has run its course. One-third of the Jewish nation still living at that time will do just that. After the inhabitants of the earth have been sufficiently punished for their sins, God will then turn to the people in hiding. This will lead to Israel's national regeneration.

The second aspect of Israel's restoration describes the punishment of Leviathan (27:1). The term "Leviathan" is a Hebrew name for Satan, who is the leader of the fallen angels of Isaiah 24:21. Satan is to be punished after the Tribulation, and in Isaiah 27:1 he is referred to by three names: "the fleeing serpent," "the twisted serpent," and "the dragon who lives in the sea." Similarly, God's "sword" is described in three ways. The "fierce" sword will punish "the fleeing serpent"; the "great" sword will punish "the twisted serpent"; and the "mighty" sword "will slay the dragon who lives in the sea." "Leviathan" also refers to Satan in other passages—Job 3:8, Psalm 74:14, and 104:26. As in the book of Revelation, after the return of the Lord and Israel's national regeneration, Satan will be confined to the abyss for the 1000

years of the millennial kingdom (Revelation 20:1-3).

The third aspect of Israel's restoration is the "Song of the Vineyard" (27:2-6). In Isaiah 5:1-17, Israel was pictured as a vineyard that brought forth wild and sour grapes. As a result, God judged the nation by leaving it unprotected and by withholding rain. This allowed it to be surrounded and choked by thorns and briars. In Isaiah 5 Israel was an unproductive vineyard, but now that will change and a different kind of vineyard song can be sung. Verse 2 introduces the song with the words "In that day," meaning the day of Israel's national regeneration. This time God will keep and water the vineyard (verse 3), and God will declare war on the thorns and briars (verses 4-5). The result is that Israel will be fruitful (verse 6) and will produce sweet grapes.

The fourth point concerning Israel's restoration is the purging of the nation's sins (verses 7-9). Verse 7 asks, in essence, "Has God ever devastated Israel the same way He has devastated Israel's enemies? Has Israel ever suffered the same type of vengeance the Gentile nations have?" The answer implied in verse 8 is no. God has never destroyed Israel, but He contended with them "in measure" (NKJV) by sending them away into the Diaspora (scattering the people among the nations). God sent the people away to punish them until they realized what their sins were. The iniquity of Jacob will be forgiven by means of the nation's punishment (verse 9). The "fruit of taking away his sin" (NKJV) speaks of the removal of Israel's idolatry. God's judgments during the Tribulation will purge the people of Israel of their sins. It is because of these judgments that Israel will come to saving faith.

The fifth point concerning the final restoration of Israel is the devastation of Babylon, described in Isaiah 27:10-11. Babylon was "the fortified city," and now it will be characterized as isolated. It is a homestead that will be "forlorn and forsaken, like the desert." It will only be good for grazing. Babylon will be as dry tree branches that are good only for use in a fire, and the inhabitants "are not a people of discernment."

The sixth and last point concerning Israel's restoration is the regathering of the people of Israel (verses 12-13). They will be regathered into all the Promised Land, of which the specific boundaries are given: the northern boundary will be the Euphrates River, and the southern boundary will be the brook of Egypt. They will be regathered "one by one" until every single Jew is back in the land of Israel and the nation is dwelling in all the Promised Land. Never before in Jewish history have the Jews possessed all the land God promised to them.

Not only will all the land be inhabited, but every Jew will be regathered from the midst of their enemies (verse 13). The sound of a great trumpet will signal the regathering and the return. The people will regather from all over, particularly from Egypt in the south and Assyria in the northeast. They will be regathered to "worship the LORD in the holy mountain at Jerusalem."

THE CRISIS OF HEZEKIAH
Isaiah 28–35

IN THE FOURTEENTH YEAR of Hezekiah the king of Jerusalem, Hezekiah foolishly, and against the advice of Isaiah, made an alliance or covenant with Egypt. He rebelled against the Assyrian Empire, which spurred the Assyrians to invade and destroy all of Judah's fortified cities. Only Jerusalem was spared because of God's judgment upon the Assyrian army—a judgment in which 185,000 soldiers were killed in one night. Much of this portion of Isaiah deals with the results of Hezekiah's covenant and the judgment that brought an end to Assyria. While these past events are history and not prophecy, they provide a backdrop for other texts that speak of a future time when Israel will again make a covenant that results in divine judgment.

ISRAEL'S COVENANT WITH DEATH
Isaiah 28:14-29

Isaiah 28:14-22 deals with the covenant of death and Sheol. Daniel 9:27 prophesies that the Tribulation will begin with a seven-year covenant between Israel and the Antichrist, and this passage in Isaiah deals with the same covenant, adding some details to the Daniel prophecy. While Daniel 9:27 presents the covenant from man's perspective, Isaiah 28:14-22 views the covenant from God's perspective. Verse 14 reveals God's view of those who enter the covenant—God calls them scoffers. He considers them mockers rather than serious leaders.

Verse 15 gives the reason for this and provides God's viewpoint of the covenant itself. Here, in vivid terms, we see why God calls the leaders scoffers. It is obvious that the leaders of Israel will go into this covenant in order to obtain some measure of security and to escape the "overwhelming scourge." The figure of a flood, when used symbolically, is always symbolic of a military invasion. The leaders of Israel believe that by entering this covenant, they will become free of any further military invasions. God warns that this is not a covenant of life, but a covenant of death. It is not a covenant of heaven, but a covenant of hell. Rather than gaining security, Israel will receive a strong measure of insecurity.

There are some who say that Israel will accept the Antichrist as the Messiah, but the Scriptures do not state such. Israel will make a covenant with the Antichrist and will place its trust for security in this covenant, but Israel will never accept the Antichrist as the Messiah.

Verse 16 speaks of those who refuse to enter into the covenant. This verse makes clear that there will be a segment of Jews, as there were in Daniel 9:27, who will refuse to have anything to do with this covenant. They will not rush to enter into it or to identify themselves with it.

Isaiah 28:17-22 mentions the same three results of the covenant as are found in Daniel

9:27. According to verses 17-18, the covenant will be broken by military invasions, which the Israelites had hoped to escape. Verses 19-20 describe desolations that fall upon the Jewish people. Rather than having security, they will have insecurity. This insecurity is pictured as tremendous discomfiture via two illustrations: that of a man trying to stretch himself out on a bed that is too short for him, and that of a man trying to protect himself from the cold with a blanket that is too small to cover all of his body. And verses 21-22 go on to describe the wrath of God.

Two Old Testament names for the Tribulation are given in this passage: God's "extraordinary work" and His "unusual act." That's because God calls for the destruction "on all the earth" (verse 22). This decree of destruction is what we see in the seven-sealed scroll of Revelation 5. With the breaking of the seals, there is massive destruction upon the earth. This decree of destruction will occur only when the covenant with the Antichrist is signed.

So the point made in Daniel 9:27 is also made by Isaiah. The Tribulation begins with the signing of the seven-year covenant between the leaders of Israel and the Antichrist. Once the covenant is signed the Tribulation begins, and a decree of destruction will be issued by God Himself.

Verses 23-29 conclude with some explanatory parables. They include a call for the people to learn the purpose and the necessity for the coming judgment and to know that God's judgment against Israel will be tempered with mercy. Isaiah compares a farmer's treatment of land with God's treatment of Israel. The first parable (verses 24-26) explains how plowing takes place before seeding. The point is that plowing does not continue forever, and the painful process of plowing is followed by sowing. This is true in God's dealings with Israel. The people must undergo a painful plowing before they will be ready for fruitful seeding. The second parable (verses 27-29) mentions light and harsh threshings. Isaiah notes that different seeds require different kinds of threshing, and while threshing is

necessary, it does not last forever. The same will be true about God's dealings with Israel. Israel will be threshed according to her need, but this threshing will not last forever because God "has made His counsel wonderful"—as confirmed by one of the messianic names in Isaiah 9:5, Wonderful Counselor.

FUTURE REGENERATION OF ISRAEL
Isaiah 29:17-24

Isaiah 29:1-16 deals mostly with Israel's spiritual condition at the time of Isaiah and verses 17-24 look to the future, predicting a time of regeneration in Israel. Isaiah prophesies that someday Israel's blindness will be removed and the people will be able to hear the Word of God and to understand what the prophets wrote. In that day they will have joy in the Lord—not a mere outward profession but the result of true regeneration. What Israel does not understand now, she will understand in the future.

DELAY OF THE RESTORATION
Isaiah 30:18-26

In Isaiah 30–31 the prophet warns Israel against any covenants and alliances with Egypt, an admonition that Hezekiah disobeyed, resulting in the Assyrian invasion of Israel. Isaiah 30 begins by describing the condition of Israel in Isaiah's day, and then verses 18-26 go on to describe the future restoration of Israel. This delay of the final restoration is caused by Israel's sins (verse 18). God is a God of justice, and people's sins must be dealt with. When Israel finally returns to God, Jerusalem will be restored (verse 19) and the people will weep no more. This prophecy was not fulfilled after the remnant returned from Babylon; rather, it will be fulfilled in the final restoration connected with the advent of the messianic kingdom. In that day, God will provide outward guidance (verse 20) through teachers who will expound the Word of God honestly. He will also give inward guidance (verse 21) through the still small voice of the Spirit, who will warn the people against turning either to the left or the right. As a result, they will walk a straight path and not deviate from the will of the Lord (verse 22). They will receive the material blessings of the land (verses 23-25), and enjoy greater light (verse 26) from the moon, which will be as bright as the sun, and the sun, which will be as bright as seven suns. This increased light will not be harmful because this will be the day of Israel's healing.

REIGN OF THE RIGHTEOUS KING
Isaiah 32

In this chapter, Isaiah reveals more details about the messianic kingdom. Verses 1-8 anticipate a good king and government. This government will consist of a righteous king who will reign in righteousness—the Messiah Himself (verse 1). This affirms the prophecies in Isaiah 9:6-7 and Jeremiah 23:5-6. The "princes" mentioned in this verse are members of the messianic kingdom who will rule in justice. For Israel to have a righteous king and righteous princes will be quite different from the nation's past experiences with kings and rulers who were not just or righteous. Isaiah goes on to mention three results of this righteous reign: People will become a source of security rather than danger (verse 2); the hardening and blindness of Israel will end, and instead of hearing stammering tongues, the people will hear clear communication of spiritual truth (verses 3-4); and the people will have a proper valuation of humanity (verses 5-8), in which fools will no longer be called noble but instead, will be removed from the land.

This righteous kingdom will be preceded by a time of tribulation (verses 9-14). While verses 9-11 were fulfilled during the Assyrian invasion, verses 12-14 were not. That which verses 12-14 describes does not match the historical details of the Assyrian invasion, but will be fulfilled during the Tribulation.

The messianic kingdom will be initiated by the outpouring of the Holy Spirit (verses 15-20). This outpouring will result in Israel's national regeneration (verse 15), which in turn will bring about the results described in verses 16-20: righteousness and justice (verse 16),

peace, safety, and quiet resting places (verses 17-18), the destruction of the enemy (verse 19), and an abundance of water and hence, an abundance of crops such that animals can eat freely of the crops without causing much damage (verse 20).

THE COMING ASSYRIAN INVASION
Isaiah 33

While some commentators claim Isaiah 33 was fulfilled in the Assyrian invasion, literal interpretation shows that the invasion did not do all that the passage requires. Thus, the passage suggests one of the biblical names for the Antichrist—the Assyrian, upon whom a woe was pronounced. While the first five woes of this segment were against Judah and Jerusalem, this one is against a Gentile leader and nation. The treacherous Assyrian who made covenants that he did not intend to keep will now himself be betrayed and destroyed. Verse 2 describes the prayer of the remnant asking God to be gracious unto them; they realize they are asking an unmerited favor. They are praying for their salvation in the time of trouble and asking to be delivered from physical endangerment. God's answer comes in verses 3-6, promising a dispersion of the invading army (verse 3), a plundering of the enemy (verse 4), and the coming of the messianic kingdom (verses 5-6).

Verses 7-12 describe the state of the nation at the time of the Gentile invasion of the land (Armageddon). The results of the invasion (verses 7-9) include the weeping of the nation—causing travel along the highways to be unsafe—and the destruction of the cities and desolation of the land. This all results from the breaking of the covenant made between Israel and the Antichrist. Later, the invaders will be destroyed (verses 10-12), for that is what God has decreed (verse 10). The enemy has planted the seeds of his own destruction (verse 11), and he can anticipate the judgment of being burned up (verse 12).

Verses 13-16 describe the state of the people at the time of the invasion. Those who put their trust in the invaders will be insecure (verses 13-14). By contrast, the faithful remnant will feel secure because they put their trust in the God of Israel (verses 15-16). Their spiritual security will come from their trust in the Lord, and their physical security from the place where they are hiding (verse 16). As reaffirmed in Isaiah 41:17-20 and 65:8-16, food and water will be provided to the remnant. This hiding place will also be "on the heights"—that is, in the mountains. It is described as "impregnable rock," meaning the nature of the place will make it easy to defend. So there are four clues about this hiding place: it will be in the mountains, in the wilderness, in a place prepared in advance, and very defensible. Micah 2:12 reveals this place to be the city of Bozrah, which is now known as Petra.

Isaiah next deals with the state of the people at the time of the restoration (verses 17-19) and points out that they will seek their Messiah and will find Him. They will also see the land extended to include all of the Promised Land, and they will see their enemy no more.

Isaiah concludes this section by pointing out the state of the nation at the time of the restoration (verses 20-24). Jerusalem will be a place of appointed feasts, characterized by quietness and confidence because the Lord dwells there (verses 20-21). As for the state of the government (verses 22-24), this kingdom will have a righteous king, the Messiah Himself, whose presence in the city will be a visible and living testimony that the enemy's goal of destroying Israel has failed.

GOD'S WRATH AGAINST ALL THE NATIONS
Isaiah 34

Isaiah issues a call and says that "the LORD's indignation is against all the nations" and against their armies in particular. They are destined to be slaughtered with the sword of the Lord (verses 1-3). Not only will there be convulsions in the earth at this time, but there will be shaking in the heavens as well (verse 4). The location of this judgment against the armies of all the nations is identified as the land of Edom (verse 5)—or more specifically,

the city of Bozrah in the land of Edom, which is now southern Jordan (verses 6-7).

Edom will become a perpetual desolation because of its sins against Israel (verse 8). Like Babylon, it will become a place of continual burning and smoke (verses 9-10) inhabited by various foul birds and animals and characterized by desolation (verse 11). It will no longer be inhabited by men (verse 12), and only animals will live there (verses 13-15). Yet real animals cannot live in a place of burning pitch and brimstone, and two clues in this text reveal that these are not literal birds and animals. The word translated "hairy goat" actually means "demons in goat form," and the word translated "night-monster" means "night demons." Like Babylon, Edom will also be an abode of demons.

This segment closes in verses 16-17 with a divine affirmation that every prophecy must have its fulfillment, and prophecies that have not been fulfilled yet must be fulfilled in the future. God views every unfulfilled prophecy like a single person who has not found his or her mate, and once the prophecy is fulfilled, the mate has been found. The point is that unfulfilled prophecy should not simply be allegorized away as if it will not be fulfilled in a literal sense. Every prophecy must be viewed as needing to be fulfilled in the future if it has not yet been fulfilled. Whatever God has commanded, the Holy Spirit will certainly carry out.

THE RESTORATION OF ISRAEL
Isaiah 35

Isaiah now describes the restoration of Israel in the messianic kingdom, and he points out there will be a transformation of the land (verses 1-2). Even the Negev Desert and the Rift Valley will blossom and become productive. The second coming of Jesus Christ will bring about these changes (verses 3-4). Other changes include the healing of all of the infirmities of the people and an abundance of water even in the desert (verses 5-7). The kingdom will also include "the Highway of

Holiness" (verses 8-10), a road on which only the righteous will walk.

The next major segment of Isaiah is the historical interlude concerning the crisis during the fourteenth year of Hezekiah's reign (Isaiah 36–39). This historical event brought on the prophecies described in the previous segment of Isaiah, and this event has been historically fulfilled.

THE REDEMPTION AND RESTORATION OF ISRAEL
Isaiah 40–66

THIS SECTION COMPRISES the epitome of Isaiah's prophecies and refers to events of his own day, events that were fulfilled after Isaiah's time, and a number of still-unfulfilled prophecies. We will examine the prophecies that have not yet been fulfilled.

ISRAEL'S FINAL DELIVERANCE
Isaiah 41:8-20

This passage begins with the reassurance to Israel that it is indeed God's chosen nation. Referring to Israel as "the descendants of Abraham My friend," Isaiah shows that Israel's status as a chosen nation is based on the Abrahamic Covenant, and on the basis of this same covenant, God will someday bring about a national salvation of Israel. Therefore, Israel has nothing to fear from humanity and has only the Lord to fear. Also, at the time of Israel's restoration, the Gentile nations that have come against Israel will be defeated (verses 11-13). Those nations characterized by anti-Semitism will cease to exist. Israel will be victorious and will thresh the nations (verses 14-16). As for the faithful remnant who survive the Tribulation (verses 17-20), God will miraculously provide water for them. Their survival will be based on God's miracles. When the people are brought back into the kingdom, the land will be reforested with seven types of trees that have great value. The purpose of God's miraculous works is to let Israel see, know, consider, and

understand who God is and that He is the One in whom they must believe and trust.

COMING OF THE MESSIAH
Isaiah 42:14-17

Next Isaiah prophesies the events of the second coming. These prophecies follow after words about the first coming of the Messiah (verses 1-13). With the second coming, God will no longer be silent. He will heal Israel's spiritual blindness and bring judgment upon the Gentiles.

REGATHERING OF ISRAEL
Isaiah 43:5-7

Isaiah 43:5-7 emphasizes the magnitude of the regathering and restoration of Israel. Jews will come from all parts of the world, and all four points of the compass are mentioned here. The magnitude is illustrated by the usage of three words: "created," "formed," and "made." These three words are used interchangeably in the creation account in Genesis 1–2. Hence, from God's perspective, the final regathering will be on the magnitude of the original creation.

OUTPOURING OF THE SPIRIT
Isaiah 44:1-5; 45:14-17

A special outpouring of the Holy Spirit upon Israel will result in Israel's national salvation. The result of Israel's salvation is that many Gentiles will align themselves with Israel because they can see that God is with His people. Thus, Israel's spiritual rebirth will lead to the rebirth of Gentiles as well.

THE SERVANT OF THE LORD
Isaiah 49

Isaiah's favorite term for the Messiah is "Servant," and there are a number of "Servant of the Lord" passages throughout his book, mostly in relation to the first coming. Some of these prophecies include second coming elements.

In verses 1-4, the Servant is discouraged because of Israel's rejection of his messianic claims (which the Messiah agonized over in the Garden of Gethsemane).

In verses 5-6 a message comes from God the Father (in Luke's account of Gethsemane it came by means of an angel) explaining that Israel's rejection of the Messiah was part of God's divine plan and did not catch Him by surprise. The point is that the Messiah was not only to be the restorer of Israel, but He was also to be a light to the Gentiles. According to God's plan, the Messiah would be rejected by Israel at His first coming, and as a result of that rejection, He would become a light to the Gentiles.

Eventually Israel will accept Jesus as the Messiah (verse 7), and that will result in Israel's final restoration (verse 8). God will also remove all obstacles to the return (verses 9-11), and the final worldwide restoration will prepare for the blessings of the kingdom.

This will lead to the consolation of Zion, showing that the city is not forsaken. It cannot be forsaken because Zion's name is engraved on the palms of God's hands. In the final restoration, God will use believing Gentiles to help bring the Jews back into the land (verses 22-23). Unbelieving Gentiles, by contrast, will be destroyed (verses 24-26). Isaiah also predicted the suffering of the Servant (52:13–53:12), which was fulfilled in Christ's death on the cross for the sins of the world.

RESTORATION OF THE WIFE OF THE LORD
Isaiah 54

Israel's restoration as Jehovah's wife is described in Isaiah 54:1-8. Isaiah declares this restored wife will now begin to bear legitimate children (verses 1-3). Israel had produced a lot more children in desolation than she produced when she was previously married to Jehovah (verse 1). In fact, Israel produced many illegitimate children and very few legitimate ones, and the ones who were legitimate were often sacrificed to foreign gods. But now all this will change. Isaiah tells Israel to enlarge her house (verses 2-3) in order to accommodate the many legitimate children about to come. The reason for this new activity and the coming

legitimate children is the reunion of the marriage (verses 4-8). Israel's former adulteries will be forgotten (verse 4), and Jehovah will once again be her husband (verse 5). God will again court His wife as He courted her when she was a youth (verse 6), and all past forsakings will now be substituted by renewed blessings (verses 7-8).

The basis of the restoration includes the Noachin Covenant (verse 9), which guarantees the assurance of God's promises, and the New Covenant (verse 10), which guarantees the continuation of God's lovingkindness toward Israel regardless of what happens to the earth.

Verses 11-17 go on to describe the messianic kingdom. A contrast is made between Israel's past condition of being afflicted, tossed with tempest, and not comforted, with a future condition when Israel will be rebuilt with costly materials (verses 11-12). Israel has been chastised by God for the purpose of bringing her back to righteousness (verses 13-14), and when this occurs, Israel's enemies will be vanquished (verses 15-17). While enemies may gather against Israel, such gathering will not be of the Lord, and those who do gather will fall because of it (verse 15). The fact is that God is the Creator of both the smith who built the fire to make the weapon and of the weapon itself. Because God created both the weapon and the one who uses it (verse 16), He can therefore dispense of the weapon-user because no weapon formed against Israel will prosper (verse 17).

MILLENNIAL SALVATION
Isaiah 56:1-8

At the time the kingdom is set up, some Gentiles may feel that because Israel is given an exalted position, the Gentiles will be excluded from receiving the benefits of millennial temple worship (verses 1-3). But this will not be the case, for the temple ministry will be open to all Gentiles who are rightly related to the King. Under no circumstances will they be excluded because they are Gentiles or because they are mutilated (verses 4-5). It is then and only then that the house of God will truly be a house of prayer for all nations (verses 6-7)—at the time of Israel's final regathering (verse 8).

ISRAEL IN THE MESSIANIC KINGDOM
Isaiah 60–61

Verses 1-3 describe the Shekinah glory that will now return to Israel. This Shekinah light will come when the darkness reaches its greatest blackness (verse 2)—that is, the darkness of the Tribulation. Afterward the Lord will "rise upon you" and the glory "will appear upon you"—these are references to the second coming. As a result, Israel will become the center of world attention (verse 3).

According to verses 4-9, the Gentiles will aid in the regathering of the Jewish people, and all the nations will be brought to Israel. This will lead to the subservience of the Gentiles (verses 10-14). The Gentiles, who will be the servants of Israel, will also be used in the building up of the millennial Jerusalem (verse 10). The 12 gates, named after the 12 sons of Jacob, will continually remain open, never to be closed throughout the messianic kingdom. The Gentile nations and kings will bring their wealth through these gates (verse 11), and failure to do so will bring swift judgment (verse 12). The Gentile nations will bow in submission to Jerusalem's authority when they pass through Jerusalem (verses 13-14).

Isaiah then describes the exaltation of Jerusalem, when nations and kings will restore their vital energies upon the city (verses 15-16). Jerusalem will be beautified with stones and be in service to the leader of peace and righteousness (verse 17). Violence and desolation will no longer exist, so the walls symbolize salvation and the gates will sing praise (verse 18), and the Shekinah glory will be the light in the kingdom (verses 19-20). Isaiah concludes with a word about the status of Israel, stating that the whole nation will be righteous (verses 21-22).

In Isaiah 61:1-11, the prophet again focuses on the Servant of Jehovah and again brings together events that were either covered by Christ's first coming or refer to His second coming. The purpose of the first coming was to fulfill the five elements mentioned in verses 1-2a. The second coming will be for the purpose of restoring Israel (verses 2b-3). It is then that the restoration of Israel will be brought about. All the wasted cities will be rebuilt (verse 4), the Gentiles will become servants to the Jews (verse 5), Israel will at long last become a nation of priests and receive the wealth of nations (verse 6), and in place of double punishment (Isaiah 40:1-2) it will receive double blessing (verses 7-8). The result is that Israel will receive Gentile acknowledgment that it is the offspring of the Lord (verse 9). Isaiah 61 concludes by describing the righteousness of Israel in that day (verses 10-11). Righteousness is given to them when they are clothed with the garments of salvation and the robes of righteousness.

REDEMPTION OF ISRAEL AND JERUSALEM
Isaiah 62

The millennial Jerusalem will be characterized by brightness and righteousness (verse 1). Her righteousness will be recognized by all the nations of the earth (verse 2a). At that time Jerusalem will be given a new name (verse 2b), the one mentioned in Ezekiel 48:35: *Jehovah Shammah*, "the LORD is there." Jerusalem will be further characterized by beauty (verse 3), never again to be forsaken or desolated by God (verse 4a). The city itself will be God's joy and delight (verses 4b-5).

Verses 6-7 mention angelic messengers positioned on the walls of Jerusalem whose entire ministry consists of reminding God of His promises to make Jerusalem the joy and praise of the whole earth. Obviously God is omniscient and does not need to be reminded of His promises. Nor does He ever forget anything. While the Bible sometimes says God will forget the sins of believers, forgetfulness and remembering do not necessarily carry the meaning of "out of mind," but rather, these terms carry the meaning that God will either act on something or not act on it.

For example, Exodus 2:24 states that "God remembered" His covenant with Abraham, Isaac, and Jacob. But how could God forget

Isaiah 61:1-4 Fulfilled in Luke 4:17-22
(Compared to Daniel's 70-week Prophecy)

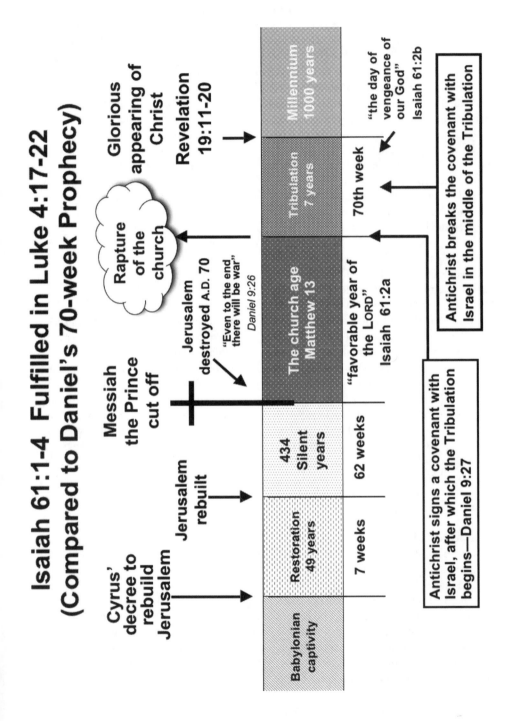

the covenant if He is omniscient? The word "remembered" in this verse means He will now act upon the promises that He made—just as forgetting our sins means He will not hold us accountable for them anymore since they have been forgiven through the blood of Messiah. That is why the angels in verses 6-7 are said to remind God of His promises. The issue is not that God might forget, but that the angels are praying for the day to come when God will act on and fulfill His promises.

The inhabitants of millennial Jerusalem are also promised that they will enjoy the fruit of their labors, for the results of their labors will never again be taken away by their enemies (verses 8-9). In addition, the redemption and salvation of Jerusalem are assured because God keeps His promises (verses 10-12).

TRIUMPHAL RETURN OF CHRIST
Isaiah 63:1-6

In a prophetic vision, Isaiah was standing on a high point or mountain in Israel looking eastward toward the land of Edom when suddenly he saw a magnificent but bloodstained figure approaching him in glory and splendor. At that point a question-and-answer session ensues between Isaiah and this marching figure. This figure is coming from the land of Edom and from the city of Bozrah, and His features reflect His glory and there is greatness in His strength. There can be little doubt that this figure arrayed with the Shekinah glory is the Jewish Messiah Himself.

Isaiah initiates a conversation with a question in 63:1. If there was any doubt as to the identity of this person, it should be resolved by now. Only one man can say, "I who speak in righteousness." Only one man has the power that is "mighty to save." This figure is Jesus the Messiah, who is marching toward Israel from the land of Edom and the city of Bozrah.

Isaiah responds to this answer with a second question in 63:2. He notices that the clothing of this individual, though radiant with the Shekinah glory, is nevertheless stained with blood. So Isaiah inquires as to how His garments became stained.

The answer is given in 63:3-6. The bloodstains were caused by a battle fought in the land of Edom at the city of Bozrah. The Messiah fought against the nations alone. In the course of trampling upon them, their lifeblood sprinkled onto His garments (verse 3). The fight was necessary in order for Him to save His redeemed people, Israel (verse 4). He fought all alone and there were none to help Him (verses 5-6).

The main point to learn from this passage is that the battle is initiated in the land of Edom at the city of Bozrah. By the time Messiah reaches Israel, His garments are stained with blood from the slaughter of the enemy.

Both Isaiah 34:1-7 and 63:1-6 state that the initial place of the second coming will be the city of Bozrah. This is reaffirmed in Habakkuk 3:3. This raises questions concerning passages that focus on His return at Jerusalem, and this will be resolved in the commentary on Zechariah 14:1-5. For now, suffice it to say that when the Messiah comes to Jerusalem, it is only after He has fought against the nations, and His coming upon the Mount of Olives is not the initial point of His return, but the final aspect of it. When He returns to Bozrah He will initiate the conflict with the armies that have come against the Jewish people, and once the fighting ends in the Valley of Jehoshaphat, He will then ascend the Mount of Olives.

PRAYER OF THE REMNANT
Isaiah 63:7–64:12

Isaiah 63:7-14 contains a remembrance of God's manifold gracious acts on behalf of Israel in the past. With confidence in God's past faithfulness, the remnant of the Tribulation will now plead for God to take note of their situation and rescue Israel from the oncoming enemy's. This plea for the second coming appears in Isaiah 64:1-12. The passage begins with the pleading for the Lord to "come down" and let the nations realize His presence (verse 1-2). The remnant of Israel will remember God's mighty works from the past (verses 3-7) and will seek those mighty works of God again (verse 8). They will also ask for the forgiveness of their sins (verse 9). The Jewish people's disastrous plight is shown by the fact that Jerusalem had been made a desolation by the nations (verses 9-10) and the temple is still defiled (verse 11). The passage ends with a plea for God to intervene lest they, too, become ruined (verse 12).

ISRAEL IN THE PLAN OF GOD
Isaiah 65:1-16

In 65:1-7, Isaiah describes the dispensation of grace, a period of time during which most of Israel has turned away from God and many Gentiles are coming to faith. Then in verses 8-16, Isaiah goes on to describe the Great Tribulation. In verses 8-12, he distinguishes between the destiny of the remnant and the nonremnant. Here the prophet describes how God will supply for the faithful remnant, whereas He will withhold provisions from those who are apostates. The passage makes it clear that apostates will be allowed to suffer and die, while the faithful remnant will receive divine protections and be given food and water. By this means the faithful remnant will be able to survive the persecutions and devastations of the Great Tribulation.

NEW HEAVENS AND EARTH
Isaiah 65:17-25

In verses 17-25, Isaiah provides some details about the new heavens and new earth. While many believe this refers to the eternal order, these new heavens and new earth are not to be confused with those of Revelation 21–22. The latter describes the new heavens and new earth of the eternal order, while the Isaiah passage describes those of the messianic kingdom, which will actually be a renovation of the present heavens and earth. Those mentioned in Revelation are not a renovation, but a brand new order.

The fact that the term "create" is used in reference to this shows that this renovation will be a miraculous one. The result of this renovation will be a continuation of many things of the old order and a number of new things. A good example of the old and the new is to be seen in what the Scriptures say about the land of Israel. Some things of the old order will remain, such as the Mediterranean Sea and the Dead Sea. But a number of things will be brand new, such as the exceedingly high mountain (the highest in the world) in the center of the country. Following this announcement about the new heavens and new earth is a description of the millennial Jerusalem (verses 18-19).

Verse 20 is especially significant, for it raises key points about life and death in the kingdom. First, there will no longer be any infant mortality in the millennium; everyone who is born in the kingdom will reach at least a certain age. Second, the reference to one dying at 100 as being a child emphasizes the blessing of longevity in the millennium. And third, those who die at the age of 100 evidently are sinners (unbelievers), for only they would be considered "accursed."

Verses 21-25 continue to describe life in the kingdom as a time of personal peace and prosperity. It will be a time of building and planting. He who builds and plants is guaranteed the enjoyment of the labors of his hands, for many of the effects of the curse will be removed (verses 21-22). Life will be characterized by longevity (verse 22), absence of calamity and turmoil (v. 23), and instantaneous response from God (verse 24). As in Isaiah 11:6-9, the members of the animal kingdom will be at peace with each other and with man (verse 25).

THE REBIRTH OF ISRAEL
Isaiah 66

Isaiah 66:1-6 deals with the rejection of the Tribulation temple. Once the temple is rebuilt, the sacrificial system stipulated in the Mosaic law will be reinstituted. However, this temple receives no sanction from God. Isaiah speaks of a house or temple being built for God which He does not sanction. It cannot refer to Solomon's temple or the temple built by Zerubbabel, because God sanctioned both of them. Nor can it refer to the millennial temple because that one will be built by Messiah, and

God will certainly sanction it. Therefore, the only temple this could refer to is the Tribulation temple. So Isaiah foresees the building of a temple that God will not sanction. God wants Israel to return to Him in faith, not merely to build Him a house.

This passage begins with a protest from God, who makes it clear that no temple built by Israel at this time will be acceptable, for God will not come and reside in this one (verse 1) as He did in the first temple. What God will require is not a new temple, but faith (verse 2). He will not accept these reinstituted Levitical sacrifices any more than He would accept human sacrifices, swine, or idolatry (verse 3). The very fact that the Jewish people build this temple shows their failure to listen to God's Word (verse 4) and come to Him by faith in Jesus the Messiah. Then Isaiah has a word of encouragement to those faithful Jews who will not participate in the rebuilding of the temple (verse 5), but are seeking to do God's will. Isaiah also states that this new temple will only end in judgment (verse 6) and not in forgiveness of sin or acceptable worship.

Two other points should be mentioned in relation to the third temple. First, the Six-Day War in 1967 set the stage for the fulfillment of this prophecy, for until that time, the temple compound was under Arab control. During the Six-Day War, the temple area fell into Jewish hands. Unfortunately, in an effort to help diffuse tensions between Jews and Arabs, Israel permitted the Muslim officials of the Waqf to have control of the structures on the Mount. The Waqf has long since restricted Jewish access, so it remains to be seen how circumstances will allow for the rebuilding of the temple.

Second, the tribe of Levi was the only tribe permitted by Mosaic law to take care of the temple and conduct the sacrificial system. It is interesting to note that while the other 11 tribes have lost their tribal identity since the temple records were destroyed in A.D. 70, the tribe of Levi has not. Unless a Jew is a member of the tribe of Levi, he is unable to know from which tribe he is a descendant. The tribe of Levi has kept their identity. Jews who have last names such as Levi, Levy, Levin, Levine, Leventhal, Levinson, Cohen, and other derivatives are members of the tribe of Levi. For the purpose of conducting temple sacrifices, only the tribe of Levi matters. It is not important to know who the members of the other tribes are, but it is very important to know who the Levites are. This contributes toward setting the stage for the temple to be rebuilt, and it is possible that it will be rebuilt before the Tribulation. If it is not, then it will certainly be rebuilt during the first part of the Tribulation. The temple must be built and functioning and have been in operation for at least a little while before the midpoint of the Tribulation because it is the temple that the Antichrist will desecrate at that time.

In any discussion of the rebuilding of the temple, the question of the Muslim Dome of the Rock arises. The Dome of the Rock is in the temple area, possibly on the spot of the previous two temples. In the opinion of some, the Dome of the Rock will have to be removed at some point. In the opinion of others, there is enough room on the Temple compound to permit the rebuilding of the Jewish temple without needing to tear down the Dome of the Rock. A novel theory that has arisen in recent years is that the Arabs might give up trying to get Jerusalem back and will simply move the Dome of the Rock to a better locality. The point missed by those who think this way is that it is not the Dome itself that is holy to Islam, but the site. According to Muslim tradition, the Dome of the Rock is built over the spot where Mohammed is said to have ascended into heaven. It is the rock that is holy and is commemorated by the building. Thus it is rather foolish to think that the Arabs would consent to moving the Dome of the Rock.

Still another novel theory of recent vintage is that the temple will be rebuilt completely away from the temple area. This is based on a misunderstanding of Jewish law and thinking. The Jews would not accept a new Jewish state anywhere but in Israel; nor will the Jews accept a new Jewish temple anywhere but on the temple compound. So the Dome of the Rock remains a problem, and there is much speculation concerning it. On this matter the Bible is silent; what we do know for certain is that the temple will be rebuilt. Only the passing of history will reveal how and where in the temple area this will come about.

Also relevant to the Tribulation temple are two other developments of recent years. One group, the Temple Mount Institute, based in the Jewish Quarter of the Old City (of Jerusalem), is in the process of making the furnishings for the next temple. A second group, located in the Muslim Quarter of the Old City, is training descendants of the Aaronic line how to perform the sacrificial rites. So while the temple itself is not yet being rebuilt, preparations are being made for the time when it will be rebuilt.

Isaiah 66:7-9 focuses on the rebirth of Israel, emphasizing the speed (verse 7), the amazement (verse 8), and the course of restoration (verse 9). This is not talking about the establishment of the state of Israel in 1948, which was a regathering in unbelief in preparation for the judgment of the Tribulation. Rather, this passage is dealing with Israel's final restoration, when the people come back in faith in preparation for the blessings of the messianic kingdom.

Verses 10-15 mention the consolation of Jerusalem and describe the peace and comfort she will enjoy in the messianic kingdom. This will be a time when lovers of Zion will rejoice with her (verse 10), and Jerusalem will receive the wealth of the nations (verses 11-12). Zion will experience comfort (verse 13) and rejoicing (verse 14) because of her experiential knowledge of the Lord. By contrast, the Gentile world will suffer the destruction of idolatry and all idolaters (verses 15-17).

Isaiah concludes his book by describing the place of the Gentiles in the messianic kingdom (verses 18-24). The Shekinah glory, which will be especially manifested in the kingdom, will be seen by many of the Gentiles (verse 18), and those who do see it will set off to travel among the Gentiles who have not seen it to tell them of it (verse 19). At the same time, Gentiles will be used to conduct the Jews back into the land of Israel and will be brought to the mountain of Jehovah's house in order to worship Him (verse 20). Furthermore, from among these Gentiles, God will choose some to serve as priests in the temple (verse 21). Not only is Israel the eternal nation, but the faithful among the Gentiles will also be eternal (verse 22), and they will have a place of worship in the temple for the Sabbath and new moon offerings (verse 23). As for the unfaithful among the Gentiles, their dead bodies and the suffering of their souls will be visible throughout the kingdom (verse 24), illustrating for 1000 years God's grace to the faithful and His severity to the lost. Isaiah's closing verse reminds us that there are two eternal destinies: heaven and hell.

JEREMIAH

Jeremiah lived during the last days of the kingdom of Judea. His ministry extended from the reign of King Josiah to that of King Zedekiah (610–586 B.C.). Most of Jeremiah's prophecies of the coming destruction of Jerusalem were fulfilled in his own lifetime. He was an eyewitness of the Babylonian siege ordered by King Nebuchadnezzar of Babylon. His book of Lamentations records his personal heartache as he watched his beloved city, Jerusalem, burning under the judgment of God.

In the book of Jeremiah are prophecies that would be fulfilled in the distant future, which include reference to the coming of the Righteous Branch and the establishment of the New Covenant. As Jeremiah looked forward in the corridor of time, he also foresaw future events of great eschatological significance.

THE COMING MESSIANIC KINGDOM
Jeremiah 3:11-25

Jeremiah 3 focuses on the precondition to setting up the messianic kingdom. Verses 11-14 issue a call to repentance, which is focused especially on Judah since, in the end, Israel has proved to be more righteous than Judah. The call is for the people to confess their sins, including their sin of disobedience to the Mosaic law. If they do, they will receive certain rewards (verses 14-18). First, they will be regathered one by one back to the land of Zion (verse 14). Second, they will be given righteous leaders who will never again be guilty of leading the nation astray (verse 15). Third, they will not so much as think of rebuilding the Ark of the Covenant (verse 16), because, fourth, God Himself in visible form, in the person of Messiah, will rule from Jerusalem. Therefore, Jerusalem itself will become the center of world attention. Fifth, and finally, the Jews will be so united as not to be split into two Jewish kingdoms again (verse 18). But before Israel can enjoy these Messianic and millennial conditions, they first must repent (verses 19-20).

The restoration described in verses 14-18 cannot happen apart from repentance, and Israel must return to God as Father and not stray from following the Lord (verse 19). Israel has been the adulterous wife of Jehovah, and just as a treacherous wife deserts her husband, so has the wife of Jehovah treacherously turned her back on her husband (verse 20).

This section closes in verses 21-25 with a prediction about Israel's future national repentance. Israel will enter a period of judgment that will bring her to the point of weeping (verse 21), and when she hears the call to repentance, she will respond (verse 22). Israel will confess her sins (verses 23-25), and finally be brought back to the Lord. That will bring about the establishment of the kingdom.

151

THE PROMISE OF ISRAEL'S RESTORATION
Jeremiah 12:14-17

THIS PASSAGE IS A MESSAGE given to the Gentiles who will help toward Israel's final restoration. The message is that just as God removed Israel from the land, He also intends to bring Israel back to the land (verse 14), and God will have compassion on Israel after the people's restoration (verse 15). In the messianic kingdom, the Gentiles who learn the ways of Israel will be blessed (verse 16), and those who do not listen will face judgment (verse 17).

THE NEW EXODUS BY GOD'S PEOPLE
Jeremiah 16:14-21

HERE, JEREMIAH POINTS OUT the magnitude of the final regathering in comparison with previous works of God. In verses 14-15, the regathering is compared to the exodus. The exodus has long been considered the high point of Jewish history, but after the final regathering, this will change (verse 14). In the future it will be the final regathering that will become the high point of Jewish history (verse 15).

In verses 16-18, God declares that He will send forth fishers and hunters to find the Jewish people because prior to the confession and restoration of Israel there must be judgment. In verse 16, he describes the fishers and hunters as fishing and hunting for the people of Israel for the purpose of punishment because Israel is the chosen people of God, and they must receive discipline for their sins (verse 18). This reaffirms a point made in Isaiah 40:1-2. Jeremiah then goes on in 16:19-21 to discuss the conversion of the Gentiles. Just as Israel's salvation is a work of God, so will the Gentile salvation be a work of God.

THE RIGHTEOUS BRANCH TO COME
Jeremiah 23:5-8

THE REIGN OF WICKED KINGS (Jeremiah 23:1-4) is contrasted with the reign of a future righteous king in Jeremiah 23:5-8. Jeremiah begins by saying in verse 5, "Behold, the days are coming," pointing forward to the prophetic future of the messianic kingdom. Then he states, "I will raise up for David a righteous Branch," emphasizing the absolute righteousness of the person (see Jeremiah 33:15). The point is that it is a descendant of David who will be characterized by absolute righteousness. Then Jeremiah states this descendant "will reign as king." This passage emphasizes both His messianic role and His kingly role. He is destined to "reign as king." When He does so, He will "act wisely, and do justice and righteousness in the land." Because the Messiah is characterized by righteousness, when He rules, He will rule righteously and justly.

Then Jeremiah states in verse 6, "In his days Judah will be saved, and Israel will dwell securely." He will extend His messianic protection over both houses of Israel. The verse concludes by revealing what the Messiah's name will be: "The LORD our righteousness." Here the Messiah is the only human being who was ever given the full name of YHVH—the name with four Hebrew letters that make up God's name, which emphasizes His deity.

According to verses 7-8, as a result of the righteous reign of the God-man descendant of David, there will be a final restoration. The words "behold, the days are coming" project outward to the prophetic future in reference to the messianic kingdom. Jeremiah points out that in that day the Jewish people will no more say, "As the LORD lives, who brought up the sons of Israel from the land of Egypt." To this day, the exodus from Egypt remains a high point of Jewish history. The Jewish people often refer to God as "the One who brought us up out of the land of Egypt." Yet the exodus will pale in comparison to the final restoration. In the future the Jews will not say, "As the LORD lives who brought [us]…from the land of Egypt," but will say, "As the LORD lives, who brought up and led back the descendants of the household of Israel from the north land and from all the countries where [God] had driven [us]." Jeremiah mentions a return from the north country, which is Babylonia. Jews will be returning from that prophetic Babylon of the future during the events of the campaign of Armageddon. They will also return "from all the countries where [God] had driven them." There will also be a regathering from all the other countries in the world as well. That final regathering will become the new high point of Jewish history. God will regather His people from all the places where He had driven them. Jeremiah then concludes with a promise from God: "Then they will live on their own soil." When they have returned to the land, they will be able to live safely in it.

A HOPE FOR THE FUTURE
Jeremiah 29:11-14

IN JEREMIAH 29:1-10, for the second time, Jeremiah predicts that the Babylonian captivity would last for 70 years. When he describes the restoration, he goes beyond the return from Babylon to the final restoration as signaled by the phrase "to give you a future and a hope" (verse 11). In that day, he prophesies, there will be a national regeneration of Israel (verses 12-13) that will then bring in the final regathering—a regathering in faith in preparation for the blessings of the kingdom (verse 14). Jeremiah does not say the people will be brought back from Babylon, but rather, that they will be regathered from all the nations where they have been scattered, which tells us this is more than just a Babylonian return.

THE BOOK OF CONSOLATION
Jeremiah 30–33

THE PROPHETIC DISCOURSE in Jeremiah 30–33 is called the Book of Consolation because that is its main theme: the consolation of Israel. Through most of his book, Jeremiah has been majoring on judgment and minoring on blessing. In these four chapters, he majors on blessing and minors on judgment.

THE RESTORATION OF ISRAEL AND JUDAH
Jeremiah 30:1-3

The Word of the Lord came to Jeremiah (30:1), and Jeremiah was commanded to write (verse 2). Literally, the Hebrew text reads, "Write for yourself." In other words, Jeremiah is asked to write for himself and for his own personal benefit "all the words which I have spoken to you in a book." Instead of receiving a mostly negative message (as in the previous 29 chapters), Jeremiah will now receive a mostly positive message, and he is to put it together in a separate book, or more correctly, a separate scroll. Verse 3 gives a summary of what these four chapters contain: "'For behold, days are coming,' declares the Lord." These words point to the prophetic future, in which God "will bring back from captivity My people Israel and Judah" (NKJV). This is the basic theme throughout the four chapters in general and the first two chapters in particular; God will again bring the Jews—both houses of Israel—back into the Promised Land. God promises a future and then makes three supporting statements affirming that promise: first, "I will bring them back"; second, He will give them the land He gave to their fathers; and, third, they will possess it.

THE TIME OF JACOB'S DISTRESS
Jeremiah 30:4-11

In Jeremiah 30:4, the prophecy regarding Israel's restoration begins in earnest. God tells Jeremiah that the words he is about to write are the words of the Lord concerning both Israel and Judah.

In verses 5-7, Jeremiah mentions the Great Tribulation. He begins with the voice of judgment (verse 5). Behold, it is "a voice of trembling, [a voice] of fear, and not of peace" (NKJV). Rather than peace, there is the pain of childbirth (verse 6). "Ask now, and see if a male can give birth." The answer is no. If that is the case, then "why do I see every man with his hands on his loins, like a woman in labor," and all faces turned pale? (NKJV). The answer is that the day of the Lord, the Tribulation, has finally arrived. Concerning the Tribulation Jeremiah states in verse 7, "Alas! for that day is great." "That day" is equal to what is elsewhere referred to as the "day of the LORD," the most common biblical name for the Great Tribulation. It is so severe that the verse states, "none [is] like it; and it is the time of Jacob's distress." The Bible has many names for what is commonly called the Great Tribulation. Here a name is given that directly relates it to the Jewish nation—it is "the time of Jacob's distress" because the Tribulation will be much more severe for Jews than for Gentiles. The reason it will be more severe for the Jews than for others is because of the principle found in Isaiah 40:1-2: Israel receives double for all her sins. As much as God punishes the Gentiles, Israel always receives double for all her sins because of yet another principle: To whomever much is given, much is required. The Tribulation will prove to be uniquely "the time of Jacob's distress." Nevertheless, there is this promise: "But he will be saved from it." No matter how bad the Tribulation may get for them, the Jews as a people, as a nation, will survive it.

Verses 8-11 provide the details of just how Israel's deliverance will be accomplished. God states He is going to break the oppressor's yoke (verse 8). "His yoke" refers to the Antichrist in that end-time period. His yoke over the Jews will be broken, and Israel will be freed. This is followed by a promise: "Foreigners will no more enslave them" (verse 8 NKJV). This prophecy is not referring to the return from the Babylonian captivity, for since that time, strangers *have* in fact made the Jews their bondmen (servants). After the Tribulation will come the final restoration, which is when this promise will be fulfilled. Though the Jews will not be enslaved, they *will* serve someone: "they shall serve [first] the LORD their God, and [second] David their king" (verse 9 NKJV). Some interpret "David their king" as being a reference to the Messiah. But there is no reason to avoid the literal interpretation of Scripture here. This should be taken as the literal David, "whom I will raise up for them." Indeed, King David will someday be resurrected, and he will be a co-regent with Jesus over Israel. This is also taught in Ezekiel 34:23-24, 37:24-25, and Hosea 3:5.

Israel is not to fear nor be dismayed for two reasons (verses 10-11). The first is that Israel is going to be regathered: "I will save you from afar and your offspring from the land of their captivity." The Jews will return; they will rest quietly and be "at ease, and no one will make [them] afraid." The second reason is that Israel is going to survive. The promise here is very graphic: God intends to eventually "destroy completely all the nations" to which God has scattered the Jewish people. But He will never make a full end of the Jewish people. He will discipline them, He "will correct [them] in justice," and He will not "let [them] go altogether unpunished" (NKJV). So the Jewish people are guaranteed to survive, as they already have throughout the centuries. Although the Tribulation will be severe for the Jews, Israel, as a nation and a people, will survive it.

THE HEALING OF ZION'S WOUNDS
Jeremiah 30:12-17

Jeremiah 30:12 describes Israel's sickly state: "Your wound is incurable, and your injury is serious." In verse 13, "There is no one to plead your cause." There is no one who can apply bandages to Israel's wounds; there is no one who can apply "healing medicines" (NKJV). The "healing" here is like that of new skin over a wound. The problem here is that new skin cannot grow. Verses 14-15 reveal that it was God who wounded Israel. He reminds the people that "all your lovers"—meaning the foreign gods with whom Israel has committed spiritual adultery—"have forgotten" them. Those nations provided no healing balm for Israel. The reason Israel has been abandoned this way is that God has done the wounding "with the wound of an enemy, with the punishment of a cruel one." The reason it was necessary for God to wound Israel is that their "iniquity is great and [their] sins are numerous."

ZION'S FUTURE
Jeremiah 30:16-17

The One who has wounded Zion intends to heal Zion. He will do so in two stages (verses 16-17). In the first stage, God intends to punish the nations who inflicted the wound upon Zion. He promises that "all who devour you will be devoured; and all your adversaries, every one of them, will go into captivity." Those who have despoiled Israel will become a spoil themselves, and all who prey upon Israel will be given for a prey. This is the principle of Genesis 12:3: "The one who curses you I will curse." In the second stage, God says, "I will restore you to health, and I will heal you of your wounds" (verse 17). The reason He will do this is because Israel's enemies "have called [Israel] an outcast"; they have called Zion a city that no man seeks. God will punish Israel's armies, and He will heal Israel by forgiving her of her sins.

THE RESTORATION OF JACOB
Jeremiah 30:18-22

Here Jeremiah speaks of Israel's return and makes four points about it in verse 18. The first point concerns their return: "Behold, I will restore the fortunes of the tents of Jacob." Note that the word "tents" is used, which always implies a temporary abode rather than a permanent one. The picture is that Jacob is in temporary abodes because, during the second half of the Tribulation, most of the Jews are no longer in their own homes, but have fled to a place called Petra or Bozrah (Micah 2:12 kjv). Therefore, they are living in tents or temporary abodes. Now God promises that

He will restore Jacob's tents. A similar statement is made in Zechariah 12:7, where the promise is made that God will save the tents of Judah first before he rescues the inhabitants of Jerusalem.

The second point in verse 18 states God will "have compassion on his dwelling places." God is going to show compassion and bring the Jews back into all the Promised Land. Third, "the city will be rebuilt on its ruin." The word "city" in the Hebrew text does not include a definite article, so it is a collective singular for all cities. All cities in the land are going to be rebuilt; each city will be rebuilt on its own ruins. In fact, the Hebrew word here for "ruin" is not the usual Hebrew word *givat,* but the word *tel,* a man-made hill that is built up of successive layers of city ruins. The point is that each city will be rebuilt on its own ruins or *tel.* And fourth, "the palace will stand on its rightful place." There will be a place for royalty as well.

Jeremiah next speaks of the effect this restoration will have on the people in verse 19. First, they will be characterized by thankfulness. Second, they will be characterized by joy and gladness. Third, they will increase numerically, for God states, "I will multiply them and they will not be diminished." And fourth, they will be glorified—they will no longer be a small nation.

Jeremiah then explains the establishment of the nation in three statements in verse 20. First, "their children also will be as formerly." As it was with the exodus, as it was with the monarchy, so it will be again. Second, "their congregation shall be established before Me." Israel will have a congregational relationship to God. Third, "I will punish all their oppressors." In keeping with the Abrahamic Covenant, God will curse those who curse Israel.

Next Jeremiah speaks of Israel's new leaders and makes two statements about them in verse 21. First, he emphasizes their Jewishness: "Their leader shall be one of them." The Hebrew word used here is *adder,* meaning "a noble one," and this was taken by the rabbis to be a messianic term. "Their ruler shall come forth from their midst." From here onward their rulers will be Jews, not Gentiles. Second is the new leader's relationship to God: "I will bring him near and he shall approach Me; for who would dare to risk his life to approach Me?" These verses may very well speak of the messianic Person. In fact, the rabbis took these verses to be exactly that.

The final result of all this is spelled out in verse 22: "You shall be My people, and I will be your God." This speaks of Israel's national salvation, which will be one of the by-products of the Great Tribulation.

THE WRATH OF GOD
Jeremiah 30:23–31:1

In this passage, Jeremiah points out that Israel must suffer the wrath of God before she reaches her national salvation. Verse 23 describes this wrath as "the tempest of the LORD," which is the "wrath [of God that] has gone forth." It is a "sweeping tempest," and "it will burst upon the head of the wicked." It describes that period of the divine wrath of God, the Great Tribulation. In verse 24, Jeremiah emphasizes the anger of God: "The fierce anger of the LORD will not turn back until He has performed and until He has accomplished the intent of His heart." The anger of God will not subside, will not be appeased, will not settle down, will not be comforted, until God has executed all the judgment that He intends to execute. This divine judgment upon the world in general—and Israel in particular—will bring about Israel's national salvation.

Jeremiah then goes on to say, "In the latter days you will understand this." With this statement he puts the event into the prophetic future. He points out that in the future they will understand it. The point of understanding is that the judgment was the means of bringing Israel to salvation. What they will understand in a future day is that God used judgment not as an end in itself, but as a means of bringing Israel back to Himself.

In 31:1, Jeremiah begins with the expression "at that time," once again speaking of the

prophetic future, the time of the Great Tribulation, when Israel comes to her national salvation. It is then, God states, that He "will be the God of all the families of Israel." The phrase "all the families" means all 12 tribes. God is going to save the whole nation of Israel, and that will include all 12 tribes. And once again He affirms, "They shall be My people."

GOD'S PROMISES TO ISRAEL
Jeremiah 31:2-6

In Jeremiah 3:12, God promises that no matter how bad Israel's situation may get, Israel will survive: "The people who survived the sword"—that is, the Jews who survive the Tribulation—"found grace in the wilderness." This "wilderness" is the same as the wilderness of Ezekiel 20:35 and of Revelation 12:6,13-14. It is the wilderness where the city of Bozrah or Petra is located and where Israel is going to be saved. Indeed, God clearly identifies who He means: Israel. The people are going to find favor and grace from God the day God moves to cause Israel to "find its rest." The rest here is the rest of salvation.

In verse 3 Jeremiah speaks of God's everlasting love for Israel, which explains the reason Israel survives: "I have loved you with an everlasting love." Because of God's eternal love for Israel, He states, "Therefore I have drawn you with lovingkindness." The Hebrew word for "drawn" speaks of the draw of love toward itself (Song of Solomon 1:4; Hosea 11:4). God will draw Israel to Himself.

In verses 4-5, God makes three promises to Israel. First, Israel is to be built: "Again will I build you and you will be built, O virgin of Israel!" The second promise is that Israel will rejoice: "Again you will take up your tambourines, and go forth to the dances of the merrymakers." The third promise is that Israel will plant: "Again you will plant vineyards on the hills of Samaria; the planters will plant, and will enjoy [the fruit]." No longer will the people have unproductive fields; no longer will others take that which they have produced. They will be able to plant and enjoy the products of their labor.

In verse 6, Jeremiah concludes the preceding verses by pointing to Jerusalem as the center of the millennial kingdom: "There will be a day [which is the kingdom period] when watchmen on the hills of Ephraim call out, 'Arise, and let us go up to Zion.'" The watchmen in the land of Ephraim are part of the northern kingdom. For a long time the northern kingdom tried to keep Jews from going to Jerusalem to worship God, but now the watchmen of Ephraim will say, "Let us go up to Zion, to the LORD our God." In the millennial kingdom, to go to Jerusalem is to go to God's presence because of what Jeremiah has already said in 3:17: God Himself will reign in a visible way from Jerusalem in the Person of the Messiah.

THE RETURN OF THE REMNANT
Jeremiah 31:7-14

Jeremiah 31:7-14. which looks at the return of the Jewish remnant, makes two main points about them. First is the regathering of the remnant, which is described in verses 7-9. Verse 7 declares the Jews are now to "sing aloud with gladness for Jacob, and shout among the chief of the nations." This verse calls upon the Gentile nations to begin rejoicing over Israel's return. "The chief of the nations" is one of Israel's titles. It is a proud term for Israel—Israel the "foremost of the nations," a title used in Amos 6:1. The Gentiles are to rejoice and shout and praise God for saving His people, the people of Israel.

Verse 8 deals with the regathering itself, which is to occur first of all "from the north country," which is Babylon, and also from "the remote parts of the earth," for this regathering will be on a worldwide scale. It will include Jews who might be blind or lame, pregnant women, and even women who are already in the process of giving birth; a great company is going to return. Verse 9 says the people will come with weeping, which points to their repentance. They will come "by supplication" and God will "lead them," the result of their prayer. "I will make them walk by streams of waters," which tells us God will provide suste-

nance for them. "On a straight path in which they will not stumble"—God will remove all obstacles. Verse 9 concludes with the reason for it all: God is a "father to Israel, and Ephraim is [God's] firstborn."

Second is the rejoicing of the remnant, which is described in verses 10-14. In verse 10 God gives a declaration, and the Gentile nations are called to respond to it: "He who scattered Israel will gather him and keep him as a shepherd keeps his flock." The point should not be missed: The very God who scattered the Jews intends to regather them. In the same way that the scattering has been literally fulfilled, so will the regathering be literally fulfilled. Verse 11 gives the reason for God's declaration: "For the LORD has ransomed Jacob and redeemed him from the hand of him who was stronger than he." God will redeem Israel from the hand of the Antichrist.

Verse 12 describes Israel's joy over God's provision, for "they [will] come and shout for joy in the height of Zion, and they will be radiant over the bounty of the LORD," and God intends to provide "grain...new wine...oil," flocks and herds. The result is that the people's "life will be like a watered garden, and they will never languish again." In verse 13 there is more rejoicing: "The virgin [the virgin of Israel] will rejoice in the dance, and the young men and the old, together, for I will turn their mourning into joy and will comfort them and give them joy for their sorrow." The section ends in verse 14 with a promise of satisfaction: "I will fill the soul of the priests with abundance, and My people will be satisfied with my goodness."

THE COMFORTING OF RACHEL
Jeremiah 31:15-22

Jeremiah 31:15-22 begins with a promise of comfort for Israel (verses 15-17). In verse 15, Jeremiah describes the weeping of Rachel: "A voice is heard in Ramah." The voice is one of "lamentation and bitter weeping." Jeremiah describes Rachel as "weeping for her children." Rachel, whose tomb was near the town of Ramah, is a symbol of Jewish motherhood. The children of this verse are the sons that are about to be taken into captivity, and Rachel is a symbol of Jewish mothers weeping for sons they will not see again. Rachel refused to be comforted "because [her children] are no more." The statement, "they are no more" could be taken in one of two ways. First, Rachel may be weeping because her children are going into captivity. Or, it may be because they are dead. Either way, the statement is accurate.

In verses 16-17, God admonishes Rachel to cease from weeping: "Refrain your voice from weeping, and your eyes from tears." The reason is that "your work will be rewarded." The promise is that the Jews will be restored from the land of their enemy. Verse 17 then adds, "There is hope for your future." This projects Jeremiah's words into the prophetic future. At a future time, the "children will return to their own territory."

Verses 18-20 tell of Israel's future confession of her sin. Israel's repentance will bring about the comforting of Rachel; Rachel will be comforted when the Jews return; and the Jews will return because of their confession. Verses 18-19 speak about the confession itself, of which God states, "I have surely heard Ephraim grieving." Ephraim will say, "You have chastised me, and I was chastised, like an untrained calf." This indicates Israel will have realized that the punishment of the day of Jacob's distress, the Great Tribulation, was a matter of divine discipline to get Israel to repent. Israel will say, "Bring me back that I may be restored, for you are the LORD my God." The point is that if God will convert the people, they will indeed be converted.

Ephraim then states, "I smote on my thigh [a token of temper]: I was ashamed [a token of shame] and also humiliated because I bore the reproach of my youth." Israel now realizes her shame because of her rejection of the Messiah. She realizes that judgment came upon her because of the sins of her youth. God's response is given in verse 20: "Is Ephraim My dear son? [Yes, according to verse 9.] Is he a delightful child? [Yes, according to verse 3.] Indeed, as often as I have spoken against him, I certainly still remember him." Though God

has pronounced judgment upon the nation, He still loves the nation: "Therefore My heart yearns for him; I will surely have mercy on him." The promise is that when Israel repents, God will respond.

This passage concludes with a call to repentance (verses 21-22). Verse 21 begins with a plea to return to the ancient paths: "Set up for yourself roadmarks, place for yourself guideposts; direct your mind to the highway, the way by which you went." God calls upon Israel to "return, O virgin of Israel"—to be repentant, to be converted. God continues, "How long will you go here and there, O faithless daughter?" (verse 22). In Hosea 1–3, the prophet Hosea speaks of Israel as a divorced wife returning to her husband. Jeremiah 2:20 speaks of Israel as playing the prostitute, and Jeremiah 3:1-10 points out that Israel was divorced by God because of her prostitution. In Hosea 2:19-20, Israel has yet to return to her husband, which will prove to be "a new thing in the earth—a woman will encompass a man" (Jeremiah 31:22). The promise is that the weak female will embrace the strong male. Israel, the wife of Jehovah, will embrace the Lord, her strong Husband, and they will have a reunion someday.

THE FUTURE PROSPERITY OF ISRAEL
Jeremiah 31:23-26

Jeremiah 31:23-26 announces the future prosperity of Israel, and three points are made. First Jeremiah prophesies of the return of an old saying: "Once again they will speak this word in the land of Judah and in its cities" (verse 23). By Jeremiah's time this saying apparently had ceased to be used. It may have seen usage in the days of David and Solomon and then died out after the kingdom split after the death of Solomon. In the future that saying will return, at a time "when [God will] restore their fortunes." In other words, when the final restoration of Israel takes place, the people will again say, "The LORD bless you, O abode of righteousness, O holy hill."

Next Jeremiah mentions two reasons for the return of this old saying. The first is that

God will bring prosperity back to Israel (verse 24). The second is that God will have satisfied "the weary ones and refresh everyone who languishes" (verse 25).

Third, in verse 26 is a puzzling interlude in which Jeremiah states, "At this I awoke and looked, and my sleep was pleasant to me." This shows that Jeremiah 30:1–31:25 was revealed to Jeremiah in a dream. He awakens at verse 26 and points out that his sleep "was pleasant" to him. For the first 29 chapters of the book he has been prophesying negative statements about his people and about his country. But now this has changed, and the Book of Consolation gives a positive rather than a negative note. Because these truths about Israel's future were so encouraging, the dream was indeed pleasant to him, and not sorrowful. In fact, earlier in the book, when God revealed to Jeremiah some of the curses to fall upon Israel, the prophet wept and complained to God. But here, in this section, he is blessed because he is able to predict sweet things.

THE PLANTING OF ISRAEL
Jeremiah 31:27-30

In Jeremiah 31:27, the prophet states that God will "sow" both houses of Israel, for both houses are destined for restoration into one nation. The words "Behold, the days are coming" put this passage into the prophetic future, and God goes on to say that He "will sow the house of Israel and the house of Judah." The concept of sowing was a figure of both judgment and blessing. Just as God has sown the houses of Israel and Judah in judgment, he will also sow them in blessing. Both of those concepts are also described in Hosea 2:21-23. Verse 28 emphasizes the watching of God, building upon God's earlier words to Jeremiah: "I am watching over my word to perform it" (Jeremiah 1:12). Jeremiah points out that God will watch over His word of judgment against Israel: "to pluck up, to break down, to overthrow, to destroy and to bring disaster." Now that is going to change. Now God is going to watch over His word of blessing as well, "to build and to plant" the houses of Israel.

THE CHANGING OF A PROVERB
Jeremiah 31:29-30

Next Jeremiah talks about the changing of a common proverb (verses 29-30). In verse 29, he talks about the proverb that is destined to be removed. Again he starts out with a timing element: "In those days," which sets the context as the prophetic future, in this case again the kingdom period. The proverb that will change is this: "The fathers have eaten sour grapes, and the children's teeth are set on edge." Apparently this was a common proverb at that time, for it is also mentioned by Jeremiah's contemporary in Ezekiel 18:1-4. The proverb refers to children being punished for the sins of their fathers, or the sins of the fathers being visited upon innocent children. But these children were not innocent, and this proverb was a misinterpretation of a principle found in the Mosaic law (Exodus 20:5; 34:7; Numbers 14:18). This principle states that God visits the sins of the fathers upon the children and upon the children's children down to the third and the fourth generations. It is true that the sins of the fathers were involved in God's judgments upon Israel, but the children were also guilty. They claimed they were innocent, but they were not. The reason the sins of the fathers are being visited upon the children is because the children were also guilty of the same sins. However, that proverb will change in the future kingdom. In verse 30 Jeremiah reveals that the new proverb is going to be based upon the principle that "everyone will die for his own iniquity." The new proverb will be that "each man who eats the sour grapes, his teeth will be set on edge."

THE REVELATION OF A NEW COVENANT
Jeremiah 31:31-34

Jeremiah 31:31-34 announces the coming of a New Covenant, and verse 31 begins with the prophetic words, "Behold, days are coming." These words push the prophecy into the time of Israel's salvation and restoration. In those days God "will make a new covenant" with both houses of Israel.

Verse 32 then mentions the Mosaic

Covenant, which was a temporary, conditional covenant. God says the New Covenant will "not [be] like the covenant which I made with their fathers." This will be a separate and distinct covenant, unrelated to the one that was made with Moses. To make it clear it is the Mosaic Covenant of which he is speaking, God refers to "the day I took them by the hand to bring them out of the land of Egypt." The covenant God made with Israel at the exodus was the Mosaic Covenant. This covenant will not continue; it will be replaced by this New Covenant. Then God explains the need for a replacement—the Mosaic Covenant had been broken. "Although [God] was a husband to them," the people of Israel broke the covenant.

Verse 33 gives more details about the New Covenant: It will be made "after those days"—that is, after the Tribulation. And the main characteristic of the New Covenant is that it is going to result in internal righteousness: "I will put My law within them and on their heart will I write it." God then says the result of this covenant is that "I will be their God, and they shall be My people." It is by the New Covenant that Israel will be remarried to God and become His wife again—thoroughly purified and thoroughly cleansed.

The result of all this is given in verse 34: the salvation of all Israel. That every Jew is included is evident because it will not be necessary for one Jew to tell another, "Know the LORD," because "they will all know me, from the least of them to the greatest of them." In other words, this covenant will mean the forgiveness of their sins. It will not be necessary in that day to witness to Jews because every Jewish person born in the kingdom will become a believer. This will not be true of every Gentile born in the kingdom, but it will be true of every Jew, from "the least of them to the greatest." God specifically states, "I will forgive their iniquity [singular], and their sin [singular] I will remember no more." One specific iniquity, one specific sin, will be forgiven. That specific sin was the rejec-

tion of the messiahship of Jesus. When the Jews believe in the messiahship of Jesus and repent, then God will forgive that particular national sin.

THE PROMISE OF ISRAEL'S INDESTRUCTIBILITY
Jeremiah 31:35-37

Jeremiah 31:35 explains the basis of Israel's indestructibility. The very Hebrew name for God, *YHVH,* emphasizes God as a covenant keeper. Because of God's covenant with Israel, the nation is indestructible. God is the One who "gives the sun for a light by day" and the One who gives the "order of the moon and the stars for light by night." He is the One who stirs up the waves of the sea "so that its waves roar." His name is "the LORD of hosts." That name, *Jehovah,* or *YHVH,* emphasizes God as a covenant keeper.

According to verse 36, Israel's national survival will never cease. There God proclaims, "If this fixed order [the sun, moon, and stars of verse 35] departs from before Me…then the offspring of Israel also will cease from being a nation before Me forever." The point is this: If any man can succeed in destroying the sun, the moon, and the stars, only then would it be possible to destroy the Jews, and only then would it be possible to cause Israel to cease from being a nation. As long as no man has the capability to destroy the sun, moon, and stars, no man will have the capability to destroy the people of Israel. Thus Israel's national survival is guaranteed.

Furthermore, not only will no one be able to destroy the Jews, but Israel's own sins cannot cause her total annihilation either. In verse 37 God states two impossibilities—"If the heavens above can be measured and the foundations of the earth searched out below"—to point out the improbable likelihood that He will "cast off all the offspring of Israel for all that they have done." Not even Israel's sins will cause her total annihilation.

Nothing outside of Israel and nothing within Israel can cause her total destruction.

THE BUILDING OF NEW JERUSALEM
Jeremiah 31:38-40

Jeremiah begins this section with a discussion on the building of the city in verses 38-39. He starts with the words, "Behold, the days are coming," once again confirming he is talking about the messianic kingdom, when "the city will be rebuilt for the LORD." Having established this, he then spells out the geography of the rebuilding of Jerusalem and makes four statements. First he talks about "the Tower of Hananel." This tower, which is also mentioned in Nehemiah 3:1; 12:39, and Zechariah 14:10, was in the northeast corner of the city near the Sheep Gate. Second, the rebuilding would go "to the Corner Gate," which is the northwest corner, mentioned in 2 Kings 14:13, 2 Chronicles 25:23, 26:9, and Zechariah 14:10. Third, in verse 39 Jeremiah says "the measuring line will go out farther straight ahead." The "measuring line" was a common figure used of rebuilding Jerusalem in the messianic kingdom (Ezekiel 40–48; Zechariah 2:1-13). And fourth, the rebuilding would extend "to the hill Gareb; then it will turn to Goah." The Hebrew word *Gareb* is the same word that is used for "leprosy," so this was probably a section where lepers were confined. The location of *Goah* is unknown, but is probably on the west side, since the north sections covered the northeast and south. The point Jeremiah makes is that all these areas that were once considered defiled—even the section where the lepers lived, which was totally unclean—are going to become ceremonially clean in the future rebuilding.

Next Jeremiah emphasizes the holiness of the city in verse 40. This holiness will include the city itself as well as the surrounding territory, such as "the whole valley of the dead bodies and of the ashes." The "valley of the dead bodies" is the Valley of Hinnom, mentioned in 2 Kings 23:10, where dead bodies were buried and also where human sacrifices were practiced (Jeremiah 7:31-33). The term "ashes" translates a Hebrew word that means "greasy ashes," referring to the fact of human sacrifices. These were committed on the western side of Jerusalem.

Not only will the section where lepers lived become holy to God, but even that section which was once cursed because it had become defiled by being used for human sacrifices will become holy.

Then Jeremiah adds that the holiness will extend to "all the fields as far as the brook of Kidron." The fields and this particular brook cover the eastern side of Jerusalem. Both the valley around the west side and the valley around the east side are going to become holy. Furthermore, this holiness will go "to the corner of the Horse Gate toward the east." This is the east side near the temple (2 Kings 11:16; 2 Chronicles 23:15; Nehemiah 3:28). By going to the east, this holiness covers all of these sides, and Jeremiah concludes by saying that all of this "shall be holy to the LORD." The point of this verse is that all of Jerusalem and its surroundings will become holy. Not only will the temple compound area be holy; the whole city will be holy down to the most mundane things (Joel 3:17; Zechariah 14:20-21). This passage concludes by again emphasizing Jerusalem's indestructibility: First, "it will not be plucked up"; and second, it will not be "overthrown anymore forever." Jerusalem, like Israel, will be indestructible when the kingdom is established.

THE PURCHASE OF HANAMEL'S FIELD
Jeremiah 32

Jeremiah 32:1-14 is historical and documents God's command to Jeremiah to redeem the property of his nephew even though property was of very little value because of the Babylonian invasion. Then comes the explanation for this command in verse 15: "Houses and fields and vineyards will yet again be bought in this land." The prophecy is of Israel's final restoration. A time will come when people will once again see the land and fields as worthy of being bought. Jeremiah's action is a test of faith. Even though the land was of little value, Jeremiah was willing, at God's command, to spend money on this land because of the assurance it would become valuable in the future.

This led to Jeremiah's prayer in verses 16-25.

He asks, in essence, "Why bother buying a field now, when the city is about to be given over to the Chaldeans?" God's answer to Jeremiah is given in two parts. The first part (verses 26-35) predicts the destruction of Jerusalem by the Babylonians. The second part prophesies the restoration of Jerusalem and begins by talking about the past (verse 36). The subject is the city of Jerusalem, the same city that God judged and that God intends to bless—though it would first be given over to the Babylonians, and the city would be destroyed "by sword, by famine and by pestilence" (verse 36).

However, there is a bright future, for there will one day be a regathering (verse 37). God intends to regather the Jewish people from all the countries where He has driven them. He intends to bring them back to "this place and make them dwell in safety." The result is Israel's national salvation (verse 38), which is described in verse 39. They will be given "one heart and one way." The word "heart" emphasizes their internal righteousness, and the word "way" refers to their external righteousness. These will be given so that the people "may fear me always, for their own good and for the good of their children."

Next Jeremiah summarizes the New Covenant and its effects, stating three things. First, it will be an everlasting covenant—an eternal, unconditional covenant. Second, God says, "I will not turn away from them, to do them good." The result of this new, everlasting covenant is that God will "do them good." And third, God says, "I will put the fear of Me in their hearts, so that they will not turn away from me." There will be a national salvation that will include every Jew, and they will never again depart from following God.

Because of the New Covenant there is the promise of future blessings (verse 41). God will rejoice over them to "do them good," and God intends to "plant them" again into their own land "with all [His] heart and with all [His] whole soul." That will lead to the reversal described in verse 42. Just as God has brought calamity upon this people, "so [He]

is going to bring upon them all the good that [He is] promising them."

Finally, God repeats the promise that was made earlier: fields will again be bought (verses 43-44). Though the land that is now being desolated has indeed lost its value (verse 43), it will someday become valuable again (verse 44): "Men will buy fields for money, sign and seal deeds, and call in witnesses." The verse closes with God's proclamation, "I will restore their fortunes."

THE FUTURE RESTORATION OF JERUSALEM
Jeremiah 33:1-9

While Jeremiah was still a prisoner in the royal court, the Word of God came to him a "second time" (33:1), the first time being in chapter 32. In verses 2-3, a call is issued for the people to turn to God. In verses 4-5, Jeremiah describes once again the present judgment of Jerusalem. Then in verses 6-9 he prophesies the future blessings of Jerusalem and states four things. First, there will be a restoration of health (verse 6). Second, there will be a return of the captives (verse 7), which includes both houses of Israel. Third, there will be a national forgiveness of all of the people's sins (verse 8):

> I will cleanse them from all their iniquity by which they have sinned against Me, and I will pardon all their iniquities by which they have sinned against Me and by which they have transgressed against Me.

Once again, in keeping with the New Covenant, the everlasting covenant, God has promised to forgive Israel's sins completely.

Fourth, that will bring certain results on Jerusalem. Jerusalem will become before God "a name of joy, praise and glory" (verse 9). This will also be true "before all the [Gentile] nations of the earth." When the nations hear the good things God intends to do for Jerusalem, they themselves will "fear and tremble" because of the good and the peace God will bring forth.

THE RETURN OF PEACE TO JERUSALEM
Jeremiah 33:10-11

Jerusalem's past was characterized by judgment—a city that was lying in waste "without man and without beast" (verse 10). What was true of Jerusalem was true of the other cities of Judah. The streets of Jerusalem were "desolate, without man and without inhabitant and without beast." The future of Jerusalem will be characterized by blessing, and Jeremiah lists several things that will once again be heard in the streets of Jerusalem (verse 11). These blessings are going to mean the removal of specific, previous judgments (recorded in Jeremiah 7:34; 16:9; 25:10). There is going to be a return of peace and joy to Jerusalem.

THE FLOCKS WILL FLOURISH ONCE AGAIN
Jeremiah 33:12-13

In Jeremiah 33:12, the prophet points out that once again there is going to be "a habitation" where the shepherds can rest their flocks. In the first part of verse 13, Jeremiah again gives a detailed geographical division of the land. The blessings mentioned in this passage will be true for all parts of the land that he lists. At the end, Jeremiah concludes with a promise: the flocks will "pass under the hands of the one who numbers them." The flocks will flourish rather than die out on account of the desolation of the land.

THE RECONFIRMATION OF THE DAVIDIC COVENANT
Jeremiah 33:14-26

Jeremiah next announces the reconfirmation of the Davidic Covenant and the Levitical priesthood in relationship to three things.

1. The Assurance of Jerusalem's Salvation
Jeremiah 33:14-18

In Jeremiah 33:14, God promises He will fulfill the prophecies regarding Israel's future. He says, "Behold, the days are coming…when I will fulfill the good word." That is, He will perform the promises made to both houses of Israel. He speaks of the Messiah's rule in relationship to all this in verses 15-16 and

states the timing of this fulfillment in verse 15: "In those days and at that time," which is a reference to the messianic kingdom. At that time, He says, "I will cause a righteous Branch of David to spring forth." There is coming a descendant of David who will be characterized by righteousness. He will "execute justice and righteousness on the earth" because He Himself is righteous. As a result, "in those days [in that prophetic future] Judah [will] be saved and Jerusalem will dwell in safety" (verse 16). Notice that here the emphasis is on Judah and Jerusalem, whereas in the first two chapters of the Book of Consolation the emphasis was on Judah and Israel. "Judah will be saved, and Jerusalem will dwell in safety." Jerusalem will be called "the LORD is our righteousness," the same name given to the Messiah in Jeremiah 23:5-6.

Verses 17-18 promise perpetuity to two things. The first is the house of David: "David shall never lack a man to sit on the throne of the house of Israel." This is in keeping with the Davidic Covenant. God has promised that the house of David will always be preserved. To this day, although we do not know who they are, there are descendants of the house of David on this earth. Someday God will reveal who they are. Furthermore, it is impossible for the line of David to become extinct because, as the previous passage promised, the line of David comes eventually to a Person who is Himself eternal: the Messiah, the God-man. Because Jesus now lives forever by virtue of His resurrection, there will always be someone to rule over the house of Israel. Jesus has been available since His resurrection, and He is the One destined to sit on the throne of David someday.

The second promise of perpetuity relates to the house of Levi (verse 18). Two facts are stated about the tribe of Levi. First, it will never become extinct. Descendants of this tribe are still alive today. Second, the tribe of Levi will have a role in the millennial temple. Part of their role is spelled out by Ezekiel 40–48, where Ezekiel points out that they will be the caretakers of the temple. One segment of the tribe—the sons of Zadok, the Zadokites—will be in charge of the sacrificial system. They will always be around "to offer burnt offerings, to burn grain offerings."

2. The Relationship to the Covenant
Jeremiah 33:19-22

The word of God comes again to Jeremiah in 33:19 with a special message that appears in verses 20-22: It is impossible to break God's covenant. Only if it were possible to break the covenant of day and night could God's covenant with David be broken. But because that is impossible, it's also impossible for God's covenant to both houses to be rendered null and void (verses 20-21).

Jeremiah then concludes by speaking of the multiplication of the houses of David and Levi in verse 22. Just as "the host of heaven cannot be counted and the sand of the sea cannot be measured," so will the seed of David and Levi be multiplied. In other words, the house of David will grow large. This promise is not limited to the fact that David has one eternal descendant, the God-man, Jesus the Messiah; this promise extends much further than that. David will have so many descendants that they will become innumerable. And what is true of David is also true of Levi. Levi will have so many descendants that they, too, will become innumerable. These things are guaranteed because God's covenant is an everlasting one.

3. The Relationship to Perpetuity
Jeremiah 33:23-26

Once again the word of God comes to Jeremiah (verse 23) because of what is being said about the two families he has been dealing with, the families of David and Levi (verse 24). God asks Jeremiah, "Have you not observed what this people have spoken" about the two families? The Gentile nations were saying that while God did choose the house of David and the Levitical priesthood, God has now cast both of them away. In saying this, the Gentiles were despising God's people. The implication

is that the Gentiles were saying Israel will no longer be a nation after Babylon has conquered the people. It is because of what these Gentile nations were saying about Israel that this new prophecy comes to Jeremiah.

Verse 25 begins with yet another impossibility: Here again God refers to the "covenant for day and night." Only if someone can break the cycle of day and night can God's covenant be broken. God also refers to "the fixed patterns of heaven and earth," or the natural laws that control the universe. Only if God is not responsible for them can God's covenant be broken.

After pointing out that it is impossible for any man to break the covenant of day and night or to cancel out God's natural laws, God then states in verse 26 that it's impossible that He should "reject the descendants of Jacob and David My servant." Because no man can cancel out the natural laws of the universe, no one can stop God from making sure that a descendant of David gets to rule over "the descendants of Abraham, Isaac and Jacob." This is a reference to the Abrahamic Covenant, a covenant confirmed through Isaac and Jacob that defines Jewishness: A Jew is any descendant of Abraham, Isaac, and Jacob. The promise is that it will be a descendant of David who is going to rule over the descendants of Abraham, Isaac, and Jacob. And because of the Messiah's eternality, because He lives forever by virtue of His resurrection, we can know this promise will one day be fulfilled.

THE RECHABITES
Jeremiah 35

JEREMIAH 35:1-19 IS an eschatological passage that mentions the Rechabites, a branch of the Kenites, a clan of the Midianites from which Moses' in-laws came. Their ancestors advised them to live a life of migration rather than settlement and live off of flocks instead of plantings. This was a commitment the Rechabites kept, and they moved to the city only temporarily due to the threat of invasion by Babylon. This is then contrasted with the Israelites' failure to keep their commitment to the Lord. Verses 18-19 tells us that because of the Rechabites' favorable commitment to a vow, God promised that the house of the Rechabites will always have descendants who will be among the elect, and furthermore, from among them, some will be chosen to be priests in the messianic kingdom. Isaiah 66:18-21 prophesied that there would be Gentile priests in the messianic kingdom, and among these Gentile priests will be the descendants of the Rechabites.

THE PROPHECIES AGAINST THE GENTILES
Jeremiah 46–51

In chapters 46–51, Jeremiah spells out prophesies against the surrounding Gentile nations. A good number of these prophecies were fulfilled in the course of the history following Jeremiah; however, there are other prophecies that speak of a future judgment against these nations, and it is this future portion of the prophecies with which we will be concerned in this section.

EGYPT
Jeremiah 46

In Jeremiah 46 God describes a massive destruction of Egypt, a massive discipline, but He will not bring total destruction. By the end of verse 26, God promises a future restoration of Egypt and, according to other passages, Egypt will have a positive future in the messianic kingdom (Isaiah 19:19-25; Ezekiel 29:13-16; Zechariah 14:16-19). In verses 27-28, after an extensive prophecy against Egypt, God concludes with words of comfort for Israel (a repetition of Jeremiah 30:10-11).

MOAB
Jeremiah 48

Moab is present-day central Jordan. Jer-

emiah 48:1-46 describes a divine judgment upon Moab that results in a partial destruction but also results in the people coming to faith. Then, in verse 47, God promises to restore the fortunes of Moab. This means there will be a saved nation called Moab in the messianic kingdom.

AMMON
Jeremiah 49:1-6

Ammon comprises northern Jordan. The prophecy here is similar to that against Moab in that verses 1-5 speak of a judgment that causes partial destruction and results in the survivors coming to faith. In verse 6, God promises the restoration of Ammon, and there will be a saved nation called Ammon in the messianic kingdom.

EDOM
Jeremiah 49:7-22

The future of Edom or southern Jordan is quite different from the future of the aforementioned nations. In keeping with other prophecies about Edom, the picture is that of total destruction—to the point that Esau has no descendants left in Edom whatsoever. Edom is in the well-protected rugged mountains of Mount Seir, nevertheless, in spite of her strong defenses, she will fall. By the time the judgment has run its course, there will be no Edomites left anywhere. Thus, there will be no country called Edom in the messianic kingdom.

When God judges the nations surrounding Israel, He will do two things: One, He will consider how closely the nation is related to Israel by blood. The closer the relation, the greater the discipline. Edom was a descendant of Esau, the twin brother of Jacob. This means that Israel and Edom have the closest blood relationship and, therefore, God holds Edom to a higher standard. For that reason, Edom's descendants will be totally wiped out.

Two, God will consider a nation's degree of past anti-Semitism. Egypt was the first anti-Semitic nation, and while Egypt will undergo a national salvation, its history of anti-Semitism cannot be easily ignored. According to Ezekiel 29:8-14, for the first 40 years of the messianic kingdom, the Egyptians will be scattered and dispersed throughout the world, and the land of Egypt will lie desolate and empty. Only after the 40 years of dispersion will the Egyptians be brought back into the kingdom. It is then that Egypt will observe the Feast of Tabernacles, according to Zechariah 14:16-21.

KEDAR AND HAZOR
Jeremiah 49:28-33

Ancient Kedar and Hazor, two Arab tribes located in what is now Saudi Arabia, are prophesied to be totally destroyed with no inhabitants left. Their lands will remain desolate throughout the messianic kingdom, with no restoration to take place.

ELAM
Jeremiah 49:34-39

Elam is an area now known as Iran. That which is true of Egypt, Ammon, and Moab will also be true of Elam. There will be a partial destruction (verses 34-38) that will result in the survivors coming to faith and will lead to the restoration of Elam in "the last days" (verse 39). Thus, there will be a saved nation called Elam in the messianic kingdom.

BABYLON
Jeremiah 50–51

Jeremiah's most extensive prophecies are against Babylon. As with Isaiah 13–14, some commentators view Jeremiah 50–51 as having been fulfilled against ancient Babylon, but the details simply do not fit the Babylon of the past. The passage can only be true of the Babylon of the future, which will be the capital of the world under the authority of the Antichrist. The description Jeremiah gives here fits that of a destruction of Babylon in the course of the war of Armageddon.

After introducing his topic (50:1), Jeremiah goes on to describe Babylon's fall and Israel's deliverance (50:2-10). The coming future destruction of Babylon will show the failure of the gods of Babylon. They will be unable to help Babylon in the invasion from the north (50:2-3). The final destruction of the Babylon of the future is often connected with Israel's final restoration, as is the case here (50:4-8).

Jeremiah specifies that at the time of Babylon's fall there will come the final restoration because of the national regeneration of Israel (verse 4), which in turn will lead to the final migration back to Israel (verse 5). This is contrasted with Israel's past condition (verses 6-7), which included their lostness (verse 6) and their becoming a prey (verse 7). Now comes a call for the Jews to leave Babylonia (verse 8) in light of her coming destruction (verses 9-10). The destroyers are described as being a company of great nations. Babylon will become a prey to armies from different parts of the world. The desolation of Babylon (50:11-16) is due primarily to Babylon's treatment of the Jews (verses 11-13), and for this reason, the nations are called to come together and destroy the city (verses 14-16).

In Jeremiah 50:17-20, Babylon's destruction is again contrasted to Israel's final regeneration and restoration. At the time of Babylon's final destruction, the iniquity of Israel will be sought, but there will be none. The sins of the people of Israel will not be found.

In 50:21-28, Jeremiah points out that Babylon, the hammer of power, will be destroyed and thus will cease to exercise strict authority over other nations. In this manner the pride of Babylon will be humbled (50:29-32). At the same time that God destroys the hammer of Babylon, He will be Israel's redeemer (50:33-34).

In 50:35-40, after Jeremiah records the sword song (verses 35-37), he explains that sword will now fall upon Babylon (verses 38-40), which will become a habitation of demons (Isaiah 13:20-22; Revelation 18:2). In 50:41-46, Jeremiah again points out that while the armies come from various directions, the attack itself comes from the north. Here he implies that the king of Babylon is not within the city when the city is destroyed. Furthermore, the armies that come against Babylon are empowered by God, and therefore their success is not of their own making. The destruction of Babylon will be so complete that there will be a great cry of mourning among the city's supporters worldwide.

In 51:1-4, Babylon is viewed as having been winnowed by the enemy, resulting in the defenders being totally slain. Once again Babylon's destruction is contrasted with Israel's survival (51:5-6), and while Babylon falls, Israel will rise again. According to 51:7-10, Babylon has been a golden cup in God's hands, a cup of the wrath of God that the nations had to drink. Now Babylon itself will drink of the divine wrath of God. The people of Israel will conclude that Babylon has fallen primarily because of Israel's turning back to the Lord.

The key power God will use to lead the conquest against Babylon will be the Medes (51:11-14)—a fact that does not fit the previous capture of Babylon, which was done by Cyrus, who was a Persian. While the Medes were allied with the Persians in that earlier incident, the Persians were the greater power and the actual leaders of that conquest.

Babylon's total collapse is then contrasted with the idolatry of Babylon (51:15-19). While previously Babylon had been the shattering hammer of God (51:20-24) used to crush the armies of other nations, now the shattering hammer itself will be crushed. The reason for this is Babylon's anti-Semitism and evil against Zion. Thus Babylon, once a destroying mountain (51:25-26), will now be a mountain destroyed. Earlier, Jeremiah pictured Babylon as being winnowed, and now he pictures Babylon as becoming a major threshing floor only to be threshed (51:27-33). This is the result of Israel's complaint to God against Babylon, and thus God judges Babylon for its crimes against the Jewish people (51:34-40). This is in keeping with the cursing facet of the Abrahamic Covenant: "I will curse them that curse you." For that reason more than any other, Babylon will become desolate (51:41-44) and the city will fall, never to rise again (51:45-49).

Jeremiah then repeats that the reason for Babylon's fall is its mistreatment of the Jewish people. On behalf of Israel, God will judge

Babylon (51:50-53) and, indeed, Jeremiah declares that Babylon will be recompensed to the full (51:54-58). The chapter then concludes with the tenth symbolic action within the book of Jeremiah, the sinking of the scroll in 51:59-64. The symbolic action itself takes place in verses 59-60.

In verse 59, the word of God came to Jeremiah, and he commanded a man named Seraiah to do something. Seraiah was the son of Neriah and the brother of Baruch, Jeremiah's scribe or secretary (Jeremiah 32:12). Seraiah was the chief chamberlain, meaning "the quartermaster," the one responsible for the supplies for the trip that King Zedekiah made to Babylon. The occasion for the symbolic action was Seraiah's trip "with Zedekiah the king of Judah to Babylon in the fourth year of his reign." Verse 60 tells us Jeremiah wrote out a scroll detailing all the disaster that will come upon Babylon. What Jeremiah wrote in this scroll is recorded in Jeremiah 50:1-58.

Then in verses 61-64, Jeremiah gives Seraiah some specific instructions, and four things should be noted. First, when Seraiah came to Babylon, he was to read publicly all the words that Jeremiah had written (verse 61). Second, he was to make his first declaration, which is a summary of the prophecies of Jeremiah concerning Babylon: It was to be cut off so totally and destroyed so totally that no one will survive, "whether man or beast" (verse 62). It will be desolate forever, including during the entire 1000-year kingdom. Neither man nor beast will live there, although it is known from other passages that demons will reside there during the kingdom period. Third, when Seraiah is finished reading the scroll, he is then to tie a stone to the scroll and throw the scroll into the Euphrates River. The weight of the stone would pull the scroll down to the bottom of the river (verse 63). And fourth, once that had happened, Seraiah was to make a second declaration: "Just so shall Babylon sink down and not rise again because of the calamity that I am going to bring upon her; and they will become exhausted" (verse 64).

This is the point of the symbolic action: Just

as the scroll will sink because of the weight of the rock, so will Babylon sink because of the weight of Babylon's sins and because of the principle of Genesis 12:3: "The one who curses you I will curse." Babylon cursed the Jews, and now God will curse Babylon. Just as the rock will keep the scroll from ever rising to the surface, so will Babylon never rise again.

The Babylon of Jeremiah 50–51 is not the ancient Babylon of history, but the future Babylon of prophecy. The Babylon of prophecy is yet to be rebuilt. It will become the economic and political capital of the world and then be destroyed in the second of the eight stages of the campaign of Armageddon. It is after this destruction that Babylon will never be built again. Instead, it will become a continual wasteland of burning pitch and brimstone, including during the 1000-year millennial kingdom. According to Revelation 18:1-3, indeed, no man will live there, no animal will live there, but demons will reside there as part of God's divine judgment.

LAMENTATIONS

THIS BOOK IS A POETIC DIRGE WRITTEN BY THE PROPHET JEREMIAH. It serves as an eyewitness account of the destruction of Jerusalem by the Babylonians in 586 B.C. Lamentations contains no future eschatology. Rather, it is an expression of the prophet's sorrow as he laments the fulfillment of his own prophecies. In a series of poignant portraits, he pictures Jerusalem as a mourning widow (chapter 1), a fallen queen (chapter 2), a broken man (chapter 3), a tarnished treasure (chapter 4), and an orphan child (chapter 5). Yet in the very heart of his lament Jeremiah triumphantly exclaims, "It is of the LORD's mercies that we are not consumed, because his compassions fail not. They are new every morning; great is thy faithfulness. The LORD is my portion, saith my soul; therefore I will hope in Him" (3:22-24 KJV). Perhaps that is the greatest prophetic hope of all. No matter what happens, God is in control!

Lamentations contains only a few passages of an eschatological nature. In 1:21 Jeremiah asks God to "bring the day which You have proclaimed," the day of God's judgment of Israel's enemies. In verse 22 Jeremiah asks God to punish those enemies.

In 3:31 Jeremiah predicts that the Lord will not cast Israel off forever. He will show compassion according to the multitude of His mercies. Following this, Jeremiah asks God to repay Israel's enemies, give them a veiled heart (see Isaiah 6:10; 2 Corinthians 3:13-16), put a curse on them, and destroy them. Then in 4:21-22 the prophet announces specifically that Edom will be judged and punished.

Next, in 5:19, Jeremiah proclaims that God and His throne will remain forever. And finally, in 5:21 he asks God to turn Israel back to Him and restore the people as a nation.

The prophecies concerning Israel's enemies will ultimately be fulfilled during the Tribulation and as Jesus Christ returns to the earth to establish His promised messianic kingdom. The throne and kingdom of Christ are eternal, as is His commitment to His covenants with Israel.

EZEKIEL

THE PROPHET EZEKIEL

Ezekiel, whose name means "God strengthens," was raised as a priest in Jerusalem until he was taken captive by Nebuchadnezzar to Babylon in 597 b.c., some 11 years before the destruction of the city and burning of the temple by the Babylonians. A contemporary with the prophets Jeremiah and Daniel, who shared the exilic experience, Ezekiel resided in the Babylonian village of Nippur (Tel Abib) beside the river Chebar, which served as Nebuchadnezzar's royal canal. In the fifth year of his exile (592 b.c.) Ezekiel was called to prophesy to his fellow exiles for about 22 years, reminding them of the reason for God's judgment of the nation and reassuring them of God's promise of future restoration. God apparently desired to use a man with priestly training to bring this unique prophetic message focused on the temple and its priestly service. As a priest, Ezekiel would have uniquely been concerned for the re-establishment of the legitimate Zadokite priesthood (1 Samuel 2:35; 1 Kings 2:26-27,35). The very fact that the Zadokite priesthood was not reinstated with the return to Jerusalem and the rebuilding of the second temple indicates that the prophecies of Ezekiel were intended for fulfillment in the eschatological (millennial) age.

THE PROPHETIC MESSAGE OF EZEKIEL

The book of Ezekiel follows the prophetic pattern of announcing ruin and then restoration for national Israel. While the whole of the book was once prophetic, from the exilic and postexilic perspective it may be divided into two divisions with respect to historical and eschatological fulfillment. The first division (chapters 4–32) contains *near-fulfillment predictions,* which were necessary to confirm Ezekiel's credentials as a prophet (Deuteronomy 18:22) as well as meet the need of the Babylonian exiles who were awaiting word concerning their nation's fate. This division may be subdivided as the judgment of Judah (chapters 1–24), the judgment of seven Gentile nations that surrounded Israel in all directions (chapters 25–32), and the judgment of those Judeans who remained in the land during the exile (chapter 33). This first section has been historically fulfilled, principally in the events of the Babylonian destruction of Jerusalem and the deportation of Judeans to Babylon (586–538 b.c.). Ezekiel's prophecies in this first section focus on Judah's cultic desecration by both priests and people alike, and Jerusalem's destruction in accord with the curses contained in the Mosaic law for national covenant violation (Ezekiel 4–24). These prophecies were communicated through symbolic demonstration (chapters 4–5), sermonic pronouncements (chapters 6–7), prophetic visions (chapters 8–11), and various prophetic signs and parabolic declarations (chapters 12–24).

God's judgment against the Gentile nations (chapters 25–32) is included to demonstrate that the divine discipline of Israel is extended justly to all sinful nations, especially because the sin of these nations had been their oppression and persecution of the people of Israel, who represented God on earth. This is noted in the opening indictment against each of these nations by the words "because you said/did (something against Israel), therefore, I will" (specifics of judgment). This formulaic expression reveals that the standard for this judgment is that found in the Abrahamic Covenant: "I will bless those who bless you [Abraham's descendants—national Israel] and the one who curses you I will curse" (Genesis 12:3). The historical record supports the accuracy of these judgments in their fulfillment.

The second division (chapters 33–48) contains more *distant predictions* of Israel's restoration in the end time and is therefore eschatological. These prophecies concern predictions of national Israel's return, regathering, rebirth, and restoration (chapters 33–39). In this section Ezekiel observes the problem of Israel's "false shepherds" and predicts the advent of the True Shepherd who will establish the New Covenant (chapter 34). Having laid this spiritual foundation, the prophet predicts the rebirth of the nation (chapters 35–36), its national regeneration (37:1–14), and its reunion in the millennial kingdom (37:15–28). This is punctuated with the prophecy of divine victory over the foreign armies in Gog's invasion of Israel (chapters 38–39). The temple is the subject of chapters 40–48, which present the design and function of the messianic temple and the revival of the sacrificial service (chapters 40–48). These chapters provide the necessary climax to the prophecy of Israel's final restoration because only the rebuilding of the messianic temple could sustain Israel's spiritual relationship under the New Covenant and fulfill its national destiny to be a kingdom of priests.

In both divisions of Ezekiel, the Jerusalem temple figures prominently as the sign of God's relationship with national Israel. Therefore the first division, which deals with the Lord's judgment on Israel, is displayed in terms of the nation's desecration of the temple and its destruction by foreign nations under the terms of discipline announced in the Mosaic Covenant. The second division deals with the reversal of the condition of exile and foreign domination of the land imposed as the result of the discipline. Return to the land with the ultimate restoration of national sovereignty and national spiritual rebirth is the promised blessing of the New Covenant, whose conclusive sign is the rebuilding of a temple to which God's own presence has been restored (Ezekiel 37:26-28; 43:1-7).

INTERPRETING EZEKIEL'S PROPHECIES

The national and spiritual restoration envisioned by Ezekiel did not occur literally with the postexilic community. The returned Jewish remnant did not even attempt to implement Ezekiel's detailed plan for a new temple (Ezekiel 40–48) when they constructed the second temple. Therefore, critical scholars argue that a literal fulfillment was never expected. Rather, they say Ezekiel's "prophetic" language was hyperbolic or exaggerated speech, common to the apocalyptic genre whose imagery served to create an inspirational fiction. Christian scholars accepting these prophecies of Ezekiel as apocalyptic (or as symbolic) have traditionally read Ezekiel's prophecy of restoration (in chapters 40–48) in light of John's vision of the church in the New Jerusalem (Revelation 21:9–22:5), claiming that just as the vision of the heavenly Jerusalem is largely symbolic, so is the vision of the earthly Jerusalem given in these chapters. However, Ezekiel complained that a symbolic understanding of his prophecies was the problem of the unbelieving constituency of his audience: "Then I said, 'Ah, Lord God! They are saying of me, "Is he not just speaking in parables?"'" (Ezekiel 20:49). Ezekiel himself gives the reader every impression that he expected a literal fulfillment of his prophecies.

Furthermore, such interpretation does violence to the literary symmetry of Ezekiel's prophecies by making the description of ruin literal and historical, but the corresponding description of restoration figurative and spiritual. Such could scarcely have been the hope of the Jewish exiles in Babylon, as the prayer of Daniel (a contemporary exile with Ezekiel) for a literal restoration of Jerusalem and a rebuilding of the temple reveals (Daniel 9:2-19). Daniel's prayer, in turn, was based on his understanding of the prophecy of Jeremiah (another exile), whose statements of geography and chronology (Jeremiah 25:11-12) had to be interpreted literally in order to be the ground of Israel's hope and Daniel's petition for restoration.

Both divisions of Ezekiel's prophecy were visionary. Therefore, it is unwarranted to treat the first division as historical (since fulfillment occurred historically with the destruction of the first temple and the exile), and the second division as symbolic (since fulfillment did not occur historically under the return and the building of the second temple). From the historical perspective of Ezekiel's audience (as well as that of Jeremiah and Daniel), the whole of the book was certainly to be understood literally (historically) as corresponding promises of the nation's punishment and pardon. Just as the first was realized in their day, so the second would also be realized in a future day.

JUDAH AND JERUSALEM'S RUIN
Ezekiel 4–24

THE INTERPRETATION THAT Israel will be restored and the temple will be rebuilt can be understood only in light of the ruin of Judah, which was tied to the problem of temple desecration. From the perspective of Ezekiel's audience, it should be obvious that the prophet's exhortation to his people of a literal national destruction would be coupled to the prophet's encouragement of a literal national restoration. Nothing less would meet the need and expectation of the vanquished nation. And nothing less would demonstrate that the Lord was the sovereign and gracious deliverer of His people. The transformation of the restoration promises by the symbolic school as merely the spiritual blessings of the New Covenant transferred to the church violates the fundamental law of biblical interpretation, which demands texts to be interpreted within their context. If national Israel received divine destruction, national Israel must receive divine restoration. This is also true of the messianic prophecies woven throughout the first division of Ezekiel (17:22-24; 21:26-27), which, though part of the church's heritage of faith, were exclusively given to national Israel.

RESTORATION UNDER THE NEW COVENANT
Ezekiel 16:60-63

THIS PROPHECY FOLLOWS Ezekiel's most severe denunciation and condemnation of national Israel (16:1-59). In these verses the prophet describes the origin of Israel (Ezekiel 16:1-5) and its moral defection (Ezekiel 16:15-34). The condition of the nation is described as "harlotry," which refers to ceremonial uncleanness communicated by contact with whatever is ritually impure or polluting—for example, illicit sexual activity (Leviticus 18:23,25,27; 19:29) and unclean animals (Leviticus 11:24-43). Sometimes the simile of a "menstruous

(unclean) woman" is employed to depict the "unapproachableness" of Israel. This condition is said to have been incurred by bad "moral conduct" and "reckless deeds." Therefore, just as the ceremonial impurity of the menstruous woman separates her from the sphere of that which is considered holy, so the conduct of Israel has caused her to be removed from the Holy Land. The analogy of menstruation occurs in Ezekiel 18:6, 22:10, and 36:17, and may have had further intention of showing the Lord's spatial separation (that is, withdrawal of the divine presence), just as a man was commanded to distance himself from a menstruating woman (Leviticus 18:19).

REGATHERING THE REMNANT
Ezekiel 20:33-44

IN THIS TEXT a time of judicial deliverance is predicted through the figure of the Lord's "mighty hand and outstretched arm." This divine intervention will result in God's theocratic rule being reestablished over Israel (verse 33; cf. Jeremiah 33:14-18). The process of reestablishing theocratic rule begins with a regathered remnant of Israel being brought to national repentance and restoration (verses 34-38) and the rebuilding of the temple on the Temple Mount and the restoring of the sacrificial service (verses 39-40). The reason for God's restored rule over a restored Israel is two-fold: 1) as a witness to Israel and the nations of God's sovereignty (verses 38,41-42; cf. Isaiah 12; Ezekiel 36:16-38; 37:15-28), and 2) to give Israel grounds for glorifying God's grace throughout the age of the millennial kingdom (verse 44; cf. Isaiah 25–26).

The time of fulfillment is in the *future* (eschatological) age rather than in the near return from the Babylonian captivity in the Persian period. This can be seen from the description of the events of redemption and restoration in verses 40-44, where the redemption is universal ("the whole house of Israel," not a portion, as in the return to Jerusalem). Also, the regathering is worldwide ("from the peoples and…from the lands," not localized, as from Babylon). Moreover, the deliverance here is not effected by a human king (such as the Persian king Cyrus), but directly by God Himself. In keeping with the primary usage of the deliverance figure in verse 33, the historical pattern for this event is the divine deliverance from Egypt (verse 36; cf. Exodus 6:6-7; Haggai 2:5-9), with its climax in the possession of the land of Israel (verse 42; cf. Exodus 6:8).

In preparation for the fulfillment of this prophecy, the Jews comprising the modern state of Israel have been brought out from the nations (verse 34) *in unbelief,* and therefore into divine judgment (verse 35), as evidenced today in the continuing Middle East conflict centered on Israel. However, the final purpose of this judgment is not to destroy, but to provoke national repentance (verses 43-44), which will bring the remnant ("the whole house of Israel, all of them," verse 40; cf. Romans 11:26) into the "bond of the covenant" (verse 37). This is the New Covenant (Jeremiah 31:31-34; cf. Ezekiel 37:25-27) that will govern Israel through the millennial kingdom. Its placement in this text after the Tribulation and Israel's national repentance further affirms the prophetic order of these events.

Finally, the *progression* of eschatological events in this prophecy clearly follows a premillennial timetable: the regathering of Israel in unbelief to the land of Israel (verse 38; cf. Jeremiah 16:14-21), followed by "the time of Jacob's [Israel's] distress" (verses 35-37; cf. Jeremiah 30:7; Daniel 12:1; Matthew 24:21), during which the rebels would be purged from the faithful remnant, resulting in Israel's national repentance (verse 43; Zechariah 12:10–13:2; Matthew 24:30), regathering (verses 40-42; cf. Zechariah 8:7-8; Matthew 24:31) and restoration to the land, and worship of the messianic king (verse 33; cf. Zechariah 14:9; Matthew 25:31), during the millennial kingdom (verse 40; cf. Zechariah 8:11-23; Matthew 19:28).

PROPHECIES AGAINST FOREIGN NATIONS
Ezekiel 25–32

Once the announcement had been received that the judgment against Jerusalem had begun,

the focus shifts from the sins of Judah to the surrounding nations. Ezekiel reveals that God will use the Babylonian Empire as an instrument of divine punishment not only against Israel but also against the foreign nations of Ammon (25:1-7), Moab (25:8-11), Edom (25:12-14), Philistia (25:15-17), Tyre (26:1–28:19), Sidon (28:20-26), and Egypt (29:1–32:32)—which in times past had been adversaries of Israel and now mockingly rejoiced over Judah's exile and Jerusalem's fall (25:3). Therefore, the prophet pronounces divine retribution on each of these nations because of their profanation of God's sanctuary and their failure to recognize that these judgments had demonstrated God's holiness and power (25:4-7). Upon the fulfillment of these prophecies the nations will recognize that Israel's God, called here by His covenantal name, Yahweh ("the Lord"), is the one and only God.

This section of judgment against the nations serves as a *prophetic preview* of the time of Jacob's trouble and the nations' attitude toward Israel in the future. Its historical fulfillment should warn those nations that will surround Israel in the future that they will likewise be destroyed if they come against her. It should inform them that despite God's continuing judgment on Israel they are not to assume that Israel has lost its covenantal status as the people of God or that God has been powerless to protect them. The nations surrounding Israel have pursued an agenda to wipe it off the map of the Middle East, arrogantly assuming that Israel's minority status is the consequence of its inferior heritage. Such intransigence will one day provoke the invasion of Israel predicted in the "Gog of Magog" war (Ezekiel 38–39) and the program of genocide launched against Israel during the Tribulation (Revelation 12:13-17; 13:7-10). For this reason the wrath of God will again be poured out on the nations, climaxing in the battle of Armageddon, during which Christ Himself returns to "strike down the nations" (Revelation 19:15; cf. Psalm 2:9).

The judgment of the aforementioned nations lays the theological foundation for understanding the future judgment of the nations at the end of the Tribulation. Their removal from a position of domination ("the times of the Gentiles," Luke 21:24) prepares the way for the regathering of Israel from "the four corners of the world" (Isaiah 11:11-12) and the restoration of Israel in the land at the beginning of the millennial kingdom. It also aids in the interpretation of Christ's judgment of the nations after He has established His rule on earth (Matthew 25:31). Without understanding the principle in Ezekiel that God holds the nations responsible for their treatment of national Israel, in whatever condition it may be found (in the Diaspora or in the land), it will be difficult to understand Christ's standard for judgment in Matthew 25:35-46.

ISRAEL'S NATIONAL REPENTANCE
Ezekiel 33

THE FINAL DIVISION of Ezekiel, chapters 33–48, contains *prophecies of hope* for the exilic community and the nation of Israel thereafter. The same righteous God who executed judgment will also mercifully grant restoration. The end of the divine purpose is to glorify His sovereign grace by acting for His own name's sake (Ezekiel 20:9,14,22; 36:21-23,32) to regather, regenerate, restore, and finally rule over Israel according to His prophetic promise. In these chapters it will be seen that the course of divine judgment during human history will come to a close with Israel's repentance (chapter 33). God will destroy all the nations who threaten Israel as a prelude to the final regathering of His people from the nations (chapters 35,38–39). Then the Messiah, Israel's true Shepherd (chapter 34), will return, regather and reunite His people as a nation, and dwell in their midst in the land of Israel and sanctify them (chapters 36–37) so they can mediate the laws of the New Covenant to the nations during the kingdom age as a kingdom of priests at the messianic temple (chapters 40–48).

Ezekiel had first been appointed by God as a "watchman" to warn the rebellious house

of Israel of the certainty of coming judgment (3:16-27). Now the prophet is reminded of his watchman role (33:1-3,7) which requires personal accountability from each person who hears the warning if deliverance is to be realized (verses 4-6). The action required of each Israelite was repentance (verses 8–20). In verse 21 the announcement of the conquest of Jerusalem was received by the prophet "in the twelfth year of [the] exile, on the fifth of the tenth month" (January 9, 585 B.C.), some six months after the city's fall to the Babylonians (Jeremiah 39:2). This announcement marked a turning point in the prophetic career of Ezekiel, removing his prior condition of speechlessness (Ezekiel 33:22) and inaugurating his new message of consolation regarding Israel's restoration (verse 23).

Ezekiel lists *six covenantal violations* that continued to condemn the nation (verses 25-26) and their consequences (verses 27-29), with an additional admonition to heed the prophetic word as truth to be obeyed (verses 30-32). The chapter concludes with a restatement of the purpose of prophetic revelation (verse 33): to authenticate the messenger (prophet) as having a message from God (prophecy). This reassertion of the validity of the prophetic program at the opening of the final division of the book—which centers on the restoration of national Israel—affirms for us that what is promised in these chapters will be fulfilled. It is not apocalyptic idealism or wishful thinking or symbols of spiritual realities, but like the former prophecies that received historical confirmation, so these prophecies made to Israel will find their fulfillment in Israel's future.

ISRAEL'S SHEPHERDS
Ezekiel 34

THE PROPHECY OF Israel's shepherds, coming at the commencement of the restoration prophecies, reproves Israel's kings (shepherds) who had, as God warned through the prophet Samuel (1 Samuel 8:11-18), been false to Israel's needs while feeding their own. The purpose of this chapter is to provide God's indictment of Israel's false shepherds (rulers) before promising to become their true Shepherd (Ezekiel 34:1-16) and regather them ("My flock," the remnant) under the rule of King Messiah (verses 17-31). As such, it corrects the abuses of leadership that had led Israel into exile and clarifies the attitude of divine leadership that will lead the nation to restoration and sustain it through the millennial kingdom. Since real restoration can come only when theocratic rule is restored, and such rule will accompany the advent of the messianic King, this chapter establishes that the whole of the restoration prophecy in this last division of the book is intended for the *eschatological* period. Therefore, Ezekiel 34 forms a foundation upon which the rest of the prophecy is built, revealing that until the unrighteous rule of man is removed, the righteous rule of Messiah will not arrive. This order again confirms the divine pattern of the overthrow of Antichrist's kingdom (Daniel 2:44; 7:23-26) before the establishment of the everlasting kingdom of the Messiah (Daniel 2:44; 7:27).

ISRAEL'S FALSE SHEPHERDS
Ezekiel 34:1-10

The Lord will remove Israel's self-seeking shepherds from their positions because they did not protect or provide for the people. The identity of these shepherds can be determined by the common use of the word *shepherd* throughout the ancient Near East and by its use in Israelite history, particularly during Ezekiel's time of writing (the exilic period). The evidence of usage of the *shepherd* motif in the ancient Near East reveals that the term *shepherd* is used of rulers of nations appointed by a deity, primarily kings. In preexilic Israelite history the term is used of a man appointed to lead Israel (Numbers 27:17), of David as a ruler over Israel (2 Samuel 5:2; Psalm 78:70-72), of evil kings whose unjust rule makes the nation like sheep without a shepherd (1 Kings 22:17; 2 Chronicles 18:16), and of the Persian ruler Cyrus (Isaiah 44:28). In the exilic period Jer-

emiah, like Ezekiel, condemns "the shepherds who are destroying and scattering the sheep of My pasture" (Jeremiah 23:1). In this text he distinguishes them from both false prophets and priests (Jeremiah 23:9-40; cf. 2:8), indicating that they must have been political leaders or kings. However, since Jeremiah (3:15; 23:4), like Ezekiel (37:24), mentions shepherds that will care for Israel in the future restoration period, during which the human office of king will have been replaced by theocratic rule, the term appears to best suit governmental rulers in Israel regardless of the era of history.

Ezekiel's indictment is against the scandalous history of wicked kings in Israel and Judah who ruled at the expense of the nation. One example is the Israelite king Ahab, who murdered Naboth in order to steal his family's vineyard (1 Kings 21). Shortly after this event the prophet Micaiah addressed Ahab and prophesied Israel as "scattered on the mountains like sheep which have no shepherd" (1 Kings 22:17). In Judah, King Manasseh "filled Jerusalem with very much innocent blood" and seduced the people of Israel "to do more evil than the nations whom the Lord destroyed" (2 Kings 21:1-16), thus sealing the divine judgment of Judah (2 Kings 23:26; 24:3).

Ezekiel's indictment also singles out the neglect of social justice and welfare, which are the duty of a righteous ruler (Ezekiel 34:4). These rulers abandoned the weakest and neediest members of the community, a clear transgression of the Mosaic Covenant (Leviticus 25:25,35,47; Deuteronomy 15:7; 24:14-15). The final fulfillment of this will be Christ's rescue of national Israel from the armies of the Antichrist in the campaigns of Armageddon (Zechariah 14:2-5; Revelation 19:11-16). In both these texts the divine deliverance is demonstrated by a declaration that the Lord's sovereign rule is replacing that of the wicked rulers (Zechariah 14:9; Revelation 19:15-16).

ISRAEL'S TRUE SHEPHERD
Ezekiel 34:11-31

In Ezekiel 34:11 the Lord announces that He Himself will shepherd His people, first by regathering them from their places of scattering and returning them to their Promised Land of Israel (verses 12-16). Even though figures of speech are employed in the metaphor of the sheep and shepherds, it is clear that a literal return from physical exile and dispersion is in view in verse 13 because of the references to the countries where they were scattered and the mountains of Israel to which they will be restored. Moreover, in the context, this promise of national regathering is *unconditional* and is therefore based on the historical unconditional covenants that promised Israel permanent possession of the land (Genesis 13:15; 17:8; cf. 2 Chronicles 20:7). Although there were conditions within the unconditional covenants, such as the Land Covenant (Deuteronomy 4:25-31; 30:2-6) requiring Israel to seek and return to the Lord, as this passage reveals, the Lord Himself will secure the necessary obedience of His sheep to fulfill this condition. He does this first by "searching" (Ezekiel 34:11) for them. The second act of grace is the Shepherd's "delivering" His sheep (from the nations) and "bringing them into their own land" (verses 12-13)—acts that demonstrate the work of a Savior.

These sheep that are called "His sheep" (verse 11) constitute the remnant of Israel who will be delivered from the Tribulation and enter into the millennial kingdom to be joined by the righteous Gentiles from the nations (Matthew 19:28; 25:34). Jesus explained that the true Shepherd was one that would seek out even one lost sheep in order to return it to the fold (Luke 15:4-6). In John 10:16 Jesus proclaimed His commitment to His sheep (Israel) and to the "other sheep" (Gentiles), whom He as the Good Shepherd would gather and guard (John 10:14,28-29).

The purpose of the Lord's shepherding activity is to reverse the conditions Israel has endured under the false shepherds. Thus, when Christ returns He will undo all the damage the false Christs have done during the Tribulation (Matthew 24:23-26), and especially the scattering and suffering experienced as a result of the greatest of these—the first beast (Revela-

tion 13:1), or the Antichrist. The Antichrist will attempt to supplant the role of Christ with Israel by conquering the nations (Revelation 13:2-4), making a covenant of peace with Israel (Daniel 9:27), building the third temple, and assuming the place of divinity within it (2 Thessalonians 2:4; cf. Revelation 13:15). The second beast (Revelation 13:11), the false prophet, may be Jewish and may claim messianic status (Revelation 13:12-14). According to Ezekiel 34:16 the Lord will destroy these false shepherds and "feed them with judgment." Indeed, Revelation 19:20 states that at His second coming Christ will judge the Tribulation's false shepherds by casting the beast and the false prophet into the lake of fire.

The nation's *political renewal* is seen as the fulfillment of the Davidic Covenant, in which David was promised an eternal dynasty on an eternal throne (2 Samuel 7:13,16). Ezekiel 37:25 contains this same promise. The identity of this one called "David My servant" who will be their prince and shepherd is debated by commentators. On one side it is argued that this is David's greatest descendant, the Messiah. The parallel reference in Ezekiel 37:24 adds that all of Israel will have "My servant David" as "one shepherd." The pairing of "God" with "My servant David" in rule over Israel in these texts implies the theological pairing of "God and Christ" in the rule over the people of God in the New Jerusalem (Revelation 21:22-23; 22:1,3).

Jesus Christ is clearly stated to be of "the house and lineage of David" (Matthew 1:1-17; cf. Luke 2:4) and is related to David in the prophetic promises of establishing the everlasting covenant (Isaiah 55:3) and ruling as the Davidic King in the millennial kingdom (Isaiah 9:7; Jeremiah 23:5; Luke 1:31-33,69; Acts 15:15; cf. Matthew 1:1; 19:28). Moreover, the rule is singular—"one shepherd" (Ezekiel 34:23; 37:24). Indeed, according to Zechariah 14:9, in the millennial kingdom "the Lord will be king over all the earth; in that day the Lord will be the only one and His name the only one." This exclusivity of rule and recognition also implies that no other one will be king except God Himself. This divine rulership points to Christ and excludes David, for the latter was only a man.

On the other side it is argued that this is King David resurrected (Daniel 12:2) to assume a role in the millennial government as ruler under King Messiah. Even though there is an emphasis on singleness of leadership in this passage and elsewhere (Jeremiah 23:6; Zechariah 14:9), David could still be considered a vice-regent ruling over Israel for the Messiah after He has established the messianic kingdom and secured Israel within it. He is called "prince" (Hebrew, *nasi*) in Ezekiel 34:24 and 37:25, a term that looks at the religious role of the leader with the people as a regent under God as in chapters 44–48. However, Ezekiel 37:24 states, "My servant David will be king (Hebrew, *melek*) over them," which has in view the political rule of the shepherd. King David, who had been chosen by God because he was "a man after [God's] own heart" (1 Samuel 13:14), had the responsibility as king to uphold God's commandments (cf. 1 Samuel 13:14; 15:28).

At David's coronation it was stated that the Lord said to him, "You will shepherd My people Israel, and you will be a ruler [Hebrew, *nagid*] over Israel" (2 Samuel 5:2). As God, the Messiah would exercise the supreme position of rule over all the earth (Psalm 2:6-9; Revelation 12:5; 19:15), receiving worship at the millennial temple in Jerusalem from both Israel and the nations (Isaiah 2:2-3; Zechariah 14:16), while David would represent Him to Israel alone. In fact, David is mentioned by name in other eschatological texts that focus on national Israel's restoration (Jeremiah 30:9; Hosea 3:5). Some would also identify David as "the prince" Ezekiel mentions later (Ezekiel 45–46); however, there are formidable reasons against this proposal (see discussion on 45:22). The term "raise up" does not refer to David's resurrection but to his royal installation, as the hiphil of the Hebrew verb *qum* was used of "establishing or setting up" ancient rulers in their office.

The phrase "covenant of peace" is a synonym for the New Covenant and describes its function of making and maintaining universal peace for Israel and also for the nations (Zechariah 9:10). The advent of the messianic King was predicted to bring an unending reign of peace, for He is the "Prince of Peace" (Isaiah 9:6-7; cf. Micah 5:5; Nahum 1:15; Luke 1:79), and peace characterizes His government (Isaiah 52:7; Jeremiah 33:9; 55:12; 60:17; 66:12; cf. Romans 14:17). Elsewhere the covenant of peace is described in terms of the cessation of war and of military disarmament (Isaiah 2:4), of exceptional agricultural prosperity in the land (Zechariah 8:12), and of the building of the Messianic temple (Haggai 2:9; Zechariah 6:13).

The description of *material renewal* in the millennial kingdom first announces the changed conditions ("there will no longer be") that fulfill the promise of blessings Israel would receive for obeying the previous covenants. Comparing these verses with Leviticus 26:4-13 demonstrates this:

Covenant Blessing	Leviticus 26	Ezekiel 34
Peace and the confirmation of a covenant	verse 6	verse 25
Rains in their season	verse 4	verse 26
Land yields its produce	verse 4	verse 27
Trees of the field will bear their fruit	verse 4	verse 27
Live securely in the Land	verse 5	verse 28
Elimination of harmful animals	verse 6	verse 25
Rest without fear from enemies	verses 6-7	verses 25,28
Covenant relationship between God and Israel	verse 12	verse 30
Bars of their former yoke will be broken	verse 13	verse 27

The *spiritual renewal* of the millennial kingdom is indicated by use of the covenantal formula in Ezekiel 34:30: "I, the LORD their God…they are My people," but with the clarification that "My people" are "the house of Israel," a reaffirmation that there will be a future for national Israel after its national repentance and return to the Lord. Verse 31 restates this covenantal relationship in terms of the shepherd/sheep motif that has distinguished this chapter. Here, too, there is a significant addition explaining that the sheep are men and the Shepherd is God. This serves as a reminder that the previous description of restoration is to be interpreted as literal conditions to be experienced by national Israel in the millennial kingdom rather than as symbols of spiritual blessings applied to the church.

EDOM'S FUTURE DESTRUCTION
Ezekiel 35

MOUNT SEIR, THE SUBJECT of the prophet's pronouncement of judgment in Ezekiel 35, is in the region inhabited by the Edomites, who are the descendants of Esau, who lost his birthright to his brother Jacob (Genesis 27:1-36). As a result, Esau's descendants were given a less fertile land (the wadi Arabah south of the Dead Sea) than the descendants of Jacob received (Genesis 27:39-40; Malachi 1:3), and Edom maintained a vendetta against Israel because of this ancient dispossession. In Psalm 83:3-6, Edom is mentioned first in the list of nations who formed a conspiracy to wipe out Israel. Edom's judgment is repeated in a number of prophetic texts (Isaiah 34:5-8; 63:1-4; Jeremiah 49:7-22; Lamentations 4:21; Amos 1:11-12; Obadiah), and Ezekiel 35:6 describes this judgment with a word play illustrating retributive judgment (judgment in kind). This is seen in the use of the term *blood* (Hebrew *'adom*), which sounds like *Edom* ("red one") and underscores that as Edom has shed blood, so it will be given over to bloodshed.

The Edomites were violently driven from their territory by the Nabataeans and disap-

peared from history with the Roman conquest of Idumea. This brought a partial fulfillment of the judgment promised in Ezekiel 35:3-4. However, the area later became reinhabited by Bedouin tribes (perhaps descendants of the Edomites) and today is part of the Bedouin Hashemite dynastic territory known as Jordan. Indeed, Edom had boasted, "We have been beaten down, but we will return and build up the ruins" (Malachi 1:4). The placement of the message in Ezekiel 35 within the eschatological division of the book of Ezekiel and the mention in verse 14 of the universal recognition of Edom's destruction, along with statements in other oracles that make the time of Edom's ultimate desolation "the day of the LORD" (Obadiah 15) and similar to the "overthrow of Sodom and Gomorrah" (Jeremiah 49:18; cf. Isaiah 34:9-15), indicates a yet future and final judgment. The Edomite territory of Bozrah is predicted as the place to which the Messiah will come during the Tribulation (Isaiah 63:1-6) and the site of divine judgment in the campaigns of Armageddon (Isaiah 34:4-6).

ISRAEL'S REBIRTH AND RESTORATION
Ezekiel 36–37

THESE ARE THE MOST theologically significant chapters in the entire section of Ezekiel dealing with Israel's restoration, if not the entire book. They provide the major eschatological motifs of the prophecy and a synopsis of Ezekiel's theology. From a *theological* perspective, the problem for Ezekiel, as well as the other prophets of the exile (Jeremiah and Daniel), was how to comfort a nation who had not only lost their land but also, as their captors boasted, their Lord. The people believed their subjugation by a foreign power symbolized the conquest of their inferior god by the victor's superior deity. The theological conclusion was that the conquered people's god was not strong enough to protect them from conquest, as Ezekiel 36:20 seems to suggest: "These are the people of the LORD; yet they have come out of

His land." But the more accurate covenantal background for this statement is the suzerain-vassal treaty, an ancient Near-Eastern form of law code made between a sovereign (the suzerain) and his subjects (the vassals). The exile demonstrated, in accordance with this established basis for national relations, that as Israel's suzerain, God was responsible to uphold the terms of His covenant by punishing Israel, His vassal, by exile for covenant violation.

However, it was the postexilic generation returning to Judah in 535 B.C. that faced the greatest theological challenge. God had brought back a remnant to rebuild Jerusalem and the temple, yet the majority of Israelites remained in exile (and continue to do so today). Were they meant to *literally* inherit the promises made by the former prophets? How could their experience of a meager return to a land still under foreign domination, while the majority of their fellow Jews remained outside the land, be considered a restoration? How could the temple they rebuilt, which was financed by a foreign government and erected under duress over an insufferable number of years, and which was pitiable by comparison to the temple of the past, fulfill the great vision they had been given? When would Messiah arrive to regather the Jews in the Diaspora, conquer Israel's enemies, and restore Jerusalem?

These were the theological questions Ezekiel's prophecies needed to address while encouraging the nation to seek the Lord and not lose heart over their present circumstances. In answer to these concerns, chapter 36 outlines the promise, purpose, procedure, and performance of the New Covenant to reverse the condition of divine profanation and vindicate the holiness of Israel's God before the world. Chapter 37 complements the theological explanation of spiritual regeneration presented in 36:25-27 with its anatomical analogy of national physical and spiritual rebirth in 37:1-14. Whereas chapter 36 is primarily concerned with the theological dilemma of restoring God's reputation through Israel despite its scandalous history, the last section of chapter

37 is concerned with the resolution of two great theological crises in Israel's history: the division of the 12 tribes into two kingdoms (Judah and Israel/Ephraim) in verses 15-25 and the loss of God's presence from the temple with the departure of the Shekinah glory (Ezekiel 11:22-23) in verses 26-28.

REMOVAL OF ISRAEL'S FOES
Ezekiel 36:1-7

Having prophesied the ultimate destruction of one of Israel's historic enemies on Mount Seir in chapter 35, the prophet now prefaces his theological explanation of Israel's national regathering, regeneration, and restoration (36:16-38) with a promise to remove *all* Israel's enemies from the mountains of Israel in preparation for its restoration under the New Covenant in the millennial kingdom (36:1-15). The past subjugation and humiliation imposed by the threat of foreign nations surrounding Israel is contrasted with the productive future that will follow the fulfillment of national restoration physically and spiritually (verses 16-38). However, the primary focus of this chapter is the restoration of God's reputation through the reversal of Israel's condition (physically and spiritually) under the New Covenant in the millennial kingdom.

In Ezekiel 36:1-3 the mountains of Israel are addressed as the place against which Israel's enemies have often launched invasions and arrogantly boasted they could desolate Israel and make her "the possession of the rest of the nations" (verse 3). Indeed "the mountains of Israel" will soon be revealed as the place that Gog and his allied nations will invade and be destroyed by divine intervention (chapters 38–39). For Israel to possess the mountains within its borders is not only vital to its military defense but also essential to its continued existence in the land. The mountains are a major source of Israel's water and fertile land for grazing animals and raising crops.

Throughout Israel's history, Assyrians, Babylonians, Medo-Persians, Greeks, Egyptians, Syrians, Romans, Turks, and "Palestinians" all have fought to possess Israel's land. However, the greater reality is that the land belongs to Israel's God ("My land," 36:5; cf. Leviticus 25:23), and the nations have in fact been warring against God (cf. Genesis 12:3). Their taunts and insults against Israel have in fact offended God (Ezekiel 36:6), and therefore He swears (takes an oath) that He will act in retributive judgment against the nations, bringing them to the same fate they intended for His people (verses 4,7). All the great empires that occupied the land of Israel in the past have vanished in the dust of conquest, and today their remnants occupy only museum shelves.

REVERSAL OF ISRAEL'S FORTUNES
Ezekiel 36:8-15

Ezekiel 36:8 addresses the mountains of Israel once again, but this time with an oracle of salvation. With the removal of Israel's foes will come the reversal of the nation's fortune. In verses 8-12 the Lord announces that the remnant of Israel ("My people") will soon be regathered and returned to its land. In advance of the restoration of the people of Israel will come the *restoration of the land* of Israel complete with revived agricultural endeavors, the multiplication of men and animals, and the rebuilding of cities and even desolated areas. Such a restoration of the land will require time, which agrees with the concept of a regathering and return to the land before the final regathering and restoration in the millennial kingdom.

The language of this portion of Ezekiel parallels that found in the next portion, which is about the millennial restoration (verses 29-30,33-38) and the reversal of Israel's fortune. The statements I "will treat you better than at the first" (verse 11), and "never again bereave them of children" (verse 12) argue for the time of the *second regathering* in the millennial kingdom. This interpretation also agrees with Ezekiel's conclusion in verses 13-15, which restates the Lord's commitment to deliver Israel permanently from the consequences of its violation of God's covenants. The threefold promise that God will no longer let Israel be depopulated (verses 13-14), disgraced, or deca-

dent (verse 15) reveals the irreversible change in status and nature that accompanies the establishment of the New Covenant for Israel in the millennial age.

THE SERIOUSNESS OF ISRAEL'S SIN
Ezekiel 36:16-21

The prophetic message ("the word of the LORD," 36:16) of divine vindication begins in verse 17 with a retrospective summary of the moral and spiritual history of the house of Israel's faithfulness to its covenantal relationship with God. The prophet had previously recounted the heathen origin of Israel (16:1-5) and its moral defection (16:15-34). This review of Israel's past not only exonerates God for His judgment against the exiles but also underscores that their future restoration is based solely on God's sovereign grace. The particular word used in verse 17 to characterize the condition of the people is "defilement" (Hebrew, *tame'*). This term, found twice in this verse and again in verses 18 and 29, means "to render ceremonially unclean." In the Old Testament this word is associated with sin that defiles or pollutes by contact.

In Leviticus, for example, *tame'* describes illicit sexual activity that has defiled the land and its inhabitants (18:23,25,27; 19:29) and ritually unclean animals that will render unclean whatever touches their carcasses (11:24-43). As a result, "the land has become defiled, therefore I have visited its punishment upon it, and so the land has spewed out its inhabitants" (Leviticus 18:25). The simile of a "menstruous [unclean] woman" (Ezekiel 36:17) depicts the "unapproachableness" of Israel (cf. Isaiah 64:6). This condition has been incurred by bad "moral conduct" and "reckless deeds." Therefore, just as the ceremonial impurity of the menstruous woman separates her from that which is considered holy, so Israel's conduct has caused her to be removed from the Holy Land.

Ezekiel 36:18-21 explains that Israel had defiled itself and its land by idolatry (verse 18), which resulted in the judgment of exile (verse 19). It also resulted in the profanation of the Lord's holy name by the nations because Israel belongs to God (verses 20-21). Verse 17 recounts Israel's moral defection, and verse 18 presents the consequence: defilement of the land, including idolatry. Ezekiel therefore reviews God's retributive judgment against Israel (cf. 14:19; 16:59; 35:6), the same form of judgment previously announced against the nations (36:7).

The prophet goes on in verse 19 to specify the nature of the judicial sentence of exile through the synonyms "scattering" and "dispersing." These particular terms are coupled in Ezekiel (12:15; 20:23; 22:15; 29:12; 30:23,26) that corresponds in thought and rhyme to the promise of return and restoration (20:34; 28:25; 34:13; 36:24; 37:21; 39:27-28). One example of a *doublet* involving both judgment and restoration appears in verses 19 and 24:

> I *scattered* them among the nations they were *dispersed* throughout the lands (verse 19)
>
> I will *take* you from the nations, *gather* you from all the lands (verse 24)...

This correspondence presents the divine intervention of Yahweh in the sovereign exercise of exile and return. It also prepares us for the remaining chapters of the book. However, it is necessary to first understand the *theological reason* the restoration must take place. Verses 20-21 show God's inseparable relationship to the people and land of Israel. From the perspective of Israel, the exile threatened the prophetic fulfillment of the historical covenants, including Israel's possession of the land. Yet a greater threat is that God's holy reputation was being profaned by Israel's behavior in the midst of the surrounding nations.

The seriousness of this offense can be seen in the meaning of the verb "profane" (Hebrew, *chalal*), which means "to pollute, defile, profane, violate, desecrate, make common." Of the 75 occurrences of the term in the Old Testament, 31 are found in Ezekiel. Of these uses by the prophet, 21 refer to treating as common those things that are consecrated as holy—such

as "holy things" (7:21; 22:26; 42:20; 44:23), "holy places" (7:24; 48:14), "the sanctuary" (23:39; 25:3; 28:18; 44:7), "holy occasions" (usually Sabbaths) (20:13,16,21-22,24; 22:8,26; 23:38), and "holy position" (for example, the king of Tyre, 28:6). The remaining ten occurrences all refer to a profanation of the Lord's holy name (13:19; 20:9,14,22,39; 36:20-23; 39:7), the highest form of profanation.

Verse 21 explains God's intent to vindicate His holy name. While no scheme is yet revealed for the recovery of the divine honor, there is introduced the general motive that underlies the specific action displayed in verses 23-32. The pivotal phrase "but I had concern for My holy name" contrasts the attitude of the nations who professed no concern for it. The word translated as "concern," "pity," or "compassion" (Hebrew *chamal*) is used in Ezekiel 16:5 (in a passage describing Israel's contemptible state at the time of her election) to indicate an attitude of active, condescending responsibility. Here it indicates God's zealous restoration of His own honor, which will require divine intervention in the future restoration of Israel (36:23-32). So assured is this future action that the verb appears as a prophetic preterite indicating that the basis of Israel's restoration has already been settled.

THE SANCTIFICATION OF GOD'S NAME
Ezekiel 36:22-32

Before the restoration of national Israel can be declared (verses 33-38), the problem of divine profanation must be resolved by *divine sanctification* (verses 22-23) through Israel's future salvation under the New Covenant (verses 24-32). However, the divine motive for restoring Israel physically and spiritually must be understood so that a proper theological foundation might undergird this future act of sovereign grace. This is given in verses 22-23, where the tone changes from explanation (verses 17-21) to declaration. This new section uses the introductory formula "thus says the Lord GOD," and the purpose is to introduce specific authoritative declarations of judgment or salvation.

God's concern for His reputation is expanded by way of declaration in verse 22 with the statement, "Not for your sake, O house of Israel, am I about to act but only for My holy name." This self-assertion removes all grounds of human arrogance and appeal, and maintains God's freedom to act sovereignly for Himself. This assertion of sovereign resolve is made through the force of the verb "act" (Hebrew, 'asah, "do, make") in the Qal active participle functioning absolutely (without an object). The sense is "I am about to do what I do," denoting the certainty and effectiveness of the action (cf. 20:9). The phrase "not for your sake" strengthens this act of self-interest by excluding Israel from any part in resolving the divine dilemma created by the nation's exile. The people did not send themselves into exile, though they were responsible for the sin that required God's judgment by exile. Israel cannot merit its restoration, and therefore it must be done by God alone. God's motive here is not Israel's need, but rather the need to vindicate His holy character before the nations (verse 22).

This vindication is necessary because God's name is "great" (verse 23) in the sense of "great in importance," which underscores the majesty and incomparability of Israel's God as opposed to the insignificance of the gods of the nations. It is not simply that God must recover the national status of a powerful local deity, but that He must be acknowledged by the nations as the only and true God (verse 23). To accomplish this requires an act greater than simply returning the Jewish people to their land. Thus the Lord will demonstrate His true nature and character "among you [Israel] in their sight." This requires a supernatural physical and spiritual restoration in Israel as a people and a land. Verses 24-31 reveal the theological and historical order of this restoration with an initial focus on the land of Israel: "I will... bring you into your own land." This confirms that there can be no fulfillment of any of the prophetic promises of the past unless Israel is restored to the Promised Land.

Verse 24 also demonstrates that the resto-

ration of Israel takes place in stages, with the first stage being a regathering from the nations and a return to the land. This is followed by the second stage, which is described in verses 25-27. *The first stage is physical:* restoration to the land. *The second stage is spiritual:* restoration to the Lord. These stages are evident in the next chapter as well, where restoration is seen in the vision of the dry bones (37:1-14) and the reuniting of the nation is seen in 37:15-28. The regathering and return of Israel to its land is seen in other prophets to be a process that begins with a partial regathering in unbelief followed by a complete regathering in belief. In other words, the fulfillment of verse 24 can take place progressively through time until both national spiritual regeneration (verses 25-27) and repentance (verse 31) take place at the end of the Tribulation (cf. Romans 11:25-27), resulting in the full and final regathering of Israel into the land for the millennial kingdom (Matthew 24:31; Mark 13:27).

In the second stage of restoration as described in verses 25-27, Israel's spiritual regeneration is presented through the ceremonial imagery of liturgical cleansing. This is in keeping with the Levitical ritual of purification from defilement.

The renewal of national Israel requires an individual *spiritual regeneration* that will prevent the loss of a ceremonial state and preserve the restoration in perpetuity. Verses 26-27 present this spiritual regeneration as a radical change in the inner disposition by the removal of that which caused ritual defilement and the implantation of a new nature. This is depicted in the original Hebrew text by the use of a chiastic arrangement (A/B/B/A pattern) in which the elements of divine activity and human change are emphasized: (A) "I will give" (B) "a new heart" (A) "a new spirit" (B) "I will put within you." The theological expression of "new" finds its place chiefly in the eschatological announcement of a New Covenant, a new covenant community, and a new creation. The "new heart" (volitional aspect) and "new spirit" (relationship aspect) therefore are inner dispositions of will and spiritual inclination that were formerly nonexistent and have been given in order to bring national Israel into the spiritual provisions of the New Covenant (cf. Jeremiah 31:33-34).

The remainder of Ezekiel 36:26 contains two important terms, "the heart of stone" and "a heart of flesh," which serve to contrast and complement the terms previously considered. The term "heart of stone" is a forcible imagery of the hardened condition of the will, the attributive genitive "stone" (Hebrew, 'even) transferring its stony quality to the heart and rendering it obdurate, insensitive, and incapable of action. By contrast, the term "heart of flesh" refers to the new sensitive and responsive will, which is ready to demonstrate obedience. While Israel's new nature qualifies it to live under the New Covenant, the additional element that defines Israel's experience of the New Covenant and secures its abiding relationship with the Lord appears in verse 27 as the bestowal of God's own Holy Spirit. God imparts the Spirit to cause Israel to faithfully fulfill the New Covenant (verse 27). The verb "walk" (Hebrew, halak) pictures Israel living according to the legal expressions of God's will, while the verb "keep" (Hebrew, shamar) indicates "keeping with observant care" or a "guarding with diligent preservation." Both terms imply the duty of covenant obedience expected of the renewed nation.

This new condition will assure Israel's *permanent residence* in the land and guarantee that God's name will never again be profaned among the nations. This connection is drawn in verse 28, where the fulfillment of God's New Covenant law results in a reestablishment of Israel in its land. The possession of this land was unconditionally promised to Israel's descendants in the phrase "and you will live in the land that I gave to your forefathers" (verse 28). God will restore the people of Israel to the land because He promised that the descendants of Abraham, Isaac, and Jacob would have it forever as an everlasting possession (Genesis 13:15; 17:8; 48:4; Joshua 14:9; 1 Chronicles 28:8; 2 Chronicles 20:7; Psalm 37:29; Isaiah 34:17; 60:21; Jeremiah 7:7; 25:5). In keeping this promise, God would restore His reputation among both Israel and the nations as "the faithful God, who keeps His covenant" (Deuteronomy 7:9; Micah 7:18).

The enjoyment of promised New Covenant blessings will provoke the nation to repentance by causing the people to remember their past iniquities (Ezekiel 36:31). A similar response is seen in Isaiah 12:1-6, a hymn of praise as Israel enters the millennial kingdom. This repentance is depicted in Ezekiel 36:31 by the words "remember," which means "a recognition or discernment which turns toward God," and "loathe," which indicates a "self-loathing." The objects of repentance are stated to be the people's "evil ways" and "deeds that were not good," terms that refer to moral action in the bad sense and the practice of wanton, evil deeds in connection with ritualistic idolatry (cf. Ezekiel 11:18,21). Thus Israel, with a new nature, the indwelling of the Spirit, and the promised blessings of the millennial kingdom, will understand its history of disobedience from the divine viewpoint and respond in repentance. Ezekiel 36:32 reminds Israel that her experience of renewal is the result of grace ("not for your sakes"), a new internalized recognition (Niphal [a major verb stem in biblical Hebrew] of *yada'*, or "know," has a reflective nuance) of the character of God, which drives the nation to a deeper experience of spiritual repentance over its failure to properly honor God.

ISRAEL'S RESTORATION
Ezekiel 36:33-38

According to Ezekiel 36:33-38, Israel's God will restore His reputation among the nations by restoring the land, repopulating its cities, and rebuilding the waste places. Having restored the people to the land, the Lord will now restore the land to the people. The announcement of this eschatological resettlement opens with the introductory formula "thus says the Lord GOD" (as done in verse 22) in order to introduce a specific declaration concerning the "salvation" of the land. This metropolitan restoration will occur "on the day that I cleanse you" (verse 33). The figure is a synecdoche using the phrase "the day" to speak of an indefinite period of time, since the rebuilding of edifices and repopulation will not be accomplished in a single day, but rather, when the time of eschatological fulfillment comes—specifically, "on the day that I cleanse you from all your iniquities" (that is, in the time of national restoration in the millennial kingdom).

At that time the Lord will "cause the cities to be inhabited [Hiphil perfect]" and the "waste places will be rebuilt [Niphal perfect]" (verse 33). The different nuances may imply that the increase in Israel's population will be the result of divine activity, while the rebuilding of waste places will be the result of human activity. However, verse 36 states that the Lord is the One who will rebuild the waste places. In either case, whether by divine fiat or by the divine increase in manpower to perform this rebuilding, the result is the work of the Lord. The "garden of Eden" (verse 35) is a simile that may imply that the newly created state of things in the millennial kingdom will be in some fashion analogous to the original state before the fall. The completion of this restoration is emphasized by the description of renewal that follows. This scene of restored order bears a testimony to the surrounding nations. If the Lord has changed the verdict of the nations concerning His land, those nations must also change their view of His sovereign power, which accomplished this restoration. Verse 36 declares that this reclamation of formerly ruined conditions will demonstrate to the nations that the Lord is God and will vindicate His name before them as He assumes His theocratic rule over all the earth.

Now that the Lord's honor has been fully vindicated among the nations, He will turn again to His people to receive honor from granting their requests (verses 37-38). The purpose behind all the Lord's actions (that is, the vindication of His name) will find its proper fulfillment in the establishment of the house of Israel. The theocratic rule will be consummated by the sovereign intervention of the Lord, and the recognition of His sovereignty will be universal (cf. Psalm 22:27-28; Isaiah 11:9; Habakkuk 2:14; Zechariah 14:9). The reflexive nuance of the Niphal, "I will be inquired of," implies that the Lord will respond to Israel's requests.

As a ceremonial flock dedicated to the praise of the Lord, the house of Israel will become priests and servants (cf. Isaiah 61:6). The flock is also distinguished as to its size. In 2 Chronicles 35:7 we read that Josiah contributed a flock of 30,000 as an offering. The imagery then is of droves of flocks crowding the narrow streets of Jerusalem at her appointed seasons or feasts, and this is offered to the remnant. To certify the metaphor as applying to Israel, verse 38 adds the clarifier "flocks of men." "Men" is a genitive in apposition, and parallels the statement of Ezekiel 34:31: "and you, My sheep, the sheep of My pasture, you are men." Israel, then, is increased as a holy flock for the divine Shepherd (cf., Ezekiel 34), which will cause the nation Israel itself to acknowledge YHWH as their sole sovereign Lord.

ISRAEL'S REGATHERING AND REBIRTH
Ezekiel 37:1-14

Ezekiel 36:16-38 gives the theological ground for the restoration of Israel and the vindication of God's reputation in the sight of the nations. Ezekiel 37:1-14 gives the mechanics of the restoration through *the vision of a valley of dry bones* that are brought to life. This account clearly states that it concerns "the whole house of Israel" (verse 11); it deals with Israel's political and spiritual rebirth (verses 12-14). Specifically, verse 12 states that God will cause His people to come up out of their graves for the purpose of returning to the land of Israel. The imagery of a physical body brought from death to life replicates the prophetic pattern of the successive stages in the process of restoration. Stage one is *physical* and portrays the political revival of national Israel through the coming together of the bones, sinews, and skin and the body standing erect (verses 5-8). Stage two is *spiritual* and portrays the regeneration of the nation (as in 36:24-25) as illustrated by "the breath" ("My Spirit") entering into the dead body and giving it life (verses 9-10,14).

The vision of a valley filled with dry bones is not meant to portray the resurrection of the individual Israelite, though this doctrine is taught elsewhere (Isaiah 26:19; Daniel 12:2; cf. Job 19:26; John 5:28-29). Here the focus is on the political life of the nation that had ended with the dissolution of the Davidic line at the commencement of the Babylonian captivity. The fulfillment of the historical covenants depended on the uninterrupted continuance of the Davidic dynasty (2 Samuel 7:10-16; Psalm 89:33-37), which was not revived in the second temple period. This served as a witness to the postexilic generation that the restoration, as envisioned by Ezekiel, had not taken place with the return from exile but would be fulfilled at some point in the future.

The establishment of the modern state of Israel seems to be part of the process of fulfillment of the political revival of the nation. The prophetic expectation was that at some time in the future a remnant of the Jewish people in the Diaspora would begin to return to the land to join their brethren who had remained there since before the destruction of the second temple. The secular return of Jewish immigrants under the Zionist movement in the late nineteenth and early twentieth centuries and the eventual creation of the independent state of Israel in 1948 is significant in this regard. Israel continues at the present time to immigrate Jews from other nations, and the possibility we are witnessing the political revival of Israel cannot be dismissed simply because the second phase of spiritual rebirth has yet to occur.

The construction of a political entity requires time, and that the first stage will take time seems to be implied in verse 8, which speaks of the bodies coming together with no breath yet in them. Not until after the bodies are together does spiritual revival take place (Ezekiel 37:9). This can be seen by the two separate calls to the prophet: the first to address the bones (verse 4) and the second

to address the breath (verse 9). While we see a time interval between the occurrence of the physical and spiritual revivals that together comprise the rebirth of national Israel, there is no interruption in this process once it has begun. Therefore, it would appear that the existing political state of Israel will continue into the Tribulation period until the second advent of Christ.

It is important to observe that one of God's primary purposes in giving Ezekiel the vision of the valley of dry bones was to underscore His sovereign ability to bring Israel's restoration to pass. The prophet was carefully shown the condition of the bones "on the surface of the valley" (verse 2). That the bones were in an unburied state indicates a condition of ritual contamination (the corpse impurity incurred by the Jewish people among the nations). That they were "very dry" indicates that the marrow (the essence of life, cf. Leviticus 17:11,14) was completely gone. The image revealed to Ezekiel was that of Israel being so defiled, lifeless, and helpless that it had no hope of restoration in itself. Its only hope was in God, and for this reason the prophet was asked the question, "Son of man, can these bones live?" (Ezekiel 37:3). In conformity with the expression of God's sovereignty in 36:16-27, the purpose of this question-answer approach was to extract from the prophet (and his reader) the admission that there was no natural hope for Israel, and to turn all hope of restoration over to the sovereign and supernatural work of Israel's God. The exilic condition seemed hopeless, but in the Lord all things are possible. The bones will not only come to life physically (the restoration of the nation), they will also come to life spiritually (the reception of the New Covenant), and Israel will be placed in its own land as a witness to Israel itself that the Lord will perform His promise (verse 14).

ISRAEL'S FUTURE REUNION
Ezekiel 37:15-25

The prophet now presents his audience with another of the symbolic acts (signs) that characterized the first division of his prophecy.

This sign (verses 15-20) is of two sticks upon which are inscribed the names of the two kingdoms into which the nation was split after the death of Solomon in 931 B.C. (1 Kings 12:16-17; 2 Chronicles 10:16-18). This schism was never healed even though representatives of both kingdoms returned to the land in 538 B.C.

During the second temple period, Israel never regained its former status with a Davidic monarchy and Zadokite priesthood. The division was caused not by mere physical geography, for the tribes had always been separated by territorial allotments. Rather, the kingdoms lacked spiritual unity. The departure of the ten northern tribes from the house of David was considered a rebellion (1 Kings 12:19; 2 Chronicles 10:19) because under the Davidic Covenant (Psalm 89:19-37), only the house of David had been given the right to rule the nation. Also, the southern kingdom had the proper place of worship (the temple), toward which prayer had to be directed in order to receive God's blessing (1 Kings 8:28-52; 2 Chronicles 7:14-15).

Every Israelite male was commanded to appear at the temple three times a year (Exodus 23:14-17; 34:23). However, the northern kingdom's rulers feared that continued spiritual devotion to the temple by their subjects would ultimately produce a political shift toward the house of David. So they constructed alternate religious centers that plunged the kingdom into idolatry (1 Kings 12:25-33). Only a restoration that reunited the two kingdoms spiritually and politically would fulfill the divine ideal.

The prophecy of the two sticks (Judah and Ephraim/Joseph) becoming one has been variously interpreted, with one modern version identifying Judah with messianic Judaism and Ephraim with Gentile Christianity and the two coming together in the church. However, the passage reveals the names to be written on these sticks. Ezekiel 37:21 identifies these two sticks with "the sons of Israel" that had been dispersed among the nations and would be regathered into their own land. Verse 22 speaks of the historic division into "two kingdoms," while verse 25 speaks of all the people

and their land in continuity with Jacob and "[their] fathers." Both of these references could apply to none but the historic Jewish people descended from the patriarchs to whom the land of Israel was given. Clearly, it is only the Jewish tribes that had been divided that would be reunited. Judah was the larger of the two tribes that gave the southern kingdom its dynastic ruler ("the house of David") and its name (1 Kings 12:22-24), and similarly the northern kingdom was named after its most prominent tribe from the house of Joseph, Ephraim (cf. Hosea 5:3,5,11-14).

The stages of regathering and reuniting are *progressive and sequential,* with Ezekiel 37:21-22 describing the physical regathering to Israel from the nations and verses 23-25 the spiritual regathering and reunification under the Davidic king in the millennial kingdom. Prophetically, this pictures Israel's return to the land as a nation and a subsequent national repentance and regeneration at the time of Christ's second advent. The purpose and result of the national rebirth (cf. Isaiah 66:7-9; Zechariah 12:10-14; Romans 11:26) will be a spiritually cleansed Israel (cf. Zechariah 13:1-2; Romans 11:27) with a new nature incapable of repeating the sins of the past that brought against them the curses of the Mosaic Covenant (Ezekiel 37:23). Under the New Covenant the people will finally fulfill their unique calling to be in special relationship to God (verse 24). The singular shepherding of the Davidic king in verses 24-25 has already been discussed in 34:23-24; however, 37:25 adds a familiar feature of the unconditional covenant with its promise of possession of the land forever (Genesis 13:15-18; 2 Chronicles 20:7).

The word "forever" is used five times in verses 25-26, 28. This repetition affirms in the strongest way the *eternality* of God's restoration and requires an eschatological projection of the divine program beyond the millennial kingdom. The word "forever" translates the Hebrew term *'olam,* which denotes "an indefinite period of time." For example, in Exodus 21:6 the term is used of an Israelite slave who has his ear pierced in token of his pledge to serve his master "permanently." In this case the duration of "permanently" is until his service is terminated by his or his master's death or by the year of Jubilee. David Friedman examined more than 80 biblical uses of *'olam* and concluded that it expresses the time element of "as long as the present heaven and earth exists" ("Israel from the Eyes of a Messianic Jew Living in the Land," p. 17). On this basis the land promise is extended to Israel for "all time," which in context would mean until the end of the millennial kingdom, at which time the present earth will be destroyed and a new earth created (Isaiah 65:17; 66:22; 2 Peter 3:10-13).

However, the Hebrew grammatical construction in Ezekiel 37:25 favors an extension of the duration of the term to an infinite degree. Verse 25 prefixes the separable preposition *'ad* to *'olam,* while verses 25-26,28 add the inseparable preposition *le.* The first of these constructions is the stronger and appears elsewhere with *'olam* in the phrase *min 'olam v'ad 'olam* ("from everlasting to everlasting" or "forever and ever"). This expression refers exclusively to God's eternal nature or rule, except in two cases where it describes Israel's possession of the land of Israel (Jeremiah 7:7; 25:5). The second construction seems to stress the future state, which, when used in the context of the millennial kingdom, would mean the eternal state. Indeed, God has promised that Israel's "offspring and name will endure" in the eternal state (Isaiah 66:22). However the outworking of God's government is to be understood in this future period, it is evident from Ezekiel's portrayal of it by the fivefold "forever" that it is meant to assure Israel that its new relationship with God will never be changed for all eternity.

THE LORD'S RETURN
Ezekiel 37:26-28

The return of Israel to the land and to the Lord is now climaxed by the return of the Lord to Israel and the land (verses 26-28). After this return the New Covenant will be enacted with Israel (Jeremiah 31:31-34), just as the Old Covenant had been put into effect when the Lord came to Israel at Mount Sinai (Exodus 19:9-25). The New Covenant is here called both a *covenant of peace* (cf. Isaiah 54:10) and an *everlasting covenant* (cf. Isaiah 55:3; 61:8; Jeremiah 32:40; Ezekiel 16:60-63). As in Ezekiel 34:25-30, where the list of millennial blessings under the New Covenant is based on the terms of the Mosaic Covenant (Leviticus 26:4-13), here the promise of "peace" for the land and the "perpetuity" of provision is drawn from Leviticus 26:4,6. The first synonym, "covenant of peace" (Ezekiel 37:26), is appropriate for describing the restored conditions of the millennial age since the Hebrew word *shalom* ("peace") denotes a comprehensive peace ("security, welfare, health, prosperity, harmony"). The second "everlasting" or "eternal covenant" (verse 26) describes the nature of God's enduring promise and the inviolability of His commitment to Israel as demonstrated by the historic covenants of the past that have now been fulfilled.

As proof of the new relationship between God and Israel, verses 26-28 announce the building of the millennial temple and the return of the divine presence to Israel. Both Hebrew terms for the sanctuary are used in verses 26-28: "and I will set My sanctuary [Hebrew, *miqdash*] in their midst forever. My dwelling place [Hebrew, *mishkan*] also will be with them; and I will be their God, and they will be My people. And the nations will know that I am the LORD who sanctifies Israel, when My sanctuary [Hebrew, *miqdash*] is in their midst forever."

The term *miqdash* ("holy place") was the usual word for the temple, whereas *mishkan* ("dwelling place") was regularly used to speak of the tabernacle. Here both terms are used (as they are of the heavenly temple in Revelation) in continuity with the previous sacred structures and to emphasize the fulfillment of the divine design to bridge heaven and earth through a theocratic government (cf. Matthew 6:9-10). Exodus 25:8 had declared that the original purpose of the sanctuary was to make possible the presence of the holy God in the midst of unholy Israel. Through the ceremonial service, Israel was kept in a state of ritual purification so it could serve the Lord as "a holy nation and a kingdom of priests" (Exodus 19:6). The return of the Lord to the tabernacle at the foot of Mount Sinai reversed the long absence of the Creator from His creation, which had resulted from the intrusion of human sin in the Garden of Eden (Genesis 3:8-19). Once constructed, the earthly sanctuary—with its Ark of the Covenant topped by cherubim—allowed God's presence to return to Israel and made possible the establishment of a theocratic form of government. Since the desecration of the first temple and the departure of God's presence, Israel has experienced the condition of exile either in part or in whole.

The capstone of the millennial kingdom and of its New Covenant is the promise of the erection of the *restoration temple,* to which God's presence will return, never to depart. Ezekiel 37:26-28 provides the template upon which the grand design of the millennial temple is detailed in chapters 40–48. God takes the initiative in building the temple: "*I will set* My sanctuary in their midst" (verse 26, emphasis added). This is one of the expected tasks of King Messiah (Zechariah 6:12-15). In the past the Shekinah glory appeared over Israel in the wilderness as a cloud by day (to provide shelter from the sun) and a pillar of fire by night (to provide illumination) and to communicate divine revelation (Exodus 13:21-22; 16:10; 40:34-38). Isaiah 4:5-6 reveals that in the future, the Shekinah glory will exist as a canopy over the millennial Jerusalem, and Revelation 21:10 describes the descent of the New Jerusalem (apparently to remain suspended over the millennial Jerusalem), in which God's glory is manifest (21:22-23), illuminating the earthly sanctuary into which the nations will bring their tribute (21:24-26; cf. Isaiah 66:18-20; Zechariah 14:16-19).

ISRAEL'S RESCUE FROM GOG AND MAGOG
Ezekiel 38–39

THE PROPHECY OF Israel's rescue by God (chapters 38–39) may be divided into three sections: the invasion of Gog (38:1-16), the defeat and disposal of Gog (38:17–39:20), and the deliverance and devotion of Israel (39:21-29). At first glance this account seems to be an intrusion into the prophetic discourse concerning the temple begun in 37:26-28, with chapters 40–48 announcing the temple's return and the explanation of its design and function. On closer examination, however, its placement between these two temple texts may imply that this event has some relationship to the eschatological temple (more on this to follow). Certainly its theological purpose is to fortify the promise that the restoration is secure, its conditions of blessing are irreversible, and no future invasion of Israel will succeed once Israel has been regathered to her land. This would have been of great concern to Ezekiel's exilic audience, which had already experienced such an invasion and suffered the loss of the temple. It would be of even greater concern to postexilic readers who, after having rebuilt the temple, were still surrounded by hostile nations (as well as hostile neighbors within their own land) and who would suffer repeated invasions of their land and the eventual destruction of the second temple. Only a prophetic guarantee that Israel's enemies would be unable to affect its future would serve to assure the nation that the promise of restoration had indeed been fulfilled.

In terms of the future, the reason this concern needs to be addressed is that before Israel will inherit these promises and experience the restoration and the millennial temple, it will go through the Tribulation. During the first half of the Tribulation Israel will see the rebuilding of the temple and probably experience a time of national revival and regathering of Jews from among the nations. If the temple is rebuilt through the covenant made with the

Antichrist (Daniel 9:27), who will be a global Gentile ruler, Israel may indeed experience an unparalleled period of international Gentile respect. Since these conditions would appear to fulfill the restoration expectations of the prophets, many Jews will undoubtedly be deceived into believing that the era of redemption has finally arrived. However, at the midpoint of the Tribulation, the temple will be desecrated and the Jewish people persecuted, ending the illusion of restoration. Therefore, before they come to this time of trouble in which all the promises of God could be called into question, thus rendering the Jewish remnant susceptible to the worldwide delusion by the Antichrist and his false prophet (see Matthew 24:24; 2 Thessalonians 2:9-12; Revelation 13:3,13-14), God will leave His people with a lesson confirming His power and purpose (in the fulfillment of Ezekiel 38–39).

THE INVASION OF GOG
Ezekiel 38:1-16

The invasion of Gog opens in Ezekiel 38:2-3 with an introduction to the aggressors, whose paired names have given rise to this prophecy popularly being called "the Battle of Gog *and* Magog." However, "Gog" (a people) is the ruler of "Magog" (a place), so it's more correct to say "the Battle of Gog *of* Magog" or "the Battle of Gog," or simply "the Gog War" (hereafter).

The name "Gog" occurs 11 times in these chapters as the title of the leader of the invasion. Since he is directly addressed several times by God (38:14; 39:1) and also called a prince (38:2; 39:1), it is evident that he is a historical figure. Although scholars (Taylor, *Ezekiel,* p. 244) have tried to identify Gog with Gyges (*Gugu*), a seventh-century B.C. Lydian king mentioned in six inscriptions by the Assyrian monarch Ashurbanipal, this ruler never led an allied invasion into Israel. The eschatological context argues against finding a past historical reference to this specific figure.

The prophecy of the Gog War begins with a list of ten proper names in 38:1-7. The names reveal an *alliance of foreign nations* from "out

of the remote parts of the north" (verses 6, 15), the land of Gog, and the prince of Rosh, Meshech, and Tubal (Ezekiel 38:2-3).

The name "Rosh" has been the subject of considerable debate among scholars. Some have taken it as a proper noun and identified it with Russia. The other alternative is to take the term as an adjective meaning "head," which would make Gog "*chief prince* of Meshech and Tubal" (*Ryrie Study Bible,* p. 1286). However, on linguistic and historical grounds, the case for taking *Rosh* as a proper noun rather than a noun-adjective is substantial and persuasive. *Rosh* appears as a place name in Egyptian inscriptions as *Rash* as early as 2600 B.C., and one inscription from 1500 B.C. refers to a land called *Reshu* that was located to the north of Egypt. As a toponym (place name), *Rosh* (or its equivalent) is found over 20 times in other ancient documents, including three times in the Septuagint, ten times in the inscriptions of Sargon, once in the record of Ashurbanipal, once in the annals of Sennacherib, and five times in the Ugaritic tablets of ancient Syria.

When Ezekiel wrote this prophecy in the sixth century B.C., several bands of the Rosh people lived in an area to the north of the Black Sea. Linguistically, the name *Rosh* was originally associated with the tribe of Ros/Rus, which lent its name to a variety of topographical features in what is now the Ukraine and Russia. On historical, geographical, and toponymic grounds it seems best identified with the modern-day Russian people (see Billington, "The Rosh People in History and Prophecy," pp. 54-64). Linguistically the very name *Russia* appears to have been derived from this term *Rosh.* This location is also confirmed by the first-century Jewish historian Flavius Josephus (*Antiquities* 1.6.1), who identified Magog (the land of Rosh) as the land of the Scythians, ancient northern nomadic tribes who inhabited the territory from central Asia across the southern steppes of modern Russia. Based on such evidence, the noted Hebrew lexicographer and grammarian Wilhelm Gesenius (*Thesaurus Linguae Hebraeae et Chaldaeae Veteris Testament:*, p. 955) stated over 150 years ago that Rosh must be "undoubtedly the *Russians,* who are mentioned by the Byzantine writers of the tenth century, under the name *the Ros,* dwelling to the north of Taurus…as dwelling on the river Rha (*Wolga*)."

Clyde Billington ("The Rosh People in History and Prophecy," pp. 59-61) has concluded,

> Historical, ethnological, and archaeological evidence all favor the conclusion that the Rosh people of Ezekiel 38–39 were the ancestors of the Rus/Ros people of Europe and Asia.… The Rosh people who are mentioned in Ezekiel 38–39 were well-known to ancient and medieval writers by a variety of names which all derived from the names of Tiras and Rosh.… Those Rosh people who lived to the north of the Black Sea in ancient and medieval times were called the Rus/Ros/Rox/Aorsi from very early times.… From this mixture with Slavs and with the Varangian Rus in the 9th century, the Rosh people of the area north of the Black Sea formed the people known today as the Russians.

Therefore, despite the objection of critics to this position, the prophecy of Ezekiel 38–39 most likely is a prophecy of a "Russian"-led invasion of Israel. Which parts of "Russia" may be a matter of debate, but Russia's involvement in this invasion is clearly indicated.

Ezekiel prophesies that three additional northern nations will be allied with Gog in the invasion (Ezekiel 38:3). Meshech and Tubal are best identified as ancient *Moschoi* and *Tibarenoi* (in Greek writings) or *Tabal* and *Musku* (in Assyrian inscriptions). Gomer (verse 6) is probably a reference to the ancient Cimmerians (Kimmerioi) who occupied part of Anatolia in the early eighth century B.C. Cognate toponyms to Hebrew *Gomer* appear as Akkadian *Gi-mir-ra-a* and Assyrian *Gimirai.* Beth-togarmah ("house of Togarmah"), "from the remote parts of the north" (verse 6), appears in various ancient texts as *Til-garamu* (Assyrian) or *Tegarma* (Hittite) and has been mentioned

previously in Ezekiel 27:14 as a nation that traded horses and mules with Tyre. All three of these ancient locations are today part of the modern country of Turkey. Attempts to identify Meshech and Tubal with Moscow and Tobolsk lack any serious linguistic support.

In the invasion, these countries will be joined by other nations (38:5) that represent the other three directions of the compass: Persia (modern Iran) from the east, Cush (northern Sudan) from the south, and Put (modern Libya) from the west. Israel will be defenseless and "surrounded" on all sides by its enemies. That these forces are overwhelming is indicated in verse 16, which describes them as "a cloud to cover the land." This impossible situation would serve to heighten Israel's need for divine intervention to rescue them from complete destruction.

Other nations that seem to object to this invasion of Israel in the last days are mentioned in Ezekiel 38:13: Sheba (Yemen), Dedan (Saudi Arabia), and Tarshish (probably located in the western Mediterranean) with its merchants (an economic union). Although the modern names of these places may change again before the fulfillment of this prophecy, all these locations are mentioned in the "table of the nations" in Genesis 10:2-7.

Ezekiel 38:8 states Gog's invasion will occur "after many days" and "in the latter years," which are designations of a future time. Verse 16 makes this future time more explicit by stating "it shall come about *in the last days*" (Hebrew, *be'archarit hayamim*), and verse 18 says "it will come about *on that day*" (Hebrew, *bayom ha-hu'*). Both phrases are common prophetic designations for the future. Therefore, in keeping with the eschatological context in which it is set, the Gog War will find its fulfillment in the final period of time known as the *eschaton* or time of the end.

A more precise timing with regard to "the latter years" is problematic. It could conceivably occur before the Tribulation, during the Tribulation, after the Tribulation (in the interim 75-day period before the beginning of the millennium—Daniel 12:11-12), or at the end of the millennium (cf. Revelation 20:8). Because this event is prophesied for Israel, it probably occurs after the church age. However, the text itself does not preclude the possibility of an earlier fulfillment during the present era. There is nothing in the text itself to indicate *when* this battle will take place. The only clear designation is in the "latter times." In like manner, the regathering of Israel to the land of Israel in unbelief can be fulfilled (and seems to be in the process of fulfillment) before the rapture without sacrificing the immanency of Christ's return.

One view is that this invasion is the same as that mentioned in Revelation 20:7-9, which refers to its participants as "Gog and Magog" (Revelation 20:8) and takes place at the end of the millennium. It cannot be doubted that the reference to "Gog and Magog" is to the invasion in Ezekiel 38–39, but only as a point of past comparison with this historic destruction of the nations by divine intervention. The differences between these two accounts make identification problematic. In Revelation it is an international army that has been deceived by Satan to join in a rebellion against God (Revelation 20:8), not an alliance of localized nations drawn by God (Ezekiel 38:2-4). In Revelation 20 the attack is "up on the broad plain" and against "the camp of the saints" (Revelation 20:9), rather than "against the mountains" and "against Israel" (Ezekiel 39:2; 38:16). It also appears that all weapons of war will have been destroyed at the beginning of the millennium (Isaiah 2:4), and universal peace among the nations is one of the distinguishing characteristics of this age (Isaiah 2:4; 9:7; 11:6-9; Micah 5:4-5), factors which contradict the conditions described for the nations in Ezekiel 38:4-7.

In Ezekiel 38:8-13 we see Israel not yet restored and threatened by the nations surrounding it, and the promise of restoration will not be fulfilled until after the defeat of Gog (39:25-29). By contrast, during the millennium, the nations are ruled by Christ with a rod of iron (Revelation 12:5) and are no longer a threat (39:26; cf. Jeremiah 23:4; Ezekiel 34:28),

and Israel has already experienced its restoration. Likewise, the defeat of Gog is followed by seven months of burials "to cleanse the land" and seven years of burning weapons, followed by the time of restoration. By contrast, the millennial kingdom begins with a cleansed land (Ezekiel 36:33-36) and the defeat of the invaders of Revelation 20 is followed by the final judgment, the creation of a new heavens and earth, and the eternal state (Revelation 20:10–21:8). Finally, in Revelation 20, there will be no need to bury the slain because the conflict will immediately be followed by the resurrection of the unjust for the Great White Throne Judgment (Revelation 20:11-15).

The *pretribulational view* of the rapture allows time for the seven months of burial and the seven years of burning up the weapons to take place before the beginning of the millennial kingdom. What's more, after the rapture, when the world will be in chaos, it's likely that a vacuum of power (especially in the west) may encourage the Gog allies of the east to launch an attack against Israel. And a subsequent divine demonstration of God's power against Israel's enemies before the Tribulation will equip the Jewish people to trust God alone throughout the Tribulation, during which Satan and the Antichrist seek to destroy Israel.

The pretribulational destruction of Gog would also eliminate a military obstacle for the Antichrist, making it possible for him to consolidate his power by the *middle* of the Tribulation—which may explain why he has both the power and the motive to make a covenant with Israel at this time (Daniel 9:27). This covenant may well make possible the rebuilding of the Jewish temple. If the seven years during which Israel will burn the weapons of these nations is the same seven years of the Tribulation (Daniel 9:27; Revelation 11:2), then this burning, along with the burial ground of Gog and the slain multitude (Ezekiel 39:11-16), will serve as a witness throughout the Tribulation to both the promise of the universal judgment of the nations and Israel's complete restoration.

The pretribulational view also finds support from a comparison between the modern situation and the conditions set forth in Ezekiel 38:8-13 concerning Israel and the nations (Fruchtenbaum, *Footsteps*, pp. 106–26). The people and land of Israel, at the time of the invasion, are described as those who have been "gathered from many nations" to a land described as having previously "been a continual waste." This land is "now inhabited," was "restored from the sword [foreign domination]," and is now "living securely" (verses 11,14) with enviable economic resources (verses 12-13). All these conditions describe the present state of Israel since 1967 when it occupied the "mountains of Israel" (verses 8,21; 39:2-3,17-19).

Today the modern state of Israel is populated by Jewish immigrants from all over the world. They have restored the barren lands in this region and live without walled cities (only the Old City of Jerusalem has a wall, and the modern city exists outside these walls). Israel's security is based on the strength of its military, which is acknowledged as one of the best in the world and has defended the country against overwhelming odds in numerous past invasions.

These modern conditions in Israel may be complemented by those concerning the nations launching the invasion. Since the collapse of the communist Soviet Union, Russia has been in an economic free fall that threatens the coherence of the central state and the ability of the government to control its arsenal of nuclear, chemical, and biological weapons as ultranationalist factions seek to usurp the present power structure. It has also maintained support of Israel's enemies, equipping them with weapons for their past invasions of the Jewish state. Six of the former Soviet republics in the south (but still north of Israel) have become independent Islamic nations: Azerbaijan, Kazakhstan, Uzbekistan, Kirghizia, Turkmenistan, and Tajikistan). All six are allied with the Islamic aim to remove the Zionist state that they claim is preventing the comprehensive unity of the Islamic world in the region. Moreover, Russia has forged alliances with most of the nations listed in Ezekiel 38:2-6, including Iran (Persia), Syria, Pakistan, Libya (Put), and Turkey (Meshech, Tubal, Gomer, Beth-togarmah). These countries are Islamic countries that, for the most part, have pledged to help destroy Israel.

These facts demonstrate that conditions at the present time are sufficient to permit the fulfillment of the Gog prophecy. In other words, there is no reason to relegate the invasion to a mid- or posttribulational setting when the present pretribulational setting already meets these conditions. Even so, the invasion probably will not take place until after the rapture of the Church.

DEFEAT AND DISPOSAL OF GOG
Ezekiel 38:17–39:20

In the opening verse of this section about the divine defeat of God, God mentions that the prophets had foretold this last-days invasion (verse 17). Though Gog is not named by the other prophets, the other prophets did make reference to the future defeat of the enemies of Israel.

The drama of Gog's miraculous defeat through divine intervention is presented in 38:18–39:8. Four different words for divine judgment are used in verses 18-19: "fury" (Hebrew, *chemah*), "anger" (Hebrew, *'af*), "zeal" (Hebrew, *qinah*), and "wrath" (Hebrew, *'ebrah*). These words express the intensity of God's display of vengeance against the invaders of His land ("My mountains," 38:21). According to 38:19-21 a divinely appointed earthquake will be so severe as to disorient Gog's multinational forces and cause them to fight each other. The earthquake will apparently set off volcanic deposits in the region, bringing down on Gog's army a hail of molten rock and burning sulphur (volcanic ash) with the result that the enemy troops are utterly destroyed before they can strike a blow against Israel (verse 22). This divine demonstration against Gog and his allies will extend even to the farthest reaches of their homelands— "Magog...coastlands" (39:6)—nullifying any reprisal or future attempts at invasion. This complete annihilation of Gog's vast army will bring God greater glory and distinguish (set apart, "sanctify") Him to the other nations as Israel's sovereign Lord (verse 23).

In 39:9-16 Israel is instructed on how to dispose of the abandoned weapons and the slain bodies of Gog and his allies (Ezekiel 39:9-16). The first instructions deal with the disposal of the weapons (verses 9-10), which are to be burned. This task will take "seven years" (39:9) and be performed by the inhabitants of nearby cities. Rather than simply destroy the weapons, they will be used for fuel and thereby benefit the Israelis. This ironic disposition of weapons designed to kill the people will be considered a "plunder of those who [intended to] plunder them" (verse 10). If this battle takes place after the rapture but before the seventieth week (the seven-year Tribulation) begins, there will be ample time and freedom even through the first half of the Tribulation (the time of pseudopeace for Israel under the Antichrist's covenant) to accomplish this job. Moreover, the statement about not needing to gather firewood from the forests (verse 10) would make more sense in such a time frame, for after the first trumpet judgment, one-third of the trees will be burned up (Revelation 8:7). If this battle were to take place at any point in the Tribulation, the people who are burning the weapons would run out of time to complete this task before the intensified persecution of the final 42 months (Matthew 24:16-22)—a persecution that drives the Jewish remnant into the wilderness to escape the Satanic onslaught (Revelation 12:6).

The next instructions (Ezekiel 39:11-20) deal with the proper disposal of the slain soldiers of the Gog army. The slaughter will have been so great that the dead bodies will fill an entire valley, blocking travelers from passing through this area (verse 11). In seeking to harmonize the need for proper burial under Jewish law (verses 12-16) with the devouring of the fallen soldiers by "every...bird and beast of the field" (verses 4,17-20), it may be that two phases of disposal are in view. The first phase of disposal is that performed by wild animals assembled to reduce the corpses to skeletons (verses 18-20). Then the bones of the enemy

will be properly buried by "all of the people of the land" (verse 13).

Because of the vast number of corpses, decontamination of the land will take "seven months" (39:12). Additional mop-up operations are to be conducted by two teams appointed to search through the land, tag, and then inter unburied bones (verses 14-15). On the basis of this verse Jewish rabbis have inferred the legal ruling (*halakha*) that *all* graves must be marked. In the modern state of Israel a group of nongovernmental Orthodox Jews known as ZAKA (Hebrew acronym for "Identification of Disaster Victims") is appointed to carefully remove all human remains after suicide bombings in order to restore order and prevent ritual impurity in the land. The reason, according to Jewish law, is that the dead must be buried immediately because exposed corpses are a source of ritual contamination to the land (cf. Numbers 19:11-22; Deuteronomy 21:1-9).

DELIVERANCE AND DEVOTION OF ISRAEL
Ezekiel 39:21-29

Allusions to the Gog War cease with verse 22, and the focus turns exclusively to God's past deliverance of His people and their devotion to Him at the time of their future restoration. Verses 21-22 are transitional and restate the divine purpose of Gog's defeat—to bring revelatory information concerning God to the nations (verse 21) and to Israel (verse 22). This revelation has consisted of a divine demonstration of God's greatness (38:22), holiness (38:23), and glory (39:13,21). However, while the nations will see the judgment of Gog (verse 21), Israel will come to know their God in a more personal and lasting manner (verse 22). Ezekiel's use of the verb plus the preposition "set in place" (Hebrew, *natan be*) with the substantive "glory" (Hebrew, *kabod*) gives the impression that a concrete object is in view.

God's glory might be thought of as the manifestation of the Shekinah glory (Exodus 16:7,10; 29:43; Numbers 14:22; Psalm 102:16) that will return to the millennial temple (Ezekiel 43:1-7; cf. Isaiah 4:5; 24:23), or even of the temple itself (2 Chronicles 7:1-2; cf. Psalm 26:8;

29:9; 63:2). However, the text does not make this clear, and it may be better to understand the statement in the terms expressed by the prophet Isaiah, who has a similar audience in mind: "For I know their works and their thoughts; the time is coming to gather all nations and tongues. And they shall come and see My glory. I will set a sign among them and will send survivors from them to the nations: Tarshish, Put, Lud, Meshech, Rosh, Tubal, and Javan, to the distant coastlands that have neither heard My fame nor seen My glory. And they will declare My glory among the nations" (Isaiah 66:18-19).

The earlier idea of something visual in the revelation of "My glory" may explain why the nations "see" rather than "know" (the usual term), since they behold something tangible in the Lord's glorious demonstration of Gog's defeat and Israel's deliverance. Verses 23-24 repeat the historical review of Israel's past sins and God's judgment as stated in 36:17-22, but with the added declaration in both verses that God "hid His face from them." This reversal is the subject of verses 25-29 which describe the national regathering and restoration of Israel and confirm the changed conditions between God and Israel with the declaration, "I will not hide My face from them any longer" (verse 29). The reason for this is because Israel has now entered the New Covenant, identified by the words, "I have poured out My Spirit on the house of Israel" (verse 29). This relates to both Israel's national repentance (Zechariah 12:10–13:1) and its new relationship with God in the land of Israel (Ezekiel 36:26-27; cf. Jeremiah 31:33-34).

THE MILLENNIAL REIGN
Ezekiel 40–48

EZEKIEL 40–48 REPRESENTS the climax of Ezekiel's prophecy and must be interpreted in light of its purpose to produce in Israel a confident trust in the sovereignty of their God to bring about the restoration promised in chapters 33–39. A regathered, redeemed, restored, and reunited Israel (chapters 33–37:23) is established in the millennial kingdom under a New Covenant (37:24-28) and forever delivered from any further threat of aggression or loss of its promised rest in the land (chapters 38–39). The time of this fulfillment must be the millennial kingdom, since these chapters elaborate on concepts previously presented which have their fulfillment in the *eschatological age*. Even though Ezekiel 40–48 lacks some of eschatological language associated with an eschatological context ("on that day," "in the latter days"), these phrases have already been used in chapters 34–37 and in the immediately preceding chapters (38–39). Moreover, the literary linkage of chapters 40–48 with other prophetic texts that concern the same theme establishes an eschatological setting. And finally, a literal fulfillment as described by Ezekiel—with immensely enlarged boundaries for the land, Jerusalem, and the temple (Ezekiel 44:1-31; 47:1-23; 48:1-35), the return of the glory of God (Ezekiel 43:1-12), and the unprecedented change from the laws of the past (for example, Ezekiel 43:17)—would require that the time of fulfillment be eschatological.

THE MESSIANIC TEMPLE OF THE MILLENNIAL KINGDOM
Ezekiel 40–43

A description of the eschatological temple would have been expected after its introduction in the restoration context of 37:26-28, as would an explanation of how God's glory (the Shekinah), which according to chapters 10–11 would depart, would be returned to the future sanctuary. In particular, 37:27-28 had stated the eschatological temple's presence in the midst of Israel would "sanctify" it before the nations. How was this to take place, and what differences could be anticipated from the form of worship in earlier temples? Answers are found in a description of the temple's design in chapters 40–42, the account of the return of the Shekinah in chapter 43:1-7, and the prophecy about the fulfillment of Israel's priestly function of bringing the nations together to worship under the New Covenant in chapters 44–46. Chapters 47–48 appropriately conclude this cultic preview of the millennial temple and worship system by describing the geographical axis of worship, the millennial Jerusalem, created for a priestly nation with the Lord at its center (48:35).

Commentators of every school of prophetic interpretation are divided in their understanding of Ezekiel's vision of the temple as given in chapters 40–48. In these concluding chapters of the prophecy, Ezekiel presents God's instructions for the construction of a new temple to be built as part of the promise of Israel's divine restoration. The concern of the exiles, as exemplified by Daniel's prayer, was for a literal rebuilding of both the city of Jerusalem and its temple (Daniel 9:3-19). Ezekiel's prophecy of the temple, delivered to these exiles, should be interpreted in light of this literal concern. It's key to recognize that the second temple, constructed by the Jewish remnant that returned from the exile (538–515 B.C.), did not implement Ezekiel's detailed plan. Futurists, therefore, interpret the literal fulfillment of this prophecy eschatologically, with the erection of this restoration temple taking place during the earthly millennial kingdom. This text is especially crucial to futurism because if literal interpretation fails with respect to this prophecy, then there is no reason to insist on a literal interpretation of any Old Testament prophecy, including messianic prophecy, which is an inseparable part of the restoration prophecies.

Despite this caution, most critical scholars and conservative nonfuturists (historicists, preterists, idealists), based on their contention that prophetic visions employ apocalyptic language that uses hyperbole (exaggerated speech) to convey idealistic or symbolic rather than literal concepts, see Ezekiel's prophecy as being fulfilled symbolically. Nonfuturists explain that the reason the builders of the second temple did not follow Ezekiel's plans for the temple was because the Jewish audience understood apocalyptic language as symbolic rather than literal.

Those who interpret Ezekiel 40–48 *symbolically* are divided on what this symbolism was intended to portray. Some believe it was meant to preserve the memory of the first temple through an idealistic remembrance, others say it idealistically describes the second temple, which was constructed after the exile (538–515 B.C.), while still others see it illustrating a spiritual ideal (God's dwelling in holiness in the midst of His people) or a spiritual reality (such as heaven, the eternal state, or the church). It is necessary to evaluate the symbolic school's interpretive theories of this pivotal text and compare them with the literal school's interpretation to determine whether the intended fulfillment is to be understood as timeless (idealistic), historical (fulfilled with the first or second temples), or future (referring to the millennial temple).

First, Ezekiel states that this vision was communicated during the captivity, not after the return (Ezekiel 40:1-2). If it was given during the exile to help unite the Israelites through a common memory of the past and assure them of God's presence, it apparently failed in its purpose. The Israelites were divided in their reaction to the construction of the second temple. The argument that God's message was only received but not delivered by the prophet in the exile cannot be sustained in view of Ezekiel 11:25, which states, "Then I told the exiles all the things that the Lord had shown me." Although this applies to the judgment section of the book, is it reasonable to assume the prophet would share only the bad news (the destruction of the first temple) and not the good news (the prophetic promise of a restored temple)?

It is clear, however, that Ezekiel did deliver his prophetic vision to the exilic community, for God commanded him to describe the plan of the temple to a still unrepentant "house of Israel" who had "defiled My holy name by their abominations" (Ezekiel 43:8). In fact, the purpose for Ezekiel's revelation of the plans for the temple was so "they may be ashamed of their iniquities" (Ezekiel 43:10-11). This is in harmony with Ezekiel's calling to deliver his message to "the sons of Israel, to a rebellious people who have rebelled against Me" (Ezekiel 2:3-4). By contrast, those who had returned to Judah to rebuild the temple displayed repentance (Ezra 1:5; Haggai 1:12; Zechariah 1:6; cf. 2 Chronicles 6:38) and therefore could not have been the original recipients of Ezekiel's message.

Second, Ezekiel did not need to give a description of the first temple, for such a description already existed in the books of Kings and Chronicles (1 Kings 5–8; 2 Chronicles 2–7). Moreover, Ezekiel's description of the temple and its services varies radically from the description of the construction of Solomon's temple. These factors argue strongly that Ezekiel's vision could not have had the first temple in view, for it was constructed according to Mosaic legislation (2 Kings 6:12; 8:56-58; 2 Chronicles 2:4; 6:16; 8:12-13).

One interpretation proposes that Ezekiel's temple is symbolic of a spiritual ideal. No consensus exists among proponents as to what these symbols signify; consequently, Ezekiel's vision has been said to represent variously the returned Israelite nation, Jesus, the church, the believing community, heaven, and the new heavens and the new earth.

Among Reformed nonfuturists the most common symbolic interpretation is that of Christ as the spiritual temple. Those who hold this view take the statement in John 2:21 concerning "the temple of His body" as teaching that the resurrected Christ would replace the physical Temple in Jerusalem.

Similarly, the view that Ezekiel's temple symbolizes the church on earth or in heaven is based on New Testament texts that speak of the church or Christians as a spiritual temple (1 Corinthians 3:16-17; 6:19; 2 Corinthians 6:16-18; Ephesians 2:21-22). Again, this analogy is said to indicate that the spiritual organism of the church replaced the material edifice of the temple as the site of the indwelling presence of God (the Holy Spirit). In particular, the interpretation of the temple as figurative of the righteous in heaven or the eternal state is based on a number of correspondences (proponents would say "parallels") between Ezekiel

40–48 and Revelation 21–22. Both accounts are visionary and deal with Jerusalem; therefore, these proponents read the new Jerusalem of Revelation back into Ezekiel's text.

Unless one has been predisposed to see the church in the Old Testament through a presupposed theological system and to view ritual language as spiritually anticipating a "New [spiritual] Israel," *nothing* in Ezekiel's prophecy corresponds to the New Testament church. As mentioned earlier, Ezekiel 40–48 offers no textual clues that it is symbolic. The entire section is devoid of the kind of unrealistic features that would indicate figurative use, a fact that contrasts dramatically with Ezekiel's prolific use of symbols in the early chapters of his book. The lack of interpretive clues in these chapters results in the many details in the text being assigned arbitrary meanings or ignored as irrelevant or meaningless by the symbolic school. Yet this result is the opposite of what the prophet himself desired: "Then I said, 'Ah Lord GOD! They are saying of me, "Is he not just speaking parables?"'" (Ezekiel 20:49). Ezekiel's concern was that people did not understand the literal interpretation of his symbolic acts (which demanded literal application), but only understood them as symbols (which would result in inaction and so spell their doom).

THE PROMISE OF A LITERAL ESCHATOLOGICAL TEMPLE

Given these objections against a symbolic interpretation, the only remaining option is to take Ezekiel 40–48 literally and to apply it to the future restoration of national Israel during the millennial kingdom. A number of arguments support the literal and eschatological interpretation of this section.

1. *The literary unity of the book requires that a literal temple be understood throughout its chapters.* Chapters 40–48 form an inseparable literary conclusion to the book. Although these chapters constitute a new vision in the prophecy, they are linked with chapters 1–39 because they repeat earlier-stated themes in a more detailed fashion. The beginnings of

chapters 1 and 40 are linked by a number of similar features. For example, Ezekiel's vision of the presence of God in Babylon (Ezekiel 1:1; cf. 8:1) finds its complement and completion in the vision in the land of Israel (Ezekiel 40:2). In like manner, the problem created by the departure of God's presence in chapters 8–11 finds its resolution with its return in this section (see Ezekiel 43:1-7). In fact, the concern for the presence of God could be argued as the uniting theme of the entire text of Ezekiel. Without chapters 40–48 there is no answer that reveals the outcome for Israel, no resolution to Israel's history of sacred scandal, and no grand finale to the divine drama centered from Sinai on the chosen nation.

2. *The context of the temple's restoration requires a literal interpretation.* These chapters open with a contextual note concerning the specific date of Ezekiel's vision: "the tenth of the month [of Tishri]" (Ezekiel 40:1). The Jewish sages saw this setting as an eschatological context, since the tenth of Tishri is reckoned as a jubilee year (Hebrew, *yovel*). The date of Ezekiel's vision was determined to be the first Day of Atonement (Hebrew, *Yom Kippur*) of the jubilee year. Together, this date prefigured Israel's day of redemption in both its physical (land) and spiritual aspects, as Rabbi Joseph Breuer notes:

> On that day, which summoned the subjugated and estranged among God's people to accept freedom and called upon all the sons of Israel to return to their God, on that day it was given to the Prophet to behold a vision of the rebuilt, eternal Sanctuary of the future and to receive the basic instructions for the establishment of the State of God that would endure forever (*The Book of Yechezkel*, p. 353).

Therefore, from the very first verse, the rabbis considered the context both literal and eschatological.

3. *The description of the temple indicates that it is to be a literal construction.* When a reader surveys Ezekiel's words, which include precise measurements; specific details about the design of the temple's courts, pillars, galleries, rooms, chambers, doors, ornamentation, and vessels; and careful instructions concerning the priestly service; the impression is that an actual temple is in view. Despite this obvious reading, Daniel Block (*Ezekiel: Chapters 25–48*, vol. 2, p. 505), one of the leading commentators on the book of Ezekiel, has contended that "the description of the temple is not presented as a blueprint for some future building to be constructed with human hands…nowhere is anyone commanded to build it." Yet Ezekiel 43:10-11 clearly states, "As for you, son of man [Ezekiel], describe the Temple to the house of Israel…and let them measure the plan…*and do them*" (emphasis added). These verses declare that those Jews who are alive at the time of the final restoration (when the prophecy will be fulfilled) are to build the temple according to Ezekiel's instructions. Later in this context (43:13-27), when the same kind of architectural measurements as given for the temple are given for the altar, it is stated that "these are the statutes for the altar on the day it is *built…*" (verse 18, emphasis added). Literary consistency (as well as logic) demands that if the altar of the temple is to be built, then so must the temple itself.

This deduction is substantiated by the wording of the command in Ezekiel 43:11, which was given to the "house of Israel." The words "observe its whole design and all its statutes, and do them" is parallel in expression to God's original command to build a sanctuary (Exodus 25:8-9). If Israel at the beginning of its national history interpreted in a literal sense God's instructions to build the tabernacle and carry out the priestly service, why would Israel not interpret the restatement in Ezekiel as literal? When a further comparison is made between the details for the construction of the temple, buildings, and the sacrificial system as given in Ezekiel and those recorded elsewhere for the construction of the tabernacle and first temple and their service in Kings and Chronicles, there is no reason to take them as less literal or historical. Would the house of

Israel be expected to interpret the instructions in any manner other than that which was historically consistent with God's previous revelation—especially in the absence of any textual guidelines for an alternate (symbolic) interpretation?

There is a suitable test that can be applied to this question. If Ezekiel 40–48 is to be interpreted literally and the temple plans are intended to function as blueprints, then it should be possible to construct an actual model based on those plans. Conversely, if the plans are merely symbolic and God never expected His people to actually build the edifice, then no such construction should be possible. The fact is, miniature-scale, three-dimensional models of Ezekiel's temple have been successfully built (see diagram on p. 202). Is it conceivable that Ezekiel would have communicated such practical instructions if God meant for them to be taken only spiritually or symbolically? Although commentators have long found symbolical and spiritual significance in the many details of the tabernacle and temple's construction and ceremonies, no such symbolism can be found in the text of Ezekiel 40–48.

4. *The eschatological interpretation of Ezekiel 40–48 is in harmony with other Old Testament prophetic passages.* As a restoration text, Ezekiel 40–48 should exhibit traits familiar to and consonant with other such texts in the prophetic corpus. For example, in examining the text that commands the house of Israel to build the temple (Ezekiel 43:10-11), we find that the time for this is stated to be after "they are ashamed of all that they have done." The nature of this national "shame" as spiritual repentance was already defined in Ezekiel 36:22-38 as part of the regenerative work of the Spirit (verse 33). The occasion of this national repentance accords with numerous references in the prophets (Isaiah 55:3-5; 66:7-9; Jeremiah 31:34; Hosea 3:4-5; Zechariah 12:10–13:2), as well as by Jesus (Matthew 24:30-31; Mark 13:26-27), Luke (Acts 3:19-21), and Paul (Romans 11:25-30).

The aforementioned Old Testament passages, in their prophetic contexts, reflect an ultimate hope for the nation, which in continuity with the New Testament writers, must be projected into an eschatological kingdom. This is especially so with respect to the description of Ezekiel's temple when compared with similar accounts of a future temple, a raised Temple Mount, and the transformed conditions enjoyed by those who worship at the temple, most of which contain eschatological time markers (Isaiah 2:2-4; 56:6-7; 60:10-22; Jeremiah 3:16-17; 31:27-40; 33:14-18; Joel 3:18-21; Micah 4:1-8; Haggai 2:7-9; Zechariah 6:12-15; 14:16,20-21). As a point of comparison we may consider the statements in Ezekiel 40–46 that speak of the sacrificial system and especially of making atonement for Israel through blood sacrifices. The symbolic school argues that interpreting Ezekiel 40–48 literally means that one must accept a future reinstatement of the sacrificial system, which they believe has been completely fulfilled by the sacrifice of Christ (Hebrews 9–10). While this theological conclusion can be debated, the immediate problem for those who take this position is that a number of other prophets also envisioned both a restored temple and sacrifices in the eschatological future:

Prophecies of a Millennial Temple	Prophecies of Millennial Sacrifices
Isaiah 2:3	Isaiah 56:6-7
Isaiah 60:13	Isaiah 60:7
Daniel 9:24	Isaiah 66:18-23
Joel 3:18	Jeremiah 33:18
Haggai 2:7,9	Zechariah 14:16-21
	Malachi 3:3-4

EZEKIEL'S TEMPLE A MILLENNIAL TEMPLE

Interpreters of the symbolic school charge that the instructions for the building of the temple and the laws that regulated its maintenance were prescribed under the Mosaic Covenant. Thus a future rebuilding of the temple would constitute a return to the Old Covenant, which has been superseded by the New Covenant inaugurated by the blood of Christ (Luke 22:20; Hebrews 8:8-13; 9:15; 12:24). This view holds that anything under the Mosaic Covenant, and especially the temple with its sacrificial system, was but a type and shadow intended to pass away and be replaced by Christ as the new and true temple.

However, Ezekiel's temple could not have been constructed at any period when the Mosaic law was in effect. The reason for this is that the instructions concerning the temple, its priesthood, and its services contradict the Mosaic law in numerous places. For example, Leviticus 21:7 forbids the high priest to take a widow or divorcée as a wife, whereas Ezekiel 44:22 extends this prohibition to *all* priests. In addition, the design of Ezekiel's temple differs from that of the first and second temples, and also conflicts with the Mosaic law in certain places. Such differences include unprecedented divergences in structure (larger dimensions), style, and ceremony, a river that flows eastward out of the temple to refresh the arid areas of the Arabah and the Dead Sea (Ezekiel 47:1-12), and instructions for the temple and its service.

Ezekiel's instruction to make the altar of burnt offering with steps (Ezekiel 43:17) violates a specific commandment in the Mosaic ceremonial legislation against such a construction (Exodus 20:26). Additional departures from the Mosaic law that commentators have noted include the absence of the Ark of the Covenant in the Holy of Holies, no mention of the table for the shewbread or lampstand in the outer Holy Place, no anointing oil within the temple or its court, and the absence of the high priesthood. Certainly Ezekiel, trained in the priesthood all his life, would have understood these violations. In fact, it appears he did understand this distinction as revealed in his words that the new temple is to be built according to "the law of the house" (Ezekiel 43:12); apparently an independent (new) law belonging to the New Covenant rather than

the old. There can be no other conclusion, and this was certainly the conclusion drawn by the Jewish sages—that Ezekiel's temple was to be built in the messianic age.

A *key misunderstanding* by those in the symbolic school is their belief that the New Covenant was made exclusively with the church (and therefore the church must replace Israel in fulfilling this covenant). On the contrary, the New Covenant was made exclusively with Israel, but its application is inclusive of the Gentiles. This is seen by the universal blessings of the New Covenant that are to be mediated by Israel to the nations, especially with respect to the temple (Isaiah 2:2-4; 11:9; 19:23-25; 49:6; 56:6-7; Micah 4:1-3; Habakkuk 2:14). What's more, Jesus is the mediator of this New Covenant for both Jews and Gentiles—that is, the church (Hebrews 9:15; 12:24).

A *second misunderstanding* is that the New Covenant is a purely spiritual covenant with no physical elements (such as a return to the land), laws, or ritual requirements such as appeared under the Old Covenant. However, just as in the church age many of the laws (or principles) of the Mosaic Covenant are repeated (such as nine of the Ten Commandments), there are many laws that were first given in the Mosaic Covenant repeated in the New Covenant. This is because they are functionally necessary for the same people (the people of Israel) in the same land (the land of Israel) in a theocratic kingdom (promised to Israel). Indeed, the promise of a return to the land of the fathers, the land of Israel, is one of the features of the New Covenant (Jeremiah 31:27-28; 32:37-41; Ezekiel 37:25-26).

Dispensationalism offers the best solution to the problem of unfulfilled prophecy by its futurist interpretation. Only a believing generation can adopt such a method of interpretation since a fulfillment in the future requires present faith in God to perform His promise. Leslie Allen (*Ezekiel 20–48*, vol. 29, p. 214), however, rejects the dispensational solution outright, declaring: "To resort to dispensationalism and postpone them to a literal fulfillment in a yet future time strikes the author as a desperate expedient that sincerely attempts to preserve belief in an inerrant prophecy." However, if the dispensational approach preserves prophetic integrity by upholding the requisite nature of prophecy as actual historical fulfillment, why should this be rejected as "desperation"? To Ezekiel's original audience, his early prophecies concerning the destruction of Jerusalem and the temple must have appeared as unbelievable as his latter prophecies of restoration appear today to a modern audience. Nevertheless those early prophecies were actually fulfilled for Ezekiel's generation and therefore cannot be denied by our generation. Why, then, shouldn't we believe that God can do in the future what He did in the past?

EZEKIEL'S VISION OF THE NEW TEMPLE
Ezekiel 40:1-4

In 40:1-4, Ezekiel receives a new prophetic vision (dated specifically to March-April 573 B.C.), some 13 years after the fulfillment of his earlier prophecies of God's judgment against Judah. For this revelation the prophet is again returned to Jerusalem (verse 1). However, the city and temple that he is now shown are not ruined, but restored. Ezekiel's vantage point affords him an initial view of the entire temple-city of the millennial age (verse 2), followed by an in-depth description from his angelic interpreter of its central feature, the temple (verse 3). The prophet is commanded to observe the structure he will be shown and to "declare to the house of Israel all that you see" (verse 4). This implies that what he was shown was not merely a symbol without substance, a fact made more explicit in 43:11, where the prophet's declarations about the structure's design and statutes are given so that the people may actually "observe its whole design and all its statutes and do them."

Some seek to interpret Ezekiel 40–48 in light of Revelation 21:9–22:5 because John says his angelic interpreter "carried me away in the Spirit to a mountain great and high, and showed me the holy city Jerusalem, coming down out of heaven from God" (21:10). They believe this proves that Ezekiel and John both saw the heavenly Jerusalem, which they assume to be symbolic. Alternately, some attempt to make the temple in Revelation 11:1 (which is clearly earthly because of the prediction it will be trampled by the nations—11:2) symbolic based on Ezekiel 40:3 because in both texts the angelic escorts have a measuring rod, and because Ezekiel's temple is assumed not to be literal. However, Ezekiel, in his vision, is taken to a literal earthly place—the land of Israel—and to a city situated on the same mountain on which he was standing. The city of John's vision was not earthly but came from heaven, and never is stated to be on earth. Furthermore, Ezekiel's angelic escort does the measuring, and the physical measurements are given in precise and reproducible detail. John's angelic escort bids him to do the measuring and no details are given, since John's measurements include the temple's "worshippers," indicating that spiritual rather than physical measurement is intended. A complete comparison of these two texts reveals numerous other differences that would require that Ezekiel and John were viewing two distinctly different structures.

DESCRIPTION OF THE TEMPLE AND ITS PRECINCTS
Ezekiel 40:5–43:27

In 40:5, Ezekiel receives the first of 318 precise measurements for the temple's design, and these measurements will continue for the next two chapters. They employ some 37 specific architectural terms that have no discernable connotation other than their normal and natural sense. The design of the temple is discussed in eight sections, and in every section, the prophet is led by his angelic escort and observes and records the temple's essential features and functions as interpreted by the divine messenger. Although the details seem tedious and repetitious, they are of fundamental importance to those who have been committed with the task of building this future temple and performing its sacred service (43:10-11). For Christians, the details provide a glimpse into the mechanics of a regulated and

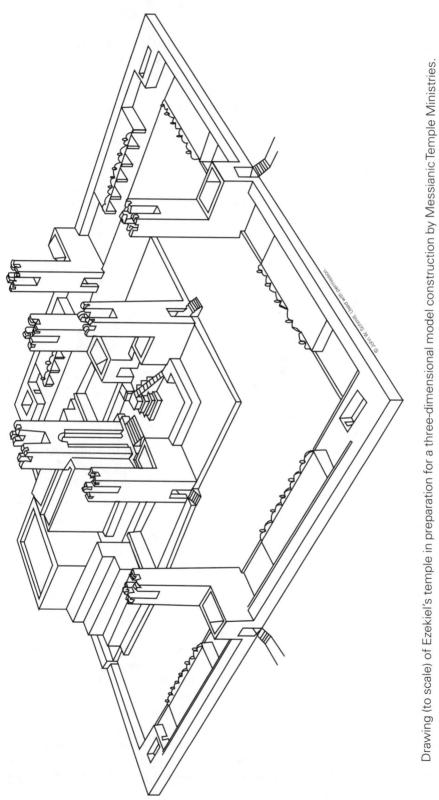

Drawing (to scale) of Ezekiel's temple in preparation for a three-dimensional model construction by Messianic Temple Ministries.

Gate Systems for All Gates
of the Outer Court

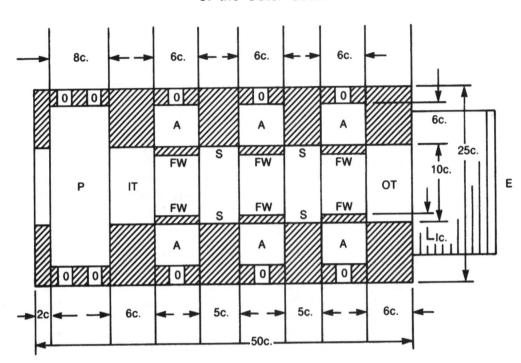

Key:

FW Wall (barriers, borders, space) (Ezek 40:12a)
A   Alcoves (side rooms, guard rooms) (Ezek 40:7a, 10a, 12b)
P   Portico (porch, vestibule) (Ezek 40:7c, 8–9, 14)
S   Walls separating alcoves (Ezek 40:7b, 10b)
OT Outer threshold of the gate (Ezek 40:6, 11)
IT Inner threshold of the porch (Ezek 40:7c)
O   Windows (parapet openings) (Ezek 40:16)
E   Steps (Ezek 40:6b, 22b, 26a)

Overall height, length, and width of the gate (Ezek 40:13–15) orderly sacred society that will characterize the millennial kingdom.

In the first section (40:5-27) the prophet saw the *outer court,* which was measured with a rod of six cubits. Each cubit was actually a cubit and a handbreadth in length (verse 5). This probably came very close to the long cubit (also Egyptian or royal cubit), which was approximately 21 inches (52.3 cm), making the rod about 10.5 feet, the height of the wall around the temple (verse 5). Next Ezekiel entered and measured the eastern gate (verse 6), one of three that led into the inner court. The eastward orientation of this gate is in continuity with the orientation of the tabernacle and the two previous temples, as well as the millennial temple (47:1), making this entrance gate the most prominent one and therefore worthy of a detailed description. Verses 7-16 go on to provide measurements for the gate's steps, threshold, guardrooms, alcoves, porches, windows, and ornamentation. Then Ezekiel moved into the outer court (verses 17-19), which is comprised of 30 chambers arranged alongside the pavement covering this area. The function for these rooms is not given, but if they mirror the use of such structures in the earlier temples (cf. Jeremiah 35:2), they may serve those who come to worship at the temple (Zechariah 14:16-17). Finally, the prophet went to the other two gates of the outer court—the northern gate (verses 20-23) and the southern gate (verses 24-27)—both of which matched the dimensions of the eastern gate.

In the second section (40:28-47) Ezekiel was led into the *inner court,* which also has three gates. The measurement between the gates of the inner and outer courts was stated in verses 23 and 27 to be 100 cubits (175 feet), and here the gates of the inner court are measured and described in detail (verses 29-37). With the description of the chambers and porches of the gates (verses 38-43) we are introduced for the first time to the fact that animal sacrifices will be offered in the millennial temple. Three types of prescribed offerings are mentioned in verse 39: "burnt offering," "sin offering," and "guilt offering." Verse 39 also mentions slaughtering

tables and hooks to support the animals while they are ritually butchered. It may seem surprising to Christian readers that the prophet gave no explanation for the restitution of the sacrificial service in a temple built after Christ has completed His atoning work. However, the incidental way in which Ezekiel mentions the sacrifices and offerings should instruct us that he and his readers accepted this reality as part of the normal worship service for the temple and expected no change in this requirement in the future, even under the New Covenant (see the discussion later at 43:12–46:24).

In the third section (40:47–41:26) the design of the *temple itself* is revealed. Ezekiel is given a preliminary view (verse 47) of the temple complex along with a first glimpse of the altar (described in more detail in 43:12-27). The primary information in this verse concerns matters of shape, size, and position, and Ezekiel reports two important details in this regard that differentiate this temple from the second temple. The first is that the shape of this temple court was square (verse 47). The shape of the platform of the first temple was also square, but in the second temple this court was changed to the shape of a rectangle as a result of Hasmonean and Herodian additions to the southern and northern sides. In the millennial temple the shape will be restored to the original design given to King David by divine revelation (1 Chronicles 28:11-12,19; cf. Exodus 25:8-9,40). The second distinction is the placement of the altar in the temple (verse 47). According to the available sources for the layout of the second temple, the altar (known as the great altar or brazen altar), while located in front of the temple, was positioned off-center to the south. But in Ezekiel's description, the altar is said to be "in front of" (Hebrew, *liphne*) the temple, implying a *direct* center alignment. That the second temple was not constructed according to Ezekiel's plan shows that Ezekiel's temple describes a yet future edifice.

The fourth section (42:1-14) contains a description of the *chambers of the outer court* (the Septuagint misreads the Hebrew *hachisona* as "inner") (verses 1-12) followed by the angelic escort's interpretation of their function (verses 13-14). The structure of the three-storied buildings (verse 3) is complex, with the roof of each at a different level, like terraces with the upper balconies set back progressively farther than those beneath them (verses 5-6). The chambers are accessed by a walkway (verse 4) that runs the entire length of the chambers (verse 9) and are separated from the outer court by a wall (verse 7) that is probably designed to protect the sanctity of the priests from onlookers while they prepared for their duties. In addition, we read of chambers located on the south that are identical to the ones to the north (verses 10-12). In verses 13-14 is an explanation of the function of these southern and northern chambers. They are set apart ("holy") for the highest order of priests. These priests serve in the inner sanctuary, and their responsibilities include the eating of their prescribed portion of certain offerings (verse 13, cf. Leviticus 2:3,10; 6:16,26-30; 7:7-10). These rooms also serve as a place where three "most holy" offerings ("grain offering," "sin offering," and "guilt offering") are stored (verse 13). The rooms are also for storing the priestly garments that must be donned and then removed and returned to the sacred chamber each time a priest completes his appointed time of service (verse 14). The functions of eating the sacred meals and storing the sacred garments will be discussed more later (44:19; 46:20).

In the fifth section (42:15-20) Ezekiel, having completed the survey of the *inside of the temple,* is taken to the outer wall of the temple complex to record the external measurements of the entire structure. The outer dimensions of the square temple complex are 500 cubits (850 feet) on each side if the text follows the *Qere* ("what is read"). If the measurement is in "reeds" following the *Kethiv* ("what is written"), then the Temple complex is about one mile on each side (some 30 times greater than its former size). However, the *Qere* reading of "cubits" has the greater support of the ancient versions (for example, the Septuagint) and is to be preferred. These measurements conform roughly to the squared area

of the present-day Temple Mount platform (less the southern and northern additions), indicating that these original dimensions have been maintained as the "sacred proportions" since the original construction of the temple in 960 B.C. Therefore the millennial temple, while not occupying the exact same *place* as the former temples, still occupies the exact same *space,* thereby maintaining a theological continuity between the different temples as the residence of the Shekinah.

In the sixth section (43:1-9) the prophet is led to the *eastern gate* of the temple (verse 1) to witness one of the most dramatic events recorded in this prophecy: the return of the Shekinah (the "divine presence" or "glory of God") to the temple. Earlier, Ezekiel had made the exilic community aware that the Shekinah, which had been in residence at the temple for 374 years, had departed before the Babylonian destruction (Ezekiel 10–11). After the temple was rebuilt, the Shekinah did not return to fill the Holy of Holies as it had the first temple (1 Kings 8:12-13), and before this, the tabernacle (Exodus 40:34-35). The traditional Jewish sources were explicit about this point as the Mishnah tractate *Yoma* explains: "These are the five things that were in the First Temple and not in the Second Temple: the Ark with the covering and angelic figures, the heavenly fire, the Divine Presence (the Shekinah), Divine Inspiration, and the Urim and the Thummim" (21b; 52b; cf. Jerusalem Talmud, *Makkot* 2:6). For this reason the sages did not believe that the restoration could have occurred with the second temple, and they looked beyond it to the eschatological period (for example, *Tosefta Yom Tov*).

Ezekiel announces the *fulfillment* of this long-awaited Jewish hope with the words "and behold, the glory of the God of Israel was coming from the way of the east" (verse 2). Ezekiel's emphasis on "the way of the east" as the direction from which the Shekinah returns is based on the precise path of previous departure. In verses 2-5 is a point-by-point description of the return that matches the order of the abandonment described in Ezekiel 10–11. The

Temple Complex

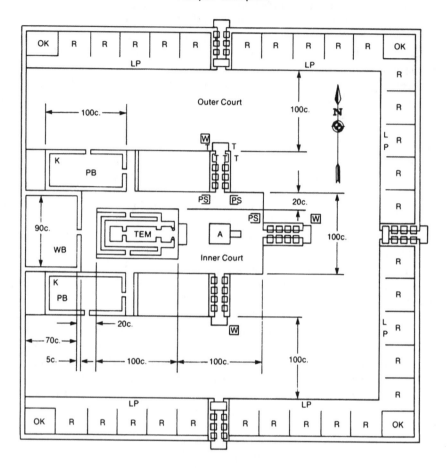

Key:

A	Altar (Ezek 40:47b)
WB	Building of the separation yard (Ezek 41:12, 13b, 15)
K	Kitchen for priests to boil sacrifices (Ezek 46:19–20)
OK	Kitchens for priests to boil people's sacrifices (Ezek 46:21–24)
LP	Pavement strip (Ezek 40:17–18)
PB	Priests' chambers (Ezek 42:1–14)
R	Rooms in outer court for storage or priests' quarters (Ezek 40:17)
PS	Rooms for singers (priests) (Ezek 40:44–46)
T	Tables for slaughter of sacrifices (two at each point) (Ezek 40:39–43)
TEM	Temple proper (Ezek 40:48–41:11, 13a, 14, 16, 23–26)
W	Rooms for washing offerings (Ezek 40:38)
	Inner court (Ezek 40:44–47a)
	Outer court (Ezek 40:17–19, 23, 27, 39–43)
	Width from outer gates to inner gates (Ezek 40:19, 23, 27)

departure of the Shekinah had started with a movement from its place within the Holy of Holies to the inner court (10:4), then from the inner court to the eastern gate (10:19), and then disappearing in the east over the Mount of Olives (11:22-23). The return of the Shekinah is a reversal of this order, beginning in the east (verse 2) and first appearing at the crest of the Mount of Olives, then moving to the eastern gate (verse 4), where Ezekiel was situated (verse 1), and finally to the inner court of the temple (verse 5) and back into the Holy of Holies (verse 7).

In the seventh section (43:10-11) Ezekiel is told to take the record of *everything* that had been revealed to him concerning the temple and describe it to "the house of Israel" (verse 10). Indeed, the plan for the building of the temple and the establishment of its priestly service has been preserved in the book of Ezekiel to this day. Moreover, this account should be persuasive and motivate Israel to obedient performance. This persuasion should make Israel "ashamed of their iniquities" (its past sins as a nation) with the result that the people repent (verse 10). Once this repentance has occurred, Israel will be permitted to build the millennial temple described by Ezekiel.

The eighth section (43:12-27) contains instructions for the ritual regulations that will enable Israel to perform the sacrificial service as a means of worship at the millennial temple. As an introduction to this section and that which follows through 46:24, verse 12 announces that the revelation about to be given, as well as the measurements already recorded, are part of the sacred "instructions" (Hebrew, *torah*) of the temple. Verses 13-27 describe the measurements (verses 13-17) and consecration (verses 18-27) of the altar of burnt offering. If the precedent of the rebuilding of the second temple is followed, the construction of the altar precedes the construction of the temple (Ezra 3:2-6), since once a functioning sacrificial service is begun, the temple may already be said to exist, even if its foundation has not yet been laid.

In Ezekiel 43:13-17 the measurements for the altar seem comparable to those of previous temples (except for the use of the long cubit, verse 13), until the word "steps" appears (verse 17). To Jews schooled in Mosaic legislation this would have been a startling revelation, for Exodus 20:26 commands, "You shall not go up by steps to My altar...." The Mosaic prohibition against building steps to the altar were part of the purification laws designed to keep Israel from imitating the pagan practices of the surrounding nations. The reference to "steps" implies a different order of events in the millennial kingdom. The best possible option is for a literal fulfillment of these details, namely, an eschatological fulfillment under the New Covenant. In the millennium the nations will also be regenerate and follow the New Covenant law of the Lord as mediated through Israel (Isaiah 2:2-3; 66:18-19; cf. Zechariah 8:22-23). Therefore, under the New Covenant, there will no longer be any reason to prohibit the building of steps to the altar. This sufficiently addresses Ezekiel's deviations from the Mosaic law in relation to the temple and its service.

In Ezekiel 43:18 the "Lord GOD" speaks directly to Ezekiel for the first time in chapters 40–48. The direct address concerns the ordinances (Hebrew, *chuqqot*) for the altar "on the day it is built" (at the beginning of the millennial kingdom following the 75 days of preparatory cleansing—Daniel 12:12). These ordinances relate to the sacrificial offerings to be made on the altar, with the requirement for only Zadokite priests to officiate over the sacrificial offerings (Ezekiel 43:19). They also include the proper consecration (decontamination) of the altar so it will be ritually acceptable for the sacred service (verses 20-27). Since Ezekiel is commanded by God to personally ensure these proceedings "on the day the altar is built," a *literal fulfillment* would require that Ezekiel be present at that time. This does not present a problem for dispensational interpreters because they understand that Old Testament saints such as Ezekiel will be part of the first resurrection at the beginning of the

Altar of Sacrifice

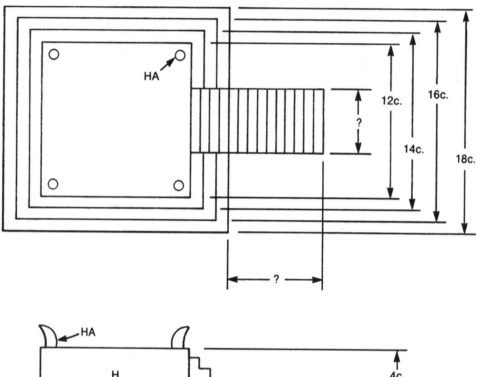

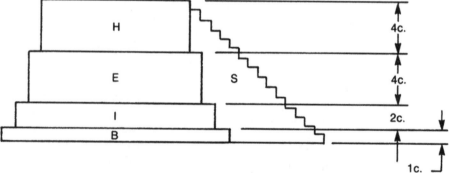

Key:

H	Altar hearth (Ezek 43:15–16)
E	Enclosure (Ezek 43:14, 17)
I	Interior (Ezek 43:14, 17)
B	Bottom (Ezek 43:13)
HA	Horns of the altar (Ezek 43:20)
S	Steps (Ezek 43:17b; cf. Ezek 40:47b)

millennium (some say the rapture) to dwell in the messianic kingdom (Daniel 12:2).

THE RESTORATION OF THE TEMPLE'S SERVICE OF WORSHIP
Ezekiel 44–46

THE SECTION RELATING TO the design of the altar of burnt offering (43:12-27) introduced the *reinstitution of the sacrificial service*. This is detailed in the subsequent chapters (44–46) with regulations regarding the Levitical priests and the various sacrifices to be offered for Israel's atonement. Although detailed instructions concerning the institution of the sacrificial system appear for the first time in these chapters, frequent references to the practice have been made since the beginning of the prophecy (40:38-43,46-47; 41:22; 42:13-14). Moreover, these references are not incidental, but *intrinsic* to the entire presentation of Ezekiel's vision in chapters 40–48. For example, every chapter but one (47) contains a statement concerning the sacrificial system. These references include "new moons and Sabbaths…all the appointed feasts" (Ezekiel 44:24; 45:17; 46:3,11-12), "daily offerings" (Ezekiel 46:13-14), "burnt offerings, grain offerings, and the libations" (Ezekiel 45:17; 46:2,4,11-15), "blood sacrifices" (Ezekiel 43:20), an "altar" for burnt offering (Ezekiel 40:47; 43:13-27), an "altar" for incense offering (Ezekiel 41:22), "boiling places" to "boil the sacrifices of the people" (Ezekiel 46:23-24); a Zadokite priesthood to "offer Me the fat and the blood" (Ezekiel 40:46; 42:13-14; 43:19; 44:15-16; 48:11), and a Levitical priesthood to "slaughter the burnt offering" (Ezekiel 44:10-11; 48:22). Furthermore, the offerings are stated to be for a sin offering (Ezekiel 43:22,25; 44:29) and to make atonement (Ezekiel 43:20; 45:25). Since the sacrifices and sacrificial personnel are so prominent throughout these chapters, the issue of sacrifices cannot be avoided.

This part of Ezekiel's prophecy has been thought to be the greatest obstacle to a dispensational interpretation of Ezekiel. Simply stated, it is believed that if the prophecy is interpreted literally, it would represent a return to the types and shadows of the Old Testament sacrificial system that found its fulfillment in the death of Christ, the Lamb of God. Reformed scholar Edmund P. Clowney ("The Final Temple," p.85) makes this understanding a test of orthodoxy, declaring:

> Jesus Christ is the only Mediator, His blood the final sacrifice. There can be no going back. If there is a way back to the ceremonial law, to the types and shadows of what has now become the bondage of legalism, then Paul labored and ran in vain—more than that, Christ died in vain.

Dispensational authors John Schmitt and Carl Laney (*Messiah's Coming Temple*, p. 181) respond to this charge by asking:

> Is it heretical to believe that a Temple and sacrifices will once again exist?… Ezekiel himself believed it was a reality and the future home of Messiah. Then, it becomes not heresy to believe that a Temple and sacrifices will exist; rather, it is almost a heresy to not believe this, especially because it is a part of God's infallible word. The burden on us is to determine how it fits—not its reality.

Dispensationalists have proposed different solutions to determine this fit. Consistent with literal interpretation, some have viewed Ezekiel's offerings as *memorial sacrifices* (Walvoord, *The Millennial Kingdom*, pp. 312-14), arguing that they will function for the millennial saints in the same way as the Lord's Supper during the church age (1 Corinthians 11:26). Others, such as the editors of *The New Scofield Reference Bible* (p. 888), have adopted the *phenomenological interpretation*, contending that the known terminology and manner of the ceremonial service is being used to describe the unexplainable manner of worship in Ezekiel's eschatological vision.

A third dispensational interpretation, known as the *ceremonial view*, makes a stronger case for the consistent literal interpretation of Ezekiel 40–48 while harmonizing the facts with

New Testament teaching. When the temple was standing, its most central function was to serve as a site for sacrificial worship. Every Jew we read about in the Bible offered sacrifices—from Abraham, the father of the Jewish nation, to Jesus, the founder of Christianity. Even Paul offered sacrifices at the temple after becoming a Christian and an apostle to the Gentiles (Acts 21:22-26; 24:16-18). He also concluded his life with the defense that he had never committed any offense against the temple (Acts 25:8).

There can be no doubt that after the finished work of Christ on the cross, after the resurrection and ascension, that Jesus' closest followers and His apostles made the temple area their sacred center. After the disciples received the Great Commission from Jesus and His blessing at the time of His ascension, they "returned to Jerusalem with great joy, and were continually in the temple praising God" (Luke 24:52-53). It was at the temple, immediately after the Holy Spirit had filled them on the day of Pentecost, that the disciples proclaimed the truth about Jesus' sacrificial death (Acts 2:1-36). The first Christians met "day by day continuing with one mind in the temple…praising God and having favor with all the people" (Acts 2:46-47). And it was on the way to prayer in the temple, at a service associated with the evening sacrifice, that Peter and John performed one of their first public miracles (Acts 3:1-11). How can it be said that those closest to Jesus—who were filled with His Spirit, preaching the gospel of His shed blood, and doing miracles by His power—were completely ignorant that continued participation in the sacrificial system was a "bondage of legalism" that made Christ's death "in vain"?

Finally, it is crucial to note that neither the building of Ezekiel's temple nor a reinstitution of the sacrificial service would constitute a return to the types and shadows of the Mosaic law. Both will have a function in the time of final fulfillment, the messianic age, when the New Covenant regulates the worship of a redeemed people under the direct rule of Christ. With the return of Christ to earth to dwell in glory in the midst of the nation of Israel (Ezekiel 37:26-28; 43:1-7; cf. Isaiah 4:4-6; Jeremiah 3:17; Zechariah 14:9-11,16-21) comes the need for His people to remain ceremonially pure as "a kingdom of priests."

The details concerning the *priestly service* in chapters 44:1–46:24 are arranged in seven sections that deal with the eastern gate (44:1-3), the Shekinah and Israel's sins (44:4-8), the specific duties of the Levitical priesthood (44:9-14), the specific duties of the Zadokite priesthood (44:15-31), the sacred proportions of the temple complex (45:1-8), the specific duties of the prince (45:9–46:18), and the places designated for the boiling of the sacrifices (46:19-24).

The first section (44:1-3) concerns the *eastern gate* and its special status in relation to the temple complex. Once the temple has been constructed at the beginning of the millennium, the Shekinah will return to fill the temple (43:1-7). The path the Shekinah will follow to reenter the temple passes through the eastern gate (43:4; 44:2). Since the restoration conditions of the people and land will prevent future desecration, the Shekinah will never again depart from the temple (43:7-9). To memorialize this fact, the eastern gate, through which the Shekinah would pass if a departure were possible (10:19), will be sealed shut and never reopened (44:2). This follows the Near-Eastern custom of showing special honor to a dignitary by restricting others from using the same gate the dignitary had used (cf. Exodus 19:9-24). Although this gate is never used again throughout the millennium, it will be used by the prince who will sit there to eat a sacrificial meal before the Lord. Yet the prince's access will be through the *porch* of the gate (44:3).

In the second section (44:4-8) Ezekiel relates his personal experience (in this vision) of seeing the Shekinah fill the temple (verse 4). Ezekiel then receives an order from the Lord to record all that had been said concerning the temple and its service (verse 5). Next there follows an admonition from the Lord for the house of Israel, which, in the first division of Ezekiel's prophecy, had been called "the rebellious ones" (cf. 2:5-6,8; 3:9,26-27; 12:3,9,25; 17:12; 24:3). At issue here is the past violation of the purification laws and the resulting desecration of the temple and nullifying of the covenant (44:6-7). The desecration, more specifically, was ritual pollution caused by the entrance of non-Levites to the priesthood (1 Kings 13:33-34) and the entrance of foreigners who were "uncircumcised in heart and flesh" (that is, non-Israelites), even "among the sons of Israel" (verse 9; cf. Jeremiah 51:51), into the sacred sanctuary (Ezekiel 44:7-8).

The third section (44:9-14) repeats an admonition previously given (verse 9, cf. verses 6-8), pronounces punishment on the Levites who defect from their office and introduce idolatry into the temple (verse 10; cf. 6:1-14; 8:1-18), and mentions the restrictions for the future heirs (from the tribe of Levi) who will serve in the new temple (44:11-14). The Levites had broad duties during the time of the first temple (cf. 1 Chronicles 15:16; 16:4; 23:28-31), but because this priestly line had been responsible for bringing about the cultic abominations that resulted in the judgment of exile (Ezekiel 44:12-13), it will no longer be allowed to perform the sacrificial service as priests who minister directly to the Lord (verse 13). Instead, they will serve the people as gatekeepers and will help slaughter animals brought for use as sacrificial offerings (verses 11,14).

In the fourth section (44:15-31) the work that the Levites have been forbidden to do is committed to the Zadokite priesthood, which will have exclusive charge over the temple's sacrificial service. Zadok was the Aaronide high priest at the time of David and Solomon (2 Samuel 8:17; 15:24; 1 Kings 1:34; 1 Chronicles 12:29), and he was given the role of chief priest because of his support for King Solomon (1 Kings 1:32-35; 2:26-27,35). Zadok and his descendants had consequently been promised by God an *everlasting* priesthood (1 Samuel 2:35; 1 Kings 2:27,33). This promise was the reconfirmation of similar promises made to Zadok's ancestor Phinehas (Numbers 25:11-13) and Phinehas' grandfather Aaron, the pro-

genitor of the Israelite priesthood (Exodus 29:9; 40:15). The Zadokite priesthood was the dominant priesthood up until the time of the Maccabean revolt, after which it was corrupted and replaced by political appointments to the priesthood under the Hasmonean dynasty. Thus, the last priests serving in the temple when it was destroyed in A.D. 70 were not of the legitimate Zadokite line. Jewish sects such as those at Qumran, which claimed to be comprised of Zadokite priests (1QS 5:2,9; 1Qsa 1:2,24; 2:3; 1Qsb 3:22), rejected the Jerusalem temple and its priesthood and expected their priesthood to regain its position of service in a future temple to be rebuilt after a climatic end-time war in which the Hasmonean priests would be punished (1QpHab 9:4-7; 4QpNah 1:11).

Seven rules are listed in verses 15-31 for the Zadokite priesthood's maintenance of the temple. The *first* of the rules concerns the priests' ceremonial attire (verses 15-19). In Exodus 28:39-41 priests had been directed that their priestly garments be made only of linen, and this regulation will remain in force for those who minister in the gates of the inner court and the temple (Ezekiel 44:17).

The *second* rule concerns the priests' physical appearance with regard to hair maintenance (verse 20). They are not to shave their heads nor let their hair grow excessively long. While it is possible this prohibition is due to shaved heads and uncut hair once having pagan associations with mourning or a cult of the dead, in the millennial kingdom, where death is uncommon and paganism no longer exists, these reasons would no longer be relevant.

The *third* rule concerns the priests' use of wine when on duty in the inner court (verse 21). Leviticus 10:9 had forbidden the drinking of wine for perhaps the same reason alcohol consumption is prohibited among police officers and similar personnel who must keep actively alert in their jobs to prevent any possibility of being hindered in the course of carrying out their duties. Likewise, priests must remain constantly focused on their need to maintain ritual purity in order to serve the

Lord without any wavering of mind or spirit (cf. Deuteronomy 6:5).

The *fourth* rule for the priests related to pure marriage relationships (Ezekiel 44:22). The Zadokites would have been sensitive about this issue because their stature as a priestly family had been hurt in part because the high priest Eli's sons had, in the performance of their duties, laid with the women who served at the entrance to the sanctuary (1 Samuel 2:22). As a result, the family's priestly position was discontinued (1 Samuel 2:27-31; 3:13-14). Priests were also prohibited from marrying any woman whose status would compromise their high position as representatives of a holy God (cf. Leviticus 21:7,14-15). Priests were allowed to marry only Israelite virgins and widows of priests (since a widow's previous marriage had been with one who was ritually pure). Here in Ezekiel 44:22 is another deviation from the Mosaic proscription for priests, which allowed marriage only to virgins of the priestly tribe and prohibited marriage to widows. This indicates the rule in Ezekiel 44:22 is for the new priestly order under the New Covenant.

The *fifth* rule for priests relates to their public role as representatives of God (verses 23-24). Verse 23 states that the priests are to help the people discern the difference between "the holy and the profane" and "the unclean and the clean." Such ritual distinctions are vital for the people to maintain their relationship with a holy God (cf. Leviticus 10:3), for they themselves are called to holiness as a nation that represents the Lord (cf. Exodus 19:6; Leviticus 11:45).

The *sixth* rule continues the focus on the priests' obligation to remain pure in regard to contact with dead bodies (Ezekiel 44:25-27). In order to avoid incurring corpse impurity and being disqualified for service, the priests are to avoid all contact with dead people who were not family members (verse 25). Corpse impurity was one of the more serious defilements that had brought ritual contamination to national Israel in the past. Some modern rabbis have sought to rectify this condition by attempting to raise a red heifer in the land,

whose ashes will purify a person from this defilement (cf. Numbers 19). They have also sought to raise priestly children from birth in a special compound that has no contact with the physical land. However, the removal of corpse impurity will occur only with Israel's national repentance and regeneration (sprinkling of clean water—Ezekiel 36:25) at the end of the Tribulation (Deuteronomy 4:27-30). The result will be a new, cleansed nation and qualified priesthood that will be able to build the millennial temple and conduct its services.

The *seventh* rule for the priests concerns their special status in relation to the Lord, the land, and people of Israel (Ezekiel 44:28-31; cf. Numbers 18:8-20). The special status for the Zadokites, in relation to the Lord, is that He is their inheritance (Hebrew, *nachala*) and possession (Hebrew, *'ahuzza*) based on the suzerain-vassal arrangement in which the former divides his land and bestows it to the latter as a grant (Ezekiel 44:28). Because the priests have a unique service to God, they are set apart to Him and require no territorial inheritance in the land for their sustenance or significance. Instead, they will be provided for through a portion of the ceremonially pure offerings (except the burnt offering) brought by the people to the Lord (verses 29-31; cf. Exodus 22:31; Leviticus 22:8). And those who provide for the priesthood in this manner will experience a divine "blessing to rest on [their] houses" (Ezekiel 44:30; cf. Numbers 6:22-27; Deuteronomy 24:19).

After the fourth section with the seven rules for the priests comes the fifth section (45:1-8), which develops more fully the subject of *priestly inheritance* just considered, as well as the *territorial possession of the prince*. As previously stated (44:28), the priests will not require a territorial possession in the land for their survival as do the other people. Rather, they will enjoy residence in a special allotment of land reserved as sacred space known as "the holy portion" (45:1), which is to be used strictly for ritual purposes. This territory contains the priests' quarters, which surround the temple in order to prevent ritual desecration from contaminating the sanctuary (verses 2-5).

Upon this allotment will be located the sacred district of the millennial kingdom—a square plateau that measures 25,000 cubits (8.3 miles) long and 20,000 cubits (6.6 miles) wide, covering an area of 50 square miles or 33,500 acres (by contrast, the present Temple Mount platform is 35 acres). This plateau will be divided into two equal rectangular portions in the north and south of 25,000 cubits (8.3 miles) by 10,000 cubits (3.3 miles). The northern portion will be reserved for the Messiah and His priests, while the southern portion will be for the Levites and the city of Jerusalem.

The sixth section (45:8–46:18) describes the *duties of the prince* and his relationship with the priests and the people. Ezekiel then contrasts this future prince with the corrupt princes of the Jewish nation in exile (previously addressed in 19:1-9; 22:25; 34:1-10), and exhorts the latter to repent of their unjust practices. The future prince will carry out his duties in Messiah's theocratic kingdom with righteousness and justice (45:8-12), and when the people pay him their taxes, he will take only what each person is able to afford based on their financial ability (verses 13-16). Moreover, he will apply the taxes properly: 1) for the maintenance of the sacrificial system ("burnt offerings," "grain offerings," and "drink offerings"); 2) at the appointed times ("feasts," "new moons," and "Sabbaths"); and 3) "to make atonement for the house of Israel" (verse 17). This last thought leads Ezekiel to discuss the roles of the priests (verses 18-21) and the prince (verses 22-25) in providing the various types of offerings for the feasts. The role of the prince continues in 46:1-15, with verses 16-18 outlining regulations for the prince.

The seventh section (46:19-24) concerns the location of special kitchens designated for boiling sacrifices. Ezekiel's angelic escort again appears and takes him on a tour of the west end of the priests' chambers, where the boiling of the guilt and sin offerings and the baking of the grain offering are to take place (verses 19-20).

The purpose for situating these functions at the end of the priests' chambers is to prevent the priests from having to go into the outer court (where the people are) and "transit holiness" that is, obliterate the distinction between that which is dedicated for the sacred service and that which is for common use (verse 20). This is in keeping with the priests' responsibility to teach the people the difference between "the holy and the profane" (44:23).

RESTORATION OF THE LAND IN THE MILLENNIUM
Ezekiel 47–48

IN THE REMAINING CHAPTERS of Ezekiel's vision (47–48) the millennial-era restoration of the land is given center stage. From the millennial temple there will burst forth a river that transforms the formerly barren and unfruitful Judean lowlands and the Dead Sea region (47:1-12). The previously revealed dimensions of the land, the sacred district, the holy portion, and the territory allocated to the prince and the priests are elaborated on and details are added concerning the territorial boundaries (47:13-23). More details are given in regard to the reorganization of the land (48:1-35), including the tribal divisions (48:1-29) and the land belonging to the restored city of Jerusalem (48:30-35). To Ezekiel's exilic audience, the news that the land will no longer be under foreign powers and will know complete restoration to the divine ideal is a powerful encouragement to trust the God of Israel, who is fully sovereign over all things and will never depart from His people (48:35).

THE RIVER FROM THE MILLENNIAL TEMPLE
Ezekiel 47:1-12

Accompanying the explanation of the topographical changes that have created the mountain of the house of the Lord with its sacred district and holy portion containing the millennial temple is the description of a river of fructified water that will flow from beneath the temple (47:1-12). Briefer accounts of this prophetic event were made before Ezekiel's time by Joel (Joel 3:18, c. 835 B.C.) and after Ezekiel's

EZEKIEL'S MESSIANIC TEMPLE

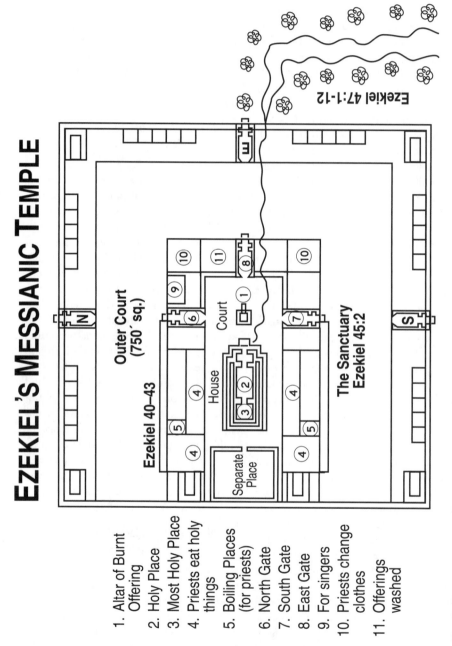

Outer Court (750′ sq.)

Ezekiel 40–43

House Court

Separate Place

The Sanctuary
Ezekiel 45:2

Ezekiel 47:1-12

1. Altar of Burnt Offering
2. Holy Place
3. Most Holy Place
4. Priests eat holy things
5. Boiling Places (for priests)
6. North Gate
7. South Gate
8. East Gate
9. For singers
10. Priests change clothes
11. Offerings washed

Taken from Randall Price, *The Temple and Bible Prophecy*, (Eugene, OR: Harvest House Publishers 1995/2005), p. 528.

time by Zechariah (Zechariah 14:8, c. 520–518 B.C.). A comparison of these texts reveals that they are independent of one another, with Joel's text stating "a spring will go out from the house of the LORD to water the valley of Shittim [an area north of the Dead Sea]," and Zechariah's adding that the "living waters" will divide and flow also "to the western sea [Mediterranean Sea]." The changes effected by this river will serve as a constant witness throughout the millennium that the source of blessing is the Lord, from whose house the waters originate.

In 47:1, Ezekiel is escorted to the main entrance of the temple, which faces east. There he observes water flowing from the front part of the temple and running beside the threshold of the door and the right (south) side of the altar (which is located directly in front of the temple—40:47). This location implies that the water is coming from God's presence from within the temple—more precisely, from beneath the throne of the Messiah within the Holy of Holies. This location would compare favorably with that in the New Jerusalem, where "the river of the water of life" flows from "the throne of God and of the Lamb" (Revelation 22:1). Ezekiel 47:12 describes "all kinds of trees" growing on each side of the river—trees whose "fruit will be for food and their leaves for healing." Similarly, Revelation 22:2 says that on "either side of the river" in the New Jerusalem is "the tree of life, bearing twelve kinds of fruit" and whose "leaves are for the healing of the nations."

THE BOUNDARIES OF THE LAND OF ISRAEL IN THE MILLENNIUM
Ezekiel 47:13-23

Here the Lord directly addresses Ezekiel and instructs him about the distribution of the land into 12 tribal divisions (Ezekiel 47:13-14). God had sworn or promised by oath (Ezekiel 20:5,15,23,42; 36:7; 44:12; cf. Exodus 6:8; Nehemiah 9:15; Psalm 106:26) to Israel's forefathers the land as "an inheritance" (Ezekiel 47:14). Therefore the historical covenants (Abrahamic, land, and Davidic) all preserved

this unconditional promise of the land not simply as a place of occupation, but as an inheritance (something passed on within a tribe to its descendants). Even though the tribal divisions had long ago been allocated, the boundaries promised to Abraham (Genesis 15:18-21) and reconfirmed to Moses (Numbers 34:1-12) never were completely realized. This time of fulfillment awaited the New Covenant (Ezekiel 37:25), and the fact that the fulfillment is in a future period is clear because the tribal divisions as given in Ezekiel are different from the divisions given in the past (Joshua 11:23; 13:7-33; 14:1–19:51; 22:1-34; 23:4; cf. Judges 18:1-31)—although the boundaries of the land, during the millennial kingdom, will be very similar to those originally given (47:15-20).

The *northern* boundary (47:15-17) will extend from the "Great Sea" (Mediterranean Sea) to the Euphrates River and incorporate the modern countries of Lebanon and part of Syria. The *eastern* boundary (verse 18) will extend from the Euphrates River down to the southern end of the Sea of Galilee at its confluence with the Jordan River and then down the Jordan Valley to the southern end of the "eastern sea" (Dead Sea). Incorporated within this boundary will be the present-day Golan Heights and portions of Lower Syria to Zedad (probably modern Sadad, about 25 miles north of Damascus). The *southern* boundary (verse 19) will extend from the southern end of the Dead Sea southward and westward to the "brook of [Egypt]" (the Wadi el-Arish—Numbers 34:5) and the Mediterranean Sea, incorporating the Negev and the "waters of Meribah Kadesh" (Kadesh Barnea—Numbers 27:14). The *western* boundary (Ezekiel 47:20) is the Mediterranean Sea running along the shoreline from the Wadi el-Arish in the south to a point opposite Lebo Hamath (the modern town of Al-Labwah in the Bekka Valley) in the north.

The land within these boundaries will be distributed to the 12 tribes for their inheritance (verse 21), and non-Israelites who desire to settle permanently and have children in the land will be permitted to do so. Under the

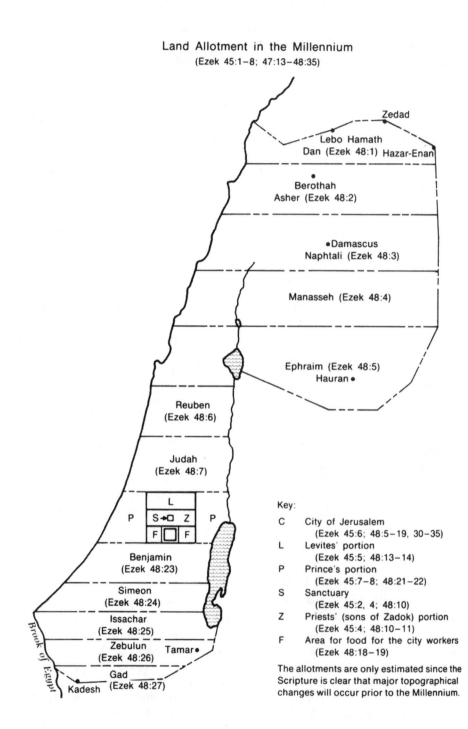

Land Allotment in the Millennium
(Ezek 45:1–8; 47:13–48:35)

Zedad

Lebo Hamath
Dan (Ezek 48:1) Hazar-Enan

Berothah
Asher (Ezek 48:2)

•Damascus
Naphtali (Ezek 48:3)

Manasseh (Ezek 48:4)

Ephraim (Ezek 48:5)
Hauran •

Reuben
(Ezek 48:6)

Judah
(Ezek 48:7)

L

P   S→□ Z   P

F □ F

Benjamin
(Ezek 48:23)

Simeon
(Ezek 48:24)

Issachar
(Ezek 48:25)

Zebulun   Tamar•
(Ezek 48:26)

Brook of Egypt

Gad
Kadesh   (Ezek 48:27)

Key:

C   City of Jerusalem
       (Ezek 45:6; 48:5–19, 30–35)
L   Levites' portion
       (Ezek 45:5; 48:13–14)
P   Prince's portion
       (Ezek 45:7–8; 48:21–22)
S   Sanctuary
       (Ezek 45:2, 4; 48:10)
Z   Priests' (sons of Zadok) portion
       (Ezek 45:4; 48:10–11)
F   Area for food for the city workers
       (Ezek 48:18–19)

The allotments are only estimated since the
Scripture is clear that major topographical
changes will occur prior to the Millennium.

Mosaic law, resident aliens were to be protected and allowed specific privileges with the native Israelites (Leviticus 19:33-36; 24:22; Numbers 15:29; Deuteronomy 14:29; 26:11). This was allowed in light of the fact that Israel had also once been residents in a strange land (Egypt).

THE DIVISION OF THE LAND OF ISRAEL IN THE MILLENNIUM
Ezekiel 48:1–29

The 12 tribes of Israel, after they are regathered, reidentified, reunited, and restored to the Lord and to the land, will be redistributed within the boundaries of the land according to their tribal allotments. The seven northern tribes will be separated from the five southern tribes by the holy portion on the mountain on which the temple rests. Moving from the north to south, the northern tribes (48:1-7) include Dan (verse 1), Asher (verse 2), Naphtali (verse 3), Manasseh (verse 4), Ephraim (verse 5), Reuben (verse 6), and Judah (verse 7). The inclusion of the tribe of Dan in the millennial distribution (48:32) seems to refute the Patristic and popular view that this tribe was cursed and therefore excluded from the 144,000 listed in Revelation 7:5-8.

The central portion of the land (48:8-22) includes the *millennial mountain* (with Jerusalem and the temple), with the precise location now revealed as south of the borders of the tribe of Judah (verse 8). In the middle of the northern division of the holy portion on the mountain is the millennial temple (verses 10,21). This holy portion (verses 12-15) also contains the millennial Jerusalem in its southern division, which will be laid out as a square of 4,500 cubits (7,875 feet) covering an area of 2.2 square miles (verse 16). The millennial Jerusalem will have "open spaces" around it that are 250 cubits (437.5 feet) wide, and "the remainder of the length alongside the holy allotment will be 10,000 cubits (3.3 miles) toward the east and 10,000 cubits toward the west (verse 18).

The holy allotment in this central portion will belong exclusively to the tribe of Levi

(the Zadokite priests and Levites) and the facilitator, the prince (verse 22). The borders of the five southern tribes (48:23-29) are described from north to south—Benjamin (verse 23), Simeon (verse 24), Issachar (verse 25), Zebulun (verse 26), and Gad (verse 27). It should be noted in this discussion that Jesus promised His 12 disciples that they would judge the 12 tribes in the millennial kingdom (Matthew 19:28).

THE MILLENNIAL JERUSALEM
Ezekiel 48:30-35

At the beginning of the millennium, topographical changes will occur in and around the city of Jerusalem. These changes will create the millennial mountain, which will be elevated above the hills (Isaiah 2:2), while all the surrounding land will be flattened into a vast plain (Zechariah 14:10). This will be done so that the site of the Lord's residence occupies the highest location in the region (and thus is always visible to the nation). This will also result in the holy district—with the millennial temple and millennial Jerusalem—becoming the new center of the land (Isaiah 2:2; Micah 4:1). The symbolic school of biblical interpretation finds the immense dimensions ascribed to the millennial mountain and its holy portion (temple and city) proof that Ezekiel 40–48 cannot be interpreted literally. However, given the extensive topographical expansion described by Ezekiel, the new boundaries and dimensions are quite realistic.

The millennial Jerusalem will have *12 gates,* each one named after one of Jacob's (Israel's) sons. Each gate will measure 4500 cubits (2.2 miles). On its northern side (verse 30) of the city, the three gates (verse 31) will be named after the tribes of Reuben, Judah, and Levi—perhaps reflecting Reuben's status as the firstborn (Genesis 35:23), Judah's past position as the site of the temple (Genesis 22:2; Exodus 15:17; Deuteronomy 12:5-6; 2 Samuel 7:10), and Levi's priestly position (Numbers 3:6). On the eastern side (Ezekiel 48:32) the gates will be named after Joseph, Benjamin, and Dan. As in Revelation 7:8, Joseph represents his sons

Ephraim and Manasseh (Genesis 48:1), who were adopted by Jacob (Genesis 48:5-6). The tribe Dan is again distinguished, confirming that its past history will not prevent its future inheritance. The gates on the southern side (Ezekiel 48:33) will be named after Simeon, Issachar, and Zebulun, whose tribal location in the south (48:24-26) meant that each tribe faced the gate bearing its name. On the western side (verse 34) the gates will be named after Gad, Asher, and Naphtali.

The fact of *theophany* (God's literal presence) distinguishes this Jerusalem from any other Jerusalem in history. The return of the Shekinah will signal the city's restoration to the divine ideal and usher in the era of its promised blessing. While the divine glory will fill the millennial temple (43:7), the extent of the glory on the entire millennial mountain is such that the millennial Jerusalem is also made glorious as "the throne of the Lord" (Jeremiah 3:17). According to Isaiah 4:5-6 the "whole area of Mount Zion" will be covered by the glory-cloud, which will be "a canopy" (literally *chupa*, like the canopy used by Jewish wedding parties) giving brightness by night (Isaiah 4:5) and shade by day as well as protection from storm and rain (Isaiah 4:6). This will also provide an independent light source for the city that will illuminate it both day and night (Isaiah 24:23; 60:19-20). The city will also be without walls, for the Lord will be a wall of fire around it

(Zechariah 2:4-5), and the city's gates will be open day and night (Isaiah 60:11).

The *restored glory* of Jerusalem is such that it can no longer be thought of without reference to the reality of God's presence. Therefore the city will be renamed "the Lord is there" (Hebrew, *YHWH Shammah*—Ezekiel 48:35). Jerusalem has had many different names in the past: Ur-Shalem, Salem, Zion, Ariel, Aelia Capitolina, and Al-Quds, but this will be its final change in name, for the Lord who defines it will never depart. In a similar way, the character of the city will also be reflected in its being referred to as "the LORD is our righteousness" (Hebrew, *YHWH Tzidikenu*—Jeremiah 33:16), and "the City of Truth" (Hebrew, *'Ir Ha'emet*—Zechariah 8:3).

This divine presence will also endue the city with perpetual holiness (Zechariah 14:20-21). For this reason, the tribal allotments have been arranged so as to make the centrality of the temple a literal, spatial reality rather than simply a theological notion (as the symbolic school contends). Ezekiel's vision has concluded (48:35) much as it began (1:4-28)—with a great and exalted vision of the Lord, whose glory appears with His people in order that they may be assured that He has desired a relationship with them and will never cease in His purpose until all of His prophecies come to fulfillment and His promises to fruition.

THE BOOK OF DANIEL HOLDS A UNIQUE PLACE IN BIBLICAL PROPHECY. It stands at the very pinnacle of Old Testament prophetic writings. Ford (*Daniel*, p. 13) observes that "New Testament scholars of almost every hue now confess that the entire eschatology of the New Testament is based on that first set forth in the Book of Daniel." The book's unique display of predictive prophecy (as evidence of the power of the God of prophecy) has also made it the subject of attacks by biblical critics who have questioned its authenticity more than any other book of the Bible. For this reason it is necessary to consider several introductory issues that relate to the book's prophetic character.

THE PROPHETIC SIGNIFICANCE OF DANIEL

The book of Daniel holds the preeminent position among the prophetic books of the Bible as the *key* to understanding prophecy. Daniel presents a sequence of prophetic events affecting Israel and the succession of nations that will dominate Israel until the advent of the messianic kingdom. According to traditional Judaism, Daniel "is also the primary source for calculating the exact date of the Final Redemption," (*Living Nach,* p. 641), which includes the coming of the Messiah. As such it connects the prophecies of the Old and New Testament, serving as a paradigm for the chronological structure of end time events in both the Olivet Discourse (Matthew 24; Mark 13; Luke 21) and the book of Revelation (6–19), while also informing the Pauline prophetic discourses.

So detailed and accurate are the prophecies in the book of Daniel that it has been the special target of criticism by those who reject the concept of predictive prophecy. In this light, two crucial issues have been raised which affect the prophetic interpretation of the book. The first of these is the date of Daniel. Those who accept the internal witness of the book that attributes authorship to the biblical Daniel during events occurring in the late neo-Babylonian and early Persian periods (605–536 B.C.) accept the book as containing predictive prophecy. And those who deny the possibility of predictive prophecy assert that the historical accuracy of these "prophecies" requires them to be *post-eventu* ("after the fact"). Those who hold to this view say the book's "prophecies" were written under the pseudonym of "Daniel" by a Jew concerned with the Antiochean persecutions some four centuries after Daniel in order to reconcile the problems of the postexilic period with God's promises to Israel.

The second issue relates to the present-day position of the book within the division of the Hebrew canon known as *Kethuvim* ("Writings"). This intentional exclusion of Daniel from the division known as *Neviim* ("Prophets") by Jewish scribes calls into question the prophetic status of the book by emphasizing pedagogy over prophecy as the key to interpretation.

Before moving on to analyze Daniel's prophetic message, it is necessary to deal with these issues.

THE DATE OF DANIEL

The book of Daniel specifically dates its proceedings and prophecies according to the regal years of certain dominant monarchs (1:1,21; 2:1; 5:31; 7:1; 8:1; 9:1; 10:1; 11:1). Moreover, Daniel is dated by named historical events such as the first deportation from Judah (605 B.C.), in which Daniel is repeatedly identified as a Judean in exile (1:1-3,6; 2:25; 5:13; 6:13). Additional confirmation for dating the book in this era comes from the historical figures with whom Daniel associated throughout his life, such as Nebuchadnezzar (1:18), Belshazzar (5:29), Darius, and Cyrus (6:28). The literary and archaeological sources confirming these figures support a literal historical setting for the book of Daniel, and the accuracy of its dates argues for a date of composition in the sixth century B.C. It is hard to imagine a second century B.C. pseudepigraphical writer having such a precise knowledge of the chronological records and cultural details that appear in Daniel.

The book specifically names the biblical Daniel as its author (12:5), as the numerous first-person references require (for example, 7:2,15,28; 8:1,15,27; 9:2,22; 10:2,7,11-12; 12:5). In addition, Daniel is mentioned in the book of Ezekiel (14:14,20; 28:3), indicating that he was recognized by Ezekiel (and Ezekiel's audience) both as a contemporary and a fellow prophet in exile.

The attack on the date for Daniel came in the eighteenth century as higher critical scholars J.D. Michaelis and J.C. Eichhorn revived Porphyry's arguments contending that the final form of Daniel was a pseudonymous product of the late postexilic Maccabean period (S.R. Driver, *An Introduction to the Literature of the Old Testament,* pp. 497-516). The Hebrew lexicographer S.R. Driver later championed this position. Driver based his arguments on the external support of philology and history, contradicting his earlier insistence that only the internal evidence of biblical books could determine the authorship and date of composition (S.R. Driver, *The Book of Daniel*). The following arguments have been made in support of the early date of Daniel (which assumes Danielic authorship and predictive prophecy).

Evidence from New Testament Usage

In the New Testament, Jesus, Paul, and John cite Daniel in support of the case they make with respect to predictive prophecy and explicitly refer to him as "Daniel the prophet." This is especially true with Matthew 24:15, where the use of the Greek preposition *dia* ("by") with the genitive cannot be construed to refer simply to a prophetic book called Daniel, but implies the personal prophetic *agency* of Daniel. Jesus' reference in these texts to Daniel's prophecy as the signal event requiring the reader to "understand" in order to act ties the prophecy in fulfillment to the events preceding His own messianic advent at the end of the age. Moreover, Jesus' interpretation of Daniel's prophecy of the desecration of the temple by "the abomination of desolation" as a still-future event opposes any date of composition in the Maccabean period, after which a supposed fulfillment (by Antiochus IV Epiphanes) would have already occurred.

Evidence from Linguistic Sources

The scholarly classification of the Aramaic language into three periods has revealed that the Aramaic used in Daniel was the official Aramaic of the courts from the seventh century B.C. onward and was used throughout the Near East (Rosenthal, *Die Aramaistiche Forschung,* pp. 66ff). This evidence led Egyptologist and linguist Kenneth Kitchen ("The Aramaic of Daniel" in *Notes on Some Problems in the Book of Daniel,* p. 33) to conclude that the Aramaic portions of Daniel (2:4–7:28) are by nature closely akin to the language of the fifth-century B.C. Elephantine papyri and of Ezra (c. 450 B.C.), and that Persian loanwords in Daniel are consistent with an earlier rather than later date. In addition, Persian period scholar Edwin Yamauchi (*Persia and the Bible,* pp. 380-82) has pointed out that Greek words are attested in the Elephantine papyri and that such loanwords in Neo-Babylonian and Persian period documents are expected due to the Grecian influence in the area from the sixth century onward.

Evidence from Extrabiblical Sources

The first-century Jewish historian Flavius Josephus, who wrote a history of the Jewish nation, stated in his *Antiquities of the Jews* that "events under Antiochus IV Epiphanes, on the other hand, had been predicted *many years in advance* by Daniel, on the basis of his visions" (10.276, emphasis added). The existence of some 20 fragments from Qumran, which date from the Maccabean period and compose nine manuscripts of Daniel, make it improbable that Daniel was composed during this same period. On the basis of paleography, these fragments are comparable to the *Great Isaiah Scroll A* and the *Pesher Habakkuk,* and therefore cannot be dated later than 125 B.C. Likewise, linguistic comparisons of Qumranic midrashim of the third and second centuries B.C. with the Aramaic and Hebrew chapters of Daniel have revealed matching traits in vocabulary, style, morphology, and syntax. From the Qumran Community's use of the Aramaic cognate of *pesher* (which appears 31 times in Daniel) along with *raz* ("mystery") in reference to Daniel's "interpretation" of dreams, it appears that the community believed that the visions of Daniel, which had not been completely fulfilled in the horrible events surrounding the persecutions of Antiochus IV Epiphanes, were still future and were to be fulfilled in their own day.

The early semicursive script of *4QDan* (*4Q114*) has been dated to the late second century B.C., within less than 50 years from the assumed autograph of Daniel. While this date, based on scribal characteristics, makes it unlikely that the original composition of Daniel took place in the Maccabean period, the Hebrew text of Daniel, when compared linguistically with the Hebrew in other Qumran scrolls, makes this impossible. Gleason Archer did a comparative analysis ("The Hebrew of Daniel Compared with the Qumran Sectarian Documents," pp. 470-81) that took into consideration syntax and morphology, postbiblical words, postbiblical pronunciation and spelling, and words with a postbiblical meaning, and he concluded, "In light of all the data adduced under the four categories just reviewed, it seems abundantly clear that a second-century date for the Hebrew chapters of Daniel is no longer tenable on linguistic grounds."

EVIDENCE FOR DANIEL AS A PROPHETIC BOOK

In the Old Testament, only one text outside of Daniel seems to affirm Daniel as a prophet (Ezekiel 14:20; cf. 28:3), ranking him with Job and Noah as a model of righteousness and wisdom to the exilic community. While this reference to Daniel is contested, in the New Testament, Daniel's position among the prophets is assumed. This is clearly reflected in Jesus' citation of Daniel 9:27 in Matthew 24:15: "...spoken of through Daniel the prophet...." The Gospel writers and Paul also allude to this Danielic motif "the abomination of desolation" (Daniel 9:27; cf. 11:31; 12:11). While they do not explicitly refer to Daniel, their dependence on Jesus' statement about Daniel and their apparent acceptance of his prophetic predictions as divine revelation indicate that they also may have considered Daniel as a prophet. For Jesus and the New Testament writers, the primary version of the Old Testament was the Septuagint, which in all manuscripts clearly placed Daniel among the prophetic writings. This is also true of all the canonical lists that appeared in early patristic literature.

In weighing this evidence, we must conclude that there is no single witness for the exclusion of Daniel from the prophetic corpus in the first half of the first millennium A.D. In all the sources of the first century A.D.—the Septuagint, the Qumran Community, Josephus, Jesus, and the New Testament writers—Daniel is reckoned among the prophets.

COMMENTARY ON THE PROPHETIC SECTIONS

Daniel's appointed task was to serve as a prophet both to the Jewish exilic community and to the Gentile rulers who exercised worldwide dominion. Since the "times of the Gentiles" (Luke 21:24) began with Babylon's conquest of Israel,

Daniel's prophetic overview of God's future program for the nations begins with the Babylonian Empire. Though Daniel's initial prophetic statements deal with world empires and their roles in the future, the focal point is still Israel, and Daniel's closing prophetic statements deal largely with Israel in the midst of the world's nations. These two periods of prophetic activity divide the book of Daniel into two sections: 1) the prophetic program for the nations during the times of the Gentiles (chapters 2–7), and 2) the prophetic program for Israel during the times of the Gentiles (chapters 8–12). The prophecies concerning the ten toes/horns, the "little horn," the seventieth seven, and the everlasting kingdom of God await future fulfillment (during the Tribulation and millennium). For the purposes of this commentary the statements concerning the nations that have already experienced prophetic fulfillment will be studied first in order to provide a consistent model for the interpretation of the prophetic statements that have yet to be fulfilled. The approach will be to provide commentary on those texts that are significant for futurist interpretation and to leave for the standard commentaries the explanation of past historical events. The chart below provides an overview of the primary context and major significance of Daniel's prophecies.

An Overview of Daniel's Prophecies

Date	Daniel's Age	Reference	Prophecy	Significance
602 B.C.	18	2:1-45	Great statue	Times of the Gentiles
553 B.C.	68	7:1-28	Four beasts, Ancient of Days	Nations, Antichrist, kingdom
551 B.C.	70	8:1-27	Ram and male goat	Nations, Antichrist
539 B.C.	82	9:1-27	70 sevens	Messiah, Tribulation
536 B.C.	85	11:2-45	Future of nations	Nations, Antichrist
536 B.C.	85	12:1-13	Future of Israel	Tribulation, kingdom

THE PROPHETIC PROGRAM FOR THE NATIONS
Daniel 2–7

BECAUSE CHAPTERS 2–7 DEAL with God's prophetic program for the Gentile nations, Daniel's original text shifts from the Hebrew language to Aramaic. Aramaic was not restricted to the Babylonians but was the common language of the day, and its usage had been extended, through conquest, to most of the world known to Daniel and his audience. Therefore, it was ideally suited as the means to communicate the prophetic program to the Gentiles.

The Gentile nations are to realize that their history is subservient to that of Israel, even though for the period of "the times of the Gentiles" they are dominant. This dominance is but the consequence of God's judicial fulfillment of His covenant with Israel and is moving progressively toward the fulfillment of the restoration of the nation of Israel, at which time the nations will submit to and worship Israel's God (Isaiah 19:19-25; 60:3-14; 66:18-21; Zechariah 14:16; cf. Revelation 15:4) and will depend on Israel's mediation for their understanding of the word of the Lord (Isaiah 2:2-3; Zechariah 8:20-23).

THE TIMES OF THE GENTILES
Daniel 2:1-45

THE FIRST OF DANIEL'S prophetic revelations is communicated through the medium of dreams. Whether to pagans (Genesis 41:1-8), patriarchs (Genesis 28:12-15; 31:11-13; 37:5-10), or potentates (1 Kings 3:5-15), only when God determined to reveal His will to Israel or His future plans for Israel had He employed this as a means. This is in no way comparable to modern psychological practices such as dream analysis (to reveal inner conflicts) or New Age dream therapy (to guide behavior and interpret the future). Such efforts are self-directed, but Daniel's dream is divinely directed. It is clear from this account that the dream was designed by God and given sovereignly for the purpose of revealing His prophetic plan (Daniel 2:28).

That a representative of the nation of Israel succeeded in interpreting the dream and the representatives of Babylon, the most powerful nation of that day, failed (verses 24-27,47) revealed that the destiny of the nations depended on Israel's God and the fulfillment of God's purpose for Israel (verses 28-30,45). One Gentile kingdom would follow another (verses 39-43), but the final and everlasting kingdom would be that promised to Israel by their God (verse 44). Prophetic revelation received in this form cannot be reduced to a spiritual message that has no corresponding reality. Daniel's visionary content of judgment and salvation points to the actual physical destruction of empires and the national deliverance of peoples. Because Daniel's prophecy speaks of a real future outcome, the interpretation of this prophecy cannot be handled subjectively but must be carefully exegeted, in context, using proper hermeneutical guidelines.

THE PROPHETIC DREAM RECEIVED
Daniel 2:1-23

Nebuchadnezzar was sent a recurring dream ("dreams" in Daniel 2:1 and "dream" in verse 3) at the beginning of his reign (verse 1) to remind him that Babylon's rank among the nations was the result of a divinely ordered program. These circumstances caused the king to realize the dream was of divine origin, making its interpretation urgent because he believed his gods were trying to communicate with him (verse 3). Since the source of the dream was supernatural, the king demanded that its interpretation follow suit. That is why he rejected the natural manner of dream analysis offered by his professional wise men (verses 4-9). Nebuchadnezzar required that his wise men demonstrate their supposed relationship with the gods rather than simply follow their trade formula for success. Understanding both the impossibility of the task and the imminence of their doom, the men confessed their inability and argued, in their defense, the unprecedented and unreasonable character of the king's request (verses 10-11). Their admission that an interpretation could not be provided without divine assistance not only highlighted the reason for the king's demand but set the stage for the polemical drama in which God's revelation to Daniel overturned the Babylonian religious worldview.

Just as Nebuchadnezzar had received his dream from God, so the dream and its "mystery" (that is, its interpretation) was revealed to Daniel by God (verse 19). This fact would force the king to see the God of Israel as distinct from his own pagan deities (verse 28), even though the king's religious worldview cannot accept this (3:12-20; 4:9). Daniel's response of praise (2:20-23) reveals his understanding of this prophecy as a revelation of "the times and epochs" (verse 21) related to the divine program for the nations. He also emphasizes that God is sovereign in the fulfillment of prophecy ("deposes...establishes kings"). He further defines prophecy in general as wisdom and knowledge granted to men, a revelation of "profound and hidden things," and light in the darkness (verses 21-22).

THE PROPHETIC DREAM REVEALED
Daniel 2:24-45

Daniel is brought to the king by Arioch (who had hoped to ingratiate himself as a result), and the prophet submits to the same strict demand the king had imposed upon the pagan wise men. In his introductory words to the king (verses 27-30), Daniel explains that prophecy is the sovereign provenance of the "God in heaven" and is the revealing of mysteries dealing with "the latter days" and "the future" (verses 27-30). Daniel's reference to "God in heaven" (cf. 2:18-19,37,44) was meant to contrast Daniel's God, the God of Israel, from the Babylonian deities. In 2:31-35 the content of the dream is described for the first time. The central image in the dream was a great statue with a head of gold, chest and arms of silver, a midsection of bronze, legs of iron, and feet of iron mixed with clay. The second image in the dream was a divinely crafted stone that struck the feet of the statue, blasting the entire statue to bits and replacing it and growing into a great mountain that fills the whole earth.

Daniel explains that the metallic image in the dream represents four successive Gentile world powers that would rule over Israel in the years ahead. *The first world empire* was *Babylon* itself, represented by the head of gold (verses 37-38). Nebuchadnezzar would have well understood this as a reference to his kingdom, whose chief deity Marduk was known as "the god of gold." In addition, gold had been employed lavishly throughout the city. Daniel then tells the king that his extensive authority had been granted not by his gods but by "the God of heaven." This revelation established the king's accountability to the God of Israel as well as the basis for God's judgment of the king in 4:31-33.

The *second world empire* in succession was depicted as two silver arms merging into a chest, indicating an empire composed of two nations (a dual monarchy). This chapter in Daniel does not give sufficient information to help determine the identity of this empire; however, other chapters in Daniel make it clear that this was the *Medo-Persian empire,* which conquered Babylon on October 11 and 12, 539 B.C. (Daniel 5:31). The Medes and the Persians had been united in 550 B.C., and the text of Daniel states that Babylon was "given over to the Medes and Persians" (5:28), whose rulers enforced "the law of the Medes and the Persians" (6:8,12,15; cf. Esther 1:19). In like manner, Daniel 8:20 identifies a ram with two horns as "the kings of Media and Persia." The ram with two horns is the single nation divided into two authorities. One horn is larger than the other because Media, the older empire, was later overshadowed by Persia (Daniel 11:2).

The *third world empire,* symbolized by the statue's midsection and thighs of bronze, was predicted to "rule over all the earth" (Daniel 2:39). The *Greek empire,* begun by Philip of Macedon and extended by his son Alexander to the farthest reaches of the then-known world, qualifies as this third kingdom. Under Alexander the empire was unified and encompassed more territory than had either the Neo-Babylonian or Persian empires, the latter conquered in 331 B.C. However, as Daniel 11:3-4 predicted, after Alexander's death, his four generals divided up his empire. Even so, only two of these divisions affected dominance over Israel: the Ptolemies (based in Egypt) and the Seleucids (based in Syria). This fits well with Daniel's division of the statue's massive midsection into two thighs. The Selucid ruler Antiochus IV Epiphanes imposed Greek culture on the Jews and desecrated the second temple, facts predicted in Daniel 11:21-35. This third kingdom was characterized by bronze, which the Greeks used extensively in their weapons of war.

The *fourth empire* in the dream (Daniel 2:40-43) was depicted as two iron legs with feet composed of a mixture of iron and pottery (verses 33,41-43) that would crush all opponent kingdoms and divide up their former territories (verse 40). Iron, which is stronger than gold, silver, or bronze, was the metal developed for weaponry by *Rome,* the one nation in historical succession that conquered all of the lands of the previous kingdoms and assimilated their people into one vast empire. Rome defeated Greece in 146 B.C. and occupied the land of Israel in 63 B.C., ending Jewish independence. In A.D. 70, Rome destroyed the Jewish temple. By A.D. 395 the Roman Empire had split into two political areas of rule: the West with its capital in Rome, and the East with its capital in Constantinople (modern Istanbul, Turkey), which included the land of Israel. This division of the empire was depicted in the statue's two legs.

The Fourth Kingdom

Higher critical scholars have rejected the futuristic view of Daniel's prophecy because of their belief that Daniel was written in the second century B.C. and because Rome did not occupy Israel until a century later. This means that if the critics agree that Rome is the fourth kingdom, they will have to admit that Daniel contains predictive prophecy. Since this school of interpretation holds that this is not the case, they terminate Daniel's prophecy with Antiochus IV Epiphanes and identify Macedonia, the progenitor of Antiochus IV's Seleucid dynasty, as the fourth kingdom. However, Josephus Flavius, the first-century Jewish historian, identified the Roman Empire as the fourth kingdom (*Antiquities* 10.10.4), as did his Jewish contemporary who authored the pseudepigraphical work 2 Esdras/4 Ezra. He wrote, "The eagle you saw coming from the sea is the fourth kingdom, which appeared to your brother Daniel. But it was not explained to him as I now explain or have explained it to you" (2 Esdras/4 Ezra 12:11-12). Likewise, the Jewish sect at Qumran seemed to have identified the end-time invaders of Israel, the Kittim, with Rome. Daniel 11:30 tells us Rome's ships came from the west past Cyprus to defeat the army of Antiochus IV Epiphanes.

The statue's strong legs of iron, which characterized Rome, became mixed with pottery at the statue's two feet and ten toes (Daniel 2:41-43). Daniel said as much about the feet and toes of the fourth kingdom as he said about all the other kingdoms combined. For this reason it is necessary to pay special attention to what is said about this final world empire. The fact the feet and toes are a mixture of iron and common pottery indicates that while they are strong, they are also easily breakable. Iron and pottery cannot be combined. Even if heated in a crucible to their melting points the two substances remain separate, and the removal of the pottery from the cooled iron leaves it porous and brittle. Verse 43 adds that the iron and pottery "will combine with one another in the seed of men." This implies that the ten toes will consist of *diverse people groups* that will be difficult to unify. Following the above analogy, some of these peoples will be strong, and others will be weak. The heat of military action will force these ten nations to forge a political union, but their unstable condition and differences will cause the union to fall apart.

That the legs of iron eventually become feet and toes of iron and clay speaks of *two stages or phases* of the Roman Empire. Since the downward movement from one section of the statue to the next represents the passage of time, this second stage was to occur sometime after the decline of the first phase of the empire. However, because a ten-nation confederation has not yet appeared at any subsequent time in history, the fulfillment of the prophecy regarding the ten toes must still be in the future. It is clear from verse 44 that God sets up His kingdom "in the days of those kings" (that is, the ten nations), which requires this to be the eschatological age or end time (Daniel 12:4,9,13). Indeed, from our vantage point, it is possible to divide verses 37-45 into those verses that deal with past history (verses 37-40) and those that deal with the future (verses 41-45). Accordingly, in the end time there is expected a revival of the Roman Empire. Although the political entity known as the Roman Empire disappeared long ago, its impact on civilization has been profound, with western law and language

Daniel's Outline of the Future

The Times of the Gentiles — Luke 21:24

612 B.C.

Israel | Church | Israel

Nebuchadnezzar's dream of the great world colossus that pictures the deterioration of Gentile power: first in quality, from gold to iron and clay; then in strength, from iron to common iron mixed with clay.

Daniel 2

The Revelation of Christ

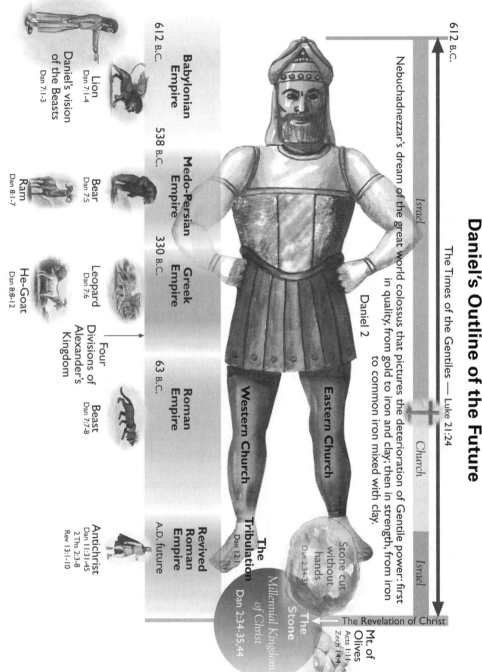

612 B.C.

Babylonian Empire

538 B.C.

Medo-Persian Empire

330 B.C.

Greek Empire

63 B.C.

Roman Empire

Western Church

Eastern Church

Daniel's vision of the Beasts
Dan 7:1-3

Lion
Dan 7:1-4

Bear
Dan 7:5

Ram
Dan 8:1-7

Leopard
Dan 7:6

He-Goat
Dan 8:8-12

Four Divisions of Alexander's Kingdom

Beast
Dan 7:7-8

Revived Roman Empire
A.D. future

Antichrist
Dan 11:31-45
2 Ths 2:3-8
Rev 13:1-10

The Tribulation
Dan 12:1

Stone cut without hands
Dan 2:34-35

The Stone
Dan 2:34-35,44

Millennial Kingdom of Christ

Mt. of Olives
Acts 1:11
Zech 14:4

Taken from Tim LaHaye and Ed Hindson, gen. eds., The Popular Encyclopedia of Bible Prophecy, (Eugene, OR: Harvest House Publishers, 2004), p. 68.

retaining the Roman imprint. Similarly, the Roman Catholic church's syncretistic adoption of Roman customs and celebrations has preserved some of the empire's religious elements, making possible a future revival of pagan religious observances in deceptive guise. The modern-day unification of Europe (the European Union) from political and economic standpoints may be setting the stage for the Roman Empire in its final form.

Daniel 7:23-25 explains this in more detail, providing both the identity of the revived Roman Empire and the time period in which it will appear. Briefly, Daniel 7 views the iron component of the ten toes and depicts them as ten horns or a confederation of ten kings who will receive their authority from the fourth beast (Antichrist) and will persecute the Jewish people ("the saints of the Highest One"—7:27) for the last half of the seventieth week (cf. Revelation 17:12). Apparently this confederation, in alliance with the Antichrist, will rule over the former territory of the Roman Empire (both East and West) during the Tribulation. Daniel 11:36-45 views the pottery component of the ten toes and further explains that this confederation will break up and be at war with one another as kings of the north, south, and east battle over control of the land of Israel.

The Fifth Kingdom

The *fifth kingdom* (Daniel 2:44-45) is said to appear in the *future* and at the time in which the ten-nation confederation will exist. This period is the seventieth week of Daniel's prophecy of the seventy weeks (cf. Daniel 7:25; 9:25-27), which will conclude at the second advent and the setting up of the millennial kingdom. According to this text the millennial kingdom is different from the preceding Gentile kingdoms in that it is established by divine rather than human means, its appearance marks the end of all human kingdoms, and its rule lasts forever. Nebuchadnezzar's dream had symbolized these characteristics of the fifth kingdom as a stone cut out of a mountain without hands that will pulverize the statue and become a great mountain and fill

the whole earth (Daniel 2:35). The mountain imagery is part of the divine polemic designed to destroy Nebuchadnezzar's religious worldview. In the Babylonian religious system the earth itself was a mountain, the "Mountainhouse," and the gods came from the sacred mountain of the earth called the "Mountain of the Lands." Marduk was the chief god and was known as the "Great Mountain," and temples dedicated to him were symbolically constructed in the shape of mountains.

God's purpose of depicting the stone as cut out of a mountain (without human assistance) and becoming a "great mountain" (verses 34-35) was to confirm to the king that his dream was of divine origin. What surprised the king was that none of earthbound Marduk's wise men were able to interpret the dream, but Daniel, a representative of the God of heaven (verses 28,37) could and did! This made it clear that God had given the dream and would fulfill it in the future. This is further emphasized by the stone reducing the statue (that is, all Gentile political dominion) to dust and "the wind" blowing away every trace that remained (verse 35). Another title for Marduk was "Lord of the Wind," based on the belief that the winds were governed by the gods. However, here the wind serves the stone by removing every vestige of human government so that the kingdom of the God of heaven could be established on earth.

The *four metals* that represent the earthly kingdoms have progressively decreasing value but progressively increasing strength. Gold (the top of the statue) is the most precious metal and iron (the bottom of the statue) the least, but iron is the strongest and gold the weakest. From a human viewpoint it would be expected that each succeeding kingdom would be stronger than that which preceded it, since successful conquest depends on superior might. However, from the divine viewpoint human governments deteriorate as time passes, and ultimately they will pass away completely when the messianic rule rises to replace them (Psalm 2:8-9; Obadiah 21; Zechariah 14:9). Thus the progressive unfolding of the divine program for the nations reveals the devolution of mankind as opposed to the evolutionary concept forming the pagan, humanistic worldview (cf. Isaiah 40:15-17,23-24). Eschatological interpretations that imagine Christianity as conquering (or having conquered) the common culture or as winning the day morally and even politically are surely idealistic and far afield from the literal historical fulfillment expected by Daniel.

A Literal, Earthly Kingdom

Those of the symbolic school of interpretation (historicism) argue that the stone that destroyed the nations was Christ, whose spiritual kingdom (effected outwardly through the church) was established at His first advent. In this interpretation, Christianity is said to have overcome (as in idealism and preterism) or be progressively conquering (as in amillennialism and postmillennialism) all nations as the gospel is extended to the world. However, it is impossible to sustain these interpretations in light of Daniel's context and actual history.

First, Daniel's interpretation of the dream clearly indicates that the stone crushed and the wind removed *every* trace of the fourth kingdom *before* the kingdom of God was established (Daniel 2:34-35). The church cannot be identified as the kingdom that replaces the fourth kingdom of Daniel's prophecy because historically the church and the fourth kingdom coexisted for many centuries. The western division of the Roman Empire continued for more than 400 years into the church age, and the eastern division for more than 1400!

Second, Daniel's interpretation does not permit the idea of a *gradual*, incomplete conquest that progressively takes dominion over time. The destruction of all of the nations represented by the statue (that is, the known world) is sudden, cataclysmic, and all-encompassing (verses 34-35,45). The text clearly states that when the stone strikes at the feet of the statue it instantly disintegrates the whole statue, reducing it to dust to be blown away immediately as was chaff from the ancient threshing floors. It is not simply that the basis for the

nations' dominion is removed; rather, the actual dominion itself is ended forever. There is also nothing in this imagery that implies a gradual *spiritual* conquest of the nations as they come under the expanding influence of Christianity.

Third, the time for the revolutionary events of verses 44-45 is stated to be "in the days of those kings." As previously stated, "those kings" refers to the last generation of Gentile power represented by the "ten toes" or ten kings/kingdoms (verses 41-43; cf. Revelation 17:12). Daniel chapter 7, which parallels chapter 2 although using different symbolism, refers to the ten toes as ten horns that are part of the fourth beast (the same as the fourth world empire—cf. 7:23-24). The fourth beast (Rome) also has a "little horn" (Daniel 7:8), which Revelation 13:1-6 describes as the beast (the Antichrist).

Daniel 7 continues with revelation of "One like a Son of Man" (verse 13), who is given an everlasting kingdom (verse 14). Just as John identified the "little horn" with the Antichrist, so Christ identified Himself as the "Son of Man" (Matthew 26:64; Mark 14:62; Luke 22:69; John 3:13). In His Olivet Discourse He cited verse 13 with respect to His second advent (Matthew 24:30; cf. 16:27-28; 19:28; 24:39,44; 25:31; Luke 9:26). Daniel 7 goes on to describe the persecution of the little horn for three-and-a-half years (verses 25), which will end with the coming of the everlasting kingdom (verses 26-27). The Olivet Discourse states that "when the Son of Man comes in His glory...He will sit on His glorious throne" and judge the nations (Matthew 25:31-32). The New Testament ties Daniel 7:13 to Christ's coming in judgment, leaving no doubt that the time of the destruction of Daniel's fourth kingdom and the establishment of Christ's everlasting kingdom occurs at the second advent.

Preterists agree with this but believe the second advent occurred in A.D. 70. Again, the problem with this interpretation is that it does not result in a literal fulfillment in which the final kingdom destroys the previous kingdoms. To make the final kingdom spiritual and heavenly when the previous kingdoms were literal and earthly goes against the contexts of Daniel 2; 7. Conversely, accepting a literal everlasting kingdom in Daniel necessitates accepting an eschatological time of fulfillment for the second advent in the Olivet Discourse and Revelation. Therefore, it may be stated—in view of the contexts in Daniel and subsequent history—that the *symbolic* school of interpretation (historicism, preterism, and idealism) has not been able to offer a reasonable explanation of the destruction of the fourth world kingdom. Only the *literal* school of interpretation (futurism) allows for a literal fulfillment of Daniel's prophecy that the destruction of the nations will be sudden and complete and followed by the establishment of Christ's kingdom at the second advent.

Daniel also predicts that following the second advent of Christ, the kingdom will be given to the people of the *saints* of the Highest One (7:18,22,27). This, however, is not the church, but the "saints" that endured the persecution of the "little horn" during the last half of the seventieth week (7:25). To Daniel's audience, the term "saints" refers exclusively to the Jewish people, a meaning found also in the Psalms (cf. Psalm 16:3; 34:9). It also refers to the Jewish people in the Olivet Discourse, which follows Daniel's understanding of the events of this period (cf. Matthew 24:15). Daniel's prophecies are messages of hope for national Israel, and the promise of the kingdom to Israel is part of this national hope, having been a theme of the former prophets (cf. Isaiah 2:1-4; 4:2-6; 11; 12; 25; 26; 27; 32; 35; 56:1-8; 60; 65:17-25; 66:7-21; Jeremiah 30–31; 33; Ezekiel 11:19-20; 16:60-63; 20:33-44; 33–48). Daniel's statement of "sovereignty, the dominion and the greatness" (7:27), connected with the possession of the kingdom, reflects the promise made by God to Israel (Isaiah 54:3; 60:11-12; cf. Zechariah 9:9-10; 14:9). Israel was given "the heritage of the nations" (Psalm 111:6; see Isaiah 54:3; 60:5-16), and it is only through Israel that the nations will be blessed (Genesis 12:3; 18:18; Zechariah 8:22-23). The kingdom that is given to the saints is the same kingdom promised to national Israel. To be sure, the redeemed nations will also share in this possession, but through the mediation of redeemed Israel, which will have finally attained the position for which it was first chosen (Exodus 19:5-6; Isaiah 60:2-3).

Although Israel will be appointed as head over the nations, the nations will enjoy equality with Israel in the spiritual benefits of the New Covenant (Joel 2:28) and be accepted with Israel as God's people (Isaiah 19:24-25) and allowed equal inheritance in the land of Israel (Ezekiel 47:22-23). In the eternal state the sons of Israel and all mankind will worship the Lord together and alike enjoy the tree of life and be His bond servants (Isaiah 66:22-23; Revelation 22:1-5). The church, by contrast, will inhabit the New Jerusalem (Hebrews 12:22-24; Revelation 21:9-10; cf. John 14:2) and will exercise co-regent responsibilities with Christ (2 Timothy 2:12) in the same way the 12 apostles will share in the rule over the 12 tribes of Israel (Matthew 19:28).

THE FOUR BEASTS
Daniel 7:1-8

BEGINNING WITH CHAPTER 7 and continuing through the end of the book, Daniel records visions that he received in the latter years of his life. In the first six chapters he spoke in the third person, but from here onward he will relate his visions in the first person. As in chapter 2, the vision in chapter 7 deals with God's program for the nations and the fulfillment of His promise to Israel of restoration and of a kingdom. For this reason the chapter focuses primarily on the period of the seventieth week, or the Tribulation period, because that is when the divine programs for the nations and Israel intersect, with the former coming to an end as the latter is restored to a new beginning. Chapter 7 covers ground already considered in chapter 2 but adds that the Son of Man is the One who will receive the kingdom and gives more details about the little horn, a symbol of the Antichrist. Both chapters 2 and 7 employ the same revelatory pattern in their imagery (see comparison chart on page

237)—in chapter 2 the imagery was of four metals, and in chapter 7 it is of four beasts.

This dream-vision was received by Daniel about 553 B.C., in the first year of Belshazzar's co-regency with his father Nabonidus, who was 60 when he ascended the throne. This occurred 14 years before the fall of Babylon and in the fifty-second year of Daniel's exile, when he was about 68 years old.

The expression "the four winds of heaven" (Daniel 7:2) generally denotes God's sovereign power to perform His purpose (cf. Jeremiah 49:36; Ezekiel 37:9; Zechariah 2:6). However, as the Aramaic term may mean either "winds" or "spirits," it may refer to the angelic forces that carry out the divine purpose among the nations (Daniel 10:13,20-21; cf. Zechariah 6:1-5; Matthew 24:31; Revelation 7:1). The four winds were "stirring up the great sea" (Daniel 7:2). The sea is often a symbol of the Gentile nations (cf. Isaiah 8:6-8; 17:12-13; Jeremiah 6:23; 46:7-8; 47:2; Matthew 13:47,49; Revelation 13:1; 17:1,15). It represented the nations in their vastness (numbers), darkness (ignorance of God), and uncontrollable nature, which also describes the fallen state of humankind (Isaiah 57:20; cf. Romans 3:10-18; Ephesians 2:2-3). This is an apt description of the chaotic conditions of the Tribulation period, also called by Daniel "a time of distress" (12:1).

Whereas in chapter 2 the great statue with its human features and polished metal image represented world civilizations from a *human* standpoint, here the term "great beasts" indicates the *divine* viewpoint of the true character and nature of these nations (cf. Genesis 6:5). And, from both viewpoints, God's judgment is the same: He will totally and permanently annihilate all human powers (Daniel 2:35,44; 7:26).

That each of these four beasts is "different from one another" (7:3) indicates they are distinct kings or kingdoms, a fact revealed in Daniel's subsequent interpretation of the vision (verse 17). The imagery of beasts coming up out of the sea (verse 3) may have in mind Isaiah's reference to "the dragon who lives in the sea" (Isaiah 27:1), and serves as the basis for John's description of the first beast (the

Antichrist) in Revelation 13:1. Since Daniel's use of "sea" indicated the national origin of the four beasts (kings or kingdoms), and the little horn (Daniel 7:8) comes up among the ten horns (or Gentile kingdoms), it cannot be doubted that John likewise understood a Gentile origin for the beast of his vision (see comments on the nationality of the Antichrist at Daniel 11:37).

The *first beast* is described as a composite animal with the body of a lion and the wings of an eagle (Daniel 7:4). This imagery describes Nebuchadnezzar, who was called a "lion from the thickets of the Jordan" (Jeremiah 49:19; 50:44) because just as lions fled from the thickets and attacked nearby villages along the Jordan when it overflowed its banks, so the Babylonian general had spread out beyond his immediate region to fiercely attack surrounding countries. Likewise, Nebuchadnezzar's army was renown for the speed with which they attacked, causing the prophet Ezekiel to describe him as having the wings of an eagle (Ezekiel 17:3,7). Moreover, the sculpted image of winged lions was an ever-present national symbol in *Babylon*. This image stood at the entrances to the Babylonian palaces, was prevalent on royal architecture and reliefs, and even flanked the monarch's throne.

The *second beast* resembles a bear with one side raised and three ribs in its mouth (Daniel 7:5). Again we see a parallel to the statue in Daniel 2, which had a chest of silver with two arms. The two-sided bear symbolizes the dual kingdom of *Medo-Persia*. The bear was considered a fearful creature (1 Samuel 17:34; Hosea 13:8; Amos 5:19), but less so than the lion. In like manner, though Medo-Persia was considered a fierce foe (Isaiah 13:15-18), it lacked the unified strength that made its predecessor so fearsome. Moreover, just as a bear moves slower than a lion, so the Medo-Persian Empire, which was larger than the Neo-Babylonian, moved slower in its campaigns of conquest. The uneven sides of the bear, with one side higher than the other, provides an additional detail not seen in the vision in chapter 2—that of the shifting dominance in the Medo-Persian Empire. Median influence governed the empire during the administrations of Cyrus and Cambyses, but within a half-century Persia gained prominence during the reign of Xerxes I (Ahasuerus). The change in political ascendancy is reflected in the change of the legal statement of royal edict from "the law of *the Medes* and the Persians" (Daniel 6:8,12,15) to "the laws of Persia and Media" (Esther 1:19). The three ribs in the mouth of the bear probably represent three of their historic conquests—Lydia (546 B.C.), Babylon (539 B.C.), and Egypt (525 B.C.).

The *third beast* was another composite animal having the body of a leopard with four heads and four wings on its back (Daniel 7:6). It corresponds to the third part of the great statue, the midsection and thighs of bronze (2:32). Everything about this creature symbolized speed: a leopard is one of the fastest animals on earth, and the four wings would make it twice as fast as the two-winged lion (Babylon) and certainly faster than the ponderous bear (Medo-Persia). Such swiftness in conquest, indicated by the statement here that "dominion was given to it," was characteristic of *Greece.* Alexander the Great invaded Asia Minor in 334 B.C. and within four years had conquered the entire Medo-Persian Empire, including Egypt, Syria, and Israel. Within six more years he had subjected more than 11,000 miles of territory from Greece in the west to the borders of India in the east. The "four heads" of this beast represent the fourfold division of Alexander's Empire among his four generals after his death in 323 B.C.

The *fourth beast,* like the fourth kingdom depicted in the statue, is different from its predecessors (Daniel 7:7). Even before providing specific details, Daniel declared that this beast was a monster that was "dreadful and terrifying and extremely strong." Daniel does not provide details about the composition of the fourth beast as he did with the previous three, except to say that it had "large iron teeth" that devoured and feet that "crushed and trampled down" whatever remained (verse 7). It would appear that John describes this same creature in his description of the first beast in Revelation 13:2 and provides the missing details of a

composite animal comprised of lion, leopard, and bear. Daniel's mention of the *iron* teeth parallels the legs and feet of iron in the statue and represents the *Roman Empire,* which conquered the territory occupied by the nations represented by the earlier three beasts.

As Daniel describes this beast, he focuses on its most distinctive feature—its *ten horns* (verse 7) and the *little horn* that arose to dominate three of the others (Daniel 7:8). The ten horns, as Daniel's interpretation later reveals (verse 24), represents ten kings and kingdoms. The little horn comes up among the other horns in relative obscurity but eventually grows to supplant three of the existing horns. It is further described as having "eyes like the eyes of a man," an idiom for human personality and especially intelligence (cf. Ezekiel 1:18; Zechariah 3:9; 4:10), and a "mouth uttering great boasts," a euphemism for arrogant and boastful things, or as Daniel later reveals, speaking against God (Daniel 7:25). John clearly understood this when he depicted, in the book of Revelation, the first beast as having a "mouth speaking arrogant words and blasphemies" (13:5-6).

The term "horn" (Aramaic, *qeren*) depicts power or authority. As verses 23-24 reveal, the ten horns represent ten kings and their kingdoms, and the little horn represents an eleventh king. Since the fourth beast represents the Roman Empire, it appears that three stages of its existence are to be understood. The first stage is when the fourth beast gains dominion (the original Roman Empire). The second stage, with the ten horns, will be a revived form of the Roman Empire. The third and final stage will occur when the little horn, the Antichrist, rises quickly to prominence by uprooting three of his competitor kings and their kingdoms in order to fulfill his ambition to dominate the entire world.

THE ANCIENT OF DAYS
Daniel 7:9-12

IN DANIEL 7:9 A DRAMATIC shift in focus occurs, moving the audience from a vision of the little horn (Antichrist) on earth to a vision of the Son of Man (Christ) in heaven. The scene of Daniel's heavenly revelation is the divine tribunal, where judgment will be decided for the nations, as indicated by the words "[judgment] thrones were set up" (verse 9; cf. Revelation 20:4) and "the court [judgment] sat" (Daniel 7:10). One of the thrones was that of "the Ancient of Days," a reference to the eternality and sovereignty of God (Deuteronomy 33:27; Isaiah 40:28; 43:13; 44:6; 57:15). As the everlasting God He has observed all the actions of the nations throughout human history, and as the Judge of all the earth He has the right to call them to accountability.

The Ancient of Days has clothes like white snow and hair like pure wool, symbolizing God's holiness and righteousness (cf. Isaiah 1:18). This description resembles John's disconcerting revelation of the glorified Christ (Revelation 1:14-17). God's position on a blazing throne with flaming wheels (Daniel 7:9) is also similar to Ezekiel's depiction of God in his first encounter with God (Ezekiel 1:4-21; cf. Psalm 97:3). The multiple mention of various forms of fire in this passage also symbolize divine judgment (cf. Numbers 14:10-12; Deuteronomy 4:24). Surrounding the throne are myriad angelic attendants (Daniel 7:10) ready to execute divine judgment upon command (cf. Deuteronomy 33:2; Psalm 103:19-21; Hebrews 12:22; Revelation 5:11). Angels appear prominently in the book of Revelation as divine agents, announcing and orchestrating the terrestrial and cosmic judgments of the end time.

When the divine Judge is seated, the court convenes and the judgment books are opened (Daniel 7:10). The opening of the books symbolizes the process of judicial review of the nations (cf. Jeremiah 17:13; Revelation 20:12), whose position and power had been assigned by God. Their accountability to Him will be realized as He weighs, according to the divine standard, their actions with respect to His people. For Daniel to describe the judgment of the nations is appropriate, for his name means "God is my judge."

The judgment of the nations falls first on the fourth beast, whose little horn had blasphemed the Ancient of Days (Daniel 7:11).

This judgment will take the form of "burning fire" with the destruction of the body of the beast corresponding to the stone striking the feet and toes of the statue and disintegrating it (2:34-35,45). This judgment in flaming fire is presented by Paul as the judgment of "the man of sin" (2 Thessalonians 1:7-9; 2:8) and by John as the destruction of the first beast (the Antichrist) when he and the second beast (the false prophet) are cast into the lake of fire (Revelation 19:20). Moreover, this judgment will occur at the second advent, when the "Son of Man" comes "in the glory of His Father" to "repay every man according to his deeds" (Matthew 16:27).

The first three beasts (kingdoms), although conquered by the fourth, were not totally assimilated, as the existence of distinct European and Middle Eastern cultures today testify. Therefore, when the revived form of the Roman Empire appears, those countries that were merged into it in its previous stage will continue to exist and will share in the divine judgment that ends the dominion of the nations (Daniel 7:12). However, these nations will not be judged at the same time as the fourth beast. Rather, their judgment will be delayed for a time. This is consistent with the New Testament account that the Antichrist and his false prophet will be judged at the second advent (Revelation 19:19-20), ending the times of the Gentiles (cf. Psalm 2:9; Revelation 19:15), but the nations' judgment will be postponed until Christ has seated Himself on His throne and gathered all the nations before Him (Psalm 2:6; Matthew 25:31-33; cf. Luke 19:27).

THE SON OF MAN
Daniel 7:13-14

JUST AS EZEKIEL SAW a vision of the One seated on the throne "with the appearance of a man" (Ezekiel 1:26), so Daniel saw in his vision of the heavenly tribunal One like a "Son of Man" (Daniel 7:13). This Son of Man is distinct from the Ancient of Days and submissive to Him, yet He is given everlasting dominion over all the nations and is worshipped by them (verse 14). He came on the clouds of heaven and is eternal. Despite these unique characteristics, higher critical scholars have understood this enigmatic figure either as the angel Michael (12:1), or (the majority view) as a corporate identity as the saints (verses 18,21-22,25) or the "people of the saints" (verse 27)—that is, the Jewish people. By contrast, Jewish apocalyptic writers clearly understood the Son of Man as an individual having divine status. Parallels to Daniel 7:13-14 appear in the Similitudes of Enoch (1 Enoch 37-71) and Fourth Ezra (4 Ezra 13).

Given this usage and interpretation by the Jewish intertestamental authors, we should not be surprised that this text is the main Old Testament reference for Jesus' use of the term "Son of Man" (Mark 8:31; John 1:51), or that He and the New Testament writers understood this figure as a heavenly or *divine Messiah* (Matthew 16:27; Revelation 1:7,13; 14:14). Jesus cited this passage when teaching about His second advent (Matthew 24:30) and during His trial before the Jewish high priest when answering a question concerning His messianic credentials (Matthew 26:63-64). For this reason, in both Jewish and Christian circles, "Son of Man" has traditionally been understood in a messianic sense. Christians, therefore, identify Daniel 7:13-14 as a central messianic prophecy that reveals a divine Messiah who not only will receive the inheritance of the nations and the messianic kingdom, but also one who is distinct from the Father (the Ancient of Days) and is connected with humanity (Son of Man). The Son of Man's "coming in the clouds" is connected with the second coming by Jesus (Mark 13:26) and the New Testament writers (Acts 1:9-11; 1 Thessalonians 4:17; Revelation 1:7).

It is evident from this text that the kingdom bestowed by the Ancient of Days upon the Son of Man will conquer and replace the previous kingdoms on earth (Daniel 7:14), and therefore it will not come until the end time (cf. Psalm 2:6-9; Luke 19:11-27). This conquest will happen at the second advent, when Christ smites the nations in "the fierce wrath of God, the Almighty" (Revelation 19:15) and "the kingdom of the world has become the kingdom of our God ['Ancient of Days'] and of His Christ ['Son of Man']" (Revelation 11:15). In the same way the third kingdom will "rule over all the earth" (Daniel 2:39), so will the kingdom (of Christ) that replaces it. This description is in harmony with the earlier vision of the great statue (2:44-45) and indicates that the messianic kingdom will be established on earth rather than be a spiritual or heavenly rule exercised through the church.

THE MILLENNIAL KINGDOM
Daniel 7:18

THE AMILLENNIAL and postmillennial interpretation of Daniel 7:18 see "the saints of the Highest One" as Christians and "the kingdom" as the spiritual kingdom. However, it is difficult to see how the saints are to "receive" and "possess" the kingdom if they are in fact the kingdom. Rather, in harmony with Old Testament texts that promised Israel an eternal inheritance in the land (Genesis 15:18-21; Exodus 32:13; Deuteronomy 1:8; Psalm 37:29; Jeremiah 7:7; 25:5; Zechariah 8:12) and Jesus' own statement concerning inheritance and rule to the Jewish nation (Matthew 5:5; cf. Psalm 37:9,11,22,29) and to His disciples (Matthew 19:27-28), it is preferable to see this kingdom as the messianic (millennial) kingdom. Daniel's exilic audience would understand "the saints" to refer to the believing remnant of national Israel. Likewise, in the New Testament, after the resurrection of Christ, the apostles continued to understand that the kingdom would be restored to national Israel (Acts 1:6; 3:19-21). However, since the fulfillment of this prophecy will occur under the New Covenant in the millennial era, "the saints" must include 1) the Old Testament saints (Daniel 12:2), 2) the martyred Tribulation saints (Revelation 20:4), and 3) the Tribulation saints who survive the Tribulation (Matthew 25:32-34).

THE FOURTH KINGDOM
Daniel 7:19-28

HAVING RECEIVED the assurance that the people of Israel will ultimately know victory in the future, Daniel now desires to know the dreadful details concerning the fourth beast (Daniel 7:19) and especially the ten horns and the arrogant little horn (verse 20). Of special concern to Daniel is the conquering character of the little horn that supersedes three of the original horns and wages war against the saints and overpowers them (verse 21) until the Ancient of Days intercedes on behalf of the saints (verse 22). The explanation given by the interpreter clearly concerns an earthly kingdom that will gain dominion over the whole earth (verse 23). Likewise, the final stage of this earthly kingdom will be comprised of ten kings and kingdoms, three of which will be subdued by a different king (verse 24) who, for three-and-a-half years, will blaspheme God, persecute the saints, and "make alterations in times and in law" (verse 25).

According to the chronology of the Tribulation period as given in the Olivet Discourse and Revelation, the conquests of the Antichrist will take place during the first three-and-a-half-year division of the seventieth week (Revelation 6:2), at which time Israel is protected from war by an agreement with the Antichrist (the Antichrist also permits the rebuilding of the temple in Jerusalem and the reinstitution of the sacrificial calendar and services—Daniel 9:27). However, at the *midpoint* of the Tribulation, the Antichrist will invade Jerusalem (Revelation 11:2), desecrate the temple (Matthew 24:15; Mark 13:14; 2 Thessalonians 2:3-4), and change the times and law by putting an end to sacrifice and offering (Daniel 9:27). Then during the last three-and-a-half-year division of the Tribulation, the Antichrist will wage a war against God and His saints by blaspheming God (Revelation 13:5-6) and persecuting the Jewish remnant (Matthew 24:16-22; Mark 13:14-20; Revelation 13:7-10). The three-and-a-half-year period spoken of

in Daniel 7:25 is therefore the final part of the Tribulation, which will culminate in the campaigns of Armageddon and the second advent of Christ.

Daniel does not give further details concerning the little horn at this point; however, the information already given about the little horn was sufficient for John to build on in his revelation of the first beast. In Revelation 13:1-10 the ascent of the first beast (the Antichrist) and his usurpation of divine prerogatives is described with allusions drawn from the career of the little horn. The literary parallels between these two texts are as follows:

Comparison of Daniel 7 and Revelation 13

"Little Horn" (Daniel 7)	"First Beast" (Revelation 13)
Beast whose power funneled into the little horn has ten horns (verse 7)	Beast has ten horns (verse 1)
Rises from the sea (verse 3)	Rises from the sea (verse 1)
Mouth speaks arrogant words (verse 8)	Mouth speaks arrogant words (verse 5)
Makes war with the saints and prevails (verse 25)	Makes war with the saints and overcomes them (verse 7)
Speaks out against the Most High (verse 25)	Opens mouth in blasphemy against God (verse 6)

The destruction of the little horn (the Antichrist) appears in Daniel 7:26. The scene here moves from earth to heaven to view the heavenly tribunals' decree of judgment. The heavenly court convenes for the specific purpose of determining the destruction the Antichrist and the removal of his dominion (cf. Revelation 6:10; 11:15-19; 19:1-3). It assumes the background previously seen in Daniel 7:13-14, where the Son of Man takes on the role of executor of the judgment that ends the dominion of the Antichrist during the final campaign of Armageddon (Zechariah 14:3-7,12-15; 2 Thessalonians 2:8-9; Revelation 19:11-21). When the Son of Man returns, He will remove the desecrator of the temple and will Himself become the consecrator of the millennial temple (Haggai 2:9; Zechariah 6:12-13).

After the Antichrist and his kingdom are removed from power, all representatives of the other kingdoms that attack the Jewish people at the final battle of Armageddon will now give their obeisance to the Jewish people, whose kingdom (the messianic kingdom) has been restored. According to Daniel 7:27, "all the dominions [nations] will serve and obey Him." Those who say this prophecy has been fulfilled must be asked how this is possible in a world in which more than half the global population (6.5 billion) has rejected Christ. That Daniel 7:27 has a future and literal fulfillment is in accord with the clear prophecies that believing nations will enter into the millennial kingdom (Matthew 25:34) and will serve Christ and His people Israel (Isaiah 60:3,12; 66:18; Zechariah 14:16; Revelation 21:24-26).

It is significant to note that after Daniel received this revelation, he was alarmed (Daniel 7:15,28). Some people have a rather irreverent attitude toward prophecy, approaching it as a pastime and reveling in figuring out complex date schemes and drawing detailed diagrams of the future. But the seriousness of prophetic truth personally affected Daniel, provoking godly fear and introspection. Rather than publish his latest prophetic insight, Daniel kept the matter to himself (verse 28). Of course, he eventually did reveal these truths to the saints by recording them under divine guidance (8:26; 12:4). Daniel's response indicates to us that the more we know about the future, the more our heart should be moved to personal purity (1 John 3:1-3), practical preparation (1 Thessalonians 1:9-10), and prayerful petition on behalf of those who may have to face the judgments to come (2 Peter 3:8-9).

THE PROPHETIC PROGRAM FOR ISRAEL DURING THE TIMES OF THE GENTILES
Daniel 8–12

In the remainder of Daniel's prophecy (chapters 8–12), the message shifts from an announcement to the nations to a concern for the future of the Jewish people. This shift back to a Jewish audience is indicated once again by a change in language, from the use of the more universal Aramaic to Hebrew, the language exclusive to Israel. Perhaps as Daniel pondered the successive dominations of world empires, he began to wonder what would happen to his people after the fall of Babylon and until the times of the Gentiles were completed. Daniel 8, then, concentrates on the second world empire—Medo-Persia—depicted as a ram (verses 3-4,20), and the third world empire—Greece—depicted as a goat (verses 5-7,21). The chapter also mentions the persecution of the Jewish people by the "small horn" (Antiochus IV Epiphanes) in verses 23-25, which serves as a type of the final persecution by the "little horn" (the Antichrist). As befits the purpose of this commentary, prophecies that have been fulfilled in past history will receive minor comment, with more attention devoted to those yet to be fulfilled. An exception is made in the case of the prophecy concerning the Seleucid ruler Antiochus IV Epiphanes, which was fulfilled in 170–165 B.C., because the description of his character and conduct serve as a typological pattern for the coming Antichrist and therefore deserves additional comment.

THE RAM, GOAT, AND SMALL HORN
Daniel 8:1-27

Daniel received the vision of the ram, goat, and small horn in 551 B.C., the third year of Belshazzar's reign (Daniel 8:1). At this time this unworthy king ruled alone (his father

Harmony of Daniel 2 and 7

Chapter 2 — Nebuchadnezzar's Dream of the Image		History	Chapter 7 — Daniel's Vision of the Four Beasts	
Prophecy		*Fulfillment*	*Prophecy*	
Dream 2:31-35	Interpretation 2:36-45	World Empire	Interpretation 7:15-28	Dream 7:1-14
2:32 Head (gold)	2:38 You—Nebuchadnezzar	Babylonian 612-539 B.C.	7:17 King	7:4 Lion with wings of an eagle
2:32 Breasts and arms (silver)	2:39 Inferior kingdom	Medo-Persian 539-331 B.C.	7:17 King	7:5 Bear raised up on one side
2:32 Belly and thighs (bronze)	2:39 Third kingdom	Grecian 331-63 B.C.	7:17 King	7:6 Leopard with four heads and four wings on its back
2:33 Legs (iron) Feet (iron and clay)	2:40 Fourth kingdom	Ancient Rome 63 B.C.–A.D. 476 (ROME)	7:7, 19 Fourth beast with iron teeth and claws of bronze	
			7:23 Fourth kingdom	
			7:24 Ten kings	7:7-8 Ten horns
		Revived Roman Empire	7:24 Different king	7:8 Little horn uttering great boasts
2:35 Great mountain	2:44 Kingdom which will never be destroyed	Messianic kingdom	7:27 Everlasting kingdom	7:9 Thrones were set up

Adapted from Thomas Ice. Taken from H. Wayne House and Randall Price, Charts of Bible Prophecy, p. 63. Copyright © 2003 by H. Wayne House and World of the Bible Ministries, Inc., Used by permission of Zondervan.

Nabonidus had gone to Arabia), and the Neo-Babylonian empire was being threatened by the rising power of the Persian leader Cyrus. In the following year Cyrus would conquer the Median Empire, thereby setting the stage for the soon invasion of Babylon (539 B.C.) by the newly combined kingdom of Medo-Persia. The vision was geographically based in the city of Susa (verse 2), located about 350 miles east of Babylon. Susa was in the province of Elam, the birthplace of the Medo-Persian empire and one of the main capitals during the Persian period. Esther and Nehemiah were among the residents of Susa (Nehemiah 1:1; Esther 1:2). Prophetically, Elam is one of the key sites from which a remnant of the Jewish people will be regathered at the time of the second advent (Isaiah 11:11) and one that will have its fortunes restored in the millennial kingdom (Jeremiah 49:39).

THE PROPHECY REVEALED
Daniel 8:3-14

Daniel first was shown the image of an all-conquering *ram* (male sheep) with two horns that was butting in westward, northward, and southward directions (verses 3-4). The angelic interpreter Gabriel explained this as the dual kingdom of Medo-Persia (verse 20), which compares to the silver chest with two arms (2:32) and the two-sided bear (7:5). The ram's butting in three directions represents the three directions of Medo-Persian military conquests: the Medes (northward), Lydia (Asia Minor) and Greece (westward), and Babylon and Egypt (southward), and compares with the three ribs in the mouth of the two-sided bear. Next a male *goat* appears from the west, and with great speed ("without touching the ground") he rushes at the ram and completely overpowers him (8:5-7). Gabriel explained that the goat represented the kingdom of Greece (verse 21). This prophecy was fulfilled when Greece, under Alexander the Great, settled in Susa in 324 B.C., having conquered all of the territory that was formerly part of the vast Medo-Persian empire.

Alexander's insistence on intermarrying with foreign women made many of Alexander's Macedonian generals rebel. After Alexander's death, four of the generals divided the empire into *four parts:* Macedonia went to Cassander, Thrace and most of Asia Minor went to Lysimachus, Syria went to Seleucus, and Egypt went to Ptolemy. Daniel predicted this four-fold division when he saw the image of "the large horn" (Alexander) of the goat (Greece) being broken and four horns (four generals) sprouting in its place toward the four winds of heaven (8:8). Out of these horns grew a "small horn" that grew great toward the land of Israel (verse 9). This small horn trampled down God's people ("the host of heaven"), made itself equal to God ("the Commander of the host"), "removed the regular sacrifice" from the temple, and brought in a horrifying transgression that remained for 2300 days before the holy place was restored (verses 10-14).

This description fits one of the most invasive and desolating figures in Jewish history, the Seleucid ruler Antiochus IV Epiphanes, who in 170 B.C. began a national campaign to end Judaism and replace it with a Hellenistic culture. To this end he deified himself, minting coins bearing the inscription *Antiochus Theos Epiphanes* ("Antiochus the god made manifest"). He also erected an idol of Zeus Olympias (the chief god of the Greeks) beside the temple's great altar; banned Jewish practices (observance of the Mosaic law, the Sabbath, and circumcision), including the regular or *tamid* (daily) sacrifice, and offered swine (unclean animals for Jews) as sacrifices on the altar in the Jerusalem temple. Antiochus also introduced foreign idolatrous images and practices to the Holy Place, bringing about "the abomination of desolation" (11:31; cf. 9:27) and resulting in ritual desecration that rendered the temple defiled, thus disrupting the ceremonial service (cf. 1 Maccabees 1:10-21).

The Jewish population's resistance to all this resulted in widespread persecution and slaughter (1 Maccabees 1:24,37,57-64; 2 Maccabees 5:11-14,23-26). The tide was turned when a revolt led by the priest Judas Maccabeus and his sons overthrew the forces of

Antiochus and reconsecrated the temple on December 25, 164 B.C. (1 Maccabees 4:52-59). The duration of time—"2,300 evenings and mornings"—until the reconsecration occurred (Daniel 8:14) has been interpreted in two ways. First, if "evenings and mornings" refers to "days," then the length of time in view here is six years and four months, the time from the beginning of the Antiochean persecution in 170 B.C. to its end in 164 B.C. Second, if "evenings and mornings" refer to the *tamid,* the daily sacrifice, then 2300 sacrifices equals 1150 days (1150 morning sacrifices + 1150 evening sacrifices). This span of three years and 55 days runs from the time of Antiochus's desecration of the temple (December 16, 167 B.C.) to the reconsecration of the temple (December 25, 164 B.C.). Regardless of how the 2300 evenings and mornings are interpreted, it's clear they were literally fulfilled by the events that took place.

The description of Antiochus IV Epiphanes as the small horn of Daniel 8:9-13,23-25 and the "despicable person" in Daniel 11:21-35 marks him out as a type of the little horn (the Antichrist). Historicists, especially those of the higher critical school, wish to see a complete identification with the little horn (7:8,20-26). However, even a cursory comparison of the two figures (see below) reveals they are not identical. In addition, the historical details of Antiochus IV Epiphanes's career cannot accommodate the symbolism of the little horn.

The Little Horn (Daniel 7)	The Small Horn (Daniel 8)
Origin is fourth kingdom (Rome)	Origin is third kingdom (Greece)
An eleventh horn that removes three of the ten horns	A fifth horn that comes out of one of the four horns
Persecutes the Jewish people for 42 months (3½ years)	Persecutes the Jewish people for 2300 evenings and mornings

According to Daniel, the little horn is an eschatological figure (the Antichrist) and is clearly identified as such by John in the book of Revelation, which was written when Rome was in power. By contrast, the small horn finds its fulfillment before the fourth kingdom of Rome arises and can be identified from historical sources as Antiochus IV Epiphanes. These differences compel us to identify two distinct individuals in these chapters. However, the similarities shared by Antiochus and the Antichrist are striking and establish a typological relationship between the two figures (see chart on page 242).

**THE PROPHECY EXPLAINED
Daniel 8:15-27**

The angelic interpreter Gabriel (8:15-16) again comes to Daniel to explain the correct meaning of the imagery Daniel had seen. *Gabriel* means "champion of God," and apparently he has a special commission from God to serve as the revelator to Israel of God's messianic program. In that capacity he will later announce the birth of the messianic forerunner, John, to his father Zacharias (Luke 1:19) and Jesus' birth to Mary (Luke 1:26). Here in Daniel, Gabriel will (13 years later) reveal to Daniel God's "seventy weeks" program for national Israel (9:20-27). Because the messianic element of God's plan for Israel will not be completed until after the times of the Gentiles has run its course, Gabriel explained that this prophecy pertained to "the time of the end" (8:17). The term "time of the end" (Hebrew, *'et-qetz*) in Daniel (8:17,19; 11:35,40; 12:4,6,9,13), as in the rest of the Old Testament, is distinct from the term "latter days" (Hebrew, *"charit hayamim*) (2:28; 10:14).

Both are eschatological expressions, but only *'et-qetz* refers exclusively to the final eschatological period or event. The paralleling of "latter days" by the expression *qetz hayyamim* ("final" or "end period") strengthens the eschatological meaning of "latter days." The combined construction *'et-qetz* ("time of the end"), which appears uniquely in Daniel and only in the latter half of the book, is strictly

THE INDIGNATION AND THE TIMES OF THE GENTILES

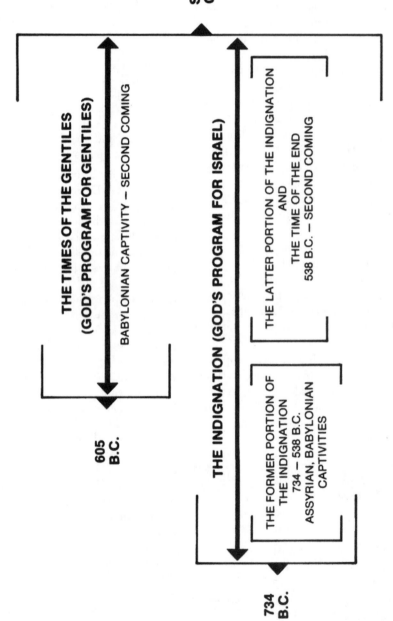

**THE TIMES OF THE GENTILES
(GOD'S PROGRAM FOR GENTILES)**

BABYLONIAN CAPTIVITY – SECOND COMING

**605
B.C.**

THE INDIGNATION (GOD'S PROGRAM FOR ISRAEL)

THE LATTER PORTION OF THE INDIGNATION
AND
THE TIME OF THE END
538 B.C. – SECOND COMING

THE FORMER PORTION OF
THE INDIGNATION
734 – 538 B.C.
ASSYRIAN, BABYLONIAN
CAPTIVITIES

**734
B.C.**

**SECOND
COMING**

Adapted from chart by Renald E. Showers, The Most High God (Bellmawr, NJ: The Friends of Israel Gospel Ministry, 1982), p. 103. Used by permission.

eschatological. Here it appears 11 times as a chronological marker of a specific eschatological period (9:21,25; 11:6,13-14,24; 12:11). Pfandl (*The Time of the End in the Book of Daniel*, pp. 213-72) notes that in Daniel 12:1-2 especially it assumes the character of an apocalyptic *terminus technicus* denoting the final period that culminates the divine program, including all the events of that time, especially the second advent.

The focus on the "end time" and the "final period of the indignation" reveals that the events pertaining to Antiochus's persecution of the Jewish people and desecration of the temple—and therefore against God, "the Prince of princes" (8:25)—would have their ultimate fulfillment with the antitype, the Antichrist, during the Tribulation. In relation to "the abomination of desolation," it is evident from Jesus' statement (based on Daniel's prophecy) that He viewed this event as yet to be fulfilled and connected it to the time of His second advent (Matthew 24:15; Mark 13:14; cf. 2 Thessalonians 2:3-4; Revelation 11:1-2). Antiochus did many of the things the future Antichrist will do, and in this way established a prophetic pattern for what is to come.

THE 70 WEEKS
Daniel 9:1-27

WHEN THE PERSIAN EMPIRE overthrew the Babylonians in 539 B.C. as predicted (5:25-31; cf. Isaiah 41:25-26; 44:26–45:3), Daniel realized the day of Israel's release was at hand. During the first year of the reign of Darius the Mede (538 B.C.) Daniel consulted the Scriptures and found his expectation confirmed by Jeremiah's prophecy that predicted the end of the Babylonian exile after 70 years (Jeremiah 25:11), the punishment of "the king of Babylon and that nation" (Jeremiah 25:12), and afterward the return of the Jewish exiles to the land of Israel (Jeremiah 29:10). Daniel further understood from Jeremiah and Ezekiel that the promised restoration depended on national repentance

(Jeremiah 29:10-14; Ezekiel 14:6; 18:30-32). Therefore, Daniel sought to personally intercede for Israel through a prayer of penitence that focused on the restoration program for Jerusalem and the Temple Mount.

DANIEL'S PRAYER
Daniel 9:3-19

Because the 70 weeks prophecy is the divine response to Daniel's prayer we should notice concerning this prayer that 1) it centers on a request for divine clemency toward the desolated sanctuary (Daniel 9:17-18), the people, and the city (verse 19) because they are God's possession and are called by His name; 2) it uses a number of terms that will be developed in verses 24-27: "desolations" (verses 17-18), "transgressions" (verse 11), "iniquity" (verses 5,13,16), "sin" (verses 5,8,11,20), "sanctuary" (verse 17; cf. verse 20), "city" (verse 19), "people" (verses 19-20), and "law of Moses" (verses 11,13); and 3) it contains vocabulary reminiscent of Jeremiah and Ezekiel's *desecration passages:* a) departure of Israel from the covenant (verses 5,10-11,13,14-15); b) judgment of the curses written in the law (verses 11,13); c) refusal to hear the prophets (verses 6,10); d) the sins of the fathers (verses 6,8,16); e) identification with the holy name (verse 19); f) exile due to cultic rebellion (verse 7); and g) the reproach from the nations caused by Israel's exile (verse 16). Therefore, verses 3-19 place the prophecy of verses 24-27 in a historical context as an *extension* of Jeremiah's historical prophecy. Consequently, as Jacques Doukhan (*Daniel: The Vision of the End*, p.8) has pointed out: "The seventy sevens' prophecy must be interpreted with regard to *history* in as realistic a way as Daniel did for the prophecy of Jeremiah."

From Daniel's prayer it appears that he expected the immediate and complete fulfillment of Israel's restoration with the conclusion of the 70-year captivity. Daniel rightly connected "the completion of the desolations of Jerusalem" (verse 2) with the end of the exile, even though Jeremiah had only spoken of desolations and of 70 years ending the exile

Development of Antichrist Typology

Antichrist typology develops from specific opponents of God and oppressors of God's people. It gains distinctive elements as each successive type adapts to the progressive historical situation. Thus, as God's relationship with the Jewish nation becomes centered on the temple, the characteristic oppressive act becomes concentrated on desecrating this divine ideal, thereby creating a paradigm for the expected antitype, the final eschatological opponent/oppressor—*the Antichrist*.

Typological Figure	Typological Activity
PHARAOH (unnamed to emphasize opponent status with God)	Opposed God (Ex 5:2) Oppressed People of God (Ex 1:11, 22)
NEBUCHADNEZZAR	**Opposed God** (Hab 1:6-11) **Oppressed People of God** (2Ki 24:14) *New Element*: Desecrated Temple of God (2Ki 24:13)
ANTIOCHUS IV EPIPHANES	**Opposed God** (Da 11:36) **Oppressed People of God** (Da 11:41) **Desecrate Temple of God** (Da 11:31) *New Element*: Abomination of Desolation (Da 11:31)
TITUS	**Opposed God** (Jn 19:7-16) **Oppressed People of God** (Da 9:26) **Desecrated Temple of God** (Da 9:26; Mt 24:2/ Mk 13:2; Lk. 21:6) **Abomination of Desolations** (Da 9:26; Lk 21:20-24) *New Element*: Roman origin (Da 9:26; Jn 11:48)
Antitype	Antitypical Activity
ANTICHRIST	**Opposes God** (Da 8:25; 11:36-39; 2Th 2:4; Rev 13:6) **Oppresses People of God** (Da 9:27; 11:41; Rev 13:7) **Desecrates Temple of God** (Da 9:27; 2Th 2:4) **Abomination of Desolation** (Da 9:27; Mt 24:15/Mk 13:14; Rev 13:14-15) **Roman origin** (Da 7:23; 9:27)

(Jeremiah 25:12) and initiating a return to the land (Jeremiah 29:10), not the end of Gentile world dominion and Israel's eschatological restoration. It is true that at the end of the 70 years a remnant returned from the exile to rebuild the Jerusalem temple, but other Jewish communities continued to remain in exile, and Jerusalem itself continued under Gentile domination.

RESPONSE TO DANIEL'S PRAYER
Daniel 9:20-23

In answer to Daniel's petition God sent the archangel Gabriel, who had interpreted Daniel's previous prophecies (Daniel 9:21). Gabriel appeared at about 3:00 P.M., the time the evening sacrifice was offered in the temple (verse 21), confirming to Daniel that his prayer for the temple ("the holy mountain of my God," verse 20) would receive an answer. Gabriel assured Daniel that he had been dispatched from the very moment the prayer had begun (verses 22-23). The answer to Daniel's prayer was the 70 weeks prophecy that reveals that Israel's restoration would be progressive and would ultimately be fulfilled only at the time of the end (cf. Daniel 12). Daniel was advised to "give heed to the message and gain understanding" (9:23), which indicates that the interpretation of this prophecy would be difficult and would require diligent effort. The history of its interpretation has demonstrated this truth and admonishes every new student to carefully consider its complicated yet critical message concerning the future of Israel.

THE 70 WEEKS
Daniel 9:24-27

In the progression of the prophetic revelation in Daniel 2-8, the prophecy in 9:24-27 of the 70 weeks (or sevens) must be considered the climax. Chapter 2 laid the prophetic foundation for the events of the Tribulation and millennial kingdom. Chapters 7 and 8 provided additional details with a focus on the Antichrist (as seen in the image of the little horn and typified by the small horn, Antiochus IV Epiphanes). Chapter 9 includes all the elements revealed in these chapters but moves its focus to the city of Jerusalem, the prophetic stage where the eschatological events will be played out. Gabriel explained (9:24) that 70 weeks were decreed as the time necessary for both Daniel's people (the Jewish people) and the holy city (Jerusalem) to complete God's prophetic program for Israel (which includes both advents of Christ). No portion of the Old Testament is as essential to unlocking the mysteries of God's future program for Israel. In this regard the late seminary president and author Alva J. McClain (*Daniel's Prophecy of the Seventy Weeks*, p. 6) stated, "…with reference to its importance, I am convinced that in the predictions of the Seventy Sevens, we have the indispensable chronological key to all New Testament prophecy."

This prophecy concerns "the times of the Gentiles" (Luke 21:24) from the perspective of Israel, defining its beginning and ending by "the desolation of Jerusalem"—the time from the Babylonian conquest to the second advent of Christ—after which Israel's time of restoration will begin (Zechariah 8:1-15; 14:3-21). Also here is the entire prophetic history of Jerusalem, with special emphasis on the Jerusalem temple, down to the end of the age. The prophecy of the 70 weeks therefore belongs to the larger corpus of *prophetic restoration texts* given to national Israel as a comfort in her captivity and as a promise of the coming messianic redemption that would take place in Jerusalem and on the Temple Mount (Isaiah 2:2-4; 40–66; Jeremiah 30–33; Ezekiel 33–48). Furthermore, the 70 weeks prophecy serves as the prophetic template for eschatological portions of the New Testament, including Jesus' Olivet Discourse (Matthew 24:3-31; Mark 13:4-27; Luke 21:7-11,25-28), Paul's "day of the Lord" discourse, (2 Thessalonians 2), and the Tribulation chapters of Revelation (6–19).

Of first concern in interpreting Daniel 9:24-27 and determining whether it has been *completely* fulfilled historically or only *partially* with the rest to be fulfilled in the eschatological period is the determination of the division

The Times of the Gentiles

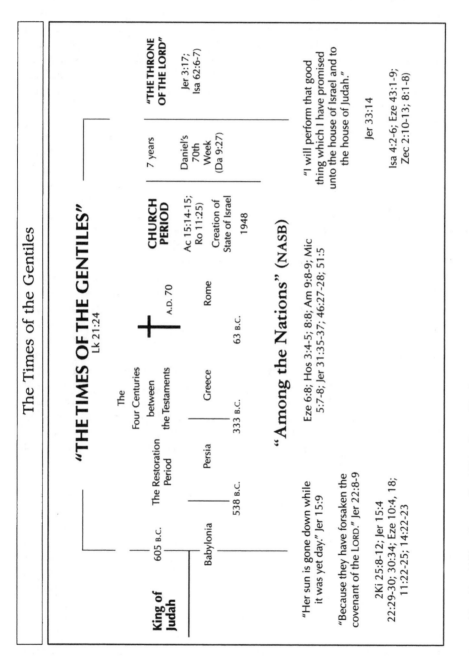

"THE TIMES OF THE GENTILES"
Lk 21:24

King of Judah

605 B.C.

Babylonia

538 B.C.

The Restoration Period

Persia

333 B.C.

The Four Centuries between the Testaments

Greece

63 B.C.

Rome

A.D. 70 ✝

CHURCH PERIOD

Ac 15:14-15; Ro 11:25)

Creation of State of Israel
1948

7 years

Daniel's 70th Week
(Da 9:27)

"THE THRONE OF THE LORD"

Jer 3:17;
Isa 62:6-7)

"Among the Nations" (NASB)

Eze 6:8; Hos 3:4-5; 8:8; Am 9:8-9; Mic 5:7-8; Jer 31:35-37; 46:27-28; 51:5

"Her sun is gone down while it was yet day." Jer 15:9

"Because they have forsaken the covenant of the LORD." Jer 22:8-9

2Ki 25:8-12; Jer 15:4
22:29-30; 30:34; Eze 10:4, 18;
11:22-25; 14:22-23

"I will perform that good thing which I have promised unto the house of Israel and to the house of Judah."

Jer 33:14

Isa 4:2-6; Eze 43:1-9;
Zec 2:10-13; 8:1-8)

Adapted from H. Wayne House and Randall Price, Charts of Bible Prophecy, p. 110. Copyright © 2003 by H. Wayne House and World of the Bible Ministries, Inc. Used by permission of Zondervan.

of the 70 sevens or weeks. The Masoretic tradition divides the 70 weeks into three separate periods: 7 weeks, 62 weeks, and 1 week. According to this interpretation the events of the 70 weeks are as follows: the *first* unit of 7 weeks (49 years) is the period of the rebuilding of the temple and the city, and at the end of this period (or during), an anointed prince or ruler will appear (verse 25). The *second* unit of 62 sevens (434 years) is a time span during which the city is restored and at the end of which another prince or ruler will be cut off, signaling the advent of troublous times (verses 25-26).

Those who disregard the Masoretic interpretation in favor of logical and contextual evidence divide the 70 weeks (49 years) into two periods that join the 7 weeks and the 62 weeks (434 years) together for 69 weeks (483 years) followed by a separate 7 (7 years). The first division is the time in which the city and temple are rebuilt (49 years) and continue (434 years) until the advent of the anointed prince, the Messiah (483 years). The purpose of keeping the 483 years together is based on the messianic perspective of this passage, which understands the period of the restoration of Jerusalem as separate from and leading to the messianic advent. After this, Messiah is "cut off" (killed), and the Roman destruction of Jerusalem takes place. Whether this occurs *after* the sixty-ninth week (483 years) or *in* the seventieth week (7 years) depends on whether the interpreter is a futurist or historicist.

Futurists understand the death of Christ and the Roman destruction of Jerusalem to have taken place *after* the sixty-ninth week and view the events of the seventieth week as occurring in the future eschatological age. During the seventieth week a covenant is made with the Antichrist (in the first half of the seven years), who will desecrate the temple (at the midpoint of the seven years) and be destroyed at the return of Christ (at the end of the seven years).

Dispensationalists have argued that verse 27 indicates a *prophetic postponement* in fulfillment of the events of the seventieth seven.

Prophetic postponement, also known as apotelesmatic interpretation, is the recognition of a delay or interruption in the fulfillment of the prophetic program. It is observed in "day of the Lord" texts where prophesied events may have a near and far (eschatological) fulfillment. It is more commonly observed in messianic contexts where events associated with the first and second advents appear together. In such cases the interpreter understands that a chronological interval separates these historical and eschatological events (cf. Genesis 49:10, 11-12; Psalm 2:7, 8; 22:1-21,22-32; Isaiah 9:1-2, 3-5; 9:6,7; 59:16,17-21; Micah 5:2-3a,6-15; Zechariah 9:9, 10; Malachi 4:5, 6). Sometimes this distinction can even be observed within a single verse. Jesus, discerning that Isaiah 61:1-2 was fulfilled in His first advent but verses 2-11 wouldn't be fulfilled until His second advent, stopped His public reading of the text in midsentence (Luke 4:16-21).

One example of such an interval was previously announced by Gabriel in relation to Jeremiah's 70-year fulfillment in Daniel's seventy weeks of years. All commentators accept the fact of this postponement—it is simply a question of the length of time involved. Similar temporal intervals also appear in Daniel chapters 2, 7, 8, and will again in Daniel 11. In this light, one might expect to find a similar occurrence in chapter 9. Setting the 69 weeks off as a distinct unit comprised of the 7 and 62 weeks implies that the events of the seventieth week are also to be treated separately. The events of the cutting off of Messiah and the destruction of the city and sanctuary by the people of the coming prince occur *after* the 69 weeks (verse 26) and are *before* the seventieth week (verse 27). If these events were intended to occur *in* the seventieth week, the text would have read "during" or "in the midst of" (cf. Daniel's use of *hetzi*, "in the middle of," verse 27). This language implies that these events *precede* the seventieth week, but do not *immediately* follow the sixty-ninth. Therefore, a temporal interval must separate the two. This is evidenced by the opening word of verse 27 (Hebrew, *higbbir*, "confirm"), which is prefixed by the *waw* consecutive, a grammatical connective that indicates the events of verse 27 are *subsequent* to those of verse 26.

Further evidence for the *eschatological interpretation* of verse 27 comes from a comparison with Jesus' interpretation of the order of the events of the seventieth week. In Matthew 24:7-14 Jesus predicts that persecution, suffering, and wars would continue to the end of the age, climaxing in a time of unparalleled distress (Matthew 24:21-22—that is, "the time of Jacob's distress," Jeremiah 30:7). Only *after* these events does Jesus make reference to Daniel 9:27 (Matthew 24:15) concerning the signal event during this time of tribulation, "the abomination of desolation." If the 70 weeks were to run sequentially, without interruption, then why does Jesus place this intervening period *before* the fulfillment of the events of the seventieth week? The text of Matthew in particular reveals that Jesus' preview of the future was to answer His disciples' questions concerning His second coming and the end of the age (Matthew 24:3). Jesus explains why His coming is necessary and when it will occur ("after the tribulation of those days"— verse 29). According to Matthew, the events described in this period prior to the messianic advent could not have been fulfilled in A.D. 70 with the destruction of Jerusalem, since these events usher in the coming of Christ.

Some critics ask dispensationalists what justification they have for stretching out the 70 weeks to 2000 years. This is an imprecise way of viewing the "sevens." The 70 weeks have *not* been extended. Rather, the fulfillment of the seventieth week has been postponed. Because the 70 weeks deal exclusively with fulfillment in connection with Israel (Daniel 9:24), and Israel's national rejection of the Messiah and divine discipline (dispersion) took place after the sixty-ninth week was fulfilled, the fulfillment of the seventieth week had to take place during the final period of Israel's discipline and deliverance, or the Tribulation and second advent. The prophecy states that 70 weeks, not 69 weeks, would be necessary to fulfill the six prophetic goals of Daniel

9:24. The fact that these goals have not been *literally* fulfilled for national Israel requires an interval and a postponed fulfillment until the seventieth week.

THE MEANING OF THE 70 WEEKS
Daniel 9:24

Gabriel stated that "seventy weeks" rather than "seventy years" (Jeremiah 25:11) was the time decreed to complete the period of indignation (Daniel 9:24). It is important to understand the meaning of the crucial chronological term "week" in order to properly interpret the prophecy. The word "week" also means "seven" (Hebrew, *shavua'*) and can mean seven of anything—days, months, or years—in the same way that the English word *dozen* can mean 12 of anything. Usually *shavua'* refers to a week of days, as attested by every appearance of the noun by itself in the Old Testament (Genesis 29:27-28; Exodus 34:22; Leviticus 12:5; Numbers 28:26; Deuteronomy 16:9 [twice],10,16; 2 Chronicles 8:13; Jeremiah 5:24). However, Gabriel's explanation in Daniel 9:25-27 makes clear that a considerably longer period is in view, and therefore the usage of *shavua'* in Daniel's prophecy must mean week of *years* or seven years. This usage is also found in Jewish apocalyptic literature (for example, the "Apocalypse of Weeks," 1 Enoch 91-104, which is to be expected because much of 1 Enoch draws its thematic material from Daniel). John Whitcomb ("The Book of Daniel," pp. 259-63) has demonstrated the validity of this usage on the basis of analogous Hebrew usage, comparative chronology, and the prophetic context.

Further assistance in determining the duration of *shavua'* in this prophecy comes from a comparison with other texts that observe a chronological scheme based on the 70 weeks. For example, Daniel 7:25 and 12:7 predict that a wicked person (Antichrist) will commit abominable acts "for a time, times, and half a time." This phrase is also used in Revelation 12:14, where it is parallel with the phrase "one thousand two hundred and sixty days" (Revelation 11:3; 12:6). This same period is mentioned in Revelation 11:2 and 13:5 as being "forty-two months." Thus, "a time, times, and half a time," according to Revelation, equals either 1260 days (42 months) or "a year and two years and a half a year" (three and a half years). Similar measurements of time also appear in Daniel 9:27: "one week...middle of the week." If *shavua'* is a "week of *years*," then *shavua' 'echad* ("one week") is a period of seven years, and *hetzi hashavua'* ("middle [or half] of the week") a period of three and a half years, which agrees with the New Testament interpretation of the phrase.

Having established that the prophecy is in weeks [sevens] of *years,* "seventy weeks" (Hebrew *shavu'im shivᵉ'im*) indicates a time span of seventy weeks [sevens] of years, or 490 years (70 x 7 = 490). This number is not merely an arbitrary one, but was based on a decreed period of discipline for Israel (the period of indignation). This determination is given in the biblical texts that explain the duration of the captivity as a sevenfold judgment based on the covenantal stipulation found in Leviticus 26:34-35,43 (cf. 25:2-5). The Jewish calendar, as given by God, was divided into seven-year periods, with every seventh year being a sabbath year. During this seventh year the people were to give the land a rest ("sabbath") by leaving it unworked. Failure to observe this covenantal obligation over a period of 490 years had resulted in a 70-year exile that allowed the land to "catch up" on the number of sabbath years it had lost (2 Chronicles 36:21).

The time period given in the passages that explain Israel's violation of the sabbatical years is 490 years. Since Daniel was studying Jeremiah to determine when the captivity would conclude, and there he learned that 490 years of sabbatical violations had resulted in 70 years of punishment (captivity), would it not make more sense that the announcement of another corresponding period of 70 weeks be 490 *years,* rather than 490 *days?* Certainly the warning of another destruction of Jerusalem and the temple only a year and a half after the end of the exile would have been of little comfort.

PROPHETIC GOALS OF THE 70 WEEKS
Daniel 9:24

Daniel 9:24 reveals that the 70 weeks (490 years) are determined for the completion of six prophetic goals for the nation of Israel. All interpretive views understand that the six prophetic goals of the 70 weeks establish the time of the prophecy's fulfillment. Nonfuturists argue that although these goals were future in Daniel's day, they were all fulfilled historically in the death, resurrection, and ascension of Jesus. Futurists contend that while some of the redemptive goals may have been fulfilled at Christ's first advent, most relate to Israel's national, spiritual, and physical restoration and will find fulfillment at Christ's second advent. These are the six prophetic goals of Daniel 9:24:

1. to finish the transgression

2. to make an end of sin

3. to make atonement for iniquity

4. to bring in everlasting righteousness

5. to seal up vision and prophecy

6. to anoint the most holy place

Before interpreting these prophetic goals, note that verse 24 states that the fulfillment of these goals relates solely to the people and land of Israel ("your people and your holy city"). In other words, the fulfillment of the 70 weeks prophecy must occur only with national Israel and in the historic city of Jerusalem. Because a Jewish remnant returned to Judah to resettle the land and to rebuild Jerusalem as was predicted to occur within the 69 weeks (483 years), the remainder of the prophecy cannot be interpreted other than in terms of literal, historical fulfillment for national Israel. In addition, the verbs used to describe the goals—"finish" (Hebrew, *kalle'* from *kalah* = "bring to an end"), "to seal" (Hebrew, *chᵉttom* from *chatam* = "seal up"), "make an end" (Hebrew, *hatem* from *tamam* = "be complete"), "bring in" (Hebrew, *habyi'* from *bw'* = "come")—indicate a finality that can only be understood of the final age or the

UNITS OF SEVENTY

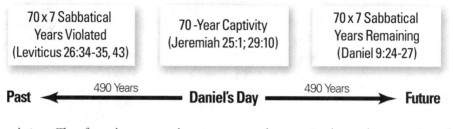

| 70 x 7 Sabbatical Years Violated (Leviticus 26:34-35, 43) | 70 -Year Captivity (Jeremiah 25:1; 29:10) | 70 x 7 Sabbatical Years Remaining (Daniel 9:24-27) |

Past ← 490 Years → Daniel's Day — 490 Years → Future

end time. Therefore, the context does not point to a fulfillment for the six prophetic goals with the church.

It is significant that in the year that the 70-weeks prophecy was given, King Cyrus freed the Jews, ending their foreign captivity and their unavoidable contact with idolatry and desecration. Although a remnant did return to Judah, idolatry and transgression continued (Ezra 9:1-2; Nehemiah 9:2) and reached its climax in the national rejection of Jesus' messiahship (Acts 7:51-52). It is clear from the apostle Paul that as a result of this rejection, the judgment of national hardening (Daniel's "period of the indignation," 8:19) will continue until the second advent, at which time Israel's national repentance will be effected (Romans 11:25-27; cf. Ezekiel 36:25-27,31-32; 37:11-14; Zechariah 12:10–13:2) and Israel's transgression will be finished (Jeremiah 31:33-34; Ezekiel 36:27-28,32). These texts support the aforementioned arguments that the first three prophetic goals in Daniel 9:24 remain unfulfilled.

That an *eschatological restoration* is in view is indicated by the fifth prophetic goal: "to seal up vision and prophecy." To "seal up" a prophecy is to preserve the prophecy until it finds its complete fulfillment or confirmation (the best sense for the verb). In context, this fulfillment would include the restoration prophesied by Jeremiah (30–33) and possibly that of his contemporary Ezekiel (because Daniel's prophecy of the seventieth week shares Ezekiel's terminology). The fulfillment of the restoration as prophesied by Jeremiah and Ezekiel could only be eschatological, since

no such restoration has yet been experienced by Israel.

The final prophetic goal, "to anoint the most holy place," also has an eschatological focus. While historicists wish to translate this goal "to anoint the most holy [One]" as a symbolic reference to Christ, the Old Testament use of the term "most holy" (Hebrew, *qodesh qodoshim*) clearly points to the Holy of Holies in the Jerusalem temple and supports the concept of the ceremonial consecration or dedication of the temple from a state of ritual defilement. This could not refer to the "anointing" of the second temple that was completed under Zerubbabel on March 12, 515 B.C., shortly after the end of the 70-year exile (Ezra 6:13-18), for the 70 sevens had not yet begun! Moreover, *Tosefta Sotah* 13:2 records that the second temple was never "anointed." Understanding this, rabbinic interpretation referred the fulfillment to the third temple (cf. *Yoma* 21b), which the messianic King will build after the regathering and restoration of Israel (Zechariah 6:12-13). Therefore, this final prophetic goal has in view the dedication of the millennial temple at the commencement of the messianic kingdom (see comments on Daniel 12:11-12).

THE CHRONOLOGY OF THE 70 WEEKS
Daniel 9:25

Gabriel again exhorted Daniel to "know and discern" the facts contained in the prophecy (cf. verse 22). Daniel petitioned the Lord to reveal the outcome of predicted events (Daniel 12:8), this exhortation indicates he still was responsible to do what he could. The primary reason, as will be revealed, is that the determination of the end of the 69 sevens should provide the exact time of the messianic advent, a matter of vital importance to the Jewish people in the second temple period, during which fulfillment was expected. However, the subsequent history of the interpretation of these verses through the ages has only confirmed the difficulty in understanding this timetable. Yet it is necessary to persevere in working through the chronological options in order to discern the accuracy of the prophecy and to employ it in a defense of the messianic interpretation.

The interpretive key for this determination appears in the opening phrase, "from the issuing of a decree to restore and to rebuild Jerusalem." The question of the *terminus a quo,* the date on which the period of 490 years begins, is essential to the accurate historical interpretation of the entire prophecy. However, determining how to calculate the 70 weeks requires a complex series of choices. At least *four different reckonings* have been proposed for calculating the 70 weeks of years: solar/tropical (365 days), lunar (354 days), solar-lunar (365 days), or "prophetic" (360 days).

In addition, four different Persian decrees to rebuild Jerusalem are recorded in the Old Testament: 1) the decree of Cyrus in the first year of his reign to rebuild the temple in 538 B.C. (2 Chronicles 36:22-23; Ezra 1:1-4; 5:13-17); 2) the decree of Darius I in the second year of his reign (confirming the decree of Cyrus) in 520/519 B.C. (Ezra 6:1,6-12); 3) the decree of Artaxerxes I Longimanus in the seventh year of his reign, 457 B.C. (Ezra 7:7-28); and 4) the decree of Artaxerxes I Longimanus in the twentieth year of his reign (445/444 B.C.), which permitted Nehemiah to rebuild the city walls of Jerusalem (Nehemiah 2:1-8,13,17). Furthermore, it is necessary to make appropriate adjustments with regard to leap years and to the Gregorian or Julian calendars. All these factors can significantly affect the calculations applied to the 70 weeks prophecy. (For an excellent discussion of these factors, see Kalafian, *The Prophecy of the Seventy Weeks of the Book of Daniel,* pp. 86-101.)

Because of the importance of demonstrating the accuracy of Daniel's prophecy in relation to Jesus' messianic identity, many Christian scholars since ancient times have attempted to produce a historical chronology of the sixty-ninth week (483 years), which terminates at the time of Jesus' crucifixion. The most famous of the attempts is that of Sir Robert Anderson, which was published in 1882. He used a 360-day prophetic year scheme and the beginning date of "the twentieth year of Artaxerxes" (assuming Nehemiah 2:1 landed on the first of Nisan, or March 14, 445 B.C. on the Julian calendar). On this basis the 483 years (x 360 days) = 173,880 days, which, added to his date for the decree and making adjustments for actual years (173,880 ÷ 365 = 476.3836), and adding 24 days from March 14 to April 6, and adding leap years (116 days), led him to determine that the date for the end of the sixty-ninth week (483 years) and for the crucifixion of Jesus was the tenth of Nisan (April 6) A.D. 32. Anderson's calculations, however, have since been shown to contain errors because he mixed up the Gregorian and Julian systems in his calculation of leap years (he was off three days).

As to the *correct* Persian decree, Daniel 9:25 states that the purpose of the decree is to "restore and rebuild Jerusalem" with a focus on refortifying it with "plaza and moat, even in times of distress." The only decree that had this intent and took place during a severe time of distress was Artaxerxes's decree to Nehemiah. The addition of 483 years to the date of this decree (the seven weeks plus the 62 weeks) will terminate in the Hebrew month of Nisan and around the year A.D. 30 (the date generally conceded by historians as the date of the crucifixion of Jesus). The important point here, even if the precise method of calculation is still debated, is that the Messiah was to arrive at the end of the second temple period, 483 years from the date the decree was given to restore and rebuild Jerusalem. The end of this time span coincided with the time period in which Jesus carried out His three-year messianic ministry. On this ground alone Jesus could understandably indict the national leadership for not recognizing "the time of your visitation" (Luke 19:44).

THE IDENTITY OF THE ANOINTED
Daniel 9:25-26

Daniel 9:25 ties the *terminus ad quem* (end) of the 69 weeks (483 years) to the appearance of an individual referred to (in the Hebrew text) as *mashiach nagid*. How this phrase is translated and whether or not it is the same person mentioned in the following verse are critical matters of interpretation for the understanding of the entire prophecy of the 70 weeks. Traditional Jewish interpreters since the advent of Christianity have adopted a historical identification in opposition to Christianity's adoption of a messianic identification. The Hebrew term *mashiach* ("anointed") is used in the Old Testament to identify a person in special relationship to God. The nontechnical use of the term simply designates one who is anointed (with oil and/or the Holy Spirit), but especially one who had been set apart by God and enabled for a special task.

The use of *mashiach* with respect to divinely appointed positions (and particularly those of prophet, priest, and king) allows for the greater embodiment of these offices by a distinctly predicted "anointed." In this light, the greater prophet spoken of by Moses (Deuteronomy 18:15), the unending priesthood of Melchizedek (Genesis 14:18-20), and the eternally enthroned seed of David (2 Samuel 7:12-16; 23:1-3,5) merge within the growing development of the messianic concept. The connection of the term *Messiah* to an anointed king appears especially strong and was used in a prophetic sense of the coming Davidic ruler. Both 2 Samuel and the Psalms refer to King David as the "anointed one" (*mashiach*) whose descendants will rule forever (2 Samuel 22:50-51; Psalm 18:50). In addition, the concept of a universal Messiah is seen in texts that give the Davidic house dominion over foreign nations (2 Samuel 22:44-51; Psalm 18:44-50; cf. Psalm 2:7-9). In the prophetic writings the Messianic concept has a special reference to God's promised Davidic ruler who will restore Israel

to the divine ideal (Isaiah 9:7; Jeremiah 23:5-6; Ezekiel 34:23-24; 37:25; Amos 9:11-12).

As to the translation of the phrase *mashiach nagid*, commentators offer two options: "anointed prince" or "Messiah the Prince." Those who seek a historical identification for this individual prefer the former translation since it allows either an Israelite (for example, Zerubbabel, or Joshua ben Josedek) or foreign ruler (such as Cyrus) to bear this title. Those who find a messianic figure (such as Jesus) accept the latter translation. The first translation is incorrect grammatically, for two masculine singular nouns in apposition should be translated as separate titles for the same person: "the anointed one, the prince/ruler." While the Old Testament may refer to a foreign ruler as "anointed" (*mashiach*), it allows a dual title or office only for one who is an Israelite (Zechariah 6:12-13). Moreover, in Daniel, a non-Israelite ruler is designated by the term "king" (Hebrew, *melek*) and never by the term *nagid* ("prince, ruler"). Therefore, this individual must be an Israelite who will bear the dual title of "anointed one" and "prince, ruler." This role is most suited to the Messiah—hence the translation "Messiah the Prince."

EVENTS PROPHESIED AFTER THE SIXTY-NINTH WEEK
Daniel 9:26

The prophecy of the 70 weeks now provides further evidence for calculating the exact time of the messianic advent by stating that it will take place *before* the destruction of the city and the temple. More precisely, it is stated that the termination of the messianic *work* occurs before this desolation transpires. Daniel 9:26 predicts that the Messiah "will be cut off" (Niphal imperfect, *yikaret*). The penal aspect is also present in the description of the Servant of the Lord's suffering in Isaiah 53:8: "he was *cut off* out of the land of the living" (even though a synonym is used). The larger context of Isaiah 53 (verses 1-12) supports a messianic interpretation and provides the only explanation for the text's seemingly anomalous death of the Messiah.

In Daniel 9:26 the phrase added after the words "cut off" may be literally rendered "not to [or for] him" (Hebrew, *'eyn lo*), or the term *'eyn* may also mean "no one." This produces the translation "[he] will have nothing" or "not for Himself." (i.e., He is dying for others as a substitution). In the former translation the meaning is that the Messiah's death would leave Him without an inheritance. Some have suggested an eschatological meaning along this line: "without inheriting the messianic kingdom."

The earliest Jewish interpretation of this text comes from the end of the second temple period from the Jewish priestly community at Qumran. This Jewish sect apparently considered Daniel's 70 weeks prophecy to be a guide that calculated the time of the messianic era, a time in which they believed they were living. They understood that during this period, the Messiah would appear and lead Israel in final triumph over its enemies. This interpretation of expected contemporary fulfillment indicates they viewed the prophecy as future (rather than as having a past fulfillment in the events of the Maccabean revolt), since they identified their present Roman occupiers with "the people of the prince that shall come" (Daniel 9:26). This implies they recognized Rome as the fourth kingdom in the vision of the great statue (Daniel 2:40). In the Dead Sea document known as 11Q13, Daniel 9:26 is found in a group of messianic texts that were linked together to reveal the status of the messianic deliverer. This corpus of prophetic texts (11Q13 2:15-20) reveals the eschatological and messianic context in which the Qumran community understood the anointed one of Daniel 9:26.

The Messiah of Daniel 9:26 is referred to as "the Anointed one of the spirit" (11Q13 2:18) and connected with Isaiah's anointed messenger (Isaiah 61:1-2) who brings the announcement of salvation (interpreted as deliverance by divine intervention—2:19), thereby comforting those who mourn. Verse 4 of this same Qumran text applies Isaiah's prophecy to "the Last Days" and concerns "the captives" (Israel under oppression). Another

text from Qumran (4Q521) commenting on this same text (Isaiah 61:1) in connection with the Messiah states that one of His abilities will be "to raise the dead" (f2ii+4:12). The final interpretation of these texts in 11Q13 is that this "Anointed one" is He who will unravel the mysteries of history "for eternity" (2:20). Evidently, this pre-Christian Jewish sect understood Daniel 9 eschatologically, viewing the time of its fulfillment for Israel to be during the time of the Roman conquest (which began in 63 B.C.). They apparently saw the anointed of Daniel 9:26 as God's supernatural end-time deliverer (the Messiah), who was decreed to appear at this same time.

The second event prophesied to occur after the sixty-ninth seven is the destruction of the city [Jerusalem] and the sanctuary [temple] by "the people of the prince who is to come" (Daniel 9:26). This was fulfilled with the Roman siege of Jerusalem and burning of the temple in A.D. 70. The phrase "the people of the prince who is to come" distinguishes this people as different from the Jewish people, since the prophecy concerns the Jewish nation (verse 24), and the Jews would hardly destroy their own city and sanctuary! Neither can this "prince who is to come" be identified with the Messiah of verse 25, since the Messiah was not a Roman ruler.

The "prince who is to come" had previously been revealed as the little horn (Antichrist). He will be part of the program for the Gentile nations and the final (revived) stage of the Roman Empire (Daniel 2:33-34,40-44). He will wage war against the Jewish people and the Most High until he is utterly destroyed by Christ at the second advent (Daniel 2:35,44-45; cf. 7:7-8,11,19-26; 11:36-45). The "people" who are related to this coming prince must therefore be Gentiles and Romans, the very people who, as members of the Roman Tenth Legion, were responsible for the destruction in A.D. 70.

Historicists (and particularly preterists) contend that the Roman destruction in A.D. 70 fulfilled Daniel 9:26-27, Daniel 11:21-45, the Olivet Discourse (Matthew 24; Mark 13; Luke 21), and the book of Revelation. However,

Daniel 9:26 includes the chronological setting, the figure of a people connected to the fourth world empire (Rome), and the clear statement of the destruction of the city and the sanctuary. Yet no such combination of parallels in time, events, nations, or persons exists in Daniel 11, the Olivet Discourse, or Revelation. In Daniel 9:27 the one who desecrates the temple by an abomination is destroyed by a decreed destruction. The Roman general Titus, who destroyed the temple, did not desecrate it by an abomination, nor was he destroyed.

The closing words of Daniel 9:26 indicate that Jerusalem will suffer warfare and desolation after the Roman destruction and until the end time. The words "war" (Hebrew, *milchamah*) and "desolations" (Hebrew, *shomemot*) refer respectively to the aggressive invasions by foreign nations and the result of warfare, or desolate conditions. This state has been determined for the city until "the end" (Hebrew, *qetz*).

In order for Daniel and his audience to understand that this has been determined it must be part of a divine decree of judgment that has been previously revealed. Daniel was told of a *period of indignation* for Israel that would run parallel with the time of the nations' domination until the end time (8:19; 11:36). This is the source of Jesus' statement in Luke 21:24 that "Jerusalem will be trodden down by the Gentiles until the times of the Gentiles be fulfilled." Despite the regathering of the Jewish people from the nations to establish the modern state of Israel, the history of the new Jewish nation has been one of continual warfare (1948, 1956, 1967, 1973, 1987–1993, 2000–?) with the Temple Mount dominated by a hostile foreign power (Islam). This condition will worsen when the event described in verse 27 commences the Tribulation and the first and second seal judgments, which will intensify warfare in the Middle East (Revelation 6:1-4).

EVENTS OF THE SEVENTIETH WEEK
Daniel 9:27

Futurists see the events in Daniel 9:25-26 as having occurred after the sixty-ninth week but not in the seventieth week, which is reserved for fulfillment in the end time. Therefore, while verse 26 was fulfilled in the late second temple period with the death of Jesus the Messiah in A.D. 30 and the destruction of Jerusalem and the temple in A.D. 70, the events prophesied for the seventieth week (verse 27) will occur during the Tribulation. Jesus cited Daniel 9:27 in His Olivet Discourse (Matthew 24:15; Mark 13:14), and Paul alluded to it in his "day of the Lord" discourse (2 Thessalonians 2:4), both of which are regarded by futurists as eschatological. If verses 25-26 were fulfilled in the past and verse 27 is yet future, then the events of the present age (church age) occupy the time in between these texts.

The justification for a *delay* in the fulfillment of the seventieth week is drawn from the structural divisions of the 70 weeks, Jesus' placement of the events described in verse 27 in an eschatological context, and the adoption of the arrangement of the seventieth week as a paradigm for the judgment section of the book of Revelation. It should also be noted that the extension of the 70 *years* of Jeremiah's prophecy to 70 *weeks of years* is an example of postponement. The restoration Jeremiah promised after 70 years (of exile) was not realized because the spiritual condition of the nation had not changed (see Daniel 9:5-14). Gabriel reveals to Daniel that though the 70-year exile would end as promised, the promise of restoration would not be fulfilled until after the seventieth week. Though a partial Judean restoration was achieved on a *physical* level (the rebuilding of the city and the temple), it could not be effected on a *spiritual* level (the New Covenant) because the nation failed to recognize and accept their Messiah. Ultimate restoration awaits national repentance toward the Messiah (Acts 3:19-21), which will not be realized until the conclusion of the seventieth week (Matthew 24:29-30; Romans 11:25-27).

Daniel 9:24 shows that verse 27 applies exclusively to national Israel. The context of the 70 weeks includes both national exile for Israel's violation of the covenant (seen in the rejection of the Messiah—John 12:39-40; Romans 11:20) and the judgment of Israel's

Gentile oppressors. This is evident in the seventieth week, which, as part of the 70 weeks prophecy, concerns the Gentile domination of national Israel and the fulfillment of the promised restoration. Verse 27 revolves around the figure of "the prince who is to come" (verse 26), whose actions are both desecrating and destructive, and who in turn will be destroyed (verse 27). While posttribulationalists would wish to see the church also in this context, the events deal *only* with Jewish concerns: the covenant made with Israel, the rebuilding of the temple and reinstitution of the sacrificial system, the desecration of the temple by the desolating abomination, and the divine vindication evidenced in retributive judgment on the desolator.

Daniel 9:27 is also significant in that it mentions the beginning, midpoint, and end of the Tribulation. The beginning is when Israel enters into a covenant with the figure known as "the prince" (Hebrew, *nagid* = "leader") that was predicted to come, and whose people (that is, Gentiles [Romans]) destroyed the (second) temple (verse 26). While this covenant is not mentioned in the Olivet Discourse or in Revelation, it is implied in the events that flow from its violation (especially in relation to Jerusalem and the temple). The idiomatic construction *higebbir berit* ("to strengthen a covenant") may be interpreted as either inaugurating ("making") a new covenant or ratifying ("confirming") an existing covenant. In either sense, the purpose for which the covenant is established—to effect a religio-political accord permitting the rebuilding of the temple—is the same.

At the midpoint of the Tribulation, the temple will be desecrated. This act forces the cessation of the sacrificial system, thereby violating the terms of the covenant that had included the institution of the temple. Jesus earmarked this act as the signal event that would tell the Jewish people that the end is coming (cf. Daniel 12:11). At the end of the Tribulation the temple desolator, the Antichrist, will be destroyed. This event corresponds to the second advent of Christ and

the Antichrist's defeat at Armageddon (cf. 2 Thessalonians 1:7-10; Revelation 19:11-21).

The seven-year Tribulation as described in Daniel 9:27 is a time of divine wrath that parallels the outpouring of judgment in Revelation 6–19. This can be seen in the fact that the seventieth week defines the beginning of the Tribulation, the commencement of the Great Tribulation, and the end of the Tribulation. Since the fulfillment of the seventieth week covers the entire period of the Tribulation, the entire seventieth week (not only the last half) should be regarded as the Tribulation. The chart on page 254 demonstrates the correlation between Daniel 9:27 and the events described in Revelation.

THE MAKING OF A FIRM COVENANT
Daniel 9:27

There are two difficulties with interpreting the phrase "and he will make a firm covenant with the many." First, the identification of who "he" is, and second, the meaning of the idiomatic expression "make a firm covenant." If the pronoun is taken as impersonal ("it"), then the subject would be the phrase "one week." However, this poetic use is without support as there is no analogy for speaking of time as making a covenant. It is also preferable to have a definite, personal subject who effects the covenant to complement the personal object of the preposition—"the many." In this case, the subject may be inferred from the previous verse (26), either as the anointed one, the messiah, or the coming prince/ruler.

Of these two options, the coming prince/ruler is the nearer antecedent and therefore grammatically preferable. It may also be the more suitable subject if it is identified with the desolator in verse 27, since "the people of the prince" in verse 26 were the agents of the destruction of the temple. Therefore, one member of the covenant-making party is the Antichrist, previously identified by Daniel as the little horn (7:8,11,20-21,24-25). Those with whom the Antichrist makes the covenant are called "the many" (Hebrew, *rabbim*). The contextual referent for this group has already

OVERVIEW OF THE TRIBULATION

Reference	Daniel 9:27a	Daniel 9:27b	Daniel 9:27c
Division	Beginning of Tribulation (3.5 years/42 months/1260 days)	Midpoint (Great Tribulation)	End of Tribulation (3.5 years/42 months/1260 days)
Status of Israel	Israel protected	Israel persecuted	Israel preserved
Relation to Antichrist	Covenant with Antichrist	Corruption of Antichrist	Condemnation of Antichrist
Event	Temple designed	Temple desecrated	Temple delivered
Revelation Correlation	Seal judgments (Revelation 6:1-17)	Invasion of city and temple (Revelation 11:1-2)	Destruction of Antichrist (Revelation 19:19-20)

been established as the people of Israel (9:24). "The many" refers to a *part* ("many") rather than the whole ("all") of the Jewish people, and to a specific group (as indicated by the definite article), which may be either the Israelite remnant, or better, in conformity with the leader (Hebrew, *nagid*) in verse 26 (and by inference, verse 27), the Israeli leadership (cf. Isaiah 52:14; 53:12). Were a different object in view clarification would have been required; otherwise, the expected object is that continued from the previous reference.

In the expression "make firm a covenant," the verb is from the Hebrew root *gabar* "to be strong, mighty," and in the *Hiphil* (perfect + *waw* consecutive) can mean "to strengthen." This makes possible the translation "to confirm a covenant" (either a new or an existing one), or "to make a strong/firm covenant." Support for the former translation, "confirm," may be had from a comparative use in the Qumran literature (1QH 8.35). The focus is upon a "new covenant" unlike any Israel has experienced in its past, since this one will result in the peaceful conditions necessary to rebuild the temple. This covenant will obviously result in a change in Israel's status since the sacrificial services appear to be reinstated as a result of its ratification.

The covenant made with the Antichrist will probably be regarded as the fulfillment of this promised covenant of peace or new covenant because many of the prophetic provisions will be realized, particularly the rebuilding of the temple. Whatever the scenario that makes possible the conditions necessary for a covenant, it appears that the opposition of Islam (or whatever power will prevent access to the Temple Mount) will have been removed. Israel will be free to exercise religious authority over the Temple Mount and rebuild the temple as required by Jewish law (Exodus 25:8). Orthodox Jews will likely announce that this event has ushered in the long-awaited messianic era of redemption. However, this covenant will bring about a *pseudo* peace that is a counterfeit of the true peace that God promised to the Jewish people.

THE STOPPING OF THE SACRIFICIAL SYSTEM
Daniel 9:27

The statement that the sacrificial system will be put to a stop of course implies the existence of a temple, apparently erected during the months following the enactment of the covenant. This likewise implies that the temple may be rebuilt as a result of the covenant made with the Antichrist. Harold Foos ("Jerusalem in Prophecy," p. 230) draws this conclusion: "...that the repossession of the Temple site and the rebuilding of the Temple with its renewed worship will be in direct consequence of the covenant that the Antichrist makes with Israel for the 'one seven,' the seven years of the Tribulation period." *Five key factors* seem to suggest this: 1) The second temple was rebuilt by the permission and power of a Gentile ruler (Cyrus), setting the precedence for the rebuilding of the third temple. 2) If a political power or leader could guarantee the rebuilding of the temple, any covenant made with Israel would be expected to include this. 3) When the covenant is broken in the middle of the seventieth week, the Antichrist takes the prerogative to cause the sacrifices to cease (Daniel 9:27; 12:11) and to occupy the temple himself (Matthew 24:15; Mark 13:14; 2 Thessalonians 2:4). This could imply that he had been involved in some prior relationship with it. 4) A pivotal event marked both the beginning and end of the first 69 weeks and the interval between the end of the sixty-ninth and the beginning of the seventieth (Daniel 9:25-26). Such an event might be expected at the beginning of the seventieth week as well, especially when it would appear to mark a revival of God's direct dealing with the nation. 5) Since the purpose of the Tribulation is to prepare Israel for the fulfillment of promises related to the millennium, in which the temple has a prominent place, and since the temple suffers with the nation during the Tribulation, its rebuilding should be connected with the beginning of the Tribulation (the signing of the covenant—Daniel 9:27).

THE ABOMINATION OF DESOLATION
Daniel 9:27

The phrase used to describe the act of desecration that ends the temple's sacrificial service is "an abomination of desolation" (Hebrew, *shiqqutz meshomem*). This phrase, occurring in the Old Testament only in Daniel (11:31; 12:11), is a combination of terms that were used separately to describe the condition of exilic punishment inflicted on Israel for covenant violation. These terms speak of the desolation or ruin and the abomination or idolatry that results from the false worship system imposed by Antichrist and the false prophet (Revelation 13:11-18). In these texts the form of the Hebrew term for "desolation" appears as the *Pol'el* participle *shomem* or *mᵉshomem* which has a range of verbal meanings ("devastate, desolate, desert, appall") with nominal derivatives ("waste, horror, devastation, appallment").

In the New Testament, the phrase appears only in the Olivet Discourse (Matthew 24:15; Mark 13:14) as a partial citation from Daniel (explicitly stated as such in Matthew 24:15). While the Greek term *eremos* ("desolation") appears in Luke 21:20, it does not have reference to the technical phrase and is used there to describe the general condition of Jerusalem (not specifically the temple). This usage is in harmony with Jesus' previous pronouncement on the city in Matthew 23:38 (where the same term is used) and Luke 19:43-44. While the second temple is in view in the pronouncement, the focus is upon its destruction (rather than desecration) as evidence that divine judgment has occurred. This is quite distinct from the desecration caused by the abomination of desolation, an act that results in divine judgment not upon the temple, but upon the one who desecrates it (Daniel 9:27). In addition, the use of the phrase in Daniel and the Olivet Discourse clearly influenced allusions in other prophetic contexts (1 Corinthians 3:17; 2 Thessalonians 2:3-4; Revelation 11:1-2).

The desecration is stated to be "on the wing of abominations." The text makes it clear that the term "wing" (Hebrew, *kᵉnaf*) has a direct association with the abomination of desolation and most likely describes the *place* where it will occur in relation to the temple. This "wing," which must be understood metaphorically, has been the subject of extensive controversy and fanciful interpretation in both ancient and modern commentaries. It is possible that *kᵉnaf* suggests the place where the abomination of desolation is placed: in the Holy of Holies in the place of the Ark of the Covenant, which was topped by winged cherubim. The Septuagint (followed by the Latin Vulgate) translated the Hebrew *kᵉnaf* as the Greek *pterugion* to designate any projecting extremity or wing-like projections.

In addition, the mention of sacrifices just before the term "wing" may imply a ritual association. For this reason it is often connected with the pinnacle of the temple (Matthew 4:5; Luke 4:9) or the horned altar of the temple. However, Paul's statement in 2 Thessalonians 2:4 that the "man of lawlessness" will seat himself in the innermost part of the temple (Greek, *naos*) may suggest another possibility. If the Antichrist follows the precedent of previous desecrators such as Manasseh, who replaced the Ark of the Covenant with an idolatrous image of Asherah (2 Kings 21:7; 2 Chronicles 33:7; cf. 35:3), such an action might be expected. Christian commentator Frederick Tatford (*Paul's Letter to the Thessalonians,* p. 90), proposed this when he wrote, "Evidently the audacious rebel will blasphemously take his seat in the *sanctum sanctorum* itself." Moreover, since the Antichrist is enthroning himself in an act of self-deification, where better for this to be done than between the wings of the cherubim atop the mercy seat of the Ark, where the God of Israel's divine presence was manifested? Paul's statement in 2 Thessalonians 2:4 that he "takes his seat in the temple of God, displaying himself as being God" may reflect this. In the days of the tabernacle and the first temple, the throne of the Lord was said to be seated above or between the cherubim (Psalm 80:1; 99:1).

The Seventy-weeks Prophecy

Daniel's "Seventy Weeks" (490 years) for the Holy City (Dan. 9:24a)

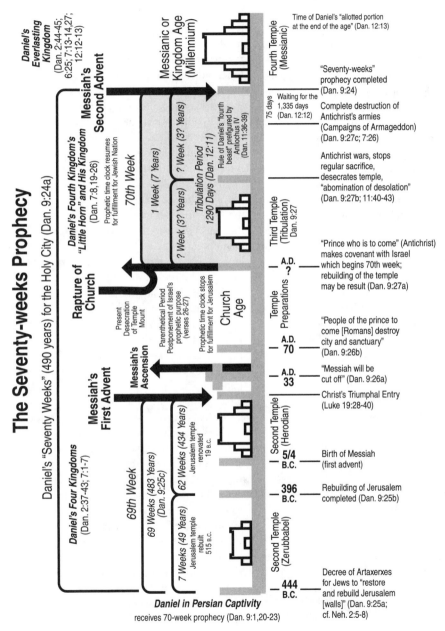

Taken from Randall Price, *Jerusalem in Prophecy* (Eugene, OR: Harvest House Publishers, 1998), p. 257. Used by permission.

THE DECREED DESTRUCTION OF THE DESOLATOR
Daniel 9:27

The interpretation of the final clause of verse 27—"a complete destruction, one that is decreed, is poured out on the one who makes desolate" (that is, the *appointed destruction* of the desolator)—is of crucial importance in establishing that this verse has an eschatological fulfillment. Two predetermined events are included in this decree: 1) the desolation of Jerusalem (of which the abomination of desolation is the nadir) has an appointed end (Zechariah 12:9; 14:2-3; Luke 21:24,28); and 2) the desolator (Antichrist) has an appointed end (7:11,26; 2 Thessalonians 2:8-9; Revelation 19:19-20). This predicted judgment for the one who desecrates the temple accords with other texts where the Lord announces the punishment of His instruments of judgment for their arrogance and self-actuated intent to destroy that which is holy (cf. 1 Corinthians 3:17).

Earlier we saw that a Messianic interpretation of Daniel 9:25-26 with a fulfillment in the second temple period requires a *literal* interpretation of those verses. Similarly, the prophetic destruction of the temple desolator in verse 27 must also be a literal event. The fact that this destruction is "decreed" (Hebrew, *necherazah*) demands that its fulfillment must be identified in Scripture as the result of divine judgment. Only the futurist interpretation, which sees the temple desolator as the Antichrist (2 Thessalonians 2:3-4; Revelation 11:1-2) and his destruction at the second advent of Christ (Daniel 2:35,45; 7:11,22,26; 2 Thessalonians 2:8-9; Revelation 19:11-20), is in harmony with this requirement of divine demonstration.

PROPHECIES CONCERNING THE NATIONS
Daniel 11:2-45

In DANIEL 10, Daniel is introduced to the archangel Michael, who is involved in the spiritual struggle to carry out God's program concerning the nations (10:13,20). The key to the vision Daniel will receive in this chapter is given in 10:14: "I have come to give you an understanding of what will happen to your people in the latter days, for the vision pertains to the days yet future." From this we are reminded of what has been previously stated (cf. 8:19; 9:24; cf. 12:1): that the prophecies of chapters 7–12 are intended to focus on national Israel and God's purpose for the nation during the times of the Gentiles and especially the end time and the conclusion of the seventieth week. In other words, the prophecies revealed in chapter 11 will deal with near-future events (those fulfilled historically)—the rise of the three kingdoms (verses 2-35)—and far-future events (those fulfilled eschatologically)—the rise of the little horn from the fourth kingdom, the Antichrist (verses 36-45).

That a *panorama of future events* from Daniel's era to the end time is in view here is indicated by the term "those times" (Hebrew *'aḥᵃrit hayyamim*) in verse 14 ("latter days" in 2:28). This chronological expression is especially prominent in the biblical prophets (for example, Isaiah 2:2; Jeremiah 23:20; 34:20; 48:47; 49:39; Ezekiel 38:16; Hosea 3:5; Micah 4:1) and is found as early as the Pentateuch (as in Genesis 49:1; Numbers 24:14; Deuteronomy 4:29-31). The Hebrew noun *'aḥarit*, which is part of the compound expression, generally describes that which takes place *after* the speaker's temporal reference, as well as that which results from a situation or an action (that is, "the end," cf. Proverbs 14:12), with context helping to determine the specific time in view in the future. The usage of the compound expression "latter days" in the Old Testament reveals it is used in the general sense of "days to come" (cf. Genesis 49:1; Numbers 24:14; Deuteronomy 31:29), but more often has the more definite sense of a time in the future.

With this in mind, as well as the progressive revelation of Gentile world history that culminates with the Antichrist, the focus on Antiochus IV Epiphanes in Daniel 11:21-35 should not be unexpected. It has already been demonstrated how this Seleucid ruler, called "the despicable person" (verse 21), having deified himself, opposed God's Word and the Mosaic law (verse 31), corrupted and persecuted the Jewish people (verse 32), and desecrated the temple (verse 31), has shared the same agenda as the coming Antichrist and therefore becomes a *type* for this future figure. In particular the abomination of desolation (verse 31), following the eschatological introduction of the concept in 9:27, indicates that an ultimate future fulfillment is in view with this figure. To limit its interpretation to Antiochus IV Epiphanes would contradict Jesus' reference to the abomination of desolation in 9:27 as having an eschatological fulfillment (Matthew 24:15; Mark 13:14). Rather, Antiochus IV Epiphanes is but another figure in a succession of antitheocratic rulers whose acts of desecration move toward a climax of fulfillment in the last days. For this reason the "latter days" of verses 36-45 move from the near (historical) vision of Antiochus IV Epiphanes to the far (eschatological) vision of his antitype (Antichrist).

THE PROPHECY OF THE ANTICHRIST
Daniel 11:36-45

FOLLOWING THE PREVIOUSLY prophesied program for the nations, Gabriel in verse 36 moves from the third kingdom and a description of Antiochus IV Epiphanes to the final phase of the fourth kingdom and a description of the dominant figure that emerges from that kingdom, the Antichrist. While 11:36-45 seems to be a continuation of the earlier description of the historical king Antiochus, the shift to an eschatological king is not unwarranted.

First, there is much in the description in verses 36-45 that does not correspond with what is known of Antiochus IV Epiphanes historically, so these verses are not a continuation of what was said about him earlier. In fact, in verse 36, the figure being described is called "the king" (Hebrew, *hamelek*), whereas Antiochus IV Epiphanes is identified earlier with "the king of the North" (verses 7,11,13,15).

In this section, "the king of the North" attacks the king being described (verse 40), so they cannot be the same individual (see further comments on verses 40-45). In terms of contrasts between Antiochus IV Epiphanes and this king, while Antiochus was "a despicable person" (verse 21) and sent forces to "desecrate the sanctuary" (verse 31), this king is a "monstrous" person (verse 36) and will establish his palace at the place of the sanctuary (verse 45), personally seating himself there (cf. 2 Thessalonians 2:4).

Second, Antiochus worshipped Greek gods and imposed Grecian culture on the Jews because of his regard for the religion of his fathers. By contrast, this king will "show no regard for the gods of his fathers or...for any other god" (verse 37). Antiochus IV Epiphanes deified himself (at least on his coins), but this king "will exalt and magnify himself above every god" (verse 36). And while Antiochus IV Epiphanes accepted "the daughter of women" (verse 17) in political marriages, this king "will show no regard...for the desire of women" (verse 37). This does not necessarily mean that the Antichrist will be a homosexual. Rather, it dictates that his self-orientation and single-minded ambition have eclipsed any desire for normal human relationships. He will regard himself as above both gods and mortal men (verse 37), and give recognition only to those who acknowledge his superior might (verse 39).

Third, the shift from Antiochus IV to another figure is indicated grammatically by the *interruption* in verse 35 that introduces an eschatological orientation to the "end time; because it is still to come at the appointed time." Verse 36 builds upon this by stating that this one will prosper "until the indignation is finished, for that which is decreed will be done." As discussed in 8:19, this refers to the period of God's judicial wrath against Israel for covenant violation (the height of which was the rejection of the Messiah). This period runs concurrent with the times of the Gentiles, for the nations' domination of Israel is part of the covenantal curse. As in 9:27 (cf. 2:35,45;

7:11,26), the final judgment of this new figure has been decreed (verse 36). Only the figure of the Antichrist fits this eschatological timetable, for his decreed demise coincides with the end of the period of indignation (cf. 2 Thessalonians 2:8-9; Revelation 19:19-20).

Fourth, even though verses 36-45 follow the description of Antiochus IV Epiphanes and bear resemblances to the former context, their language goes beyond what could be properly stated about the Seleucid king. Either the description has become hyperbolic, or we have here a greater future figure of evil that accords with the character and career of the Antichrist. Such movement in prophetic texts from historical to eschatological persons and events is common. Old Testament examples include the shifts in Isaiah 14 between the king of Babylon (verses 4-11,18-21) and Satan (verses 12-17) and in Ezekiel 27–28 from the King of Tyre (27:2–28:12) to Satan (28:13-19). A New Testament example is Jesus' shift in Luke 21 between the time of the Tribulation (verses 8-19,25-28) and the A.D. 70 destruction of Jerusalem (verses 20-24). In like manner, the shift in Daniel 11 moves from Antiochus IV Epiphanes (verses 21-35) to the Antichrist (verses 36-45). Similarly, shifts from a near (historical) fulfillment to a far (eschatological) fulfillment occur in "day of the Lord" texts (see examples in discussion on 9:27).

THE CHARACTER OF THE ANTICHRIST
Daniel 11:36-39

The description of the Antichrist's character in verses 36-39 reveals he will do as he pleases and exalt himself (verse 36), blaspheme the true God (verse 36), abandon natural feelings for people, even for the opposite sex (verse 37), magnify himself above all gods (verse 37), and care only for military might and conquest (verses 38-39). This description is thought by some to reveal a distinct ethnic origin of the Antichrist and has provoked prophetic students to try to discover his nationality. In the historical disputations between Jews and Christians, the nationality of the Antichrist has played a major role as both theological polemic and in ecclesiastic and political reaction to the Jewish community. Therefore, the determination of this question is not simply an academic issue. Four types of arguments have generally formed the substance of the debate over the nationality of the Antichrist.

The first is the *logical argument.* This states that the Jewish people believe there is coming a day when the Messiah will rebuild the temple (cf. Zechariah 6:12-13). So when the Antichrist makes it possible for the temple to be rebuilt, the Jewish people will accept him as the Messiah. If the Antichrist is accepted as the Messiah, and the Messiah is Jewish, the Antichrist must also be of Jewish origin. After all, would the Jewish people allow a non-Jew to be involved in rebuilding the Jewish temple? However, the pagan Persian Cyrus, who made possible the rebuilding of the second temple (2 Chronicles 36:22-23; Ezra 1:1-11) was called a "messiah" (Isaiah 45:1). Thus, the mere reference to someone as a messiah does not necessarily require the person be of Jewish origin.

The second argument is the *lexical argument,* a deduction based on the statement in Daniel 11:37 that the Antichrist will not "regard the God of his fathers" (KJV). Since the term "God of the fathers" is used elsewhere to refer to the God of Abraham, Isaac, and Jacob (the Jewish patriarchs or "fathers"), this must indicate that the Antichrist is an apostate Jew (this was the identification of such conservative dispensational commentators as J.N. Darby and Arno Gaebelein). However, the translation here could as easily read "the gods of his fathers," which is followed by most modern versions. The reason for this is because the form of the Hebrew word (*'elohim*) used here is a plural and may be applied to both the true God as well as to false gods. For example, *'elohim* is translated "God" as a proper name when used in reference to the God of the Bible, and translated "gods" as a generic term for deity when used with reference to angels (Psalm 8:5), men (Psalm 82:6), judges (Exodus 21:6), but especially of foreign or pagan deities (Genesis 31:30; Exodus 12:12).

The problem of how to translate this term in the context of Daniel may be observed in 3:25, where the Babylonian king Nebuchadnezzar makes a statement concerning an unexpected companion who has joined the three Jewish exiles Shadrach, Meshach, and Abednego in their fiery punishment in a furnace. In the NKJV translation the king exclaimed, "I see four men loose, walking in the midst of the fire; and they are not hurt, and the form of the fourth is like *the Son of God.*" The Aramaic equivalent of *'elohim* is used here and therefore the same sentence could be rendered "a son of the gods." Since this exclamation comes from the mouth of a pagan with polytheistic theology, the translation "gods" is preferable. The construct form in 3:35 ("son of the gods") is identical to that in 11:37, and in verses 37-38 the singular form *'eloah* ("god") appears twice, supporting the use of the plural here as "gods of the fathers."

Following this fact, the context of verses 36-39, which speaks of the Antichrist's exaltation of himself above all gods (verses 36-37), his blasphemous words against the true God (verse 37), his use of "a foreign god" for his own ends (verse 39), and the statement that his god is "a god of fortresses" (verse 38) makes it clear that this king is a pagan who reveres only military might. Moreover, his attack on Israel (verse 41) implies that he has no kinship with the Jewish people, but rather, intends to control and ultimately destroy them. These are not usually the actions of a conqueror toward his own people. Historically it has been non-Jews who have pursued occupation of Israel and persecuted the Jewish people. Because the Antichrist is the final figure in the succession of these non-Jewish nations, his actions are consistent with the Gentile powers revealed in Daniel's visions. Therefore, lexically, the expressions of deity are in a pagan context and do not support a Jewish identity.

Third is the *linguistic argument,* which contends because of the Greek preposition *anti* (with the nuance of substitution) in the word *Antichrist,* the Antichrist is a "counterfeit" of Jesus the Messiah. Jesus was Jewish, and this argument reasons that the Antichrist must also be Jewish in order to claim a Messianic identity. However, there is nothing in the use of the preposition *anti* in Antichrist that linguistically requires the Antichrist to be a "counterfeit Christ." The preposition *anti* can denote 1) *equivalence*—one object set over against another as its equivalent (Matthew 5:38; 1 Corinthians 11:15); 2) *exchange*—one object opposing or distinct from another, or one object given or taken in return for the other (Romans 12:17; John 1:16); and 3) *substitution*—one object given or taken instead of the other (Matthew 2:2; Luke 11:11). While the idea of *replacement* may be understood in this last nuance, the idea of *counterfeit* is not. Such a determination must be derived from the context, and there is no context that states that the purpose or program of the Antichrist is to counterfeit Christ.

Fourth is the *contextual argument,* which considers the nationality of the Antichrist in those texts that speak of his relationship to the Gentile nations and his intense opposition to the Jewish nation. Daniel 2 and 7 have already shown that the program for the nations is a succession of Gentile world kingdoms headed by Gentile rulers who dominate and oppress the Jewish people. This period of Gentile world dominion, "the times of the Gentiles" (Luke 21:24), will end with the Antichrist as the final ruler in the succession of nations. It would be contrary to the prophetic sequence revealed in Daniel to have a Jew rise to the status of a world ruler at a time when only Gentiles can have the preeminence and before the appointed time for the Jewish kingdom (Daniel 2:32-45; Romans 11:25). In Daniel 2 and 7, all the Gentile rulers mentioned come from the boundaries of their empires. Why would not the figure of the Antichrist, whose roots appear in the Roman Empire not also be circumscribed by these boundaries? While it is true that the eastern division of the Roman Empire includes the Middle East, the dominant rulers of this region from ancient times to modern have been Gentiles.

Also relevant is that the little horn (Antichrist) emerged from "the ten horns," which are all Gentile kings/kingdoms (7:8,24).

Although he is "different from the previous [kings]," this difference is his superior power to subdue them (7:24), not his ethnic origin. In addition, Revelation 13 depicts two different beasts described as arising respectively from the sea (verse 1) and the earth (verse 11). The sea is a literary image that often pictures the Gentile nations (cf. Daniel 7:2-3). If so, the nationality of the first beast from the sea (the Antichrist) is Gentile and the nationality of the second beast, the false prophet, is Jewish.

THE CONQUESTS OF THE ANTICHRIST
Daniel 11:40-45

In Daniel 11:40-45, the focus of the biblical text moves from the maleficent character of the Antichrist to his military conquests. Throughout this section the personal pronouns "he" and "him" refer to "the king" (Antichrist) who was the subject of verses 36-39. It is necessary to carefully note this fact—otherwise, as many commentators have demonstrated, there will be confusion as to who attacks whom and who invades Israel. Earlier verses have established that the Antichrist's military ambition will be all-consuming, and that he will exalt himself above all men and gods in order to have the highest station. This, of course, is the intended goal of Satan (Isaiah 14:13-14), who will give the Antichrist his authority—that is, his military prowess and conquests (Revelation 13:2,4).

The Antichrist's military campaign will ultimately center on the land of Israel (Daniel 11:41), but he will have to overcome a two-pronged attack by both the king of the South and the king of the North (verses 40-44) before he can achieve his objective (verse 45). Apparently, these two kings/nations will form an alliance against the Antichrist and will launch a joint attack against him (verse 40). The time of this attack is stated to be "in the end time"—it probably takes place in the first half of the Tribulation. The identity of these two kings/nations may be revealed in Isaiah 19:24-25, which records that believers from Egypt and Syria (Assyria)—perhaps because of this opposition to Antichrist's attempt to control the Middle East and especially Israel—will receive special recognition alongside Israel in the millennial kingdom.

After the Antichrist secures the region from further defiance to his authority, he will next assert his control over Israel by *politically* dominating its capital city of Jerusalem (Revelation 11:2) and *religiously* desecrating its central shrine, the temple (Daniel 9:27; Matthew 24:15; Mark 13:14). Daniel 11:45 explains that upon his return to Israel after the battle with Syria he will establish his royal palace at "the beautiful Holy Mountain" (verse 45). These events will lead to the erection of his mysteriously animated image (Revelation 13:15). They are part of the Antichrist's usurpation of the divine prerogative of residence in the Temple (2 Thessalonians 2:4).

After his desecration of the Holy of Holies (Matthew 24:15; Mark 13:14), which will cause the cessation of the sacrificial service (Daniel 9:27), Antichrist will establish his headquarters on the Temple Mount (11:45). Then the false prophet will declare him to be the sole recipient of the world's worship (Revelation 13:12,15). As a result, the Jewish people will realize the deception, and many will flee from Jerusalem (Matthew 24:16-20) to avoid persecution when Antichrist's armies take control of the city (Revelation 11:2). Others will remain in the city to fight against Antichrist during his assault upon and dividing of the city (Zechariah 14:2).

Daniel 11:45 also proclaims the destruction decreed for the desolator of the temple (as in Daniel 9:27). Here it is stated that "he will come to his end, and no one will help him." When the Antichrist arrogantly returns to Jerusalem in the last of his Armageddon campaigns to destroy the Jewish remnant, his armies will be met by the Messiah, who will fight for Israel, rescue the remnant, and completely massacre Antichrist's forces (Zechariah 14:3-4). When this destruction occurs there will be no support for his armies, for "the great day of their wrath has come, and who is able to stand?" (Revelation 6:17). In this great day of "the fierce wrath of God, the Almighty" (Revelation 19:15), the Antichrist and his false prophet will be "thrown alive into the lake of fire" (Revelation 19:20).

PROPHECIES CONCERNING ISRAEL
Daniel 12

DANIEL'S AMAZING PROPHECIES trace the rise and fall of multiple world empires, but in the end, the focus returns to where it all began—in the Middle East and the land of Israel. This region that saw the dawn of mankind will also witness its final judgment. The land of Israel saw the beginning of human redemption through the chosen people, and will once again be the site of salvation when "the day dawns and the morning star arises" (2 Peter 1:19; cf. Isaiah 25:9). The main point of Daniel 12 is to assure Daniel that the terrible events revealed to him, including Israel's suffering during the times of the Gentiles, will result in salvation. There will be a time of distress, but also a day of deliverance (verse 1). Verses 1-3 prophesy Israel's deliverance both in this age (verse 1) and the age to come (verses 2-3), and the rest of the prophecy (verses 4-13) deals with Israel's destiny being sealed up until the end time (verse 4), the Tribulation period (verses 5-10), and the millennial kingdom (verses 11-13).

Because Daniel 12 represents the conclusion of the revelation of the divine program for both Gentiles and Jews, it is appropriate that the chapter opens with an explanation about the point at which Gentile history and Jewish history, which have been progressing on parallel lines, converge (the time of the Tribulation). If Israel can be saved at this time, its salvation is truly assured (Romans 11:26), the prophecy can be sealed up until the end time (Daniel 12:4,9), and Daniel can go to his rest (verse 13) in the knowledge that the divine plan will be fulfilled as promised.

THE PROPHECY OF ISRAEL'S DELIVERANCE
Daniel 12:1-3

The opening words of verse 1 establish the time frame for the text that follows: "Now at that time...." These words force us back to

the previous context for the temporal setting, which 11:40 stated was "the end time" and which verses 40-45 revealed was the time of the seventieth week, or the Tribulation period. That the end time is in view here is also confirmed in verses 2 and 13, which mention the resurrections of the righteous at the second advent (Revelation 20:4) and of the wicked at the end of the millennium (Revelation 20:5). The dire conditions predicted in Israel during the Great Tribulation explain why Gabriel's fellow archangel, Michael, will arise at that time on behalf of "the sons of your people" (Israel, verse 1).

Because the Antichrist's attack on Israel takes place at the midpoint of the Tribulation, it would be expected that this is when Michael will arrive on the scene. His help will be most needed during the Great Tribulation, for that is when Satan will launch his attempt to eradicate the remnant of Israel (Revelation 12:12-17) with the help of the armies of the world in a final onslaught on Jerusalem (Zechariah 12:2-3; 14:2). Michael, whose name means "who is like God," apparently has the specially appointed task of serving as the guardian or protector of the remnant of national Israel, as implied by the words "the great prince who stands guard over" (verse 1, cf. Daniel 10:13-21; Jude 9). This Jewish remnant is further defined as "your people, everyone who is found written in the book" (verse 1). This remnant represents the "all Israel" who will be saved at the time of the second advent (Romans 11:26-27).

Gabriel then announced to Daniel that "there will be a time of distress such as never occurred since there was a nation until that time" (Daniel 12:1). As the modifying phrase makes clear, this time of distress will be unlike any previously experienced or that will yet be experienced under Gentile dominion. Because of the importance of this concept to this prophecy as well as to the correct interpretation of the Olivet Discourse and Revelation, it is necessary to take time to consider the usage of Daniel's Tribulation terms in both the Old and New Testaments.

The term employed here by Daniel is the Hebrew phrase 'et sarah ("time of trouble, tribulation"). That a future period is in view is understood by the opening phrase of verse 1—"at that time" (Hebrew, ba'et hahu') which has as its antecedent the eschatological term 'et qetz ("the end time") in 11:40. This same eschatological referent appears in this context in verses 4 and 9. Since the concern here is Israel's experience of this time of distress, only the last three-and-one-half years of the Tribulation is in view (verse 7). In the phrase "time of distress," the word "distress" (Hebrew sarah) is derived from the root sarr, which expresses a condition or experience of "suffering distress or trouble."

Daniel's use of the phrase 'et sarah ("time of distress") is evidently borrowed from Jeremiah 30:7 (cf. 14:8; 15:11), since this book had been informing Daniel's interpretation of the 70 weeks (Daniel 9:2) as well as his prayer for Israel's restoration from Gentile dominion (Daniel 9:3-19). Jeremiah spoke decisively of "the time of Jacob's distress" and that "he [the remnant] will be saved [delivered] from it" (30:7).

When the Old Testament prophetic references to the time of Israel's trouble are compared to specific references in the New Testament, we can see that the same period of tribulation is in view.

The chart on the next page makes it clear that the Old Testament references to the Tribulation, in every case, has its expected fulfillment in the end time. The scope of the judgment, in most cases, is unparalleled and requires salvation (physical deliverance)—an indicator of the severity of this event. That these contexts involve idolatry in some form—whether in relation to false prophets or to the Antichrist and the abomination of desolation—accords with the frequent mention of the temple. This comparison also demonstrates that the New Testament doctrine of the Tribulation was developed from Old Testament texts.

The second realm of deliverance for Israel will also come at the end time, and will concern Israelites who have already died. Apparently the magnitude of the "time of distress" was so great and fearful that Gabriel had to include a word of assurance about the fate of those Jews who would perish during the Tribulation. This word of assurance is the promise of bodily resurrection, which here is described as a dead (and disintegrated into "dust") body (not soul) awakening from sleep (verse 2).

Jesus affirmed the resurrection in a dialogue with some Jewish religious leaders known as Sadducees (Matthew 22:29-32; cf. John 5:28-29). Daniel 12:2 is one of the most significant Old Testament texts on the resurrection and is enlarged upon in Revelation chapter 20. According to this chapter, the righteous who died before the church age and during the Tribulation will be resurrected at the beginning of the millennial kingdom (Revelation 20:4), but the wicked dead will not experience resurrection until the conclusion of the millennium (verse 5). The former will share in the blessings of the kingdom (verse 4), while the latter will face the Great White Throne Judgment and the lake of fire (verses 11-15).

Daniel 12:2 says much the same things in an abbreviated manner. The righteous will receive a resurrection body that will be able to enjoy all of the pleasures of "everlasting life" (Hebrew, chayye 'olam, cf. Psalm 16:11), while the wicked ("others") will receive a resurrection body to experience the pains of "disgrace and everlasting contempt." Those who died during the church age will be resurrected at the rapture (1 Corinthians 15:51-56; Philippians 3:20-21; 1 Thessalonians 4:13-17) and return with Christ at the second advent to reign with Him during the millennium (cf. Matthew 19:28-29).

PROPHECIES CONCERNING ISRAEL'S DESTINY
Daniel 12:4-13

Daniel is instructed to "conceal these words and seal up the book until the end of time" (12:4). These prophecies concern Israel's destiny and were apparently given to assure Israel that what has been promised will be fulfilled. The terms "conceal" (Hebrew, satam) and "seal up" (Hebrew, chatam) do not mean Daniel

Comparison of Tribulation Texts in the Old and New Testaments

Biblical Text	Dt 4	Jer 30	Da 9	Da 12	Mt 24/Mk 13	2Th 2	Rev 6-19
Event	Tribulation (sar) (v. 30)	Tribulation (sar) (v. 7)	seven-year covenant (v. 27a)	Tribulation (sar) (v. 1b)	Tribulation (thlipsis) (24:21; 13:19)	revealing of Antichrist (vv. 3, 8)	Great Tribulation (7:15)
Time reference	after previous exiles, latter days (v. 30)	great day, that day (vv. 7, 8)	70th week (v. 27)	end time (11:40)	those days, immediately prior to Second Advent (Mt 24: 22, 29)	Day of the Lord (v. 2), in his time [i.e., day of Antichrist] (v. 6)	great day of wrath (6:17), hour of judgment (14:7), great day of God (16:14)
Scope	has anything been done like this? [ref. to Exodus] (v. 32)	none like it (v. 7), complete destruction (v. 11)	complete destruction (v. 27c)	such as never occurred (v. 1)	such as never occurred nor ever shall (24:21; 13:19)	"bring to an end" [complete destruction] (v. 8)	such as had not been since man came on earth (16:18)
Religious context	idolatry (vv. 25, 28)	false prophets (29:24-32)	prince that will come (Antichrist), abomination of desolation (v. 27)	Antichrist (11:36-45), wicked (12:10)	false prophets' signs and wonders (24:24; 13:22)	Antichrist, false signs and wonders (vv. 4-9)	Antichrist, false prophets' signs and wonders (13:1-14)
Temple activity	promise of spiritual restoration (v. 30)	promise of spiritual restoration and theocracy (v. 9)	temple desecrated (v. 27)	temple desecrated (v. 11)	temple desecrated (24:15; 13:14)	temple desecrated (v. 4)	temple desecrated (11:1, 2)
Salvation message	you will return (v. 30)	saved from time (v. 7)	implied in destruction of desolator (v. 27)	[elect] rescued (v. 1)	elect saved (24:22; 13:20)	day will not come [upon you], elect saved (vv. 3, 13)	bondservants of God saved (19:1, 2)

is to conceal these prophecies or keep them secret. Rather, because the revelation is now completed, he is to "keep intact" and "carefully preserve" the prophecies for future generations of his people. In reference to Jesus' citation of Daniel's prophecy about the abomination of desolation in His Olivet Discourse, Matthew wrote, "Let the reader understand" (Matthew 24:15). This statement reveals that the Lord expected His people to discern Daniel's intended meaning. Yet Jesus' words were for the generation that would be alive at the time of the abomination of desolation and, upon understanding Daniel's context, would realize they need to flee the coming persecution by the Antichrist (Matthew 24:16-21). In like manner, Daniel is told that the clearest understanding of these prophecies will come only as people approach and enter the end time.

Daniel 12:11-12 explains the *prophetic time-table* that will take these Tribulation saints from the midpoint of the Tribulation (when "the regular sacrifice is abolished and the abomination of desolation is set up") to the end of the seventieth week and the second advent. This time was previously revealed to be 1260 days, but Gabriel says there will be 1290 days (verse 11). Likewise, verse 12 exclaims, "How blessed is he who keeps waiting and attains to the 1335 days!" Apparently these additional periods of 30 days and 45 days, which total a time of 75 more days, indicate there will be an interim period between the second advent and the commencement of the millennial kingdom. Since the judgment of the nations follows the second advent and precedes the entrance of the

saints into the kingdom (Matthew 25:30-34), it must occupy this interim period.

Other events may also occur within this time frame, such as the elevation of the millennial Jerusalem and the building of the millennial temple (cf. Isaiah 2:2-3; Ezekiel 40–43; Zechariah 14:10). The dedication of the millennial temple will require that a functioning priesthood be resident at the site, so it's likely the work on the temple will take place once the kingdom has commenced. The reason the one who makes it to the end of the 1335 days is so blessed is because this date will mark the first day of the millennial kingdom and his entrance into it.

The concluding command to Daniel is actually a commendation and encouragement to this saint who has served so faithfully and for so long (Daniel 12:13). Daniel is to continue his duties and devotion to God until his death ("the end"), after which he will enter into the "rest" of the afterlife (the reward of the righteous) and then "rise again for your allotted portion at the end of the age" (see comments on 8:17). Daniel may have been relieved to know he would miss the terrible time of Tribulation that he so feared (7:28; 8:27), and overjoyed to learn that he, like other righteous Israelites, will have an appointed function to fulfill in the millennial kingdom. Just as he was assured through the prophecy that this time would come for Israel, now he has been personally assured it will also come for him as well. Thus, Daniel's prophecy ends with words of hope for the future.

THE MINOR PROPHETS

HOSEA

HOSEA IS ONE OF THE MOST autobiographical of all the prophets. He bares his soul as he tells the story of his personal heartache over the unfaithfulness of his wife, Gomer. After she betrayed him, be bought her back from slavery and degradation. Based on his personal testimony, Hosea then predicted God's willingness to forgive, redeem, and restore wayward Israel. Ultimately, his prophecies will be fulfilled in the eschatological future when all Israel will be saved, redeemed, and restored during Christ's millennial reign.

CONCERNING HIS WIFE AND CHILDREN
Hosea 1:2-9

HOSEA IS OFFICIALLY CALLED into the prophetic office and given a direct revelation from God (1:2). This first revelation is his commission, in which he is told to "take to yourself a wife of harlotry." This means he is to marry a prostitute. Some have thought this is not possible, for if it were, God would be asking Hosea to do something contrary to the law of Moses. Actually, only the Levites were forbidden to marry prostitutes (Leviticus 21:7,14). Hosea, however, was neither a priest nor a Levite; he was a member of one of the tribes in the northern kingdom of Israel. Therefore, the prohibition in the law of Moses did not apply to Hosea.

Not only does God ask Hosea to marry a prostitute, He also tells him to take the children "of harlotry"—that is, children already born to the prostitute before the marriage (verse 2). Since the word "children" is used, this particular prostitute had already given birth to at least two children. God then explained the reason for this symbolic action: "For the land commits flagrant harlotry, forsaking the LORD." Just as Hosea's wife is a prostitute, so is God's "wife," or Israel, a prostitute. Hosea's wife symbolized the nation of Israel as a whole, and the children symbolized the specific individuals within the nation.

Hosea's obedience is recorded in verse 3: "So he went and took Gomer the daughter of Diblaim." The prostitute's name is *Gomer,* meaning "perfection" or "completion." Her father's name is *Diblaim,* meaning "double fig cakes." The term "fig cakes" was an erotic symbol throughout the ancient world of this period and it is used in this way in the Song of Solomon. Putting the two names together gives the meaning that Gomer was a "perfect daughter of pleasure." She was devoted to not just her own pleasure, but the pleasure of those who used her. This is the kind of woman God asks Hosea to marry.

By the way, Hosea is warned not to expect a happy marriage. He is told in advance to marry someone who will cause him grief. Hosea still obeys the Lord anyway and marries Gomer and adopts her children.

In the early years of Hosea's marriage to

Gomer, Gomer gives birth to three more children. The first child is a son named *Jezreel* (verses 3-4). *Jezreel* can have two meanings: "God scatters," and "God sows." Throughout these first three chapters of Hosea, Jezreel is used in both senses—sometimes in the sense of God scattering, sometimes in the sense of God sowing.

God then states that He "will avenge the blood of Jezreel upon the house of Jehu" (verse 4). Jehu had led a revolt against King Ahab and destroyed the entire family of Ahab, including Jezebel. God had condemned the family line of Ahab to total destruction because of their sinfulness (2 Kings 9:7-10). So, while Jehu's act itself was the will of the Lord, his motivation for destroying the family of Ahab was improper. Jehu's motivation was not a desire to reestablish the worship of Jehovah, but to gain full power and authority. While he destroyed Ahab and did away with Baal worship, he did not reinstitute the worship of Jehovah as the only proper worship. Instead, he went back to the sins of Jeroboam, which involved the worship of the golden calf (2 Kings 12:25-33).

Although Jehu's act was right, because his motivation was improper, God promised judgment would come (verse 5). God states that a day will come when He "will break the bow of Israel in the valley of Jezreel." To "break the bow" meant that He would break up the kingdom. The "valley of Jezreel" is the place where "the bow of Israel" or the kingdom would be broken. This, in turn, will result in the scattering of Israel, thus fulfilling the first meaning of Jezreel—God scatters.

The second child, a daughter, is named *Lo-ruhamah*, which means "no mercy" (verse 6). The significance of her name is that there would no longer be mercy for Israel, or the northern kingdom. Judah, the southern kingdom, will be spared (verse 7). The reason is that Judah has been more faithful than Israel and has had some righteous kings, while Israel has had none. As a result, Judah will be spared destruction by the Assyrians. God further points out He will rescue Judah not by means

of another military power, but "by the LORD their God." Judah will "have mercy" and Israel will have "no mercy," for the latter is destined for destruction.

Then Gomer gives birth to a third child, a son named *Lo-ammi*, which means "not my people." The application to Israel was that, for a period of time, Israel would be *Lo-ammi*, or "not God's people." Positionally speaking, on the basis of the Abrahamic Covenant, the people of Israel are always the people of God, and according to Romans 11:29, "the gifts and the calling of God are irrevocable." Therefore, God will not reject His people (Romans 11:1-2). But experientially, Israel cannot enjoy the benefits of being God's people unless she is in a state of obedience. For a long time Israel will be *Lo-ammi*, "not my people," and the people will not experience the various blessings that belong to those who are God's people.

FUTURE REVERSAL AND RESTORATION
Hosea 1:10–2:1

THE JUDGMENT DESCRIBED in Hosea 1:2-9 will one day be reversed. First, there will be a reversal of *Jezreel* from "God scatters" to "God sows" (verse 10). In the sense of judgment *Jezreel* means "God scatters," and God will scatter His people out of the land. In the sense of blessing *Jezreel* means "God sows," and He would someday "sow" them in the land. As a result there will be a tremendous increase in Israel's population.

Second, Hosea predicts a national conversion (verse 10). Israel, who was once *Lo-ammi*, "not My people," will again become *Ammi*, "My people." Because of this concept of going from "not My people" to "My people," these verses are used by Paul to illustrate the salvation of Gentiles in Romans 9:24-26. The Gentiles also were for a long period of time "not My people," but now have become "My people." Peter also quotes Hosea in 1 Peter 2:9-10 when he speaks about the believing Jewish remnant.

Before these Jews were believers, they were *Lo-ammi,* or not God's people. But as believers in Jesus the Messiah, they become *Ammi,* or God's people.

Hosea then goes on to prophesy a future national reunification (verse 11). The kingdoms of Israel and Judah will again be reunited under one national leadership. There will be one head, which will be the Messiah, with David as the co-regent. Then "the day of Jezreel" will come, which will be a national day of sowing of the people of Israel in the land (verse 11).

The third reversal is mentioned in 2:1. In this reversal, the name *Lo-ruhamah,* meaning "no mercy," is changed to *Ruhamah,* meaning "having mercy."

APPLICATION TO ISRAEL, THE WIFE OF JEHOVAH
Hosea 2:2-23

In Hosea 2 appears a more detailed application of Hosea's marriage and children to Israel as the wife of Jehovah. Israel was guilty of adultery (verses 2-5). This adultery has led to a separation between husband and wife (verse 2). The wife, Israel, must put away her adultery. Idolatry is spiritual adultery, so the putting away of adultery means putting away idolatry (Genesis 35:2; Joshua 24:14; 2 Kings 18:4; 23:19).

There were two results of Israel's adultery (verses 3-5). The first result emphasizes the *Lo-ammi,* "not My people," aspect of God's judgment (verse 3). Hosea predicts the stripping of Israel by God, meaning that she will be treated as an adulteress. Women in those days who were guilty of adultery were stripped naked. This pictures how Israel would be stripped of its productivity and become a "wilderness…like desert land" (verse 3). The second result emphasizes the *Lo-ruhamah,* "no mercy," aspect of God's judgment (verses 4-5). There will be no mercy upon the children (the individuals of the nation), and there will be no mercy on the mother herself (the nation as a whole) because she misinterpreted where her gifts had come from. Rather than recognizing them to be gifts from her husband, Jehovah, she assumed that these gifts came from other gods, and for that she will be punished.

The adultery of Israel will lead to the punishment of Israel (2:6-13). God states that He will throw a "hedge" around Israel (verse 6). Elsewhere, the throwing up of a hedge is used with a good connotation (see Job 1:10; 10:11-12). But the result of this hedging (verse 7) is that Israel will not be able to find her lovers, the gods with whom she committed adultery, and they will prove themselves to be nonentities. She will eventually see her need to return to her first husband, God. The reason for the hedging (verse 8) is her failure to recognize the true source of her material benefits. Because of her disobedience, Israel's material blessings will be withheld. Israel had assumed these material blessings came from other gods, but they had not, and she is about to recognize this.

Furthermore, these material gifts that Jehovah gave Israel were used by her as worship gifts to the other gods, especially the god Baal. The throwing up of the hedge involved the stripping of Israel, which is the taking away of material blessings. Israel will be stripped of food and clothing, resulting in "her nakedness," or the land becoming barren (verses 9-10). The result of the punishment will be a cessation of "all her gaiety" and festivities (verse 11). These festivals were ordained by God and refer to Jewish festivals: the new moons, the Sabbaths, and the solemn assemblies. Instead of using these festivals as acts of worship directed to God, Israel used them as acts of worship for the god Baal. Thus, God is going to take them away from her.

The "vines and fig trees" are symbols of security (verse 12). Israel assumed they were gifts from her lovers, and because of that wrong conclusion, these gifts will now be taken away. The "days of the Baals" (verse 13) are the days mentioned in verse 11, the days of proper festivals, which Israel used improperly for the worship of Baal. The worship of Baal throughout "the days of the Baals" resulted in Israel forgetting her true husband, Jehovah (verse 13).

In verses 14-23, Hosea describes the restoration of Israel. Jehovah, the husband, will once again court His wife (verse 14). He will woo her in the "wilderness," the wilderness of Revelation 12:6,13-14 and Micah 2:12-13, the wilderness of the land of Edom, specifically the city of Bozrah or Petra. There God will court Israel and bring her back to Himself. Israel's response will be to return to the Lord as in "the valley of Achor" (verse 15). The valley of Achor is where Achan committed his sin (Joshua 7:24-26) that resulted in Israel's defeat at Ai, so it became known as the "valley of troubling." As a result of the removal of Achan's sin, it became a "door of hope" of new victory and conquest. Achor will once again be a "door of hope" when Israel returns.

Upon Israel's return, five things will happen (verses 16-18). First, there will be the removal of all idolatry (verse 16). Second, there will be a change in Israel's vocabulary (verse 17). Israel will no longer address God as *Baali*, but only as *Ishi*. *Baali* and *Ishi* both mean "my husband." *Baali* means "my husband" in the sense of "my master," and *Ishi* means "my husband" in the sense of "my man." Both are valid forms and are used interchangeably throughout the Old Testament. But because *Baali* sounds so much like the name Baal, one of the gods with whom Israel committed adultery, the term *Baali* will be dropped from the Hebrew vocabulary in the kingdom. The Jews will no longer address God as *Baali* but only as *Ishi* to erase any possible remembrance of the god Baal; all remembrance of idolatry will cease.

Third, peace and security will be restored, with no threat of harm from the animal kingdom or from war (verse 18). Fourth, there will be a new betrothal (verses 19-20). Several characteristics of a new betrothal are mentioned in verse 19—it will last forever, and it will be marked by righteousness, justice,

lovingkindness, and mercy. The result will be a faithful marriage (verse 20).

Finally, there will be a reversal in the names of Hosea's children (verses 21-23). In verses 21-22, *Jezreel*, which first meant "God scatters" in the sense of judgment, will now mean "God sows" in the sense of blessing. God will sow the people in the land and there will be fruitfulness in the land, with heaven and earth cooperating to give great production. *Lo-ruhamah*, which means "no mercy," will now be *Ruhamah*, meaning "obtaining mercy." And in verse 23, in place of *Lo-ammi*, "not My people," it will be *Ammi*, "My people."

HOSEA RESCUES HIS WIFE
Hosea 3:1-3

HOSEA'S SECOND COMMISSION is to rescue Gomer from the slave market. After Gomer had given birth to her third child, she abandoned Hosea and began to seek the lovers she had known in relationships before her marriage to Hosea. Whereas before she was a prostitute, now she had become an adulteress. She had lost her appeal, and no one wanted her anymore. She had fallen into debt and had been sold into slavery. Hosea is now told to rescue her from the slave market, for she is "loved by her husband," Hosea. Hosea is commissioned to take Gomer back and love her still.

The application is that God still loves Israel in spite of her loving other gods and in spite of her loving "raisin cakes" (which were an erotic symbol [Song of Solomon 5:2] and used in the worship of idols [Jeremiah 7:18; 44:19]). Hosea purchases Gomer for 15 pieces of silver plus one and one-half homers of barley, which is also equal to 15 pieces of silver. He purchases her back for the total price of 30 pieces of silver, the value of a dead slave (Exodus 21:32). When he brings her home, she is to be deprived of two things: She is no longer to "play the harlot," nor to play the wife. She would have no conjugal rights until there is complete restoration of love between the two, at which point the physical relationship will be restored.

APPLICATION TO ISRAEL, THE WIFE OF JEHOVAH
Hosea 3:4-5

JUST AS GOMER IS TO SUFFER deprivation (3:3), Israel is also to suffer (3:4). First, Israel will be deprived of civil authority—"without king or prince." After the destruction by Babylon, Israel was deprived of a king and after the destruction by Rome, Israel was deprived of a prince. Second, Israel will be deprived of true worship—"without sacrifice…and without ephod." The term "without sacrifice" tells us Israel will be without the temple. The term "without ephod" tells us Israel will be without the priesthood. Both of these have been true since the Roman destruction in A.D. 70. Third, Israel will be deprived of the false worship of idolatry—"without…sacred pillar…or household idols." Israel will no longer worship false temple gods (sacred pillar) or household gods. This has been true since the Babylonian destruction in 586 B.C.

The restoration of Israel (verse 5) will come "afterward"—that is, after a period of "many days" (verse 4), Israel will be restored to her relationship as the wife of Jehovah. This verse transitions into the prophetic future. In that day, Israel will do three things. First, Israel will undergo a national regeneration and will again become the wife of Jehovah. Second, Israel will seek two persons: the first will be "the LORD their God," or more specifically, the Messiah, and the second will be "David their king," who will be the Messiah's co-regent over Israel in the messianic kingdom. And third, Israel will be faithful to the Lord from then on. As a result of the nation's faithfulness and obedience, the people will experience the material goodness of God and never be deprived of this goodness again.

In summary, the kingdom and the nation are to be "scattered" (*Jezreel*), "without mercy"

(*Lo-ruhamah*), and experientially "not God's people" (*Lo-ammi*). But in the future, they will be "sown" to the Lord (*Jezreel*), become "God's people" (*Ammi*), and will "obtain mercy" (*Ruhamah*).

PREREQUISITE OF THE SECOND COMING
Hosea 5:15–6:3

IN 5:1-14, HOSEA SPELLS OUT a broad sweep of prophecy that has now been fulfilled. In this prophecy, sometimes the focus is on Judah, sometimes it is on Israel, and sometimes it is on both. This overview includes what was fulfilled through the Assyrian captivity, the Babylonian captivity, and the events of A.D. 70.

God, who does all the speaking throughout chapter 5 of Hosea, concludes by saying in verse 15, "I will go away and return to My place until they acknowledge their guilt and seek My face; in their affliction they will earnestly seek Me."

There are certain presuppositions behind the understanding of this verse. Before anyone can return to a place, he must first leave it. In this passage, God states that He is going to go back to "my place," which is heaven. Before God can go back to heaven, He must first leave it. The question is, When did God ever leave heaven? At the incarnation, in the Person of Jesus of Nazareth. Then, because of one specific offense (the word is singular) committed against Him, God returned to heaven at the ascension from the Mount of Olives. Hosea 5:15 further states that God will not come back to the earth until the offense that caused Him to return to heaven is acknowledged or confessed.

What is that Jewish national offense committed against the Person of Jesus? This does not refer to killing Him, for the actual killing of Jesus was done by Gentile, not Jewish, hands. He was condemned and sentenced by a Gentile judge. He was crucified by Gentile soldiers. But all this is ultimately irrelevant, for regardless of Jewish acceptance or Jewish rejection, Jesus would have had to die anyway to become the sacrifice for sin. The national offense of Israel was the rejection of His messiahship. According to Hosea 5:15, only when this offense is acknowledged or confessed will Messiah return to the earth.

Note that Hosea 5:15 concludes with a warning: "In their affliction they will earnestly seek Me." The term "affliction" is one of the common Old Testament names for the Tribulation in general and Armageddon in particular. Indeed, in the context of Armageddon, the Jewish people will begin to search for the Messiah earnestly. There are two prerequisites, then, to the second coming: First, there must be the confession of Israel's national sin (Leviticus 26:40-42; Jeremiah 3:11-18); and second, there must be a pleading for the Messiah to return (Zechariah 12:10; Matthew 23:37-39).

This will take place when the armies of the Antichrist are at the city of Bozrah, in the last three days of the campaign of Armageddon.

The first three verses of Hosea 6 are actually a continuation of Hosea 5 and contain the acknowledgment of sin that is demanded in 5:15. Verses 1-3 are a call issued by the Jewish leaders exhorting the nation to repent of their national sin. Only then will the physical blessings Israel once enjoyed be restored to her, and the leaders of Israel will finally recognize the reason why the Tribulation has fallen on them. Whether this will happen through the study of the Scriptures, or by the preaching of the 144,000, or through the testimony of the two witnesses of Revelation 11, or by the future ministry of Elijah is not clearly stated. Most likely, it will be a combination of these things. But the leaders will come to a realization of the nation's sin in some way.

In the three days mentioned in Hosea 6:1-3, the confession of Israel's national sin will take place during the first two days. This confession appears in Isaiah 53:1-9 and admits that the nation had looked upon Jesus as nothing more than another man, a criminal who had died for His own sins. However, on this occasion they will recognize that Jesus was no ordinary man,

but the perfect Lamb of God, the Messiah Himself. Then on the third of the three days, the people as a nation will be saved, fulfilling the prophecy of Romans 11:25-27.

GOD'S LOVE FOR ISRAEL
Hosea 11:1-11

HOSEA 11:1-7 SHOWS how Israel turned her back on God's love for her. Even in the face of Israel's rejection, God states that He could not possibly give up on Israel nor destroy Israel totally as He did Admah and Zeboiim, two cities destroyed with Sodom and Gomorrah (Genesis 14:8 with 19:25). On the contrary, God clearly feels compassion for Israel. Therefore, He will not extend the fullness of His anger (Hosea 11:9), and although He must judge Israel for Israel's sins, He will not judge the people to total destruction. He will judge them for the purpose of correction. Once they do come back to Him, only then will they experience the final regathering and the restoration of the land (verses 10-11). The fact that the regathering is not only from the north and south but also from the west is certainly possible after A.D. 70. The return from the captivity was from the east.

ISRAEL'S SIN AND GOD'S SALVATION
Hosea 11:12–14:8

THE PROPHECIES IN this passage intermix past and future fulfillment. Hosea begins by contrasting the nation of Israel with Jacob, the father of Israel (11:12–12:14). Whereas Jacob sought after God and His blessing, Israel sought idolatry and, for that reason, calamity came upon the land (13:1-16). However, the judgment upon Israel, which will be a judgment of destruction, will not be total (13:14), for God declares that death and Sheol will not win, and God intends to ransom Israel from Sheol and death. When God declares that "compassion will be hidden from My sight" (13:14), He is saying that He will not change His mind about the future salvation of Israel. Therefore, it will indeed come.

Hosea concludes with a look at Israel's future and final salvation (14:1-8). He begins with a call to repentance (verses 1-3), which is followed by God's promise that once Israel does repent, God will indeed respond (verses 4-5). This, in turn, will lead to Israel's future fruitfulness (verses 5-8). Thus, in the messianic kingdom, Israel will be a fruit-bearing nation that will benefit the Gentiles as well. With that positive note, Hosea concludes his book by confessing his great impression of the wisdom of God, just as the apostle Paul does in Romans 11:33-36.

JOEL

THE PRINCIPAL FOCUS OF THE BOOK OF JOEL, written about 825 B.C. in Judah, is a coming day of judgment—"the day of the LORD" (1:15). This day will bring both punishment for sin and deliverance from its consequences. The punishment of the nation is pictured as analogous to a locust invasion that devastates the land. The language depicts the future period known as the Great Tribulation, when a Gentile army will invade Israel and be destroyed by God. God then intervenes on behalf of Israel following its repentance—an intervention to be fulfilled at the end of the Tribulation. The "day of the LORD" is not merely a day of God's wrath, but also a day when God will save and deliver a remnant, for in that day "whosoever calls on the name of the LORD will be delivered" (2:32). It is at this time that Christ will return to reveal Himself in judgment and salvation.

THE DAY OF THE LORD
Joel 1:2–2:17

THIS FIRST MAJOR SEGMENT of the book of Joel shows that "the day of the LORD" (1:15) will be a time of invasion. There are two subdivisions, of which the first, 1:2-14, deals with the historical invasion of locusts. It is this invasion that gave rise to the prophecy as a whole, as Joel prophesies of future invasions. Since this locust invasion was historical, we will turn our attention to the prophecy in the next section.

The second subdivision, 1:15–2:17, describes the devastation that is going to occur during the Day of the Lord, the Great Tribulation. Having described the devastation caused by the locusts and pointing out that this was the worst that had ever occurred until that day, Joel now points out that a day is coming when things will get even worse. During the Day of

the Lord, the Great Tribulation, there will be an invasion that will prove to be even more devastating than the locust invasion that has just occurred.

Joel introduces his new theme in 1:15-20. In verse 15, Joel announces the coming Day of the Lord, a time of destruction from the Almighty. It is God's judgment upon this earth. When that day comes, it will result in a massive devastation even worse than that which occurred from the recent locust invasion. The crops will be destroyed (verses 16-17), and as a result, there will be no sustenance for the temple (verse 16) or the people (verse 17). Livestock will be affected too, for they will have nothing to eat (verses 18-20).

In 2:1-11, Joel begins to detail the account of the invasion. He begins by sounding the alarm in 2:1: "Blow a trumpet in Zion, and sound an alarm on My holy mountain! Let all the inhabitants of the land tremble: for the day of the LORD is coming; surely it is near." In the ancient world, an alarm was sounded to announce an approaching army (Numbers 10:9). Here an alarm will sound from the holy mountain, Mount Zion, upon which the temple stands. When this alarm sounds, it will point out that the Day of the Lord has arrived with full force. In verse 2, Joel says this day will be a time of darkness, gloominess, and clouds. These are typical descriptions of the Day of the Lord or the Great Tribulation (Isaiah 8:22; 60:2; Amos 5:18-20; Zephaniah 1:14-16). Joel concludes his description with the words, "as the dawn is spread over the mountains…." In other words, just as dawn is sudden and widespread, so will be the Day of the Lord. It will come not only upon the land of Israel (though that is Joel's particular focal point), but extend to all parts of the world.

Next, in Joel 2:2-9, the prophet describes the invading army. This invasion will have some similarities to the locust invasion, yet there will be some crucial differences. Verses 2-3 describe their approach and emphasize that "there has never been anything like it." Verse 3 describes the coming devastation, which will be massive. The land before this army is like the Garden of Eden, but after the invasion passes through, all that will remain is a desert wilderness.

Verses 4-9 describe the army itself. Joel says "their appearance is like the appearance of horses; and like war horses, so they run" (verse 4). They make a noise like chariots (verse 5), they cause terror (verse 6), they are fast (verse 7), they are disciplined (verse 8), and their attack will be pervasive (verse 9). While this sounds similar to the locust invasion, this army has certain characteristics (horse-like characteristics) that point out that they are not locusts, though the devastation they cause is similar.

This invasion will have two major results: There will be tremendous convulsions of nature, and there will be no light that penetrates to the earth from the sun, moon, or stars (verse 10). Verse 11 explains why all these things have occurred: the judgment of God. Joel states

that God is able to execute His word, and He will execute it during the great and terrible Day of the Lord. What Joel describes in these verses is the same thing that John describes in Revelation 9 when John wrote of two demonic invasions (9:1-11 and 9:13-21).

After the locust invasion in chapter 1, Joel encouraged the nation and the priests to fast and repent and call on the Lord in prayer. The same thing will occur in the future. As a result of this demonic invasion, there will be an exhortation and a call to fasting and prayer (2:12-17). The exhortation is in 2:12-14. In verses 12-13, Joel states that the people's requirement in that future day will be to turn and repent. The repentance is to come with fasting, weeping, and mourning. This time the people are not to rend their garments but to rend their hearts. Where there is true repentance, God will respond in grace (verses 13-14). Indeed, toward the end of the Tribulation, the whole nation will repent in just this way, and God will respond in grace.

The call to fasting and prayer is in 2:15-17. In verse 15, a trumpet is sounded once again. When the trumpet sounded in 2:1, it was a warning that the invading army had arrived. This time the alarm is sounded for the purpose of calling a solemn assembly. That, too, was a biblical use of the trumpet (Numbers 10:10). Once again the trumpet will sound from Mount Zion, and verse 16 emphasizes the totality of the call. All should come to repentance in the nation of Israel: the old men and the children, the bridegroom and the bride. According to verse 17, there will be a special calling upon the priests to weep and cry for help that the chosen people would be spared and not be a reproach among the Gentiles. Psalm 79 describes Israel calling upon the Lord in the closing days of the Tribulation, and Psalm 79:10 makes a similar plea as Joel 2:17—that the Jews not remain a derision among the Gentiles. Ultimately, the invasion Joel describes will be one of several catalysts that will lead Israel to true repentance in the closing days of the Great Tribulation.

THE SALVATION AND RESTORATION OF ISRAEL
Joel 2:18–3:21

THE SECOND MAJOR SEGMENT of the book of Joel deals with the salvation and restoration of Israel. Indeed, among the results of the Great Tribulation (as taught in many places in Scripture) is the fact that Israel will be saved. This, in turn, will lead to Israel's restoration to all the Promised Land. There are four subdivisions in this section of the book.

THE RESTORATION OF THE LAND
Joel 2:18-27

The first subdivision deals with the restoration of the land. In verses 18-20, Joel writes about God's answer. The first segment of the book ended with Israel mourning and lamenting in repentance. These verses describe God's response to that repentance in three ways. First, He responds in mercy (verse 18). God's mercy arises out of His jealousy for His land and pity for the Jewish people. Second, He responds by removing their reproach (verse 19). In verse 17, they had asked that the reproach of the Gentiles against the Jews might be removed, and so it will be. Third, God will remove the invading army (verse 20). The main part of the army will be destroyed in the deserts of the Negev in the south part of Israel, and the stench from the dead bodies "will arise." The armies of the Antichrist that come against the Jews in the campaign of Armageddon will be destroyed to the south, east, and west of Israel. The north is not mentioned because the army will come from the north.

In verses 21-27, God then promises the restoration of material blessings. The land itself will be glad and rejoice because God "has done great things" (verse 21). The beasts who had earlier suffered because of the devastation of the land will also rejoice because the pastures and wilderness will spring up again, and there will once again be sufficient food and water (verse 22). The people of Israel will rejoice as well, according to verses 23-26.

Five reasons are given for this rejoicing. First is the teacher of righteousness (verse 23). English translations normally refer to "former rain" or "early rain" because that seems to make more sense in the context. But the Hebrew literally reads "the teacher of righteousness." This teacher of righteousness is the Jewish Messiah Himself. So the people are rejoicing over the presence of the teacher of righteousness, the Messiah. The second reason is that the rains will come in their proper seasons, which will mean an abundance of crops (verse 23). The third reason is the abundance of grain, wine, and oil (verse 24) that will result from the rains coming in their proper seasons. The fourth reason Israel will rejoice is that there will be a restoration of all the losses Israel suffered in earlier plagues, such as the locust plague of Joel's day (verse 25). God will provide so abundantly in the messianic kingdom that all of the previous losses will be more than made up for. The fifth reason for this rejoicing will be the removal of shame (verse 26). The reproach the people felt among the Gentiles, which they prayed might be removed (2:17), will be removed.

So the land, the animals, and the people of Israel will rejoice over the restoration of the material blessings. The result of all this is given in verse 27: They will really and certainly know that Jehovah is indeed the God of Israel and that He is in their midst.

THE OUTPOURING OF THE HOLY SPIRIT
Joel 2:28-32

In the Hebrew Bible, Joel 2:28-32 comprises one individual chapter, the third chapter of the book, which implies the importance the rabbis ascribed to this passage. Israel's national salvation is frequently connected to the outpouring of the Holy Spirit. Joel describes the outpouring of the Holy Spirit in verses 28-29. Verse 28 specifies the timing of this outpouring with the word "afterward." After what? After what the preceding context has been dealing with. After the judgments of the Great Tribulation—after Israel's repentance—will come an outpouring upon the whole nation that will lead to the nation's salvation. This outpouring will occur during the last three days of the Great Tribulation (Hosea 5:15–6:3).

Verses 28-29 describe the universality of this outpouring and its results. It will be poured out upon all mankind. The "all mankind," in this context, is Jewish flesh. Joel does not mean that there will be an outpouring upon the whole world in general, but rather, upon the whole nation of Israel in particular. The use of the word "your"—your daughters, your young men, your old men—shows he is speaking of Israel and not the church. In this outpouring, there will be no distinction of age, sex, or social status. The whole nation will receive this outpouring, and it will result in prophetic dreams and visions. Joel's promise to Israel is later used by Peter to explain the outpouring of the Spirit at Pentecost (see commentary on Acts 2).

In verses 30-31, Joel points out two signs that will precede this outpouring of the Holy Spirit. God will "display wonders in the sky and on earth" (verse 30), and there will be a massive blackout (verse 31). No light from the sun, moon, or stars will penetrate to the earth. Evidently this blackout will occur "before the great and awesome day of the LORD comes." Sometime before the Tribulation starts, the first of five blackouts will occur. The events in verses 30-31 are signs that the final salvation of Israel will soon come.

In verse 32, Joel gives the one prerequisite to Israel's salvation: Israel must call on the name of the Lord. The remnant of Israel will do precisely that.

THE JUDGMENT OF THE GENTILES
Joel 3:1-17

The remainder of Joel, or the third segment, comprises the fourth chapter of Joel in the Hebrew Bible and deals with the judgment of the Gentiles. Following Israel's national salvation, there will be a judgment of all living Gentiles. This is the same judgment as that described in Matthew 25:31-46.

Verses 1-8 give the announcement of that coming judgment of the Gentiles, which will occur at the time of the final restoration of Israel (verse 1). It will take place in conjunction with Israel's regathering, after the second coming, and before the kingdom is officially set up. Verse 2 names the place of the judgment: the Valley of Jehoshaphat, also known as the Valley of Kidron. This is one of two valleys that surround the Old City of Jerusalem, and it separates the Old City from the Mount of Olives. Verses 2-3 give the basis of this judgment: how these Gentiles treated the Jews during the Great Tribulation. Many of these Gentiles will be guilty of three anti-Semitic acts: first, scattering Israel; second, dividing the land among themselves, a land that belongs to the Jews; and third, enslaving the Jews. Verses 4-6 give an example of the sins of which these Gentiles are guilty.

Joel mentions three examples of the sins committed against the Jews. First is the sin of vengeance against the Jews (verse 4). Joel speaks of the recompense of Tyre and Sidon and Philistia. Those living in the area of the Philistine and Phoenician countries will be particularly guilty. The Philistine country today includes the Gaza Strip, comprised mostly of Palestinian Arabs, and Phoenicia today is Lebanon. Apparently these two areas will be especially vengeful against the Jews, and at this time they will be repaid by vengeance from God. Second, they will be guilty of spoiling the temple (verse 5). Third, they will be guilty of selling Jews as slaves to the Greeks (verse 6).

In verses 7-8 Joel makes two points. First, the Jews who were sold afar off will be brought back to the land. Second, the sellers themselves will be sold "far from their territory." The anti-Semites will be slain in this judgment (Revelation 16:16; 19:19-21) and ultimately sent to hell (Revelation 20:11-15). In that sense they are indeed sent far off.

After describing this call for the judgment of the Gentiles, Joel next gives the occasion of the judgment in verses 9-13. The crime is that these Gentiles had gathered themselves for war against the Jews. Verses 9-11 describe the gathering of the nations of the world against the Jews for the campaign of Armageddon. According to Revelation 16:12-16, the Antichrist will be responsible for gathering these armies together. What's more, the armies that join the Antichrist will not do so merely out of a sense of necessity, but will be enthusiastic about it (verse 10). Their enthusiasm will be seen in two ways: first, they will form weapons of war from peaceful materials; and second, the weak and cowardly will be self-deceived to believe they are strong and courageous.

Verse 11 describes the armies' speed in coming together. They cannot wait to begin killing the Jews. But God will send His own mighty ones, the angels, to carry out His own purposes against Satan or the Antichrist. When the nations gather together to annihilate the Jews, they will do so in the Valley of Jezreel, the Valley of Megiddo. But just as the Antichrist will gather all the nations for war against the Jews, God will now gather all the nations in another valley, the Valley of Jehoshaphat, for judgment (verses 12-13).

Verse 12 marks the beginning and the end of the campaign of Armageddon. In verse 13, the nations are pictured as undergoing reaping and treading. The reaping results in salvation because many Gentiles are pro-Semites, and they are reaped to salvation (this is also found in Revelation 14:14-16). The treading results in the destruction of the anti-Semites and is also described in Revelation 14:17-20, which speaks of this treading taking place just outside the city (the Valley of Jehoshaphat is just outside the east walls of Jerusalem). The pro-Semites are not saved because they were good to the Jews. It is because they are already saved that

they are good to the Jews. Their pro-Semitic acts show their faith.

In Joel 3:14-17, Joel describes the execution of God's judgment. This judgment will be the outworking of "the day of the LORD" (verse 14). In verse 15 another blackout is described. This one happens after the Tribulation and is also mentioned in Matthew 24:29. According to verse 16, this is a war of judgment against the Gentiles, for God is a refuge for Israel. Following the judgment of the Gentiles, the kingdom will be established (verse 17). The judgment of the Gentiles described in Joel 3:1-17 is the very same judgment that is described in Matthew 24:31-46, the judgment of the sheep and the goats.

THE MESSIANIC KINGDOM
Joel 3:18-21

In 3:18-21, Joel states five facts about the messianic kingdom. First, there will be much water in the land, and the land will never lack water again (verse 18). Second, there will be a special millennial river (verse 18). This river is also mentioned in Zechariah 14:8 and Ezekiel 47:1-12. Third, there will be a desolation of Egypt and Edom (verse 19). The desolation of Egypt is limited to only 40 years—the first 40 years of the messianic kingdom, according to Ezekiel 29:8-14. But Edom will be desolate throughout the 1000 years of the millennial kingdom. The reason that Egypt and Edom (southern Jordan) will be desolate is because of their earlier violence against the Jews. Fourth, Israel will live in security (verse 20). And fifth, Israel will experience a national salvation (verse 21).

AMOS

Amos, who was from Tekoa, southeast of Bethlehem, conducted his prophetic ministry in the northern kingdom of Israel about the year 760 B.C. His book has nine chapters, and much of it deals with God's judgment on the people of Israel. Amos accused them of greed, immorality, selfishness, and oppression. Their worship of God was more form than substance.

Amos warned God's people to repent of their sin and seek God and His will. They were to return to the precepts of the law of Moses. Failing this, they would fall into severe punishment from God—a day of darkness and sorrow for the nation. The book then closes with a section in which Amos prophesies the future restoration of Israel (Amos 9:11-15).

THE RESTORATION OF ISRAEL
Amos 9:11-15

Amos makes five key points about the future restoration of Israel. First, the throne of David will be restored (verse 11). Using the common prophetic phrase "in that day," God promises to raise again the tabernacle of David, which has fallen. The Hebrew word for "booth" refers to a hut, and in this case, a broken-down one. The point is that at the time of Messiah's coming, the house of David will be a broken-down dynasty, which Isaiah also points out (Isaiah 11:1). In fact, this verse is the origin of the Talmudic name for the Messiah as *Ben Naphli,* which means "the son of the fallen one." Now this broken-down hut is to be repaired, meaning that it will be restored to its former glory. In Acts 15:16-17, James applies Amos 9:11 to the present day of Gentile salvation. James is not saying that Amos 9:11 had been fulfilled. He is merely pointing out that it was necessary to have a period of Gentile salvation before the final restoration of the tabernacle of David, and the prophecy will be fulfilled only when that occurs.

Second, Amos emphasizes Israel's future supremacy over the Gentiles (verse 12). This will be true of the nations in general and of Edom in particular.

Third, there will be increased production in the land (verse 13)—so much so that the reaping will take place at the same time as the planting. This verse may be a quotation of Joel 3:18.

Fourth, there will be a restoration of the land (verse 14). God will restore the people to the land and restore the land to the people, and Israel will finally possess all of the Promised Land.

Fifth, this restoration will be perpetual (verse 15). God promises that following the final restoration, the people will never again "be rooted out from their land which I have given them." Statements such as these show that this prophecy was not fulfilled by the Babylonian captivity, as some claim. The wording is such that it's clear Scripture is speaking of a restoration after which the people cannot be forced from the land again. That has yet to be fulfilled, and it will take place in the messianic kingdom.

OBADIAH

OBADIAH IS ONE OF THE SHORTEST BOOKS IN THE SCRIPTURES, containing only one chapter. The theme of the book is the doom of Edom. The Edomites were the descendants of Esau, the twin brother of Jacob. The Jews came from Jacob, and the Edomites came from Esau. In this sense Israel and Edom were brother nations; but because Edom was characterized by an unbrotherly attitude toward Israel, the prophets condemned Edom (today southern Jordan) rather severely. One of the first prophets to do so was Obadiah.

Obadiah can be divided into four main divisions.

THE DESTRUCTION OF EDOM
Obadiah 1-9

THE FIRST DIVISION DESCRIBES Edom's destruction, and is comprised of three smaller units. The first unit is in verse 1, which contains a call to the nations. An ambassador ("envoy") is sent out to the nations. The Hebrew word translated "envoy" is a word that normally means "angel." An angel is sent out to stir up the nations against Edom. God frequently uses angels to carry out His will among the nations, and that is the case here. After this angel has done his work, the nations will say, "Arise and let us go against her for battle" (verse 1). The nations will call for war against Edom.

The second unit, verses 2-4, announces that the pride of Edom will be destroyed. Edom's population is to be greatly reduced as a result of divine judgment (verse 2). Obadiah points out that Edom's pride was in her security: she dwelled among the rocks (verse 3). The two major cities in Edom, Sela and Bozrah, were located in a range of mountains in Edom known as Mount Seir. These mountains rise up sud-

denly from the plain and are very majestic. It would have been very difficult for an enemy to execute a full-scale onslaught against these cities in the clefts of these rocks. It was because of Edom's protective place in the mountains that the nation was proud. But Obadiah says that Edom's pride will be brought down (verse 4). Even the seemingly invincible Mount Seir could not protect the people from God's judgment.

In the third unit, verses 5-9, Obadiah emphasizes the totality of Edom's destruction. Obadiah begins by contrasting the incomplete and the complete (verses 5-6). First he addresses the incomplete (verse 5). When robbers break into a home, they do not take every single item in the house; some things are always left behind. Even when people glean the fields they do not manage to get all the crop. Inevitably, little bits are left here and there. But that won't happen with Edom's judgment (verse 6). The city will suffer complete destruction. There will be nothing hidden that will escape. Those who will despoil the Edomites will take everything until nothing is left.

In verse 7, Obadiah speaks about Edom's deceptive alliances. The peoples who are confederated with Edom will be the ones who will destroy Edom. The very ones with whom Edom has a covenant are the ones who will bring about her destruction. The expression "send you forth to the border" refers to an ancient custom. When an ambassador from one nation came to visit another nation, he would, after the state visit was completed, be escorted to the border as a sign of loyalty and as a visible assurance that all agreements would be kept. When the ambassadors of Edom come to these other nations with whom they have treaties and covenants, the other nations will escort the Edomite ambassadors to the border as a sign of loyalty; but it is all deceptive and a ploy to catch Edom off guard so that Edom can be destroyed.

As a result of the deception by Edom's allies, the wisdom of Edom will be deceived (verse 8), and the courage of Edom will collapse (verse 9). Again, the emphasis is on the totality of destruction: "Everyone may be cut off from the mountain of Esau by slaughter." Not just some, or even a majority, but *everyone* will be cut off.

THE REASON FOR JUDGMENT
Obadiah 10-14

IN THE SECOND MAJOR DIVISION of the book, Obadiah reveals the reason for the destruction of Edom. Why is God rendering such havoc upon the Edomites? Why is He so adamant about bringing total destruction? In verses 10-14, Obadiah spells out six reasons.

The first reason is Edom's violence against brother Jacob (verse 10). The violence of Edom against Israel is the violence of a brother against a brother. That makes the crime much more hideous. The result of this crime is that Edom will be shamed by being "cut off forever" (verse 10). This again emphasizes Edom's total destruction.

The second reason is Edom's hostile attitude toward the Jews as evidenced when Edom stood back and failed to help the Israelites when foreigners attacked, sacked, and despoiled Jerusalem. The Edomites should have come to Isra-

el's rescue. Instead, they cast lots for Jerusalem. They wanted to share in the spoil. While they were not actually a part of the fighting force, once they saw the Jews losing the battle, the Edomites began planning to join the enemies in partaking of the spoil. Obadiah says, "You too were as one of them" (verse 11). While Edom was not involved in the actual attack and war, she participated in the looting. For all practical purposes, she was just as guilty as those who instigated the sacking of Jerusalem.

The third reason Edom is to suffer is because of her glee over the fall of Jerusalem (verse 12). Not only were the Edomites characterized by a hostile attitude, but they were delighted and rejoiced over the collapse of Jerusalem. Although the Edomites were told, "Do not gloat...do not rejoice...do not boast in the day of their distress" (verse 12), they were guilty of all these things.

The fourth reason for God's judgment is that the Edomites joined in on the spoiling of Jerusalem (verse 13). Although they were not to enter into the gate of God's people during the day of their calamity, they entered in anyway. Although they were not to look on the affliction of Jerusalem, they looked with glee anyway. Although they were to lay no hand on the Jews' wealth, they joined in on the spoiling of the city.

The fifth reason Edom is destined for a total destruction is that the Edomites had blocked the escape routes for the Jews who were fleeing Jerusalem (verse 14). The Edomites did not let the Jews pass by; instead, they blocked the escape routes so the Jews could not escape.

The sixth reason for God's judgment against Edom was that the Edomites had captured the fleeing Jews and turned them over to the enemy, who made them slaves.

THE DAY OF THE LORD
Obadiah 15-16

THE THIRD MAJOR DIVISION of Obadiah states when the prophecy of Edom's total destruction will be fulfilled: the Day of the Lord. The time of retribution—the time of this judgment of the total destruction of the Edomites—will be during the Day of the Lord (verse 15). Whenever the Scriptures speak of the Day of the Lord, this is the most common biblical title for what is known as the seven-year Tribulation. In other words, the destruction spoken of in verses 1-9 will be fulfilled in its totality during the Tribulation. Verse 15 also points out that what the Edomites had done to Israel would now be done to them.

In verse 16, Obadiah gave yet another reason why Edom is destined for destruction: The Edomites had swallowed wine and gotten drunk on Mount Zion. After they despoiled the city, they celebrated by getting drunk on Mount Zion. Because of this, they too will be swallowed up. Again, the emphasis is on totality. A similar imagery appears in Zechariah 12:2-3, where Zechariah prophesied that the enemies of Jerusalem would become a "cup that causes reeling to all the peoples around." It is a cup the nations will drink, only to find themselves reeling with drunkenness afterward. Edom will share in that reeling.

A RESTORATION OF ISRAEL
Obadiah 17-21

IN THE FOURTH MAJOR DIVISION of the book, Obadiah concludes with the restoration of Israel and makes five points.

First, he speaks of the remnant: They will escape, meaning they will survive; they will be holy, for this is the saved remnant; and they will repossess all the land they had lost and will get back even more (verse 17).

Second, whereas the remnant returns, is saved, and enjoys the land, Edom will be destroyed by Israel (verse 18). During the Tribulation the house of Israel will become like fire while the house of Esau becomes like stubble. When fire is applied to stubble, the stubble quickly burns. One of the means by which God will bring about the destruction

of Edom mentioned in verses 1-9 is the people of Israel. This same point is taught in Ezekiel 25:12-14. Edom's destruction will be total, and Esau, from whom the Edomites came, will not have a single descendant left alive. Not only did Obadiah teach this, but other prophets taught it as well (Isaiah 34:5-15; Jeremiah 49:14-20; Ezekiel 35:14-15).

Third, Israel will possess the Gentile nations (verse 19). In this verse, Obadiah makes four points. First, the people of the Negev will possess the Mount of Esau. "Those of the Negev" were the tribe of Simeon, and this tribe will someday possess the "mountain of Esau," or Mount Seir. Second, "those of the Shephela" will possess the Philistine plain. Many of the tribe of Judah dwelled in the area known as the Shephela, and they will possess the coastal plain. Third, the ten tribes of Israel will possess Samaria and Ephraim as they did in the past. And fourth, the tribe of Benjamin will possess Gilead. The tribe of Benjamin was small and, except for the tribe of Dan, received the smallest amount of territory. But in the future, this tribe will possess not only the land on the west bank of the Jordan, it will also possess land on the east bank of the Jordan where Gilead is located.

The fourth point regarding the restoration is there will be a return of the captives (verse 20). Obadiah refers to "the exiles of this host of the sons of Israel." The captivity mentioned in verse 20 is probably the same captivity in verse 14. If that is true, then this refers to the Great Tribulation. What Obadiah speaks of here is what Zechariah spoke of in Zechariah 14:1-2—that many Jews will be taken into captivity as part of the Armageddon war. But the captivity will conclude after the day of the Lord, when the Jews are gathered once again. After the Great Tribulation, Israel's dispersion will come to an end and the Jews will be brought back together. The "exiles of this host of the sons of Israel" will be reunited. And all the Jewish captives who were taken as slaves during the Tribulation, such as those in Zechariah 14:1-2, will now be freed. They will possess Zaraphath, which is in Lebanon, and

Lebanon will become part of the Jewish state in the messianic kingdom. Furthermore, the Jews "in Sepharad" will possess and dwell in the land of the Negev (verse 20). *Sepharad* is the modern Hebrew word for Spain, and Obadiah might mean that the Jews of Spain will possess what is now known as the Negev Desert, which is in the southern part of Israel. This means that Jews who will come back from Spain, the Sephardic Jews, will possess and dwell in the land of the Negev.

Fifth is the establishment of the kingdom (verse 21). When the messianic kingdom is established, saviors will come to Mount Zion and "judge the mountain of Esau." God will bless Mount Zion and judge the Mount of Esau. This judgment will be so severe that, as Obadiah has pointed out several times already, not a single descendant of Esau will be left.

And the kingdom will belong not to Edom or to Israel, for the kingdom "will be the LORD's."

JONAH

THE PROPHECIES OF JONAH BASICALLY DEAL WITH God's warning of impending judgment upon Nineveh, the capital of the Assyrian empire. The experience of the prophet, however, prefigured the resurrection of Christ after three days and three nights. Jesus' reference to this event indicates His confidence in the historicity of the story of Jonah and the great fish.

THE SIGN OF JONAH
Jonah 1:16-17

GOD CALLED THE PROPHET JONAH from northern Israel to preach judgment upon Nineveh. Instead of going to Nineveh, Jonah fled in the opposite direction and was eventually swallowed by a great fish for three days and three nights (1:17). In the New Testament, Jesus refers to this event as the "sign of Jonah the prophet" (Matthew 12:39), using it to illustrate His miraculous resurrection after three days and three nights in the grave. The actual period of time that Christ was in the grave was either, at minimum, from Friday evening to Sunday morning, covering parts of three days, or at most, from Wednesday evening until Sunday morning. Regardless, Jonah's experience in the great fish was a prophetic type or picture of Christ's experience.

THE WARNING TO NINEVEH
Jonah 2:1-9

HAVING BEEN GIVEN a second chance, Jonah goes straight to Nineveh and announces that it will be overthrown unless the people repent. To the prophet's amazement and frustration, they repent, God relents, and Nineveh is spared. In the closing verses of the book, Jonah is rebuked by God because of his anger over the response of the people. Jonah had hoped they would be condemned and protested that he knew God would be merciful to his enemies (Jonah 4:1-3). As much as any Old Testament book, Jonah highlights the universal appeal of God's love and mercy—even to the unlovely and the unmerciful.

MICAH

THE PROPHET MICAH WAS AN EARLY CONTEMPORARY OF ISAIAH, prophesying chiefly between 735 and 710 B.C. He was from the small town of Moresheth (1:1), located southwest of Jerusalem. Jeremiah later mentioned him (Jeremiah 26:18), and Isaiah apparently knew his writings (see Isaiah 2:2-4). One of Micah's interests was the poor and oppressed people of Judah, but his principal emphasis, like that of Isaiah, was to warn of punishment for sin if the nation did not repent. Micah predicted the destruction of the northern kingdom (722 B.C.), and then used this as a stern illustration of what could happen to Judah, the southern kingdom.

The book of Micah has three broad divisions, with the first division comprising 1:1–2:13, where Micah describes the judgment that will come upon Israel and Judah at the hand of the Assyrians. Micah plays word games with the meaning of the cities he mentions in chapter 1. This is difficult to demonstrate in English, but it is quite obvious in the Hebrew text. Much of what he says has already been fulfilled, but he closes the section with a prophecy that is still future (2:12-13).

THE CITY OF REFUGE
Micah 2:12-13

MICAH 2:12-13 EXPLAINS where the remnant of Israel will be hidden during the Tribulation and where they will be at the time of the second coming. Micah 2:12 pinpoints the place exactly:

> I will surely assemble, O Jacob, all of you; I will surely gather the remnant of Israel; I will put them together as the sheep of Bozrah, as a flock in the midst of their pasture; they shall make great noise by reason of the multitude of men (ASV).

The remnant will be gathered together "as the sheep of Bozrah." Since the sheep of Bozrah are not any different from other sheep, this gathering together "as the sheep of Bozrah" simply means that Israel, the flock of God, is to be gathered in Bozrah.

The ancient city of Bozrah was located in the region of Mount Seir. Mount Seir is a very rocky range of mountains, and its name means "the hairy mountains," which fulfills the requirement of Matthew 24:15-16. It is located in the wilderness section of ancient Edom and so fulfills the requirement of Revelation 12:6,13-14. And Mount Seir is easy to defend, fulfilling the requirements of Isaiah 33:16. Mount Seir is located on the western side of ancient Edom, extending from southeast of the Dead Sea down to the city of Akaba. It towers over the Arabah, part of the rift valley from the south shore of the Dead Sea to the Gulf of Eilat. Today this area is in southern Jordan.

A key issue is the exact location of Bozrah in the mountain range of Mount Seir. Two places have been suggested. One is the present-day Arab village of Buseira, which seems to retain the name of Bozrah. This is the main argument in favor of it. Another suggestion is the city now known as Petra. Both cities meet all the aforementioned requirements, but Petra stands out as more likely because it is located in a basin within Mount Seir and is totally surrounded by mountains and cliffs. The only way in and out of the city is through a narrow passageway that extends for about a mile and can be negotiated only by foot or by horseback. The city is easy to defend, and its surrounding high cliffs give added meaning and confirmation to Isaiah 33:16. Only a few abreast can enter through this passage at any one time, giving this city even greater protection.

The name *Bozrah* means "sheepfold." Ancient sheepfolds had narrow entrances so that the shepherds could count their sheep more easily. Once inside the fold, the sheep had more room to move around. Petra is shaped like a giant sheepfold, with its narrow passage opening to a spacious circle surrounded by cliffs. This is not true of the town of Buseira. Furthermore, by modern Petra is a site known as Butzeira, which retains the Hebrew *Botzrah* better than Buseira.

Regardless of which of the two cities is to be considered as Old Testament Bozrah, the general area of Mount Seir remains the same. But is there any other reason that this area is chosen besides its natural defensibility? There is an indication of such in the context of Daniel 11:40-45. This passage concerns the conquests of the Antichrist in the middle of the Tribulation as he begins his worldwide political takeover. Verse 41 states that when the Antichrist will conquer the world, three nations will escape his domination: Edom, Moab, and Ammon. All three of these ancient nations currently comprise the single modern kingdom of Jordan The city of Bozrah in

Mount Seir is located in ancient Edom or southern Jordan Since this area will escape conquest by the Antichrist, it is logical for the Jews to flee to this place. Thus, God will provide a city of refuge outside the Antichrist's domain for the fleeing remnant. It will be an easily defensible city located in Mount Seir (regardless of which of the two sites one might pick). Furthermore, as the Jews flee and while they are living there, food and water will be miraculously provided to them.

As Micah 2:12 notes, this is where the remnant of Israel will be gathered together. Verse 13 points out this will be the place of the second coming. The "breaker," the "king," and the Lord are all the same person in this verse. At the second coming, the Messiah will enter into battle against the forces of the Antichrist who are gathered at this city. Placing the second coming here is in agreement with Habakkuk 3:3, Isaiah 34:1-7, and Isaiah 63:1-6.

THE CONSOLATION OF ISRAEL
Micah 4–5

THE SECOND MAJOR PART of Micah deals with the condemnation and the consolation of Israel in 3–5. In chapter 3 the focus is on the condemnation of Israel, and the major point Micah makes is that the nation's leaders are guilty of leading the people astray. This point is a common theme among the prophets as well as in the New Testament. Jeremiah 26:1-19 shows that the Jewish leaders rejected the message of the prophets, and Zechariah 11:4-14 presents a clear prophecy that the leaders would reject the ministry of the Messiah. Indeed, in Matthew 12:22-24 Israel rejects the Messiah on the false charge of demon possession, and in John 11:47-53, after Jesus resurrected Lazarus back to life, the Sanhedrin planned to put Jesus to death. In Matthew 23:13-36, Jesus closed his public ministry with a public denunciation of the scribes and Pharisees, who were the spiritual leaders of Israel in that day. Jesus concludes in verses 37-39 by pointing out that it was the leaders of Israel who led the nation to reject Him, and there will come a day when the Jewish leaders exhort the nation to accept Him. This is the precondition to the second coming—indeed, the fulfillment of this precondition will lead to the fulfillment of the prophecies of Micah 4–5.

Micah deals with the consolation of Israel in 4–5. He begins by describing the messianic program (verses 1-5). The verses in Micah 4:1-3 are the same as those found in Isaiah 2:2-4 and speak of the mountain of Jehovah's house becoming the center of attention for the world's Gentile population, the kingdom being characterized by a time of messianic teaching, and universal peace permeating the entire messianic kingdom. After quoting this much from Isaiah's book (see the commentary on Isaiah 2:2-4 for further details), Micah adds that the kingdom era will also be a time of personal peace and prosperity (verse 4), with Israel's total allegiance being to God (verse 5).

In 4:6–5:1, Micah mentions the messianic people, describing the restoration of Israel in verses 6-8. The regathering is prophesied in verses 6-7, with the opening phrase "in that day" pointing to the future. God will regather the very people He scattered. Those who were afflicted will be made strong and, in that day, the Lord Himself will be their king and rule over them from Mount Zion. Micah goes on to make a clear promise for the future kingdom of Israel (verse 8), promising that the Davidic sovereignty will one day be restored. He mentions Migdal-eder, a reference to Bethlehem, where the Messiah was born. He also mentions the "hill of the daughter of Zion," which is where Messiah died and will also be the city from where Messiah will rule.

In 4:9–5:1, Micah points out that before a final restoration comes, there will be a time of tribulation, a time of painful birth pangs (verses 9-10) followed by the Armageddon campaign (4:11–5:1). The nations will assemble against Jerusalem (verse 11) for the purpose of destroying it, but in the course of doing so, these nations will become like sheaves on a threshing floor (verse 12), and the Jewish

forces will thresh them thoroughly. However, the battle will be lost, and the Gentiles will capture Jerusalem, which is symbolized by the smiting of Jerusalem's leader on the cheek (verse 1). After the heavy fighting and great losses, the soldiers of the Antichrist will plunder the Jewish homes of Jerusalem and ravish the women (Zechariah 14:2).

In summary, Micah makes three points: first, all the nations that are against Jerusalem will be gathered together in order that God may destroy them; second, the enemies will suffer great losses at the hand of the Jews because God will energize the Jewish forces; and, third, Israel will fall and the judge of Israel will be smitten with a rod upon his cheek—an ancient symbol of defeat and surrender.

At that point Micah introduces Israel's spiritual and physical Savior (5:2-15). Micah begins by mentioning the origin of the Messiah (verse 2), noting that He has both a human origin (Bethlehem) and a divine origin (from everlasting), thus indicating the Messiah is the God-man. Messiah's relationship to Israel is described in verse 3, and two basic stages of this relationship are spelled out. First, "He will give them up." Because the Messiah was rejected by the Jewish leaders of Israel, the people were dispersed from the land with their city and temple destroyed. Second, this was only a temporary measure, "until the time when she who is in labor has borne a child." This is a reference back to 4:9-10 and speaks of the time when Israel's leaders will lead the nation back to faith and belief in the Messiah. The people's return to the Lord will have two major results: the reunification of Israel and Judah as one people and nation, and the establishment of Messiah as the One who will rule over the kingdom (verses 3-4). This will finally lead to the coming of peace (5:5-15). God will defend Israel from her enemies (verses 5-6), and Israel will be empowered to overcome her enemies (verses 7-9). Indeed, Israel's salvation will result in a unique purging of the nation (verses 10-15) that will include the purging of weapons, fortified cities, the practice of the occult, and idolatry. At the same time, God will execute vengeance upon the Gentiles (verse 15).

THE TRIBULATION AND RESTORATION
Micah 7

THE THIRD SEGMENT of Micah deals with God's controversy with Israel (chapters 6–7). The controversy itself involves Israel's failure to obey the law and the judgments resulting from that failure (chapter 6). In 7:1-6, the judgment leads to the lamentation of the people, who finally come to admit that indeed, tribulation has come, and what the prophets had predicted about family disunity has now come to pass. In fact, Jesus prophesied that such disunity would result from His coming to earth and Israel's rejection of His messiahship (Matthew 10:34-36). This problem will reach its height during the Tribulation. In fact, according to Malachi 4:5-6, a major reason for Elijah's return is to restore the Jewish family unit so that the name of Jesus ceases to be a point of division. The remnant alive during the Tribulation will exercise hope during this time of judgment (Micah 7:7-10), and this hope will be twofold, with each aspect followed by a special message against the enemy. The first hope is the hope of salvation (verse 7), followed by a word for the enemy not to rejoice when Israel falls because within Israel's time of darkness, God will provide light (verse 8). The second hope is the hope of deliverance (verse 9), followed by a warning to the enemy that at the second coming, they will be destroyed (verse 10).

Micah then presents God's promise of restoration (verses 11-17), in which the Lord responds to the hopes expressed earlier. The walls of Jerusalem will be rebuilt (verse 11), and the Jews will be regathered, particularly from Egypt and Assyria—the main areas of the exile when the state falls at the midpoint of the Tribulation (verse 12). Once again the phrase "in that day" points out that the final restoration will be preceded by a time of judgment (verse 13). However, Israel is to be regathered in order to possess the land (verse 14), and its final regathering in faith will be accompanied by miracles (verse 15). When the Gentiles see this, they will stop reproaching the Jews and will have reverential fear. They will at long last submit to the God of Israel (verses 16-17).

Micah concludes his book with a response of praise (verses 18-20). God's covenantal love for Israel will cause Him to pardon and to pass over the sins of the people, and He will return to them in compassion (verses 18-19). He will do so on the basis of the Abrahamic Covenant (verse 20), especially as it is developed in the salvation aspect of the New Covenant.

NAHUM

Lᴵᴋᴇ ᴛʜᴇ ᴘʀᴏᴘʜᴇᴛ Jᴏɴᴀʜ, Nᴀʜᴜᴍ ᴄᴏɴᴄᴇʀɴs ʜɪᴍsᴇʟꜰ ᴡɪᴛʜ the nation of Assyria and Nineveh, its capital city. Many years have now passed since Jonah's preaching, and Nineveh is again warned of the coming judgment of God. This time there is no repentance, and Nineveh eventually falls to the Babylonians in 612 ʙ.ᴄ. Israel's northern kingdom had already fallen to the Assyrians when Nahum delivered his prophecy. It is of interest to note that only two Old Testament books end in a question mark—Jonah and Nahum. And these same two books contained messages of warning to Nineveh.

HABAKKUK

THE BOOK OF HABAKKUK WAS WRITTEN DURING the reign of King Josiah, one of the few good kings of Judah. This was a time of great outward prosperity, but inwardly the people were corrupt. Although Josiah's own heart was right, much of his reformation for the nation was merely external conformity rather than internal devotion. On the international scene, the Assyrians were no longer an immediate threat to Judah, but they were still a strong power.

The book of Habakkuk is unusual in that it records a theological-historical discussion between Habakkuk and God rather than announcements from a prophet acting mainly as a spokesman for God. Through this discussion the prophet learns that the principle by which God deals with humanity is that "the righteous will live by his faith" (2:4), whereas the wicked will perish (2:4-20).

The first two chapters of this book deal with the prophet's complaints and God's answers.

THE PROPHET'S COMPLAINTS
Habakkuk 1–2

THE PROPHET'S FIRST COMPLAINT, in essence, is this: "How long can God continue to tolerate sin among His people? His silence seems to be making matters worse!" (verses 1-4). God answers that He would not tolerate the sins of the people forever. Eventually the Chaldeans will rise out of obscurity and swiftly punish the people of Judah for their sins (1:5-11).

God's answer frustrates Habakkuk even more. This leads to a second complaint. It is true that Judah was wicked, but the Chaldeans or Babylonians are even worse. How could God use the wicked Chaldeans to punish the Jews (1:12–2:1)?

God responds by saying that yes, He could use a more sinful nation to punish the less sinful people of Judah. But the Chaldeans would not get off without judgment. Eventually they will suffer an even more terrible destruction because of the principle that sin carries within itself the seed of its own destruction. The righteous one who lives by faith will accept God's way of doing things and will accept that the Judge of all the earth will do right (2:2-20).

THE ANTICIPATION OF VICTORY
Habakkuk 3:1-2

AFTER RECEIVING DIVINE ANSWERS to the dilemmas presented in chapters 1–2, Habakkuk writes a poetic prayer of victory in chapter 3.

This is a prayer to God to fulfill that final judgment for sin that will occur at the second coming of the Messiah. The prophet pictures himself living in those last days and seeing what is taking place.

Verse 1 introduces Habakkuk as the writer of this victory prayer. Habakkuk was transported, in a vision, to a prophetic period many years in the future to a time just before the second coming. In this vision, Habakkuk sees himself as a member of the faithful remnant during the Tribulation. Representing this faithful remnant, Habakkuk says, "I have heard the report." This "report" is the good news of the second coming of the Messiah, as the context clearly shows. In the context of the book of Revelation, the faithful remnant could have heard this report from two possible sources. One is the preaching of the 144,000 Jews of Revelation 7, who will be evangelizing during this period. They will be preaching the gospel of the messianic kingdom to be established at the second coming. The other possible source is the testimony of the two witnesses in Revelation 11.

Habakkuk then says, "I fear" because in conjunction with this report, he knew there were more judgments to come before the second coming. He then adds, "O Lord, revive Your work in the midst of the years." Many believe the word "years" refers to the seven years of the Tribulation. The expression "in the midst of the years" refers to the middle of the Tribulation, during which there will be a temporary cessation of the divine judgments of God. The seal judgments of Revelation 6 and the trumpet judgments of Revelation 8–9 will be poured out during the first half of the Tribulation. In the middle of the Tribulation there will be this temporary calm, like the proverbial eye of the hurricane, during which no divine judgments will be poured out of heaven. Then there will be a third series of judgments toward the latter part of the second half of the Tribulation. These are the bowl judgments of Revelation 16. Speaking on behalf of the faithful remnant who had heard the report of these coming judgments, Habakkuk is now praying for God to revive His work, the bowl judgments, because they will bring His wrath to an end. But at the same time, Habakkuk is fearful, and he pleads, "In wrath remember mercy" (verse 2).

THE COMING OF THE MESSIAH
Habakkuk 3:3-15

In Habakkuk 3:3-15, Habakkuk talks about five elements of the second coming: the place, the Shekinah glory, the effects upon the nations, the oath of God, and the campaign of Armageddon.

First, in verse 3, Habakkuk points out the *place* of the second coming. Teman is a city located in Mount Seir, within the land of Edom or southern Jordan, just north of the city of Bozrah or Petra. Mount Paran is in the southern Negev, across the Arabah from Mount Seir. According to Micah 2:12-13, Isaiah 34:1-6, and Isaiah 63:1-7, the initial place of the second coming will be the city of Bozrah (its Hebrew name), or Petra (its Greek name). This verse describes the route that the Messiah will take. He will first go north of Bozrah or Petra until He comes to Teman. Then from Teman He will make His way down Mount Seir, cross the Arabah proper into the Negev Desert, come by way of Mount Paran, and then enter the land of Israel from the southeast. He will return to Israel from the direction of Teman in Edom and Mount Paran in the southern Negev.

Second, at the second coming, the *Shekinah* glory will appear (verses 3-5). Matthew 24:29-31 points out that this is the sign of the second coming. Habakkuk says five things about the Shekinah glory: 1) the glory will cover the earth; 2) the brightness will be like the sun; 3) rays will issue from the Lord's hand; 4) there will be a bright light that will hide His power; and 5) the glory will be destructive against the armies of the Antichrist. Zechariah 14 describes the second coming in similar terms.

Third, the Messiah's return will have two

effects upon the Gentile nations that have come against the Jews at Bozrah. The first is that the nations will be driven asunder (verse 6 KJV). The second is that fear will take hold of them as the Messiah moves against them. Two nations are mentioned specifically in this regard: Cushan and Midian (verse 7).

Fourth, God must move because of an *oath* He has made (verses 8-11). God's judgment will affect the waters of the earth, so the question will be raised, "Was it against the waters that the judgment of the second coming came?" The answer will be no (verse 9). Rather, the judgment came because of God's oath to save the tribes of Israel. In the course of these judgments being poured out on the enemy, certain physical elements of the earth—the rivers, oceans, and mountains—will be affected (verse 10). Not only that, but the celestial sphere—the sun, moon, and stars—will also feel the effects. The second coming will affect the earth, the heavens, and outer space.

The fifth aspect Habakkuk mentions about the second coming is the campaign of Armageddon (verses 12-15). Here Habakkuk makes four points:

1. The Messiah will march through the land "in indignation" and trample the nations "in anger" (verse 12). This verse summarizes a more graphic description found in Isaiah 63:1-6, where the Messiah is pictured as trampling on the enemy in the process, and being splattered by the enemies' blood.

2. The key reason He will thresh the nations is "for the salvation of Your anointed"—He threshes the nations on behalf of Israel. Before Christ comes, Israel will be saved spiritually, and when He comes, Israel will be saved physically from its enemies (verse 13).

3. Habakkuk describes the fall of the Antichrist in two statements: "You struck the head of the house of evil," and "You pierced with his own spears the head of his throngs" (verses 13-14). The

word "head" is singular, so there is only one ruler over all the armies of all the nations. This one head will be the Antichrist himself, who will receive a fatal wound. According to 2 Thessalonians 2:8, the Antichrist will be the very first casualty of the second coming.

4. Habakkuk says the campaign of Armageddon will lead to the fall of the Gentile nations (verses 14-15). After the death of the Antichrist, the nations that he led against the faithful remnant will be destroyed. Their purpose was to scatter Israel, but instead, they will be scattered, trampled, and dispersed. According to Revelation 14:17-20, this will result in bloodshed so great that it flows to the depth of a horse's bridle.

After seeing this, Habakkuk deals with the fear and the faith of the faithful remnant (verses 16-19). The message concerning the campaign of Armageddon will cause tremendous fear. Still speaking on behalf of the faithful remnant, Habakkuk states the reason for the fear: "I must wait quietly for the day of distress, for the people to arise who will invade us" (verse 16). He realizes that these prophecies have been given unconditionally by God, and therefore, they must be fulfilled. These promises include not only the good things about the kingdom, but also the bad things about the judgments that will precede the kingdom. Again, the prayer, in its prophetic context, occurs in the middle of the Tribulation, so Habakkuk knows he must wait for the enemies' invasion before he will see the Messiah return. Although this fills him with great fear, it is not the kind of fear that chases away faith.

THE FAITHFUL REMNANT
Habakkuk 3:17-19

HABAKKUK MAKES THREE statements about the faith of the faithful remnant (3:17-19). First, although all sources of livelihood and sustenance will be cut off, this will not turn him against the Lord (verse 17). Second, he says, "I will rejoice in the God of my salvation" (verse 18). This is the same kind of faith Job expressed when he said, "Though He slay me, I will hope in Him" (Job 13:15). Habakkuk is speaking not only for himself, but also for the future faithful remnant. And third, he promises that ultimately, God will have the victory (verse 18). The feet of the faithful remnant will be like "hinds' feet," meaning they will be sure-footed; and they will be in "high places," meaning they will have total confidence. This speaks of total confidence of victory (2 Samuel 22:34; Psalm 18:3).

Although Habakkuk cannot understand everything about the way God works, and although he has questioned God's use of a more sinful nation to punish a less sinful one, Habakkuk has learned two things. First, the just will live out his life by faith, even when he cannot understand why God does things the way He does. And second, all injustices will be rectified and settled once and for all with the second coming of the Messiah.

ZEPHANIAH

THE BOOK OF ZEPHANIAH HAS TWO MAIN PARTS. The first (1:2–3:8) covers the Day of the Lord, and the second (3:9–20) presents the restoration of Israel.

THE DAY OF THE LORD
Zephaniah 1:2–3:8

ZEPHANIAH BEGINS BY describing a judgment that will consume all things (verse 2) and destroy all types of life (verse 3), the categories of which are detailed in the book of Revelation.

The prophet then focuses on the judgment of Judah (1:4–2:3), noting how the sins of the past will bring on the divine judgments of the future. He speaks out against Judah's religious practices (verses 4-6) and social practices (verses 7-13). He clearly announces the coming "day of the LORD" (1:7), a term used for the Great Tribulation, which will be a time of judgment upon both civil and religious authority accompanied by massive destruction (verses 10-11). God intends to remove sinners from the earth so thoroughly that every part of Jerusalem will be searched to make sure no sinners have survived (verse 12). The final result will be the total plunder and desolation of their wealth, homes, and crops.

In 1:14-18, Zephaniah gives a rather vivid description of "the great day of the LORD" (verse 14). It is God's day and God's tribulation. It is a day that is promised to come, and no matter how long it may take before it arrives, the people are to live in anticipation of it because it will indeed come. Zephaniah

goes on in verse 15 to describe that day using five negative descriptions: "a day of wrath," "a day of trouble and distress," "a day of destruction and desolation," "a day of darkness and gloom," and "a day of clouds and thick darkness." This is quite similar to what Joel 2:2 describes. It is a day that is pictured only in negative terms throughout Scripture.

The day of the Lord is a day of war, a "day of trumpet and battle cry" against all of Israel's fortified cities (verse 16). The prophet Joel described these elements using similar terminology (2:1). Zephaniah notes this is also a day of judgment against sinners (verse 17), resulting in their death and total removal. He also describes how the whole land will suffer and be devoured, and how no one's wealth will be able to save him from these judgments (verse 18).

In chapter 2, Zephaniah uses the word "before" three times in the Hebrew text, noting an event that must precede the arrival of the Day of the Lord. Before the period of wrath arrives, there must be a regathering of the Jewish people back into the land. However, it is a regathering in unbelief because they are not yet ashamed of their sins, and the purpose of this regathering is specifically for the judgments of the Day of the Lord to finally bring them to turn away from their sins. Then they will finally come to faith and bring in the second coming and the kingdom. While the severe judgment will come upon the nation as a whole, the message to the remnant (verse 3) is to seek out the God of Israel, to seek righteousness and meekness, so that they will be "hidden in the day of the LORD's anger." In other words, the believing remnant will be protected during the Tribulation, and here Zephaniah makes a play on words by using his own name, which means "Jehovah hides."

In 2:4-15, Zephaniah warns the Gentile nations that if God fulfilled His prophecies of judgment against these nations in the past, then they can surely expect Him to fulfill His warnings of judgment in the future Day of the Lord. This he proclaims to Philistia in the west (verses 4-7), Moab and Ammon in the east (verses 8-11), Ethiopia in the south (verse 12), and Assyria in the north (verses 13-15).

God will use the Tribulation to judge the Gentile nations for their anti-Semitism, but He will also use it to judge Israel in general and Jerusalem in particular (3:1-7). God's destruction of the Gentile nations is meant to serve as a warning to Israel that He is taking disciplinary action to bring about correction. In the past, such action has failed to bring correction and resulted in further judgment, and a major reason the Tribulation will come upon Israel is the people's failure to repent.

Zephaniah then speaks again to the remnant and encourages them to wait for the Lord, "for the day when I rise up as a witness" (verse 8)—that is, until God moves into the final judgment of the Tribulation. God will gather all the nations against Israel and then destroy those nations at Armageddon. This will bring about Israel's national salvation and, in turn, Israel's national restoration.

THE DAY OF RESTORATION
Zephaniah 3:9–20

ZEPHANIAH PROPHESIES the future conversion of the Gentiles (verse 9), who in turn will help with Israel's final regathering (verse 10). He then describes the regeneration of Israel (verses 11-13), which will include the removal of sin and the sinners (verse 11), the saving of the remnant who seek refuge in the Lord (verse 12), and a remnant free from deceit and duplicity (verse 13). In the messianic kingdom the remnant will finally have security in the land.

That will, in turn, result in Israel's final regathering (verses 14-20). The nation is called on to rejoice (verse 14) because God's judgment has been removed and Israel's enemies have been cast out (verses 15-17). God Himself will rejoice over Jerusalem (verse 17) and gather those "who grieve about the appointed feasts" (verse 18). Again Zephaniah reiterates that God will punish those who afflicted Israel (verse 19) and promises a final worldwide regathering in faith in preparation for the blessings of the messianic kingdom (verse 20).

HAGGAI

Haggai prophesied to the returned exiles after the Babylonian captivity. The major focus of his preaching was to urge the Jews to finish the task of rebuilding the temple of God in Jerusalem. Most of his prophecies in this regard were fulfilled within his own lifetime, as the temple was completed and dedicated in 515 B.C. But Haggai also predicted the connection between Zerubbabel and Jesus Christ. The rejected signet ring of Jehoiachin (Coniah) predicted in Jeremiah 22:24 would be restored to the Davidic line through Zerubbabel (Haggai 2:23), an ancestor of Jesus (Matthew 1:12).

THE FUTURE TEMPLE
Haggai 2:6-9

The main goal of Haggai's prophecies was to encourage the Jewish people to complete the building of the temple, for no work had been done since the foundations were laid 15 years earlier. After reviewing the past (1:2–2:5), Haggai now presents God's promise for the future. Three statements are made concerning this promise (2:6-9).

First, Haggai prophesied God would "shake the heavens and the earth" (verse 6). This future shaking will be done in preparation for the messianic kingdom. The Hebrew words used here are the same ones used elsewhere to speak of the final upheaval of nations in the last days in conjunction with the second coming of the Messiah (see Isaiah 13:13; 14:16). The shaking will occur during the Great Tribulation.

Second, God promises that "with the wealth of all nations" the Gentiles will beautify the temple. After the shaking of the Tribulation will come the kingdom, which will include a millennial temple that will be beautified by

the Gentiles. This was also predicted by Isaiah 60:5-7. And when God says "this house," we must keep in mind that from His perspective, it has always been only one house—whether the Solomonic temple, the second temple, or the millennial temple.

Third, God promises the millennial temple will be filled with the Shekinah glory (see also Ezekiel 43:5). God tells the people they should not be discouraged about the poorer materials they are using to construct the temple because He will one day beautify the temple in a greater way—by a new manifestation of the Shekinah glory, the visible manifestation of God's presence (verse 7). The millennial temple will be built not by the hands of man, but by God Himself. And though the millennial temple is far in the future, the temple these people were building was part of God's overall prophetic program.

Then God made a promise about the temple that was being built (verse 9). While the temple the people were then building was less glorious than the Solomonic temple in many ways, a day will come when God Himself will build a temple that is superior to the Solomonic temple. Indeed, the temple of the millennium will be far superior to the Solomonic temple, and the details of this structure are given in Ezekiel 40–48. Yet the temple the people were building was part of God's divine plan. Before that great future temple can come into being, the temple they were working on must fulfill God's program. God then promised that the "latter glory of this house [the temple the people were then building] will be greater than the former [the Solomonic temple]" (Haggai 2:9). The glory of the former temple was the Shekinah glory that authenticated Solomon's temple by taking up residence within the Holy of Holies.

This promise was eventually fulfilled in two ways. First, the temple the people were then building was later reconstructed and refurbished by Herod the Great. By the time Herod the Great was finished with the remodeling, the temple did indeed supersede the Solomonic temple in beauty and glory. In fact, the Jewish rabbis of that era said, "He who has not seen Herod's temple has not seen beauty in all his life." The second way God's promise was fulfilled is this: While the Solomonic temple had the Shekinah glory in the form of a cloud, this later temple was the one in which Jesus ministered—so this temple knew the Shekinah glory in a greater way. The many times that Jesus ministered in the temple compound fulfills God's promise that "in this place I will give peace" (verse 9). Indeed, one of the names of the Messiah is *Sar Shalom,* which means "the Prince of Peace." In conjunction with His work in the temple and the once-for-all sacrifice of His own blood, He made possible spiritual peace in the hearts of believers. And ultimately, when He returns, He will provide physical peace, too.

THE SHAKING AND THE KINGDOM
Haggai 2:20-23

In Haggai 2:20-22, God sends a special message to be given to Zerubbabel, saying that there will be a shaking of the nations in preparation for the coming kingdom. The shaking of the nations will mean the fall of the Antichrist and his army. Verse 22 declares, "I will overthrow the throne of kingdoms" (NKJV). The word "throne" is singular, but the word "kingdoms" is plural. Normally one would expect the text to read "thrones [plural] of kingdoms"—that is, every kingdom has its own throne. However, during the last half of the Great Tribulation, the Antichrist will rule all the kingdoms of the world. There will be one throne, the throne of the Antichrist, ruling over all the kingdoms. And God's shaking of the nations will lead to the fall of the Antichrist and his armies.

As a result of this shaking, God will accomplish three things (verse 22). First, He will "overthrow the throne of the kingdoms" (NKJV). That is, He will destroy the Antichrist and his armies. Second, He will "destroy the power of the kingdoms of the nations." He will render the Gentile nations powerless, causing the "times of the Gentiles" to come to an end (Luke 21:24). Third, He will "overthrow the chariots and their riders, and the horses and their riders will go down." God will destroy the armies of the Antichrist in the campaign of Armageddon, and one of the ways He will do this is "everyone by the sword of another"—that is, the many different nationalities in the Antichrist's armies will begin to fight among themselves and kill each other.

Haggai concludes by describing Zerubbabel's place in the kingdom (verse 23). The phrase "on that day" puts this event into the prophetic future, following the shaking that occurs in verses 21-22. Verse 23 describes Zerubbabel's place in the kingdom; he will be "like a signet ring." A signet ring was a sign of authority, and those who had signet rings did not easily part with them. In the messianic kingdom, Zerubbabel will be in a position of authority, and he will have been chosen by God for this unique place. According to Isaiah 32:1 and Ezekiel 45:8, one of the positions of authority over Israel in the messianic kingdom will be that of "princes." And according to Haggai 2:23, Zerubbabel will be one of those princes. Who the other will be is not known.

ZECHARIAH

THIS BOOK BEGINS BY SUMMARIZING ZECHARIAH'S CALL to the prophetic office (1:1-6) and then divides into four main parts: the eight visions (chapters 1–6), the question of fasting (chapters 7–8), the first burden of the word of the Lord (chapters 9–11), and the second burden of the word of the Lord (chapters 12–14). All four sections include both historical and prophetic material.

THE EIGHT VISIONS
Zechariah 1–6

ZECHARIAH RECEIVES AND describes eight specific visions, makes some key points, and then draws some conclusions at the end of chapter 6.

GOD'S PLAN FOR ISRAEL
Zechariah 1:7-17

The main point of Zechariah's *first vision* (1:7-17) is that God has a plan for Israel. The angel of the Lord, in the midst of a degraded and deprived people, expresses His loving and yearning intercession for them and makes promises of future blessing. The message that the angel of the Lord receives from the other angelic beings is that in the whole earth nothing is moving toward the fulfillment of God's divine plan for Israel (verses 7-11). At that point, the angel of the Lord speaks up (verses 12-17), making specific promises to the people, the land, and the city. He begins by praying for God to bring about the fulfillment of His promises of Israel's restoration (verses 12-13), and the message given in verses 14-17 contains seven specific declarations. First, God is jealous for Jerusalem with a great jealousy, and that jealousy must burn against those who attack the object of His love (verse 14). Second, He

is very displeased with the Gentiles now at ease (verse 15). Though He used these Gentile nations to punish Israel, they have helped "further the disaster" by going beyond what God had intended in order to carry out their own goals rather than the goals of the Lord. Third, He will now return to Jerusalem with mercies (verse 16a). Fourth, He will rebuild His house (verse 16b). Fifth, a line will be stretched out over Jerusalem as a symbol of building (verse 16c). Sixth, God will cause the cities of Israel to overflow with prosperity (verse 17a). Seventh, God will comfort Zion and choose Jerusalem (verse 17b). Zechariah's subsequent visions elaborate on some of these points.

GOD'S SOVEREIGNTY OVER ISRAEL
Zechariah 1:18-21

Zechariah's *second vision* (1:18-21) makes the point that God is in control and elaborates on what He said in 1:15. God takes into account everyone who lifts up his hands against the Jewish people and has complete knowledge of the condition of the Jewish people. Zechariah then describes the four horns (verses 18-19), which represent the four Gentile empires that were detailed by Daniel the prophet. He then goes on to describe the four craftsmen (verses 20-21), which he identifies as those who were sent to punish the four horns. The four craftsmen therefore would be Cyrus, who brought down the Babylonian Empire, Alexander the Great, who brought down the Medo-Persian Empire, Pompey, who placed Israel into the Roman Empire, and the Messiah, who at the second coming will destroy the Antichrist, the last ruler of the fourth Gentile empire.

THE FUTURE OF JERUSALEM
Zechariah 2

Zechariah's *third vision* (2:1-13) states that Jerusalem will become the capital of the millennial earth and elaborates on what was stated in 1:16-17. The passage begins by introducing a man with a measuring line (verses 1-5), and his purpose is to measure Jerusalem in its restoration state. Jerusalem will someday be well populated and inhabited as a city without walls, for it will be too great and contain too many people to be confined by walls. On the other hand, God Himself will be "a wall of fire around her," and will be "the glory in her midst" (verse 5). The Shekinah glory will permanently protect the messianic city for the messianic kingdom.

The explanation of the vision (verses 6-13) has an immediate application: The Jews are called to leave Babylon and return to the land (verses 6-7), but then Zechariah projects the vision into the future in relation to the coming of the Messiah. By means of the Messiah, God will punish those who have mistreated the Jewish people. Here, Zechariah spells out the important principle that whoever touches Israel touches the apple of God's eye; those who do so will find themselves becoming a spoil (verses 8-9). Following the punishment of Israel's enemies, God will then inhabit the city of Jerusalem (verses 10-13), ruling the world from the city to which Gentiles will be in submission and making Judah His possession. In light of God's promise to fulfill certain blessings for Israel, the whole world is commanded to remain silent as a sign of respect.

THE KINGDOM OF PRIESTS
Zechariah 3

Zechariah's *fourth vision* (3:1-10) reveals

that God will cleanse Israel so that the nation can become a kingdom of priests. Before the blessings mentioned in the earlier visions can be given to Israel, there must be a spiritual transformation. For the near future, God's intent is to restore the people's confidence in the priesthood in light of the fact that it was the priesthood's sins that led the nation into captivity. The vision begins in a courtroom (verses 1-5), where Joshua, the high priest, represents Israel, the angel of the Lord is the judge, and Satan is the prosecuting attorney. Regardless of what accusations Satan brings against the Jewish people, he is rebuked by God not because the accusations may or may not be true, but because God has chosen Jerusalem and therefore intends to save Israel. In this scene, Joshua is clothed with filthy garments, and the Hebrew word used to speak of this refers to filth of the most loathsome character (Isaiah 4:3-4; 64:6). This renders the high priest ceremonially unclean. But, by the judge's orders, the clothing is exchanged for clean garments, marking the forgiveness of sins and being clothed with salvation.

In verses 6-10 the angel of the Lord tells Joshua that the responsibility of the priesthood is to maintain the ethical, moral, and spiritual standards of the temple compound, and says that the priests are a sign that God intends to bring in His "servant the Branch" (verse 8). This is an Old Testament messianic name or title that will be discussed further in the commentary on 6:12.

The angel of the Lord points out that the branch is a stone (verse 9), and often when the word "stone" is used symbolically, it refers to the Messiah. The fact that the stone has seven eyes tells us that He is all-seeing—He is omniscient and omnipresent. The key promise to note is that God intends to "remove the iniquity of that land in one day," and the land here is the holy land of 2:12. Because Israel's national regeneration will occur in one day (Hosea 6:1-3), the iniquity of the land will also be removed in one day. The passage concludes with a scene from the millennium (verse 10), during which everyone will sit under his vine and his fig tree—a common symbol of security and of prosperity. Such will be the conditions in the messianic kingdom.

ISRAEL'S WITNESS TO THE WORLD
Zechariah 4

Zechariah's *fifth vision* (4:1-14) points out that through the work of the Holy Spirit, Israel will become a witness to the world. This is a personal message to Zerubbabel, a ruler of the returnees from Babylon, who led in the rebuilding of the second temple. The vision goes well beyond Zerubbabel, describing the final restoration of Israel. The vision, which is in verses 1-3, contains several elements that Zechariah already understands because of previous revelation, but there is one key element that he does not understand. In this vision he sees a seven-branch lampstand (menorah)—the kind that will stand in the new temple being rebuilt in his day and that serves as a symbol of Israel. Over the lampstand is a bowl, and on each side of the lampstand is an olive tree. Zechariah sees a pipe emptying olive oil into the bowl, and from the bowl are seven smaller pipes or ducts providing oil to each one of the seven lamps. There are a total of 49 such smaller pipes. The fact that the oil comes straight from its source, the tree, emphasizes an inexhaustible supply of oil. In fact, the one common element in the whole vision is that of oil from the olive tree, the spouts, the bowls, the 49 ducts, and the seven lamps. Furthermore, oil is commonly used in Scripture to symbolize the Holy Spirit.

Zechariah then gives the main purpose of the vision, which is encouragement to Zerubbabel (verses 4-10). Following Zechariah's request for the interpretation (verse 4), the first message to Zerubbabel (verses 5-7) is that the same person who laid down the foundation of the temple, which he did about 15 years earlier, will also be the one to complete it. And, ultimately it is not Zerubbabel who is responsible for making this happen but God Himself—Zechariah points out that it will happen "not by might nor by power, but by my Spirit" (verse 6). Thus the temple will be completed because of divine enablement and not human planning. Israel laid the foundation and will also lay the capstone, which will mark the completion of the second temple. Yet when that happens, the people will shout, "Grace, grace," recognizing that God did this and not man.

Zechariah then gives a second message to Zerubbabel (verses 8-10). Although the temple he was then building was not as great as the one Solomon built, the latter glory of the temple will supersede the former glory. Indeed, Herod the Great will totally remodel this temple and make it more significant than the one Solomon had built. Again, Zechariah understood most of this vision because of previous revelation, but there was one new element in the vision that he had never seen before, and this is the two olive trees. Zechariah thus requests a clear interpretation of the meaning of the two olive trees (verses 11-14). After making his request (verses 11-13), he receives a rather cryptic answer (verse 14). They represent "the two anointed ones who are standing before the Lord of the whole earth." All he is told for now is that the two olive trees represent two anointed ones through whom Israel's national salvation will come so Israel can finally fulfill its calling to be a light to the Gentiles.

Exactly how much Zechariah understood we cannot be sure, but the answer about the olive tree is finally provided in Revelation 11:3-13, where we read about the two witnesses of the Tribulation period. John clearly identifies them as being "the two olive trees," using a definite article, which refers to specific ones. The way these witnesses become the source of Israel's salvation is that at the end of their ministry, at the midpoint of the Tribulation, they will be killed by the Antichrist and their bodies will lie unburied in the streets of Jerusalem for three and a half days. Then, in the sight of all, their bodies will be resurrected, and the two witnesses will then ascend into heaven. According to Revelation 11:13, the resurrection and the ascension of the two witnesses will lead to four results: a great earthquake will hit the city, a tenth of the city will be destroyed, 7000 people will die, and "the rest [will be] frightened and [give] glory to the God of heaven." The resurrection and ascension of the two witnesses will lead to the salvation of many Jews in Jerusalem shortly before they have to flee the city because of the abomination of desolation (Matthew 24:15-16). That will begin a process that three and a half years later will lead to the rest of Israel being saved (Isaiah 5:15–6:3; Zechariah 13:8-9; Romans 11:25-26).

THE FLYING SCROLL
Zechariah 5:1-4

Zechariah's *sixth vision* (5:1-4) speaks of a day when God will punish sinners with a divine judgment. The vision begins with a flying scroll (verses 1-2) that represents the Mosaic law and cites violations of the third and eighth commandments. Thus the scroll is a curse against the lawbreaker, and now the curse is carried out in the lives of the lawbreakers (verses 3-4). The major purpose of the Tribulation is to remove sin and sinners from the earth.

WICKEDNESS REMOVED
Zechariah 5:5-11

The *seventh vision* (5:5-11) says that in the Tribulation, God will remove national wickedness. In the vision itself (verses 5-7), Zechariah sees an ephah, a standard of weight used to weigh dry goods. However, because a talent of lead was inserted into the ephah, it provided a false measure of weight, and the true measure and standard were corrupted. Zechariah also sees a woman who symbolically represents a religious entity—in this case, a false one that is somehow united with an economic symbol. Then comes the interpretation (verses 8-11). The woman clearly represents wickedness (verse 8) in both religious and economic affairs. The ephah was placed into a large basket, which was carried away to the land of Shinar (verses 9-11). Shinar is the land of Babylonia and Babylon, where false religions had their beginning (Genesis 11:1-9). False religion and economics will eventually be sent

back to where they all began—to the future rebuilt city of Babylon—which, in turn, will become the world capital under the Antichrist. This is further elaborated in Revelation 18, which describes Babylon as both the political and economic capital of the world.

THE MESSIANIC KINGDOM
Zechariah 6:1-8

Zechariah's *eighth vision* (6:1-8) reveals that before God establishes the messianic kingdom, He will judge the Gentile nations that oppress Israel. Zechariah sees four chariots between two mountains, probably the mountains of Moriah and Olives (verses 1-3). Between the two mountains is the Valley of Jehoshaphat, which is the place of the judgment of the Gentiles (Joel 3:1-3). The fact that the mountains are made of brass confirms this is a place of judgment. Here Zechariah sees four chariots that are about ready to go out. In his first vision, these chariots came to this place to report on the stillness of the Gentile nations, and here in the eighth vision, they are sent back to carry out God's judgment against the Gentiles. These four chariots are divine agencies now sent out to the four Gentile empires to begin the fulfillment of all the preceding visions (verses 4-8). Thus, the first chariot with the black horses is sent to the north against Babylon, and is followed to the north by the white horses going against the Medo-Persian Empire. The grizzled horses take their chariot to the south against the Hellenistic Empire as symbolized by Egypt, which controlled Israel after the division of the Greek Empire. The red horses take their chariot throughout the world, for the fourth empire, under the Antichrist, will rule the whole world. Then comes a message that the first group, which went north, had finished their work by appeasing God's wrath against Babylon (verse 8). This shows that God's prophetic program was now moving forward.

The eight visions can be summarized as follows: First, they reaffirm God's goal to restore Israel and His anger against the Gentile nations. Second, He is angry with the Gentile nations because of Israel's dispersion among them. Third, He promises the restoration of Jerusalem, and the fourth through seventh visions are all preparations for that restoration. The fourth vision restores the confidence in the priesthood with a renewal of Israel's priestly ministry. The fifth vision restores confidence in civil authority and presents the Messiah as the future priest and king. The sixth vision focuses on the removal of sinners and judgment against covenantal disobedience. The seventh vision focuses on the removal of sin and the fact that wickedness will return to Babylon, its point of origin. The eighth vision puts everything into force, showing that ultimately, God will exercise authority over the entire world.

THE COMING BRANCH
Zechariah 6:9-15

Zechariah's eight visions come to a conclusion in 6:9-15. The passage begins with a symbolic act (verses 9-11) in which Zechariah is to take gold and silver donations from certain men who have come back from the Babylonian captivity, make them into crowns, and place the crowns upon the head of Joshua, the high priest. Two lessons come from this symbolic act.

The first lesson is for the distant future (verses 12-13). Here again Zechariah brings up the Branch doctrine, which is a common motif of the Messiah. This is the second time Zechariah has mentioned the concept of Messiah the Branch, although this time he makes a different point.

The Branch doctrine can be summarized as follows: Zechariah 3:8 teaches that the Branch is a servant, which happens to be the theme of the Gospel of Mark. In Zechariah 6:12 the Branch is a man, which is the theme of the Gospel of Luke. The Branch is also a king (Isaiah 11:1; Jeremiah 23:5; 33:15-16), which is the theme of the Gospel of Matthew. Finally, the Branch is also God (Isaiah 4:2; Jeremiah 23:5-6; 33:15-16), which is the theme of the Gospel of John. The point of this passage is that the Branch (the Messiah) will be a man, and He will also build the temple of

the Lord, but the temple He will build is the one revealed by Ezekiel (chapters 40–48), the millennial temple.

Zechariah also shows that the Branch will have two functions. First, He will "sit and rule on His throne," which shows He will have kingly functions; and second, He will also "be a priest on his throne," which shows He will have priestly functions. He will be both priest and king. Joshua could never be both, for the king had to come from Judah and the priest had to come from Levi. But the Messiah, functioning under the Melchizedekian priesthood and under kingdom law, will be both priest and king. In this way the "counsel of peace will be between the two offices" of king and priest.

There is also a lesson for the immediate future (verses 14-15) in that these crowns were not to remain upon Joshua's head, but were to be placed inside the new temple as a memorial to the generosity of the men of verse 10. Because this would happen in the near future, shortly after the temple is completed, this would authenticate that Zechariah was indeed a prophet of God. Also, the fulfillment of the prophecy for the immediate future would provide assurance that someday the distant prophecies would also be fulfilled.

THE QUESTION OF FASTING
Zechariah 7–8

THE SECOND MAJOR PART of Zechariah's book deals with the issue of fasting. As a result of Jerusalem's destruction by the Babylonians in 586 B.C., the Jewish people had inaugurated new fasts that were not previously practiced. Now that the Babylonian captivity had ended and the temple was being rebuilt, the question now being raised is whether these fasts should continue.

This section begins by dealing with the real issue concerning fasts (7:1-7). The question about whether to continue the fasts is not directly answered. After all, if the people had obeyed the prophets who warned them in the past, there would have been no Babylonian captivity, no new fasts would have been inaugurated, and the questions about fasting would not have been raised. Furthermore, these fasts were never commanded by God but were instituted by the people themselves because Jerusalem was destroyed.

Zechariah then points out that the real issue was the people's disobedience to past prophets (7:8-14). For that reason, God's judgment came. The people were concerned about that which was not commanded (new fasts) when they should have been concerned about that which God had commanded. The people were concerned with whether to follow human traditions rather than following divine law.

Zechariah then describes the future restoration and prosperity of Jerusalem (8:1-8). As in the first vision (1:14), God again expresses His great jealousy over Jerusalem. Indeed, since the fall of the Jewish commonwealth, Jerusalem has been overrun about 50 different times, and no indigenous government was established there until 1948. Until then, Jerusalem was always ruled from somewhere else. Now God reaffirms His promise that He will someday dwell in Jerusalem, and which will then be called "the City of Truth" (verse 3). The city will be inhabited by the very old and the very young (verses 4-5) and because believers themselves will not die (Isaiah 65:20), those who survive as believers from the Tribulation until the millennium will live the entire 1000 years of the kingdom era. By the end of this time, there will be people on earth who are 1000 years old. God promises to bless and restore the remnant back into the land (verses 6-8), and when the final restoration comes, it will not be the result of following traditions but of coming to the Lord in faith and obeying the commandments of the Lord.

God then gives a message to Zechariah's own generation (8:9-17), calling on the people to be obedient, reminding them of the difficulties in the land before they returned, and promising them blessing if they are obedient. He repeats and summarizes what the former

prophets taught regarding obedience and the blessings for obedience.

Not until the final segment of chapter 8 does God give an answer to the question of fasting (8:18-23). He makes three key points:

First, someday all these fasts will be turned into feasts (verses 18-19). As far as God is concerned, because these fasts were not commanded by Him, it is irrelevant whether or not the people continue fasting. And in the future, when the messianic kingdom is established, there will be no fasts, but rather, "cheerful feasts" (verse 18).

Second, Jerusalem will become the center of worldwide attention (verses 20-22). Not only will Jewish people want to migrate to Jerusalem to observe the rituals of the millennial temple, but Gentiles will also come to implore God's favor.

Third, God will become the center of Gentile attention (verse 23). Ten Gentiles will take hold of the clothing of a Jew and say, "Let us go with you, for we heard that God is with you." Throughout much of Jewish history, when ten Gentiles took hold of the clothes of a Jew, it was for very negative reasons. But when Israel becomes a regenerated people and is restored to the land, the Gentiles will recognize that Israel is indeed a chosen nation and the Jews are a chosen people. They will wish to go with the Jews and learn God's ways from them. Those Gentiles will turn back to the Lord on the basis of Jewish restoration and regeneration.

THE FIRST BURDEN: REJECTION OF THE SHEPHERD
Zechariah 9–11

THIS THIRD MAJOR SEGMENT of Zechariah can be summarized in three main points: first, Israel's rejection of the true Shepherd leads to the subsequent turning over of Israel into the hands of the Gentiles; second, eventually judgment will come upon the Gentile world; and third, Israel will be strengthened to withstand the Gentile invasion until its physical and spiritual redemption by the true Shepherd.

This section begins with a prophecy that was fulfilled by the conquest of Alexander the Great in the year 332 B.C. (9:1-7), followed by a promise that Jerusalem will be protected from that invasion (9:8). Historically, it is known that Alexander did not destroy Jerusalem and did not require the city to pay him tribute. But the prophecy of verse 8 apparently goes well beyond Alexander's time, for the promise is that "no oppressor will pass over them anymore." Many oppressors have gone through Jerusalem since the time of Alexander, which means the promise must have a future fulfillment.

Zechariah then announces the coming of the messianic king, blending together prophecies of both the first and second comings of Messiah (9:9-10). The first coming is described in verse 9 and was fulfilled with the triumphal entry of Jesus into Jerusalem on a donkey. Verse 10 has yet to be fulfilled and awaits the second coming, when Messiah will remove all weapons of war from the land and bring peace to all the nations.

Next, Zechariah deals with the redemption, salvation, and restoration of Israel (9:11–10:12). The passage begins with the redemption of Israel (9:11-17) and is a fuller exposition of the fulfillment of verse 10. He promises that Israel will be freed (verses 11-12), a deliverance that is based on the Abrahamic Covenant. Isaiah stated (40:1-2) that Israel would receive double punishment for her sins, and this is reaffirmed by Zechariah, who says the double punishment will give way to double blessing. On the one hand, Israel will be empowered to withstand the Gentile attacks (Zechariah 9:13), but ultimately the Gentiles will be defeated by God Himself (verses 14-16). God will intervene on behalf of Israel (verse 14), defend Israel (verse 15), and deliver Israel (verse 16). The rest of the passage deals with the redemption of Israel, and Zechariah concludes by praising God for the redemption that will someday come (verse 17).

Zechariah then describes the salvation of Israel (10:1-7) and mentions that someday there will be a restoration of the blessing of rain—the early rains, the main body of rains, and the latter rains, all of which will make the land much more productive (verse 1). The people will recognize their failure due to idolatry and listening to false prophets, which ultimately caused the dispersion of the flock of Israel (verse 2). Furthermore, they will recognize the failure of their previous shepherds, who did not free them from bondage to the Gentile nations (verse 3). Now, God will finally empower Israel to withstand the Gentiles (verses 3-5). Israel will be saved not only spiritually but also physically because God Himself will do the rescuing (verses 6-7).

Zechariah goes on to describe the restoration of Israel (10:8-12) and the final regathering in faith in preparation for blessing, which is a result of redemption (verses 8-9). The regathering will take place from the Gentile world, but the main focus is on the lands of Egypt and Assyria (verses 10-11) because the next exile that takes place will be limited to the nations of the Middle East. This is similar to the promise of Isaiah 11:15-16. Ultimately, the most important thing is Israel's spiritual restoration, which will be characterized by the people walking "in His name" (verse 12).

This segment ends with the account of the rejection of the true Shepherd (11:1-17). Here, Zechariah deals primarily with events that were fulfilled by the first coming and shortly thereafter. He describes a massive devastation of the whole land from north to south (verses 1-3), which is the result of the two Jewish revolts against Rome in the years A.D. 66–70 and A.D. 132–135. He gives two reasons for this devastation: the rejection of the true Shepherd, the Messiah (verses 4-14), which brought about the devastation of A.D. 70; and the people's acceptance of a foolish shepherd (verses 15-17), which was the first of many false messiahs. This foolish shepherd was Simon Bar Kochba, who brought about the devastation of A.D. 135.

Israel's rejection of the Messiah led to its worldwide dispersion, which remains true to this day. But that is not the future God has planned for Israel. A final restoration is coming, and that is the focus of the last segment of Zechariah.

THE SECOND BURDEN: REDEMPTION OF ISRAEL
Zechariah 12–14

ZECHARIAH 12–14 DEALS WITH the final worldwide campaign against Israel, when Israel will be purged, saved, and redeemed from her enemies. That will result in the second coming, the final restoration, and the establishment of the messianic kingdom. Here, Zechariah provides more details about how some of the prophecies of chapters 9–11 are going to be accomplished. Some call these chapters the Little Apocalypse of Zechariah.

THE CAMPAIGN OF ARMAGEDDON
Zechariah 12:1-3

Zechariah begins a new theme in 12:1: "the burden of the word of the LORD concerning Israel." This is the second "burden" in the book of Zechariah. The Hebrew word for "burden" means "a heavy weight." God's message through Zechariah was heavy for two reasons. First, because it was "the word of the LORD," and second, because it contained prophetic truth that was both negative and positive.

Zechariah also says this was "the word of the LORD concerning Israel"—this message concerned Israel. Other nations are mentioned, but only in connection with their relationship to the people of Israel. Zechariah then affirms God's control over all things in three ways (verse 1). First, "the Lord...stretches forth the heavens." He controls outer space. Second, He "lays the foundation of the earth." He controls the physical earth. And third, He "forms the spirit of man within him." He controls human life.

Because of who God is, what He has done, and what He is able to do, all the prophecies

in this "burden of the word of the LORD concerning Israel" will surely be accomplished.

THE ATTACK ON JERUSALEM
Zechariah 12:2-3

As Zechariah described the nations coming against Jerusalem, God made two statements about the city. First, Jerusalem will become a *cup of trembling,* or "a cup that causes reeling" (verse 2). Jerusalem is pictured here as a vast bowl around which the Gentile nations will gather to drink. In the majority of cases when the word "cup" is used symbolically in the Old Testament, it refers to divine judgment (Psalm 75:8; Isaiah 51:17,21-23; Jeremiah 25:15-16; 51:7). As these Gentile nations come against Jerusalem, they will begin to drink from this vast cup, hoping to derive pleasure from it. But after drinking, they will run away reeling and staggering, no longer in control as they thought they would be.

Notice in Zechariah 12:2-3 the distinction the prophet makes between the Jews of Judah and the Jews of Jerusalem. Not only will the Jews in Jerusalem suffer in this "siege…against Jerusalem," but the Jews in Judah will also suffer. By this time, the majority of the people of Judah will no longer be in Judah; they will have been scattered out of the land to Bozrah. There will be a number of Jews still living in Jerusalem, and the armies of the Antichrist will come against them in this siege; but, in due course, the Jews of Judah, who are in Bozrah, will also feel the effects of the siege.

Second, God declares that Jerusalem will become *a burdensome stone,* or "a heavy stone." The phrase "it will come about in that day" means this will happen during the campaign of Armageddon. Jerusalem is pictured here as a heavy stone, not one that is smooth, but rather, one that has many sharp, jagged edges. Those who "lift it will be severely injured" or lacerated. Those who try to lift this stone with their hands will be able to raise it just a little bit; but as they do so, the stone will be so heavy that it will slip through their hands, cutting their hands to shreds. Verse 2 ends, "All the nations of the earth will be gathered against it." The campaign of Armageddon will not be one group of nations fighting a second group of nations. Rather, all the Gentile nations of that day will come together against Israel and Jerusalem.

Thus Jerusalem will become two things to the Gentile nations in the campaign of Armageddon: "a cup that causes reeling" that will cause them to stagger, and "a heavy stone" by which they will be "severely injured."

THE BATTLE FOR JERUSALEM
Zechariah 12:4-9

The ways in which Jerusalem will become "a cup that causes reeling" and "a heavy stone" are described next, as well as the physical deliverance of Jerusalem.

"In that day," or during the campaign of Armageddon, as Jerusalem's enemies come against her on their horses, God will strike "every horse with bewilderment and his rider with madness" (verse 4). Under the Mosaic Covenant, God said that these judgments would come on the Jews for disobedience (Deuteronomy 28:28). What God once pronounced upon the Jews He will now pronounce upon the Gentiles because of their movement against the Jews. This is an outworking of the principle of Genesis 12:3: "I will bless those who bless you, and the one who curses you will I curse." Because the horses will be stricken with blindness (Zechariah 12:14), the Gentile armies will rush to their own destruction. Yet God says that His eyes will "watch over the house of Judah"—not merely to see where they are, not merely to see how things are going, but to look out for their protection. He will keep His eyes on Judah in order to protect it from the Gentile armies.

The source of Judah's strength is given in verse 5, and once again the separation of Judah and Jerusalem should be noted. The Jews of Jerusalem are still in the land, while the Jews of Judah are in Bozrah or Petra, outside the land. The "clans of Judah" will receive moral and spiritual strength from the way the "inhabitants of Jerusalem" are staunchly withstanding the enemy.

Verse 6 says God will so energize the Jewish forces that they will become "like a firepot among pieces of wood and a flaming torch among sheaves." The Gentiles are pictured as dry wood and sheaves that burn quickly when touched by fire. There are two results from God's energizing of the Jewish forces: First, "they will consume…all the surrounding peoples." Second, "the inhabitants of Jerusalem [will] again dwell on their own sites in Jerusalem." To a certain degree, Judah will help in rescuing Jerusalem.

The order in which salvation comes to Jerusalem is revealed in verse 7. God is not going to save the inhabitants of Jerusalem first; instead, He will "save the tents of Judah first." By using the expression "the tents of Judah," Zechariah is pointing out that the people of Judah will no longer be living in permanent abodes; rather, they will be living in temporary dwellings outside the land. According to Micah 2:12-13, the location of the majority of the Jewish remnant will be Bozrah or Petra. And according to Zechariah 12:7, God will first deliver the Jewish remnant in Bozrah; then He will rescue the Jews in Jerusalem. This is the reason the prophet has made a distinction between the Jews in Jerusalem and Judah. Furthermore, the reason God will "save the tents of Judah first" is so two other groups would not be magnified above Judah: "the house of David and…the inhabitants of Jerusalem." The fact that the Messiah will come to save the Jewish remnant in Bozrah is also brought out in Habakkuk 3:3 and Isaiah 34:1-7; 63:1-6.

In Zechariah 12:8 the prophet points out the means God will use to rescue the Jews of Jerusalem. First they will be energized such that the "feeble among them," the weakest people, "in that day will be like David" (that is, bold to fight). Second, those who are like King David will be able to fight like "the angel of the LORD." This is not a common, ordinary angel, but the second person of the Trinity, the Messiah Himself. So the Davids among the Jews will be able to fight with the power of the Messiah Himself.

This segment concludes with the statement that God is going to pass judgment upon the Gentiles (verse 9). God declares His intention "to destroy all the nations that come against Jerusalem." Once again, this emphasizes the principle of Genesis 12:3.

The order in which this judgment takes place is that God will first rescue the Jews in Bozrah or Petra, destroying many of the foreign armies there. Second, He will rescue the Jews of Jerusalem. When He does, He will destroy the final portions of the Antichrist's armies just outside Jerusalem in the Valley of Jehoshaphat.

THE DELIVERANCE OF ISRAEL
Zechariah 12:10–13:1

The third main unit of the Little Apocalypse of Zechariah deals with the salvation and spiritual deliverance of Israel in two areas: their mourning for the Messiah to return, and the spiritual cleansing of Jerusalem.

The Plea for the Messiah to Return
Zechariah 12:10-14

The basis of Israel's pleading for the Messiah to return is given in verse 10. This mourning will be a result of the outpouring of the Holy Spirit upon the entire nation. This outpouring of "the Spirit of grace" leads to salvation; the outpouring "of supplication" will move the people to plead for the Messiah's return. Elsewhere the Bible predicts an outpouring of the Holy Spirit upon the nation of Israel in Isaiah 32:13-20; 44:3-5, Joel 2:28-32, and Acts 2:16-21. There are two groups upon whom the Spirit will fall: "the house of David" and "the inhabitants of Jerusalem" (verse 10). When the Holy Spirit is poured out upon all Israel, Israel as a nation will be spiritually regenerated and saved.

The result of this spiritual salvation is given in verse 10: "They will look on Me whom they have pierced." They will begin to mourn for the Messiah to return so that He can rescue them physically as was predicted earlier in verses 2-9. The Hebrew word translated "pierced" is a strong word that means "to be thrust

through." This is a reference to the spear that pierced the Messiah's side (John 19:37). The time is coming, after Israel is saved and the Spirit has been poured out upon the nation, that the people will begin to look to the One whom they have thrust through.

The King James Version erroneously reads, "They shall look upon me whom they have pierced." Because of the mistranslation of the Hebrew word al as "upon," many have interpreted this to mean that Jesus will come first, and after the Jews have seen Him, then will they be saved. However, the Hebrew word used here does not mean "upon" but "unto" because of where He is—"aloft" or "on high." When believers look unto the Lord, they do not visibly see the Lord. This passage should be interpreted as saying that when the Holy Spirit is poured out upon the whole house of Israel, they will then look unto—not upon—the One "whom they have pierced," mourning for Him to return. Only then will He return. After they have looked unto Him they are saved, resulting in His return. Israel's national salvation is the prerequisite to the second coming.

The intensity of Israel's mourning is emphasized in verse 10. In the world of that day, there was greater mourning for the loss of a firstborn son than for the loss of any other child. The mourning for the Messiah is not only a mourning related to loss, but also a mourning in hope that this Son might come back and be restored to life. This is the kind of mourning that the Jewish people will have for the Messiah. They will mourn over the fact that Israel rejected His messiahship at His first coming, and they will also mourn so that He might come back. Indeed, in this case, He will come back.

The Mourning for the Messiah
Zechariah 12:11-14

According to Jeremiah, Israel mourned the loss of King Josiah because he was such a good king. Jeremiah himself mourned because he knew that Josiah was the last of the good kings and that Judah was now destined for a series of wicked kings who would bring about the destruction of the kingdom of Judah. The national mourning for the Messiah will be similar to the "mourning of Hadadrimmon in the plain of Megiddo" (verse 11), when King Josiah was killed in a war against the Egyptians (2 Chronicles 35:22-25). The Valley of Megiddo is the same as the Valley of Jezreel. The specific place in this valley where Josiah was killed was Hadadrimmon. Just as the people mourned bitterly for King Josiah, so they will mourn bitterly for the Messiah to return.

Three different groups of people will be mourning for the Messiah (verses 12-14). The first group mentioned is the royal house from "the house of David," the greatest, to "the house of Nathan," the least (verse 12). Although the house of Nathan never saw any kings upon the throne, it was from this lineage that the Messiah comes. The second group mentioned is the priestly house from "the house of Levi," the greatest, to "the Shimeites," the least (verse 13). The third group mentioned is "all the families that remain," who will also be mourning (verse 14). In keeping with the Jewish custom of mourning, the sexes will be separated so that nothing can distract them from the main business of mourning.

The Cleansing of Jerusalem
Zechariah 13:1

Zechariah 13 opens with the phrase "in that day," which tells us the following is also part of the campaign of Armageddon (verse 1). Zechariah says that at that time, a fountain will be opened. In the Old Testament, a fountain was a symbol of cleansing. The fountain in the tabernacle and the fountain in the temple compound were the means of cleansing one's self from ceremonial uncleanness. Here the word "fountain" symbolizes the outpouring of the Holy Spirit and the people's faith in the Lord (John 7:37-39). This fountain will be opened to the house of David and the inhabitants of Jerusalem. As a result of the outpouring of the Holy Spirit, the nation will be saved and look to the Messiah. The purpose for the opening of this fountain is to remove two types of spiritual problems: sin and impurity (verse 1).

The word "sin" refers to judicial guilt resulting from violation of the law, whether the Mosaic law or the law of the Messiah, and this requires justification. As a result of this fountain of the Holy Spirit, Israel will be justified, judicial guilt will be removed, and the people will be declared righteous. The word "impurity" has to do with moral guilt, which requires sanctification. As a result of the outpouring of the Holy Spirit and of Israel's national salvation, when the people look to the Messiah, they as a nation will be sanctified.

THE SPIRITUAL CLEANSING OF THE LAND
Zechariah 13:2-6

After Israel's spiritual and physical deliverance will come the cleansing of the land. Two matters are addressed in Zechariah 13:2-6: the judgment against pollution, and the removal of the false prophets. The phrase "it will come about in that day" means that what is about to be prophesied will happen in conjunction with Israel's national salvation. Zechariah then mentions three sources of the pollution in the land: idolatry, false prophets, and demons (verse 2). Idolatry will be removed once and for all when the image of the Antichrist (Daniel 12:11) is destroyed. False prophets and demons will also be removed from the land. During the messianic kingdom, all demons will be confined to one of two places: some will be confined in Babylon (Isaiah 13:21-22; Revelation 18:2), and others in Edom (Isaiah 34:8-15). Both places will be continuously burning wastelands. Throughout the messianic kingdom, all sources of spiritual pollution will be removed from the land.

THE REMOVAL OF THE FALSE PROPHETS
Zechariah 13:3-6

In conjunction with Israel's national regeneration, the people of Israel will have such a great zeal against the sins in which they once participated that they will be zealous to rid themselves of false prophets. The phrase "if anyone still prophesies" shows that there will still be false prophets who rebel against God even after the majority of the people have come to realize the truth. Verse 3 goes on to state the consequences: "Then his father and mother who gave birth to him will say to him, 'You shall not live, for you have spoken falsely in the name of the LORD.'" Indeed, the Old Testament law clearly demanded that false prophets be destroyed (Deuteronomy 13:6-10; 18:20-22). They are to "pierce" (Zechariah 13:3) false prophets—and the word translated "pierce" in 13:3 is the same word that is translated "pierced" in 12:10. Just as the Messiah would be thrust through, so these false prophets were to be thrust through by a sword or spear. In fact, the parents of the false prophets are the ones who are to thrust them through.

Zechariah 13:3-6 describes the hunt that will flush out the false prophets in the land. Because their prophecies will not come true, they will be shamed (verse 4). That their prophecies never came to pass is one of the key evidences of false prophets.

One key distinguishing mark of a prophet was the wearing of a hairy robe (1 Kings 19:13; 2 Kings 1:8; 2:8,13; Matthew 3:4; Mark 1:6). The false prophets described in Zechariah will wear a hairy robe in order to deceive people. When they become ashamed of their unfulfilled prophecies and realize that they are being sought out to be executed, they will discard their hairy robes so that they will no longer be identified as prophets.

Verses 5-6 conclude this section with a dialogue between the false prophets and those seeking to kill them. These false prophets who once claimed to be true prophets will deny that they ever were prophets. When someone is suspected of being a false prophet but is no longer wearing a hairy robe, he will say, "I am not a prophet; I am a tiller of the ground [a farmer]" (verse 5).

While a false prophet can remove his hairy robe, there are certain marks a false prophet cannot remove from himself. It was a practice of false prophets in those days to mark their bodies and cause scars. This is something true prophets never did. For example, in the contest between Elijah and the prophets of Baal, the prophets of Baal cut themselves (1 Kings 18:28).

The false prophets will be able to cast away their hairy robes, but they will not be able to remove the scars from their bodies. They will try to say that these wounds came from partying in the house of friends (Zechariah 13:6), but such deceit will not succeed in deterring the searchers; these prophets will lose their lives anyway.

Sometimes Zechariah 13:6 has been pulled out of context and been made to refer to the Messiah. But "a text apart from its context is a pretext." The context of verse 6 is false prophets, a topic that began in verse 2. Verse 6 is also part of the dialogue that began in verse 5. Therefore, verse 6 is not a reference to the true Messiah; it is a reference to the false prophets of the Tribulation who will be executed at that time as part of the spiritual cleansing of the land.

ISRAEL'S RELATIONSHIP TO THE MESSIAH
Zechariah 13:7-9

At the end of chapter 13, Zechariah summarizes Israel's relationship to the Messiah with three points.

Zechariah begins in verse 7 by stating, "Awake, O sword." The word "sword" is a symbol of death and not the manner of execution, pointing out that the Messiah will be killed by violent means. The "sword" is to awake "against My Shepherd." By calling Him "My Shepherd," God is emphasizing the humanity of the Messiah. The verse then states, "And against the man, My Associate." The phrase "the man" once again emphasizes Messiah's humanity. He is also called "My Associate," which literally means "my equal" or "my companion." This emphasizes Messiah's deity as God's equal. Literally the passage reads, "Awake, O sword, against My Shepherd and against the Man that is My equal." For this One to be God's equal means that He must be God Himself. The One who is going to be killed is the Good Shepherd, and He is both God and Man. So this verse speaks of the rejection of the Messiah at His first coming—a rejection by means of a violent death.

The first result of this rejection is the scattering or dispersion of the flock: "Strike the Shepherd that the sheep may be scattered; and I will turn My hand against the little ones." This is a summary of 11:4-14, where Zechariah gave a detailed, pictorial prophecy concerning the Good Shepherd, who is rejected. As a result of the rejection of the Good Shepherd, the sheep, the flock of Israel, were scattered. The Shepherd was smitten in A.D. 30, He died a violent death, and the sheep were scattered in A.D. 70. This verse is applied directly to the scattering of the disciples when Jesus was arrested in the Garden of Gethsemane (Matthew 26:31-32), but its primary reference is to the great dispersion by the Romans in A.D. 70. The statement "I will turn my hand against the little ones" means that even the innocent, common people will suffer as a result of the rejection of the true Shepherd by their leaders.

The second result of the rejection is the death of two-thirds of the flock (verse 8). Here, Zechariah summarized what he detailed in 11:4-14. This will be fulfilled during the Great Tribulation, when Israel will suffer tremendous persecution (Matthew 24:15-28; Revelation 12:1-17) and two-thirds of the Jewish people will be killed. This will happen "in all the land." The Hebrew word for "land" is *eretz,* which can be translated as either "earth" or "land," but in this context, earth fits better. In all the earth, two-thirds of the world's Jewish population who are alive at the beginning of the Great Tribulation will not survive to the end of it. However, the verse ends with a promise: "But the third will be left in it." One-third of the Jewish population will survive. This is the "all Israel" of Romans 11:26—the nation that is going to experience salvation.

The third point in 13:7-9 concerns the one-third of the Jewish population that will survive. God makes three statements about how this remaining third will come to salvation. He will "bring the third part through the fire," "refine them as silver is refined," and "test them as gold is tested." The fires that will refine the Jewish remnant are the judgments of the Great Tribu-

lation. By means of these judgments, they will learn righteousness and come to salvation. God says, "They will call on My name, and I will answer them." The surviving remnant will turn to the Lord and call upon Him in saving faith. God will respond, "They are My people." The Jews have always been God's people positionally, but they experience what this means only when they are in a right relationship with Him. They will say, "The LORD is my God"—that is, they will accept the one true God and Jesus, the Jewish Messiah.

THE CAMPAIGN OF ARMAGEDDON
Zechariah 14:1-5

In chapter 14, Zechariah returns to the physical aspect of the salvation of Israel and gives details that were not covered in the earlier passage on the campaign of Armageddon. Zechariah again mentions the Gentile armies that will gather against Jerusalem and repeats some of what he said in chapter 12. Concerning these nations he makes two main points. First, is the dividing of the spoil (verse 1). Zechariah introduces the timing of this event in a little different way: "Behold, a day is coming for the LORD...." Before he used the phrase "the day," but this time he says "a day," referring to one specific part of the day of Jehovah or the Great Tribulation. It is "a day" toward the end of the second half of the Great Tribulation, when the campaign of Armageddon takes place, that "the spoil taken from you will be divided among you." Second, the city will be captured (verse 2). Zechariah reiterates what he said in 12:2-3 about the nations coming against Jerusalem. He says "the city will be captured" by the Gentiles, "the houses plundered," "the women ravished," "half of the city exiled," and "the rest of the people will not be cut off from the city." Those who are still left in the city will experience the rescue described in the following verses.

Zechariah also prophesies that the Gentile armies will suffer tremendous losses (as stated in 12:4-9), for God will supernaturally energize the Jewish forces. But in spite of the supernatural energizing and the tremendous losses that the Jewish forces inflict upon the forces of the Antichrist, in the course of time, the city will fall. The same point is made in Micah 4:9–5:1.

In 14:3-4, Zechariah states the Messiah will come to fight on behalf of Israel. Note that the fighting from Bozrah to Jerusalem will precede Messiah's standing upon the Mount of Olives. Too often teachers of prophecy have taught that at the second coming, Jesus will come first to the Mount of Olives to fight against the enemy. However, that is not the order given in Scripture. To begin with, the second coming will occur not upon the Mount of Olives initially, but at the city of Bozrah or Petra (Isaiah 34:1-7; 63:1-6; Micah 2:12-13). Messiah will begin fighting against the forces of the Antichrist, who have come down to Bozrah or Petra to try to destroy the Jewish remnant located there. Zechariah 12:7 already stated that the people of Judah will be saved before the inhabitants of Jerusalem are saved. The fighting will finally end in the Valley of Jehoshaphat (Joel 3:12-13), where the winepress of blood is located (Revelation 14:19-20).

Zechariah 14:14 says, "In that day His feet will stand on the Mount of Olives." This occurs after the fighting in verse 3. One should not picture Jesus descending to the Mount of Olives at the second coming. Rather, after He finishes the fighting in the Valley of Jehoshaphat, He will then ascend the Mount of Olives. This will conclude the campaign of Armageddon. The result of the victory ascent upon the Mount of Olives will be a tremendous earthquake that will split the mountain in two, "from east to west by a very large valley" (verse 4). This geographical change to the Mount of Olives is not the only one that will occur during this time.

According to 14:2, after the capture of Jerusalem, half of the population will remain in the city. They will flee through this newly created valley to escape from the city before it collapses as a result of the earthquake (verse 5). This "valley of the mountains will reach unto Azel," which means it will move in the direction of the Jordan Valley. The phrase "as

you fled before the earthquake in the days of Uzziah king of Judah" compares this flight to the one that took place during Uzziah's reign, when a massive earthquake caused the Jews to flee Jerusalem (Amos 1:1). Zechariah concludes with the words, "Then the LORD, my God, will come, and all the holy ones with Him!" (verse 5). These "holy ones" who return with Jesus will include the angels (Matthew 16:27; 25:31), and the church saints (Jude 14).

RESULTS OF THE SECOND COMING
Zechariah 14:6-11

The seventh unit of the Little Apocalypse of Zechariah mentions five results of the second coming. The first result will be a change in the light sources (verses 6-7). The phrase "in that day" means this will happen in conjunction with the second coming. And the words "there will be no light" mean there will no longer be an interchange between day and night. That "the luminaries will dwindle" indicates that our natural sources of light will somehow be blanked out. At that time there will be "neither day nor night" (verse 7). In the millennial kingdom, whether it is considered daytime or nighttime, there will be no darkness. The same truth is taught in Isaiah 30:26.

The second result of Messiah's return will be the new millennial river (verse 8). "In that day" tells us this will happen during the kingdom era. The millennial river is described as "living waters [that] will flow out of Jerusalem." This river will begin at the threshold of the temple, and it is also mentioned in Joel 3:18 and Ezekiel 47:1-12. By combining all three of these passages we can see that the millennial river will gush out from the threshold of the millennial temple, which at that time will be located approximately 35 miles north of Jerusalem. Initially the river will flow eastward from the threshold of the temple, but then it will turn south and make its way to Jerusalem. When it reaches Jerusalem it will split in two—half of it will flow "toward the eastern sea," the Dead Sea, and the other half will flow "toward the western sea," or the Mediterranean Sea. Today the Dead Sea is just that—a dead sea so thick with minerals that it cannot sustain life. Not even saltwater fish can survive there. This millennial river of living water will change the nature of a specific area of the Dead Sea, so that an area along the western shore will support a major fishing industry (Ezekiel 47:10).

The third result is that the Lord "will be king over all the earth" and will be the one and only God (verse 9). The "LORD" spoken of here is the same as "the LORD…[who] will come" of verse 5, and the Messiah of verses 3-4. Again the Messiah is God Himself, and He will be the "king over all the earth." He "will be the only one, and His name the only one." During the kingdom period, no other god will be worshipped, and He will not be referred to by any false names.

The fourth result will be a number of topographical changes (verse 10). Zechariah states, "All the land will be changed into a plain from Geba to Rimmon south of Jerusalem." Today this area is mountainous, but in the kingdom, it will become flat. This will further emphasize the exaltation of Jerusalem, for the city "will rise" and be exalted above all. Today Jerusalem is not the highest city in the world, but in that future day, Jerusalem will sit atop the millennial mountain of Jehovah's house, the highest mountain in the entire world (Isaiah 2:2; Ezekiel 40:1-2; Micah 4:1). Zechariah then mentions some strategic points in the city that are no longer identifiable because Jerusalem has undergone some major changes since the prophet's time. He mentions "the gate of Benjamin unto the place of the first gate" and the site where "the Corner Gate" was located. He also mentions "the tower of Hananel" and "the king's wine presses."

The fifth result of the second coming will be the safety of Jerusalem (verse 11). "There will no longer be a curse, for Jerusalem will dwell in security. Nothing will threaten the safety of the city ever again.

DESTRUCTION OF THE ENEMY
Zechariah 14:12-15

In 14:12-15 Zechariah gives more details about how Israel's enemies will be destroyed

at Armageddon. God will use four means to destroy the Antichrist's forces at His second coming.

First, God will send a plague that causes human flesh to rot (verse 12). As the enemies are standing on their feet, their skin will melt away from their bones and their eyes will melt within their sockets. Just how this will occur is given in detail in Habakkuk 3:4, which discusses the events of the second coming and mentions the death rays that will emit from the Messiah's hand.

Second, God will send civil strife. Israel's enemies will begin fighting among themselves because of "a great panic" created by the Lord. The sudden confusion that results from the second coming will cause the army of many nations to begin fighting among themselves. Through this civil strife and chaos, they will destroy one another.

Third, God will supernaturally energize the Jewish forces (verse 14). Many of the Judeans who were rescued at Bozrah will come up to Jerusalem with Jesus and help with the rescue of Jerusalem. When this happens, "the wealth of all the surrounding nations will be gathered, gold and silver and garments in great abundance." The Jewish people will collect the spoils rather than become the spoils of the enemy.

Fourth, God will send a plague on all the animals that are in the camps of the invading armies. Perhaps this will make the animals unusable for food and all domesticated functions, and severely restrict the invaders' ability to conduct war.

THE MESSIANIC KINGDOM
Zechariah 14:16-21

This ninth and final unit of the Little Apocalypse of Zechariah deals with the messianic or millennial kingdom. Zechariah does not say much about the messianic kingdom, for that is discussed by many other prophets, particularly Isaiah and Ezekiel. Zechariah does, however, touch upon two major truths concerning this future kingdom.

CELEBRATION OF THE FEAST
OF TABERNACLES
Zechariah 14:16-19

Zechariah 14:16 reveals it will be obligatory not only for the Jews but also for the Gentile nations to celebrate and observe the Feast of Tabernacles. Every year throughout the 1000-year kingdom, it will be mandatory for every Gentile nation "that went against Jerusalem" to send a delegation to Jerusalem in order to observe the Feast of Tabernacles. This makes sense because the kingdom is the fulfillment of the Feast of Tabernacles. The purpose of this attendance is twofold: "to worship the King, the LORD of hosts, and to celebrate the Feast of Booths."

The punishment for refusing to observe the feast is given in verse 17. Should any nation fail to send a delegation to Jerusalem, God will punish that nation by inflicting a plague of drought for that year. Egypt is then cited as an example (verses 18-19). It is interesting that God chose to bring up the Egyptians, for if any nation is likely to be tempted to dispense with observing the Feast of Tabernacles in the kingdom, it would certainly be Egypt. The Feast of Tabernacles was one of the seven holy seasons of Israel inaugurated as part of the observance of God's deliverance of Israel from the land of Egypt. Perhaps one day the Egyptians will say to themselves, "Why should we send a delegation to Jerusalem to observe a festival that commemorates an Egyptian defeat?" If that happens, then God will punish the Egyptians by withholding rain from the nation. Although Egypt is singled out as an example, the warning applies to all other Gentile nations as well.

HOLINESS OF THE LAND
Zechariah 14:20-21

The second major truth Zechariah reveals about the messianic kingdom is that *everything* in the land will be holy, not just the vessels in the temple compound. The Mosaic system distinguished between that which was for holy use and that which was for mundane, earthly, secular, or common use. Zechariah first mentions that even the bells of the horses will bear the inscription, "HOLY TO THE LORD" (verse 20). Before, this phrase was emblazoned only on the miter of the high priest. But in the millennial kingdom, even the bells that hang around horses' necks will be considered holy.

This holiness will also extend to "the cooking pots in the LORD's house," which "will be like the bowls before the altar" (verse 20). Everything within the temple compound will be equally sanctified, including the pots used for boiling and the bowls used for pouring out the blood of the sacrifices on the altar. Under the Mosaic law, these implements were not considered to be equal, but they will be considered equally holy in the kingdom.

Zechariah says that even "every cooking pot in Jerusalem and in Judah will be holy to the LORD of hosts" (verse 21). All domestic utensils throughout the land will be considered holy so that "all who sacrifice will come and take of them and boil in them." It will not matter which pot people bring; they will all be equally holy.

Zechariah closes his book by stating, "There will no longer be a Canaanite in the house of the LORD of hosts in that day." "In that day" refers to the millennial kingdom. God had long ago commanded the Jewish people to totally exterminate the Canaanite population because of their extreme degree of sinfulness. But never in the history of Israel were the Jewish people able to accomplish this. There were Canaanites living in the land after Joshua died, and also during the days of David and Solomon. In fact, David and Solomon had agreements with the Phoenicians, who were Canaanites.

Not until the kingdom is established will God's wish be carried out to its fulfillment. There will be no more Canaanites anywhere in the land, let alone "in the house of the LORD of hosts." As a result of this total extinction, everything in the land will be holy, including the bells on the horses and the pots and pans in every Jewish kitchen.

MALACHI

MALACHI WAS THE LAST OF THE HEBREW PROPHETS and his book is usually dated about 430 B.C. He gives a call to repentance and obedience, with a warning of judgment on those who rebel against God. The people of Judah had become complacent in sin, and God sent this messenger to proclaim that He would come to punish the wicked, deliver the righteous, and cleanse the land.

In form, Malachi does not simply present messages from God, but rather asks questions to priests and others, then disputes their answers, giving proofs for his responses. The reforms that had been introduced by Ezra (457 B.C.) and Nehemiah (444 B.C.) were stagnating as priests became corrupt, Jews divorced their spouses and intermarried with Gentiles, tithes to God's temple and priesthood were neglected, and the poor were oppressed. Malachi's first prophetic statement deals with the nation of Edom or the descendants of Esau.

EDOM AND ISRAEL
Malachi 1:4-5

THE ISRAELITES RECOVERED from the Babylonian captivity, but the Edomites never did. And, according to God, Edom is destined to become "the wicked territory, and the people toward whom the LORD is indignant forever" (verse 4). During the millennial kingdom there will be no inhabitants in Edom; it will be a land of burning pitch and brimstone, a land indwelt by demons. It will not be beautified as other parts of the world will be. The phrase "beyond the border of Israel" means that the Lord will be magnified among the Gentiles. Israel recovered from Babylonian captivity and rebuilt Jerusalem and the temple, but Esau's land will never recover.

THE MESSIANIC KINGDOM
Malachi 1:11

MALACHI 1:11 POINTS OUT something that is yet future. In the messianic kingdom, Gentiles will honor God's name and will bring "incense" and an "offering that is pure" to God. A day will come when the entire Gentile world will worship the God of Israel (Zechariah 14:16-21).

THE COMING MESSIAH
Malachi 3:1-6

MALACHI 3:1-6 IS SIMILAR TO Zechariah 9:9-10. In both passages, the first and second comings of the Messiah are blended together in such a way that no hint is given of a gap of time between the two comings.

Malachi here answers the question in 2:17, "Where is the God of justice?" He begins by announcing the coming of a forerunner to the Messiah in verse 1: "Behold, I am going to send My messenger, and he will clear the way before Me." This same prophecy appears in Isaiah 40:3-5, and the messenger who fulfilled this prophecy was John the Baptist.

Malachi then mentions the first coming of the Messiah: "The Lord, whom you seek, will suddenly come to His temple; and the messenger of the covenant, in whom you delight, behold, He is coming" (Verse 1). This temple, built by Zerubbabel, is the second temple (Ezra 1:2-6)—the one that Haggai and Zechariah had encouraged the people of Israel to complete. By Malachi's time, it had been completed and was functioning, although the priesthood had been corrupted. During Jesus' time on earth, the second temple was being remodeled by Herod. Nevertheless, after the forerunner came, the Messiah Himself suddenly came to "His temple." The pronoun "His" emphasizes that the Messiah is the owner of the temple. Indeed, during His first coming, Jesus fulfilled this prophecy at the first Passover of His public ministry when He went to the temple and threw out the money changers and the merchants selling sacrificial animals (John 2:13-22). By so doing, He claimed ownership of the temple. In fact, He said the temple was "My Father's house" (verse 16).

The temple belonged to God the Father, and because Jesus is the Son of God, He shares in that ownership. By doing this "suddenly" (Malachi 3:1) Jesus performed a function of cleansing the temple. He repeated this action at the last Passover of His public ministry (Matthew 21:12-13; Mark 11:15-18; Luke 19:45-47). Furthermore, this "messenger of the covenant" is the Messiah Himself (Malachi 3:1). One way He is the messenger of the covenant is that He is the One who will fulfill the covenants God has made with Israel. He will fulfill the Abrahamic Covenant, the Land Covenant, and the Davidic Covenant. He is also the One who is going to make a New Covenant; therefore, He is the "messenger of the covenant." In fact, Isaiah had already prophesied that when the Messiah came, He would be "a covenant to the people" (Isaiah 42:6; see also 49:8). This is the Messiah of that covenant.

Malachi 3:1 relates to the first coming, but verses 2-5 have to do with the second coming. Three things will be accomplished at the second coming of the Messiah. First, He will refine the people; He will cleanse them of their sins (verse 2). Second, "he will purify the sons of Levi," the priesthood, so that they will then offer righteous offerings (verse 3). As a result, the millennial sacrifices will be acceptable. Earlier in the book, Malachi emphasized that God was not accepting the people's sacrifices because they were offering weak and sickly animals that were spotted and blemished. God asked for someone to shut the doors of the temple so that no more unacceptable offerings could be brought to Him (1:10). Third, there will be a judgment of sinners (verses 4-5). Malachi states that sorcerers; adulterers; perjurers; oppressors and cheaters of hirelings, widows, and orphans; and sojourners are all going to suffer judgment. This will give a final answer to the skeptical question of 2:17, "Where is the God of justice?" Someday He will come, and justice will be meted out.

Verse 6 concludes with the eternal covenantal promise, "I, the LORD, do not change; therefore you, O sons of Jacob, are not consumed." God is the unchanging One. This is the uniqueness of perfection—there is no need to change anything; He is the perfect One; He is the changeless One. If God makes a promise, He will keep it. That is why the "sons of Jacob" "are not consumed." Because of who God is, the Jews, as a people, are indestructible. Individuals may be destroyed, but the people as a nation cannot be destroyed on account of the promises of the unchanging God.

THE DAY OF THE LORD
Malachi 4:1-4

MALACHI 4:1-3 MENTIONS the day of the Lord, which is the most common single term used throughout the Scriptures for the Great

Tribulation. In the judgments of the Great Tribulation, God is going to fulfill His promise of sparing the remnant (3:17). In 4:1-4, Malachi describes the day of the Lord and makes two points.

The first point is that the wicked will be destroyed in the Tribulation (verse 1). One of the motifs the Old Testament commonly uses to describe the Great Tribulation is a fiery furnace. That motif is used here. Indeed, a good number of the judgments of the Great Tribulation found in the book of Revelation—such as the seal judgments, the trumpet judgments, and bowl judgments—include fiery judgments. God will turn "all the arrogant and every evildoer [to] chaff" (4:1). When even just a spark of fire is applied to dry chaff, it all burns instantly. When the divine judgments of the Tribulation have finally run their course, "neither root nor branch" will be left, emphasizing the totality of God's judgment.

The second point is that during this time of massive annihilation of the wicked, God will preserve a believing remnant (verses 2-3). In verse 2 God addresses the remnant directly, saying, "You that fear my name…." Those who feared Jehovah were already mentioned in 3:16, and He promised them that they would be placed into "a book of remembrance." Being put into that book meant they would be protected from His fiery judgments. The "sun of righteousness" is the One who will protect the believing remnant, and the "sun of righteousness" of 4:2 is the same as "the messenger of the covenant" in 3:1—none other than the Messiah Himself. The forerunner was like the morning star that announces the coming of day. Both the forerunner of the first coming and the forerunner of the second coming are like daystars that announce the coming of "the sun of righteousness," or the Messiah, who will preserve the remnant.

Furthermore, the sun of righteousness will come "with healing in its wings" (4:2). The Hebrew word translated "wings" means "rays" or "beams." This figure is also used in Psalm 107:20, which speaks of deliverance from destruction. In other words, the sun's

rays will bring healing. Malachi is not referring to the literal sun, but the Son of God, the Messiah. And the healing that will come is spiritual healing from sin. The context here is spiritual sickness, so Malachi is speaking of spiritual healing. With the coming of the sun of righteousness will come spiritual healing that makes the remnant strong. The phrase "and you will go forth and skip about like calves from the stall" means the people will jump about like young calves who have been released from a pen.

We also learn that this remnant "will tread down the wicked" (verse 3). They will conquer the wicked ones. This victory will occur in the days of the Tribulation.

Malachi then urges the people to remember the law of Moses (verse 4). This is his final call for Israel to keep the law. Malachi had emphasized this to his people in the earlier chapters of his book. He calls upon the people to obey "even the statues and ordinances" that God commanded in Horeb. Horeb is in the same area as Mount Sinai. It was because of the people's disobedience to the law that curses had come and that they had not experienced the blessings promised under the Mosaic law.

THE COMING OF ELIJAH
Malachi 4:5-6

MALACHI 4:5-6 ANNOUNCES the coming of Elijah and the purpose of his coming. In 3:1, the prophet proclaims the coming of a forerunner before the first coming of the Messiah, but does not reveal a name. The New Testament tells us this forerunner was John the Baptist. Now in 4:5 Malachi announces a forerunner before the second coming of the Messiah, and this time he names the person—someone who has been here once before: "Elijah the prophet." There is no reason to spiritualize this verse away. Malachi simply states, "I am going to send you Elijah the prophet," and so Elijah will come. The timing of Elijah's coming is "before the coming of the great and terrible day of the LORD" (verse 5). Again, the expression "day of the LORD" is the most common Old Testament term used to speak of the last half of the seven-year Tribulation. So before the Great Tribulation starts, Elijah will return, perhaps as one of the two witnesses (Revelation 11:3-14). The Tribulation will begin with the signing of a seven-year covenant between Israel and the Antichrist. Before that covenant is signed, Elijah the prophet will return. The primary purpose for his coming is to restore the Jewish family unit, which is known for its closeness and togetherness (verse 6). The one thing that has divided Jewish families is the issue of whether Jesus is the Messiah. Even in a close-knit Jewish family, if one member becomes a believer in Jesus, there is instantaneous division in that family. Indeed, when the Messiah came the first time, He pointed out that He would become a point of division in the Jewish world and family unit (Matthew 10:34-37). Some would believe and some would not, and this would result in father being against son, son against father, daughter against mother, and so on.

To this day, the issue of Jesus' messiahship is a point of contention in Jewish families. The purpose for Elijah's return is to help restore the family unit, to work in such a way that Jesus will no longer be a point of division. This, in turn, will lead to Israel's national salvation, which is a prerequisite to the second coming. If Elijah were not to succeed, God would "smite the land with a curse." But as other passages indicate, Elijah will succeed in his ministry (Matthew 17:11; Mark 9:12).

The Old Testament ends with reference to a curse, known as *cherem*. It is the worst type of curse, one of utter destruction. Today's rabbis do not like to conclude the reading of Malachi with a curse, so after they read verse six, they repeat verse five so that the book will not close with a curse. But regardless of how anyone might try to euphemize it away, the curse is a curse, and the judgment of the day of the Lord still stands. Ultimately, the perversion of the Mosaic law that came about through Pharisaism and Sadduceeism will lead to the Great Tribulation. And according to Zechariah, the Tribulation will compel Israel toward national regeneration and restoration.

Although the Old Testament ends with a curse, it sets the stage for the blessings of the fulfillment of chapter 3:1 with the coming of John the Baptist, the forerunner at the first coming of the Messiah. Eventually the second forerunner, Elijah the prophet, will come, and that will be followed by the second coming of the Messiah.

NEW TESTAMENT
PROPHECIES

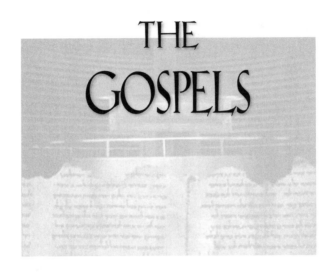

THE
GOSPELS

THE GOSPELS

The four Gospels (Matthew, Mark, Luke, and John) provide a biblical portrait of Jesus Christ. In these four books we are introduced to an array of prophecies that find their fulfillment in Him alone. We are also introduced to a series of eschatological or end-times predictions about future events from the lips of Jesus Himself.

Because many of these prophecies are repeated in the four Gospel accounts, we have arranged them in chronological order based on A.T. Robertson's *Harmony of the Gospels*. Each prophecy is identified both topically and textually for the purpose of clarifying and simplifying the reader's study.

THE ANNUNCIATION OF JOHN THE BAPTIST'S BIRTH
Luke 1:5-25

The first prophecy of the New Testament was the prediction of the birth of John the Baptist, the forerunner of the Messiah. John's parents were Zacharias and Elizabeth, two righteous individuals who were advanced in years, with Elizabeth barren and unable to have children (verses 6-7). While Zacharias, a priest, was performing his priestly functions in the temple (verse 8), an angel of the Lord (Gabriel) appeared to him (verse 11) and related how his wife would become pregnant and bear a son named John, which means, "Yahweh has been gracious" (verse 13).

John would be great in God's sight, be filled by the Holy Spirit (verse 15), and be instrumental in turning "back many of the sons of Israel to the Lord their God" (verse 16). He will be the forerunner of the Messiah and serve "in the spirit and power of Elijah" (verse 17), though he was not that prophet who would yet come later. He would do a similar work

as Elijah for the first coming of Christ (Isaiah 40:3-5), while Elijah would come from heaven and herald the second coming of Christ to reign and rule (Malachi 4:5-6). As prophesied, with the first and second comings of Christ, both John and Elijah would "turn the hearts of the fathers back to the children, and the disobedient to the attitude of the righteous; so as to make ready a people prepared for the Lord" (Malachi 4:6; Luke 1:17).

Zacharias argued with Gabriel over this revelation, claiming that he and Elizabeth were too old to bear children (Luke 1:18). As a sign that the prophecy was true, Zacharias was struck dumb until the words of this promise were "fulfilled in their proper time" (verse 20). When Zacharias came out of the temple, he was unable to speak. The people realized that he had seen a vision while inside the temple (verse 22). When the couple returned back to their home, which was probably not far from Jerusalem, Elizabeth became pregnant and remained secluded for five months (verse 24)—possibly because she felt embarrassed and disgraced for having a child at such an old age (verse 25). She may have been a cousin or a relative of Mary because Mary stayed with her for some time when both women were pregnant (verses 39-40).

It is interesting to note that it is prophesied that John would be making "smooth in the desert a highway for our God" (Isaiah 40:3), and Elijah would be, according to Luke, preparing a people "for the Lord" (Luke 1:17). Christ is God incarnate, and He is the Lord of the Old Testament! God, in the person of the Lord Jesus, would be coming to earth as had been prophesied in so many passages in the Old Testament.

THE ANNUNCIATION OF CHRIST'S BIRTH
Luke 1:26-38

THE ANGEL GABRIEL, who had appeared to Zacharias (verses 11,19), now came to Mary six months after Elizabeth became pregnant and announced to her, "Hail, favored one! The Lord is with you" (verse 28). Mary and Joseph were at the time living in the northern Israelite city of Nazareth (verse 26). Mary was a virgin (Greek, *parthenos*) who was engaged to Joseph (verse 27). In Jewish culture the betrothal period is considered binding upon the couple as if they were already married, though sexual relations had not yet taken place. It was by the mysterious work of the Holy Spirit that Mary would conceive (verse 35). This would make Jesus the "adopted" son of Joseph. His virgin birth was a unique and miraculous work of God in which the Son of God was "birthed" into the world.

The *virgin birth of Christ* fulfills the cryptic prophecy of Genesis 3:15 that describes how the seed of the woman will bruise (crush) the head of the serpent. The snake was embodying Satan in the temptation of Eve in the garden (verses 1-13). In Revelation 12, John the apostle writes concerning this far-distant event and describes Satan as "the great dragon…the serpent of old who is called the devil and Satan, who deceives the whole world" (verse 9). Genesis 3:15 foresees the ultimate triumph of Christ (the seed of the woman) over Satan.

The virgin birth was prophesied hundreds of years earlier in Isaiah 7:14: "Therefore the Lord Himself will give you a sign: Behold, a virgin will be with child and bear a son, and she will call His name Immanuel," which means "God is with us." The Hebrew word for "virgin" is *'almah,* which describes a young girl of marriageable age who could be betrothed and who is also physically a virgin. This clearly applies to Mary. In biblical Hebrew the word *bethulah* is more commonly used to speak of a virgin, but the word is less precise and can mean anything from a young girl to a young widow (see discussion on Isaiah 7:14). *Bethulah* may in some cases miss the implication that the woman was of marriageable age. The Hebrew lexicographer Gesenius (*Gesenius' Hebrew and Chaldee Lexicon,* p. 634) describes the word *'almah* as meaning "of the nubile state and puberty." *'Almah* is rendered by the Septuagint (LXX) as *parthenos,* which *always* carries the meaning of "a virgin" (the Septuagint is a Greek translation of the Hebrew Old Testament produced during the second and third centuries B.C.).

Mary was troubled by Gabriel's greeting and "kept pondering what kind of salutation this was" (Luke 1:29). She was to name her son Jesus (*Yeshua*), which means "the Lord is salvation." He would be great and called "the Son of the Most High" (verse 32), fulfilling Psalm 2. The Lord God "will give Him the throne of His father David" (Luke 1:32; Isaiah 11:1; cf. 2 Samuel 7:12-17; Psalm 89:3-4). Mary was told that someday He would "reign over the house of Jacob forever, and His kingdom will have no end" (Luke 1:33; cf. Daniel 2:44; 7:14). Jacob is the father of the 12 tribes of Israel, and these promises were made to the Jewish people. In no way can these messianic promises be transferred to the church. Mary would have understood these words in their literal, normal, and obvious meaning. The church does not replace Israel in the kingdom promises that God gave to the Jewish people!

Though Mary did not fully understand the

great mystery that was about to take place, she answered, "Behold, the bondslave of the Lord; may it be done to me according to your word" (Luke 1:38).

ELIZABETH'S SONG
Luke 1:39-45

MARY JOURNEYED TO WHERE Elizabeth lived and shared Gabriel's good news with her (verses 39-40). When Elizabeth heard the news, "the baby [who would be named John] leaped in her womb," and at that moment she "was filled with the Holy Spirit" (verse 41). Prompted by the Spirit, Elizabeth cried out, "Blessed are you among women, and blessed is the fruit of your womb" (verse 42). She then added, "And how has it happened to me, that the mother of my Lord would come to me?" (verse 43). This can only mean that Elizabeth realized that Mary's child would be the promised Messiah in fulfillment of Psalm 110:1. This was further confirmed when Elizabeth's baby leaped in her womb for joy at the sound of Mary's voice (Luke 1:44). Both women now realized the significance of what was about to transpire. God was using them in a most miraculous way! Speaking about Mary, Elizabeth added, "And blessed is she who believed that there would be a fulfillment of what had been spoken to her by the Lord" (verse 45).

MARY'S HYMN
Luke 1:46-56

MARY NOW RESPONDS to Elizabeth's words with a poem that reveals how much the Old Testament was known and loved in the homes of pious and godly Jews who were awaiting the birth of the Messiah. Often called the Magnificat, this poem includes some 15 discernable prophecies and quotations from the Old Testament.

Mary describes how her spirit exalts in the Lord, who is "God my Savior" (Luke 1:47;

see Psalm 34:2; 106:21). She realizes that the Lord had looked upon her with favor, and that all future generations would count her as blessed (Luke 1:48). The fact she was blessed, however, does not mean she was perfect and without sin. This is why she speaks of God as "my Savior."

Mary said that God was merciful to her as He is "from everlasting to everlasting on those who fear Him" (Psalm 103:17). He has scattered the proud (Luke 1:51), brought down rulers, and "has exalted those who were humble" (verse 52). He has filled the hungry with good things (verse 53) and has given help to His servant Israel "in remembrance of His mercy" to them (verse 54). She then made direct reference to the root of blessing for Israel and the nations, the promises "to our fathers, to Abraham and his descendants forever" (verse 55; cf. Genesis 12:1-3; 17:19; Psalm 132:11; Galatians 3:16). Mary understood that the starting point for the blessings God promised in Scripture is the Abrahamic Covenant. The "forever" promises have their focal point in the person of the Lord Jesus Christ.

JOHN THE BAPTIST'S BIRTH
Luke 1:57-80; John 1:6-8

JOHN WAS BORN in fulfillment of Gabriel's predictive announcement. After his birth, Zacharias and Elizabeth's neighbors assumed he would be given the name of his father (Luke 1:59), but Elizabeth answered, "No, indeed; but he shall be called John" (verse 60). God had been gracious and granted them a son in their old age, and He would use their son to herald the arrival of the promised Messiah! Zacharias, who still could not speak, confirmed what his wife said and wrote out on a tablet, "His name is John" (verse 63). With that, Zacharias began to speak and gave praise to God (verse 64). The neighbors were still confused and wondered out loud what the son would do, not fully realizing that the hand of the Lord was upon him (verse 66).

Filled with the Holy Spirit, Zacharias gave a poetic prophecy, which began with a blessing for the Lord (verse 68). God was accomplishing a redemption "for His people" and had raised up a "horn of salvation for us in the house of David His servant" (verse 69). This is similar to how Hannah praised God when the much-wanted Samuel was born to her. However, she added that the Lord "will give strength to His king, and will exalt the horn of His anointed," a reference to the future birth of the Messiah (1 Samuel 2:1, 10; Psalm 2:2). "Horn" is a metaphor for power, as with the horn of a powerful animal.

In his prophecy, Zacharias refers to God's political salvation of Israel "from the hand of all who hate us" (Luke 1:71). The enemies nearest in time would be the Romans, but in the final chapters of world history, the enemies will include the kingdom of the Antichrist, who will come against the Lord's people in the Tribulation. Zacharias also proclaimed that God will show mercy toward the ancient fathers and remember His "holy covenant, the oath which He swore to Abraham our father, to grant us that we, being rescued from the hand of our enemies, might serve Him without fear, in holiness and righteousness before Him all our days" (verses 72-75).

Zacharias's son John will be the prophet "of the Most High" who will "go on before the Lord to prepare His ways" (verse 76; Isaiah 40:3). John will be the "voice calling" that the way is to be clear for the Lord "our God." This has to refer to God the Son, who would come to the earth to bring salvation. In fact, Zacharias continued his words of praise and added that John would "give to His people the knowledge of salvation by the forgiveness of their sins" (Luke 1:77). Zacharias seems to be alluding to Christ when he says, "the Sunrise from on high will visit us" (verse 78). Malachi 4:2 speaks of those who fear God's name—on them "the sun of righteousness will rise with healing in its wings." This sunrise will "shine upon those who sit in darkness and the shadow of death, to guide our feet into the way of peace" (Luke 1:79; Isaiah 9:1).

John grew up "strong in spirit, and lived in the deserts until the day of his public appearance to Israel" (Luke 1:80). "Strong in spirit" may refer to a determined temperament that became rightly critical of all of the spiritual apostasy in the nation at that time. Because of this, John refused to associate with the priests in Jerusalem. Instead, he remained secluded in order to study and pray for the mission that was before him. Later, there would be some confusion as to who John was and what his task was all about. John was "sent from God" and came to bear witness to Christ, "the Light." All who trusted in Christ would find salvation (John 1:6-8).

THE ANNUNCIATION TO JOSEPH AND THE VIRGIN BIRTH OF CHRIST
Matthew 1:18-25; Luke 1:26-38; 2:1-7

MARY WAS BETROTHED to Joseph (Matthew 1:18). When he found out she was pregnant, he became concerned that perhaps she had been unfaithful. Joseph, a godly and righteous man, did not want to disgrace Mary, so he was willing to break off the engagement quietly (verse 19). While he was considering this possibility, an angel of the Lord appeared to him in a dream to remind him that he was a "son of David" and to reveal that Mary's conception was the work of the Holy Spirit (verse 20). Since the Lord Jesus would be Joseph's "stepson" or adopted son, Joseph could pass on to Him all the legal privileges and rights inherent in King David's lineage. Thus, Christ's legal right to the Davidic throne would come through Joseph. Most scholars believe that Luke was attempting to connect the genealogy of Mary to the line of David in the lineage recorded in 3:23-38, though many believe the focus is still on Joseph. One suggestion is that Eli (verse 23) may be Mary's father. Mary then would be the natural descendant of David through whom Christ would come. One fact is certain: Christ's lineage is traced all the way back to Adam, through whom He could represent the entire human race (verse 38).

Both Mary and Joseph were told by the angel of the Lord to name the child Jesus because He "will save His people from their sins" (Matthew 1:21; Luke 1:31). *Jesus* comes into the English language through the Greek *Iesou*, which translates the Hebrew *Yeshua*. *Jesus* means "Jehovah saves." This is confirmed in dozens of places in the Old Testament, including "the God who is our salvation" (Psalm 68:19). To "save His people from their sins" is also alluded to in the prophecy of the Suffering Messiah, which appears in Isaiah 53:1-12. "He Himself [will bear] the sin of many, and [will intercede] for the transgressors" (verse 12). Matthew adds, in his account of the virgin birth, that the son's name would be Immanuel, which means "God is with us," indicating the incarnation of the divine Christ in human flesh (Matthew 1:23; Isaiah 7:14).

Mary was also informed that her son would "be called the Son of the Most High," and that "the Lord God will give Him the throne of His father David" (Luke 1:32). This means that He is the prophesied Messiah who would become king over Israel, or over the house of Jacob (Jacob, whose name was changed to Israel, was the father of the 12 tribes—Genesis 49). This reign has an unending quality; it is "forever" because it is the messianic kingdom that "will have no end" (Luke 1:33). Mary took these promises in a normal, literal way, understanding that the prophecies would be fulfilled in history. She did not see these promises in some allegorical or nonliteral sense. None of the Jews of her day would have taken them that way either. It was further explained to Mary that because her son was "the Son of the Most High," the Most High, by His power, would send His Holy Spirit to come upon her, and "the holy Child shall be called the Son of God" (verse 35). The expression "the Most High" is a reference to the Lord (Daniel 7:18,22,25).

Before Jesus was born, Joseph and Mary were made to travel from Nazareth to Bethlehem because of a decree from Quirinius, the governor of Syria and northern Israel. The Roman emperor was Caesar Augustus (Luke 2:1-2). Quirinius was apparently the governor of Syria from 4 B.C. to A.D. 1 and then again in A.D. 6. Because of his decree, the Jews were forced to travel to the city of their birth to register for the tax, so Joseph and Mary had to travel to Bethlehem.

The term "virgin" in Matthew 1:34 relates Mary the mother of Jesus to Isaiah 7:14. Matthew uses the Greek word *parthenos* to translate the Hebrew word *'almah*. His contextual usage of "fulfill" shows that he understood the Isaiah passage to contain a definitely predictive element. He recognizes the prophecy as coming from God (the Greek preposition *hypo* [by] introduces the direct agent with a passive verb, whereas *dia* [through] introduces the mediate agent). The Lord is the source of the prophecy, and the prophet is his mouthpiece. God is the cause, and the prophet is the instrument that He uses. The quotation of Isaiah 7:14 follows the Septuagint's rendering of the passage, where *parthenos* is also used to translate the Hebrew *'almah*. Perhaps no prophetic prediction has created a greater controversy than Isaiah's prediction of a virgin-born Son, which Matthew clearly claims was fulfilled in Christ's birth.

Without a doubt, the Greek term *parthenos* is always to be translated "virgin" (Arndt and Gingrich, *A Greek-English Lexicon of the New Testament*, p. 632). The real question is whether the Septuagint is correct in its translation of the Hebrew *'almah*. Since the weight of scholarship supports the translation of the Hebrew word *'almah* as being the most accurate word possible for "virgin," one can only conclude that the LXX translators were correct in their interpretation. The Dead Sea Scroll copy of Isaiah indicates the same usages. For a thorough discussion of the Old Testament usage of *'almah*, see E.J. Young, *The Book of Isaiah*, vol. 1, pp. 284-91; E.J. Young, *Studies in Isaiah*, pp. 143-98; and E. Hindson, *Isaiah's Immanuel*.

The virgin birth of Christ is undoubtedly the most essential doctrine underlying His deity. The prediction in Isaiah 7:14 of a virgin-born son calls His name "Immanuel, which being interpreted is, God with us." This is a title describing the deity of the Son of God rather than a name. It implies God will come to dwell among His own people. For a discussion of the significance of the virgin birth of Christ see R. Gromacki, *The Virgin Birth: Doctrine of Deity;* and J.G. Machen, *The Virgin Birth of Christ.*

By now Joseph was comfortable with what God was doing in his life and in Mary's. After the angel of the Lord had spoken to him about the miracle of Mary's pregnancy, Joseph arose from his sleep and immediately took Mary "as his wife" (Matthew 1:24). Mary remained a virgin until after Jesus was born (verse 25). But God "kept her a virgin until she gave birth to a Son." Matthew makes it clear that she remained a virgin…implying that normal marital relations began after that time. The fact that Jesus' brothers and sisters are spoken of numerous times in the Gospels (including Matthew 12:46; 13:55-56; Mark 6:3) prove that Mary did not remain a virgin perpetually, as some claim" (MacArthur, *Matthew 1–7,* p. 22).

To fulfill the prophecy that Christ would be born in Bethlehem (Micah 5:2), Mary and Joseph, under God's providence, were led to make the journey south to Bethlehem. There, Mary gave birth "to her firstborn son, and she wrapped Him in cloths, and laid Him in a manger, because there was no room for them in the inn" (Luke 2:7).

THE ANGELS' AND SHEPHERDS' PRAISE
Luke 2:8-20

NEAR BETHLEHEM, SHEPHERDS were keeping watch over their flocks the night Jesus was born (verse 8). An angel of the Lord (Gabriel) stood before them, "and the glory of the Lord shone around them; and they were terribly frightened" (verse 9). Gabriel announced that the Savior (Matthew 1:21), who is the Christ (Greek, *christos,* "anointed"), "has been born for you" (Luke 2:11). This was "good news of great joy which will be for all the people" of Israel (verse 10). God is to receive the glory, and

peace is to be "among men with whom He is pleased" (verse 14). This fulfills the prophecy made by Jacob to his sons that the Messiah would come through the tribe of Judah and would be designated as "Shiloh" ("peaceful, peacemaker") (Genesis 49:10). It also fulfills the prophecy that the Messiah would be called "Prince of Peace" (Isaiah 9:6).

The angels' dramatic appearance to the shepherds was more than convincing. When the angelic host departed, the shepherds determined to "go straight to Bethlehem" to see what had happened (Luke 2:15). After finding Mary and the child, they reported what the angels told them (verses 16-17). Then the shepherds returned to their fields "glorifying and praising God for all that they had heard and seen, just as had been told them" (verse 20).

JESUS' CIRCUMCISION
Luke 2:21

As WAS THE CASE FOR all male Jewish babies, Jesus was circumcised on the eighth day (verse 21). But before the circumcision was accomplished, He was formally given His name *Jesus,* as the angel of the Lord commanded (1:31; Matthew 1:21). *Jesus* means "Jehovah saves." In Hebrew, the name is *Yeshua.* In the narrow sense, *Jesus* is prophetic of what He would do at His first coming. He would be the Savior of the world! This was what Gabriel had told the shepherds (Luke 2:11). Later, Christ's own testimony to some Samaritan villagers led them to realize that "this One is indeed the Savior of the world" (John 4:42).

Circumcision was a sign of the Abrahamic Covenant (Genesis 17). All the males of Israel were later commanded to be circumcised (Exodus 12:48; Leviticus 12:3). Circumcision was a hygienic procedure, but it had spiritual connotations. It symbolized that the Jews were to be morally and spiritually pure because they belonged to God. Circumcision was also a sign that their offspring were to be uniquely dedicated to God.

THE PRESENTATION AT THE TEMPLE
Luke 2:22-38

Following Jesus' circumcision and the 33 days required for Mary's purification, the family went up to Jerusalem to give the required ceremonial offerings. As required by the Law, Christ, the firstborn male who opened His mother's womb, was "called holy to the Lord" (verse 23; Exodus 13:2). And because the family was poor, they presented a pair of turtledoves for the ceremonial offering (Luke 2:24; Leviticus 12:8).

In Jerusalem the family met Simeon, a righteous man who was looking for "the consolation of Israel" (Luke 2:25). In the Greek text, "looking for" (Greek, *prosdechomai*) can better be translated "to welcome, receive, expect, wait for." "Consolation" (Greek, *paraklasis*) means "comfort, help" and refers to the coming of the Messiah and the establishment of the Davidic kingdom. Inspired by the Holy Spirit, it was prophetically revealed to Simeon that he would not die until he had seen the Lord's Christ, the promised Anointed One (verse 26; Psalm 2:2). When Simeon saw the baby Jesus, he took Him in his arms and blessed God (verse 28) and proclaimed that he could now depart from this world in peace because God's word had been fulfilled (verse 29). The prophecy of Isaiah 52:10 had come to pass. "For my eyes have seen Your salvation, which You have prepared in the presence of all peoples" (Luke 2:30). The coming of Christ would bring blessings to the Gentile nations. He would be "a light of revelation to the Gentiles, and the glory of Your people Israel" (verse 32; Isaiah 42:6). Christ is declared here to be the blessing to both Gentile and Jew; His provision of salvation would be available to all.

It was also prophesied to Mary by Simeon that Jesus was "appointed for the fall and rise of many in Israel, and for a sign to be opposed—and a sword will pierce even your own soul—to the end that thoughts from many hearts may be revealed" (Luke 2:34-35). There would be those who rejected the Messiah and those who accepted Him. And what happened to Him would bring great grief and sorrow to His mother.

The 85-year-old elderly widow Anna, who was a prophetess and a servant at the temple, also realized that the Messiah had been born. Seeing Jesus, she began "giving thanks to God, and continued to speak of Him to all those who were looking for the redemption of Jerusalem" (verses 36-38). The words of both Simeon and Anna give the impression that many at that time were looking for the Messiah. The nation of Israel was filled with anticipation! Yet later, when Jesus began His ministry, many chose to reject Him.

THE VISIT OF THE WISE MEN
Matthew 2:1-12

Several months after Jesus was born, magi arrived in Jerusalem from the east, traditionally identified as Persia, looking for the child who had been born "King of the Jews." Herod the Great was in power over the nation of Israel at the time, under the authority of the Roman Empire. He was not of the kingly royal family but was a nominal Jew, an Edomite and a usurper who had been placed on the throne of Israel by the favor of the Roman government. He ruled with an iron fist, and the Jewish people despised him greatly.

Upon arriving in Jerusalem, the magi asked, "Where is He who has been born King of the Jews?" (verse 2). Herod and all who had been placed in power by him in Jerusalem were troubled (verse 3), because Caesar Augustus had given Herod the title "King of the Jews." Now an old man, Herod was in the last days of his long and cruel reign. History portrays him as a paranoid tyrant who even executed his own wife and sons to protect his throne.

If there was now another King of the Jews, Herod and his associates would certainly be removed from their positions of authority. Herod inquired of the chief priests and the scribes where the Christ should be born (verse 4), and he was told "in Bethlehem" (verse 5). The leaders quoted Micah 5:2, which cites His birthplace and said that from that city would come forth "a Ruler, who will shepherd My people Israel" (Matthew 2:6). The verse in Micah also speaks of His deity: "His goings forth are from long ago, from the days of eternity." This refers to the Lord's preincarnate, divine nature—He has always existed. The same is said of God the Father: "Are you not from everlasting, O LORD, my God, my Holy One?" (Habakkuk 1:12).

The magi were led to Jerusalem by a star on the western horizon, which they could see from somewhere in the east (Matthew 2:2,7-9). Herod sent them on their way to search out the Christ child so "that I too may come and worship Him" (verse 8). The star that guided the magi finally stopped over Bethlehem (verse 9), leading them to the place where Joseph, Mary, and Jesus were living at the time. The magi worshiped the child and brought costly royal gifts of gold, frankincense, and myrrh (verse 11).

The question is often raised as to the role of the star seen by the magi. The star relates to the prophecy of Moses that such a divine sign would come out of Israel, out of Jacob, along with a king's scepter that will rise from Israel (Numbers 24:17). Unger wrote,

> The "Scepter" envisions the Lord coming to rule the earth as absolute King and Lord (Rev. 19:16). The "Scepter" is owned first in Zion (Psalm 110:2) and extends to the ends of the earth when Shiloh comes (Gen. 49:10; Psalm 45:6-17; Isa. 11:9-10). Although the royal insignia "star" and "scepter" include David, they only find their fulfillment in the greater David at His second advent and Kingdom (*Unger's Commentary on the Old Testament*, p. 219).

THE ESCAPE TO EGYPT
Matthew 2:13-18

IN A DREAM, the Lord came to Joseph and told him to go to Egypt because Herod wanted to kill the Christ child (verse 13). Joseph, Mary, and Jesus remained in Egypt until the death of Herod, which fulfilled the statement by the prophet Hosea, "Out of Egypt I called My son" (11:1). Stanley Toussaint makes a fine point that Matthew did not say a "prophecy was fulfilled" but that "what had been spoken by the Lord through the prophet" might be fulfilled (Matthew 2:15). The point Toussaint is making is that Hosea 11:1 seems to refer to Israel, yet in a theological way it is applied to Christ (Toussaint, *Behold the King*, p. 54). Toussaint says, "Thus that which God accomplished in delivering Israel [from Egypt in the Exodus] is confirmed in His workings with His Son. All this was not left to haphazard circumstances. The flight into Egypt (verse 14) is looked at as a purposeful fulfillment of Hosea 11:1" (*Behold the King*, p. 55).

Realizing he was tricked, Herod sent troops to the Bethlehem region with orders to kill all the male children aged two years and under, presumably because this covered the period of time it took for the magi, following the star, to travel to the Holy Land (Matthew 2:16). This brings to mind a fulfillment of Jeremiah 31:15, where Jeremiah in poetic imagery describes Rachel, representing Jewish motherhood, as weeping for the Israelites who are being deported from Ramah to Babylon. What happened in Jeremiah 31 was typological of the slaughter of the innocent children: "Rachel weeping for her children; and she refused to be comforted, because they were no more" (Matthew 2:18).

JESUS RAISED IN NAZARETH
Matthew 2:19-23; Luke 2:39-40

AFTER THE DEATH OF HEROD, Herod's son Archelaus assumed the throne. Joseph, still in Egypt, was told in a dream that the family could return back home to Israel (Matthew 2:19-22). Afraid to travel the route that would lead through Jerusalem, he was warned by the Lord to depart "for the regions of Galilee" and to Nazareth (verse 22). This fulfilled the prophecy of Isaiah 11:1 that the Messiah would be called a *Nazarene*. *Nazareth* comes from either the Hebrew word *nasar*, "to watch" or "guard," or the word *neser*, "sprout" or "branch." The city sits on the Galilean hillside 15 miles west of the Sea of Galilee, where it commands a spectacular view of the Valley of Jezreel (Armageddon). What makes this prophecy amazing is that during the days of Isaiah, there was no city called Nazareth. The city's name is a play on the word "roots" as found in the messianic passage Isaiah 11:1: "Then a shoot will spring from the stem of Jesse [David's father], and a branch [*netzer*] from his roots will bear fruit."

It was prophesied of the Messiah that He would be "like a tender shoot, and like a root out of parched ground" (Isaiah 53:2), and that He would be the Lord's servant "the Branch" (Zechariah 3:8). The Lord further prophesied that in the millennial kingdom the "man whose name is Branch...will branch out from where He is; and He will build the temple of the LORD" (6:12). And He "will...bear the honor and sit and rule on His throne. Thus, He will be a priest on His throne" (verse 13). Jesus grew up in Nazareth and became "strong, increasing in wisdom; and the grace of God was upon Him" (Luke 2:40).

THE MINISTRY OF JOHN THE BAPTIST
Matthew 3:1-6; Mark 1:2-6; Luke 3:3-6

DURING HIS LATER formative years, John had "lived in the deserts" (Luke 1:80), probably contemplating God's calling on his life. He would begin "his public appearance to Israel" by preaching in the wilderness (verse 80). He apparently lived a solitary and reclusive existence, wearing "a garment of camel's hair,

and a leather belt" and eating "locusts and wild honey" (Matthew 3:4). He was designated "the Baptist," a reference to the fact that he would spend much of his ministry calling Israel to repent and then be baptized. Those who repented demonstrated this fact by the "washing" of baptism (verses 1-2) in the Jordan River (verse 6). *Repentance* (Greek, *metanoeo*) means "to change the mind." The implication is that the Jews were to change their minds about their sinful ways, and to turn back to God. This seems to be proven by what Peter said to the Jews during Pentecost: "Repent and *return*," which implies returning to God (Acts 3:19).

John, as the forerunner of the Messiah (Mark 1:2-3; Isaiah 40:3), preached that "the kingdom of heaven is at hand" because the King was about to make His presentation (Matthew 3:2). The spiritual life of Israel must have been like a dry well, for people eagerly came from Jerusalem, all Judea, and "the district around the Jordan" (verse 5; Mark 1:5) to hear John, confess their sins, and be baptized (Matthew 3:6; Mark 1:4). John described Christ in an extraordinary manner: "After me One is coming who is mightier than I, and I am not fit to stoop down and untie the thong of His sandals" (verse 7). It was clear that the Lord Jesus would save the Jews from their sins, as prophesied in Isaiah 40:5 and quoted in Luke: "And all flesh will see the salvation of God" (Luke 3:6). Neither John nor the Jews fully understood all of what was happening at this point, but it was clear that Christ had come to deal with the issue of sin, and also that someday He would reign as King over Israel and the world.

THE BAPTISM OF THE HOLY SPIRIT
Matthew 3:7-12; Mark 1:7-8; Luke 3:15-18

THE PHARISEES AND THE SADDUCEES came down from Jerusalem to the Jordan River to criticize the work of John the Baptist (Matthew 3:7). John revealed their motives and called them a "brood of vipers" who, if they were sincere, should show repentant hearts by bringing fruit "in keeping with repentance" (verse 8). He knew they thought they were saved because Abraham was their father (verse 9). The priests and the Levites also journeyed from Jerusalem and asked, "Who are you?" (John 1:19). John made sure they knew he was not "the Christ" (verse 20), nor Elijah (Malachi 4:5), nor "the prophet" Moses prophesied about (Deuteronomy 18:15). John added that God was about to bring down the Jewish people because of their evil: "The axe is already laid at the root of the trees; therefore every tree that does not bear good fruit is cut down and thrown into the fire" (Matthew 3:10). If this generation did not repent, judgment was certain. Christ's own people, the Jews, "did not receive Him" (John 1:11), but for those who did, "He gave the right to become children of God, even to those who believe in His name" (verse 12).

John's baptism was with water and reflected the idea of a purification brought by repentance, but Christ would baptize "with the Holy Spirit and fire" (Matthew 3:11; Mark 1:8; Luke 3:16). The inner work of the Holy Spirit was prophesied in Ezekiel 36: "Then I will sprinkle clean water on you, and you will be clean; I will cleanse you from all your filthiness and from all your idols.… I will put My Spirit within you…you will be My people, and I will be your God. Moreover, I will save you from all your uncleanness" (verses 25-29).

People could choose either a blessing by the baptism of the Holy Spirit, or the judgment of fire (Matthew 3:11). As with a "winnowing fork" (grain rake), the Messiah will one day "thoroughly clear His threshing floor; and He will gather His wheat into the barn, but He will burn up the chaff with unquenchable fire" (verse 12). The gathered wheat represents the Jews who trust Christ and will be baptized by the Spirit. The chaff represents those Jews who reject Him. Christ reminded His disciples of these words before His ascension: "John baptized with water, but you shall be baptized with the Holy Spirit not many days from now" (Acts

1:5). This prophecy was fulfilled at Pentecost according to Peter (10:47; 15:8).

While John's message did not reveal the final form of the gospel—the death, burial, and resurrection of Christ (1 Corinthians 15:1-6)—it was still the gospel (Greek, *euangelion*, "good news") in its initial seed form to the Jewish people at that time. "So with many exhortations [John] preached the gospel to the people" (Luke 3:18). At that time, Israel had every opportunity to receive the rightful King.

JESUS' BAPTISM
Matthew 3:13-17; Mark 1:9-11; Luke 3:21-22; John 1:29-34

As JOHN THE BAPTIST was preparing the nation of Israel for the kingdom of heaven and its King, the Lord Jesus came down to the Jordan River and told John that He too must be baptized, "for in this way it is fitting for us to fulfill all righteousness" (Matthew 3:13-15). John was reluctant at first, for he knew who Jesus was. Nevertheless he complied and "permitted Him" to be baptized (verse 15). Since water baptism was intended for those who repented of their sins, why did Christ have to be baptized? Scholars have pondered this question for centuries. The answer may be found in Isaiah 53:12, which says the Messiah would pour "out Himself to death, and was numbered with the transgressors; yet He Himself bore the sin of many, and interceded for the transgressors." Christ by baptism then could be identifying or associating Himself with sinners and therefore could serve as a substitute for them under the wrath of God. It was prophesied that He would be "pierced through [in substitution] for our transgressions" (verse 5) and "for the transgression of my people, to whom the stroke was due" (verse 8).

Following His baptism, John saw the Spirit of God "descending as a dove, and coming upon Him" and heard the Lord's voice from heaven saying, "This is My beloved Son, in whom I am well-pleased" (Matthew 3:16-17;

Mark 1:9-11; John 1:33-34). This is a reference to Psalm 2:7, where the Lord prophetically referred to His "begotten" Son. Luke wrote that the Spirit descended "in bodily form" (Luke 3:22). The meaning is that Christ would be controlled by the Holy Spirit, or He would be embodied by the Spirit. This was prophesied in Isaiah 11:2, where it is written that "the Spirit of the Lord will rest on Him."

It is also recorded that when Christ approached John, the prophet said, "Behold, the Lamb of God who takes away the sin of the world!" (John 1:29,36; cf. Isaiah 53:6-7; 1 Peter 1:17-19). John also somehow recognized an aspect of deity in Christ, for he said, "After me comes a Man who has a higher rank than I, for He existed before me" (John 1:30). "Existed" in the Greek text appears in the imperfect or past tense and implies that Christ was always continually existing in the past.

CHRIST'S FIRST DISCIPLES
John 1:35-51

Upon realizing that Jesus was the promised Messiah, some of John's disciples began following the Lord (1:35-39). This may indicate that many godly and pious Jews knew their Old Testament Scriptures and were at that time anticipating the coming of Israel's King. In the days to come, others would also follow Christ and become part of His inner circle of apostles.

Andrew sought out his brother Simon Peter and told him that he had discovered the Messiah (the Anointed One), "which translated means Christ" (verse 41). Andrew's words were a direct quote of Psalm 2:2. The Lord then called Philip to "follow Me" (John 1:43). Philip too realized that the Old Testament prophecies were being fulfilled in Christ and told Nathanael, "We have found Him of whom Moses in the Law and also the Prophets wrote, Jesus of Nazareth, the son of Joseph" (verse 45, cf. Deuteronomy 18:15; Isaiah 11:1). Nathanael's protest about Nazareth in John 1:46 was either

personal or based on the absence of any reference to it in the Old Testament.

Nathanael realized who Christ was when the Lord stated He had seen Nathanael while he was sitting under a fig tree (John 1:48). Quoting Psalm 2:6-7, Nathanael answered, "Rabbi, You are the Son of God; You are the King of Israel" (John 1:49). Christ was not only the Son of God ("the Son related to God") but He also made it known to His fledgling disciples that He was the Son of Man ("the Son related to mankind") (verse 51), a distinct messianic description that comes from Daniel 7:13. In Daniel 7:9-28 we read the vision of Christ entering the throne room of God the Father following His ascension to glory. He comes before God, "the Ancient of Days," and is presented as the One who is victorious in His work on earth. Therefore, Christ is "presented before Him" (verse 13) and given "a kingdom, that all the peoples, nations and men of every language" might serve Him (verse 14). This is His future messianic reign!

The "angels of God ascending and descending" on Christ (John 1:51) are reminiscent of the vision of Jacob's ladder in Genesis 28:12-19, where the Lord demonstrated to the patriarch His care over him. In the same way, the Lord would provide for His Son during His ministry on earth.

JESUS CLEANSES THE TEMPLE
John 2:12-22

During the first Passover described in the Gospels, the Lord was at the temple in Jerusalem and observed the money changers and the sellers of sacrificial animals doing business in the temple's inner courts (verse 14). The money changers apparently had been given permission by the temple authorities to move their shops to within the inner temple grounds. Christ became angry and, with righteous indignation, "overturned their tables" (verse 15), saying "to those who were selling the doves...'Take these things away; stop making

My Father's house a house of business'" (verse 16). Later, the disciples remembered "that it was written, 'Zeal for Your house will consume Me'" (verse 17; Psalm 69:9). Not all of Psalm 69:9 is quoted; the rest of it says, "And the reproaches of those who reproach You have fallen on me." In other words, the deep hatred or resentment some people had against God was transferred to the Son. "As a result of the Messiah's glowing ardor for God's honor, the reproaches aimed at God fell upon Him; this part of the verse is quoted in Romans 15:3 to demonstrate that Christ did not please Himself" (Unger, *Unger's Commentary on the Old Testament*, p. 844)

The Jews then questioned Jesus and asked what sign (meaning some Old Testament indication) He was giving them by expressing His anger against the animal merchants (John 2:18). Jesus knew their hearts and how their hatred of Him would begin to grow. He then prophesied of the day they would kill Him and added, "Destroy this temple, and in three days I will raise it up" (verse 19). Unable to think outside of the physical realm, the people thought Jesus was talking about the historic temple that up to that time had taken 46 years to build (verse 20). "But He was speaking of the temple of His body" (verse 21). Again, the disciples later remembered this and understood Jesus was speaking of His resurrection (verse 22; Luke 24:7-8), according to the Scriptures (Psalm 16:10).

Because Christ knew what was in the hearts of the leaders at the temple, and others as well, He refused to entrust Himself to men.

JESUS AND NICODEMUS
John 3:1-21

CONTRARY TO POPULAR THOUGHT, the doctrine of being "born again" was not new in Jesus' day. It had been predicted in Ezekiel 37. Nicodemus, an orthodox Jewish leader who was a Pharisee and a member of the ruling Sanhedrin, should have known of this truth. Out of fear of criticism, Nicodemus came to Christ at night to express his belief that the Lord was a rabbi and a teacher "come from God" because no one else could do the signs He was performing unless "God is with him" (verses 1-2). Nicodemus realized that the Lord was the prophesied Messiah who would usher in the kingdom of God, but Jesus startled Nicodemus when He said, "Truly, truly, I say to you, unless one is born again, he cannot see the kingdom of God" (verse 3).

Taking the Lord's words very literally, Nicodemus thought Christ was talking about coming forth from a mother's womb a second time (verse 4). But Christ was speaking of spiritual birth and not physical (verse 6). That is why He said, "Truly, truly, I say to you, unless one is born of water and the Spirit, he cannot enter into the kingdom of God" (verse 5). Much controversy has been generated about the "water" in this passage. Some believe it is referring to 1) water baptism, 2) being born again by the Word of God, or 3) the water that accompanies physical birth. In any case, one must be born again by the Spirit in order to experience citizenship in the kingdom of God.

Nicodemus then asked, "How can these things be?" (verse 9). Christ answered, "Are you not the teacher of Israel, and do not understand these things?" (verse 10). That is, Nicodemus could have known about being born again from Ezekiel 37:25-28. God had said that someday, He would sprinkle clean water on the Jewish people, give them a new heart, and put His Spirit within (verses 25-27). The spiritual washing and the receiving of the Spirit seem to coincide and function together. This is the prophesied baptism of the Holy Spirit (Matthew 3:11) that would be given to believers after Christ's ascension (Acts 1:5; 11:15-16). The Holy Spirit, then, is the dynamic of the New Covenant that brings about forgiveness of sins.

In the same way that the Old Testament children of Israel who were dying from the scourge of snakes in the wilderness were delivered by looking upon the golden snake raised up on a pole (Numbers 21:9), so would Christ one day be raised up so "that whoever believes in Him would have eternal life" (John 3:15). He would die as Israel's Messiah (verses 14-16), the Son of Man (Daniel 7:13), and also as the divine Son of God (Psalm 2:7). The world can now be saved by trusting in Him who is the "only begotten Son" (John 3:16,18). "Only begotten" comes from the Greek term *monogeneses,* which communicates that Jesus is "the unique, or only born One" who came down to earth from God the Father. Whoever believes in Him now and comes to the light will not be judged (verses 19-20). To "practice" the truth is to come to the truth and come to Him who gives spiritual light (verse 21).

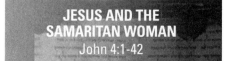

JESUS AND THE SAMARITAN WOMAN
John 4:1-42

As Christ continued His ministry He showed mercy even to those who were considered outcasts, such as the Samaritans who lived north of Jerusalem. These people were half-breeds, the result of Jews and Assyrians who had intermarried. When the Assyrians invaded Israel in 722 B.C., some settled in the northern regions (2 Kings 17:24) and brought their gods with them. While many of these who intermarried turned to Israel's God, they did so without fully accepting all of the Old Testament's teaching. By Christ's time, this mixed people were considered heretics by the Jews.

In John 4 we read that Jesus and His disciples passed through Samaria, and stopped at the city of Sychar, which Jacob had given to his son Joseph (John 4:1-5). Sitting by a well, Jesus began a spiritual conversation with a woman who had come to draw water (verses 6-12). Speaking to her directly, the Lord spoke of the "gift of God" and the fact that He could grant her "living water" (verse 10). With this water one would never thirst again; within the individual this water would be "springing up to eternal life" (verse 14).

When Jesus, who had never met the woman before, told her the secrets of her sordid life (verses 16-18), she realized He was a prophet

(verse 19). When she pointed out the theological conflicts between the Jews and the Samaritans (verse 20), Jesus reminded her that "an hour is coming when neither in this mountain [of Samaria] nor in Jerusalem, will you worship the Father" (verse 21). Salvation is of the Jews (verse 22), and everyone must worship the Father "in spirit and truth" (verses 23-24).

The woman then admitted she knew that the Jewish Christ was to come and "declare all things to us" (verse 25). Jesus answered, "I who speak to you am He" (verse 26). With this the woman rushed into the city and told everyone to come see the one who told her "all the things that I have done, this is not the Christ, is it?" (verse 29). The people of the area wanted to hear Jesus speak, so He stayed with them for two days (verse 40), and "many more believed because of His word" (verse 41). The people proclaimed, "This One is indeed the Savior of the world" (verse 42).

Some time earlier the prophecies about the Messiah had penetrated this land of the Samaritans. They knew of the coming Christ, the Anointed One (Psalm 2:2), and they knew that He would one day bring salvation not only to Israel but also to all people.

THE KINGDOM OF GOD IS AT HAND
Matthew 4:17; Mark 1:14-15; Luke 4:14-15

When Jesus began His ministry, His message was the same as John the Baptist's: "Repent, for the kingdom of heaven is at hand" (Matthew 4:17; cf. 3:2). This means "the kingdom that comes down from heaven." This undoubtedly refers to the messianic kingdom, the Davidic rule that will be based in Jerusalem but will have sovereignty over all the nations of the earth. "John came, then, heralding an event, and that event was the drawing near of the kingdom. In proclaiming this event, John was acting as a forerunner for the King, preparing the way ahead of Him" (Toussaint, *Behold the King,* p. 59). Now the King is presenting Himself!

Mark called this message "the gospel of

God" (Mark 1:14), meaning the "good news" about the King and the kingdom. Christ added, "The time is fulfilled, and the kingdom of God is at hand; repent and believe in the gospel" (verse 15). Ministering in the power of the Spirit, the "news about Him spread through all the surrounding district" (Luke 4:14), and so "He began teaching in their synagogues and was praised by all" (verse 15).

CHRIST REJECTED IN NAZARETH
Luke 4:16-30

Initially Jesus was heard and accepted throughout the region of Galilee (4:14-15), but a different scenario developed when He went to the synagogue in His hometown of Nazareth (verse 16). Given an opportunity to present Himself, He opened the book of the prophet Isaiah and read Isaiah 61:1-2. The passage says of the Messiah that the Spirit of the Lord will come upon Him, and He will be anointed to "preach the gospel to the poor" and bring spiritual sight, freedom, and release to those less fortunate (Luke 4:18-19).

When Jesus finished reading, those in the meeting place were taken aback and fixed their eyes on Him (verse 20). Was He claiming to be the Messiah? Without giving any opportunity for doubt, He said, "Today this Scripture has been fulfilled in your hearing" (verse 21). The people began "wondering at the gracious words which were falling from His lips; and they were saying, 'Is this not Joseph's son?'" (verse 22). Could the boy who grew up in our town be the Messiah? While their questions seemed innocent enough, Jesus knew the people were doubtful, and He sensed their opposition. They wanted to see some kind of physical sign or miracle done in their own city (verse 23), yet they did not want to accept the spiritual words of a prophet from their own circles (verse 24). Jesus then cited the story of Elijah and the widow of Zarephath (1 Kings 17:8-24). Many widows suffered in a three-and-a-half-year famine, but only one received help (Luke 4:25-26). And Elisha cleansed only one

leper, Naaman the Syrian (verse 27; 2 Kings 5:1-19).

The crowd in the synagogue rejected Jesus' claim to be the Messiah. They resented His refusal to do a miracle for them and tried to push Him off a cliff into the adjacent Valley of Jezreel (verses 28-29), but Jesus miraculously slipped through their midst (verse 30).

PROPHECY OF CHRIST'S MINISTRY IN GALILEE
Matthew 4:13-16

When Christ heard that John the Baptist had been arrested by Herod the tetrarch (14:1-12), He went to the region of Galilee, as He often liked to do (4:12). He passed through Nazareth and traveled on to Capernaum, where He settled in to minister (verse 13). This ministry was prophesied in Isaiah 9:1-2. The prophecy mentions the tribal territorial areas of Zebulun and Naphtali "by the way of the sea, beyond the Jordan, Galilee of the Gentiles" (Matthew 4:15). Though these were Jewish regions, many Gentiles had settled here also.

The prophecy continues: "The people who were sitting in darkness saw a great light, and those who were sitting in the land and shadow of death, upon them a light dawned" (verse 16). These areas were more blessed by Jesus than the southern territory of the land and the city of Jerusalem. Christ spent more time in the Galilee than other places, and the people were more receptive to His ministry and His teaching. He would bring spiritual light to both Jew and Gentile (John 1:9; 12:46).

DEMONS RECOGNIZE THE SON OF GOD
Matthew 8:14-17; Mark 1:21-34; Luke 4:31-41

Capernaum was the home of the apostle Peter. When Jesus was visiting, He saw Peter's "mother-in-law lying sick in bed with a fever"

(Matthew 8:14). Jesus touched her hand, and she was cured and was able to arise from her bed and wait on the Lord (verse 15). That evening, many people began bringing demon-possessed individuals to Christ. Demons (Greek, *daimonion*) may have been angels, the "stars of God" over whom Lucifer wished to have dominion (Isaiah 14:13), a third of whom he swept from heaven with him—who are now active on earth as evil spirits (Revelation 12:4). "Demon-possessed" (Greek, *daimonizomai*) means "to control" or, "to be demonized" (Matthew 8:16). When Jesus cast out demons, those possessed by them were healed. This healing fulfilled Isaiah 53:4: "He Himself took our infirmities, and carried away our diseases" (Matthew 8:17). At the synagogue in Capernaum the leaders were amazed that Christ had authority "not as the scribes" (Mark 1:22), and He could command "even the unclean spirits, and they obey Him" (verse 27).

Demons could control the whole person physically and emotionally. They could also speak through the possessed. At Capernaum, with a collective voice, multiple demons spoke through one possessed person and said to Christ, "What business do we have with each other, Jesus of Nazareth? Have You come to destroy us? I know who You are—the Holy One of God!" (Luke 4:34). Jesus commanded the spirit (singular) to "be quiet and come out of him!" Collectively they did and left the man unharmed (verse 35).

CHRIST: THE SON OF GOD, THE SON OF MAN
John 5:22-29

When Christ explained that He was doing the very same work as God His Father (verse 17), the Jews sought to kill Him because He "was calling God His own Father, making Himself equal with God" (verse 18). The Lord continued to explain to them His relationship with the Father: "Whatever the Father does, these things the Son also does in like manner"

(verse 19). As the Father raises the dead "and gives them life, even so the Son also gives life to whom He wishes" (verse 21). The judgment of the Father has been given to the Son (verse 22), and as the Father is honored, so is the Son (verse 23). Because Christ now does the same work as the Father, whoever hears Christ's word "and believes Him who sent Me, has eternal life, and does not come into judgment, but has passed out of death into life" (verse 24). The Son will call forth the dead (verse 25) because, just as the Father has life in Himself, "even so He gave to the Son also to have life in Himself" (verse 26).

Christ is also the "Son of Man" with authority to "execute judgment" (verse 27), even over those coming forth from the tombs in "a resurrection of life" as well as over the evil who come forth to "a resurrection of judgment" (verses 29-30). "The Son of Man" is one of the *strongest messianic designations*, meaning "the Son related to mankind," whose coming kingdom will encompass "all the peoples, nations and men of every language" (Daniel 7:13-14).

PRAYER FOR THE KINGDOM TO COME
Matthew 6:1-13; Luke 11:1-4

In the Sermon on the Mount, Christ proclaims moral and spiritual principles that had been overlooked and even denied by His generation of the Jewish people. He was direct in His rebuke and called the people "hypocrites" who said one thing and practiced something else (Matthew 6:1-7).

In Luke's account, the disciples seemed to have a conviction about prayer and said, "Lord, teach us to pray just as John also taught his disciples" (Luke 11:1). Telling them not to use vain repetition as the Gentiles do (Matthew 6:7), Jesus urged them to pray directly to God the Father, who is in heaven and whose name is holy (verse 9). "Your kingdom come. Your will be done, on earth as it is in heaven" (verse 10) is in the aorist imperative mood in the Greek text, and it is in the third person singular and should be translated as a statement of wish or desire: "Let Your kingdom come. Let Your will be done...." The requests are eschatological and cannot be spiritualized. The last clause of verse 10 is "an appeal for God's sovereignty to be absolutely manifested on earth" (Toussaint, *Behold the King*, p. 110).

The rest of the prayer is personal and has to do with forgiveness (verse 12) and the need to be kept from temptation and evil (verse 13). The last sentence in verse 13 does not appear in the best ancient manuscripts, though its tone certainly fits the nature of this prayer: "For Yours is the kingdom and the power and the glory forever. Amen."

CHRIST, THE PROPHESIED SERVANT
Matthew 12:14-21

THOUGH THE PHARISEES BEGAN counseling to "destroy" Christ (verse 14), He continued healing many who followed Him (verse 15). Because His healing ministry had become so controversial, He urged the people He healed "not to tell who He was" (verse 16). This fulfilled the prophecy of Isaiah 42:1-4.

Isaiah records that God called the Messiah His chosen Servant, the "Beloved in whom My soul is well-pleased." On Him God would place His Spirit, and through Him "He shall proclaim justice to the Gentiles" (Matthew 12:18). The Messiah will go about quietly and will not even break off a battered reed or put out "a smoldering wick" (verses 19-20). Justice will have victory through Him, "and in His name the Gentiles will hope" (verse 21). The Lord Jesus is a servant to God and is especially chosen for this task.

In Isaiah 42:1-4, "the Messiah's task is broadly indicated: 'He will bring forth justice to the nations,' in a sense by His redemptive work and gospel at His first advent, but principally by His earthly rule and Kingdom at His second advent" (Unger, *Unger's Commentary on the Old Testament*, p. 1255—see

Psalm 72:4,11-14; Isaiah 9:7; 11:3-5; Revelation 19:15-16; 20:4).

JESUS AND JOHN THE BAPTIST
Matthew 11:2-19; Luke 7:18-35

JOHN THE BAPTIST was thrown into prison when he rebuked Herod Antipas for marrying the wife of his half-brother Philip, her uncle (Matthew 14:1-12), thus committing incest (Leviticus 18:16). John would later be killed and his head given to Herod's wife, Herodias (Matthew 14:6-11). While in jail, John sent word by his disciples to Jesus, asking, "Are You the Expected One, or shall we look for someone else?" (11:3). Some have speculated that John may have had doubts because Jesus had not yet used His authority to begin His kingdom reign. "Perhaps his being in prison, a place which was certainly incongruous for the herald of the King, reinforced his doubts" (Toussaint, *Behold the King*, p. 148). John's humanity is revealed in his question, and Jesus set the record straight.

The phrase "Expected One" in the original Greek text is the present participle of *erchomai* and should be translated with the article as "the One who is coming." This can only mean the promised Messiah of the Old Testament. Christ answered John by reminding him of His miracles, which no one could do but the promised King. "The blind receive sight and the lame walk, the lepers are cleansed and the deaf hear, the dead are raised up, and the poor have the gospel preached to them" (verse 5; Isaiah 35:5; 61:1). Jesus then turned to the crowds and asked them what they saw when they looked at John as he preached: a weakling, or a man dressed in fine clothes? (Matthew 11:7-8). They saw a prophet who would prepare the way for the Messiah (verse 9-10; cf. Isaiah 40:3; Malachi 3:1). If the Jews had accepted Christ, the kingdom of heaven ("the kingdom from heaven") would have come and it would be as if they had believed John, who would have been prophesying like Elijah, who was to come (Matthew 11:14; cf. Malachi 4:5).

Those who trusted in Christ would be greater even than John the Baptist. They would be "in the kingdom of God…greater than he" (Luke 7:28). Those who had come to Christ "acknowledged God's justice, having been baptized with the baptism of John" (verse 29). Jesus' comments here make a clear dispensational distinction between Old Testament believers (such as John) and the New Testament believers of the church age.

The detractors and the doubters, however, could not be pleased. They rejected John, who was an esthetic and did not eat bread nor drink wine (verse 33). And they called Christ a "gluttonous man, and a drunkard, a friend of tax collectors and sinners!" (verse 34).

JESUS AND BEELZEBUL
Matthew 12:22-37

As the Pharisees continued their attack against Jesus, they began to accuse Him of performing miracles, such as the casting out of demons (verse 22), by the power of "Beelzebul the ruler of the demons" (verse 24). This was done to blunt the inquiries of many who thought Jesus might be the promised King, "the Son of David" (verse 23). *Beelzebul* was a name for Satan derived from Baal-Zebub, the god of the Philistine city of Ekron (2 Kings 1:2). The name can imply "lord of the flies," "god of the dung heap," or "lord of the high places" (Barbieri, Jr., "Matthew," *Bible Knowledge Commentary*, p. 42) The Pharisees were not denying Christ's miracles; rather, they were assigning Christ's work to Satan!

Christ points out that this makes no sense. How could Satan be using Jesus to cast out his own demonic servants? (Matthew 12:25-30). The Holy Spirit was the power working within Jesus that was causing such miracles! By contrast, the Pharisees said that Satan was behind them. This was a blasphemy that could not be forgiven, though all other sins can be (verse 31). It was possible even to speak a word against Christ, the Messiah and the Son of Man. But to attribute to Satan an obvious and clear miracle is blasphemous, and it "shall not be forgiven him, either in this age or in the age to come" (verse 32). The reference to "the age to come" could mean that a person who commits such blasphemy cannot enter the messianic kingdom, or it could refer to the day of the final judgment.

Christ then used the same description of the Pharisees that John did—they are a "brood of vipers" (verse 34; 3:7). Within them is an "evil treasure [that] brings forth evil things" (verse 35 NKJV). The Pharisees will bear the responsibility for the "careless word" and "account for it in the day of judgment" (verse 36). Before others a person is "justified," and "by your words you will be condemned" (verse 37). This is not a "works" justification before God but a justification before men for what one has said or done (see James 2:14-26).

THE SIGN OF JONAH
Matthew 12:38-45

Though the scribes and Pharisees may have seemed sincere when they said, "Teacher, we want to see a sign from You" (verse 38), their real motive was to try to prove Jesus wasn't the Messiah. Jesus answered that an evil and adulterous generation wants a sign, but the only sign they will see is "the sign of Jonah the prophet" (verse 40). "Jonah was three days and three nights in the belly of the sea monster," and so will the Messiah, the Son of Man, "be three days and three nights in the heart of the earth" (Matthew 12:40). This present generation of Jews, Jesus said, is so evil that even the pagans of Nineveh to whom Jonah witnessed will rise up and judge Israel! The men of Nineveh repented at the preaching of Jonah (Jonah 3:5), and now one greater than Jonah was in their midst (Matthew 12:41). (On the sign of Jonah, see also Matthew 15:39–16:4.)

Even the "Queen of the South" (the queen of Sheba) will judge this doubting Jewish generation (12:42; 1 Kings 10:1; 2 Chronicles 9:1). She came to hear the wisdom of Solomon, but now someone "greater than Solomon is here."

Just as an evil spirit leaves a man but returns to embody him with seven other spirits "more wicked than itself," in the same way "it will also be with this evil generation" (verses 43-45). This generation will never admit its sin; it will only become more and more sinful and hardened in its rejection of the Lord.

PARABLES OF THE KINGDOM
Matthew 13:1-53;
Mark 4:1-34; Luke 8:5-18

THERE ARE THREE BASIC VIEWS about the parables Jesus taught in the passages cited above: 1) They were simply given to further blind those who already were rejecting the truth; 2) they are prophecies about this present church age; or 3) they are "mysteries of the kingdom of heaven"—that is, they were used by Christ to describe deeper spiritual aspects about the millennial kingdom that had not yet been revealed.

If the parables present truths about the kingdom of heaven in this present age, they bring about a strange mixture of the church and the messianic kingdom reign. If the expressions "kingdom of heaven" and "kingdom of God" are always messianic descriptions, then they are prophecies of spiritual truths about this future state not before given. They were previously hidden "mysteries" (Matthew 13:11).

Some view the parables as representing the church age in an allegorical manner. Pentecost says, "We come to see that the time period covered by the parables in Matthew 13 extends from Israel's rejection until its future reception of the Messiah. Thus this new program begins while Christ was still on the earth, and it will extend until His return to the earth in power and great glory" (*Prophecy Knowledge Handbook*, p. 220).

That the parables are meant to reveal new truths concerning the messianic kingdom is held by Toussaint, Stallard, Couch, and others. Toussaint (*Behold the King*, p. 175) writes that this approach "states that the King is giving new revelation concerning the kingdom prom-

ised to the Jews. The truths relate to the time of the establishing of the kingdom, the preparation for it, and other such material which has never before been revealed."

Stallard ("Hermeneutics and Matthew 13, Part 2," p. 358) points out that one cannot escape the conclusion that the word "kingdom," in the context of the Gospels, always refers to the coming messianic reign. The parables are spiritually preparatory to the beginning of the kingdom and possibly are focusing on the Jews who turn to Christ during the Tribulation.

Couch (*Biblical Theology of the Church*, pp. 214-15) gives five reasons the parables of Matthew 13 are about the messianic kingdom: 1) In the context of the chapter [Matthew 13] and in the previous chapter, Jesus pronounces a judgment on the hardheartedness of the Pharisees and the Jewish people in general. 2) The expressions "kingdom of heaven" and "kingdom of God" are always used in reference to the messianic kingdom and are never applied to the church. 3) In Matthew 13, Christ is clearly speaking about the spiritual blindness and deafness of Israel, especially in His quoting of Isaiah 6:9-10. 4) Christ quotes Daniel 12:3 in Matthew 13:43, which is an obvious reference to the future Jewish millennial kingdom. And finally, 5) in more than one place the messianic expressions "the Son of Man" and "His kingdom" are used (verses 37-41).

The parable of the sower (13:3-9,18-23). When truth is spread as a farmer scatters seed, no one knows for sure what the crop will be like. Many do not understand the "word of the kingdom" (verse 19). Though some hear and rejoice, the rocky soil gives no firm footing for the truth. And when trials come "because of the word," the hearer "falls away" (verses 20-21).

The parable of the wheat and tares (13:24-30). After a landowner sows good wheat seeds in his field, an enemy comes at night and sows tares. As the seeds grow, the landowner and his servants can see the difference between the wheat and the tares but decide to wait until harvest time before separating the wheat from the tares and gathering the crops into barns (verse 30).

The parable of the mustard seed (13:31-32).

The seed of a mustard plant is as small as a grain of sand, but when the plant is fully grown, its branches and leaves are larger than those of most other plants. The kingdom of heaven is like a mustard seed: The truth about the kingdom starts so small that men pay little attention to it. But as the seed matures, or when the kingdom actually arrives, it will be all-pervasive and dominate everything.

The parable of the leaven (13:33). A little bit of leaven can cause an entire lump of dough to rise or swell up. Again, when the kingdom arrives, it will quickly dominate the whole earth.

The parable of the hidden treasure (13:44). The truth about the kingdom is precious. To the Jews and to all who love Christ, the glories of the kingdom should be a most valuable and consuming spiritual truth. The kingdom should be eagerly anticipated and prayed for.

The parable of the pearl of great price (13:45-46). This parable is similar to the parable of the hidden treasure. The kingdom of heaven is like a valuable pearl that compels a person to give up everything he has in order to possess the pearl.

The parable of the dragnet (13:47-50). This parable is similar to the parable of the wheat and tares. The kingdom of heaven is like a fishing net that sweeps into it both good and bad fish. At the end of the Tribulation, or at the beginning of the kingdom, the wicked will be removed from among the righteous (verse 49) and will be cast into the furnace of fire, where there is "weeping and gnashing of teeth" (verse 50).

The parable of the householder (13:51-52). Jesus said that every scribe of the kingdom of heaven, or every student of kingdom truth, will bring out of his storehouse (vault of safe-keeping) valuable things (treasures) that are both new and old. The new treasures are, at least in part, taught in these parables. And they were meant to be understood by the disciples (verse 11).

The parable of the lamp (Mark 4:21-25). A lamp is not to be hidden; it is not to be put under a basket. Nothing will remain hidden or kept secret; everything will be brought to light (verse 22). The messianic kingdom, then, should be shared and made understandable.

The parable of the growing seed (Mark 4:26-29). The kingdom of God is likened to the seed cast down that grows quickly overnight, and the sower does not know how it happens (verse 27). The growth begins with the blade, then the head, then the mature grain in the head (verse 28). Then it is time to use the sickle "because the harvest has come" (verse 29). In other words, events will develop quickly to bring the kingdom to pass.

Psalm 78:2 prophesied that Christ would speak in parables: "I will open My mouth in parables; I will utter things hidden since the foundation of the world" (Matthew 13:35). Strangely, parables were meant to keep the truth about the kingdom from mockers and even to blind them. Christ spoke in parables "in order that while seeing, they may see and not perceive; and while hearing, they may hear and not understand, otherwise they might return and be forgiven" (Mark 4:12; cf. Isaiah 6:9).

SHEEP WITHOUT A SHEPHERD
Matthew 9:35-38

JESUS WAS TRAVELING to all the cities and villages in Galilee, teaching and preaching "the gospel of the kingdom, and healing every kind of disease and every kind of sickness" (verse 35). Seeing the multitudes and their problems, He had great compassion for them. They were "distressed and dispirited like sheep without a shepherd" (verse 36). As the prophesied Messiah, He would Himself bear their griefs (Isaiah 53:4). Turning to the disciples, He said, "The harvest is plentiful, but the workers are few. Therefore beseech the Lord of the harvest to send out workers into His harvest" (Matthew 9:37-38).

Christ's work was reminiscent of what Moses did when he selected Joshua to lead the people of Israel so that they "will not be like sheep which have no shepherd" (Numbers 27:17-18). God castigates those false shepherds of Israel who do not feed the flock but instead feed themselves (Ezekiel 34:8). The Lord God is the true Shepherd of Israel (verses 11-31), and Christ took on that role when He walked among the Jews. In the future kingdom, God's servant David will be a prince among the people, and he will feed them and act as one of their shepherds (verses 23-24).

THE PROPHET PREDICTED BY MOSES
John 6:14-15

WHEN JESUS MULTIPLIED the fishes and the loaves (verses 1-13), the people were amazed. They saw His miracle as an indication that He was the great Prophet foretold by Moses to come into the world (verse 14). The crowds wanted to take Jesus by force and make Him king at that moment. Because their motives were wrong, the Lord "withdrew again to the mountain by Himself alone" (verse 15). Moses predicted the coming of the Prophet who would be one of their countrymen, and they were to listen to Him (Deuteronomy 18:15,18). When John the Baptist began his ministry, the crowds thought that he was that prophesied Prophet (John 1:21). The apostle Peter connected Moses' prediction about the Prophet to Christ (Acts 3:22), and he added that "every soul that does not heed that prophet shall be utterly destroyed from among the people" (verse 23).

THE PROPHECY AGAINST THE HYPOCRITES
Matthew 15:7-9

JESUS DEALT CONTINUALLY with the hypocritical religious leaders of Israel. The nouns hypocrisy (Greek, hupokrisis) and hypocrite (Greek, hupokritees) are mentioned by Him in the Gospels 23 times, especially with reference to those in the synagogues (Matthew 6:2) and those who were scribes and Pharisees (15:13-14). After answering these leaders about certain moral issues, the Lord accuses them of invalidating "the word of God for the sake

of your tradition" (15:6). It was prophesied in Isaiah 29:13 that when Christ came, there would be hypocrites who served God only with lip service (Matthew 15:7). "This people honors Me with their lips, but their heart is far away from Me. But in vain do they worship Me, teaching as doctrines the precepts of men" (verses 8-9). The disciples seemed concerned that the Lord had brought embarrassment to the Pharisees. They said, "Do You know that the Pharisees were offended when they heard this statement?" (verse 12). Jesus chided His disciples for "lacking in understanding" (verse 16) and not realizing that it is that which comes out of the mouth that defiles a man (verse 18). The Pharisees were duplicitous and hypocritical!

JESUS AND THE SYRO-PHOENICIAN WOMAN
Matthew 15:21-28

WHEN JESUS TRAVELED to the Gentile regions of Tyre and Sidon (verse 21), He encountered a Canaanite woman whose daughter was demonically controlled. The woman cried out, "Have mercy on me, Lord, Son of David; my daughter is cruelly demon-possessed" (verse 22). Frustrated, the disciples tried to stop the woman and urged Christ to send her away (verse 23). Testing her, the Lord said that He had come "only to the lost sheep of the house of Israel" (verse 24). At this the woman bowed down and begged, "Lord, help me!" (verse 25), with the result that the girl "was healed at once" (verse 28).

This amazing story reveals that many Gentiles believed that Jesus was the promised Messiah, the prophesied Son of David. In fact, Christ stated that this particular woman's faith was great, and He said to her, "it shall be done for you as you wish" (verse 28). Pious Jews and Gentiles had realized that the Son of David was the promised Messiah of Isaiah 53 and that one of the signs that He had arrived was His ability to heal. Using the prophetic present tense, Isaiah says in verse 4, "Surely our griefs He Himself bore, and our sorrows He carried."

Concerning such miraculous healings, Isaiah's words were quoted in Matthew 8:17 to show that Jesus was the prophesied Messiah.

JESUS PREDICTS THE CHURCH
Matthew 16:13-28

Jesus' greatest prediction was that He would build His church (Greek, *ekklesia,* "assembly"), and He made this announcement when He took His disciples to the remote Gentile region of Caesarea Philippi. Upon their arrival in northeastern Galilee, Jesus asked the disciples, "Who do men think I am?" Verse 14 shows that public opinion placed Him on the highest human pedestal possible by identifying Him with such national heroes as Elijah, Jeremiah, or even John the Baptist. But when Jesus asked the disciples who they thought He was, Peter responded, "You are the Christ, the Son of the living God" (verse 16).

Upon hearing Peter's confession, Jesus announced, "I will build My church" (verse 18). The Greek word used for "rock" (Greek, *petra*) is played against the name Peter (*petros*) in the original text. The Roman Catholic interpretation of this passage is that Peter was the foundation stone of the church, that he had a primacy among the apostles, that he became the bishop of Rome, and that his primacy was passed on to his successors, the popes. But the verse scarcely bears the first of these propositions, and certainly none of the others.

Protestant interpreters, with some support from the early church fathers (Chrysostom, Justin Martyr, and Augustine), have tended to identify the rock with Peter's faith or confession, or with our Lord Himself. The most straightforward interpretation seems to be that Jesus' reference to the "rock" alludes to Peter but indicates that Peter is not the exclusive foundation of the church. Paul said that the church was built on the foundation of the apostles and prophets (Ephesians 2:20; cf. Revelation 21:14). The words that Jesus spoke to Peter in Matthew 16:19 were addressed to all the disciples in Matthew 18:18. Therefore, the rock or foundation of the church is the confession (ultimately, the doctrine) of the apostles, which became normative for the church.

The word here translated "church" (Greek, *ekklesia*) means literally "a chosen or called out assembly." Thus the use of the word as a technical term for an assembly or group of believers in Christ is quite natural. Externally, it is not viewed as an organization, denomination, or hierarchical system. The New Testament church, therefore, is a congregation or assembly of believers, which is a "church" in and of itself. This is the first occurrence of the word in the New Testament, and it is used in prophetic anticipation.

Jesus' prediction, "I will build," could be translated, "I shall continue to build" (progressive future tense). Since the commission in Matthew 10 sent the apostles only to the "house of Israel," and no further commission was given until chapter 28, there was no worldwide task for the disciples until the physical manifestation of the church at Pentecost.

Jesus promised that the "gates of hell would not prevail" against the church (assembly). Some have viewed this as the inability of hell to overpower the church and see the church as being on the defensive against Satan. However, the phrase "shall not prevail" may be understood as meaning "shall not stand against." The imagery would then picture the church being on the attack against the gates of hell. Here, hell (Greek, *hades*) probably represents the kingdom of Satan, not just death and the grave. While Jesus' resurrection certainly will overcome the sting of death, it will also enable His church to aggressively and offensively attack the gates of hell by snatching victims out of the darkness and into His glorious kingdom of light. One does not attack with gates; he defends. The church is on the attack, and hell is on the defensive.

Our Lord then promised to Peter and the other apostles "the keys of the kingdom." This means that Peter would have the right to enter the kingdom himself and would have general authority therein, symbolized by the possession of the "keys," and preaching the gospel would be the means of opening the kingdom of heaven to all believers and closing it to unbelievers. The book of Acts shows us this process at work. With his sermon on the day of Pentecost (Acts 2:14-40), Peter opened the door of the kingdom for the first time. The expressions *bind* and *loose* were common Jewish legal phrases that meant to declare forbidden or to declare allowed. Peter and the other disciples (see 18:18) were to continue on earth the Word of Christ in preaching the gospel and declaring God's will to men, and they were armed with the same authority He Himself possessed. Christ in heaven ratifies what is done in His name and in obedience to His Word on earth.

The original Greek text literally reads, "I will [future tense] give you the keys of the kingdom of heaven; and whatever you should bind [aorist, active, subjunctive] on earth shall itself have been bound [perfect, passive, participle] in heaven, and whatever you should loose [aorist, active, subjunctive] on earth shall itself have been loosed [perfect, passive, participle] in heaven" (Couch, *Biblical Theology of the Church*, pp. 203-04).

By the use of two perfect, passive participles, the Lord seems to be saying that what Peter does here on earth is but following through with what God has already determined in heaven. "These were decisions Peter was to implement as he received instruction from heaven, for the binding and loosing occurred there first. Peter simply carried out God's directions" (Barbieri, "Matthew," *Bible Knowledge Commentary*, p. 58). The principle of the binding and loosening is found in Isaiah 22:20-23.

After Peter's confession that Christ was the Son of God, the Lord began to share with him and the other disciples that He would die and rise again after three days (Mark 8:31). But Peter rebuked the Lord after taking Him aside (verse 32). Christ turned to the other disciples and showed them that Peter's rebuke was actually coming from Satan: "Get behind Me, Satan; for you are not setting your mind on God's interests, but man's" (verse 33). Jesus then warned them to tell no one that He was "the Christ of God" (Luke 9:20)—probably

because He did not want anyone to view Him as a conquering hero, which is not the reason for His first coming.

THE PREVIEW OF THE KINGDOM OF GOD
Matthew 16:27-28; Mark 8:38–9:1; Luke 9:26-27

When Christ returns as the Messiah, the Son of Man (Daniel 7:13), He will call to account how each person responded to the truth while on earth. "What will a man give in exchange for his soul?" (Matthew 16:26). When Jesus comes back to reign "in the glory of His Father with His angels," He will serve judgment and "repay every man according to his deeds" as people enter the millennial kingdom (verse 27; 24:40-51; Psalm 62:12). The "glory" Jesus spoke of was about to be shown to some of the disciples at that time. They would "not taste death until they see the Son of Man coming in His kingdom" (verse 28). Here the Lord was referring to His transfiguration (17:1-9; Mark 8:38–9:1; Luke 9:26-27). All three of the synoptic Gospels tell of the dramatic transfiguration happening immediately following this prediction by the King and the revelation of His kingdom. Peter, James, and John were the ones who saw this preview of the coming kingdom glory.

THE TRANSFIGURATION OF CHRIST
Matthew 17:1-8; Mark 9:2-8; Luke 9:28-36

Peter, James, and John were the ones who would see "the Son of Man coming in His kingdom" (16:28), a revelation event that took place in 17:1-8. In verse 2, the word "transfigured" is the Greek term *metamorphoomai,* which means to be changed in form, or in the case of Christ, to be glorified. Christ's face "shone like the sun, and His garments became as white as light" (verse 2). He was seen by the three apostles in His kingdom brilliance, and with Jesus were Moses and Elijah, talking with Him (verse 3). They were discussing with Christ what was about to happen to Him when He departed for Jerusalem for the final time (Luke 9:31). Impetuous Peter wanted to make three tabernacles (tents)—one for Jesus and one each for Moses and Elijah (Matthew 17:4). The disciples then could bask in the light of the kingdom blessing with Christ and these respected prophets of the Old Testament.

Why Moses and Elijah? Moses was the great leader through whom God brought the covenant of the law, and Elijah is to be the herald who announces Christ's coming to establish His kingdom reign (Malachi 4:4-5). The voice of God the Father (Mark 9:7) was again heard from heaven, saying, "This is My beloved Son, with whom I am well-pleased; listen to Him!" (Matthew 17:5; cf. 3:17; Psalm 2:7). The disciples fell on their faces (Matthew 17:6) and had to be lifted from the ground by the Lord (verse 7). Looking around, the disciples no longer saw Moses and Elijah. This event brought confirmation to these leading apostles that one day, Christ will come to earth in full glory to reign and rule!

In a spiritual sense, the word "transfigured" is used to describe the transformation that takes place "by the renewing" of the believer's mind in order to prove in his life the will of God (Romans 12:2). It is also used to describe how, by the glory of the Lord, believers "are being transformed into the same image [of Him] from glory to glory, just as from the Lord, the Spirit" (2 Corinthians 3:18).

ELIJAH WILL HERALD THE COMING OF CHRIST
Matthew 17:9-13; Mark 9:9-13

MORE THAN ONCE the Gospels mention that Elijah the prophet will herald the coming of the messianic king (Matthew 11:14; 17:11; 16:14; cf. Malachi 4:4-5). "Elijah is coming and will restore all things"—meaning the theocratic kingdom, with the millennial reign, to the nation of Israel (Matthew 17:11; Mark 9:12).

But Christ adds that "Elijah already came," referring to the ministry and message of John the Baptist (verse 12; cf. Isaiah 40:3; Malachi 3:1-3). Did the Lord mean that John the Baptist had replaced Elijah and that Elijah would no longer come?

John the Baptist came as the forerunner of Christ for His first coming. John came in "the spirit and power of Elijah" to prepare the way of the Lord's first coming (Luke 1:17). And Elijah will herald Christ's second appearance as Israel's king. The Jews did not recognize the spiritual work of John as being in the likeness of Elijah's future work. Instead, the Jewish people rejected John and did to him "whatever they wished." "So also the Son of Man is going to suffer at their hands" (Matthew 17:12). When Jesus said this, the "disciples understood that He had spoken to them about John the Baptist" (verse 13). The description of the two witnesses in Revelation 11:1-13 indicates they are probably Moses and Elijah, the same two witnesses who appeared at the transfiguration.

PROPHECY OF CHRIST'S DEATH AND RESURRECTION
Matthew 17:22-23; Mark 9:30-32; Luke 9:43-45

TOWARD THE END of His ministry the Lord spoke more and more of His coming suffering and death (Matthew 17:12), and in these passages, He speaks more specifically as to what is about to happen (verses 22-23). At the end of His discussion about the coming of Elijah (verses 9-12), He tells all His disciples that "the Son of Man is going to be delivered into the hands of men; and they will kill Him, and He will be raised on the third day." With this announcement, the disciples "were deeply grieved" (verses 22-23), though in another sense they did not fully understand His words and "were afraid to ask Him" (Mark 9:32). In the wise providence of God, the comprehension of this fact "was concealed from them so that they would not perceive it" (Luke 9:45). Even when He mentions His death again to the disciples in the Upper Room Discourse (John 16:16-19), they said, "We do not know what He is talking about" (verse 18). Only after Jesus' resurrection did the disciples begin to put it all together. And some had to have their eyes opened progressively as He came to them in His resurrection body (Luke 24:13-35).

CHRIST, THE SEED OF DAVID
John 7:37-44

ON THE LAST DAY OF THE Feast of Tabernacles (or Booths), Christ cried out, "If anyone is thirsty, let him come to Me and drink" (verse 37). On this seventh and final day of the festival, a priest came down from the temple to the pool of Gihon and filled a gold pitcher with water while the temple choir sang (see Isaiah 12:3). The ritual reminded the people of the water God brought forth from the rock when Israel was in the desert (Numbers 20:8-11; Psalm 78:15-16). It also spoke prophetically of the coming time of the Messiah (cf. Zechariah 14:8,16-19).

Jesus said of those who trust Him that "from his innermost being shall flow rivers of living water" (John 7:38). Here Jesus was speaking about the Holy Spirit, "whom those who believed in Him were to receive; for the Spirit was not yet given, because Jesus was not yet glorified" (verse 39). The water Jesus spoke of represented the cleansing work of the Spirit. Christ told His disciples following His ascension, "John baptized with water, but you shall be baptized with the Holy Spirit not many days from now" (Acts 1:5). Speaking of the Scripture, Jesus could have been referring to Psalm 78:15-16; Zechariah 14:8 (cf. Ezekiel 47:1-11; Revelation 22:1-2). The argument continued as to whether Jesus was "the Prophet" spoken of by Moses (John 1:21; 7:40; cf. Deuteronomy 18:15,18) or the prophesied Christ (John 7:41). He was both! Some questioned, "Surely the Christ is not going to come from Galilee, is He?"

Many rightly asked whether the Messiah would be the offspring of King David and

come "from Bethlehem, the village where David was?" (verse 42). In their endeavor to discern Jesus' identity, they were putting together the many prophecies about David's son. The offspring of David, through Solomon, would be the Messiah (2 Samuel 7:12), and His birthplace would be Bethlehem (Micah 5:2). That Jesus was this one was fully confirmed by the angel Michael when Mary was told, "He will be great and will be called the Son of the Most High, and the Lord God will give Him the throne of His father David" (Luke 1:32).

JESUS IS THE I AM
John 8:51-59

JESUS' CLAIMS TO BE THE MESSIAH were really getting to the Jewish religious leaders! They began character assassination by suggesting He had a demon (verses 48-49). He responded that "if anyone keeps My word he will never see death" (verse 51). Not understanding that Jesus was speaking of spiritual eternal life rather than physical life, the leaders said Jesus must have a demon because Abraham and the prophets had died, which made it impossible for Jesus to say, "If anyone keeps My word, he will never taste of death" (verse 52). The leaders then said Christ couldn't be greater than Abraham and the prophets (verse 53).

Jesus replied that it would be God the Father who would glorify Him (verse 54) and told the Jews He was speaking with that they did not know God the Father (verse 55). Coming back to the issue of Abraham, He added that the Jewish patriarch "rejoiced to see My day, and he saw it and was glad" (verse 56). Writing about Abraham and other great men of the Old Testament, the author of Hebrews said that they received the promises of God, "having welcomed them from a distance, and having confessed that they were strangers and exiles on the earth" (Hebrews 11:13).

When the Lord said Abraham rejoiced to see His day, the Jews responded in anger: "You are not yet fifty years old, and have You seen Abraham?" (John 8:57). Jesus then gave a powerful confirmation of His deity. He quoted Exodus 3:14, where God told Moses, "I AM WHO I AM…I AM has sent" Moses to the children of Israel to deliver them from Egypt. Using this verse, Jesus said to the Jews, "Truly, truly, I say to you, before Abraham was born, I am" (John 8:58). The Jews got the point; they knew Jesus was claiming to be God and picked up stones to "throw at Him." Christ then hid from them "and went out of the temple" (verse 59). This, along with many other passages, confirms Christ's deity (cf. 5:17; 10:30).

CHRIST, THE GOOD SHEPHERD
John 10:1-21

WITH THE PHARISEES IN MIND, Jesus talked about the thief and the robber who enter the sheep door to harm or steal the sheep (verses 1-2,8). But the sheep hear the voice of their shepherd, "and he calls his own sheep by name and leads them out" (verse 3). The true sheep will not follow the stranger but will flee from him (verse 5). "The thief comes only to steal and kill and destroy; I came that they might have life, and have it abundantly" (verse 10). In another analogy that also communicates care and protection, Christ said He is "the door; if anyone enters through Me, he shall be saved, and will go in and out and find pasture" (verse 9).

Like the legalistic Pharisees, the hireling "is not concerned about the sheep" (verse 13). He will allow the wolf to come in and snatch, destroy, and scatter the flock (verse 12). But Christ said of Himself, "I am the good shepherd, and I know My own and My own know Me" (verse 14). In an intimate relation, the Father knows His Son, and the Son knows His Father. The Father loves the Son because He lays down His life "that I may take it again" (verses 15,17). Christ has the very attribute of the Creator; He has the power of life and can lay down His life on His own initiative. "I have authority to lay

it down, and I have authority to take it up again" (verse 18).

As Christ spoke of Himself as the good Shepherd, He referred to the fact that God is the Shepherd over His flock, the Jews, according to Ezekiel 34. The Lord said, "I will 'search for My sheep and seek them out'" (verse 11) and restore those who are scattered (verse 12). When the Lord brought Israel out of Egypt, "He led forth His own people like sheep and guided them in the wilderness like a flock" (Psalm 78:52). Christ is the Great Shepherd (Hebrews 13:20-21) who arose from the dead to care for His sheep. As the Chief Shepherd, (1 Peter 5:4), He will return again to regather His sheep.

THE SON OF GOD IS RELATED TO GOD THE FATHER
John 10:22-39

DURING THE FEAST OF DEDICATION (or of Lights, or Hanukkah), the Lord was in Jerusalem walking in the portico of Solomon in the temple (verse 23). This feast dedicates and commemorates the cleansing and reopening of the temple after its spiritual desecration by the Syrian ruler Antiochus Epiphanes in 168 B.C. (Daniel 11:31; 1 Maccabees 4:52-59). The Jews confronted Jesus and said, "How long will You keep us in suspense? If You are the Christ, tell us plainly" (John 10:24). Jesus reminded them that He had already told them the truth, and if they did not believe Him, they should believe the works that He did in His Father's name (verse 25). Those works bore witness to who He was. Those who did not believe Jesus were not His sheep and thus didn't follow Him (verse 26). His own sheep, however, knew His voice and followed Him (verse 27), and to them He gave eternal life. These "will never perish; and no one will snatch them out of My hand" (verse 28), nor can they be snatched out of the Father's hand (verse 29) because "I and the Father are one" (verse 30).

The Jews picked up stones to kill Jesus (verse 31) because He had made Himself "out to be God" (verse 33). In response, Christ quoted Psalm 82:6, where God said, "You are gods" (verse 33). Psalm 82 refers to Israel's unscrupulous judges, who showed partiality (verses 1-2). They had no spiritual understanding (verse 5), and the Lord called them "gods" (Hebrew, *elohim*) only in the sense that they had high authority and responsibility (verse 6). Christ quoted Psalm 82 to make a point of going from the lesser to the greater. If God the Father could call the judges of Israel *elohim,* why did the Jews standing before Him have trouble calling Him "the Son of God" (John 10:36)? After all, He was doing the very same works as the Father, and He said that "the Father is in Me, and I in the Father" (verses 37-38).

The Jews were so blinded by hatred for Jesus that they could not understand spiritually or intellectually what He was saying. Jesus had to go away again because they attempted to seize Him. "He eluded their grasp" (verse 39).

THE BLESSINGS AND CURSES OF THE KINGDOM
Luke 13:22-35

To BE SAVED IS TO ENTER a narrow door (verses 23-24). In the same way, there will be a narrow entrance for those who enter the millennial kingdom. The Lord will say to many that He did not know where they were from (verse 25). They will claim to have drunk in the Lord's presence and taught in His streets (verse 26), yet He will say to them, "I do not know where you are from; depart from Me, all you evildoers" (verse 27, cf. Psalm 6:8). When the pretenders see "Abraham and Isaac and Jacob and all the prophets in the kingdom of God," there will be weeping and gnashing of teeth because they are outside the kingdom (verse 28).

Gentiles from the east, the west, the north, and the south will enter the millennial kingdom (verse 29). As if overlooking what Jesus had just said, the Pharisees came up and warned Him to flee because Herod Antipas was trying to kill Him, as he had John the Baptist (verse 31). In reply, the Lord said He would not stop ministering until He had reached His goal (verse 32), which was to carry on to Jerusalem (verse 33). The infamous heritage of this city was that it had killed many prophets, but the Lord was more than a mere prophet. He wanted to gather the inhabitants of the city as a hen gathers her brood, but they would not have it (verse 34).

When Christ made His final appearance in Jerusalem just before His arrest and crucifixion, the Jews who believed in Him gave a messianic welcome (19:38) and quoted Psalm 118:26-27. Their hopes that Christ would establish His kingdom were premature, and their expectations were dashed when the Lord went to the cross. But in Luke 13:35, Jesus quoted Psalm 118 and said to those standing around and listening, "Behold, your house is left to you desolate; and I say to you, you will not see Me until the time comes when you say, 'Blessed is he who comes in the name of the Lord!'" The reality of Christ's entering Jerusalem as the Davidic king and reigning as Israel's monarch is yet future. The "house left desolate" refers to that generation of Jews who had rejected the Lord and were about to be judged.

JESUS RAISES LAZARUS FROM THE DEAD
John 11:1-44

When Christ, who was in Jerusalem, heard that His friend Lazarus was sick, He tarried two more days before going to Bethany, where Mary, Martha, and their brother Lazarus lived (verse 6). When Jesus told His disciples that Lazarus was only sleeping and must be awakened, they thought He meant Lazarus had simply fallen asleep (verses 11-12), though He was speaking of the fact that Lazarus had died (verse 13). When Jesus arrived, the sisters said Jesus could have made Lazarus better if He had arrived earlier (verse 21), though they also realized that Jesus could receive any request He made of His heavenly Father (verse 22).

Getting straight to the point, Jesus told Martha, "Your brother will rise again" (verse

23). She agreed, though she was thinking of the future prophesied resurrection that will take place "on the last day" (verse 24). Jesus took this moment to tell Martha that He had the power of resurrection and of life itself: "I am the resurrection and the life; he who believes in Me will live even if he dies, and everyone who lives and believes in Me will never die. Do you believe this?" (verses 25-26). Martha realized by these words that Jesus was the promised Anointed One, "Christ, the Son of God, even He who comes into the world" (verse 27; cf. Psalm 2:2). By her response, she was admitting the Messiah would have power over life and death.

With the stone removed from Lazarus's tomb, Jesus reminded Martha that as a believer she would see the glory of God in what was about to happen (John 11:40) even though Lazarus had been in the grave for four days (verse 39). Jesus thanked the heavenly Father that He had heard His Son's request (verse 41) and prayed that the people standing around would believe "that You sent Me" (verse 42). With a loud voice Jesus cried out, "Lazarus, come forth" (verse 43), which Lazarus did while still bound in grave cloths (verse 44). Though the raising of Lazarus was a kind of prototype and a rehearsal of the final resurrection for all believers, Lazarus still possessed his natural body and eventually died again. Some skeptics have alleged that Lazarus's resurrection was actually nothing more than a resuscitation.

The promise of the future resurrection of believers is given in many Old Testament passages (Job 19:25-27; Ezekiel 37:9-14; Daniel 12:2-3), and it is a promise that gives us assurance for today.

CAIAPHAS'S PROPHECY
John 11:45-54

THOUGH MANY JEWS came to believe in Christ through the raising of Lazarus (verse 45), many others went away and reported this incident to the Pharisees (verse 46). A council followed in which the chief priests and Pharisees asked, "What are we doing? For this man is performing many signs" (verse 47). In other words, we must stop Him from doing these miracles; otherwise, we are in trouble! For "if we let Him go on like this, all men will believe in Him, and the Romans will come and take away both our place and our nation" (verse 48). One would think the Jewish religious leaders would be rejoicing over Christ's works, but this was not the case!

The high priest for that year, Caiaphas, chided the leaders for not understanding what was happening: "You know nothing at all" (verse 49). In other words, "You are not getting it!" Unwittingly, and probably unknowingly, Caiaphas then reached back and quoted Isaiah 53:8, where the death of the Messiah was prophesied: "that one man should die for the people, and not that the whole nation should perish" (John 11:50 NKJV). In His arrests and trials, Christ would come before Caiaphas (18:14). One would think this man would have recalled his statement to the Jewish leaders and his reference to the Old Testament messianic prophecies, but apparently that didn't happen.

When Caiaphas uttered this statement, he did so not "on his own initiative, but being high priest that year, he prophesied that Jesus was going to die for the nation" (verse 51).

As the high priest, Caiaphas pointed to the last sacrificial Lamb in a prophecy he did not even know he made. Caiaphas meant Jesus had to be killed, but God intended the priest's words as a reference to His substitutionary atonement. Jesus' death would abolish the old system in God's eyes by fulfilling all its types and shadows. His death was not only for Jews but also for the world (Blum, "John," *Bible Knowledge Commentary,* p. 315).

PROPHECY OF CHRIST'S RETURN AND JUDGMENT
Luke 17:22-37

THE JEWISH PEOPLE in Christ's day would not see God's kingdom with signs that were observable (verse 20) because it was already in their midst (verse 21). The king was in their presence, but they didn't recognize Him. Some translations of the Bible, such as the KJV, say the kingdom "is within you," but the Greek phrase *entos umon* is a present participle with a personal plural pronoun, and it should read that the kingdom "is existing in the midst of all of you." That the kingdom of God was postponed because of the people's unbelief, and that the kingdom is not the church, seem clear from verse 22. Christ established the fact that the disciples would long to see "just one" of the days of the Son of Man (Daniel 7:13), or the earthly messianic reign, but they will not see it in their own generation.

When the messianic kingdom comes, it will arrive suddenly (Luke 17:24). But before that happens, the Lord "must suffer many things and be rejected by this generation" (verse 25). In the days of Noah, the people on earth lived without regard for impending judgment, and "the flood came and destroyed them all" (verses 26-27). The same happened in the days of Lot to the city of Sodom: "It rained fire and brimstone from heaven and destroyed them all" (verses 28-29). So it will happen when the Son of Man, the Messiah, arrives (verse 30). Those reading Christ's words need to take heed and flee (verse 31) and "remember Lot's wife" (verse 32), who turned into a pillar of salt (Genesis 19:26).

When the Lord returns to earth to establish His Davidic rule, some will be ready and others won't. While some view this as a reference to the rapture, when one will be removed while the other is left, the context does not appear to have the rapture in mind. Some will be taken before the Lord and judged—like one taken from bed and the other left (verse 34), or one taken from the grinding at the mill with the other left (verse 35), or one removed from the field and the other left (verse 36). The disciples asked where the people were taken. His answer: To judgment! "Where the body is, there also will the vultures be gathered"—meaning they will be taken away and destroyed for their disbelief that He is coming back (verse 37). This is repeated in Matthew 24:29–25:46. The Son of Man will return to reign on His "glorious throne" (25:31). He will come at an hour not expected (24:44) and remove the faithless slave who was not looking for his master to come back at that time (verse 45-51). The doubters will be killed, and "weeping shall be there and the gnashing of teeth" (verse 51). This story has a special application to a future generation of Jews who will not be anticipating the coming of their promised Messiah.

CHRIST WILL AVENGE HIS ELECT AT HIS COMING
Luke 18:1-14

As JESUS AND THE DISCIPLES were journeying toward Jerusalem for the last time, He urged them "to pray and not to lose heart" (verse 1). He told them the story of the oppressed widow who went to a judge for protection (verses 2-5). The judge granted her request because she was so persistent (verse 5). God will do more for those who are His children. He will "bring about justice for His elect, who cry to Him day and night, and will He delay long over them?" (verse 7). When the King comes, He will "bring about justice for them quickly. However, when the Son of Man comes, will He find faith on the earth?" (verse 8). "Speedily" is the Greek word *tachei,* which means "in a hasty way or manner, with rapidity of execution." Jesus' arrival will not be immediate, but when it takes place, it will happen quickly as He comes with haste from heaven.

To "find faith on the earth" refers to finding people who have trusted in God, have believed in His promises, and are righteous in heart. To illustrate this, Jesus tells the story of the Pharisee and the tax-gatherer who go up to the temple to pray (verses 9-14). The Pharisee trusted in his good works (verse 9), but the tax-gatherer, who knew he had sinned, cried to God to "be merciful to me, the sinner!" (verse 13). Jesus then asked His listeners which man went home "justified," or "legally acquitted" (Greek, *dikaioo*) before God. The Pharisees should have caught on as to what Jesus meant by justification. Isaiah had prophesied that the

Messiah would "justify the many" (53:11). The tax-gatherer was justified because "everyone who exalts himself shall be humbled, but he who humbles himself shall be exalted" (Luke 18:14). In the Tribulation period, only those who trust the Lord will be welcomed into the millennial kingdom by the Son of Man.

THE KINGDOM OF GOD REQUIRES SIMPLE FAITH
Matthew 19:13-15;
Mark 10:13-16; Luke 18:15-17

GOD REQUIRES FAITH AND TRUST from those who want to enter the kingdom of heaven. They must have a sincere trust, like that of a small child (Matthew 19:14). The kingdom of heaven "belongs to such as these."

When children were brought to Christ, they "rebuked them" (Mark 10:13). Jesus was indignant with the disciples' rebuff (verse 14) and said, "Whoever does not receive the kingdom of God like a child will not enter it at all" (verse 15; Luke 18:17). "Christ is not saying that children are the only ones who inherit the kingdom, but He is saying that childlike trust and humility are essential for entrance…. [Matthew] uses the character of children to sharply contrast the distinction between their faith and humility and Israel's unbelief and blindness" (Toussaint, *Behold the King*, pp. 225-26).

ENTERING THE KINGDOM OF GOD
Matthew 19:16–20:16; Mark 10:17-31; Luke 18:18-30

CONTRARY TO WHAT MANY of the Jews in Jesus' day thought, obtaining eternal life is not about keeping the law (Matthew 19:16-20). To enter the kingdom of heaven requires faith, and that faith can be tested to ascertain if it is genuine. Here, Jesus says that giving up all and following Him shows where our heart is (verse 21). And we also see that riches can

keep a person from true faith-commitment (verses 23-24).

Those who follow Christ will sit with Him on His glorious messianic throne in the kingdom, even "judging the twelve tribes of Israel" (verse 28). True faith made them leave all, even family, to follow Him. Their reward will be eternal life (verse 29). Those willing to give up everything were willing on this earth to be last. In the kingdom, "the last shall be first, and the first last" (20:16). In telling people to give up everything, Christ was not speaking about a form of "works salvation." Rather, He was saying that the true faith within them would be evident in their actions.

Peter was not complaining but simply stating a fact when he said to the Lord, "Behold, we have left our own homes and followed You" (Luke 18:28). Jesus answered, "Truly I say to you, there is no one who has left house or wife or brothers or parents or children, for the sake of the kingdom of God, who will not receive many times as much at this time and in the age to come, eternal life" (verses 29-30).

CHRIST PREDICTS HIS RESURRECTION
Matthew 20:17-19;
Mark 10:32-34; Luke 18:31-34

AS JESUS AND THE DISCIPLES approached Jerusalem, the Lord told His disciples what was coming. The Son of Man would "be delivered up to the chief priests and scribes, and they will condemn Him to death" (Matthew 20:18). The Gentiles—meaning the Roman authorities—would mistreat Him "and crucify Him, and on the third day He will be raised up" (verse 19). Many of these events had been written by the prophets but were now about to be fulfilled (Luke 18:31). Though the disciples heard Jesus' words, they "understood none of these things, and the meaning of this statement was hidden from them, and they did not comprehend the things that were said" (verse 34).

The great prophecy of Psalm 16:9-10 about the Lord's resurrection is not alluded to, or mentioned by the disciples, until after His ascension. Then Peter expounds on it in detail before the great crowd of Jews gathered for Pentecost (Acts 2:22-36). Peter said the Christ "was neither abandoned to Hades [the grave], nor did His flesh suffer decay. This Jesus God raised up again, to which we are all witnesses" (verses 31-32; cf. Psalm 16:10).

THE KINGDOM AND SELFISH AMBITION
Matthew 20:20-28; Mark 10:35-45

THE MOTHER OF THE DISCIPLES James and John (the sons of Zebedee, Matthew 4:21) came to Christ and virtually commanded Him to place her two sons at the right and left sides of His kingdom throne (20:20-21). He asked them if they were able to drink the cup that He was about to drink (meaning His death), and they answered, "We are able" (verse 22). The Lord then explained that the cup of sorrow He was about to drink was not His to give, but it is prepared by the heavenly Father (verse 23). Likewise, when it came to reigning with Jesus, that was the Father's choice "for those for whom it has been prepared" (Mark 10:40). He further said that whoever wished to become great had to first become a servant (Matthew 20:26). In the same way, "the Son of Man did not come to be served, but to serve, and to give His life a ransom for many" (verse 28; Mark 10:45).

This conversation shows that the earthly millennial kingdom is not simply a political kingdom, but one that is driven by spiritual qualities. Trust, humility, and servitude will characterize this kingdom. And just as we are to serve Christ faithfully during the church age, so we are to serve Him faithfully in the future age.

JESUS AND ZACCHEUS
Luke 19:1-28

CHRIST'S FIRST COMING WAS for the purpose of dying for the sins of the world. Not until His second coming will He reign on the earthly throne of David.

While passing through Jericho, Jesus told inquisitive Zaccheus, who had climbed a sycamore tree to better see Him (verse 4), "Zaccheus, hurry and come down, for today I must stay at your house" (verse 5). Jesus then explained, "Today salvation has come to this house, because he, too [Zaccheus], is a son of Abraham. For the Son of Man has come to seek and to save that which was lost" (verses 9-10). The Son of Man is a kingly title also found in Daniel 7:13. His work of salvation fulfilled the prophecy of the Suffering Servant, the Righteous One, of Isaiah 53:11, which says He will bring salvation and justification to many.

JESUS' TRIUMPHAL ENTRY INTO JERUSALEM
Matthew 21:1-11,14-17; Mark 11:1-11; Luke 19:29-44; John 12:12-19

ENTERING JERUSALEM FOR HIS final week on earth, the Lord ordered the disciples to bring to Him a donkey with her colt, saying, "The Lord has need of them" (Matthew 21:3). This fulfilled the words of Zechariah 9:9: "Say to the daughter of Zion, behold your king is coming to you, gentle, and mounted on a donkey, even on a colt, the foal of a beast of burden" (Matthew 21:5). When the crowds announced that Christ was coming, many spread their garments and tree branch cuttings on the road (verse 8). This was a symbolic gesture indicating that the people wanted to make the king's ride more comfortable on the rough highway. The multitudes cried out to Jesus the song of greeting of the son of David from Psalm 118:26: "Hosanna to the Son of David;

blessed is He who comes in the name of the Lord; Hosanna in the highest!" (Matthew 21:9). The Hebrew word *hosanna* means "save now!" Mark adds to their greeting, "Blessed is the coming kingdom of our father David; Hosanna in the highest!" (11:10).

This greeting seems to confirm that many in Israel believed that Jesus was the Messiah prophesied in the Old Testament. The crowd was made up of pilgrims who had come to Jerusalem from other regions, including the northern part of Israel, where the Lord was accepted and believed to be the Messiah. The Jews in the city of Jerusalem, as a whole, were not believers. When Christ entered the city, the population "was stirred, saying, 'Who is this?'" (verse 10). The multitudes who were coming into the city for Passover answered, "This is the prophet Jesus, from Nazareth in Galilee" (verse 11). Some of the Pharisees tried to silence Christ's followers, but He declared, "I tell you, if these become silent, the stones will cry out!" (Luke 19:40). With this the Lord began to weep because the truth of who He was had been hidden from the eyes of many of the people (verse 42), and judgment was certain to come (verse 43). Jesus added, "You did not recognize the time of your visitation" (verse 44).

After entering Jerusalem and visiting the temple, Jesus looked around and "left for Bethany with the twelve, since it was already late" (Mark 11:11). Bethany was only a few miles away by foot on the southwest side of the Mount of Olives.

PROPHECIES OF CHRIST'S IMPENDING DEATH
John 12:20-50

CHRIST MADE IT CLEAR to His disciples that His time was coming. His death would result in His glorification: "The hour has come for the Son of Man to be glorified" (verse 23). By this Jesus meant that after His crucifixion and resurrection, He would ascend to heaven, where He would enter the throne room of the heavenly Father and be introduced as "the Son

of Man" (Daniel 7:13), meaning, "the Son who is related to mankind." This would result in His glorification, in which He would be given all "dominion, glory and a kingdom, that all the peoples, nations and men of every language might serve Him" (verse 14).

By His death "judgment is upon this world," and the ruler of this world (Satan) "will be cast out" (John 12:31). By His death He would draw all men to Himself (verse 32), meaning that He would die a humiliating death, for this is how the people perceived it (verse 33). The crowds who heard Jesus speak knew more about the coming of the Messiah than imagined. They said, "We have heard out of the Law that the Christ [the Anointed] is to remain forever; and how can You say, 'The Son of Man must be lifted up?' Who is this Son of Man?" (verse 34). The eternality of the Messiah is mentioned in Psalm 110:4, Isaiah 9:6, and Micah 5:2.

Regardless of what the Lord said, many of the people refused to believe in Him (John 12:37). This fulfilled the prophecy of Isaiah 53:1: "Who has believed our report? And to whom has the arm of the Lord been revealed?" (John 12:38). Those who did not believe did so because of the judicial blindness God had placed on the nation. In Isaiah 6:10 it is prophesied that the Lord "has blinded their eyes, and He hardened their heart; so that they would not see with their eyes and perceive with their heart, and be converted and I heal them" (John 12:39). To show that the rebellion of the Jews had to do with their rejection of God, Christ said, "He who believes in Me does not believe in Me but in Him who sent Me" (John 12:44).

THE FINAL REJECTION OF CHRIST BY ISRAEL'S LEADERS
Matthew 21:23–22:14; Mark 11:27–12:12; Luke 20:1-19

AS JESUS CAME INTO THE TEMPLE during the Passover season, the chief priests and the elders asked Him where He received His authority for the things He did (Matthew 21:23). The Lord asked in return where John the Baptist got his authority. This put the Jewish leaders in a difficult spot. If they said John the Baptist got his authority from heaven, then Jesus would ask, "Why do you not believe him?" (see verse 25). If they said he got it from men, the people would react against them because the crowds believed John was a prophet (verse 26). Realizing they were stumped, the leaders simply answered, "We do not know" (Mark 11:33). Those who claim they serve God as a son but in reality do not are not doing the will of the Father (Matthew 21:30), but those who respond to the Lord, such as humble tax-gatherers and harlots, will enter the future kingdom of God (verse 31). John came in the "way of righteousness," and yet the leaders did not believe him, but the lowliest of people did (verse 32).

By way of explanation, Jesus told a parable about a landowner who sent his servants to harvest his vineyard, but the vine-growers drove them out, even killing some (verses 33-36). When the landowner sent his son, thinking the vine-growers would respect him, the vine-growers said, "This is the heir; come, let us kill him and seize his inheritance" (verse 38). Jesus then warns that the owner of the vineyard will exact vengeance on those who killed his son (verses 40-41). Quoting Psalm 118:22, Christ said, referring to Himself, "The stone which the builders rejected, this became the chief corner stone; this came about from the Lord, and it is marvelous in our eyes" (Matthew 21:42). This prophecy is quoted elsewhere in the Gospels (Mark 12:10; Luke 20:17) and by other New Testament writers (Acts 4:11; Romans 9:33; 1 Peter 2:7). Those who fall on the stone "will be broken to pieces" (Matthew 21:44), and the Jewish leaders understood that Christ was speaking of them (verse 45).

Jesus added to this that "the kingdom of God will be taken away from you and given to a people, producing the fruit of it" (verse 43). Some believe the word "nation" (Greek, *ethnos*) refers to the church, but biblically, *nation* is never used to describe the church age. Rather, it is a reference to a future generation or nation of Jews who will be granted the blessings of the kingdom. When the Jewish leaders "sought to seize [Jesus], they feared the people, because they considered Him to be a prophet" (verse 46). So "they left Him and went away" (Mark 12:12). From a human standpoint, Jesus' fate was sealed!

Jesus then told another similar parable about the kingdom of heaven. A king prepares a wedding feast for his son (22:1-14). No one comes; in fact, some of the invited guests even kill the servants who bid them to come to the banquet (verses 2-6). The king sends more servants to the highways and byways to gather in wedding guests (verses 7-9). These later guests fill the wedding hall, but then imposters, probably those who rejected the earlier invitation, crash the wedding hall without proper wedding clothes (verses 11-12). They are rejected to outer darkness, where there is "weeping and gnashing of teeth" (verse 13), "For many are called, but few are chosen" (verse 14). God is the sovereign Master of His kingdom, and rejection is certain for those who disdain His Son and His dominion!

MARRIAGE AND THE RESURRECTION
Matthew 22:23-33; Mark 12:18-27; Luke 20:27-40

To trick Jesus, the religiously liberal Sadducees, who did not believe in the doctrine of the resurrection, questioned Him about a command in Deuteronomy 25:5. Since a man can marry his brother's widow (Matthew 22:24), what happens if he has seven brothers, all of whom marry her and then die, one at a time? (verses 25-27). To which man will she belong at the resurrection? (verse 28). The evil intention of the Sadducees was to force the Lord to somehow misquote or misrepresent the Scriptures. But Jesus answered them head-on using Scripture: "You are mistaken, not understanding the Scriptures nor the power of God" (verse 29). He went on to say there is neither marrying nor giving in marriage in the resurrection because the redeemed are "like angels in heaven" (verse 30). The resurrected are "sons of God, being sons of the resurrection" (Luke 20:36), and there will be no marriage.

The Lord then said, "Have you not read what was spoken to you by God: 'I am the God of Abraham, and the God of Isaac, and the God of Jacob? He is not the God of the dead but of the living'" (Matthew 22:31-32; cf. Exodus 3:6). "If God is able to make one's spirit exist after death, then He is certainly capable of a resurrection.... The resurrection is the means by which many would enter the kingdom" (Toussaint, *Behold the King*, p. 258). The patriarchs will experience the resurrection because God is the God of the living, as stated in Exodus 3:6. Christ then rebuked the Sadducees: "You are greatly mistaken" (Mark 12:27). The multitudes who heard this verbal exchange "were astonished at His teaching" (Matthew 22:33).

THE MESSIAH IS THE LORD
Matthew 22:41-46; Mark 12:35-37; Luke 20:41-44

WHILE TEACHING in the temple (Mark 12:35), the Lord questioned the Pharisees, asking, "What do you think about the Christ, whose son is He?" They answered, "The son of David" (Matthew 22:42). Then Jesus asked, "How does David in the Spirit call Him 'Lord'"? (verse 43). That is, how can David call the Messiah "Lord" (Greek, *Kurios*) if He is David's son? Jesus then cited Psalm 110:1, one of the most quoted Old Testament prophecies: "The Lord said to My Lord, 'Sit at My right hand, until I put Your enemies beneath Your feet'" (Matthew 22:44). At the ascension, Christ entered the throne room of the God of heaven, and He is now seated and waiting until God has subdued all of His enemies. The heavenly Father will extend His "strong scepter from Zion" and command Him to rule "in the midst of Your enemies" (Psalm 110:2).

In Psalm 110:1, the Hebrew word for "LORD" is *Yahweh,* and the second appearance of the word "Lord" is *Adonai.* Both names are used to describe the God of the Bible. *Yahweh* means "the Ever-existing One," and *Adonai* is the term for "Master" or "Lord."

Jesus put the Pharisees into a quandary and they could not answer. "No one was able to answer Him a word, nor did anyone dare from that day on to ask Him another question" (Matthew 22:46). No matter how the Pharisees tried to answer, they would have had to admit that Jesus was the Messiah and that somehow He was related to deity. They didn't want to do that.

DENOUNCING THE SCRIBES AND PHARISEES
Matthew 23

SPEAKING DIRECTLY TO the crowds following Him in the temple, the Lord gave a warning concerning the high-and-mighty scribes and Pharisees, who had placed themselves in the seat of Moses with their authority (verses 2-4). They loved their honored positions and showed off their piety by prominently displaying the boxes of Scripture they wore on their heads and arms (the phylacteries—Exodus 13:9; Deuteronomy 6:8; 11:18) and their prayer tassels on their garments (Matthew 23:5). Christ then warned these leaders and called them hypocrites who "shut off the kingdom of heaven from people; for you do not enter in yourselves" (verse 13). They would not escape the "sentence of hell" (verse 33). A judgment would fall on that generation (verse 36), and their house would be left desolate (verse 38).

Christ prophesied that He would be sending "prophets and wise men and scribes" to the doubters. He said, "Some of them you will kill and crucify, and some of them you will scourge in your synagogues, and persecute from city to city" (verse 34). Many of the early church disciples suffered this very persecution (Acts 8:1-4), as did the apostles, who had the special task of spreading the gospel (Matthew

10:17,23). After Jesus' death, burial, resurrection, and ascension, the nation of Israel will not see Him again until they hear the messianic cry, "Blessed is He who comes in the name of the Lord!" (Matthew 23:39, cf. Psalm 118:26).

THE OLIVET DISCOURSE
Matthew 24–25;
Mark 13; Luke 21:5-36

THESE CHAPTERS ARE some of the most important in the Gospels because they spell out the scenario of 1) the days of vengeance on Israel, 2) the coming of the days of Tribulation, and 3) the coming of the Messiah to reign on earth. This discourse takes place on Passover eve, and it begins with the disciples asking questions of the Lord on the Mount of Olives (Matthew 24:1-2). When the disciples point out the temple buildings to Jesus, He uses the moment to tell them that all the stones will one day be thrown down (verse 2). This was shocking news to Jesus' Jewish disciples. Privately they ask Him three questions: 1) When will this happen, 2) what is "the sign of Your coming," and 3) what is the sign of "the end of the age?" (verse 3). They had in mind the revealing of His messianic kingship and the possibility He would overthrow the Roman rulership.

Jesus' answers are important to the entire scope of biblical prophecy. Amillennialists and preterists see His answers being fulfilled either in church history or during the 30 to 40 years following Jesus' pronouncement. Some preterists even say that Christ's second coming took place in some mysterious, spiritual manner when the city of Jerusalem and the temple were destroyed in A.D. 70. But when the Lord answers the disciples' questions, for the most part, His answers are projected forward to the end times, or the end of world history as we know it.

It is important to note that the contexts of Jesus' answers are Jeremiah 30 and Daniel 9. In those chapters, certain things must first take place before Christ returns, and these things have not happened yet. In Matthew

24:8,21, the Lord refers to Jeremiah 30 in a very distinct way, thus establishing the context of the Olivet Discourse in light of Old Testament prophecy.

The fulfillment of the prophecies of Jeremiah 30 will take place when God has brought back to the land the descendants of both kingdoms, Israel and Judah (verse 3). The Lord says, "I will also bring them back to the land that I gave to their forefathers, and they shall possess it." After they return, the pains of childbirth fall on the people (verse 6), for "Alas! For that day is great, there is none like it; and it is the time of Jacob's distress" (verse 7). Christ quotes this in Matthew 24:8,21 as coming upon the Jews. In these verses, He is telling the disciples about "the beginning of birth pangs" (verse 8), when a future generation of Jews will be delivered up "to tribulation" and be killed and hated by the nations for His name's sake (verse 9).

Jesus further alludes in verse 13 to Jeremiah 30:7, saying Israel (Jacob) "will be saved from" this terrible day, though this does not mean all the Jews, for only an elect number will be spared and delivered (Matthew 24:22). The prophet Jeremiah was referring to the seven-year Tribulation prophesied in Daniel 9:24-27. This is the "one week" (or seven years) of verse 27. During this time, "this gospel of the kingdom shall be preached in the whole world for a testimony to all the nations, and then the end will come" (Matthew 24:14). The "gospel of the kingdom" is the good news about the fact that the promised King is coming, though of course embedded in this message is the good news of personal salvation made possible by the death and resurrection of the King!

That future generation of Jews will also see the temple desecrated by "the abomination of desolation" (verse 15; Daniel 9:27). This will happen when the beast, "the prince" or the Antichrist, enters the temple and proclaims himself to be God (2 Thessalonians 2:3-9). When the Antichrist makes his move against the temple, the second half of the Tribulation begins (Revelation 13). Walvoord says, "Those who see the Great Tribulation will also see the

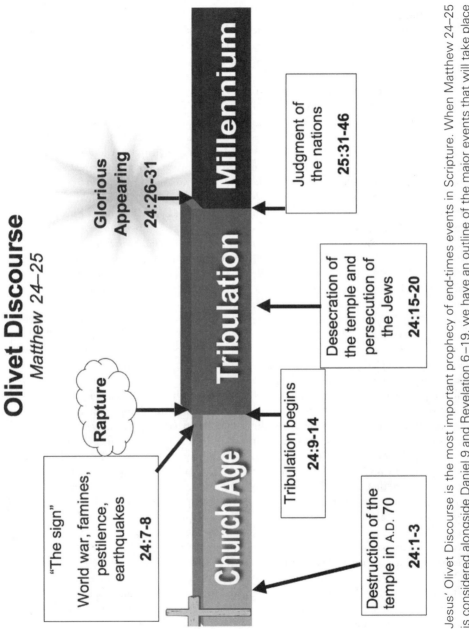

Olivet Discourse
Matthew 24–25

Rapture

Glorious Appearing
24:26-31

Church Age

Tribulation

Millennium

"The sign"
World war, famines, pestilence, earthquakes
24:7-8

Tribulation begins
24:9-14

Desecration of the temple and persecution of the Jews
24:15-20

Destruction of the temple in A.D. 70
24:1-3

Judgment of the nations
25:31-46

Jesus' Olivet Discourse is the most important prophecy of end-times events in Scripture. When Matthew 24–25 is considered alongside Daniel 9 and Revelation 6–19, we have an outline of the major events that will take place in the future.

coming of the Lord" (*Prophecy Knowledge Handbook,* p. 391). Preterist attempts to limit "this generation" to the generation of Jesus' day disregard the context of Jesus' remarks. The Messiah, the Son of Man, will come quickly (Matthew 24:27) amid catastrophic and cosmic signs (verse 29; cf. Isaiah 13:10; 24:23; Ezekiel 32:7; Amos 5:20; 8:9; Zephaniah 1:15). The world will see His arrival and mourn (Matthew 24:30), and He will gather His elect of Israel "from the four winds, from one end of the sky to the other" (verse 31). These things did not happen in A.D. 70 when the Romans destroyed Jerusalem.

The generation that sees all the terrible events Jesus describes "will not pass away until all these things take place" (verse 34). His words are sure! (verse 35). As in the days of Noah when the flood came, few will be expecting His sudden arrival (verses 36-39). The unfaithful Jews who were not expecting His coming will be brought before Him and executed, while the faithful will be blessed (verses 42-51). The unfaithful will be assigned "a place with the hypocrites; in that place there will be weeping and gnashing of teeth" (verse 51).

At the time of Christ's return, many Jewish people will be caught by surprise. They will be like the foolish virgins (the bridesmaids) who had not prepared their oil lamps for the wedding processional when the bridegroom arrived (25:1-10). They will not be given entrance to the wedding (verses 11-12) because they were not alert for the day nor the hour (verse 13). The Jewish people are responsible for the message of the coming of their King. Like responsible servants, they were allotted talents of silver to invest wisely for their departed master (verses 14-18). When the master returned, he found that one servant had not done anything with the stewardship entrusted to him (verses 19-29). Such unfaithful servants will be cast into outer darkness (verse 30). "No one in Scripture spoke more of judgment than Jesus.... No pictures of judgment are more intense and sobering than those Jesus portrayed" (MacArthur, *Matthew 24–28,* p. 111).

Most of what Christ teaches in the Olivet Discourse is far future prophecy. However, in the book of Luke, He does refer to the coming destruction of Jerusalem in A.D. 70. The narration of the coming Tribulation events makes a shift in Luke 21:12-24. This section begins, "But before all these things..." (verse 12). He then addresses the persecution that will come upon the disciples and other believers (verses 12-21) because these are the "days of vengeance, so that all things which are written will be fulfilled" (verse 22, cf. Hosea 9:7,17; 10:3). The "vengeance" is God's visit of anger upon Israel for their rejection of Jesus. This will be the "great distress" that will come upon the land with wrath that will fall upon the Jewish people. This happened when the Romans turned against the Jewish nation and destroyed the temple and the city of Jerusalem. This began the final stage of the Jewish Diaspora, when the people were killed, scattered, or put into slavery. Jesus said the people "will fall by the edge of the sword, and will be led captive into all the nations; and Jerusalem will be trampled underfoot by the Gentiles until the times of the Gentiles are fulfilled" (Luke 21:24).

The ultimate sign of the second coming will be the appearance of Christ Himself in the sky as He returns to earth in triumph (Matthew 24:30; Mark 13:26; Luke 21:27). This return is described in detail in Revelation 19:11-16. Walvoord observes, "It should be noted that Matthew was not talking about the Rapture of the Church" (*Prophecy Knowledge Handbook,* p. 389). The Olivet Discourse focuses on the return of Christ at the *end* of the Tribulation. During the Tribulation, people will be fainting for fear "and the expectation of the things which are coming upon the world; for the powers of the heavens will be shaken" (verse 26). Then "they will see the Son of Man coming in a cloud with power and great glory" (verse 27; Daniel 7:13). Those who will go through the Tribulation are told here to look up at this time "because your redemption is drawing near" (Luke 21:28). That generation is to "be on guard" (verse 34) and "keep on the alert at all times" (verse 36), for the Tribulation "will come upon all those who dwell on the face of the earth" (verse 35), but the righteous who are ready for His return will "stand before the Son of Man" and be blessed (verse 36). "Only by being watchful at all times, through fervent prayer and consecrated living, can one escape the terrors of that day, and thus, by God's sovereign grace, take his stand, without fear, before the Son of man" (Hendriksen, *The Gospel of Luke*, p. 944).

PARABLE OF THE FIG TREE
Matthew 24:32-35; Mark 13:28-31; Luke 21:29-33

JESUS TAUGHT THE PARABLE of the budding of the fig tree to reveal when the time of his return would be near, even "right at the door" (Matthew 24:33). In the context of the Olivet Discourse, He stated that the generation who saw this happen would not pass until "all these things take place" (verse 34). Some have insisted that the fig tree represents Israel, but not one verse in the Bible substantiates this idea. Many of these interpreters also assume that since Israel returned to the Promised Land in 1948, Jesus will return in this present generation.

Israel's return to the land in 1948 is certainly significant and indicative of the fact that we are moving closer to the time of Christ's return. But the parable of the fig tree cannot be used to prove that we are now living in that generation. Besides, after 2048 (at the longest), such speculation will be redundant. Those who suggest the fig tree symbolizes Israel overlook three significant facts: 1) Scripture never refers to Israel as a fig tree; 2) the parallel passage in Luke 21:29 says "the fig tree and all the trees" blossoming are the sign of Christ's return; and 3) the context of the passage in Matthew 24 is the Tribulation.

Walvoord wrote, "The sign in the passage is not the revival of Israel, which is not the subject of Matthew 24, but rather the details of the Great Tribulation which occur in the three and a half years preceding the Second Coming" (*Prophecy Knowledge Handbook*, p. 391). Thus, the generation living during the Tribulation will see all "these things" fulfilled. The budding of the fig tree, or any other trees, merely illustrates the fact that in the same way that tree blossoms indicate summer is coming soon, so does the appearance of these signs indicate that Christ is coming soon.

JUDGMENT OF THE NATIONS
Matthew 25:31-46

WHEN THE SON OF MAN comes in glory, "and all the angels with Him, then He will sit on His glorious throne. And all the nations will be gathered before Him; and He will separate them from one another, as the shepherd separates the sheep from the goats" (verses 31-32). The nations that treated the Jews ("these brothers of Mine") with kindness during the Tribulation will be the "righteous" who will "inherit the kingdom prepared for you from the foundation of the world" (verse 34). The goats on the left are those who mistreated the Jews, and they will be cast "into the eternal fire which has been prepared for the devil and his angels" (verse 41). The unrighteous will "go away into eternal punishment, but the righteous into eternal life" (verse 46). The righteous will then enter the millennial kingdom, in which Christ will reign over the world for 1000 years (Revelation 19:11–20:6).

JUDAS'S BETRAYAL OF JESUS
Matthew 26:14-16; Mark 14:10-11; Luke 22:3-6

JUDAS'S BETRAYAL OF CHRIST (Matthew 26:1-16) was prophesied in Zechariah 11:12-13. After Satan entered Judas (Luke 22:3), Judas went to the chief priests and asked, "What are you willing to give me to betray Him to you?" (Matthew 26:15). The price agreed upon was 30 shekels of silver, or the price of a slave. Judas then began to look for a good opportunity to betray Jesus (verse 16). Realizing what was about to happen to Christ after His arrest, Judas "felt remorse" (27:3), saying that he had "sinned by betraying innocent blood" (verse 4). The Jewish leaders had no sympathy for Judas.

In disgust, Judas threw the silver into "the temple sanctuary and departed; and he went away and hanged himself" (verse 5). Because the blood money could not be put back into the temple treasury (verse 6), it was used to buy "the Potter's Field as a burial place for strangers" (verses 7-8). This fulfilled the words of Zechariah 11:12-13 (Matthew 27:9-10).

The details of the betrayal were spelled out while Christ and the disciples were at the Passover meal. The apostles did not realize who the betrayer was (26:17-25; Mark 14:17-21; John 13:21-22). "[Jesus] does not expose Judas but reveals the act of Judas and then states its effect upon Judas himself; and this is done so as to bring the most powerful pressure to bear upon" him (Lenski, *The Interpretation of Mark's Gospel*, p. 614).

THE WASHING OF THE DISCIPLES' FEET
John 13:1-20

BEFORE THE PASSOVER MEAL, Jesus knew that "His hour had come" and that He would soon return back to the Father (13:13). And during the supper, He arose and began washing the disciples' feet (verses 4-5). The Lord explained how the disciples were clean all over (though this did not include Judas) (verse 10), but they still needed to wash their feet because their feet got dirty from walking in the world (verses 11-15). The words "washed all over" are a picture of a person's positional justification, which is never repeated, and the washing of the feet symbolized the experiential sanctification believers undergo constantly because of the polluting influences of the world.

At first when Jesus washed the disciples' feet, Peter objected that Jesus would do a chore normally done by lowly slaves. What Peter didn't understand was that Christ was demonstrating both the need for a servant's heart and for His followers to keep themselves cleansed from the sinful influences of the world. Christ concluded by saying, "I say to you, a slave is not greater than his master, nor

is one who is sent greater than the one who sent him. If you know these things, you are blessed if you do them" (verses 16-17). By this show of servitude, the Lord was prophesying how believers would relate to each other, and to their daily sin problems, during the church age. Jesus then prophesied again of Judas's betrayal by quoting Psalm 41:9: "He who eats My bread has lifted up his heel against Me" (John 13:18). "Because of His omniscience, Jesus had never trusted Judas and had warned the disciples of his action a year earlier (6:70-71). The expression 'lifted up his heel' is based on the metaphor of a sudden kick of a mule or a horse" (Towns, *Gospel of John*, p. 133).

IDENTITY OF THE BETRAYER
Matthew 26:21-25; Mark 14:18-21; Luke 22:21-23; John 13:21-30

WHILE RECLINING WITH His disciples at the Passover meal, Jesus mentioned that one of them would betray Him (Matthew 26:21). This was followed by puzzlement from the men eating with Him (verse 22). The Son of Man, the Messiah, would be betrayed by the one who dipped in the bowl (of lamb gravy) with Him (verse 23). Judas denied he was the one by saying, "'Surely it is not I, Rabbi?' Jesus said to him, 'You have said it yourself'" (verse 25). Christ added, "It would have been good for that man if he had not been born" (Mark 14:21). "But he was born, and is in the process of committing the gruesome deed.... We know that he did not repent. Hence he faces everlasting damnation (see Matthew 25:46)" (Hendriksen, *The Gospel of Mark*, p. 571). The fact that Jesus named His betrayer in advance indicates His divine omniscience and serves as a fulfillment of the prediction of the betrayal in Psalm 41:9 and Zechariah 11:12-13.

The so-called "Gospel of Judas," a nonbiblical Gnostic text, attempts to represent Judas in a more positive light, whereas the biblical Gospels present him as the "son of perdition" (John 17:12). The heretical manuscript first appeared at the end of the second century

A.D. and has no historical claim to being early enough to have been written by Judas.

PETER'S DENIAL
Matthew 26:31-35; Mark 14:27-31; Luke 22:31-34; John 13:36-38

THE PREDICTION OF PETER'S DENIAL of Christ is recorded in all four Gospels. Jesus had just announced that all the disciples would "fall away" from Him "this night" (Matthew 26:31). In response, Peter insisted that he would "never fall away" (verse 33). But Jesus looked at him and said, "This very night, before a rooster crows, you will deny Me three times" (verse 34).

Despite the fact that Peter and the other disciples insisted they would not deny Him, all but John forsook Him before the night was over. Despite the disciples' failures, Jesus went to the cross to die for their sins and for ours.

The reference to the rooster crowing may be taken literally or in relation to a particular watch of the night. Either way, Jesus meant that Peter would deny Him before daybreak. Even then, Luke 22:61 makes it clear that Peter did not realize what he had done until "the Lord turned and looked" at him. It was the look on Jesus' face that broke Peter's heart and caused him to weep.

ISRAEL'S REJECTION OF CHRIST
Matthew 26:31-35; Mark 14:27-31; Luke 22:31-38; John 13:31-38

WHILE PREDICTING THAT Peter will deny Him three times before the cock crows (Matthew 26:34), Christ quotes in Matthew 26:31 the prophecy from Zechariah that predicts the Lord's "Associate," the Shepherd, will be stricken down and the sheep will be scattered (Zechariah 13:7). Zechariah explains that there is coming a future restoration when one-third of the Jews will pass through the refiner's fire and be tested, and many will call on the Lord's name, and He will answer them. The refiner's fire is the seven-year period

known as the Tribulation. He will say when they come through this crucible, "'They are My people,' and they will say, 'The LORD is my God'" (verse 9).

Peter disavowed his role in the coming rejection of Christ: "Even though all may fall away, yet I will not" (Mark 14:29). He added, "Lord, with You I am ready to go both to prison and to death!" (Luke 22:33). Jesus then explained from Isaiah 53:12 that He must die and be accounted with sinners: "And He was numbered with transgressors," which referred to Him and had to be fulfilled (Luke 22:37). Peter still did not understand and assumed that with the help of swords, Christ's rendezvous with death could be prevented (verse 38).

Peter's statement in Mark 14:29 "is one of the most unfavorable specimens on record of the dark or weak side of this great apostle's character, because it exhibits, not mere self-sufficiency and overweening self-reliance, but an arrogant estimate of his own strength in comparison with others, particularly with his brethren and associates in the apostolic office" (Alexander, *Commentary on the Gospel of Mark*, p. 384).

THE NEW COVENANT
Matthew 26:26-29; Mark 14:22-25; Luke 22:17-20

CHRIST'S COMING DEATH on the cross would ratify the prophesied New Covenant given in Jeremiah 31:31-34 (Luke 22:20). The cup of suffering He was about to drink, "which is poured out for you is the new covenant in My blood." This New Covenant would replace the Mosaic Covenant, the law, which in itself could never bring a permanent forgiveness of sin (Jeremiah 31:34). When the Lord poured the cup of blessing at the Passover meal, He told His disciples, "Drink from it, all of you; for this is My blood of the covenant, which is poured out for many for forgiveness of sins" (Matthew 26:27-28). The New Covenant seems to be an extension and an expansion of the blessing promises first prophesied in the Abrahamic Covenant (Genesis 12:1-3).

The New Covenant was first prophesied as a blessing for the nation of Israel (Jeremiah 31:31-36). The nation rejected Christ and therefore did not benefit from His death. When God, in the future, restores the Jews to their former blessing, the New Covenant will bring them salvation. In the messianic kingdom, the disciples will again drink the "fruit of the vine" of the New Covenant (Mark 14:25). The church presently benefits from the New Covenant in the gifts of salvation and forgiveness. When the Holy Spirit was poured out at Pentecost, this was a sign that the New Covenant had been inaugurated (Acts 2:1-13; 10:47; 11:15-16; 15:8).

This does not mean, however, that the church fulfills the New Covenant. The land blessings of the covenant are not passed on to the church, only the benefits of personal salvation and the indwelling of the Holy Spirit. "Just as the covenants of old were sealed with the shedding of animal blood, so now Jesus said this new covenant had been sealed with His own blood" (Barbieri, "Matthew," *Bible Knowledge Commentary,* p. 315).

THE UPPER ROOM DISCOURSE
John 13–17

IN THE UPPER ROOM DISCOURSE, the Lord Jesus predicts what is coming in regard to His death and His return to the Father in heaven. He also discusses the new relationship believers will have with Him in the church age. Some of Jesus' words in the Upper Room Discourse relate specifically to the work of His disciples after His departure, and other words relate to all believers (particularly in relation to the Holy Spirit).

After prophesying of Judas's betrayal and then departing from the Passover meal (13:21-30), Christ predicted His messianic glory: "Now is the Son of Man glorified, and God is glorified in Him" (verse 31). The Father will also be glorified (verse 32). The cross is a tragic yet glorious event in which the Father and the

Son bring finality to the curse of sin. As a result of Christ's work on the cross, someday all the disciples and all the other believers will follow Christ into heaven (John 13:36).

THE RAPTURE OF BELIEVERS
John 14:1-6

IN JOHN 14:1-6, JESUS DESCRIBES the rapture and the promise of our future home with Him. Though the disciples did not experience the rapture, that doesn't mean Jesus was wrong. Jesus' words apply to a future generation of believers who will go to heaven and not face death. When Christ left earth, it was "to prepare a place for you" in heaven (verse 2). He promised to come again "and receive you to Myself, that where I am, there you may be also" (verse 3). This is the first prediction of the fact that Jesus will return to earth to take believers home with Him to the Father's house (heaven). Notice that this promise was given to the disciples *after* Judas had left the room. In 1 Thessalonians 4:13-17, Paul gives more details about the rapture, in which the "dead in Christ will rise first," and then "we who are alive and remain will be caught up [Greek, *harpazo*] together with them in the clouds to meet the Lord in the air."

Meanwhile, until that day, the apostles and other believers are to serve the Lord and testify of the grace of God in the salvation provided by Christ's death, burial, and resurrection. And whatever we ask in the name of Christ, that the Father may be glorified, the Lord will do (John 14:13-14).

PROMISE OF THE SPIRIT
John 14:16-31; 15:1-11; 16:5-15

JESUS PROMISED THAT WHEN He ascended to His Father, He would send the "Helper" (Greek, *Parakletos,* which means "counselor"), who will abide within the believer (John:14:16). Also, the Father and the Son will dwell within the child of God (verses 18,20,23). To the

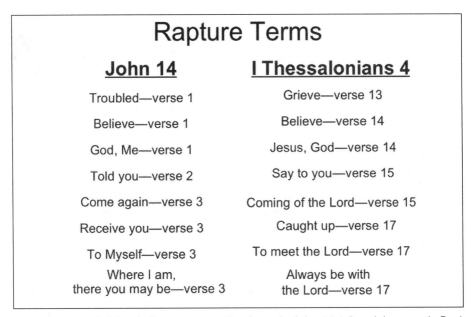

Rapture Terms

John 14	I Thessalonians 4
Troubled—verse 1	Grieve—verse 13
Believe—verse 1	Believe—verse 14
God, Me—verse 1	Jesus, God—verse 14
Told you—verse 2	Say to you—verse 15
Come again—verse 3	Coming of the Lord—verse 15
Receive you—verse 3	Caught up—verse 17
To Myself—verse 3	To meet the Lord—verse 17
Where I am, there you may be—verse 3	Always be with the Lord—verse 17

A comparison of eight similar terms used by Jesus in John 14:1-3 and the apostle Paul in 1 Thessalonians 4:13-18 reveals that both passages are describing the rapture. The details in Matthew 24:29-31 and Revelation 19:11-21 are different, which makes it evident those passages are describing the glorious appearing of Christ—a different event.

disciples Jesus promised, "[The Holy Spirit] will teach you all things, and bring to your remembrance all that I said to you" (verse 26). The Spirit would be sent by Christ from the Father, and He would "testify of Me" (15:26). The Lord would also impart peace, give comfort to troubled hearts, and remove fear (14:1,27). Notice that the promise to send the Spirit is predicated on the promise that Christ will someday come back (verse 28).

If the believer "abides" (Greek, *mino*) with Christ in fellowship, he will bear much fruit (15:1-8). This is not an issue of salvation but of remaining in relationship with Christ so that fruit can be produced. The Father is the vinedresser (verse 1) who will remove dead branches from a believer's life or will prune the branches so that more fruit can be produced (verse 2). No spiritual fruit can be harvested unless a believer remains close to Christ in the same way that branches abide in a vine (verse 5). Not only does God judge Christians who are fruitless, the world does, too, because even the world hates hypocrites! The world

will also automatically hate believers as it has hated Christ and even God the Father (verses 18,23). It was written of Christ in prophecy, "They hated Me without a cause" (verse 25; Psalm 35:19; 69:4).

When the Helper, the Holy Spirit, comes, He "will convict the world concerning sin and righteousness and judgment" (verse 8). To "convict" (Greek, *elenxei*) means "to present or expose the truth." The world must face the fact of Christ's death for sin; humanity must accept His offer of deliverance or perish. To find righteousness, the world has to turn to Christ. His righteousness is the measure against which all human righteousness will be scrutinized.

The Lord's hour of departure was imminent, in which He would return to the Father (John 16:16-17). For a while, the disciples would weep, but their sorrow "[would] be turned into joy" when they realized He had risen from the grave (verse 20). Christ warned the disciples they would be scattered (verse 32), but "these things I have spoken to you, so that in Me you may have peace. In the world you have tribulation, but take courage; I have overcome the world" (verse 33). The baptism of the Spirit would ignite their souls and commence the church age, which begins at Pentecost and ends with the rapture.

In John 17 is Jesus' prayer to the Father in which He asks that the Father glorify His Son, and that the Son may glorify Him (verse 1). Christ has been given authority over "all flesh" so that all who belong to Him may now have eternal life (verse 2). As the Father had sent the Son into the world, so now the Son sends His disciples into the world (verse 18). They are to be "sanctified" in the truth of the Word (verse 17). The relationships between believers will be as strong as the relationship between the Father and the Son (verse 21). "And the glory which You have given Me I have given to them, that they may be one, just as We are one" (verse 22).

JESUS' ARREST IN GETHSEMANE
Matthew 26:30,36-46; Mark 14:26, 32-42; Luke 22:39-46; John 18:1

COMING TO THE MOUNT OF OLIVES after the Passover meal, Christ predicted His disciples would fall away because of what was coming: "I will strike down the shepherd, and the sheep of the flock shall be scattered" (Matthew 26:31; Zechariah 13:7). Jesus asked the disciples to stay awake while He prayed, but they fell asleep. After three episodes of this (verses 36-44), the Lord said, "the hour is at hand and the Son of Man is being betrayed into the hands of sinners" (verse 45). When Judas arrived with a great multitude and the chief priests and the elders, Christ reminded them that He could call down 12 legions of angels to save Him if He wished (verse 53). Instead, He asked, "How then will the Scriptures be fulfilled, which say that it must happen this way?" (verse 54). All that was taking place in connection with Christ's arrest had already been prophesied and was now being fulfilled.

CHRIST BEFORE CAIAPHAS
Matthew 26:57-68; Mark 14:53-65; Luke 22:54,63-65; John 18:24

JESUS WAS BROUGHT BEFORE Caiaphas the high priest as well as the scribes and elders of the Sanhedrin. They put Jesus on trial, even though it was illegal for them to do this at night. False witnesses were summoned who accused Jesus of saying He would destroy the temple of God and rebuild it in three days (Matthew 26:61). They were referring to a statement Jesus made earlier in His ministry in regard to His death and resurrection (John 2:19-21). Jesus did not answer the false witnesses, but instead kept quiet (Matthew 26:62-63).

The high priest knew the issues, and he knew also the many prophecies that predicted the coming of the Messiah. He said, referring to Psalm 2, "You tell us whether You are the Christ, the Son of God" (Matthew 26:63). In response Jesus quoted Psalm 110:1 and Daniel 7:13: "I tell you, hereafter you will see the Son of Man sitting at the right hand of power, and coming on the clouds of heaven" (Matthew 26:64). The high priest knew Jesus was claiming deity and "tore his robes" and accused Christ of blasphemy (verse 65). Jesus was then spat upon and beaten in fulfillment of Isaiah 50:6 and 52:14. Then the council took Jesus to Pilate in order to have Him crucified (in fulfillment of Psalm 22:16 and Zechariah 12:10).

JESUS BEFORE PILATE
Matthew 27:2,11-14; Mark 15:1-5; Luke 23:1-5; John 18:28-38

PILATE, THE ROMAN GOVERNOR, asked Christ, "Are You the King of the Jews?" From Psalm 2:6, it was common knowledge that the Son of God (verse 7) would be Israel's king. Because Pilate did not want to further anger the Jewish leaders, he was cautious in what he said about Christ. He referred to Jesus as the one "who is called Christ" (Matthew 27:17,22). *Christus* is the Greek translation of the Hebrew

HaMaschioch (the "Anointed") of Psalm 2:2. When the mob called for Jesus' crucifixion (Matthew 27:22-23), Pilate answered that he was innocent of the Lord's blood (verse 24). The people shouted a prophetic cry, "His blood be on us and on our children" (verse 25 NKJV).

Later, as the disciples began to preach the risen Christ, the Sanhedrin must have remembered the words of Pilate. They told the disciples to stop speaking about Jesus because "you have filled Jerusalem with your teaching and intend to bring this man's blood upon us" (Acts 5:28).

THE FIRST THREE HOURS ON THE CROSS
Matthew 27:35-44; Mark 15:24-32; Luke 23:33-43; John 19:18-27

THE CRUCIFIXION FULFILLED the Old Testament prophecies of the Messiah being "pierced" (Psalm 22:16; Zechariah 12:10). When the Lord was on the cross, the people again flung at Him their misquotation about destroying the temple and rebuilding it in three days (Matthew 27:40; John 2:19-21). Mockingly, they called Him the Son of God and Israel's king (Matthew 27:40-42; Psalm 2). And with some sense of biblical insight, they quoted the messianic prophecy in Psalm 22:8: "'He trusted in God; let Him deliver Him now if He will have Him; for He said, 'I am the Son of God'" (Matthew 27:43). The people were not ignorant of the great messianic passages, yet sadly, they didn't recognize that Jesus was the very Messiah they had long waited for.

THE THREE HOURS OF DARKNESS
Matthew 27:45-50; Mark 15:33-37; Luke 23:44-46; John 19:28-30

AS A GREAT DARKNESS FELL on Jerusalem (Matthew 27:45), Jesus neared death on the cross and cried forth the exact words of Psalm 22:1: "Eli, Eli, lama sabachthani," which means

"My God, My God, why have You forsaken Me?" (Matthew 27:46 NKJV). Because Jesus spoke in Aramaic, many of the people could not understand Him. Some thought He was crying out for Elijah to rescue Him (verse 47). One man responded by giving Jesus some sour wine on a reed (verse 48). Others mocked and said, "Let us see whether Elijah will come to save Him" (verse 49). In the end, Jesus announced, "It is finished" (John 19:30), indicating the atoning nature of His death. With this, Christ "yielded up His spirit" (verse 50) as prophesied. He had said that no one would take His life, and indeed, He gave it up voluntarily (John 10:18).

THE BURIAL OF CHRIST
Matthew 27:57-60; Mark 15:42-46; Luke 23:50-54; John 19:31-42

CHRIST WAS BURIED IN THE TOMB of a rich man (Matthew 27:57-60) in fulfillment of Isaiah 53:9: "His grave was assigned with wicked men, yet He was with a rich man in His death." The rich man was Joseph of Arimathea, a member of the Sanhedrin who "was waiting for the kingdom of God" (Mark 15:43). He "gathered up courage and went in before Pilate, and asked for the body of Jesus." Joseph was "a good and righteous man" (Luke 23:50). Though he was a member of the Sanhedrin, he had not consented to the council's plan to kill the Lord (verse 51).

THE TOMB AND THE RESURRECTION
Matthew 27:61-66; Mark 15:45; Luke 23:55-56

THE LORD HAD PREDICTED that He would be in the tomb for three days, and then He would rise again. The Jewish leaders remembered this statement (Matthew 27:63; cf. 16:21) and gave orders for the grave to be made secure with guards and a large stone over the door

(Matthew 27:66). Jesus' prediction of His own resurrection was His greatest prophecy because it would take an absolute miracle for it to be fulfilled.

THE WOMEN AND THE ANGELS AT THE EMPTY TOMB
Mark 16:2-8; Luke 24:1-12; John 20:1-10

WHEN THE WOMEN ARRIVED at the empty tomb, they were met by two angels, "men" who "stood near them in dazzling clothing" (Luke 24:4). The angels asked, "Why do you seek the living One among the dead?" (verse 5). They reminded the women what the Lord had said when He was still in Galilee, "saying that the Son of Man must be delivered into the hands of sinful men, and be crucified, and the third day rise again" (verse 7). When this was said, the women "remembered His words" (verse 8). The "Son of Man" is a messianic reference that refers to the ascension, when the Messiah returns to the throne room of the heavenly Father. He comes before the throne of glory as "the Son related to Mankind" (see Daniel 7:13). As the "living One," death could not hold Him, as prophesied in Psalm 16:10: "You will not abandon my soul to Sheol; Nor will You allow Your Holy One to undergo decay."

THE APPEARANCE ON THE EMMAUS ROAD
Mark 16:12-13; Luke 24:13-32

FOLLOWING CHRIST'S RESURRECTION, two of the Lord's followers were on the road to Emmaus, a village seven miles from Jerusalem (Luke 24:13). One was Cleopas, and the other is unnamed (verse 18). When the risen Christ joined them, by God's providence, "their eyes were prevented from recognizing Him" (verse 16). They began to tell Him "the things about Jesus the Nazarene, who was a prophet mighty in deed and word in the sight of God and all the people" (verse 19). Their hope, they said,

was that He would "redeem Israel" (verse 21), meaning He would be the political savior who would rescue the nation from the tyranny of the Romans.

Jesus then interrupted them and said, "O foolish men and slow of heart to believe in all that the prophets have spoken!" (verse 25). Was it not true, He went on, that the Christ had to suffer these things "to enter into His glory?" (verse 26). Then from Moses and all the prophets Christ "explained to them the things concerning Himself in all the Scriptures" (verse 27). Staying with them for a time in their house, Jesus broke bread with them (verse 30), which made them realize who He was (verse 35). Suddenly their eyes were opened and they recognized Him, only to see Him vanish from their sight (verse 31). The verification of who He was became solidified when, as they said, "He was explaining the Scriptures to us" (verse 32).

Jesus taught these disciples about Himself, explaining the prophecies of the Old Testament that He had fulfilled. Pointing to the law, the prophets, and the psalms, Jesus referred to the threefold division of the Hebrew Bible. In doing this, He was saying that the Old Testament was all about Him. All the prophecies of the Old Testament about the first coming of the Messiah had been confirmed—everything from His birth to His resurrection! These two disciples returned to Jerusalem and explained to the 11 what they had seen and heard, saying, "The Lord has really risen, and has appeared to Simon" (verses 33-34). That Simon Peter was a key witness to the resurrection of Christ is confirmed by the apostle Paul in 1 Corinthians 15:5.

The verses in this passage give rare insight from Jesus Himself regarding Jesus' place in prophecy. He taught these disciples that He is the subject of prophecy from Moses through the prophets, and in this manner we today are able to "open the Scriptures." Anyone who studies the messianic prophecies (of which there are at least 321 passages in Scripture) will get a full portrait of Jesus the Messiah, and the result will be "our hearts will burn within us."

THE GREAT COMMISSION
Matthew 28:16-20; Mark 16:14-16; Luke 24:44-49

MEETING WITH THE 11 disciples again, Jesus showed them that He could be touched, that He had flesh and bones, and that He was not simply a spirit (verse 39). His glorified resurrected body was indeed a real body. He chided them for being so troubled and for having doubts in their hearts (Luke 24:38). He reminded them that He had taught them "all things which are written about Me in the Law of Moses and the Prophets and the Psalms must be fulfilled" (Luke 24:44). He added, "Thus it is written, that the Christ would suffer and rise again from the dead the third day, and that repentance for forgiveness of sins would be proclaimed in His name to all the nations, beginning from Jerusalem" (verses 46-47; cf. Matthew 28:19).

The Lord then promised them that He would send forth the promise of His Father upon them so that they would be "clothed with power from on high" (Luke 24:49). Here He was prophesying the sending of the Holy Spirit (John 14:26; 15:26), who would impart His power upon them so they could be His witnesses "both in Jerusalem, and in all Judea and Samaria, and even to the remotest part of the earth" (Acts 1:5,8).

In Matthew 28:19-20 and Mark 16:15, Jesus made it clear that they were to "go into all the world" and "make disciples of all the nations." He promised to go with them and empower them until the "end of the age" (Matthew 28:20).

With His ascension (Acts 1:9-11), the Lord Jesus entered the throne room of His heavenly Father as the Son of Man (Daniel 7:13), where He is now seated at the Father's right hand (Psalm 110:1). There, He is the Advocate for the children of God when they sin, "Jesus Christ the righteous" (1 John 2:1). He is also "the propitiation" (Greek, *hilasmos,* meaning "place of satisfaction") "for our sins; and not for ours only, but also for those of the whole world" (verse 2). Though Christ's glorified body is now in heaven, He is still omnipresent. He and His heavenly Father will come and abide within every believer forever through the indwelling of the Holy Spirit (John 14:23).

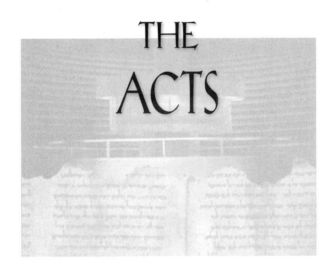

THE ACTS

ACTS

WRITTEN BY LUKE THE PHYSICIAN, THE ACTS OF THE APOSTLES has been called the book of transition between the dispensations of the law and the church age. At the first, the apostles Peter and John are key players. As the transition develops, Paul comes on the scene and becomes the great apostle of evangelism to the Gentile world.

Great portions of prophecy are scattered throughout the book, but no prophetic message dominates so heavily as in 2:14-36. Peter gives to a Jewish audience, on the day of Pentecost, a masterful oration of the prophecies of Christ. The Holy Spirit was promised to come (verses 14-21), and Jesus is Israel's Messiah who was prophesied to rise from the grave and be seated at the right hand of the Father in heaven (verses 22-35). Peter's conclusion is that Christ is now proclaimed as being both the prophesied Lord and the Christ (verse 36). These messages start the book of Acts and convict the hearts of many Jewish people, who asked Peter, "What shall we do?" (verse 37).

Acts closes with a great prophetic indictment by the apostle Paul against the nation of Israel for its dullness of heart in rejecting the Lord Jesus as Savior and King (28:17-31). In this way the stage is set for the setting aside of Israel temporarily and the development of the church age to reach the world for Christ.

THE BAPTISM OF THE HOLY SPIRIT
Acts 1:5-8

LUKE RELATES TO the recipient of Acts how Jesus, after His resurrection, appeared to His disciples over a period of 40 days, "speaking of the things concerning the kingdom of God" (1:3). The "kingdom of God" is not a reference to the church but to the promised messianic reign of the Lord at some future date. More than likely Jesus was explaining to them that the kingdom was yet to arrive in the future, but not now. In fact, the disciples asked, "Lord, is it at this time you are restoring the kingdom to Israel?" (1:6). Jesus replied, "It is not for you to know times or epochs which the Father has fixed by His own authority" (1:7).

Before His ascension, described in verses 9-11, Jesus gathered His followers together and reminded them of the promised arrival of the Holy Spirit (verse 4). Jesus had prophesied to them about this in John 14:26 and Luke 24:49. In the Upper Room, the Lord had said, "The Helper, the Holy Spirit, whom the Father will send in My name, He will teach you all things, and bring to your remembrance all that

I said to you" (John 14:26). Jesus also said, "I am sending forth the promise of My Father upon you; but you are to stay in the city until you are clothed with power from on high" (Luke 24:49).

Christ reminded the apostles, "John baptized with water, but you will be baptized with the Holy Spirit not many days from now" (verse 5). For the Jews, baptism was a picture of spiritual cleansing, but for the Christians it became the symbol of their union with Christ. In a sense, Christ deflected the thinking of His followers, who were still thinking about the promised Davidic kingdom. The disciples' question about the coming of the kingdom reflected their anticipation of a literal earthly kingdom. It must be remembered that Israel lived under kings who came from the line of David, so what is to come is indeed a *restoration,* except that the son of David, the Messiah, will be reigning on His earthly throne. The word "times" (Greek, *kronos*) refers to "the seasons," and the word "epochs" (Greek, *kairos*) has in mind "definite fixed times." Barnes observes: "The difference between these two words is, that the former denotes any time or period that is indefinite or uncertain; the latter denotes a fixed, definite, or appropriate time" *(Barnes' Notes on the New Testament,* 10:5). Only the Father knows when the kingdom will come!

Jesus did not deny the reality of a future earthly kingdom for Israel. Rather, He simply told them it was not going to come now, and that the time of its arrival had been set by the Father. What's more, Jesus did not tell the disciples that the church would replace Israel. Rather, He redirected their attention to the promise of the Spirit, whose coming would initiate the church age. And when the Spirit came, the disciples would "receive power," and they would be Christ's "witnesses both in Jerusalem, and in all Judea and Samaria, and even to the remotest part of the earth" (verse 8). The disciples did travel far and wide with the gospel, and their followers went even farther to carry the truth throughout the world.

THE BODILY RETURN OF CHRIST PROPHESIED
Acts 1:9-11

IMMEDIATELY AFTER the Lord's promise of the coming Holy Spirit, He was "lifted up," and "a cloud received Him out of their sight" (verse 9). Suddenly "two men in white clothing" stood beside the apostles (verse 10). Virtually all commentators agree these men were angelic beings sent to interpret the Lord's departure back to heaven. The angels asked the disciples why they were gazing into the sky. Then the angels said, "This Jesus, who has been taken up from you into heaven, will come in just the same way as you have watched Him go into heaven" (verse 11).

Christ departed from the Mount of Olives, and when He returns He will come back to the same place. Zechariah 14:4 says, "In that day His feet will stand on the Mount of Olives, which is in front of Jerusalem on the east; and the Mount of Olives will be split in its middle from east to west by a very large valley." Then the Jewish people who will inhabit Jerusalem (12:6) will mourn and weep because it was they who pierced Him (verse 10). At this time some nations will come to war against Jerusalem, and the Lord will come to defend the inhabitants of Jerusalem (verse 8) and will "set about to destroy all the nations that come against Jerusalem" (verse 9). This will happen at the end of the Tribulation, just before Christ establishes His earthly rule in Jerusalem.

Acts 1:9-11 is a powerful response against those who say that Christ returned in A.D. 70 in a literal yet spiritualized sense. Note that the angels said the Lord "will come *in just the same way* as you watched Him go into heaven" (verse 11). In other words, Christ's return will be a literal, physical one. We are told that when He comes,

> he shall come in the same flesh, in the same human nature; he shall come in the clouds of heaven, and shall be attended with his mighty angels, as he

now was; he shall descend himself in person, as he now ascended in person; and as he went up with a shout, and with the sound of a trumpet...so he shall descend with a shout, with the voice of the archangel, and the trump of God, and, it may be, he shall descend upon the very spot from whence he ascended; see Zech. xiv.4 (Gill, *Gill's Commentary*, 5:801).

This did not happen in A.D. 70! It has yet to happen, and we are still waiting for Christ to return—literally and bodily—just as He left! (The fact that the glorious return of Christ will be literal and visible is also emphasized in Matthew 16:27; 24:30; 25:31; and Revelation 1:7.)

THE PREDICTION OF JUDAS'S BETRAYAL
Acts 1:16-20

PSALM 41 PREDICTED Judas's betrayal of Jesus: "Even my close friend in whom I trusted, who ate my bread, has lifted up his heel against me" (verse 9; Acts 1:16). Judas was paid 30 pieces of silver to point Christ out to the authorities who arrested Him, though afterward, in bitterness of soul, he tossed the coins back into the temple sanctuary and "went away and hanged himself" (Matthew 27:3-5). The leaders of Israel were afraid to put the money into the treasury because it had become blood money (verse 6). So they used the funds to buy a burial place in the Potter's Field, which was where poor people who had no family plots were laid to rest (verses 7-9). This fulfills several scriptures that Matthew pieces together in a prophetic pattern about the death of Judas (Jeremiah 18:2; 19:2,11; 32:6-9; Zechariah 11:12-13).

There is no contradiction when Luke records that Judas fell headlong and "burst open in the middle and all his intestines gushed out" (Acts 1:18). Such a fall would have happened after he hanged himself. The people of Jerusalem called

this place where he died *hakeldama*, which means "field of blood" (verse 19). Luke also adds that two other prophecies were fulfilled by Judas's betrayal: Psalm 69:25 and 109:8 NKJV. They read, "Let [his] dwelling place be desolate" and "Let another take his office." Kistemaker observes that the psalmist "pronounces a curse upon God's enemies and implies that the expression...includes all the material possessions a man owns.... Peter applies the expression to Judas's name, family, and earthly possessions, which are cursed. Then [Peter] thinks of the apostolic place Judas occupied during Jesus' ministry and quotes Psalm 109:8" (*The Interpretation of the Acts of the Apostles*, p. 63).

Psalm 109:8 was fulfilled when the disciples chose a replacement for Judas to be a "witness with us of [Christ's] resurrection" (Acts 1:22). Setting two men before them, Barsabbas and Matthias (verse 23), the apostles prayed over them, asking the Lord who should "occupy this ministry and apostleship from which Judas turned aside to go to his own place" (verses 24-25). The lot drawn "fell to Matthias; and he was added to the eleven apostles" (verse 26). Some argue that this position should have later been given to Paul, but the verses in Acts confirm that the apostles were led of the Lord in their choice.

THE PROPHECY OF JOEL 2
Acts 2:14-21

FEW PASSAGES IN the New Testament engender such controversy as Peter's quote of Joel 2:28-32 as recorded in Acts 2:17-21. Long ago, Joel had prophesied that the Holy Spirit would be poured out "on all mankind" at the end of the Tribulation, when the kingdom of Israel is reestablished in Jerusalem. The Tribulation is described as "the great and awesome day of the Lord" (verse 31). At the end of the Tribulation there will be "survivors" (Joel 2:32) who call upon the name of the Lord (Joel 2:32).

At the Feast of Pentecost, the disciples "were all filled with the Holy Spirit" and began speaking in foreign languages (Acts 2:4-11), proclaiming what had happened to Christ some weeks earlier. Thousands of Jews and proselytes had made the pilgrimage to Jerusalem for Passover and Pentecost. These people from other areas spoke other languages, and they heard the disciples speaking the gospel message in their own languages. Thus, they heard scriptural truth they would otherwise have not known.

Lenski observes, "Peter uses excellent psychology, he meets the questioning of his auditors squarely, without circumlocution. His authoritative tone is enforced by the full impact of what he says. He even uses excellent homiletics" (*The Interpretation of the Acts of the Apostles*, p. 72). Peter announced that what the people had witnessed was not a sign of drunkenness, as some people thought, but a miracle of the Holy Spirit. He explained, "This is what was spoken of through the prophet Joel" (verse 16).

What did Peter mean by this reference to Joel? Some say Peter was simply using the Joel reference 1) as an *illustration* of what was happening at Pentecost. Others argue that Joel 2 was 2) fulfilled in Acts 2, and that Joel 2 is really describing what would happen in the new church age. Another view says that 3) Peter is focusing strictly on Joel's reference to the outpouring of the Holy Spirit. In the same way the Spirit will be given to the Jews when the messianic kingdom begins, He is given here to the church. A better view seems to be that 4) the New Covenant is now launched as prophesied in the Old Testament, and that the Holy Spirit is the dynamic initiator of that covenant.

This does not mean that the church is replacing Israel, but rather, that the prophesied covenant has begun, and it will have its ultimate fulfillment among the Jewish people in the future kingdom. Presently, the church benefits from this covenant but is not fulfilling it. The New Covenant was prophesied to replace the Mosaic Covenant by the prophet Jeremiah (31:31-37). It was ratified by the death of Christ and by His blood (Luke 22:20), and was then launched at Pentecost.

This is confirmed in the writings of Paul. He compares the circumcision of the Spirit over against the "letter," meaning the letter of the Mosaic law (Romans 2:29). He repeats this in Romans 7:6, where he wrote, "Now we have been released from the Law, having died to that by which we were bound, so that we serve in newness of the Spirit and not in oldness of the letter [of the law]." He wrote similarly in 2 Corinthians 3:4-7 that God has made us "adequate as servants of a new covenant, not of the letter, but of the Spirit; for the letter kills, but the Spirit gives life."

Steve Ger seems to have captured the intent of Peter's quoting of Joel 2 best when he writes,

> Some have described Peter's use of Joel 2 as the launching of the New Covenant, but not as a fulfillment in the normal sense. However, this preliminary fulfillment is only in reference to the first portion of the prophecy that deals with the Holy Spirit's outpouring (Acts 2:17-18).... Peter did not state that these numerous prophetic expectations had been completely fulfilled at Pentecost.... The Pentecost experience was merely a "down payment" on Joel's prophecy.... There is a much more extensive fulfillment of this prophecy still to be "tapped" at a later date (*The Book of Acts*, pp. 45-46).

THE PROPHECY OF MESSIAH'S RESURRECTION
Acts 2:22-36

As Peter continued his message to the crowds gathered at Pentecost, he focused on the issue of "Jesus the Nazarene" (verse 22), who was "attested by God" by "miracles and wonders and signs." God was working through Him by a predetermined plan to send Him to the cross, where He was slain by godless men (verse 23). The Lord, in raising Him, ended "the agony of death" since the power of death could not hold Him (verse 24). Peter added that David the prophet gave this prediction in Psalm 16:8-11. MacArthur states that by using the phrase "the Nazarene," Peter "identified Him with His hometown of Nazareth; in fact, the phrase is sometimes translated 'Jesus of Nazareth,' which was the name on the inscription on His cross (John 19:19)" (MacArthur, *Acts 1–12*, p. 59).

In prophetic words, the Messiah said through David, "Thou wilt not abandon My soul to Hades," or to the grave in permanency. The reason is that God would not "allow Your Holy One to undergo decay" (verse 27). Being the Son of God, the Lord Jesus is forever holy and sinless—He "knew no sin" (2 Corinthians 5:21). Before His physical birth, the angel told Mary, "The Holy Spirit will come upon you, and the power of the Most High will overshadow you; and for that reason the holy Child shall be called the Son of God" (Luke 1:35).

Peter reminded his Jewish brothers that Psalm 16 was not about David, because David was still buried, and his tomb "is with us to this day" (Acts 2:29). Rather, David was speaking as a prophet, and God had revealed to him by an oath that one of his descendants would be seated upon his throne (verse 30). Christ will be able to take David's throne because He was not abandoned to the grave, and His flesh did not suffer decay (verse 31). Christ is now "exalted to the right hand of God" (verse 33); this exaltation took place at Christ's ascension and fulfills Psalm 110:1, one of the most often-quoted Old Testament passages in the New Testament: "The LORD [*Yahweh*] says to my Lord [*Adonai*]: 'Sit at My right hand until I make Your enemies a footstool for Your feet.'" *Yahweh* refers to the Father, and the word *Adonai* is also used to describe God. Here the same name is used of the Messiah, and He is David's Lord!

In this passage, then, God the Father is addressing God the Son. This is the same passage that Christ used to stump the Pharisees (Matthew 22:41-46). After quoting the words to them He asked, "If David then calls Him 'Lord,' how is He [David's] son?" (verse 45).

Christ will remain at the right hand of the Father until the Lord will "stretch forth Your strong scepter from Zion, saying, 'Rule in the midst of Your enemies'" (Psalm 110:2). Jesus will then be in heaven on the throne of God the Father until the time of the messianic kingdom. Then after His return and after He subdues His enemies, He will reign from Jerusalem (2:5-7; Matthew 25:31-46).

Peter continued his sermon before the Jews and, toward the end, directly quoted Psalm 110:1, a passage very familiar to the Jews (Acts 2:34-35). His conclusion is very important to our understanding of who Christ is. He said, "Therefore let all the house of Israel know for certain that God has made Him both Lord and Christ—this Jesus whom you crucified" (verse 36). The Greek word for "made" (*poieo*) is best translated "designate, establish." The resurrection of Jesus made it very clear that He is both the Lord of Psalm 110:1 and the Christ, or the Anointed One (Hebrew, *Meschioch,* Greek, *Christos*), of Psalm 2:2. From a human and earthly standpoint, this is the One "whom you crucified." Ger observes,

Jesus' true identity has now finally been revealed. The Jewish people had believed Him to be a mere man, indeed, one worthy of an ignoble execution. However, now, through His exhibition of power in His resurrection and glorious exaltation to the right hand of God, it was clear that Jesus is the reflection of God's essential nature. He is, therefore, supremely worthy of both titles, "Lord" and "Christ" (Ger, *The Book of Acts,* pp. 50-51).

THE RESTORATION OF ALL THINGS
Acts 3:12-26

A DAY OR SO AFTER THE EVENTS of chapter 2, Peter and John were walking up to the temple and encountered a beggar who had been lame from birth (verses 1-2). As the man was begging for alms, Peter said to him, "I do not possess silver and gold, but what I do have I give to you: In the name of Jesus Christ the Nazarene—walk!" (verse 6). In response to the amazement of the eyewitnesses to this miracle, Peter took the occasion to remind them again who Christ is: "The God of Abraham, Isaac and Jacob, the God of our fathers, has glorified His servant Jesus" (verse 13). Peter then added that the Jewish people had "disowned the Holy and Righteous One" (verse 14) and "put to death the Prince of life, the one whom God raised from the dead" (verse 15).

Taking his audience back to the Old Testament, Peter paraphrased the prophets, saying that what "God announced beforehand by the mouth of all the prophets, that His Christ would suffer, He has thus fulfilled" (verse 18, cf. Psalm 22:11-18; Isaiah 53:4-8). Alexander comments that to the Jews, Peter said, "The death of Christ, although a crime on your part, was the execution of a divine purpose as predicted by the ancient prophets.... The obvious meaning is that the point, to which the whole drift of prophetic revelation tended, was the death of Christ" (*Commentary on the Acts of the Apostles*, pp. 112-13).

Peter spoke much as John the Baptist had, telling the Jews that if they repented, their sins would be "wiped away [Greek, *aleipho*, 'washed away'] in order that times of refreshing may come from the presence of the Lord; and that He may send Jesus, the Christ appointed for you" (Acts 3:19-20). This is a reference to the promised messianic kingdom. When the Jews repent, the kingdom will arrive. However, as Scripture tells us, they will not repent until the end of the Tribulation.

Peter then said Christ would remain in heaven "until the period of restoration of all things about which God spoke by the mouth of His holy prophets from ancient time" (verse 21). "Restoration" means "to again set in order." It is a reference to the restoration of the kingdom of the Jews. "The 'all things' are not limited just to spiritual blessings. 'All things' means all things. This is the long anticipated 'age to come' (Is. 11:1-12), the coming kingdom which will be

the final realization of all the promises God had made to the Jewish people through the prophets" (Ger, *The Book of Acts*, p. 65).

Peter then said Christ was the great Prophet that Moses spoke about concerning this day (Acts 3:22; 7:37; Deuteronomy 18:15), and the souls of the Jews who do not heed Him "shall be utterly destroyed from among the people" (Acts 3:23). Beginning with Samuel, all the prophets together had "announced these days" (verse 24). Peter was saying that it was Samuel the prophet who first prophesied that the Messiah would come through the house of David (2 Samuel 7:12-17; Psalm 89:26-27). This blessing has its roots in the fathers of Israel, beginning with Abraham, to whom God said, "In your seed all the families of the earth shall be blessed" (Acts 3:25; Genesis 22:18). The Messiah, God's Servant, descended from Abraham through the line of David. Peter then concluded, "God raised up His Servant and sent Him to bless you by turning every one of you from your wicked ways" (Acts 3:26).

The Jews, especially the liberal Sadducees, who denied the doctrine of the resurrection, were furious with Peter's sermon. They were "greatly disturbed because [Peter and John] were teaching the people and proclaiming in Jesus the resurrection from the dead" (4:2).

THE REJECTION OF THE MESSIAH
Acts 4:10-11,23-28

EVEN THOUGH THE temple authorities and the Sadducees threw Peter and John in prison, some 5000 men believed their message about the resurrection of Christ (verses 1-4). When Peter and John were brought from prison before the rulers and the scribes, Peter, "filled with the Holy Spirit," spoke to them with great boldness (verse 8). Using the healing of the lame man as a firmly confirmed miracle (3:1-10), Peter pointed out that this happened "by the name of Jesus Christ the Nazarene, whom you crucified, whom God raised from the dead" (4:10). He then added that Jesus, by His crucifixion, "is the stone which was rejected by you, the builders, but which became the chief corner stone" (verse 11; Psalm 118:22; cf. Matthew 21:42). Hackett states, "The Jewish rulers, according to the proper idea of their office, were the builders of God's spiritual house, and as such should have been the first to acknowledge the Messiah and exert themselves for the establishment and extension of his kingdom" (*Commentary on Acts,* p. 68).

Peter was direct with the Jewish rulers and elders about Jesus, saying, "There is salvation in no one else; for there is no other name under heaven that has been given among men by which we must be saved" (Acts 4:12).

The Jewish leaders then ordered Peter and John not to speak any more "or teach at all in the name of Jesus" (verse 18). After they were threatened, the disciples were let go (verse 21). When the disciples reported back to other believers what the chief priests and the elders had said, they lifted their voices and praised God for His sovereignty, quoting Psalm 146:6: "O Lord, it is You who made the heaven and the earth and the sea, and all that is in them" (Acts 4:24). They continued praising Him and, quoting prophecy, they said that the nations would turn against the Lord and against His Christ (verses 25-26; Psalm 2:1-2).

Though the nations will rebel, God is in charge! In His mysterious providence Christ was crucified for the sins of humanity. This was all a part of God's plan; it was not an accident. As Peter said, "Truly in this city there were gathered together against Your holy servant Jesus, whom You anointed, both Herod and Pontius Pilate, along with the Gentiles and the peoples of Israel, to do whatever Your hand and Your purpose predestined to occur" (Acts 4:27-28).

STEPHEN'S PROPHETIC SUMMARY OF ISRAEL'S PAST
Acts 7:1-53

STEPHEN WAS THE FIRST deacon chosen for the church in Jerusalem (Acts 6:5). He was the first one mentioned to be a significant helper in the newly formed congregation in Israel. He was "full of faith" and "full of grace and power, was performing great wonders and signs among the people" (verses 5,8). Polhill observes that Stephen's argument shows "the beginnings of the fulfillment of God's promises to Abraham," continuing into the story of the patriarchs (*Acts,* p. 191). Since a reference to circumcision would remind them of the birth of Abraham's son (Genesis 17:10-14), "the circumcision of Isaac confirms that God kept His promise" to Abraham's seed (Genesis 21:4). The Jewish authorities accused Stephen of speaking "blasphemous words against Moses and against God" (Acts 6:11), and of speaking against the holy temple, "and the Law" (verse 13). Questioned by the high priest (7:1), Stephen responded by giving the longest sermon recorded in Acts, with the conclusion that this generation of Jews "are doing just as your fathers did" in rejecting God's messengers (verse 51).

Stephen's sermon includes many references to *Old Testament prophecies,* beginning with the call of Abraham out of Mesopotamia (verses 2-3). God gave Abraham the promise of a land, and said this would be the possession of his offspring (verse 5). But the Lord also gave a prophecy that his children would be strangers for 400 years in a foreign land, Egypt (verse 6). Mentioning prophecy after prophecy and citing their fulfillments, Stephen showed how God was faithful in all of His promises to the Jewish descendants of Abraham (verses 7-45). Coming down to the story of David and Solomon, he related how God commanded that the great "house" or temple be constructed by Solomon (verses 46-48). Yet God cannot be contained in a building made "by human hands." Quoting Isaiah 66:1, Stephen showed that "heaven is [God's] throne, and earth is the footstool of My feet" (Acts 7:49). No earthly temple could hold God (verse 50).

At this point in his message, Stephen set forth an indictment against his own generation. To the Jews, the present temple was the beginning and the end of their theology. God was left out of their thinking. Stephen called those standing before him stiff-necked and uncircumcised, with heart and ears "always resisting the Holy Spirit; you are doing just as your fathers did" (Acts 7:51). He added that all of the prophets of the past were persecuted, and the people even killed "those who had previously announced the coming of the Righteous One [the Messiah], whose betrayers and murderers you have now become" (verse 52). He also said his listeners bragged about keeping the law, but did not actually keep it (verse 53).

This was the last straw to the leaders hearing Stephen speak. "They were cut to the quick, and they began gnashing their teeth at him" (verse 54). Covering their ears, they cried out with loud voices and rushed on him (verse 57). God was merciful and filled Stephen with the Holy Spirit, and Stephen looked upward "into heaven and saw the glory of God, and Jesus standing at the right hand of God" (verse 55). There he saw the resurrected and ascended Christ, "the Son of Man," standing at the right hand of God (verse 56). The Scriptures say that Christ is now seated on His Father's throne (Psalm 110:1-2), but here, we read that Christ is standing at the right hand of His Father. Christ in glory was honoring Stephen, who gave a powerful testimony of the Lord Jesus Christ to the Jewish leadership. For this Stephen was stoned to death, during which he pleaded, "Lord Jesus, receive my spirit!" (Acts 7:59). With a loud voice, Stephen's final words were "Lord, do not hold this sin against them!" (verse 60).

That the Lord Jesus is now with His Father on His throne in heaven is continually quoted in the New Testament. There He makes intercession for His saints, and He is waiting until all His enemies are subdued before He comes to reign on earth on the Davidic throne in Zion (Psalm 110:1-2; see also Matthew 26:64; Mark 16:19; Ephesians 1:20; Colossians 3:1; Hebrews 1:3; 8:1; 10:10-14; 12:2).

THE ETHIOPIAN EUNUCH AND ISAIAH 53
Acts 8:26-40

An angel of the Lord instructed Philip, one of the first deacons in the Jerusalem church (6:5), to "go south to the road that descends from Jerusalem to Gaza" (8:26). There, Philip had an encounter with an Ethiopian eunuch, or court official, who represented the queen of the ancient land of Nubia. The name "Candace" (verse 27) was a descriptive title for all the queens of that nation. Philip found the man, who was on his way back to North Africa, sitting in his chariot reading Isaiah 53 (verse 28). The Spirit of God instructed and guided Philip to "go up and join this chariot" (verse 29), which was apparently parked or moving slowly along the desert road. When Philip asked the eunuch if he understood what this chapter was about (verse 30), the eunuch answered "Well, how could I, unless someone guides me?" And with that, he invited Philip to join him in the chariot (verse 31).

The eunuch was studying Isaiah 53:7-8, which prophesies, "He was led as a sheep to slaughter; and as a lamb before its shearer is silent, so He does not open His mouth. In humiliation His judgment was taken away; who shall relate His generation? For His life is removed from the earth" (Acts 8:32-33). When the eunuch asked who this was (verse 34), Philip began to preach Jesus to him from this Scripture (verse 35). Seeing some water, the man instantly asked Philip what would prevent him from being baptized (verse 36). Philip responded, "If you believe with all your heart, you may." The man answered, "I believe that Jesus Christ is the Son of God" (verse 37). Coming out of the water, Philip was snatched away by the Spirit of the Lord, and the man went away rejoicing (verse 39).

This event shows how important Isaiah 53 was in Jewish theology at that time. The Jewish rabbis recognized this passage as messianic in nature. It was obvious that the verses were prophesying the substitutionary death of Christ, as a sacrificial lamb, for the sins of Israel. This story also shows it was common knowledge that the lamb of Isaiah 53 was the Son of God of Psalm 2:7. The encounter also illustrates that it was commonly held by the Jews that water baptism was a sign of inner conversion and repentance. An inner cleansing had taken place by the confession of Jesus as the Son of God! It is not necessarily a coincidence that the eunuch was reading Isaiah 53 when he did. Journeying from Jerusalem, this man had more than likely heard much about the death and resurrection of Christ. Many other people who heard about these events also connected them with the Old Testament prophecies that foretold of these things.

This incredible story shows the extraordinary measures God will go to to bring the truth about Jesus to one lost soul.

PAUL'S CONVERSION
Acts 9:17-20

SAUL WAS STANDING nearby in hearty agreement when Stephen was slain by the angry Jews (Acts 8:1). On the day of Stephen's death there began a great persecution that scattered the Christians of Jerusalem "throughout the regions of Judea and Samaria," though the apostles remained in the city. Saul became the "district attorney" of the Jewish leadership commissioned to root out all those following the name of Christ. He ravaged the church, "entering house after house, and dragging off men and women, he would put them in prison" (8:3).

Saul was driven to persecute all Christians. Armed with letters of authority from the high priest (9:1), he started on his way to the synagogues in Damascus to capture any who belonged to "the Way," that is, those who claimed to be believers in Christ (verse 2). Couch writes, "The theological concept of the Way begins in Christ's statement in John 14:6: 'I am the way, and the truth, and the life; no one

comes to the Father, but through Me'" (*Bible Handbook to the Acts of the Apostles,* p. 272).

Saul was suddenly interrupted on his journey by a flash of light from heaven. He fell to the ground and heard a voice calling to him, "Saul, Saul, why are you persecuting Me?" (verses 3-4). Crying out, he asked, "Who art Thou, Lord?" Christ answered, "I am Jesus whom you are persecuting, but get up and enter the city, and it will be told you what you must do" (verses 5-6). Those traveling with Paul were speechless, having heard a voice but having seen no one (verse 7).

Saul continued on to Damacus and waited there three days, sightless and neither eating nor drinking (verse 9). The Lord then appeared to a disciple in the city named Ananias, who heard his name spoken and answered, "Here I am, Lord" (verse 10). God instructed him to find Saul (verse 11) and lay hands on him so that he might regain his sight (verse 12). The Lord told Ananias, "Go, for he is a chosen instrument of Mine, to bear My name before the Gentiles and kings and the sons of Israel; for I will show him how much he must suffer for My name's sake" (verses 15-16). Upon regaining his sight and being filled by the Holy Spirit (verse 17), Paul immediately "began to proclaim Jesus in the synagogues, saying, 'He is the Son of God'" (verse 20).

Saul was "called as an apostle, set apart for the gospel of God" (Romans 1:1). This calling was "by the will of God" (1 Corinthians 1:1), who sent him as an apostle not "from men…but through Jesus Christ and God the Father" (Galatians 1:1). The full understanding of the gospel did not come through men, nor was Saul taught it by men. Rather, he said, "I received it through a revelation of Jesus Christ" (verse 12).

PAUL'S MINISTRY
Acts 13:4-11

THE CHURCH AT ANTIOCH was full of "prophets and teachers" (verse 1) who were ministering to the Lord, fasting, and waiting for guidance as to how the work of evangelizing should be carried out. The Holy Spirit revealed that Barnabas and Saul were to do the work to "which I have called them" (verse 2). Hands were laid upon them and prayers were said, and the men were sent out by the Spirit to Seleucia and Cyprus (verses 3-4), and then on to Salamis (verse 5). Here the apostle, whose Jewish name was Saul and who was also known as Paul, would exercise the gift of foretelling the future in a confrontation with a warlock, an evil magician name Elymas.

This encounter took place on the island of Cyprus at Salamis, where "they found a magician, a Jewish false prophet whose name was Bar-Jesus" (verse 6). He was a personal friend of the island's proconsul, Sergius Paulus, "a man of intelligence" who had summoned Paul and Barnabas in order to hear the Word of God (verse 7). About the word "magician," MacArthur states, "The term originally referred to the hereditary priestly tribe within the Median nation. They were well versed in astronomy and astrology, agriculture, mathematics, and history. They were involved in various occult practices and were famous for their ability to interpret dreams (cf. Dan. 2:1ff.)" (*Acts 13–28*, p. 8).

When Elymas realized that the proconsul was being spiritually influenced by these men, he sought to turn him away from the faith (verse 8). Elymas wanted to keep to himself the power of influence over a government authority in order to carry out his evil purposes!

Paul, full of the Holy Spirit, "fixed his gaze upon him" (verse 9) and with the strongest words said, "You who are full of all deceit and fraud, you son of the devil, you enemy of all righteousness, will you not cease to make crooked the straight ways of the Lord?" (verse 10). Then speaking prophetically, Paul said, "Behold, the hand of the Lord is upon you, and you will be blind and not see the sun for a time" (verse 11).

Paul was confirmed as an apostle and prophet of the Lord because immediately "a

mist and a darkness fell upon [Elymas], and he went about seeking those who would lead him by the hand" (verse 11). This miraculous judgment, which came through Paul, had a great impact on the proconsul "when he saw what had happened." He was amazed at the "teaching of the Lord" spoken to him by Paul and Barnabas (verse 12). Such prophetic miracles verified that God was working through the apostolic authority of Peter, Paul, and the other apostles who were being led by the Holy Spirit.

PAUL'S REVIEW OF ISRAEL'S HISTORY
Acts 13:16-50

IN A MESSAGE SIMILAR TO that which Stephen spoke to the Jewish authorities (7:1-53), Paul preached on the Sabbath in a synagogue at Pisidian Antioch (in Asia Minor). Paul addressed the synagogue officials when they asked if he had any exhortation for the people gathered there (13:13-15). Beginning with the call of the fathers of Israel and the sojourn in Egypt, Paul showed how God led His people from slavery into the 40-year exodus in the wilderness, and finally into the land of Canaan (verses 17-19). Bruce says, "Paul's exhortation takes the form of a historical retrospect, as Stephen's defense did. Paul's retrospect surveys the course of God's dealings with his people Israel from his election of the patriarchs and deliverance of the nation from Egypt on to the accession of David and the establishment of his dynasty" (*Book of Acts*, pp. 252-53). After God removed King Saul, whom the people had asked for, "He raised up David to be their king, concerning whom He also testified and said, 'I have found David the son of Jesse, a man after My heart, who will do all My will'" (verses 21-22; 1 Samuel 13:14).

Wasting no time in his dialogue, Paul moved immediately to the call of Christ. "From the descendants of this man [David], according to promise, God has brought to

Israel a Savior, Jesus" (Acts 13:23). John the Baptist brought repentance to Israel (verse 24) and was the herald of Christ, the promised King. "Brethren, sons of Abraham's family, and those among you who fear God, to us the message of this salvation is sent out" (verse 26), but the people of Jerusalem and their rulers did not recognize Him nor the utterances of the prophets concerning Him (verse 27). He was executed (verse 28), raised from the dead (verse 30), and Paul now preached to them "the good news of the promise made to the fathers" (verse 32). God fulfilled His promise when He raised up Jesus, as confirmed in Psalm 2:7: "You are My Son; today I have begotten You" (Acts 13:33).

Paul added that the Lord promised that Christ would never return to decay, according to Isaiah 55:3: "I will give you [the Messiah] the holy and sure blessings of David" (Acts 13:34), meaning that the Messiah would live and inherit all the promises made to His earthly father David. Paul then cited Psalm 16:10, which says, "You will not allow Your Holy One to undergo decay" (Acts 13:35). Paul reminded his audience that these words through King David were not about himself but David's future son, the Lord Jesus. David "fell asleep" and "underwent decay" (verse 36), but Christ Jesus "did not undergo decay" (verse 37). Now, "through Him forgiveness of sins is proclaimed to you, and through Him everyone who believes is freed from all things, from which you could not be freed through the Law of Moses" (verses 38-39).

When Paul finished, many who heard wanted to know more, including many of the "Jews and of the God-fearing proselytes," who attended the synagogue (verse 43). The next week, "the whole city assembled to hear the word of God" (verse 44). The Jews, who were jealous, didn't like the reactions of the Gentiles and "began contradicting the things spoken by Paul, and were blaspheming" (verse 45). Speaking out boldly, Paul and Barnabas reminded the Jews that they should hear the truth first, but if they repudiated it and became "unworthy of eternal life," then Paul and Barnabas would be "turning to the Gentiles" (verse 46). Many Gentiles believed and were glorifying the Lord, "and as many as had been appointed to eternal life believed" (verse 48). "And the word of the Lord was being spread through the whole region" (verse 49). Though persecution followed (verse 50) and the disciples left the city and shook the dust from their feet (verse 51), still, they "were continually filled with joy and with the Holy Spirit" (verse 52).

It was the prophetic Word of the Old Testament rehearsed by the apostle Paul, coupled with the undeniable historic events of Christ's crucifixion, that elicited both stubborn rejection and belief in the truth.

THE JERUSALEM COUNCIL
Acts 15:1-21

THIS IS CONSIDERED the first formal church council that met to address important issues related to doctrine and policy. The arguments took place at the church at Antioch, but the council was held in Jerusalem around A.D. 49. The council was called because "some men came down from Judea" and began arguing that men could not be saved who were not circumcised (verse 1). Paul and Barnabas challenged these men, while others decided that these two disciples should go up to Jerusalem "to the apostles and elders concerning this issue" (verse 2). Paul and Barnabas's views were reinforced on the Jerusalem journey because they passed through the regions of Phoenicia and Samaria and witnessed the conversion of the Gentiles, with the result that this was "bringing great joy to all the brethren" (verse 3).

At Jerusalem, Paul and Barnabas reported what God was doing outside of the nation of Israel (verse 4). But some in the sect of the Pharisees who were believing on Christ objected and said, "It is necessary to circumcise them and to direct them to observe the Law of Moses" (verse 5). After much debate,

Peter stood up and said that God had been touching the hearts of the Gentiles through Peter's testimony, and many were believing the gospel (verse 7). He shared how the Holy Spirit fell on the Gentiles in Cornelius's house, with many believing and receiving forgiveness of sins (verse 8; see also 10:23-48). He described how the Gentiles received the Holy Spirit upon conversion, just as the disciples had at Pentecost (11:15-18; see also 2:4).

Peter argued at the council that *faith alone* saves, no matter whether that faith is exercised by Jew or Gentile (15:8). God makes no such distinction, "cleansing their hearts by faith" (verse 9). The yoke of the law, which the Jewish fathers had not been able to bear, should not be placed on the Gentiles (verse 10), because "we believe that we are saved through the grace of the Lord Jesus, in the same way as they also are" (verse 11). All the audience with the apostles and elders sat silent, listening to how God was using Paul, Barnabas, and Peter with "signs and wonders" and bringing Gentiles to Christ (verse 12).

The well-respected apostle James stood up and put his stamp of approval on what Peter said (verse 13). God was at that time taking "from among the Gentiles a people for His name" (verse 14). James then quoted Amos 9:11-12, saying that when God is finished among the Gentiles, He will return and begin working again with the Jewish people. He will rebuild "the tabernacle of David which has fallen," the temple, through which the rest of mankind "may seek the Lord"—that is, all of the Gentiles who are called by the name of the Lord (Acts 15:16-17). James finished by quoting the prophecy in Isaiah 45:21, where the Lord said He will make these things known from of old (Acts 15:18).

The point James was making is that it was prophesied that the Lord will use the restoration of the temple to draw the Gentiles to salvation in the millennium. Since this is so, He certainly can at that time reach the Gentiles. Because this was God's work, James added, the Gentiles should not be troubled by Jewish ceremonial issues (verse 19). However, in order to not offend the Jewish brethren, the Gentiles should not eat anything contaminated by idols or eat animal meat that had been strangled and still contained blood (verse 20). Since the law of Moses is read in the synagogues every Sabbath in the Gentile cities, the Jews would be incensed by these actions (verse 21).

James realized that the Lord was fulfilling great prophecies by saving Gentiles. While he may not have realized it at the moment, from this point forward it will be clear that God is uniting Jew and Gentile in this new thing called the church. "The apostles, elders and the collective church, [are] now in unified agreement" as to how Gentiles should be accepted into the body of Christ (Ger, *The Book of Acts*, p. 214).

THE MACEDONIAN CALL
Acts 16:6-10

PAUL AND SILAS TRAVELED through Lystra and Iconium, where they picked up a young disciple named Timothy, who was of Jewish and Greek heritage (15:40–16:2). Paul had him circumcised before they traveled on to Mysia and Troas (verses 7-8). During their journey they spoke and taught at various places, strengthening the churches and seeing their numbers increase (verse 5). As they passed through the Phrygian and Galatian regions, the Holy Spirit forbade them to speak the Word of God in that area of Asia Minor (verse 6). Also, at Mysia the "Spirit of Jesus did not permit them" to teach and preach the truth (verse 7).

By a prophetic vision that appeared to Paul in the night, a certain man of Macedonia "was standing and appealing to him, and saying, 'Come over to Macedonia and help us'" (verse 9). Ger writes, "Free of qualm or quandary in interpreting the vision as a divine directive to evangelize Macedonia, the missionaries made immediate plans to sail from Troas to Europe" (*The Book of Acts*, p. 227). This was a clear prophetic message that told Paul, "God had called us to preach the gospel to them" in that region (verse 10). After the vision, Paul and his companions immediately sought to travel into Macedonia. Much pain and persecution would follow when they arrived at Philippi, a city in the district of Macedonia. Though they would know the joy of Lydia's conversion (verse 14), Paul and Silas would later be thrown into prison for the disturbance that followed over the casting out of the spirit of divination in the slave girl (verses 16-24). But their imprisonment made it possible for the jailer and his household and many others to come to Christ (verses 25-34).

Johnson writes that just as "Peter was drawn to the edge of Palestine before being shown that he was to preach to Gentiles, so is Paul given a vision of a 'certain Macedonian man' who implores him for help. On the basis of that [prophetic] vision, Paul and his companions decide that God is 'summoning them' to preach the gospel also in Europe" (*The Acts of the Apostles,* p. 290).

PAUL AT MARS HILL
Acts 17:22-34

WHEN PAUL ARRIVED in Athens, he was greatly moved in spirit at the idolatry in the city. He divided his time between speaking to the Jews and the God-fearing Gentiles in the synagogue and to any who would listen to him in the open marketplace (verses 16-17). The Epicurean and Stoic philosophers accused him of being an "idle babbler" who was proclaiming strange deities because he "was preaching Jesus and the resurrection" (verse 18). Taking him up to the Areopagus, the venerable council that was in charge of the religious and educational matters in Athens, they gave Paul an opportunity to teach and to explain what he was proclaiming (verse 19).

With great boldness, and also subtlety, Paul reminded the people of Athens they had an altar inscribed "To an Unknown God," which they worshiped in ignorance (verse 23). Paul then spoke of this God, who made the "world and all things in it, since He is Lord of heaven and earth," and does not dwell in temples made by hands (verse 24). This God is not served by hands, but instead, gives life and breath to all (verse 25) and has determined the "appointed times and the boundaries" of the habitation of all (verse 26). The nations should seek Him because He is not far away (verse 27), and "in Him we live and move and exist." Even some Gentile poets admit, "We also are His children" (verse 28).

With the revelation of the resurrected Christ, "all people everywhere should repent" (verse 30) because God has appointed a judgment day "in righteousness through a Man whom He has appointed, having furnished proof to all men by raising Him from the dead" (verse 31). Some reacted to Paul with sneers, but others said, "We shall hear you again concerning this" (verse 32). All judgment has been placed in the hands of Christ (John 5:22) and will come to pass at the end of the millennial reign of Christ (Revelation 20:11-15). Christ is now proclaimed "the Son of God with power" because of His resurrection from the dead and because He is the holy One of God (Romans 1:4). This message drove Paul to witness to both the Jews and Gentiles.

THE WARNING TO THE EPHESIAN ELDERS
Acts 20:17-32

THE APOSTLE PAUL PROPHESIED to the Ephesian elders that from among their own ranks some "will arise, speaking perverse things, to draw away the disciples after them" (verse 30). Therefore they were instructed by Paul to "be on the alert, remembering that night and day for a period of three years I did not cease to admonish each one with tears" (verse 31).

Paul knew his days were short, and that is why he summoned the elders of the church to meet him at Miletus (verse 17). However he was mistaken about his death, living some ten or more years before he was martyred in

Rome between A.D. 65 and 67. He rehearsed with the Ephesian elders his ministry since the day he set foot in Asia (verse 18). During this ministry Paul testified "to both Jews and Greeks of repentance toward God and faith in our Lord Jesus Christ" (verse 21). It was prophesied to Paul by the Holy Spirit that persecution awaited him as "bonds and afflictions" (verse 23). These things came about as predicted.

Paul had taught the Ephesians about the kingdom and the future millennial reign of Christ, which all the believers at that time were still eagerly waiting for (verse 25). The kingdom has been presently postponed while people worldwide are being added to the body of Christ during this dispensation known as the church age. In his teaching, Paul also declared to the Ephesians "the whole purpose of God" (verse 27). The word "purpose" is the Greek word *boulee,* which means "will" or "council." Paul was teaching the full spectrum of important doctrine that ranges from the Old Testament all the way to the New Testament.

PAUL'S TESTIMONY TO AGRIPPA
Acts 26

AGRIPPA II, THE GRANDSON of Herod the Great, had murdered James the apostle some 15 years earlier (12:2). Agrippa had been given a modest kingdom, and from A.D. 50–56, his rule had been expanded to encompass the region of greater Galilee and northern Judea. As Paul faced charges from the Jews that he was preaching a form of insurrection, Agrippa expressed enthusiasm in personally hearing from Paul and even seemed open-minded when he said to Paul standing before him, "You are permitted to speak for yourself" (26:1). Paul explained that from his youth he spent his life as a faithful Jew living in Jerusalem (verse 4), and that he lived as a strict Pharisee, which was confirmed even by his enemies (verse 5). He described how he had hated Christians

and agreed with Jewish authorities when they were put to death (verses 9-11). But then Christ appeared to him on the Damacus road and said, "Saul, Saul, why are you persecuting Me? It is hard for you to kick against the goads" (verse 14).

Christ said He appeared to Paul in order "to appoint you a minister and a witness not only to the things which you have seen, but also to the things in which I will appear to you" (verse 16). He would be sent to open the eyes of the Gentiles to bring to them light and release them "from the dominion of Satan to God, that they may receive forgiveness of sins and an inheritance among those who have been sanctified by faith in Me" (verse 18).

Paul told Agrippa how he proclaimed to Israel the Christ who suffered and who would be resurrected in order "to proclaim light both to the Jewish people and to the Gentiles" (verse 23). Prophecy played a key role in Paul's defense; he reminded Agrippa that he was testifying "both to small and great, stating nothing but what the Prophets and Moses said was going to take place" (verse 22), and that Christ was going to suffer as predicted in Isaiah 53 (Acts 26:23). Ger comments:

> Everything Paul testified to was in strict accord with the ancient promises of Moses and the prophets contained in Hebrew Scripture of how the Messiah would suffer and die and as the first fruits of the resurrection (1 Cor. 15:23) would spiritually enlighten Jews and Gentiles alike. One need not look further than Isaiah's description of the suffering servant of God to locate the Scriptural origins of Paul's assertion (Is. 52:13-53:12) (*The Book of Acts,* p. 296).

PAUL'S INDICTMENT OF THE ROMAN JEWS
Acts 28:17-31

WHILE UNDER HOUSE ARREST in Rome, the apostle Paul was allowed to stay by himself (verse 16) and to have visitors who came to hear him teach. While there, Paul called together the Jewish leaders in order to clarify the reason he had been arrested (verse 17). He pointed out that he had done nothing against the Jewish people, and that when officials examined him in a court setting, they could find no ground for putting him to death (verse 18). Therefore he had appealed to Caesar, though he was not bringing any accusation against his own people (verse 19).

Those listening to Paul responded that they wanted to hear about this sect of Christianity, which "is spoken against everywhere" (verse 22). Paul was given a full day to explain and testify to them about the kingdom of God, and he tried "to persuade them concerning Jesus, from both the Law of Moses and from the Prophets, from morning until evening" (verse 23).

Some of the Jewish leaders were persuaded, while others rejected the message (verse 24). As a group, they could not agree with one another on the issues concerning Christ (verse 25). Paul became frustrated with their slowness of heart and rebuked them, saying, "The Holy Spirit rightly spoke through Isaiah the prophet to your fathers" (quoting Isaiah 6:9-10). A future generation would hear but not understand, and see but not perceive (Acts 28:26). God said their hearts would become dull, their ears would barely hear, and their eyes would be closed, "lest they should see with their eyes and hear with their ears, lest they should understand with their heart and turn, so that I should heal them" (verse 27 NKJV). Paul applied this prophecy of rejection to those standing before him, as well as to the majority of the Jews of his generation.

Because of the spiritual hardness manifest among the Jews, the gospel would go to the Gentiles, who were willing to listen (verse 28). The Jews in Paul's house departed, arguing among themselves (verse 29). Many came to Paul, and he welcomed them, "preaching the kingdom of God and teaching concerning the Lord Jesus Christ with all openness, unhindered" (verses 30-31). The "kingdom of God" is neither the church nor the church age, but it is the promised future messianic reign of Christ that will take place in Jerusalem and have a worldwide dominion.

THE
LETTERS

ROMANS

THE BOOK OF ROMANS IS PAUL'S EPISTOLARY MASTERPIECE. In it, the apostle lays out the fullest explanation of the doctrine of salvation in all the Bible. Starting with the opening verses of the first chapter, Paul connects our salvation with the prophecies of Scripture. God had promised the gospel beforehand through the Old Testament prophets (1:2-3). As prophesied, Christ was born of the seed of David (verse 3) and declared the Son of God by the resurrection (verse 4). Through Him the gospel has come to both Jew and Gentile (verses 16-17). For Paul, the doctrine of salvation in Jesus Christ is the greatest prophecy of all.

The book of Romans has been characterized as a court trial in which the people of earth are judged and found guilty (1:18–2:16). A charge is presented and the case is heard before the Lord's tribunal. For sin all the world stands guilty and is due a future judgment and wrath from the Judge, who is the Lord (3:9-20). However, God provides a full pardon, a legal acquittal, for those who trust Christ (verses 21-31). That is, the Lord Jesus steps up to the judicial bar and takes upon Himself the burden of sinful humanity. Salvation is assured to those who trust Him (5:1-21). In fact, the guilty are made heirs and sons of God through Christ's work on the cross.

Later in the book, Paul deals with the Jewish people's rebellion (Romans 9–10). Eventually they will be restored to God's favor (Romans 11). While the book reveals the situation as it stood at the time of the apostles, it establishes the major doctrines for the dispensation of the church (Romans 12–16). Much of what Paul wrote has future implications and fulfillment.

THE FUTURE JUDGMENT FOR SIN
Romans 2:5-16; 3:19

AFTER STATING THE THEME of the epistle and a glorious declaration about the gospel and its power to save (1:16), the apostle Paul explains why the saving grace of Christ is so important (verses 18-32). Humanity is condemned because of the rejection of the knowledge of God as revealed in nature (verses 18-23). In fact, people actually "exchanged the glory of the incorruptible God for an image in the form" of man and animals (verse 23). Because of this, God gave the world over to "the lusts of the heart" to carry out the most abominable of sins and evil actions (verse 24-32).

Paul then launches into the arguments of the moralists, who attempt to defend the actions of humanity and even argue for some kind of reprieve from God for their evil actions. He adds, "The judgment of God rightly falls" (2:2). He finishes this section and its indictment against the world with the fact that "God will judge the secrets of men through Christ Jesus" (verse 16). "There have been days of sinning, and days of acting, and days of suffering. Why should there not be a day of reckoning and of retribution?" (Plumer, *Commentary on Romans,* p. 105).

Writing to Gentiles, Paul reminds them of their "stubbornness and unrepentant heart," by which they are "storing up wrath for [themselves] in the day of wrath and revelation of the righteous judgment of God" (verse 5). This is not the wrath of the Tribulation (1 Thessalonians 1:10; 5:9) but the wrath of the final judgment of the lost (2 Thessalonians 1:5), the judgment of the great day (Jude 6). The Lord will execute judgment "upon all, and…convict all the ungodly of all their ungodly deeds which they have done in an ungodly way" (Jude 15).

These Gentiles judge others, but they are condemning themselves, "for you who judge practice the same things" (Romans 2:1). The Lord's judgment is a right judgment, and it will fall "upon those who practice" sin (verse 2). One cannot "suppose" (Greek, *logizomai,* or "logically calculate") that they can pass judgment on others, do the same things themselves, and then "escape the judgment of God" (verse 3). To do so is to think "lightly of the riches of His kindness and tolerance and patience, not knowing that the kindness of God leads you to repentance" (verse 4). Paul's point is that God's kindness *should* lead one to repentance, but because of the "stubbornness and unrepentant heart," only wrath is stored up (verse 5).

The apostle has already made it clear that "the wrath of God" hangs over the heads of all men who practice "ungodliness and unrighteousness," who press down or suppress "the truth in [by] unrighteousness" (1:18). If the world rejects the grace of God as found only in the Lord Jesus Christ and His work on the cross, there is no other recourse except that

God "will render to each person according to his deeds" (2:6). Paul quotes here the second half of Psalm 62:12, though the first part of the verse reminds the reader of God's grace and lovingkindness. The Lord prefers dispensing mercy and grace rather than executing a just recompense for the sins that one has done.

For those who turn from their sins and "seek for glory and honor and immortality, eternal life" will be given (Romans 2:7). Those who do not follow the truth of salvation as given freely in Christ and who "obey unrighteousness" will experience the future "wrath and indignation" (verse 8). By spurning the offer of salvation provided in the gospel of Christ (1:16), everyone, both Jew and Greek, will face "tribulation and distress" (2:9). The one who "does good" receives "glory and honor and peace" (verse 10). Paul is not teaching salvation by good works. To do good, in this context, is to "do the right thing" by accepting the work of Christ at the cross. Some Jews asked Christ, "What shall we do, so that we may work the works of God?" (John 6:28). Jesus answered, "This is the work of God, that you believe in Him whom He has sent" (verse 29).

At the final judgment of the lost there will be no partiality with God (Romans 2:11). If a Gentile sins without knowledge of the law, he will perish without the adjudication of the law; but the Jew who sins under the law will be judged by the law (verse 12). At the Great White Throne Judgment, all of the lost will be judged on the basis of their deeds (Revelation 20:12-13). No one can work his or her way to heaven. For the Gentile, the heart condemns, and for the Jew, the law condemns. Human effort and all forms of human works can never be enough to cancel sin from one's personal record. As Isaiah 64:6 says, "All of us have become like one who is unclean, and all our righteous deeds are like a filthy garment; and all of us wither like a leaf, and our iniquities, like the wind, take us away."

Condemnation comes because of what one has done that is sinful. Paul is using a hypothetical situation that argues that one could "earn" salvation if he indeed could live a perfect life. But of course, no one can do such a thing. In fact, Paul summarizes by quoting Psalm 14:1-3: "There is none righteous, not even one; there is none who understands, there is none who seeks for God" (Romans 3:10-11). To seal this issue once and for all, he adds that "by the works of the Law no flesh will be justified in His sight; for through the Law comes the knowledge of sin" (verse 20). The law was not given to save, but to condemn. The greater purpose of the law is "to lead us to Christ, so that we may be justified by faith" (Galatians 3:24).

On that future day of judgment, the backdrop of the judicial process will be the gospel (Romans 2:15-16). The gospel stands in contrast to human efforts for salvation. Even the "secret thoughts of men" will be judged by God. Because Paul says this will happen "through Christ Jesus," many hold that the One on the Great White Throne will be Christ Himself, who will judge humanity for His Father. After all, the Lord Jesus died for humanity; it is logical that He will judge humanity. Jesus said, "Not even the Father judges anyone, but He has given all judgment to the Son" (John 5:22).

Walvoord concludes, "The unsaved...will not be judged finally until after the millennial kingdom.... The final judgment determines the ultimate destiny of the soul" (*Prophecy Knowledge Handbook,* p. 446). The Bible describes this event as the Great White Throne Judgment (Revelation 20:11-15). At this judgment, all the lost of all time will be condemned and cast into the lake of fire.

THE PROMISE OF SALVATION AND LIVING WITH CHRIST
Romans 5:9-11; 6:8; 8:1

PAUL SETS FORTH the practical benefits of salvation and justification in 5:1-8. Justification is by faith alone and not by works. The believer receives peace with God "through our Lord Jesus Christ" (verse 1). This is because believers have been reconciled to God (verse 10). Christ introduces us by faith into the grace of God, in which the believer now stands positionally (verse 2). Standing in Christ brings about "perseverance" (Greek, *hupomone*), the ability to abide under pressure (verse 3), and this brings about "proven character" (verse 4), which leads to "hope [that] does not disappoint" (verse 5). All of this comes about "because the love of God has been poured out within our hearts through the Holy Spirit who was given to us" (verse 5).

Christ died for the helpless and the ungodly (verse 6). While some may be willing to die to save a righteous person (verse 7), God the Father sent Christ to earth to die for the unrighteous—even us, "while we were yet sinners" (verse 8). God's plan and provision has a future connotation to it. *Present* salvation puts the believer into a right relationship with God the Father and makes for peace because the issue of sin has been settled at the cross. But there is more to come! The apostle prophesies of a *future* salvation, when the believer will stand justified in glory and will have been completely redeemed from the wrath of God that will be poured out on the earth (verse 9).

Reconciliation (Greek, *katallasso*) involves a change in a relationship. It is the coming together of two (or more) parties in which a conflict has been resolved. Christ resolved the conflict believers had with God the Father because of their sin, and Jesus brought about this reconciliation. Sinners could not bridge the barrier that separated them from God, and Christ's reconciliation accomplished this for them (Romans 5:10-11; 11:15). God brought about this reconciliation by the death of His Son (2 Corinthians 5:18), who reconciled the world to Himself (verse 19). God no longer counts the trespasses against the sinners but views the sinners as redeemed by Christ.

Because of this reconciliation, we have the guarantee of future salvation. Now being "justified by His blood, we shall be saved from the wrath of God through Him" (Romans 5:9), and we "shall be saved by His life" (verse 10).

Because the old life was crucified with Christ and died with Him, it is certain that in a positional sense we are "freed from sin" (Romans 6:6-7). Newell says, "How utterly marvelous, then, to know that we have been justified *from sin itself*. Not only has it lost all right and power over us, but we are declared righteous from the hideous thing itself" (*Romans Verse by Verse*, p. 219).

Since believers died with Him, "we shall also live with Him" in heaven (verse 8). In a positional way, we are dead to sin "but alive to God in Christ Jesus (verse 11). Even though this body will die, the future promise of our final salvation means we will never, in an actual sense, die. Christ said, "I am the resurrection and the life; he who believes in Me will live even if he dies, and everyone who lives and believes in Me will never die" (John 11:25-26).

Salvation is a finished work, completed by the death of Christ on the cross. But there is also our future salvation, the completion or the finishing of the process of redeeming the believer and finally bringing him or her home to heaven.

BECOMING HEIRS AND SONS OF GOD
Romans 8:12-39

TRUE BELIEVERS IN THE LORD JESUS are characterized as having no condemnation against them (verse 1). Though this position does not automatically produce a perfect moral and spiritual life, it shows that believers are now living under the new nature instead of the old one (verse 13). The present experience of salvation is the first stage of that which is prophesied. Since we are now sons of God (verse 15), we have the assurance that we will also be heirs of God (verse 17).

The fact that Christians can call out "Abba! Father!" shows that they have been given "a spirit of adoption" (verse 15). "Abba" is an Aramaic word meaning "Daddy." As a little child

calls for his father, so believers can call upon the heavenly Father for help. The Holy Spirit witnesses to the fact that we are "children of God" (verse 16) and "heirs also, heirs of God and fellow heirs with Christ" (verse 17).

Prophetically speaking, a *future glorification* awaits believers (verse 17), a glory yet "to be revealed" (verse 18) and a full revelation coming of "the sons of God" (verse 19). "This 'revelation' has the connotation of a disclosure, or 'unveiling'; Christians, suffering (verse 18) and weak (verse 26) like all other people, do not 'appear' in this life much like sons of God, but the last day will publicly show our real status" (Moo, *Romans 1–8*, p. 550). This is when the plan of redemption is completed and believers will stand as trophies of God's grace. Creation will then be absolutely free from the curse placed upon it by the fall of Adam (Genesis 3:17-19). It "will be set free from its slavery to corruption into the freedom of the glory of the children of God" (Romans 8:21).

This prophecy will not be finalized until the universe is purged, restored, and renovated (2 Peter 3:10-14; Revelation 21:14). Believers "await eagerly" for the resurrection of the body, when the full adoption as sons will be completed and finalized—that is, "the redemption of our body" (Romans 8:23). Witmer observes:

> The verb for "eagerly awaits" (*apek-dechomai*) is used seven times in the New Testament, each time to refer to Christ's return (Rom. 8:19, 23, 25; 1 Cor. 1:7; Gal. 5:5; Phil. 3:20; Heb. 9:28). The revealing of the sons of God will occur when Christ returns for His own. They will share His glory (Rom. 8:18; Col. 1:27; 3:4; Heb. 2:10), and will be transformed (Rom. 8:28). All of nature (inanimate and animate) is personified as waiting eagerly for that time (Witmer, "Romans," *Bible Knowledge Commentary*, p. 472).

In verses 24-25, Paul describes the two kinds of salvation. By faith in Christ, believers already "have been saved" (verse 24). Yet the final stage of redemption is still ahead—that is, when one dies or is suddenly transformed and given a new body by being raptured to glory without having to experience death (1 Thessalonians 4:13-18). Believers "hope" (Greek, *elpizo,* "anticipate") for this great event. The child of God "wait[s] eagerly" for this because it cannot presently be seen. "There is something in the very expectation of future good, and especially of such good, the glory that shall be revealed in us, to produce not only patient but even joyful endurance of all present suffering" (Hodge, *Romans,* pp. 277-78).

Meanwhile, because believers are earthbound, suffer weaknesses, and have limited understanding, God sends us the Spirit, who "intercedes for us with groanings too deep for words" (Romans 8:26). While a Christian may not know how to pray under stressful and painful circumstances, the Lord promises that the Holy Spirit will pray before the Father as his Intercessor (verses 26-27). The Spirit of God intercedes on the behalf of the child of God "according to the will of God" (verse 27). The persons in the Godhead are working in a sovereign way to bring God's purposes to fruition in the lives of His children. In this way the Lord causes "all things to work together for good to those who love God, to those who are called according to His purpose" (verse 28).

Next Paul reviews the divine steps that brought about the salvation of the believer. Whom God *foreknew* in an intimate and personal way in the eternal past, He *predestined* the same to "become conformed to the image of His Son," that the Son might be the "firstborn among many brethren" (verse 29). (In this passage, the word "predestined" means that in eternity past God gave a destiny to those who would receive God's mercy. This destiny is to be "conformed to the image of Christ" through salvation and sanctification.) And those predestined were in time called and justified (verse 30). But there is more. Those justified (legally acquitted) are already *glorified* in heaven! God is not bound by time. He sees all things as a whole. In the original Greek text, the main nouns (*foreknew, predestined,*

called, justified, glorified) are in the aorist tense, meaning that the action *is completed.* What is surprising is that this includes the *glorification* of the believer! In God's mind, this has already been accomplished. Those who know Christ are already "blessed...with every spiritual blessing in the heavenly places in Christ" (Ephesians 1:3). This is why the apostle Paul can end Romans 8 with this great promise: Nothing "will be able to separate us from the love of God, which is in Christ Jesus our Lord" (verse 39).

GOD'S PROPHETIC PLAN FOR ISRAEL
Romans 9

In Romans 9–11, the apostle Paul shows the significance of the nation of Israel in the earthly plan of God. Though the church is the new dispensation for this age, God is not finished with the Jewish people! The earthly kingdom is yet to come. The theocracy of the Davidic kingdom has been temporarily set aside but will someday be restored, fulfilling hundreds of Old Testament prophecies.

Paul tells his readers he has a great spiritual concern for his Jewish brethren and kinsmen "according to the flesh" (9:2-3). He wishes that he could be accursed if this would bring salvation to them. He makes sure his readers know of the importance of the Jewish people, who "are Israelites, to whom belongs the adoption as sons, and the glory and the covenants and the giving of the Law and the temple service and the promises" (verse 4). They are related to the "fathers" of old, from whom comes the Christ "according to the flesh, who is over all, God blessed forever. Amen" (verse 5). These verses establish the place of the Jewish people in divine history. However, at the time of Paul's writing to the Romans, there was a great spiritual failure among many in Israel. Nevertheless, the mysterious sovereignty of God in His earthly plans cannot be questioned or ignored (verses 6-33).

When God gave the prophecies about His program to the patriarch Abraham (Genesis 12:1-3), He later showed that the promises would not be for all of his descendants. The promises were for the line of Isaac (Romans 9:7,9) and not Ishmael (Genesis 17:15-19), through Jacob (Romans 9:10-12; Genesis 25:23) and not Esau, Jacob's older twin (Romans 9:23; Genesis 25:33-34). God drew the boundaries of His covenant line and passed it along to whom He pleased. Not all Jews who are "the children of the flesh" are "children of God," but only those whom the Lord called in order to work out His plan. Paul revealed God's choices concerning Esau and Jacob when he wrote, "Though the twins were not yet born and had not done anything good or bad, so that God's purpose according to His choice would stand, [God elected Jacob over Esau] not because of works, but because of Him who calls" (Romans 9:11).

God has a right to reject sinners from His plans. Esau, the first of the twins out of Rebekah's womb, as a grown man, "despised his birthright" and gave it to his brother Jacob (Genesis 25:34). This is why the Lord later said, "Jacob I loved, but Esau I hated" (Malachi 2:1; Romans 9:12). No one can fully explain this. Though people are held fully responsible for the choices they make, still, God's mysterious plans and purposes in various people's lives defy human understanding.

The apostle Paul uses this as a launching pad to go on to a bigger subject: God is the One who determines the course of history. It is He who has mercy on whom He will have mercy (verse 15). It is clear that humans cannot fully grasp God's providence. On this issue Paul asks an important question and then gives the answer: "There is no injustice with God, is there? May it never be!" (verse 14). God deals justly and mercifully with all men, and when we refuse His grace and mercy, we bring condemnation on ourselves.

The end of history will bring a great demonstration of the grace of God. He will show His power by what He has done with the vessels "prepared for destruction" and the vessels "prepared beforehand for glory" (Romans 9:22-23). He is in charge of history. At the end of time, the merciful God will again extend His mercy to Israel.

In the prophetic master plan, the Lord has called both Jews and Gentiles (verse 24). The Lord foretold this through His prophet Hosea (Hosea 1:10; 2:21). From a future generation of Jews He will call out those who once were in rebellion (Romans 9:25) to become the "sons of the living God" (verse 26). They will reply "You are my God!" (Hosea 2:23). The larger context of these verses in Hosea refers to when the Jews are sown back "in the land" (verse 23) during the kingdom age. Paul adds that the same thing was predicted in Isaiah 10:22-23 about future Israel. Though the nation is large in number, only a future "remnant...will be saved; for the Lord will execute His word on the earth, thoroughly and quickly" (Romans 9:27-28). Paul quotes the prophet Isaiah, who speaks for ancient Israel (Isaiah 1:9): "Unless the Lord of Sabaoth [the Lord of hosts] had left to us a posterity, we would have become like Sodom, and would have resembled Gomorrah"—totally destroyed (Romans 9:29)!

After Paul describes how the Jews will finally be redeemed, he turns to the issue of how Gentiles were now turning to Christ, in contrast to the Jews, who thought they could be saved by law keeping (verses 30-33). The Gentiles, the pagans of the world, "did not pursue righteousness," but now have "attained righteousness, even the righteousness which is by faith" (verse 30). The righteousness of Christ must be applied to the believer in order for salvation to be complete. Abraham, the father of the Jewish people, "believed in the LORD; and He reckoned it to him as righteousness" (Genesis 15:6). By giving His Son, God the Father demonstrated His love for the entire world, not just for Israel (John 3:16). The Jews tried to find righteousness by keeping the law and doing good works (Romans 9:31), and not by faith (verse 32).

The Lord prophesied in Isaiah 28:16 that the Jewish people would stumble over the coming of Jesus their Messiah, who would become to them a "stone of stumbling and a rock of offense." But the one "who believes in Him will not be disappointed" (Romans 9:33).

Taken in its entirety, Romans chapter 9 sets forth the extension of the gospel to the Gentiles since the nation of Israel, as a whole, refused to accept Jesus Christ by faith. From here, the apostle writes about Israel's present situation and opportunity (chapter 10), and the nation's future restoration (chapter 11).

JEWISH SALVATION IN THE AGE OF GRACE
Romans 10

THE APOSTLE PAUL KNEW that many Jews would not receive Christ in the present dispensation of the church. Nevertheless, he still had an emotional affinity to his own people. He had a heart's desire and a prayer for their salvation (10:1). But the salvation of the larger number would not happen. They refused God's imputed righteousness and set out "seeking to establish their own" right standing with God (verse 3). They failed to understand that Christ "is the end of the law for righteousness to everyone who believes" (verse 4). By "end" (Greek, *telos*) he means that Christ is the completion, the summing up of the law for all who trust in Him. Therefore, righteousness before God must come as a gift by faith (verse 6).

The apostle quotes various expressions from Deuteronomy 30:12-14 to show the connection between what one says with the mouth and believes in the heart. The two should be the same: "'The word is near you, in your mouth and in your heart'—that is the word of faith which we are preaching" (Deuteronomy 30:14; Romans 10:8). The Jewish people cannot simply give lip service to the person of Christ. With all the promises given them by the prophecies proclaimed by their own prophets, they could not simply believe that He was just a good man, a clever rabbi, or an esteemed prophet. They had to face the

evidence that He was the promised Lord of Daniel 7 and Psalm 110. "If you confess with your mouth Jesus as Lord, and believe in your heart that God raised Him from the dead, you will be saved" (Romans 10:9).

For both Jew and Greek, "the same Lord is Lord of all, abounding in riches for all who call upon Him; for 'Whoever will call on the name of the Lord will be saved'" (verses 12-13). So that both Jew and Gentile then might believe, a preacher must be sent to bring the glad tidings of salvation (verses 14-16). But the question is still asked: "Have the Jews really had an opportunity to trust Christ?" Paul answers, "Indeed they have" (verse 18). God prophesied that they would hear but that they also would deny the truth about their own Messiah. To prove this, Paul quotes four Old Testament prophecies. The psalmist wrote that the words of preachers would go "to the ends of the world" (verse 18; Psalm 19:4). Moses predicted the Jews would be made jealous and angry "by those who are not a nation," probably meaning the Gentile peoples collectively (Romans 10:19; Deuteronomy 32:21). Isaiah prophesied that God would be found by those who did not ask for Him, meaning the Gentiles (Romans 10:20; Isaiah 65:1), and finally, "as for Israel [God] says, 'All the day long I have stretched out My hands to a disobedient and obstinate people'" (Romans 10:21; Isaiah 65:2).

God's promises to the nation of Israel have not been transferred to the Gentiles. Paul focuses on the fact that, for the present time, the Jewish people have been set aside, and the Lord is reaching out to the Gentile nations. But this does not eliminate His promises to Israel through the prophets.

THE GLORIOUS FUTURE OF THE NATION OF ISRAEL
Romans 11:1-32

THE QUESTION ARISES whether God is forever finished with the Jewish people. Are His promises about the messianic kingdom void?

In a certain spiritualized or allegorical way, do the kingdom promises become promises for the church? The answer to these questions is no.

Though Israel as a theocracy, with Christ reigning on the throne of David, has been set aside, this is temporary. "God has not rejected His people, has He?" Paul asks (11:1). The word "rejected" (Greek, *apotheo*) means "to push away, to shove away from, to repudiate." In the original Greek text, this term appears in the aorist middle indicative, and thus the question can be translated, "Has God Himself finished His work with His people?"

Paul was living proof that the Lord was saving some of the Jewish people. Paul was "an Israelite, a descendant of Abraham, of the tribe of Benjamin" (verse 1). God has not permanently rejected His people, whom He *foreknew* in a planned and intimate way (verse 2), though it may seem as if He has. The Old Testament prophet Elijah thought that all the Jewish people had turned away from God. He cried out, "Lord, they have killed Your prophets, they have torn down Your altars, and I alone am left, and they are seeking my life" (verse 3; 1 Kings 19:10). But God responded, "I have kept for Myself seven thousand men who have not bowed the knee to Baal" (Romans 11:4; 1 Kings 19:18). Paul thus shows that God has always saved a remnant, even when it seemed to some individuals as if only a few faithful Israelites were left.

Though the nation as a whole has rejected her Savior and King, the Lord Jesus Christ, "at the present time a remnant according to God's gracious choice" is being saved (Romans 11:5). There will be a saved remnant who will enter the kingdom at the end of the Tribulation (9:27), and a remnant now is saved by grace and not by works (11:6).

The word for "hardening" (Greek, *poroo*) means "to render insensitive." The Jews became insensitive to the Lord and His law. Such moral insensitivity brought about a judicial penalty. They were given "a spirit of stupor" (verse 8; Deuteronomy 29:4), and as King David predicted, a table that became a trap, along with a stumbling block (Romans 11:9; Psalm

69:22). The table is a reference to the table of blessing and provisions that God bestowed upon His people. In other words, Israel would turn against God's goodness and His care of the people. What was meant for good became a curse. David added, "Let their eyes be darkened to see not, and bend their backs forever" (verse 23; Romans 11:10). Kroll observes that these quotes give "reference to the unseeing eyes and unhearing ears of those who refuse to recognize the truth of God. Each of the gospel writers used this expression to indicate the Jews' failure to recognize Jesus as the Messiah (cf. Matt. 13:14; Mark 4:12; Luke 8:10; John 12:40)" (*The Book of Romans*, p. 178).

The spiritual and national fall of Israel are not permanent (Romans 11:11). The riches of God's grace will be shown for a time to the Gentiles (verse 12), and Paul argues that his people will be moved to jealousy as a result, causing them to turn to Christ and be saved (verse 14). So the Jews' rejection of their promised Messiah brings about a reconciliation of the Gentile world with God. It is as if the Gentile acceptance of Christ is "but life from the dead" (verse 15).

Paul here gives an illustration of an olive tree and its roots. It is often asked what the tree and its roots represent. Water and nourishment comes from the ground into the roots and on up into the branches. The roots then, represent God's blessings that supplied the Jews, the natural "branches," with spiritual blessings (verse 17). These natural branches were broken off (the Jews' rejection of Christ), and the wild olive branches (the Gentiles) were grafted in among the Jewish remnant (verse 17). Because the Jewish branches were broken off in unbelief (verse 19), the Gentiles must not become conceited, but must remain humble and stand in their faith (verse 20). Some scholars believe the roots represent the blessings that flowed to the Jewish people from Abraham and the covenant God made with him (Genesis 12:1-3). Since the passage does not say that, it might be just as simple to see the roots as the means, or the instrument, of the flow of God's blessing.

The apostle then warns the Gentiles of "the

kindness and severity of God; to those who fell, severity, but to you, God's kindness, if you continue in His kindness; otherwise you also will be cut off" (Romans 11:22). Paul is not speaking of the loss of one's salvation, but rather, of the departure of the Gentiles away from the grace that has come to them. With the warning comes these prophetic reminders: 1) God is able to graft the Jews back into a place of blessing (verse 23); and 2) when the wild olive tree (the Gentile nations) has rejected the truth, the natural branches (the Jews) will be "grafted into their own olive tree" (verse 24). This is a "mystery," something that has not previously been completely revealed. It leads to a prophecy about God's providential work with all the nations of the world. Eventually a change among the nations is going to take place: "A partial hardening has happened to Israel until the fullness of the Gentiles has come in" (verse 25).

The phrase "the fullness of the Gentiles" has been interpreted many different ways. Some believe this could progressively be taking place now—that is, God is winding down His work with the nations of the world. The Gentiles are hardening themselves toward the gospel, and God is working again with the Jewish people, who have been brought back in unbelief to the Holy Land. But this phrase may also refer to the end of the worldwide Tribulation, when the Messiah comes from heaven and completely restores the Jews both in terms of salvation and in reference to the peace that takes place in the land with His presence. The nations will be judged and will be, to a degree, subservient to God's earthly people, the Jews. Kroll believes the fullness of the Gentiles is to some degree about the present age and that the renewed times for Israel will take place during the Tribulation. He writes, "Eschatologically, the nation of Israel will remain hardened to the gospel until God's Church is complete and the New Testament saints are raptured to heaven at the close of this present age. Then, during the Tribulation period, God will again focus His attention on Israel in order to restore the Jewish people to a place of blessing" (*The Book of Romans,* p. 183).

Paul then says, "All Israel will be saved" (verse 26). What does this mean? Paul is probably alluding to Jeremiah 30, where the Lord prophesies of the Tribulation and the redemption of Israel from it. The Lord says the Tribulation (Jeremiah 30:6) is an awful period—"it is the time of Jacob's distress, but he will be saved from it" (verse 7). The patriarch Jacob here represents the entire nation of the Jews. Jeremiah is saying the nation as a whole will be saved from it. Jacob, or Israel, will be "saved...from afar," and "Jacob will return, and will be quiet and at ease" (verse 10). Though not every Jew will be saved, there will be a remnant, a group of survivors who will constitute the whole of the people as represented by the singular noun Jacob.

Paul then quotes Isaiah 59:20-21, a prophecy that speaks of the coming of the Messiah. The "Deliverer will come from Zion, He will remove ungodliness from Jacob" (Romans 11:26). Neither Zion nor Jacob can be construed as the church. What is prophesied here has to do with the national restoration of Israel and the establishment of the earthly Davidic kingdom.

In verse 27 the apostle quotes Isaiah 27:9 and says that the nation of Israel will be blessed by the New Covenant, which takes away the sins of those Jewish people who choose to trust in Christ as their Savior. The New Covenant comes out of the promise of blessing through Abraham. God promised him, "I will bless you, and make your name great; and so you shall be a blessing, and I will bless those who bless you, and the one who curses you I will curse" (Genesis 12:2-3). The New Covenant is made with all of the Jewish people, the descendants of the houses of Israel and Judah (Jeremiah 31:31-37). In this covenant God will "forgive their iniquity, and their sin I will remember no more" (verse 34). Christ made it quite clear that by His death on the cross, His blood "is poured out for you [in] the new covenant" (Luke 22:20). Though the church now benefits by the New Covenant and receives the forgiveness of sins by the blood of Christ (2 Corinthians 3:1-8), the covenant will have its ultimate and complete fulfillment for the Jews as they are blessed in the land.

Romans 11:28-32 makes it clear that God has not finished His work with the Jews. While the Jewish people are in conflict with the Gentiles who have accepted Christ ("they are enemies for your sake"), "from the standpoint of God's choice they are blessed for the sake of the fathers." By this Paul means that the Lord had made covenant promises to Abraham, Isaac, and Jacob on the basis of His sovereign election, and He will not go back on those promises. In fact, at the present, while the Jews are denying Christ, they are still loved by God (verse 28). The "gifts and the calling of God are irrevocable" (verse 29)—that is, they are not to be taken back.

Just as the Gentile nations were "disobedient to God" but now have been shown mercy because of the Jews' disobedience (verse 30), they shall in the future be given mercy when the Gentiles disobey the truth (verse 31). God designed a plan of salvation that would show mercy to everyone: "For God has shut up all in disobedience so that He may show mercy to all" (verse 32).

Paul summarizes this great mysterious work of God in verses 33-36. The Lord's judgments are unsearchable (verse 33); no one has been His counselor in the matters concerning His providence (verse 34). No one can buy off the Lord (verse 35), "for from Him and through Him and to Him are all things. To Him be the glory forever. Amen" (verse 36).

LIVING IN LIGHT OF HIS COMING
Romans 13:11-14

ROMANS 13 CAN BE DIVIDED into two parts: 1) how believers are to relate to the government and civil authorities (verses 1-7), and 2) how believers are to relate to each other (verses 8-14). Christians need to be aware of what they are doing in the Christian walk. They are to be "awake" and not asleep, "for now salvation is nearer to us than when we believed" (verse 11). When Paul refers to sleep, he isn't necessarily talking about sinning. He may simply be saying that believers should not be drifting in their Christian life but should remain aware of what is happening in the sinful environment around them. He states a similar thought in 1 Thessalonians 5:5-9, where he urges Christians to "be alert and sober" (verse 6).

In Romans 13:11-13, Paul uses the pronouns *us, you,* and *we* to remind his readers that the final salvation they hoped for could come upon them while they are alive on earth. This, then, is a rapture passage, in that this "salvation" event could come at any time. This is similar to what Paul says in 1 Thessalonians 5:9: "God has not destined us for wrath, but for obtaining salvation through our Lord Jesus Christ." Though the rapture has not yet happened, we are always to live as if it could occur at any time.

The apostle Paul realized that this life is short, and that the opportunity for believers to serve is limited. He says, "The night is almost gone, and the day is at hand" (Romans 13:12 NKJV). Believers are to walk with meaningful spirituality, conscious morality, and a sense of duty. They are to "lay aside the deeds of darkness and put on the armor of light" (verse 12), and "behave properly as in the day, not in carousing and drunkenness, not in sexual promiscuity and sensuality, not in strife and jealousy" (verse 13). Instead, they are to "put on the Lord Jesus Christ, and make no provision for the flesh in regard to its lusts" (verse 14). Believers are to *dress themselves* with Christ so that He is seen in them as they go about in life. Here, Paul has the believer's progress in sanctification in view (Haldane, *Commentary on Romans,* p. 599). Therefore, before the rapture, or even before natural death, the Christian is to be careful how he lives the Christian life, as if "the day is at hand"—that is, the day of going home to be with the Lord.

THE BEMA JUDGMENT SEAT
Romans 14:8-12

ONE OF THE MORE COMMON Greek words used to describe judgment in the New

Testament is *bema*. The apostle Paul, in these verses and elsewhere, reminds believers that we all must stand before the *bema* of Christ to be judged for the works done in the Christian life. Because the Christian's position in Christ is a completed work (Romans 8:1), this judgment is not in regard to our salvation, but rather, is to determine our rewards for faithful service (see 1 Corinthians 3:10-15; 2 Corinthians 5:10).

The *bema* portrays a seat or raised platform upon which a judge sits to adjudicate a case (Matthew 27:19; John 19:13; Acts 18:12). The same word is used to describe the platform upon which a referee sat during the Olympic games in Greece or the Isthmian games at Corinth. It was at this platform that the winners of the various athletic events received their rewards. The *bema* judgment of believers should not be confused with the Great White Throne Judgment described in Revelation 20:11-15. This latter judgment is the general judgment of all unbelievers from all generations. Because the blood of Christ does not cover their sins, they must answer for all "their deeds" in life. All of those who stand before the Lord at this judgment are cast into the lake of fire (verse 14), which is the conclusive spiritual "second death."

In the larger context surrounding Romans 14:8-12, Paul discusses how believers should relate to each other (verses 1-7). They are not to judge others over "doubtful things," such as whether one eats only vegetables (verse 2). Each "stands or falls" before the Lord (verse 4) as to their conviction in their own mind (verse 5). Whatever one does in such matters, that person must give thanks to God (verse 6), for "not one of us lives for himself, and not one dies for himself" (verse 7) because all are accountable to God.

Paul then reminds believers, "We will all stand before the judgment seat [*bema*] of God" (verse 10). He then quotes Isaiah 45:23 in verse 11: "As I live, says the Lord, every knee shall bow to Me, and every tongue shall give praise to God." The reason is that "each one of us will give an account of himself to God" (Romans 14:12). Because this *bema* judgment will call all believers to account for their actions, Paul commands, "let us not judge [Greek, *krino*] one another anymore, but rather determine this—not to put an obstacle or a stumbling block in a brother's way" (verse 13).

The *bema* judgment is for rewards done in the Christian life for Christ's sake. "Each one may be recompensed for his deeds in the body, according to what he has done, whether good or bad" (2 Corinthians 5:10). "Recompense" (Greek, *komizo*) conveys the idea of receiving pay or wages. The Greek middle voice may better read, "He should receive to himself wages." The word "bad" is the Greek word *phaulon* and can mean "worthless, of no account, base, wicked."

Believers labor for Christ's name. Christ is the foundation upon which a child of God is placed to build or construct a new life (1 Corinthians 3:11-12). On this foundation a Christian may build with "gold, silver, precious stones." Or, the child of God may choose to build with "wood, hay, straw," or temporal works that are worthless. These latter works will not stand the scrutiny of the Lord at the *bema* judgment. Those believers who wasted their opportunities to serve wisely will suffer loss, "but he himself will be saved, yet so as through fire" (verses 13-15). This "fire" is not applied to the believer but to his works.

When does the *bema* judgment take place? Some believe it takes place in heaven just before the marriage feast of the Lamb (Revelation 19:7-9). In a similar vein, some think it happens anytime in heaven while the seven-year Tribulation is taking place on earth. But some evidence indicates that it will happen soon after the rapture of the church, when all of the church saints are gathered in glory. The rapture and the *bema* judgment seem to be in view in 1 Corinthians 4:5, where Paul writes, "Do not go on passing judgment before the time, but wait until the Lord comes who will both bring to light the things hidden in the darkness and disclose the motives of men's hearts; and then each man's praise will come to him from God." The apostle James writes similarly, "Do not complain, brethren, against one another," because "behold, the Judge [Christ] is standing right at the door" (James 5:9).

The concept of the *bema* judgment is related to the Greek games; rewards are to be distributed to the saints in Christ for their service in relation to His name. When speaking of the believer's judgment, Paul uses the figure of the victorious athlete who is rewarded for his accomplishments.

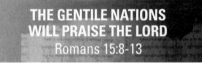

THE GENTILE NATIONS WILL PRAISE THE LORD
Romans 15:8-13

BY MEANS OF HIS DEATH on the cross, Jesus Christ became a servant to the Jewish people to confirm the covenant promises the Lord gave to their fathers (verse 8). He also brought a blessing "for the Gentiles to glorify God for His mercies" (verse 9).

While it is true that in Old Testament times many Gentiles who lived around Israel were blessed by the witness concerning God, Paul quotes verses that point to a future worldwide praise coming from the nations who will be blessed by the rule of Israel's Messiah in the kingdom age. He illustrates the fact that in the past, many Gentiles saw God's glory as He blessed Israel. He quotes David's prayer: "I will give thanks to You, O LORD, among the nations, and I will sing praises to Your name" (15:9; 2 Samuel 22:50; Psalm 18:49). Even before the children of Israel entered the Holy Land after the sojourn in Egypt, Moses urged the Gentiles, "Rejoice, O nations, with His people [the Jews]" (Romans 15:10; Deuteronomy 32:43). Paul then quotes from Psalm 117:1: "Praise the Lord all you Gentiles, and let all the peoples praise Him" (Romans 15:11).

The apostle then goes on to quote Isaiah 11:10, which is a distinct messianic prophecy: "There shall come the root of Jesse, and He who arises to rule over the Gentiles, in Him shall the Gentiles hope" (Romans 15:12). Jesse was the father of King David, and the Messiah

is a "shoot" ("twig"), a "stem" ("stump"), a "branch" that comes from him to bear spiritual fruit (Isaiah 11:1). As a root from Jesse (and then David), the Messiah "will stand as a signal [flag] for the peoples; and His resting place will be glorious" (verse 10). It is clear that Isaiah 11:10 is about the kingdom reign of Christ and not about the present church age. Christ is not presently acting as a king upon the earth, ruling from Jerusalem in a political sense over the nations of the world. The key to the passage is that He will "rule" over the nations.

David prophesied that God will install His King "upon Zion, My holy mountain" and that the nations will be His inheritance, and the ends of the entire earth will be His possession (Psalm 2:6,8). He will rule these nations with a "rod of iron" or "scepter" (verse 9; 110:1-2). While it is clear that the Gentiles are presently being blessed in a spiritual sense in the church age, both the Jews and the Gentiles will be blessed in the millennial kingdom. For now, Paul urges both Jew and Gentile to enter the full blessing of their fellowship one with the other and their enjoyment of God's mercy and grace. He writes, "Now may the God of hope fill you with all joy and peace in believing, so that you will abound in hope by the power of the Holy Spirit" (Romans 15:13).

THE PROMISE THAT SATAN WILL BE CRUSHED
Romans 16:20

IN ROMANS 16:1-16 the apostle greets various Christians in Rome and exhorts them to serve the Lord with full hearts. Then he adds, "The God of peace will soon crush Satan under your feet" (verse 20). Paul is alluding to the prophecy given in Genesis 3:15, where, after Adam and Eve were tempted and fell into sin, the Lord told Satan that the seed of the woman "shall bruise you on the head, and you shall bruise him on the heel." This is a cryptic prophecy not fully explained in Genesis, but later generations would understand that it was in reference to the virgin birth of the Messiah, who would enter the human race as the seed of the woman. "Bruise" should read *crush*. To crush the heel is but a limiting wound, but the snake—that is, Satan—will be once and for all conquered by Christ—the crushing of the head—when he is cast into the lake of fire for eternity (Revelation 20:10).

What does Paul mean when he says God will crush Satan under the feet of the believers? Many commentators think he is referring to the ultimate triumph of the church over the power of the devil. But it's more likely Paul is thinking about something specific that would take place with the Roman Christians. Nicoll observes that Romans 16:17-18 reminds them to be aware of those who cause "dissensions and hindrances"; from these they should turn away ("Romans," *Expositor's Greek Testament,* 2:723).

It could be that the Roman church at that time would rebuff the work of Satan coming against the congregation and would, as Christ will ultimately, crush Satan under their feet (verse 20) by rejecting false teaching. Either way, the crushing of Satan is pictured as taking place in the future, meaning it was not completed at the cross but would be completed in the future *eschaton,* when God brings true peace to the world. Nicoll adds, "The false teachers may come and cause dissension, but it will not be long till peace is restored" ("Romans," *Expositor's Greek Testament,* 2:273).

Seen in its entirety, the epistle to the Romans not only "sets forth the great doctrines of sin, salvation, and sanctification, but also how this affects Israel in the present age and in the future where Israel's restoration is assured" (Walvoord, *Prophecy Knowledge Handbook,* p. 457). Romans predicts the triumph of the believer in Christ, the salvation of Gentiles in the church age, and the final restoration of Israel.

1 CORINTHIANS

There are many prophetic sections in the book of 1 Corinthians. One of the most important has to do with the future judgment and reward of believers for their works (3:11-15). The Christian life is pictured as a building whose foundation is the Lord Jesus Christ. Believers are to build upon Him that which is spiritually worthwhile. That which is spiritually worthless will be burned away at the *bema* judgment seat of Christ.

The other major prophetic section is chapter 15. In one of the longest chapters in the New Testament, Paul answers the critics who are skeptical of the resurrection from the dead. The apostle argues that if there is no such thing as a resurrection, then Christ was not raised. But since He did rise from the dead, this is a guarantee that those who place their trust in Him will be given new life. In 15:51-53 Paul introduces a mystery, something not before revealed, which is the rapture of the church saints.

Both the resurrection and the rapture are used of God to bring final and complete victory over death. Because of the prophecies regarding the resurrection and future rewards, believers can serve with full assurance knowing that their "toil is not in vain in the Lord" (verse 58).

SECURITY OF BELIEVERS
1 Corinthians 1:4-9

Though the people in the church at Corinth had a host of problems, the apostle Paul starts out his letter by describing what the Lord did to save them. In Christ Jesus, "in everything you were enriched in Him" (1 Corinthians 1:5). The testimony about Christ being their Savior "was confirmed" (Greek, *bebaioo*) in them (verse 6), meaning they were unreprovable, steadfast, firm in their standing in Christ. This is a statement about their position in Christ, not about their walk with Him (though Paul does address their walk throughout most of this letter). Paul and the writer of the book of Hebrews use this word to affirm the believers' relationship to Christ (1 Corinthians 1:8; 2 Corinthians 1:21; Colossians 2:7; Hebrews 2:3; 13:9).

The result of this salvation "confirmation" is that believers "are not lacking in any gift," and are "awaiting eagerly the revelation of our Lord Jesus Christ" (verse 7). This *waiting* of the believer for Christ's revelation shows that this is a rapture passage. "Thus they could eagerly wait (*apekdechomenous;* used seven times in the NT of the return of Christ: Rom. 8:19, 23, 25; 1 Cor. 1:7; Gal. 5:5; Phil. 3:20; Heb. 9:28) for Him" (Lowery, "1 Corinthians," *Bible Knowledge Commentary,* p. 508). That generation was in a waiting mood, eagerly so, expecting that Christ could come at any time. This is not about His coming to reign and judge the world, which takes place at the end of the Tribulation, but His coming at any time to take the children of God home before the wrath of the Tribulation comes upon the earth. The language here is almost identical to that in the rapture passage in Philippians 3:20: "Our citizenship is in heaven, from which also we eagerly wait for a Savior, the Lord Jesus Christ."

Paul then makes a prophecy about a future confirmation of the believer. Positionally, in Christ, believers *were confirmed* (aorist tense, passive voice—1 Corinthians 1:6). Now there is a future confirming (future tense) that will carry the believer "to the end" in the "day of our Lord Jesus Christ" (verse 8). Paul concludes his thought by saying, "You were called into fellowship with His Son, Jesus Christ our Lord" (verse 9). The Greek word for "confirm" in verse 8 is like the word "confirmed" in verse 6 (aorist tense, passive voice). Together they could read, "In the past you were *confirmed* into a state of fellowship with God's Son, but you shall also be *confirmed* in the future all the way to the end." Paul's point is that there will be a future finishing and completion of the believers' salvation when they are called home to glory.

Finally, the expressions "the day of the Lord Jesus" (2 Corinthians 1:14) and "the day of our Lord Jesus Christ" (1 Corinthians 1:8), have to do with the final future program God has for His church (5:5; Philippians 1:6,10; 2:16; 2 Thessalonians 2:2). Mitchell writes, "The Day of the Lord is a more general term for God's future judgment upon Israel and the nations—including the Tribulation period (Zech. 14:1-4)" (*Book of 1 Corinthians,* p. 21).

THE POWER OF THE CROSS
1 Corinthians 1:17-19

INFLUENTIAL VOICES IN CORINTH may have been attempting to destroy the biblical teaching about salvation and the cross of Christ. Paul made it clear to this church that he was driven by one message—he came to them "not in cleverness of speech, so that the cross of Christ would not be made void" (1 Corinthians 1:17). He was not going about debating the issue of the crucifixion of Christ, nor was he promoting water baptism as somehow inflated in importance (verses 13-16). In fact, he says that he was not sent by the Lord "to baptize, but to preach the gospel" (verse 17). He would tell the Corinthians later that Christ's death, burial, and resurrection (15:3) are the core of the gospel, the very gospel he preached to them (verse 1).

When Paul writes about "the word of the cross" (1:18), he uses the Greek term *logos* in the singular for the noun "word." By this he means a specific doctrinal teaching about the death of the Lord on the cross. He is not trying to make the word "cross" (Greek, *stauros*) somehow mystical in its implication, but he is fortifying the importance of the death of Christ for sinners. The apostle writes elsewhere about "the offense" of the cross (Galatians 5:11) and the persecution that believers will face because of it (6:12). He warned of enemies of the cross (Philippians 3:18) and of a shame that the world heaps on the idea of Christ's crucifixion (Hebrews 12:2). However, only through Christ's substitutionary death on the cross can people find peace with God. God the Father made it possible "through Him to reconcile all things to Himself, having made peace through the blood of His cross" (Colossians 1:20).

The cross is "foolishness" (Greek, *moria*) to those who are "perishing" (present passive participle of the Greek word *apollumi,* or "presently destroying themselves"). But to the child of God who is being saved, "it is the power of God" (1 Corinthians 1:18). Paul then

Judgment by Fire

1 Corinthians 3:12-15

BAD WORKS

1. **Good works done with evil motives**
   Matthew 6:2

2. **Hidden counsels**
   1 Corinthians 4:5

3. **Unconfessed sin**
   1 John 1:9

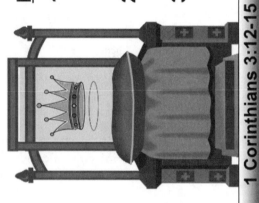

1 Corinthians 3:12-15

Judgment Seat of Christ

GOOD WORKS

Ephesians 2:10

1. **Quality**
   Matthew 25:14-30

2. **Quantity**
   Luke 19:11-27

3. **Time**
   Matthew 20:1-16

Those who are faithful servants of Christ while on earth will hear Him say, "Well done, good and faithful servant" (Matthew 25:21 NKJV). He will reward them for their good works done with the right motives. But those who do their works in ways unpleasing to the Lord will have their work "burned up," though they will still "be saved, yet so as through fire" (1 Corinthians 3:15).

quotes Isaiah 29:14, where the Lord says, "I will destroy the wisdom of the wise, and the cleverness of the clever I will set aside" (1 Corinthians 1:19). At a future time the Lord will settle all accounts. Human wisdom will be exposed at the judgment as wanting and impotent (Revelation 20:11-15). The unrighteous dead will be resurrected and stand before the "great white throne," and they will have no place to hide (verse 11).

For now, before the final judgment, human wisdom is made foolish by the Lord (1 Corinthians 1:20), and by it the world cannot know God (verse 21). "It was the same with all human wisdom, whether of the esteemed Jewish scholar or Greek philosopher. The brilliance of man cannot appreciate the plan of God (Isaiah 55:8-9)" (Lowery, "1 Corinthians," *Bible Knowledge Commentary,* p. 509). Both Jew and Gentile seek after human wisdom (verse 22) and reject Christ, who to the Jews is a "stumbling block" and to the Gentiles is "foolishness" (verse 23). What seems to the world as foolish God has chosen "to shame the wise" (verse 27). God has chosen the despised cross in order "that He may nullify the things that are, so that no man may boast before God" (verses 28-29).

THE BEMA JUDGMENT
1 Corinthians 3:10-15

THIS PASSAGE IS TIED together with Romans 14:10-11 and 2 Corinthians 5:10-13, which describe the *bema* judgment for the works of believers done during their life on earth. While the Greek word *bema* was used to describe a criminal court hearing in the ancient world, it was also used to refer to the podium or dais where rewards were given out for meritorious achievement. Every believer will someday stand before the "judgment seat of God" (Romans 14:10) and "give account of himself to God" (verse 12). Because "there is therefore now no condemnation for those who are in Christ Jesus" (8:1) in the positional sense, this *bema*

judgment does not determine one's spiritual destiny. That has already been settled at the cross and by the believer's trust in that sacrifice of Christ for his sins. Instead, the *bema* judgment is about rewards and about what the believer has done for the Lord in this life.

Paul urges: "Each man must be careful how he builds on" the foundation "which is laid, which is Jesus Christ" (1 Corinthians 3:10-11). The Christian life starts with Him. Each "man's work will become evident" and will be tested as to its spiritual quality (verse 13). It will be either "gold, silver, precious stones," or "wood, hay, straw" (verse 12). Those works done for Christ's glory will remain, and "he will receive a reward" (verse 14). Those works done for selfish reasons will be "burned up" and the believer, though suffering loss, "himself will be saved, yet so as through fire" (verse 15). By this Paul does not mean that the child of God just barely squeaks into heaven. He means that after all a believer's worthless works are consumed "so as" by fire, the soul is still intact because Christ died for this person and he is a member of the body of Christ (12:13). "The stress in this entire passage is not on an individual's relationship to Christ, but on service. It does not suggest that one might be in danger of losing his or her salvation, but it does give a stern warning with respect to one's ultimate accountability (see also Amos 4:11; Jude 1:23)" (Mitchell, *Book of 1 Corinthians,* p. 55).

Every believer must "appear before the judgment seat [Greek, *bema*] of Christ" in order to be recompensed for "what he has done, whether good or bad" (2 Corinthians 5:10). While there is no fear of loss of salvation, there should be a fear of accountability before the Lord. There should be a moral and spiritual persuasion because we will be "made manifest to God" (verse 11).

BELIEVERS' MOTIVES
1 Corinthians 4:1-5

PAUL CONTINUES HIS DISCUSSION about responsibility and accountability in these verses. Knowing that many in the Corinthian church were criticizing him, he reminds the congregation that he, and those ministering with him, are servants of Christ and stewards "of the mysteries of God" (1 Corinthians 4:1). It is understood that servants must "be found trustworthy" (verse 2); therefore, the critics have no right examining Paul. Rather, he must examine himself as to his servitude and faithfulness (verse 3). All believers must carry out an ongoing self-examination, though ultimately, "the one who examines" us "is the Lord" (verse 4). "As a moral agent, as a believer, and as a minister, Paul felt himself accountable to Christ. This inward allegiance of the conscience is the highest form of worship" (Hodge, *Commentary on the Epistle to the Romans*, p. 67).

Believers are not to go around "passing judgment" on one another "before the time" (verse 5), meaning before the *bema* judgment comes. We must all wait "until the Lord comes who will both bring to light the things hidden in the darkness and disclose the motives of men's hearts; and then each man's praise will come to him from God" (verse 5). This praise will come after the *bema* judgment of Christ for our works. Because of the praise that the Lord will give, this is not about the Great White Throne Judgment, which has to do with a person's eternal destiny (Revelation 20:1-4). Rather, it is about a Christian's accountability to God in this life. Since believers are urged to "wait until the Lord comes," this coming must certainly be the rapture of the church. The *bema* judgment will then take place, in which "the motives of men's hearts" will be exposed (see also Romans 14:10-12; 2 Corinthians 5:10-13).

THE CONSEQUENCES OF SIN
1 Corinthians 5:1-7

THE COMING OF THE LORD JESUS and the *bema* judgment loom large in Paul's theology. He is concerned that believers recognize the consequences of what we do as Christians. Here he continues addressing the issue of sin in the Corinthian congregation and what this will mean "in the day of the Lord Jesus" (1 Corinthians 5:5).

It was reported to Paul that there was a man in the assembly who was having illicit relations with his stepmother (verse 1). The church had become insensitive and "arrogant" (Greek, *thusioo*) over the issue, failing to mourn over the evil and to remove the man from their midst (verse 2). Though Paul was not there, he "already judged" the man in spirit (verse 3). In the name of Christ, the apostle decided "to deliver such a one to Satan for the destruction of his flesh, so that his spirit may be saved in the day of the Lord Jesus" (verses 4-5). Paul is saying that he had decided to set the man outside the protection of the fellowship of believers so that Satan could be used to discipline him and cause him to drop the sin of the flesh that was so destructive. The word "destruction" (Greek, *olethros*) means "to bring to ruin, nullify" and cause to end, in this case, his vile and gross carnality.

By setting the man outside the assembly, his fellowship with other believers is broken. At the *bema* judgment following the coming of "the day of the Lord" (verse 5), the offender will have no rewards, though his spirit will be saved. The arrogance and boasting of the congregation "is not good" because a little leaven of sin "leavens the whole lump of dough" (verse 6). Such open sin seen by all will corrupt the entire congregation. The "old leaven" of sin must be cleaned out because believers are now a "new lump" of "unleavened" and sanctified dough. In fact, Christ was sacrificed and became the Passover Lamb for the child of God (verse 7). Believers can no longer live as they did in the past. The offender "is assumed to be saved; otherwise he would not be contemplated as being present at the 'day of the Lord Jesus'" (verse 5). And indeed, in most cases of this sort, since they involve members of the local church, this would be the assumption. But salvation is not the issue being addressed here—it is fellowship" (Mitchell, *Book of 1 Corinthians*, p. 79).

THE JUDGMENT OF THE LOST
1 Corinthians 5:13

Aᴏ̈ᴛᴇʀ ᴅɪsᴄᴜssɪɴɢ the flaunted sin of the brother in verses 1-7, Paul now addresses the issue of the person in the church who does not know Christ as Savior. The church is not to associate (Greek, *sunanaginnumi*, aorist passive infinitive) with "any so-called brother" (verse 11) who is living in sin. The verb can read as meaning we are not to be mixed together. By saying "so-called brother," Paul is referring to pretenders, or those who *confess* but do not *possess* faith in the Lord Jesus Christ. Such a one is described as "an immoral person, or covetous, or an idolater, or a reviler, or a drunkard, or a swindler" (verse 11). The believer is "not even to eat with such a one" (verse 11). The church will someday judge the world as a system of evil. At present it judges only those who profess to be brothers and sisters.

Since these people are not believers, Paul makes it clear that he has no reason to be "judging outsiders," though judgment within the congregation is legitimate (verse 12). It is God who will judge those who are outside the assembly. However, as with the Jewish people when they were sojourning in the wilderness, the congregation should "remove the wicked man from among yourselves" (verse 13; Deuteronomy 13:5; 17:7). He was to be cast outside the camp. At the Great White Throne Judgment, righteousness will finally prevail (Revelation 20:1-4). But even now, "the wrath of God is revealed [presently] from heaven against all ungodliness" (Romans 1:18). Mitchell observes,

> It is true, as the apostle John has said, that "the whole world lies in the power of the evil one" (1 John 5:19). But it will not do to simply curse the darkness. It is the task of the believer to proclaim the positive truth of the gospel. The saints are obligated to be faithful stewards; as for the world, God will take care of it (*Book of 1 Corinthians,* p. 84).

THE DESTINY OF THE RIGHTEOUS AND THE UNRIGHTEOUS
1 Corinthians 6:9-11

Tʜᴇ ᴅᴇsᴛɪɴʏ ᴏꜰ ᴀʟʟ ʙᴇʟɪᴇᴠᴇʀs of all generations is to be with Christ in His earthly 1000-year messianic kingdom. Believers from all generations past, including those now living in the dispensation of the church, will enjoy His triumph over evil. Those of the past, including church age believers, will be on earth in their new, eternal bodies. The resurrected Jews of the Old Testament will also share in Christ's kingdom rule, when He possesses the nations as His inheritance as well as the very ends of the earth (Psalm 2:8).

The apostle Paul makes it clear that the "unrighteous will not inherit the kingdom of God" (1 Corinthians 6:9-10). Is Paul referring to those who practice unrighteous works, or does he have something else in mind? In the context of this statement and the earlier verses (verses 1-8), he is concerned about the church saints—believers—taking their fellow Christians to court (verse 6) "before the unrighteous and not before the saints" (verse 1). Problems among believers should be settled by fellow believers in Christ and not before unbelievers (verses 5-6). A church has come to a pretty sad state "when its members believe that they are more likely to get justice from *unbelievers* than from their own brothers" (Barrett, *First Epistle to the Corinthians,* p. 138).

Paul then makes an important distinction between the believer and the unbeliever. The unbeliever is *the unrighteous* as a spiritual group, while *the righteous,* the saint, is the brother in Christ. It's possible for believers to walk as carnal Christians (3:3), but from a positional standpoint, they are righteous before God and "sanctified in Christ" (1:2). The lost are the unrighteous whose sins are not covered by the blood of Christ. They openly practice all manner of heinous and debauched acts (6:9-10), and they will not inherit the kingdom of God (verse 10).

To explain further the distinctions between

the saved and unsaved, Paul writes, "Such were some of you; but you were washed, but you were sanctified, but you were justified in the name of the Lord Jesus Christ and in the Spirit of our God" (verse 11). Those who are saved by faith will be with Christ in His kingdom rule, and will be joint-heirs with Him, whereas the wicked will have no share in that future kingdom of God because they are not related to Christ, the Heir (cf. Mark 12:7). "The wicked will someday be judged by the saints (1 Cor. 6:2)" (Lowery, "1 Corinthians," *Bible Knowledge Commentary,* p. 515). This will probably take place at the beginning of the kingdom era.

THE FUTURE PRIZE FOR SERVICE TO CHRIST
1 Corinthians 9:24-27

Paul tells the Corinthians he is "under compulsion" to preach the gospel of Christ to a lost world (1 Corinthians 9:16). He does this ministry "without charge" (verse 18), making himself "a slave to all, so that I may win the more" to Christ (verse 19). In order to be effective, he adjusted himself to all classes of people, becoming "all things to all men, that I may by all means save some" (verse 22). "Paul holds himself up as an example. To the weak he became as weak; he accommodated himself to their prejudices that he might win them over to better views. And he wished the Corinthians to do the same" (Hodge, *First Corinthians,* p. 166).

Paul then discusses his future reward for service by using the example of the athlete who gives himself totally to winning a race. "Do you not know that those who run in a race all run, but only one receives the prize? Run in such a way that you may win" (verse 24). With these words Paul states the fact that all believers are in the race of service to the Lord. Just as self-control is necessary in order to compete in athletic games, self-control is essential in the spiritual race. We must exercise spiritual

and moral determination in order to fare well in the race. The world expends its energy on "a perishable wreath, but we an imperishable" (verse 25). To run and win, discipline is required (verse 26) in order to make the body a slave to the endeavor, "so that, after I have preached to others, I myself will not be disqualified" (verse 27). The Greek word *adokimos* ("disqualified") suggests it is possible for a believer to fail in the spiritual race. When Paul speaks of failure he is not addressing the issue of salvation, but how we live the Christian life. Mitchell writes that Paul's "subject is…Christian liberty, and his point is that sometimes the mature Christian will have to restrict himself for the sake of the work" in front of him (*Book of 1 Corinthians,* p. 139).

Thus believers are to receive a reward (verse 17), a prize (verse 24), an "imperishable" wreath (verse 25). It would only be logical that such a reward will be given at the *bema* judgment, when the works believers have done for Christ are acknowledged (Romans 14:10-12; 1 Corinthians 3:10-15; 2 Corinthians 5:10-13).

THE FUTURE REVELATION OF FULL KNOWLEDGE
1 Corinthians 13:9-13

In 1 Corinthians 13 Paul discusses the issue of godly love (verses 1-7) and concludes that, in the Christian experience, "love never fails." The gifts of prophecy, tongues, and knowledge will someday "be done away" (verse 8). They will no longer be operative, but love will not disappear. For the present, believers in Christ know and prophesy only "in part" (verse 9)—that is, with limitation. However, in the future, "when the perfect comes, the partial will be done away" (verse 10). What does the apostle mean when he refers to "the perfect" (Greek, *teleios*)? Edwards writes, "The temporary character of the Charismata is proved by their essentially partial nature.… It will, therefore cease, not because it has been absorbed in something better, but as sounds which have no music in

The Believer's Rewards

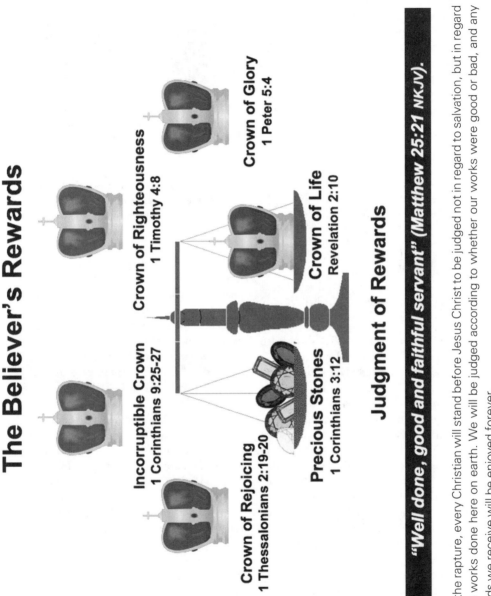

Incorruptible Crown
1 Corinthians 9:25-27

Crown of Righteousness
1 Timothy 4:8

Crown of Glory
1 Peter 5:4

Crown of Rejoicing
1 Thessalonians 2:19-20

Precious Stones
1 Corinthians 3:12

Crown of Life
Revelation 2:10

Judgment of Rewards

"Well done, good and faithful servant" (Matthew 25:21 NKJV).

After the rapture, every Christian will stand before Jesus Christ to be judged not in regard to salvation, but in regard to the works done here on earth. We will be judged according to whether our works were good or bad, and any rewards we receive will be enjoyed forever.

them die away in the air and do not live in ideas" (*Commentary on the First Epistle to the Corinthians*, p. 349).

Some believe Paul is here referring to the *completion* of the New Testament canon, when all the revelations and commandments for the church age are made known. After the book of Revelation is written by John the apostle (A.D. 90–95), there will be no need for the "communication gifts" within the body of Christ, such as prophecy, tongues, and knowledge. Others believe Paul is simply saying that none of the gifts will need to be in operation when the church age is completed or has fully matured. Mitchell writes,

> The body growing up as a perfect, or mature adult (cf. Eph. 4:12-13) will eventually outgrow the need for certain things associated with immaturity, as verse 11 shows. This becomes a metaphor for the "Church triumphant," where the physically challenged will stand once again on their own (Mitchell, *Book of 1 Corinthians*, p. 190).

At this time the church will be shepherded by the Great Physician and will no longer need pastors and elders. Full maturity will be in place, for "we will be like Him, because we will see Him just as he is" (1 John 3:2). For now, we think and act with certain limitations, as children and not as those who are grown (1 Corinthians 13:11). Believers see "dimly" as if looking into a polished bronze mirror that gives but limited clarity. But in the future believers will see "face to face" and shall, as Paul puts it, "know fully just as I also have been fully known" (verse 12). This refers to the resurrection, when all believers will stand together in their new, glorified bodies and enjoy the company of each other and the Lord.

There are many today who exalt and overemphasize the gifts given to the church. Yet "the gifts are fragmentary and serve only as a means to an end. Paul's advice is to keep your eyes on the goal and not on the means toward achieving it" (Mitchell, *Book of 1 Corinthians*, p. 191). For now, certain spiritual qualities are

to be in place in the life of the believer: "faith, hope, love, abide these three...the greatest of these is love" (verse 13).

THE PROMISE OF THE RESURRECTION
1 Corinthians 15:12-19

FIRST CORINTHIANS 15 has been called Paul's great resurrection chapter. After defining and describing the gospel in verses 1-11, he gives a detailed analysis of the doctrine of the resurrection.

In this section (verses 12-19), Paul points out that the *resurrection of Christ* is central to Christianity. He begins by noting that without the promise of a resurrection, "not even Christ has been raised" (verse 13).

The truth concerning the resurrection was revealed in the Old Testament. In fact, it is mentioned in the book of Job, which may be the oldest book in the Old Testament, written about the time of the patriarch Abraham (2000 B.C.). Job said that he knew that his Redeemer lives, "and at the last He will take His stand on the earth" (19:25). Even though Job's body will decay, "yet from my flesh I shall see God; whom I myself shall behold, and whom my eyes will see and not another" (verses 26-27).

David spoke of the resurrection of the Messiah when he wrote, "You will not abandon me to the grave, nor will You let Your Holy One see decay" (Psalm 16:10). David specifically saw his own resurrection when he said, "As for me, I will see Your face in righteousness; I shall be satisfied when I awake in Your likeness" (17:15 NKJV).

One of the most powerful statements on the resurrection is given in Isaiah 26:19: "Your dead will live; their corpses will rise. You who lie in the dust, awake and shout for joy, for your dew is as the dew of the dawn, and the earth will give birth to the departed spirits." And Daniel prophesied of the resurrection when he said, "Many of those who sleep in the dust of the ground will awake, these to everlasting life, but the others to disgrace and everlasting contempt" (12:2).

The doctrine of the resurrection was well-known by the pious Jews who witnessed the raising of Lazarus. His sister Martha told the Lord, "I know that he will rise again in the resurrection on the last day" (John 11:24). This gave Jesus the opportunity to reveal how and why the righteous will come forth from the grave with a new body. He said to Martha, "I am the resurrection and the life; he who believes in Me will live even if he dies, and everyone who lives and believes in Me will never die" (verse 25).

The theme of *future resurrection*, then, runs through Scripture, and its importance is emphasized here in 1 Corinthians 15 with these well-known words by Paul: "I delivered to you as of first importance what I also received, that Christ died for our sins according to the Scriptures, and that He was buried, and that He was raised on the third day according to the Scriptures, and that He appeared to Cephas, then to the twelve" (1 Corinthians 15:3-5). If Jesus did not rise from the dead, Paul wrote, "your faith also is vain" (verse 14). And all who saw Christ after His resurrection are false witnesses, "because we testified against [about] God that He raised Christ, whom He did not raise" (verse 15). If the Lord did not come out of the grave, Christians are still in their sins (verse 17), and those who have "fallen asleep in Christ have perished" (verse 18). The believer's hope in the Lord Jesus Christ is not simply in this life; otherwise, Christians are "of all men most to be pitied" (verse 19). Or as Stanley puts it, "We are more wretched than all who are not Christians. We have fallen from the greatest of hopes, which we have purchased at the greatest of costs" (*The First Epistle of St. Paul to the Corinthians*, p. 313).

The Lord "presented Himself alive after His suffering, by many convincing proofs, appearing to [the disciples] over a period of forty days" (Acts 1:3). Stephen saw the risen Christ in heaven before he was stoned to death (7:56), and Paul encountered Him personally on the Damascus road (9:1-7). And the apostle John, in the last book of the Bible, was given a vision of the glorified Lord in His heavenly majesty (Revelation 1:12-20). The Lord told John, "Do not be afraid; I am the first and the last, and the living One; and I was dead, and behold, I am alive forevermore, and I have the keys of death and of Hades" (verses 17-18).

If there were no resurrection the Gentile pagan world could rightly speak of the "foolishness of the cross" (1 Corinthians 1:18). Men like Paul and others would have suffered needlessly for the gospel (4:9-13), and for this could only be pitied.

THE ORDER OF RESURRECTION
1 Corinthians 15:20-28

PAUL GIVES AN ORDER to the resurrection, though this order is not complete. His words are meant to comfort the church as to the main events concerning the resurrection. Despite the denials of the pagan world, the fact is that Christ came forth from the dead, and He is the "first fruits" or the first crop of "those who are asleep" (verse 20). Whereas Adam brought death to the human race, the Lord Jesus Christ brought new life by "the resurrection of the dead" (verse 21). Because the entire human race comes from Adam, all in him must die, just as Adam died. The divine commandment brought upon him the sentence of death threatened in Genesis 2:17. "Adam's sin marked the historic entry of death as a phenomenon—his own death" (Barrett, *First Epistle to the Corinthians*, pp. 351-52). But all who are "in Christ...will be made alive" (verse 22).

The *order of resurrection* begins with Christ. He is "the first fruits," but then follow those "who are Christ's at His coming" (verse 23). The discussion here is confined to the church saints who had "fallen asleep in Jesus" (1 Thessalonians 4:14), the "dead in Christ" who will rise from the grave at the sound of God's trumpet (verse 16). It will also include the bodily transformation of those who are alive on earth at the time (1 Corinthians 15:51-52), who will be changed and "caught up together with them in the clouds to meet the Lord in the air" (1 Thessalonians 4:17).

The apostle then moves to "the end, when He [Christ] hands over the kingdom to the God and Father, when He has abolished all rule and all authority and power" (1 Corinthians 15:24). During the kingdom reign, Christ will put all His enemies under His feet (Psalm 2:8-9; 110:2,5-6), and then at the end, He will abolish the last enemy—death (1 Corinthians 15:26). This final subjugation, when God will "put all things under his feet" (Psalm 8:6-7; 1 Corinthians 15:27), will bring about a complete dominion over all things by Christ, the Son of Man, as prophesied in Daniel 7:13. "To Him was given dominion, glory and a kingdom, that all the peoples, nations and men of every language might serve Him. His dominion is an everlasting dominion which will not pass away; and His kingdom is one which will not be destroyed" (verse 14).

When all things are rightfully given to the Son, "the Son Himself also will be subjected to the One who subjected all things to Him, so that God may be all in all" (1 Corinthians 15:28). What does this mean? Barrett answers, "It is not the absorption of Christ and mankind, with consequent loss of distinct being, into God; but rather the unchallenged reign of God alone, in his pure goodness" (*First Epistle to the Corinthians,* p. 361). God receives the final glory through the work of His Son at the cross and because of His Son's victory over all things. In the Trinity, the Son is still subservient to the Father, who receives the final and eternal honor for His great plan of redemption. The beneficiaries are the church saints, who will experience the blessing of being resurrected to eternal life with Christ.

THE RESURRECTED BODY
1 Corinthians 15:35-50

How WILL THE DEAD BE RAISED, and what will the resurrection body be like (1 Corin-

thians 15:35)? The old body must be sown in the ground; it must die (verse 36). It is like wheat that begins as a grain or a kernel and is later turned into something else (verse 37; John 12:24). To the grain that turns to dust, the Lord had given "a body just as He wished," but now "to each of the seeds a [distinct] body of its own" (1 Corinthians 15:38).

In life, each species has a different flesh—"all flesh is not the same flesh" (verse 39). Human beings, animals, birds, and fish—all possess a different kind of flesh. "The inanimate bodies in space such as the sun, the moon, and the stars, likewise have different qualities (verses 40-41)" (Walvoord, *Prophecy Knowledge Handbook,* p. 463). So also will the resurrected "heavenly" body be different from the "earthly" body in which believers once existed (verse 40). "It is sown a perishable body, it is raised an imperishable body" (verse 42). It will be raised in glory, in power, and as a spiritual body (verses 43-44). This heavenly spiritual body will be re-created by the Lord from a heavenly source and not an earthly one. However, it is still a real and tangible body, yet without "dishonor," "weakness," and earthly limitations.

The resurrection body is specifically empowered by the new man, the Lord Jesus Christ. Referring to Genesis 2:7 Paul writes, "The first man, Adam, became a living soul," but the last Adam, Christ, "became a life-giving spirit" (verse 45; Romans 5:14). The spiritual man comes after the natural man (verse 46), and "the first man is from the earth, earthy; the second man is from heaven" (verse 47). Believers have the certain promise that "just as we have borne the image of the earthy, we will also bear the image of the heavenly" (verse 49). "The one partakes of temporality, the other of eternality. . . . Thus, the human body, instead of becoming an argument against the resurrection, becomes an argument in its favor" (Mitchell, *First Corinthians,* p. 224).

The church saints cannot enter into the kingdom of God in their natural, earthly bodies. "Flesh and blood cannot inherit" this future millennial realm, "nor does the perishable inherit the imperishable" (verse 50).

Believers in this church age who are still alive on earth at the time of the resurrection must be "changed" by the rapture. And those who have fallen asleep in Jesus will experience the resurrection of the new body when the trumpet sounds (verse 52; 1 Thessalonians 4:16-18).

THE RESURRECTION AND THE RAPTURE
1 Corinthians 15:51-58

In these verses and in 1 Thessalonians 4:13-18, the apostle Paul mentions both the resurrection and the "change" (Greek, *alasso*) that describes the rapture of the church. The rapture is also called a "mystery" (Greek, *musterion*) that has to do with the fact that "we will not all sleep, but we will all be changed" (1 Corinthians 15:51). This great event was not revealed in the Old Testament.

First Corinthians 15:52 is virtually the same as 1 Thessalonians 4:16-17, which is a well-known rapture passage. There, the trumpet is sounded and the resurrection of the dead in Christ takes place. Then the believers who are alive on earth "shall be caught up together with them to meet the Lord in the air." The "change" takes place followed by the "catching up." This is the imparting of the new, glorious and heavenly body Paul wrote about earlier (verses 40-44).

With both the resurrection and the rapture, "change" must take place, "for this perishable must put on imperishable, and this mortal must put on immortality" (verse 53). Though the context of these verses has to do with church believers of all generations, Paul quotes from Isaiah 25:8 and Hosea 13:14 that the gen-

eral promise of resurrection is for all peoples of all dispensations. Paul writes "O death, where is your victory? O death, where is your sting?" (verse 55). "The sting of death is sin," he adds (verse 56). Death is like a fatal sting, and everyone who is so afflicted dies, which means, of course, the entire human race.

Paul then goes on to say that that which amplifies "the power of sin is the law" (verse 56). "The Law, which epitomized the command of God, was thus the mirror against which human rebellion and disobedience was starkly portrayed. Like the first Adam, all who followed him rebelled (cf. 1 Cor. 2:14)" (Lowery, "1 Corinthians," *Bible Knowledge Commentary*, p. 546). The law represents the righteous demands of a holy God. No one can keep it, and therefore, all stand under its judgment and penalty. The whole world stands condemned under the curse of the law (Romans 3:19), for "by the works of the Law no flesh will be justified in His sight; for through the Law comes the knowledge of sin" (verse 20). Only the righteousness of God through faith in Jesus Christ can save (verse 22), and justification comes only as a gift "by His grace through the redemption which is in Christ Jesus" (verse 24).

The final triumph over death and sin comes through the victory that only Christ can bring (1 Corinthians 15:57). Because of this, the believer has a great hope even in this life that his efforts in serving Christ are not for nothing. Believers can serve steadfast, immovable, "always abounding in the work of the Lord." This toil "is not in vain in the Lord" (verse 58). "Now we can *invite* Death to do its worst, knowing that the final victory will be ours in Christ" (Mitchell, *Book of 1 Corinthians*, p. 225).

2 CORINTHIANS

Apart from the prophecy of the judgment seat of Christ and the promise of an eternal home in heaven for the believer (5:1-10), this letter contains only two additional *major* prophetic sections. The first has to do with the fact that Paul will be proud of the Corinthian believers when the rapture takes place (1:14). The day of the Lord, in this context, is a reference to the rapture, which the apostle had written about in 1 Thessalonians 4:13-18. Paul also writes about his own resurrection in 2 Corinthians 4:14—that is, if he dies before the rapture takes place.

THE DAY OF THE LORD JESUS
2 Corinthians 1:14

Many of the Corinthian believers were suspicious of Paul's ministry. They often did not give him the full honor due to him as an apostle, and they often challenged his authority. Paul made it perfectly clear that he was "not in the least inferior to the most eminent apostles"—that is, the original 12 (2 Corinthians 11:5). Without charge he preached to the Corinthians the pure gospel of God (verse 7).

With this in mind he reminded them that in "the grace of God" he conducted himself with honor toward this church (1:12). He desired that the assembly thoroughly understand his apostolic mission, but if not, he hoped they "partially did understand" his work. He pleaded for mutual respect, showing that "we are your reason to be proud as you also are ours, in the day of our Lord Jesus" (verse 14). The "day of our Lord Jesus" would be when the Corinthians, and all believers of the church dispensation, would stand before the Savior to give an account for their service.

The children of God are "awaiting eagerly the revelation of our Lord Jesus Christ, who will also confirm [us] to the end, blameless in the day of our Lord Jesus Christ" (1 Corinthians 1:8). The apostle desires that the work that the Lord began in believers He "will perfect...until the day of Christ Jesus" (Philippians 1:6).

The church in Corinth had many moral and maturity issues Paul had to deal with. But he hoped they would assent to what he was writing to them, and by this, that they would someday wholeheartedly accept and endorse fully what he was doing. David K. Lowery observes that the apostle "was confident of the genuineness of their conversions (cf. 1 Cor. 9:1-2). And he felt they would eventually come to vindicate him and even boast of (*kauchema,* 'exult over') him in the day of the Lord Jesus (cf. Phil. 2:16), that is, at the judgment seat of Christ (cf. 2 Cor. 5:10-11)" ("2 Corinthians," *Bible Knowledge Commentary,* p. 556).

Some scholars incorrectly think that the "day of Christ Jesus" is a reference to "the Day of the Lord" referred to so often in the Old Testament. But the day of the Lord, a day that is still future, has to do with the seven-year period of wrath and tribulation on earth (1 Thessalonians 5:1). What Paul is speaking of here in 1:14 has to do with the *bema* judgment that occupies an important part of his two Corinthian letters (1 Corinthians 3:10-16; 2 Corinthians 5:10-13; cf. Romans 14:10-13). On 2 Corinthians 1:14, Hodge writes,

> Paul believed that in the day of the Lord Jesus the Corinthians would rejoice over him as he would rejoice over them. In that day they would appreciate the blessedness of having had him for their teacher, as he would rejoice in having had them for his converts. The joy, however, which he anticipated in its fullness when Christ should come, was in a measure already theirs (*Second Epistle to the Corinthians*, p. 16).

Though the *bema* judgment is not until the end of the church age (1 Corinthians 1:8), Paul puts "we are to be proud" in the present tense to show that he is already involved in the "eschatological event" (Kistemaker, *II Corinthians*, p. 56). Christians are urged to walk in the light of that coming day (Romans 13:12-13).

THE RESURRECTION OF BELIEVERS
2 Corinthians 4:14-18

WHILE BELIEVERS MAY be afflicted and persecuted and perplexed in this life (2 Corinthians 4:8), they will not be forsaken (verse 9). They are constantly "being delivered over to death for Jesus' sake" (verse 11). But they can walk about "having the same spirit of faith," trusting in the fact that what is spoken about God's faithfulness and about eternal life will come to pass (verse 13). The child of God can know for certain that "He who raised the Lord Jesus will raise us also with Jesus and will present us with you" (verse 14). The apostle makes the message of the resurrection one of the key doctrines in his theology (1 Corinthians 15:12-58; 1 Thessalonians 4:13-18). The resurrection will culminate in the presentation of all believers together before the Lord in heaven

(2 Corinthians 4:14). Meanwhile, God's grace is spreading to more and more people everywhere, causing "the giving of thanks to abound to the glory of God" (verse 15).

The *hope* of the resurrection is so certain that the fact the believer's physical outer man will decay should not disturb us. "Our inner man is being renewed day by day" (verse 16), and the temporary and momentary "light affliction is producing for us an eternal weight of glory far beyond all comparison" (verse 17). Christians should not look at the things which are seen, but the eternal things "which are not seen" (verse 18). These things are the "spiritual and heavenly, among them being those of the inner man. Ordinary eyes and unenlightened minds cannot see them and hence never regard them and, when they are told about them, imagine them to be folly" (Lenski, *I and II Corinthians*, p. 993).

The joys of heaven are eternal joys. "There shall be no interruption; no night; no cessation; no end" (Barnes, *Notes on the New Testament*, 11:95). The Savior, who is eternal, is the believer's everlasting friend, and all our fellow believers will live with us in heaven for all eternity. There will never again be a time of separation!

ABSENT FROM THE BODY, AT HOME WITH THE LORD
2 Corinthians 5:1-9

THE APOSTLE PAUL reminds believers that this "earthly tent," or our present "house," will someday be torn down (2 Corinthians 5:1). In its place, Christians "have a building from God, a house not made with hands, eternal in the heavens." In this passage, Paul continues his discussion about the future, the hope (or confident expectation) of the resurrection, and the destiny given to believers in glory. This "house," the present body, is groaning with infirmity (Romans 8:23), and we are "longing to be clothed with our dwelling from heaven" (2 Corinthians 5:2).

Human beings are meant to be corporeal, or to have a body to reside in (verse 3). But because we are in a body that is cursed and limited, "this tent," we are groaning, "being burdened" (Greek, *bareo* or "weighed down"). Desiring then to not exist "unclothed," our hope is that this "mortal will be swallowed up by life" (verse 4), and it is only Christ who can give eternal life to those who trust in Him. Jesus said, "Everyone who beholds the Son and believes in Him will have eternal life, and I Myself will raise him up on the last day" (John 6:40). He added, "I am the resurrection and the life; he who believes in Me will live even if he dies" (11:25; cf. 14:6).

For those who belong to Christ, God has given "the Spirit as a pledge" (2 Corinthians 5:5). The Spirit of God Himself is the "pledge" (Greek, *arrabon*), the first installment, the guarantor that the believer has an inheritance that leads to eternal life (Ephesians 1:14). Because of this, the child of God can be "always of good courage," knowing that while at home in this body "we are absent from the Lord," though preferring "to be absent from the body and to be at home with the Lord" (2 Corinthians 5:6,8). Believers do not see all of this working out as yet because "we walk [now] by faith, not by sight" (verse 7). These verses assure that at death, Christians pass directly and instantly into the very presence of the Lord. There is no "soul sleep," unconsciousness, or delay. While death may not bring about the sudden experience of the resurrection, "it does make us at home with Christ among the souls who wait for the resurrection" (Ellicott, *Ellicott's Commentary on the Whole Bible*, 8:379).

THE JUDGMENT SEAT OF CHRIST
2 Corinthians 5:10-11

BASED ON WHAT PAUL SAID in 2 Corinthians 5:1-9, he reminds his readers again of the judgment seat (Greek, *bema*) of Christ (verse 10). He wrote of this in his previous letter (1 Corinthians 3:10-15) and also in Romans 14:10-12.

All believers must appear at this place of judgment. This judgment does not determine the believer's eternal destiny; that issue was settled at the cross. "There is now no condemnation for those who are in Christ Jesus" (Romans 8:1). Lowery states, "Salvation is not the issue here. One's eternal destiny will not be determined at the judgment seat of Christ. Salvation is by faith (Eph. 2:8-9), but deeds issuing from that faith (1 Thes. 1:3) will be evaluated" ("2 Corinthians," *Bible Knowledge Commentary*, p. 566). The purpose of the believer's standing before the *bema* is to "be recompensed for his deeds in the body, according to what he has done, whether good or bad" (2 Corinthians 5:10). In a positional sense, those "in Christ" have become new creatures, with the old things passing away and being replaced by "new things" (verse 17).

While the *bema* is a place where rewards are given (1 Corinthians 3:14), it will be a sobering experience. Believers are to "fear" because their thoughts and actions will be made manifest before the Lord (2 Corinthians 5:11). The Christian builds his new experience on Christ Jesus, who is the foundation of the new life (1 Corinthians 3:11). The believer's works done for the Lord will be exposed and tested as to their "quality" (verse 13). The worthless works of "wood, hay, straw" (verse 12) will be burned up, with the believer suffering loss, though "he himself will be saved, yet so as through fire" (verse 15).

This *judgment seat of Christ* cannot be confused with the other judgments mentioned in Scripture, such as the judgment of the nations (Matthew 25:31-46), the judgment of the nation of Israel (Ezekiel 20:33-38), the judgment of the righteous Jews who are waiting for Christ's second coming (Daniel 12:1-2), or the judgment of the lost (Revelation 20:11-15). Walvoord states, "The Judgment Seat of Christ is peculiar in that it relates only to Christians and, apparently, is limited to those who have been saved between Pentecost and the Rapture" (*Prophecy Knowledge Handbook*, p. 467).

GALATIANS

THE BOOK OF GALATIANS IS LARGELY OCCUPIED with the law and legalism in relation to the Christian life, and prophecy is a rather minor subject in the book. However, Paul points out that Christ came to save sinners, and He did this by securing the blessings of the Abrahamic Covenant (3:16-29). This is important for Jew and Gentile because so much that is involved in this covenant has to do with the blessings and promises that God has pledged to keep.

Galatians 6 includes the prophecy of judgment for sowing to the flesh (verses 7-10). Even under grace, the believer does not inherit the crop he has not sown. The harvest may not come in this life, but the believer will certainly be rewarded at the judgment seat of Christ.

ESCHATOLOGY OF THE CROSS
Galatians 1:4

THE LOVE OF GOD is demonstrated by the fact that the Lord *sent* His Son to die for sinners (John 3:16), but Christ also *"gave* Himself for our sins" (Galatians 1:4). He voluntarily became a substitute for the sinner under the wrath of God. Isaiah prophesied that as a sacrificial lamb, the Messiah would be "pierced through for our transgressions" (Isaiah 53:5) and that the Lord would cause "the iniquity of us all to fall on Him" (verse 6).

By becoming a sacrifice, Christ would "deliver" (Greek, *exaireo,* "pluck out, pull out, set apart") us out of "this present evil age" (Galatians 1:4). "Out of this present age of evil," in the Greek text, is "out of the age the present evil." *Poneros* is the Greek word used to describe a most filthy and malicious generation in the moral sense. It carries the connotation of the grossest of sexual evil.

Christ died in order to remove His own from such an environment.

The first stage of deliverance is spiritual in that the believer no longer is part of this world culture, but rather, is a citizen of heaven (Philippians 3:20). Until the rapture or death, the child of God lives "in the midst of a crooked and perverse generation" (2:15). A believer's removal from earth is the second stage of deliverance, for in heaven, "there will no longer be any death; there will no longer be any mourning, or crying, or pain; the first things have passed away" (Revelation 21:4).

This deliverance comes about "according to the will of our God and Father" (Galatians 1:4). Martin Luther wrote, "This knowledge maketh the heart cheerful, so that it steadfastly believeth that God is not angry, but that he so loveth us poor and wretched sinners, that he gave his only begotten Son for us.... and that by the good will of the Father" (*Commentary on Galatians,* p. 56).

CHRIST DIED TO SAVE GENTILES AS WELL AS JEWS
Galatians 3:13-14

IT WAS PROPHESIED that the blessing of Abraham would come upon the Gentiles so that they might also receive the promise of the Holy Spirit through faith (Galatians 3:14). To be hanged upon a tree was mentioned in the Old Testament as an ignominious punishment and death; Deuteronomy 21:23 says, "Cursed is everyone who hangs on a tree." Christ took upon Himself this curse in order to redeem His own "from the curse of the Law" (Galatians 3:13).

In the covenant made with Abraham (the Abrahamic Covenant), God prophesied that through Abraham "all the families of the earth will be blessed" (Genesis 12:3). This prophecy was in seed form in Genesis 12, but the full implication would unfold with the passage of time as God revealed more and more of His plan for humanity. Paul quotes Genesis 12:3 and offers an explanation in Galatians 3: "The Scripture, foreseeing that God would justify the Gentiles by faith, preached the gospel beforehand to Abraham saying, 'All the nations will be blessed in you'" (verse 8). To everyone who trusts Christ, whether Jew or Gentile, "it was reckoned to him as righteousness" (verse 6), by which believers become "sons of Abraham" (verse 7) and are "blessed with Abraham, the believer" (verse 9).

Within the New Covenant is a promise in which God told the Jewish people, "I will put My Spirit within you and cause you to walk in My statutes" (Ezekiel 36:27). The church is not the beneficiary of this promise, but it does benefit from the New Covenant. Christ reminded the disciples just before His ascension that "you will be baptized with the Holy Spirit not many days from now" (Acts 1:5).

These verses are not co-mingling Israel and the church, as taught by amillennialists. God was simply prophesying, through Abraham, the master plan of how the world would be blessed by Abraham and his descendants, the Jewish people.

CHRIST SECURES THE BLESSINGS PROMISED TO ABRAHAM
Galatians 3:16-29

PROMISES AND PROPHECIES about spiritual and physical blessings were made to Abraham and to his seed. Yet at the same time, the Lord also prophesied about Abraham's future "seed" (Hebrew, zera) in the singular sense, not "referring to many, but rather to one, 'And to your seed,' that is, Christ" (Galatians 3:16; Genesis 22:17). The Hebrew word zera can be singular or plural, and Paul picks up on the fact that in Genesis 22:17 it is used in the singular sense, pointing to one specific seed of Abraham. This One would be victorious as a conquering hero as illustrated by the fact that He would possess the gate of His (singular) enemies (verse 17). Unger says this is an "expanded blessing centered in Christ, the coming seed (see Gal. 3:16; cf. John 8:56), and could only be realized in Him" (Unger's Commentary on the Old Testament, p. 71).

Though the law was given 430 years after the children of Jacob (Israel) entered the land of Egypt, it did not nullify the promise made to Abraham (Galatians 3:17). (Jacob entered Egypt around 1875 B.C., and Moses led the Israelites out about 1445 B.C.) Israel did not receive the prophecies about blessings on the basis of the law but rather, on the Abrahamic Covenant (verse 18).

Why, then, did God give a law through Moses? And did this law override the Abrahamic promises? It was added alongside of the Abraham Covenant "because of transgressions...until the seed would come to whom the promise had been made" (verse 19). The law does not contradict the promises of God, nor does it provide life imparted by righteous works (verse 21). Instead, the law condemns and shuts up everyone under sin, keeping them in custody under the law, "that the promise by faith in Jesus Christ might be given to those who believe" (verses 22-23).

Many Jews tried to find life and salvation by law-keeping. But faith in Christ "was later to be revealed" (verse 23). The law then was but a "tutor" (Greek, *paidagōgos,* "child leader"), a servant who supervised the learning of the master's child. This law tutor then leads us "to Christ, that we may be justified by faith" (verse 24). Because of this, believers are "no longer under a tutor," the law (verse 25). To be "justified by faith" means to be legally acquitted before God's bar of justice by having received the righteousness of Christ. The result for believers is that they "are all sons of God through faith in Christ Jesus" (verse 26).

The apostle Paul saw how the promises that came through the Abrahamic Covenant would bless "the nations" (verse 8). He concludes: "There is neither Jew nor Greek, there is neither slave nor free man, there is neither male nor female; for you are all one in Christ Jesus. And if you belong to Christ, then you are Abraham's descendants, heirs according to promise" (verses 28-29).

THE PROMISE OF REDEMPTION
Galatians 4:4-6

WHEN THE HEIR DESCRIBED in Galatians 3:29 was a child, he "was taught only faint outlines of spiritual truth suited to his capacity" (Eadie, *Galatians,* p. 296). But he would someday have full freedom, privilege, and understanding under the gospel.

In order to create spiritual heirs, at just the right moment God sent His Son into the world to accomplish redemption. Paul puts it this way: When "the fullness, maturity [Greek, *to plaroma*] of the time [Greek, *tou kronou*]" had arrived, "God sent forth His Son" (4:4). The Son previously existed eternally with the Father (John 1:1; 8:58; 17:5; Romans 8:3) but now took upon Him human flesh yet without sin (Hendriksen, *Galatians and Ephesians,* p. 158). As prophesied, He was "born of a woman, born under the Law"

(Galatians 4:4). Paul here is addressing the fact Christ was born of a "virgin" (Hebrew, *alma;* Greek, *parthenos*) (Isaiah 7:14; Matthew 1:25; Luke 1:27), and born of physical flesh as the son of David (Matthew 1:25; Luke 1:27; Romans 1:3). The far-distant cryptic prophecy of "the seed of the woman" crushing the head of the serpent, Satan, was first mentioned in Genesis 3:15. Unger says the Lord's "redemptive work was initiated by the first announcement of the gospel (Lat. *protevangelium,* 'original evangel'), which envisioned the tremendous opposition of Satan and his agents to the good news of God's redeeming grace. God declared He would put 'enmity' between Satan and the woman and between her descendants and Satan's descendants" (*Unger's Commentary on the Old Testament,* p. 19). Unger then adds, "Since 'the seed of the woman' focuses on an individual, whose miraculous birth gave Him a preeminent title to be called 'the seed of the woman' (see Gal. 4:4), the designation constitutes the first great prophecy of the coming virgin-born, incarnate Son of God and Savior."

The reason Christ came was that "He might redeem those who were under the Law, that we might receive the adoption as sons" (Galatians 4:5), making it possible for believers to be adopted into a new family and become sons of God (3:26; Romans 8:14). Because of this adoption, God "has sent forth the Spirit of His Son into our hearts, crying, 'Abba! Father!'" (Galatians 4:6; Romans 8:15). The word *Abba* is an Aramaic word of affection that means "father" (possibly equivalent to "daddy"). As sons, believers now have full possession of all they can receive from God. And even more, the child of God now has an intimate relationship with the heavenly Father, which he did not have before.

THE JUDGMENT OF THE FLESH
Galatians 6:7-10

THESE VERSES FOCUS ON one's personal eschatology. Prophetically speaking, what one does in the Christian walk will bring on consequences that are just as certain as the fulfillment of other prophecies made in Scripture.

The apostle Paul is very concerned that the child of God may easily "be deceived" in the way he lives out his moral and spiritual life (Galatians 6:7). The Greek word here, *planao,* means "to be led astray, to be led into error." This word is used in the present passive sense, warning the believer that such deception could be continually coming upon him and clouding his judgment as to how he lives. Paul also uses the word *muktarizō* ("mock"), which means "to deride, to sneer at, to turn up the nose." If the believer thinks that he can snub what the Lord has said, he is being led into error, and there will be a price to pay. Paul's point is that the believer will not get away with sneering at God's commands. There will be consequences, "for whatever a man sows, this he will also reap" (verse 7).

Sowing to one's flesh will produce spoiled or rotten crops—"corruption" (Greek, *phthora,* "decomposition as with a dead body, decay") (verse 8). Bruce observes the works of the flesh being committed by the Galatians were sins that had to do with being quarrelsome and showing envy (5:15,26) (Bruce, *Galatians,* p. 265). By contrast, sowing to the Spirit brings forth crops that are compatible with eternal life (6:8). "It is obvious, however, that even under the grace of God, a Christian does not inherit a crop that he has not sown. The harvest may not be in this life; it may be in the life to come

at the Judgment Seat of Christ" (Walvoord, *Prophecy Knowledge Handbook,* p. 469).

The believer is urged by the apostle to not lose heart "in doing good" nor grow weary as if doing right will not be rewarded or recognized, for "in due time we will reap if we do not grow weary" (verse 9). At every opportunity, the believer is to practice good "to all people, and especially to those who are of the household of the faith" (verse 10). We are not to be kind "when it is convenient; or when it will advance the interest of a party; or when it may contribute to our fame; the rule is, that we are to do it when we have the opportunity" (Barnes, *Notes on the New Testament,* 11:395). This injunction makes Christianity unique. Kindness and charity should be lived out in an almost equal sense to both the lost and to the saved. Hendriksen says, "The believer has been placed on this earth for a purpose. The best way to prepare for Christ's second coming is to use to the full every opportunity of rendering service. Moreover, this service should be rendered to everybody" (*Galatians and Ephesians,* p. 238).

Eadie observes that these verses speak of "duties which spring out of love, the fruit of the Spirit [5:22-26], and are themselves forms of spiritual beneficence or well-doing—duties, however, which one may be tempted to neglect, or regard only in a negative aspect, so far as not to be acting in direct opposition to them" (*Galatians,* p. 444). Right living and good works will someday be rewarded (Romans 14:10-12; 1 Corinthians 3:10-15; 2 Corinthians 5:10-11).

EPHESIANS

Most prophecies in Ephesians have to do with the dispensation of the church, though Paul begins by saying that all things will be summed up in Christ (1:9-10). The church saints will have an inheritance (verse 14) and will be seated someday in heaven with the Lord. Meanwhile, Paul's desire is that the church will come to maturity in Christ. Paul also writes about the wrath of God, which will fall on those who do not accept the message of the gospel (5:5-6). And believers, the members of Christ's body, can anticipate future glory with Him. The church will also receive rewards from Him for faithful service (6:7-9).

SUMMING UP ALL THINGS IN CHRIST
Ephesians 1:9-12

After citing many of the gracious processes that bring about salvation (1:3-8), Paul writes about being blessed "in the heavenly places" (verse 3), being chosen and presented "blameless before Him" (verse 4), being predestined (verse 5), and being given redemption and forgiveness "of our trespasses, according to the riches of His grace" (verse 6).

The Lord performed this marvelous work of salvation "with a view to an administration suitable to the fullness of the times, that is, the summing up of all things in Christ, things in the heavens and things on the earth" (verse 10). The Greek word *oikonomia* means "house law, economy, administration, or dispensation." More than likely the apostle Paul is not referring to the various earthly dispensations but to the time when all of history is concluded in the Lord Jesus Christ. He sees the present church dispensation as the next-to-the-last period before eternity. The "summing up" is probably not a reference to the last dispensation, the kingdom, but to the eternal state. This is so because Paul says that this summation includes both "things in the heavens and things upon the earth." There may be some disagreement on this. For example, Walvoord writes, "Paul revealed that it is an important part of God's ultimate purpose of bringing all things under Christ" (*Prophecy Knowledge Handbook*, p. 469).

Others believe the "summing up" at this time, in this dispensation mentioned here, is about the Davidic kingdom and not eternity. Harold Hoehner writes, "This dispensation is the millennial kingdom when 'the times' in God's purposes will be completed (fulfilled), and all things both spiritual and material will be under Christ and His rule (cf. 1 Cor. 15:27; Col. 1:20)" ("Ephesians," *Bible Knowledge Commentary*, p. 618).

Whichever may be correct, believers in the present dispensation of the church are given an inheritance concerning salvation in Christ, "having been predestined according to His

423

purpose who works all things after the counsel of His will" (Ephesians 1:11). This inheritance is already in the possession of believers but is brought to fruition in the future when God brings about the final bodily redemption, either at the resurrection of the body or at the rapture (verse 14). Hodge writes that the "influences of the Spirit which believers now enjoy are at once a prelibation...of future blessedness, the same in kind though immeasurably less in degree; and a pledge of the certain enjoyment of that blessedness" to come (*Ephesians*, p. 65). The dispensation of the church gives the children of God a special relationship with Christ. Paul says believers are now "in Christ," "in Him," and are "sealed in Him" (verses 10,12-13). In the future the Lord Jesus will be seen as the inheritor of the Davidic throne and King over Israel. He will be recognized as well as the head over the church (5:23).

of Christ at the cross. Through Him, believers are justified and have the promise of someday being glorified (Romans 8:30).

To make sure the readers of this letter understand that God is honored and recognized in giving to Him "the praise of His glory," Paul makes this point three times (Ephesians 1:6,12,14). Salvation in Christ came about because of the eternal plan "which [God] purposed in Him" (verse 9). Redemption came by "the riches of His grace which He lavished on us" (verses 7-8). The apostle Paul cannot say enough about the grace of the Lord, which saves even the most wretched of sinners. The church is part of the grand purpose of God in Christ, and salvation is the great redemptive scheme that would bring deliverance to both the Jew and to the Gentile (3:6-8). This deliverance is available to any individual who chooses to call upon the name of the Lord (Romans 10:13).

OUR ETERNAL INHERITANCE
Ephesians 1:13-14; 4:30

AFTER LISTENING TO THE TRUTH, the gospel of salvation, those who believed are "sealed in Him [in Christ] with the Holy Spirit of promise" (Ephesians 1:13). This "sealing" (Greek, *sphragizo*) is accomplished at the moment of belief. The illustration used here is that of an official government wax seal used to close a scroll that can only be opened by the recipient to whom it is addressed. Believers "were sealed for the day of redemption" (4:30). The coming of the Spirit was prophesied or promised to the disciples just before the ascension of Christ (Acts 1:4; 2:33), and not only would the Spirit spiritually baptize all believers "into one body," the body of Christ (1 Corinthians 12:12-14), but He would also be "a pledge" (Greek, *arrobon*), a surety, the guarantor of our inheritance, "with a view to the redemption of God's own possession, to the praise of His glory" (Ephesians 1:14). The security of a child of God is not based on his or her goodness or perfection, but on the work

THE GLORY OF THE LORD JESUS CHRIST
Ephesians 1:15-22

PAUL TELLS THE BELIEVERS in Ephesus that he does "not cease giving thanks" for them, "making mention [of them] . . . in [his] prayers" (Ephesians 1:15-16). His desire for them is that "the Father of glory, may give to you a spirit of wisdom and of revelation in the knowledge of Him" (verse 17). The apostle wants believers to be fortified with certain spiritual truths about Christian living. He wants them to have been "enlightened" (Greek, *photizo*) in order that they may know 1) the hope of God's calling (verse 18), 2) the riches of the glory of His inheritance (verse 18), and 3) the surpassing greatness of His power toward the child of God (verse 19). The knowledge of these workings of the Lord in the lives of believers "are in accordance with the working of the strength of His might" (verse 19).

Such blessings have taken place because of Christ, whom God the Father raised from the dead and "seated...at His right hand in the heavenly places" (verse 20). This exaltation of Christ was predicted in Psalm 110:1-6, where it was written that the Lord said to Him, "Sit at My right hand, until I make Your enemies a footstool for Your feet" (verse 1). Paul adds that Christ will be seated "far above all rule and authority and power and dominion and every name that is named, not only in this age but also in the one to come" (Ephesians 1:21). This is a reference to what happened when the Lord Jesus ascended back to His Father. He entered the heavenly throne room as the "Son of Man" and presented Himself to God, who is described by Daniel as "the Ancient of Days," the One whose existence is eternal (Daniel 7:13).

In this heavenly presentation, Christ was "given dominion, glory and a kingdom, that all the peoples, nations and men of every language might serve Him" (verse 14)—this is what the apostle was referring to in Ephesians 1:21. Paul then quotes Psalm 8:6, which says God "put all things in subjection under His feet, and gave Him as head over all things to the church, which is His body, the fullness of Him who fills all in all" (Ephesians 1:22). While Christ has been bequeathed all authority over the entire universe, His rulership has yet to take place (Hebrews 2:8-9), though He has now been granted rule over the church, "which is His body" (Ephesians 1:23). His rulership over all things will begin when He comes to earth to reign as "the Word of God" and the "KING OF KINGS AND LORD OF LORDS" (Revelation 19:11-16). Hoehner says,

> Christ is both the originator and sustainer of all creation and the head over everything in the church. This also coincides well with Eph. 5:23-24 where it states that the church is under the headship of Christ.... God has subjected everything in creation under Christ's feet; and...God gave Christ to the church as head over everything, which thus implies that he is head over the church ("Ephesians," *Bible Knowledge Commentary*, pp. 289-290).

The child of God is privileged to be related to the Son of God by His work in salvation. And there are additional privileges yet to come when the Christian joins the Lord Jesus Christ in His glorious splendor as the sovereign Ruler of the universe!

SEATED WITH CHRIST IN HEAVEN
Ephesians 2:5-7

BY GRACE THE LORD JESUS CHRIST saved us "when we were dead in our transgressions" (Ephesians 2:5). We have been made alive in Him, and spiritually, we have been raised up with Him and seated "with Him in the heavenly places" (verse 6). Because of this new relationship "in the ages to come," Christ will someday "show the surpassing riches of His grace in kindness toward us" (verse 7). Prophetically speaking, believers will be trophies of His matchless grace. This salvation came about "because of His great love with which He loved us" (verse 4).

What are the "ages to come"? Since the Greek word for "ages" is plural (*aiōsin*), this could mean many periods of time that lead on into eternity. It could begin with the resurrection of the saints who have died and are asleep and the believers who are alive on earth, all of whom will be transformed and meet the Lord in the air at the rapture (1 Thessalonians 4:13-18). It would certainly also include the period of time when believers are in glory and awaiting the revelation of Christ as king upon the earth. The book of Revelation has the church saints in mind when we read about the great company in heaven "from every tribe and tongue and people and nation" (Revelation 5:9) who are "thousands of thousands" (verse 11) crying with a loud voice, "Worthy is the Lamb that was slain to receive power and riches and wisdom and might and honor and glory and blessing" (verse 12).

The "ages" can also include eternity, when the "new heaven and new earth" begin (Revelation 21:1). Then the tabernacle of God will be with men, and "He shall dwell among them, and they shall be His people, and God Himself shall be among them" (verse 3). Hodge says, "When the saints are raised up in glory, and not before, will the kindness of God towards them be revealed" (*Ephesians,* p. 117). Throughout time, and on into eternity, the church is a society of pardoned sinners and rebels designed by God to be the masterpiece of his goodness. O'Brien writes, "What God has done for those in Christ is a reality, but only in the coming ages will it be fully seen for what it is. In the light of God's gracious saving work, believers point men and women from themselves to the one to whom they owe their salvation" (*Letter to the Ephesians,* p. 173).

THE MATURITY OF THE CHURCH
Ephesians 4:7-16

As a conquering general the Lord ascended the heights, freed the captives, "and He gave gifts to men" as if bestowing favor on His own followers (Ephesians 4:8). Christ came to earth to free the captives (verse 9), but after His resurrection He ascended "far above all the heavens, so that He might fill all things" (verse 10). He is now the Sovereign who rules over the church, giving some as apostles, prophets, evangelists, pastors, and teachers (verse 11). With these gifted leaders Christ will nourish the believers who are part of His spiritual body (1 Corinthians 12:12-14). As a result, He will be "equipping...the saints for the work of service, to the building up of the body of Christ" (Ephesians 4:12).

Ephesians 4:13-16 shows that the Lord has a plan that may not always be seen with the physical eye. He is building His church, but this does not mean that simply numbers are in view. He is growing the church to be "a mature man, to the measure of the stature which belongs to the fullness of Christ" (verse 13). The church is to be fully grown and mature like the Lord, who is the measure and standard for spirituality.

As this growth takes place, believers are "no longer to be children, tossed here and there by waves and carried about by every wind of doctrine, by the trickery of men, by craftiness in deceitful scheming" (verse 14). Faith and knowledge are living qualities that must produce results. "To know only something about Christ, God's Son, is not enough, it is not the full oneness with our fellow saints, not full-grown manhood. We must apprehend all that our faith and our knowledge are able to understand" (Lenski, *Epistles to the Galatians, Ephesians and Philippians,* p. 537). Without the fullness of Christ, believers have nothing left but self-righteousness and a mere imitation of spirituality.

Growth comes about by the speaking of the truth (God's Word) in love. By this "we are to grow up in all aspects into Him who is the head, even Christ" (verse 15). As in a physical body, the "proper working of each individual part causes the growth of the body for the building up of itself in love" (verse 16). The prepositional phrase "in love" is instrumental and should be translated "with love, by means of love." Hoehner says, "Love with truth that enables individual believers to grow harmoniously with other members of the body with the resulting growth of the whole body" ("Ephesians," *Bible Knowledge Commentary,* p. 565). This is the great desire of the Lord—that the body of Christ might grow up, mature, and function as it was intended to.

These verses reveal the ideal plan for the church. Because of carnality and human frailty, the outward work of the church will fail. There will be apostasy in the church before the end of the age (1 Timothy 4:1-3; 2 Timothy 3:1-5). Despite this, the Lord will accomplish His ultimate and final purposes with His church.

THE CERTAINTY OF GOD'S WRATH
Ephesians 5:5-6

Believers in Christ are not to walk in the old way, in immorality and impurity, "which are not fitting" (Ephesians 5:4), but are to walk "as is proper among saints" (verse 3). They are to be "imitators of God, as beloved children" (verse 1). Christians are to walk in love, just as Christ loved and gave Himself for us. Believers no longer have an interest in the immoral and impure affairs of the lost. The unsaved are cut off and shall never see the glory of the Lord in eternity.

Children of God have an *inheritance* with Christ that is far greater than any human inheritance (1:11,14,18). The lost cannot share in this. "For this you know with certainty, that no immoral or impure person or covetous man, who is an idolater, has an inheritance in the kingdom of Christ and God" (5:5). Christians should not be fooled into believing they can live however they please. They should not be deceived with empty words; "because of these things the wrath of God comes upon the sons of disobedience" (verse 6).

The kingdom described here is more than likely the millennial reign of Christ. Believers in the church age have a place in this kingdom, though the central people will be the Jewish nation that has trusted Christ and entered into His promised millennial glory. Paul uses the present tense "has an inheritance," indicating that the believer *has* a place kept for him in that prophesied future kingdom. Just as that inheritance is absolute, so is the wrath that will fall upon the lost. "Comes upon" is also in the present tense, indicating the certainty of a future fact.

Hoehner fortifies this idea when he writes that the present tense of the verb "comes"

> signifies "a solemn present." It is both present and future. In Romans Paul states that the present wrath of God is revealed from heaven (Rom. 1:18) and that there is a future wrath for those who are hard-hearted and who continue to store up wrath for the day of God's judgment (2:5). This present and future notion applies also to the kingdom mentioned in the preceding verse. We are presently in the kingdom (Eph. 5:5; Col. 1:13) and counted as

fellow heirs ("Ephesians," *Bible Knowledge Commentary,* p. 664).

In these verses it is clear that Paul is emphasizing the state of human beings in both the present and the future. The believer has hope in the glorious inheritance awaiting him, but the lost can only anticipate his doom under the coming wrath of God.

THE FUTURE GLORY OF THE CHURCH
Ephesians 5:25-27

CHRIST'S CARE FOR THE CHURCH is the supreme example of the way husbands are to relate to their wives. Christ cherishes the church (Ephesians 5:29), gave Himself for her (verse 25), and makes the individual believers "members of His body" (verse 30). In a wedding, the father generally presents the bride to the bridegroom, but Christ will present the church to Himself "in all her glory" (verse 27). Lenski states, "This sanctification which presents the believer in the perfection of holiness, when every stain and wrinkle of the flesh are finally removed, is explained in more detail in the rest of verse 27. It is Christ's ultimate final purpose" (*Epistles to the Galatians, Ephesians, and Philippians,* p. 632).

The completion of the *wedding analogy* is yet in the future, when the church, in glory, will have "no spot or wrinkle or any such thing;" but will be "holy and blameless" before Him (verse 27). This will happen when all things are brought to final fruition and completion, when the church saints are all taken home by the resurrection and the rapture. "When the church is resurrected, or translated, individual believers will have bodies that are without sin and suited to serving the Holy God throughout eternity future" (Walvoord, *Prophecy Knowledge Handbook,* p. 472).

It is best to understand the word "glorious" in verse 27 as the eschatological radiance of God's presence on the final day rather than the glory in which the church currently participates. A close parallel is found in 2 Corinthians 11:2, where the apostle writes about the Corinthian congregation as a "pure virgin" to Christ. While this passage has present-tense connotations, it is best understood as referring to what will happen at the resurrection and the rapture (O'Brien, *Letter to the Ephesians*, p. 424).

REWARDS FOR FAITHFULNESS
Ephesians 6:7-9

SLAVERY AND OWNERSHIP OF SLAVES was part of the culture of Paul's day, and in the Bible, Christian slaves and masters are given guidance as to how they should relate and respond to each other. While the Bible does not condone slavery, it offers a moral imperative that governs how slaves and masters should act. Slaves are to be obedient according to the flesh, show respect ("fear and trembling"), and serve from a sincere heart, as if serving Christ (Ephesians 6:5). They are not simply to please the master in what they do, but they are to carry out their duties as if serving Christ, "doing the will of God from the heart" (verse 6). Their service is to be done "as to the Lord, and not to men" (verse 7).

The ultimate reward for the Christian slave will be receiving back from the Lord (verse 8). This principle is true for either the "slave or free." The principle applies to *all*, though Paul is emphasizing a special responsibility on the part of slaves. Paul then says masters must "do the same things to [slaves] and give up threatening, knowing that both their Master and yours is in heaven, and there is no partiality with Him" (verse 9). To do "the same things" is to "deal in like manner with them." This literally reads "act by them, as they are bound to act by you." The book of James, which also addresses partiality and favoritism, warns believers about complaining against and mistreating one another (James 2:1-4). Like Paul, James warns of a future judgment. He writes, "Do not complain, brethren, against one another, so that you yourselves may not be judged; behold, the Judge is standing right at the door" (5:9).

In summary, Paul places the actions of both the slave and the master on a higher plane. The slave must work "as to the Lord," and the slave owner must relate in a kind manner, knowing that the heavenly Master is watching and will reward according to one's motives and actions. Hoehner says, "It is only the Lord who can accurately and impartially judge the performance and motivation (cf. 1 Peter 1:17)" ("Ephesians," *Bible Knowledge Commentary*, p. 642). Special rewards will be given to Christian slaves and masters at the *bema* judgment (Romans 14:10-12; 1 Corinthians 3:10-15; 2 Corinthians 5:10-11).

PHILIPPIANS

In Philippians, Paul looks forward to the "day of Christ Jesus" (1:6,10), the rapture of the church. Though not wanting to die, still he looks forward to the day he can be with Christ. In light of this, he says to die is but gain (verse 21). When death comes, the believer will then be fully perfected (3:11-14). By contrast, the lost will perish and be forever cut off from God (verses 18-19). The child of God is a citizen of heaven (verses 20-21) whose name is written in the book of life (4:3).

THE DAY OF CHRIST JESUS
Philippians 1:6,10

The "Day of the Lord" is a technical expression used in Scripture to speak of the coming seven-year Tribulation (1 Thessalonians 5:2-3), whereas the "day of Christ Jesus" refers to the rapture of the church, which comes before the terrible Day of the Lord (4:13-18). Sometimes the "day of the Lord" refers to some tragic event and judgment that is coming upon the nation of Israel or her enemies, as in the case of Obadiah 15: "The day of the Lord draws near on all the nations." In that same prophecy, other expressions are used to describe this terrible visitation: the "day of misfortune," the "day of destruction," and the "day of disaster" (verses 12-13).

In Philippians 1:6, we can see that the apostle Paul is describing a *blessed event* for the church, not judgment. He writes that he is "confident of this very thing, that He who began a good work in you will perfect it until the day of Christ Jesus." The word "perfect" (Greek, *epiteleō*) is in the future tense and could be translated "to mature, make complete." What the Lord has started with the believers He will finish or complete when the rapture comes.

Given that context, the phrase the "day of Christ Jesus," which appears with various wordings elsewhere, clearly has to do with the rapture of the church. It does not refer to the judgment of the world. When Paul writes about "the day of the Lord" in 1 Corinthians 5:5, the context tells us he is clearly talking about the rapture. He tells the Corinthian church that they do not lack any spiritual gift while they are "awaiting eagerly the revelation of our Lord Jesus Christ, who will also confirm you to the end, blameless in the day of our Lord Jesus Christ" (1:7-8). Paul urges the Philippians to be "holding fast the word of life, so that in the day of Christ I will have reason to glory" because this church maintained its spiritual integrity in its witness (Philippians 2:16; cf. 1:10; 2 Corinthians 1:14).

Though the wording may differ in the context of these references, the rapture is in view rather than the seven-year period of wrath known as the Day of the Lord. This Day of the Lord, however, does begin after the resurrection of the church saints and the rapture of believers who will be alive at that time. The purpose of the rapture is to *remove the* church from the earth before God's wrath is poured out upon the earth in the Tribulation. The Day of the Lord will extend through the Tribulation, and some say it will even continue on to the end of the millennial kingdom. In that sense, then, the Day of the Lord is both a judgment but also a beginning of a time of blessing on the earth under the reign of the Lord Jesus Christ.

THE CERTAINTY OF LIFE TO COME
Philippians 1:19-24

THOUGH PAUL WAS PROBABLY in prison in Rome when he wrote to the Philippians, his imprisonment was a benefit in that it emboldened other believers to speak "the word of God without fear" in various places (Philippians 1:14). While some preached from good will, others preached the truth from envy and strife—probably because they were jealous of or disagreed with Paul (verse 15). Yet even then Paul rejoiced because it didn't matter to him how the truth was proclaimed (verse 18).

While Paul was a special servant of the Lord, we can tell from the upcoming verses that he was still very human. He struggled with whether it was better for him to live yet suffer, or die and be with Christ. On the one hand he wished to remain alive in order to keep his work going, which would mean "fruitful labor" (verse 22). On the other hand, he said he had "the desire to depart and be with Christ, for that is very much better" (verse 23). Ultimately it was Paul's "earnest expectation and hope" that he would be used "whether by life or by death" (verse 20). He lived by the principle, "For to me, to live is Christ, and to die is gain" (verse 21). Prophetically, he was convinced he should remain so he could continue his ministry to others "for your progress and joy in the faith" (verse 25). His prophecy came to pass, and he lived for another four to seven years. If he wrote the letter to the Philippians at the end of A.D. 60, then he survived until at least A.D. 64 or 66.

Putting all these verses together, it is clear that Paul knew intuitively and prophetically—by the indelible conviction of the Holy Spirit—that he would be set free (verse 19). Gromacki observes that Paul

> viewed his imprisonment and legal appeals from the standpoint of the divine will and human necessity. Paul's knowledge manifested itself in two predictions. He knew he would remain alive ("I shall remain," Greek, *menō*), and he knew he would return to Philippi ("continue with you all"). The Greek verb here literally means "to remain with them beside them" (Greek, *sumparamenō*). It was one thing to get out of prison; it was another to be able to travel to their city once again (*Books of Philippians and Colossians,* pp. 42-43).

CHRIST'S EXALTATION
Philippians 2:8-11

THE LORD JESUS IS BOTH human and divine. As is sometimes said, He is "very Man, and very God"! He is not two persons but one—His two natures come together perfectly in His incarnate state. And though He is human, He was without sin. The apostle Paul touches on this great miracle in what is called his *kenosis* (emptying) passage (Philippians 2:5-8). Verse 7 tells us that Jesus "emptied Himself, taking the form of a bond-servant, and being made in the likeness of men." The Lord Jesus did not surrender His immanent attributes in any way; He was continually and perfectly holy, just, merciful, truthful, and faithful. "The emptying was not a subtraction but an *addition....* The 'emptying' of Christ was taking on an additional nature, a human nature with its limitations. His deity was never surrendered" (Enns, *Moody Handbook of Theology,* pp. 228-29).

The Lord took on the "outward appearance" (Greek, *schēmatos*) "as a man" and humbled Himself "by becoming obedient to the point of death, even death on a cross" (verse 8). The prophecy of the exaltation of the Messiah as stated in Daniel 7:13-28 was fulfilled: "Also,

God highly exalted Him, and bestowed on Him the name which is above every name, so that at the name of Jesus every knee will bow, of those who are in heaven, and on earth, and under the earth" (verses 9-10).

Paul paraphrases Psalm 110:1-2 as another important prophecy about the *name and the title of the Messiah:* There is coming a day when "every tongue will confess that Jesus Christ is Lord, to the glory of God the Father" (Philippians 2:11). In Psalm 110:1, the Messiah is called David's Lord (Hebrew, *Adonai*), who now sits at the right hand of His Father's throne in glory. He awaits the establishment of the Davidic kingdom, in which God will "make Your enemies a footstool for Your feet." *Adonai* will then rule from Zion in the midst of His enemies (verse 2). Christ Jesus is the exalted Lord who will someday establish His earthly reign and subdue the nations (Psalm 2). Paul also alludes to Christ's prophesied lordship in Romans 10:11-13, where he writes that Christ "the Lord is Lord of all" (verse 12). In Romans 14:9, Paul says Christ is "Lord both of the dead and of the living."

Those "under the earth" (Philippians 2:10) probably refers to Satan and his demonic host, and even the souls in hell. "Willingly or unwillingly, every tongue will confess the lordship of Jesus Christ, and this will bring glory to God the Father" (Walvoord, *Prophecy Knowledge Handbook,* p. 474). God has given to Jesus a designation that distinguishes Him from all others. He outranks all by this title of Lord. "All authority in heaven and on earth were his by nature as well as by gift (Mt. 28:18; cf. Eph. 1:20-21)" (O'Brien, *Commentary on Philippians,* p. 238).

ATTAINING TO THE RESURRECTION FROM THE DEAD
Philippians 3:11-14

BELIEVERS IN CHRIST HAVE BEEN given the righteousness of Christ, not through the law, but through the exercise of faith (Philippians 3:9), with the goal of knowing Him "and the

power of His resurrection and the fellowship of His sufferings" (verse 10). The ultimate purpose, as Paul says, is to "attain to the resurrection from the dead" (verse 11). Though all believers have been justified by Christ, they have not yet experienced the benefit of Christ's resurrection, nor have they "already become perfect" or "complete" (Greek, *teleioō*), though they are still pressing on, finally and completely, with the resurrection, to be "laid hold of by Christ Jesus" (verse 12). Vine states that the Greek word "*katalambano* properly means to lay hold of, and then to do this so as to appropriate a thing to oneself, possess as one's own (cp. 1 Cor. 9:24, 'attain')" (*The Collective Writings of W.E. Vine,* 2:315).

Paul's thought, in terms of his final redemption, is that it is "not as though I were now perfected," or that he has arrived on the other side of the bodily resurrection (Lightfoot, *Epistle to the Philippians,* p. 152). Ultimately, when that day arrives, Paul and all believers can say, "I do not regard myself as having laid hold of it yet; but one thing I do: forgetting what lies behind and reaching forward to what lies ahead, I press on toward the goal for the prize of the upward call of God in Christ Jesus" (Philippians 3:13-14). The imagery Paul uses is of a runner who keeps his eyes fixed on the finish line. He leans forward and runs a straight course "and will not allow himself to be distracted or turned aside" (O'Brien, *Commentary on Philippians,* p. 430). Paul's goal is to finish his course in this life, and to be resurrected. He waits for the final "victory through our Lord Jesus Christ" (1 Corinthians 15:57). Because of the absolute certainty of the future resurrection, he urges believers to live "steadfast, immovable, always abounding in the work of the Lord, knowing that your toil is not in vain in the Lord" (verse 58).

THE FINAL DESTINY OF THE LOST
Philippians 3:18-19

THE APOSTLE IS MOVED emotionally when he thinks about the lost and those who live as enemies of the cross (Philippians 3:18). He confessed to the Philippians that this hurt him to the point of "weeping." Their final end is "destruction" and their god is their appetite (verse 19). The Greek text here literally reads, "whose god the stomach" (*he koilia*), or "intestines." What does Paul mean by this?

Vine comments, "This suggests the combination of sensual self-indulgence with a glorying in a sort of religion, by which the vilest influence is exerted, and which turns liberty into license" (*The Collective Writings of W.E. Vine*, 2:317). The word "destruction" is *apoleia* and is based on the same Greek word stem that is used for such words as *perish* and *lost* (as in Luke 19:10). The apostle is prophesying the final spiritual destruction of the unsaved. They have denied the "Master who bought them, bringing swift destruction upon themselves" (2 Peter 2:1), and will face an eternal separation from God in the lake of fire (Revelation 20:15).

"The unsaved treat the message of the cross with intellectual contempt because they already are perishing (1 Cor. 1:18)" (Gromacki, *Books of Philippians and Colossians*, p. 96). These who despise the cross will have a certain human "glory" coming to them, but it will be "their shame, who set their minds on earthly things" ("the upon-earth things," Greek, *epigeia*, Philippians 3:19). The lost are earthbound; their minds cannot rise above the physical and the earthly. "Those Paul warned against were perhaps profligates in incipient Gnosticism who trusted in their own attainments and not in the sufficiency of Christ alone" (Lightner, "Philippians," *Bible Knowledge Commentary*, p. 662).

OUR HEAVENLY CITIZENSHIP
Philippians 3:20-21

In contrast to the lost, who are doomed for destruction (Philippians 3:19), the believer looks forward to his heavenly "citizenship" (verse 20). The word "citizenship" in the Greek text is *politeuma,* a word related to the Eng-

lish *politics.* The Greek word *polis* means city. This citizenship is *in* the heavens, and it is from heaven that believers "eagerly wait for a Savior, the Lord Jesus Christ" (verse 20). The expression "eagerly wait" is a verb made up by the apostle Paul that contains the prepositions *from* (Greek, *apo*) and *out* (Greek, *ek*), along with the verb *to receive* (Greek, *dechomai*). "We" refers to believers who may be alive, including Paul, when this may happen, though no apostle knew the specific time when the rapture of the church might take place. This "verb stresses an earnest longing, an eager expectation, and an anxious waiting. It connotes an imminent coming, a possibility in one's own lifetime" (Gromacki, *Books of Philippians and Colossians,* p. 98).

The Lord Jesus will "transform the body of our humble state into conformity with the body of His glory" (verse 21). The word "transform" (Greek, *metashēmatizo*) speaks of complete change from one appearance to another. Using this word, Paul says 1) that false teachers can transform themselves into apostles of Christ (2 Corinthians 11:13); 2) that Satan can transform himself into an angel of light (verse 14); and 3) that Satan's ministers (the demons or those who represent him in false religions) are able to appear as if they are ministers of righteousness (verse 15).

In this transformation, Paul says, believers will change from their present weakened and limited human bodies to conformity with Christ's glorious body. The expression "the body of our humble state" is better translated "the body of our humiliation." That is, our body exists in a low estate because it is subject "to sufferings and indignities and all the effects of sin" (Vine, *The Collective Writings of W.E. Vine,* 2:318). But it will be conformed (Greek, *summorphos*) to His body "by the exertion of the power that He has even to subject all things to Himself" (Philippians 3:21).

While Paul here has the rapture in mind, which could take place while his readers are still living, this same transformation will take place in the dead in Christ, who will arise and precede the living when the rapture takes place. Both those who are changed while alive and those who are resurrected "will be caught up together…in the clouds to meet the Lord in the air, and so we shall always be with the Lord" (1 Thessalonians 4:17).

Christ's resurrection is the guarantee of the believer's resurrection. According to O'Brien, "his resurrected body is the prototype and paradigm of theirs. So in place of earthly bodies characterized by frailty, physical decay, weakness, and mortality, believers will have bodies that are suitable to the life of heaven (1 Cor. 15:38-49), and thus imperishable, spiritual, glorious, and powerful" (*Commentary on Philippians*, p. 465).

THE BOOK OF LIFE
Philippians 4:1-3

THE APOSTLE DEARLY LOVED the believers in the church at Philippi. Twice in Philippians 4:1 he calls them his "beloved." Because of their special place in his heart, he says that they are his "joy and crown." Paul generally felt this way about all his converts (1 Thessalonians 2:19-20). That they were his "crown" (Greek, *stephanos*) means they were a victory wreath to be worn on the head, as done by winners in the Greek games (1 Corinthians 9:24-25). At the judgment seat of Christ, the *bema*, believers will receive various crowns for their service to the Lord (2 Corinthians 5:10). For Paul, these saints represented his joy of victory because they were proof that his work in Philippi had not been in vain (Philippians 2:16).

In 4:2 Paul has to put out a "brush fire" between two women, Euodia and Syntyche, who apparently were not relating together in Christian harmony "in the Lord." They may have been among the women Paul met outside of the city on a Sabbath day when he first began his work in Philippi (Acts 16:13). Paul urged these women to live in harmony and to think the same things when it comes to living out the Christian walk (Philippians 2:2; 3:16).

Paul then asks that these women be helped because they are worthy. They aided Paul in his struggles for the gospel, along with someone by the name of Clement (4:3). Paul wants the same recognition extended to "the rest of my fellow workers, whose names are written in the book of life" (verse 3). What is meant by the book of life? And can a believer's name be stricken from the book of life? The Bible teaches elsewhere that this will not be the case.

Some ask about Revelation 3:5, where the Lord Jesus said to the church at Sardis, "He who overcomes will thus be clothed in white garments; and I will not erase his name from the book of life." Robert L. Thomas observes, "Interpreters could take the 'blotting out' as an example of *litotes,* a figure of speech in which an affirmative is expressed by the negative of a contrary statement. Coming by way of denial of the opposite, this is an understatement to express emphatically the assurance that the overcomer's name will be retained in the book of life" (*Revelation 1-7*, p. 261). The apostle John adds that believers' names were "written in the book of life from the foundation of the world" (17:8) (Couch, *Revelation*, p. 168).

Finally, the names of these saints "were in the Book of Life, meaning that they had received eternal life from God through faith in His gracious provision by Jesus Christ (Luke 10:20; Rev. 20:15)" (Gromacki, *Books of Philippians and Colossians*, p. 103).

THE PROMISE OF GOD'S PEACE AND PROVISION
Philippians 4:5-7,19

THE APOSTLE PAUL URGES the Philippian Christians to demonstrate their "forbearing spirit" (Greek, *epieikas*) or sweet and reasonable attitude "to all men" (Philippians 4:5). The reason is that "the Lord is near." The Greek word for "near," *eggus,* refers to a closeness, either in time or space. It can refer to the imminence of the Lord's return for the saints

(James 5:7-8). This would make sense in that Paul had just discussed the blessed hope that believers will one day receive new bodies (Philippians 3:20-21). Christians are to look up and ahead in anticipation of the Lord's soon return. However, it is also true that the Greek word *eggus* could be referring to the closeness of the Lord in that Christ is omnipresent, and that He abides with each believer. The Lord never leaves His own, and He is aware of everything a believer does and thinks.

Because of the assurance of Christ's closeness, the believer is not to be anxious in the affairs of life, but is to continue in prayer and supplication with thanksgiving and let "requests be made known to God" about all the struggles and doubts he experiences (4:6). This exhortation comes with a personal "prophecy" or promise that assures spiritual results: "And the peace of God, which surpasses all comprehension, shall guard your hearts and your minds in Christ Jesus" (verse 7). The Greek word for "guard," *phroureō,* is in the future tense and assures, by supplication and prayer, that the believer will be fortified and protected both emotionally and mentally, in Christ Jesus, during the course of the Christian life. "The peace of God is designed to guard from evil all these inner activities, and all 'in Christ Jesus,' for peace can be enjoyed only in realized communion with Him, the living one" (Vine, *The Collective Writings of W.E. Vine,* 2:322).

Christ said that anxiety about physical needs is characteristic of the pagan world (Matthew 6:25-34), and here in Philippians, Paul states Christians shouldn't exhibit anxiety. To do so is to show a lack of confidence in the Father's care for His children (verse 32). If He feeds the birds, how much more will He care for those who are His (verse 33)?

Paul then writes about how the Lord "shall supply all your needs according to His riches in glory in Christ Jesus" (Philippians 4:19). This is a promise of God's ongoing care for His own children. The apostle begins the verse with the words, "My God." "The pronoun [*my*] is especially expressive here: 'You have supplied *my* wants (verses 16, 18); God *on my behalf* shall supply all *yours*'" (Lightfoot, *Epistle to the Philippians,* p. 167). The phrase "in Christ Jesus" speaks of union with or incorporation into Christ Jesus. Is Paul writing about something distinctly future? Is he discussing physical or spiritual riches?

Vine believes the apostle is talking about something far richer than simply physical comfort. "This fullness is in the heavenly sphere, where His attributes and power are in unceasing manifestation, as emanating from His own person. This glory shines into the hearts and lives of His people, expressing to and in them all that centers in Himself" (Vine, *The Collective Writings of W.E. Vine,* 2:326). While many believe Paul is discussing physical supply in this passage, it could just as well be about the great spiritual riches that truly sustain a believer even when he has lost all his material riches.

COLOSSIANS

SOME OF THE PROPHECIES WRITTEN IN EPHESIANS are also found in Colossians. Paul speaks about the hope that is laid up for the believer in heaven (1:4-5), where the inheritance is kept for the saints on earth (verses 12-14). As with Ephesians 2–3, the church is a mystery not mentioned in the Old Testament but revealed in the New (Colossians 1:24-28). The Old Testament rituals, ceremonies, and laws were prophetic signs of blessings to come because of Christ (2:16-17). And finally, Christ is now seated at the right hand of God, and the believer is secure in Him (3:1-4).

HOPE LAID UP IN HEAVEN
Colossians 1:4-5

THE CHURCH IN COLOSSAE HAD a great outpouring of love not only for the saints in their own congregation but apparently also for believers throughout the growing Christian community spreading out everywhere (Colossians 1:4). They also held firmly to the hope (Greek, *elpis*) that was laid up for them in heaven. This heavenly hope (or confident expectation) was set forth "in the word of truth, the gospel" (verse 5). This shows that part of the good news was the anticipation of going home to be with the Lord someday. "Faith and love came into their hearts because of the great hope they had heard, heard from the start...in the Word, the Word that was marked by divine truth" (Lenski, *Colossians,* p. 24). This same gospel was bearing good works and fruit and "increasing, even as it has been doing in you also since the day you heard of it and understood the grace of God in truth" (verse 6).

Believers in Christ have the *prophetic promises* of glory and being with the Lord in heaven. The world does not share in this hope (1 Thessalonians 4:13) because this hope is found only in the gospel, which the world does not accept (Colossians 1:23). God is "the God of hope" (Romans 15:13), and in His Son is the hope of glory (Colossians 1:27). Christ's return to catch away His own is called "the blessed hope and the glorious appearing" (Titus 2:13 NKJV). This hope is "set before us" (Hebrews 6:18) and includes a living hope by the resurrection from the dead (1 Peter 1:3). Peter adds that it is God "who raised [Christ] from the dead and gave Him glory, so that your faith and hope are in God" (verse 21).

The word of the truth of the gospel alone reveals the certainty of future and celestial blessings. The glories of heaven are in no way connected to the earth that moves only through time and space and is so matter bound! These forms of the earthly sphere can never lead to the discovery of heaven. Every blessing that the gospel makes known has the future ultimately as its goal. "The gospel takes the believer beyond the present horizon" (John Eadie, *Colossians,* p. 12).

THE INHERITANCE WITH THE SAINTS
Colossians 1:12-14

Salvation was planned by the heavenly Father and carried out by the sacrifice of the Son. Paul gives thanks to God the Father "who has qualified us to share in the inheritance of the saints in light" (Colossians 1:12). The Greek word *hikanoō,* translated "qualified" means "to make one sufficient, render fit, make adequate." Through the sacrifice of Christ, God has made believers adequate for salvation. Mortals who by faith trust Christ as Savior now can share in the glory that they could otherwise not attain to.

The apostle writes much about the "inheritance" (Greek, *klēronomia*) believers have in Christ. The Greek term means "to be legally called, appointed." Paul uses this word in his writings 17 times, and that includes the word "heir" (Greek, *klēronomos*). The Holy Spirit is the earnest of our inheritance (Ephesians 1:14), and Paul points out that the eternal inheritance (Hebrews 9:15) cannot come by keeping the law (Galatians 3:18). While believers now have the guarantee of this inheritance of everlasting life, its completion is yet future. Believers who now exist as children of God are "heirs also, heirs of God and fellow heirs with Christ" (Romans 8:17). They are "waiting eagerly for our adoption as sons, the redemption of our body" (verse 23). With patience the child of God waits eagerly for this to take place (verse 25).

Believers are now called "the saints in Light" (Colossians 1:12)—that is, sons of the day and not of the darkness (1 Thessalonians 5:5). The Christian now has a new status, a new position because God the Father "rescued us from the domain of darkness, and transferred us to the kingdom of His beloved Son" (Colossians 1:13). The word "rescued" (Greek, *ruomai*) is a strong word and means that God "caused to

escape, rescued, drew to" Himself those who were helpless. Believers were delivered out of the "domain" (Greek, *exousias*) or the power of darkness and were placed or "transferred" (Greek, *methistami*) into another category, "the kingdom of His beloved Son." There are three views on this kingdom: 1) It is the church here described as *the* kingdom; 2) it is simply referring to a different realm of spiritual reality; 3) it is a reference to the future millennial Davidic kingdom of the Lord Jesus that lasts 1000 years. The second view is certainly possible, though the third view is more in keeping with what both the Jews and the church saints anticipated. If the third view is the right view, then Christians are already seen as residents of the millennial kingdom even though it has not yet arrived upon the earth. Citizenship in the kingdom is guaranteed by the fact of the believer's conversion (Nicoll, *Expositor's Greek New Testament,* 3:501).

On the issue of the kingdom, Vine writes that the believer's "allotted portion is the future condition and possessions of believers in the new and eternal order of things to be ushered in at the return of Christ" (Vine, *The Collective Writings of W.E. Vine,* 2:338). He adds, "This removing takes place when a person receives Christ by faith. It is an immediate transference from one spiritual region or kingdom to another" (Vine, *The Collective Writings of W.E. Vine,* 2:339). The apostle Paul further writes that it is Christ "in whom we have redemption, the forgiveness of sins" (verse 14). This is the wonderful result of having the new inheritance. "This emancipation is enjoyed only because of the tremendous cost Christ paid on the cross (cf. Romans 3:24-26)" (Geisler, "Colossians," *Bible Knowledge Commentary,* p. 672).

THE MYSTERY OF THE CHURCH AGE
Colossians 1:24-28

Paul uses the Greek word *mustērion* 20 times in his writings. He uses the word most often in the sense of "that which is not before revealed." He writes about the dispensation of the church age and the union of believers with Christ as a mystery. He reminds the Colossian church that he has been made "a minister according to the stewardship from God bestowed on me for your benefit" (Colossians 1:25). The word "stewardship" is the Greek word *oikonomia*, which is translated "dispensation" in many Bible versions. Paul is referring to the new dispensation of the church, "the mystery which has been hidden from the past ages and generations; but has now been manifested to His saints" (verse 26). The great truth not shown in the Old Testament, but now seen in this dispensation, is that "Christ would indwell the believer" (Walvoord, *Prophecy Knowledge Handbook*, p. 477).

Some scholars argue that this simply means that the church age was mentioned in the Old Testament but not made clear until Acts 2. It was then revealed most specifically to the apostle Paul. But it is better to understand the mystery as "Christ in you, the hope of glory" (verse 27). That believers, especially Gentiles along with the Jews who trust in Christ, would form a *new body*, the spiritual body of Christ, now called "the church," is something new in God's program. It is in this church dispensation that this great miracle takes place. Old Testament saints were not thus united to Christ the Savior, though they are certainly ultimately saved by His death at the cross.

Gromacki writes, "The Old Testament both depicted and predicted Gentile salvation through faith in the redeeming God of Israel, but it never revealed that Jews and Gentiles would become spiritually one in Christ and that Christ would dwell in both (Eph. 3:6)" (*Stand Perfect in Wisdom*, p. 160). Now everyone who accepts the Lord Jesus is presented "complete in Christ" (Colossians 1:28). Eadie comments, "The apostle felt an undying interest in every man, whatever his character or creed—every man, whatever his race or lineage—every man, whatever his colour or language—every man, whatever his class or station; every living man on earth" (*Colossians*, pp. 103-4).

In the parallel passage in Ephesians 2:19–3:21, the apostle elaborates further on this great truth. God has built a *new building*, a holy temple, "built together into a dwelling of God in the Spirit" (2:22). It is the new "stewardship" (3:2) or "administration" (verse 9) (or "dispensation," Greek, *oikonomia*) that is the mystery revealed to Paul (verse 3). Paul adds, "to be specific…the Gentiles are fellow heirs and fellow members of the body, and fellow partakers of the promise in Christ Jesus through the gospel" (verse 6). By "fellow heirs" he means joint heirs with the present believing Jews—both Jew and Gentile form a new and unique body, the spiritual body of Christ. Paul repeats the fact that this "mystery which for ages has been hidden in God…[is now] made known through the church to the rulers and the authorities in the heavenly places" (verses 9-10). This present church dispensation is "the eternal purpose which He carried out in Christ Jesus our Lord" (verse 11).

THE BLESSING OF THINGS TO COME
Colossians 2:16-17

THE CHURCH AT COLOSSAE was familiar with the Jewish festivals and feasts and the foods proscribed for such occasions. The Pharisees also had legalistic restrictions on food and on ceremonies that forced people to bathe a certain way and to ceremonially wash their hands before eating (Mark 7:1-23). However, under the law, there were dietary regulations that the Jews had to abide by (Leviticus 11; Acts 10:14). As well, many Jews also kept the feasts of the new moon (Numbers 10:10) and the Sabbath, which was part of the old Mosaic law covenant (Exodus 20:8-11; 31:12-18). "Christians, however, should remember the work of spiritual creation by gathering in the local church on Sunday, the day on which Christ rose from the dead (Acts 20:7; 1 Cor. 16:2)" (Gromacki, *Stand Perfect in Wisdom*, p. 186).

Nevertheless, many Jews were attempting to force legal rules on the congregation of the Colossians. They wanted to force morality and spirituality on this church by law-keeping. Paul says, "No one is to act as your judge in regard to food or drink or in respect to a festival or a new moon or a Sabbath day" (Colossians 2:16). Attempting to measure up via the law only produces a sense of moral guilt and side-tracks believers from the loving and gracious provision of the Lord found only in Christ (Galatians 3:24). What was the purpose, then, of the law and its commands?

Paul says that the commandments were a "shadow of what is to come, but the substance belongs to Christ" (Colossians 2:17). The apostle is arguing that the law and all of its types and ceremonies were but a prophecy of the coming work of Christ on the cross. Gromacki states,

> The sacrificial calendar produced pictures or types of what Christ would accomplish in His death and resurrection (Heb. 9:13-14; 10:1). He is the Passover lamb for believers (1 Cor. 5:7) and the open veil into the very presence of God (Heb. 10:19-20). In real life, one embraces the body, not the shadow (*Stand Perfect in Wisdom,* p. 187).

Since the *substance* belongs to Christ, it is foolish for Christians to long for the shadow. The shadow, the law, gave the prophecy; Christ gave the fulfillment. Nicoll says, "All that the most sanguine hoped to attain by asceticism and ceremonialism was possessed immediately in the possession of Christ" (*Expositor's Greek New Testament,* 3:531). Paul scorns the fictitious safety and superiority of the law "with the absolute completeness and superiority of the gospel, with the infinite supremacy of the God-man [Christ], the utter fullness and completeness of his saving work, and the fullness (verse 10) which he has bestowed upon us" (Lenski, *Colossians,* p. 124).

CHRIST SEATED ABOVE IN THE HEAVENS
Colossians 3:1-4

One of the more frequently quoted prophecies in the Old Testament is Psalm 110:1-2, which predicts that the Messiah would someday be seated at the right hand of God the Father. There, David wrote, "The Lord says to my Lord: Sit at My right hand until I make Your enemies a footstool for Your feet." Christ used this passage to confound the Jews who denied that He was the Son of God. They admitted that the Christ (the Messiah) was the son of David (Matthew 22:42), and Christ went on to ask them in verse 45 about why David called the Messiah his Lord if the same Messiah was his son. The Pharisees could not answer Jesus, and never asked Him another question (verse 46).

Psalm 110:1 is quoted 13 times in the Gospels and Acts. Paul quotes it three times in his epistles (Romans 8:34; Ephesians 1:20; Colossians 3:1). In Colossians 3:1 the apostle quotes Psalm 110:1 this way: "If then you have been raised up with Christ, keep seeking the things above, where Christ is, seated at the right hand of God." In a spiritual sense, believers have been united in Christ's death and burial. By being spiritually baptized and united with Him, the child of God is "also raised up with Him through faith in the working of God, who raised Him from the dead" (2:12).

Because of the spiritual work of God the Father in salvation, the believer is instructed to "set your mind on the things above, not on the things that are on earth. For you have died and your life is hidden with Christ in God" (Colossians 3:2-3). Since the believer's life is now eternally tied to the Lord Jesus, when He comes and is revealed, "then you also will be revealed with Him in glory" (verse 4).

This revealing relates to the resurrection of the saints who have died as well as the immediate transformation of those still alive on earth. All the church saints will be "caught up together with them [the resurrected] in the clouds to meet the Lord in the air, and so we shall always be with the Lord" (1 Thessalonians 4:17). This being "revealed with Him in glory" (Colossians 3:4) is the first stage of Christ's return and is distinguished from His second coming, in which He comes to reign upon the earth. In the rapture, or the coming for the church, believers will experience a marvelous change. John the apostle says, "When He appears, we may have confidence and not shrink away from Him in shame at His coming" (1 John 2:28), and "when He appears, we will be like Him, because we will see Him just as He is. And everyone who has this hope fixed on Him purifies himself, just as He is pure" (3:2-3).

When Paul writes that believers are *hidden in Christ* (Colossians 3:3), he "implies both concealment and safety; both invisibility and security. [The believer] is not yet glorified, but he is secure and safe in Christ. In fact, Christ is his very life. Christ said He was going where 'the world will not see Me anymore' (John 14:19)" (Geisler, "Colossians," *Bible Knowledge Commentary,* p. 680). This gift of life, "along with its medium and its destiny, are hidden in the Giver, as the infinite source" of eternal life (Eadie, *Colossians,* p. 218).

THE CERTAINTY OF GOD'S WRATH
Colossians 3:5-6

THERE IS NO QUESTION THAT the wrath of God will come upon all those who live as the old man or "old self" (Greek, *palaion anthrōpon*) instead of as the "new self," who is born again by the work of Christ (Colossians 3:9-10). Those who are born again are the sons of light and the sons of day, not sons of the night and of darkness (1 Thessalonians 5:5). While the child of God has a new position in Christ, it is still possible for him to sin. Yet he can say no to sin (Romans 6:12-13) and is exhorted to "put on the new self" (Colossians 3:10).

Upon the lost, or the "sons of disobedience," "the wrath of God will come" (Colossians 3:6). This wrath "is revealed from heaven against all ungodliness and unrighteousness of men who suppress the truth in [by] unrighteousness" (Romans 1:18). For those who live out sin as part of who they are, there is a judgment prophesied. Paul further writes in Romans, "We know that the judgment of God rightly falls upon those who practice such

things" (2:2). Wrath is being stored up for "the day of wrath and revelation of the righteous judgment of God" (verse 5). God will not only judge the acts of the lost but "according to my gospel, God will judge the secrets of men through Christ Jesus" (verse 16).

By contrast, those who are *in Christ* will be "justified as a gift by His grace through the redemption which is in Christ Jesus" (3:24). They must put aside the works of the old self, such as "anger, wrath, malice, slander, and abusive speech from your mouth" (Colossians 3:8), and be renewed spiritually "to a true knowledge according to the image of the One who created him" (verse 10). The final and ultimate renewal will happen when the believer is taken home to be with Christ in glory.

THE REWARD OF AN INHERITANCE
Colossians 3:18-24

HERE, PAUL ADDRESSES the social and moral conduct of the Christians in the church at Colossae. What he says is applicable to all believers for all time. Paul is concerned that wives be subject to their husbands (Colossians 3:18), that husbands be loving to their wives (verse 19), that children be obedient to their parents (verse 20), and finally, that fathers be fair with their children (verse 21).

Paul also commands that slaves should do their work heartily, "fearing the Lord" (verses 22-23). And finally, he wants masters to treat their slaves with justice and fairness, "knowing that you too have a Master in heaven" (4:1). As for Christian slaves, they are to work "as for the Lord rather than for men, knowing that from the Lord you will receive the reward of the inheritance. It is the Lord Christ whom you serve" (verses 23-24). Some scholars look at Paul's words as almost a warning. For example, Nicoll writes, "We should interpret the verse[s]…as a warning to the Christian slave not to presume on his Christianity, so as to think that God will overlook his misdeeds or idleness" (*Expositor's Greek New Testament,*

3:543). But most take Paul's thoughts in a positive and encouraging sense.

The apostle writes often about the "inheritance" (Greek, *klēronomos,* or legal designation) of eternal life (verse 24) given to all those who trust Christ as Savior. In the New Testament, the word "heir" is a related term. Paul writes that the Holy Spirit is the earnest (down payment) of the inheritance (Ephesians 1:14), and that the inheritance is the riches of the glory that will come in eternity (verse 18). Further, believers are now called the children of God (Romans 8:16), "and if children, heirs also, heirs of God and fellow heirs with Christ" (verse 17). The inheritance of eternal life that believers now possess will not be finalized until glory.

Why did Paul specifically mention the inheritance as a reward only to Christian servants, and not to all those who trust in Christ?

Paul is not excluding all classes of believers from being so blessed. He is simply amplifying and punctuating the fact that lowly servants have something that is spiritual and greater to look forward to than material rewards. Interestingly, Paul calls the inheritance of eternal life here a "reward," though he certainly is not saying that salvation is earned by good works! Vine states,

> The *klēronomia* is an inheritance, not in the sense of anything hereditary, but a sanctioned, settled possession. The slave was not paid for his work and could not, strictly speaking, have a possession, but to the converted slave Christ is everything; he has Christ in him "the hope of glory," a present reality and the pledge of an eternal recompense (*The Collective Writings of W.E. Vine,* 2:369).

1 THESSALONIANS

THIS LETTER TO THE CHURCH AT THESSALONICA is possibly Paul's first to the growing churches to which he was ministering. Paul started this congregation on his second missionary journey, during which he spent three Sabbath days proclaiming the gospel to those who would listen. Wanting to give hope and encouragement to the Thessalonians in their new-found faith, Paul wrote two letters to them. In these letters he emphasized the doctrines of the resurrection, the rapture of the church, and the Day of the Lord, the wrath from God upon a rebellious world.

Believers have a firm certainty of entering someday into the very presence of the Lord (1:3). The Thessalonian church, while serving the Lord, was waiting for His arrival to deliver them from the "wrath to come" (verse 10). Though the believer will go to glory in the rapture, there is also the return to earth to be in the kingdom with Christ (2:10-12).

Paul also deals with the prophecies about the resurrection of those in Christ and the rapture of believers who are alive on earth when He comes (4:13-18). The rapture will rescue the living saints of the church before the arrival of the terrible Day of the Lord, or the Tribulation (5:1-11). In the end, Christ will complete the believers' salvation (verses 22-24).

THE HOPE OF THE RAPTURE
1 Thessalonians 1:3

FIRST THESSALONIANS WAS WRITTEN around A.D. 51, which means this letter contains Paul's first mention of the rapture of the church (1 Corinthians, which also mentions the resurrection and the rapture in chapter 15, was written around A.D. 56).

Paul commends this suffering church for their "work of faith and labor of love and steadfastness of hope in our Lord Jesus Christ in the presence of our God and Father" (1 Thessalonians 1:3). In many places the Greek word for "hope," *elpis,* is used in an eschatological sense (see Romans 8:25; 15:13; 1 Corinthians 9:10; 13:7; 15:19; Ephesians 1:12; 4:4; 1 Timothy 4:10; Titus 2:13; Hebrews 11:1; 1 Peter 1:13). It also contains a spirit of confidence in that the believer's "hope" is a confident expectation of Christ's ultimate coming to take us to His Father's house as He promised in John 14:1-3. This hope is the anticipation of going home and being with the Lord Jesus Christ. First Thessalonians 1:3 better reads, "hope concerning our Lord Jesus Christ *in the face of* [Greek, *emprosthen*] our God and Father" (on *emprosthen,* see also 2:19 and 3:13). The word can be translated "before, as in front of something or someone"—in this case, in front of the Father (Couch, *Christ's Return,* p. 50). Believers have a firm certainty of entering the very presence of Christ and the heavenly Father. This could take place at death or at the rapture of the believer, though here, more than likely Paul is referring to the rapture. The Thessalonians were able to endure because of their hope of the Lord's return.

WAITING FOR CHRIST FROM HEAVEN
1 Thessalonians 1:9-10

THE CHURCH AT THESSALONICA was under tremendous persecution from Gentile and Jewish critics (1 Thessalonians 1:6), yet the people continued to spread the "gospel of God amid much opposition" (2:2). But they had something else that the apostle Paul commended: They had "turned to God from idols to serve a living and true God" (1:9). They were also waiting "for His Son from heaven, whom He raised from the dead, that is Jesus, who rescues us from the wrath to come" (verse 10).

There are clues that tell us these verses are about the rapture of the church. First, there was an immediate hope with this church about the return of Christ. They were waiting for His arrival; it was an "any moment" expectation. Second, Paul writes that Christ will deliver us from the coming wrath. The apostle puts himself into the hope of Christ's coming. He says He will deliver "us," meaning he includes himself. The word "delivers" is the Greek present participle of *ruomai*. Some scholars make it descriptive; the expression could read "the One who rescues us," or "Jesus, our Deliverer" (Alford, *The Greek Testament,* 3:253). The word "wrath" (Greek, *orges*) is a reference to the seven-year Tribulation, the Day of the Lord, which is described in 5:1-11. Paul says that the church saints "are not in darkness, that the day would overtake you like a thief" (verse 4). God "has not destined us for wrath" (verse 9).

The verb "to come" is a present participle of the Greek word *erkomai* with an article. It could read "the wrath absolutely coming," "which is already coming," with the full-blown meaning "the wrath is on its way to the world"

(Ellicott, *Ellicott's Commentary on the Whole Bible,* 4:131). The "coming wrath" is an essential feature in Paul's argument. It emphasizes the certainty of the event (Milligan, *Epistles to the Thessalonians,* p. 15). This Tribulation wrath takes place before the Messiah's kingdom is set up on the earth. God will afflict the world's inhabitants with an unparalleled pouring out of physical torment because of its rejection of Christ and of the Lord's will (Matthew 3:7; 24:21; Luke 21:23; Revelation 6:16-17).

Some critics of the Bible believe the early church thought that Christ would absolutely return at that time, or that indeed He did come back spiritually or in a metaphorical way in A.D. 70, at the time of the destruction of the city of Jerusalem and the temple. But the hope or expectation of the rapture should be likened to a couple who is planning to get married; their union is certain though the date has not been set. The early church had great anticipation, but they did not know when Christ would come back for them. Believers still wait today because they know the "marriage" is sure, but "the when" is still unknown (Couch, *Christ's Return,* p. 60).

THE CALL TO THE COMING KINGDOM
1 Thessalonians 2:10-12

THE THESSALONIAN CHURCH was a witness to how Paul and his fellow ministers behaved—they had acted "uprightly and blamelessly" toward the believers in that congregation (1 Thessalonians 2:10). Paul gently urged this assembly in the midst of persecution by "exhorting and encouraging and imploring each one of you as a father would his own children" (verse 11). He commanded them to "walk in a manner worthy" of God's call. That call would ultimately be "into His own kingdom and glory" (verse 12), the final destination of the church saints. Though the rapture of the church saints takes them to heaven, these same believers will return with Christ at His second coming to share in His rule on earth.

Rapture Passages

John 14:1-3	2 Thessalonians 2:3
Romans 8:19	I Timothy 6:14
I Corinthians1:7-8	2 Timothy 4:1
I Corinthians15:51-53	2 Timothy 4:8
I Corinthians16:22	Titus 2:13
Philippians 3:20-21	Hebrews 9:28
Philippians 4:5	James 5:7-9
Colossians 3:4	I Peter 1:7,13
I Thessalonians 1:10	I Peter 5:4
I Thessalonians 2:19	I John 2:28
I Thessalonians 4:13-18	I John 3:2
I Thessalonians 5:9	Jude 21
I Thessalonians 5:23	Revelation 2:25
2 Thessalonians 2:1	Revelation 3:10

Second Coming Passages

Daniel 2:44-45	Luke 21:25-28
Daniel 7:9-14	Acts 1:9-11
Daniel 12:1-3	I Thessalonians 3:13
Zechariah 12:10	2 Thessalonians 1:6-10
Zechariah 14:1-15	2 Thessalonians 2:8
Matthew 13:41	I Peter 4:12-13
Matthew 24: 15-31	2 Peter 3:1-14
Matthew 26:64	Jude 14-15
Mark 13:14-27	Revelation 1:7
Mark 14:62	

When reading the Bible's 320-plus references to the second coming, one must read the contexts carefully to discern whether a specific passage is describing the rapture or the glorious appearing.

Writing to the church at Thyatira, the apostle John says that the believers who overcome will be given authority over the nations to co-rule with Christ (Revelation 2:26-27). The Lord says they will "sit down with Me on My throne, as I also overcame and sat down with My Father on His throne" (3:21; Psalm 110:1-2). It is clear from 1 Thessalonians 2:12 that the church is not the kingdom, for the believers Paul is writing to are already "in the church." All believers in the present church dispensation can look forward to the 1000-year reign of Christ, when righteousness will rule and the glory of Christ will fill the whole earth (Zechariah 14:9) (Couch, *Christ's Return*, p. 75).

THE COMING WRATH
1 Thessalonians 2:14-16

HERE, PAUL MENTIONS HOW the Gentile believers in the Thessalonian church are suffering hateful persecution "at the hands of your own countrymen," even as believing Jews suffered at the hands of unbelieving Jews (1 Thessalonians 2:14). Paul is probably referring here to the persecution that began in Jerusalem with the death of the first martyr, Stephen (Acts 7:54–8:4). This persecution brought about a scattering "throughout the regions of Judea and Samaria" (8:1). Fortunately, those who were scattered continued to preach the Word (verse 4).

The Jews who killed Christ and many of the New Testament prophets pursued Paul, and as he said, were "hindering us from speaking to the Gentiles so that they may be saved" (1 Thessalonians 2:16). Those who were hostile to the gospel were filling up to the fullest measure their sins. Milligan writes, "In acting as they were doing the present Jews were but carrying forward to its completion the work which their fathers had begun...and which had now brought down upon them God's judicial wrath" (Milligan, *Epistles to the Thessalonians*, p. 31). Because of their sins, "wrath has come upon them to the utmost" (verse 16). The verb "has come" (Greek, *phthano*) means "to attain, to come upon, to be unhindered."

Some have taken this to mean that the Jews who were turning against the gospel would soon fall under the wrath of the Roman authorities and be persecuted. Persecution was coming down on the Jews at this time under the reign of the Roman emperor Claudius (Nicoll, *Expositor's Greek New Testament*, 4:29). It seems better to take this as meaning that a particular judgment awaits these Jews when they stand before God condemned for their rejection of the Savior and King.

Thomas Constable writes,

> Possibly Paul was thinking of the wrath of God that is on every individual who fails to believe in Christ (John 3:36). Or the wrath may refer to the Tribulation which will assuredly come upon them because of their rejection of Jesus Christ. This was probably his thought since in other contexts in this epistle where he speaks of the wrath to come he has the Tribulation in mind ("1 Thessalonians," *Bible Knowledge Commentary*, p. 696).

The expression "to the utmost" is *telos* in the Greek text. The prophesied wrath will come upon the Jews "with finality" at the very end (Lenski, *I and II Thessalonians*, p. 270). At the second coming of Christ, when the Lord's feet touch the Mount of Olives, the Jewish remnant in the Holy Land will see the One whom they pierced, "and they will mourn for Him, as one mourns for an only son, and they will weep bitterly over Him" (Zechariah 12:10).

of exultation," especially when he would stand with them "in the presence of our Lord Jesus at His coming" (verse 19). He further says that this church was to him and his companions "our glory and joy" (verse 20).

In the context of the Thessalonian letters, this "coming" (Greek, *parousia*) is the rapture, and it is very similar to what we read in 3:13. This coming is not about Christ's arrival to take over the Davidic kingdom. It has to do with the church, when the believers are suddenly brought face to face with Christ. There is no crescendo of judgment and wrath here as when He arrives on earth to subdue His enemies and judge the nations (Matthew 25:31-46). In the spiritual sense Paul will be proud of his offspring, the faithful believers who stood so tall spiritually under persecution in Thessalonica.

That this is a rapture passage is evident because the Lord Jesus could have come and taken that very generation of saints, including the apostle Paul, unto Himself. The phrase "in the presence" (Greek, *emprosthen*) means "in front of [Him]." "In effect [Paul] asked what would be the greatest blessing he could possibly receive at the judgment seat of Christ. They were! They were everything that was worth anything to Paul" (Constable, "1 Thessalonians," *Bible Knowledge Commentary*, p. 697). Paul's life was filled with joy because of these believers, and he couldn't wait to present them to Christ when the church goes home to be with Him.

BELIEVERS PRESENTED TO CHRIST AT HIS COMING
1 Thessalonians 2:18-20

THE APOSTLE PAUL HAD A SPECIAL love for the Thessalonian church and for many months wanted to come back and visit the people, though he was thwarted by Satan (1 Thessalonians 2:18). He had great hope in these believers. To him, they were his "joy or crown

BELIEVERS PRESENTED TO THE FATHER AT CHRIST'S COMING
1 Thessalonians 3:11-13

IN THESE VERSES THE APOSTLE PAUL encourages this church to remain pure, mature, and grounded in the faith all the way until they are taken home to glory to be with God. Paul expresses his desire to return to this church in order to minister to the people more (1 Thessalonians 3:11). But he also wants them to mature and become more sensitive toward the needs of their fellow believers. He writes, "May the Lord cause you to increase and abound in love for one another, and for all people, just as we also do for you" (verse 12).

Paul then gives a similar parallel statement that is a rapture passage very much like 2:19. He wants the Thessalonian Christians to grow and establish their hearts "without blame in holiness before our God and Father at the coming of our Lord Jesus with all His saints" (verse 13). In the Greek text the two verses read like this:

"In the presence of the Lord [our] Jesus in the [of Him] coming" (2:19).

"In the presence of God and Father [our] in the coming of the Lord [our] Jesus with all the saints [of Him]" (3:13).

First Thessalonians 3:13 is a rapture passage because the event it describes could happen at any time to the believers Paul is writing to. It also pictures the believers being ushered into the very presence of God the Father immediately. This is tied to Christ's coming, though this is clearly not referring to Christ's arrival to reign, but rather, His taking up of the church saints to heaven to be with Himself and the heavenly Father. Coming with "His saints" has to do with bringing the souls of those who have gone before in order to give them a new body and usher them into glory in that resurrected state. This is exactly what Paul says in detail in 4:13-18. Constable states, "The holy ones accompanying Christ at His coming are probably the souls of the saints who have departed this life and gone to be with Christ, whose bodies will be resurrected when He comes (4:16)" ("1 Thessalonians," *Bible Knowledge Commentary,* p. 700).

While many scholars believe the *bema* judgment (Romans 14:10-12; 1 Corinthians 3:10-15; 2 Corinthians 5:10-11) of the saints takes place in Revelation 19:7-10, others hold that it takes place here upon arrival in glory. This view has some merit because the Greek word *emprosthen* ("in the presence of") can carry the thought to appear before a judge (Matthew

25:32; 27:11; Luke 21:36; 2 Corinthians 5:10). Paul seems to be picturing the judgment seat of Christ in 1 Thessalonians 2:19. There is no contradiction between 2:19 and 3:13. The unity of the Father and the Son is certain and the two passages allow for a joint judgeship at the *bema* judgment. Walvoord writes that in heaven the saints' "holiness and faithfulness to God will be especially evident before God the Father and before saints and angels" and that "this verse is commonly related to the Rapture of the church" (*Prophecy Knowledge Handbook,* p. 481).

THE RAPTURE OF THE CHURCH EXPLAINED
1 Thessalonians 4:13-18

THIS CENTRAL PASSAGE PROVIDES one of Paul's most detailed descriptions of the doctrine of the rapture of the church. Along with 1 Corinthians 15:51-58, this passage is one of the more crucial revelations about the end of the church age. While the Old Testament and the synoptic Gospels reveal much concerning the second coming of Christ, the rapture is not developed until the writings of the apostle Paul. The rapture was first mentioned cryptically by Christ Himself in John 14:1-3 when He explained that He would return to take believers home to the "Father's house." Paul writes, "Behold, I tell you a mystery; we will not all sleep, but we will all be changed, in a moment, in the twinkling of an eye, at the last trumpet; for the trumpet will sound, and the dead will be raised imperishable, and we will all be changed" (1 Corinthians 15:51-52).

Paul wanted the Thessalonian believers to be informed about the rapture. He did not want them to grieve about "those who are asleep" in the same way the lost grieve because they have no hope (1 Thessalonians 4:13). Constable observes, "This is not the sleep of the soul, however, because Paul wrote elsewhere that a Christian who is absent from his body is present with the Lord (2 Cor. 5:8; cf. Phil.

The Second Coming of Christ

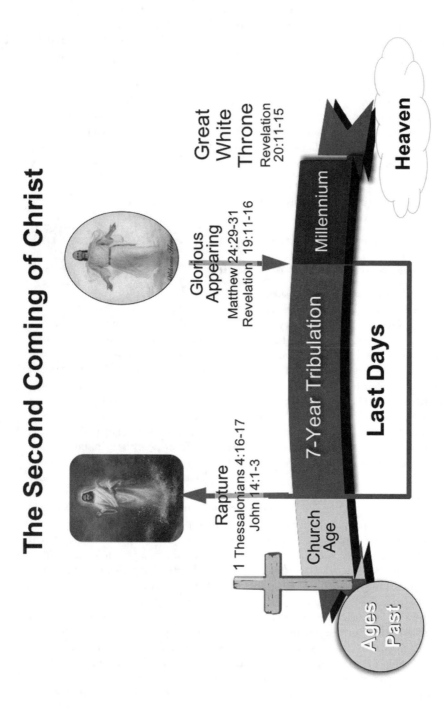

Rapture
1 Thessalonians 4:16-17
John 14:1-3

Glorious
Appearing
Matthew 24:29-31
Revelation 19:11-16

Great
White
Throne
Revelation
20:11-15

Church
Age

7-Year Tribulation

Millennium

Last Days

Ages
Past

Heaven

The second coming of Jesus Christ is prominent in Scripture—it is mentioned 320-plus times, second only to the doctrine of salvation. An examination of all these passages shows they fall into two categories: the rapture, which takes place in the air before the "hour of testing" (Revelation 3:10) from which Christians are exempt, and the glorious appearing, which occurs on earth immediately after the Tribulation and just before the Lord establishes His millennial kingdom.

1:23; 1 Thess. 5:10). It is rather the 'sleep' of the body in the earth until it is resurrected, changed into a glorious body, and reunited with the soul (1 Cor. 15:35-57; 2 Cor.5:1-9)" ("1 Thessalonians," *Bible Knowledge Commentary,* p. 703).

On the basis of Christ's death and resurrection, "God will bring with [Jesus] those who have fallen asleep in Jesus" (1 Thessalonians 4:14). The souls of believers will come from heaven with Christ, and instantly, as "the dead in Christ," will be given a resurrected and imperishable body (verse 16).

"We who are alive and remain until the coming of the Lord, will not precede [go before] those who have fallen asleep" (verse 15). Christ will come from heaven, a *shout* will be heard, along with the *voice* of the archangel and the *trumpet* of God, and the dead will rise first (verse 16). They will be drawn upward to Christ along with believers who are still alive on earth. Their bodies will then be changed and transformed. "Then we who are alive and remain will be caught up together with them in the clouds to meet the Lord in the air, and so we shall always be with the Lord" (verse 17). In order for those alive to be transported bodily to heaven, "this perishable must put on the imperishable, and this mortal must put on immortality" (1 Corinthians 15:53).

The *description of the rapture* in 1 Thessalonians 4:17 is vivid. In the Greek text it reads, "Then with them [the resurrected] we shall be snatched away, caught up, in the clouds." The words "caught up" come from the Greek word *harpazo.* The idea is that with sudden force, believers are instantly carried away "to meet the Lord in the air." "To meet" is a prepositional phrase—"into *[eis]* a meeting" (Greek, *apantesis*) with the Lord (Couch, *Christ's Return,* p. 128). Milligan adds, "It was towards this goal, a life of uninterrupted…communion with his risen and glorified Lord that St. Paul's longings in thinking of the future always turned"(*Epistles to the Thessalonians,* p. 62). Believers will never again be away from the presence of their Savior; they "shall always be with the Lord" (verse 17).

Some have claimed the doctrine of the rapture has no practical or personal significance, but the truth is just the opposite. Paul closes this passage by saying, "Comfort one another with these words" (verse 18).

These verses have all the markings of a rapture passage and not a passage about the second coming of Christ to earth. First, the events described could happen at any time. Second, they could have happened in Paul's day because he says this might happen to "us" or "we." Third, Paul talks about the church saints—those "asleep in Jesus," "the dead in Christ." This miraculous event happens only to the church saints and not to the Old Testament saints, who are not described as those "in Christ." And as Walvoord notes, "Unlike passages that deal with the second coming of Christ and trace the tremendous world-shaking events which shall take place in the years preceding it, the Rapture of the church is always presented as the next event and, as such, one that is not dependent on immediate preceding events" (*Prophecy Knowledge Handbook,* p. 481).

Being *taken up suddenly* into the sky is clearly distinct from Jesus coming down to establish His kingdom. The church saints are going upward. The reason is clear in 5:9—they are being taken up to escape the wrath that will fall upon the earth (Couch, *Christ's Return,* p. 128).

THE COMING TRIBULATION
1 Thessalonians 5:1-11

BECAUSE THE CHURCH SAINTS will be removed from the earth by the rapture, they will be spared the horrible judgments of the Day of the Lord. Paul says the church was "uninformed" about the rapture (1 Thessalonians 4:13), but believers were already aware of the Day of the Lord (5:1) because it is mentioned multiple times in the Old Testament. The Thessalonian congregation knew "full well

Events of the Rapture

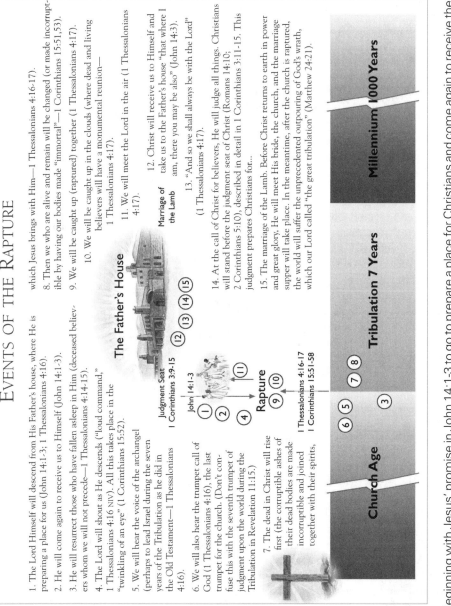

1. The Lord Himself will descend from His Father's house, where He is preparing a place for us (John 14:1-3; 1 Thessalonians 4:16).

2. He will come again to receive us to Himself (John 14:1-3).

3. He will resurrect those who have fallen asleep in Him (deceased believers whom we will not precede—1 Thessalonians 4:14-15).

4. The Lord will shout as He descends ("loud command," 1 Thessalonians 4:16 NIV). All this takes place in the "twinkling of an eye" (1 Corinthians 15:52).

5. We will hear the voice of the archangel (perhaps to lead Israel during the seven years of the Tribulation as he did in the Old Testament—1 Thessalonians 4:16).

6. We will also hear the trumpet call of God (1 Thessalonians 4:16), the last trumpet for the church. (Don't confuse this with the seventh trumpet of judgment upon the world during the Tribulation in Revelation 11:15.)

7. The dead in Christ will rise first (the corruptible ashes of their dead bodies are made incorruptible and joined together with their spirits,

which Jesus brings with Him—1 Thessalonians 4:16-17).

8. Then we who are alive and remain will be changed (or made incorruptible by having our bodies made "immortal"—1 Corinthians 15:51,53).

9. We will be caught up (raptured) together (1 Thessalonians 4:17).

10. We will be caught up in the clouds (where dead and living believers will have a monumental reunion—1 Thessalonians 4:17).

11. We will meet the Lord in the air (1 Thessalonians 4:17).

12. Christ will receive us to Himself and take us to the Father's house "that where I am, there you may be also" (John 14:3).

13. "And so we shall always be with the Lord" (1 Thessalonians 4:17).

14. At the call of Christ for believers, He will judge all things. Christians will stand before the judgment seat of Christ (Romans 14:10; 2 Corinthians 5:10), described in detail in 1 Corinthians 3:11-15. This judgment prepares Christians for...

15. The marriage of the Lamb. Before Christ returns to earth in power and great glory, He will meet His bride, the church, and the marriage supper will take place. In the meantime, after the church is raptured, the world will suffer the unprecedented outpouring of God's wrath, which our Lord called "the great tribulation" (Matthew 24:21).

The Father's House

Marriage of the Lamb

Judgment Seat
1 Corinthians 3:9-15

John 14:1-3

Rapture

1 Thessalonians 4:16-17
1 Corinthians 15:51-58

Church Age

Tribulation 7 Years

Millennium 1000 Years

Beginning with Jesus' promise in John 14:1-3 to go to prepare a place for Christians and come again to receive them to Himself, we find at least 15 successive "events" believers will participate in during and after the rapture while the world goes through the Tribulation.

that the day of the Lord will come just like a thief in the night" (verse 2).

Most of the Bible's references to the Day of the Lord have to do with the seven-year Tribulation. There are seven main passages. This day will come upon the world (Isaiah 2:12-22), will fall upon the wicked (13:6-16), will devastate many of the nations of the Middle East (Ezekiel 30:1-9), will affect the vegetation of earth (Joel 1:15-20), will bring ruin to Edom, or present-day southern Jordan (Obadiah 20), will be a time of darkness and distress (Zephaniah 1:14-18), and will come suddenly when the world will be saying "peace and safety" (1 Thessalonians 5:3) (Couch, *Dictionary of Premillennial Theology,* p. 88).

When this awful period arrives, the church will be gone (1 Thessalonians 1:10; 4:13-18). Believers are "not in darkness, that the day would overtake [them] like a thief" (5:4). Those who have trusted Christ are sons of light and of the day, and "not of night nor of darkness" (verse 5). Furthermore, "God has not destined us for wrath, but for obtaining salvation through our Lord Jesus Christ" (verse 9). While the word "salvation" (Greek, *sotēria*) is often used to speak of spiritual redemption, Paul is using the word here to describe being rescued or delivered from the wrath to come in the Day of the Lord.

The Day of the Lord is called the "birth pangs" (verse 3) and is first mentioned in the Old Testament in Jeremiah 30:6. When this day arrives, the world and the Jewish people who have not trusted Christ during the church age "will not escape" (1 Thessalonians 5:3). Rather, they will enter the horrible seven-year Tribulation. Christ quoted Jeremiah 30 extensively in relation to this day. He referred to the birth pangs (Matthew 24:8; Jeremiah 30:6), and called that day "great" and said that there is none like it (Matthew 24:21; Jeremiah 30:7). He added that some will be saved out of it (Matthew 24:13; Jeremiah 30:7). In Jeremiah 30 the Lord says He will "destroy completely all the nations where I have scattered" the Jewish people (verse 11), and He will punish all of Israel's oppressors (verse 20).

Walvoord writes, "Because Christians are forewarned that the Day of the Lord is coming and should not be surprised, they should live in the light of God's divine revelation" (*Prophecy Knowledge Handbook,* p. 487). The trumpet that will call for the dead in Christ to rise and those who are alive to be taken up could sound even today (1 Thessalonians 4:16). "So then let us not sleep as others do, but let us be alert and sober" (5:6). All believers are of the day and not of the night, though in the daily Christian experience they may be "awake or asleep" morally and spiritually (verse 10). Couch states:

> All of our sins have been purged at the cross; our position in Christ is based on His complete work of redemption. Thus, the promise says that, although our experience in Christ may be weak and may need strengthening, all believers should be longing for the return of their Savior. And if the trumpet sounds tomorrow, all who are physically alive, who belong to Him, will join the resurrected in meeting Him in the air (*Christ's Return,* p. 143).

CHRIST WILL COMPLETE THE BELIEVERS' SALVATION
1 Thessalonians 5:23-24

PAUL CONCLUDES THE LETTER with a desire, a wish, that God Himself may sanctify these believers, and that He may preserve them completely "without blame at the coming of our Lord Jesus Christ" (1 Thessalonians 5:23). The word "may" indicates the Greek optative mood, which shows a desire on the apostle's part. While he is not necessarily indicating this as a prayer, it could be considered close to that. "The coming of our Lord Jesus Christ" can only mean the rapture of the church. Paul desires that the Lord continually do His sanctifying work in believers to bring about maturity up until the time Jesus returns for His own (4:13-18).

Three Views of the Rapture

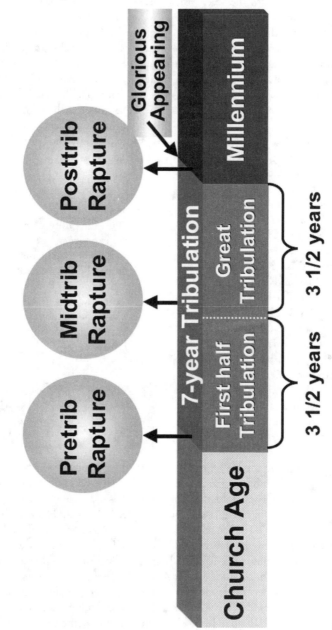

There are basically three views on when the rapture will take place—before, in the middle of, or at the end of the Tribulation. The majority of evangelical Christians (as well as the authors and contributors of this book) believe that the preponderance of second-coming passages in the Bible support the view that the rapture of the church will take place before the Tribulation (see in this commentary under Romans 5:9, 1 Thessalonians 1:10 and 5:9, and Revelation 3:10, as well as the entry on the rapture in Tim LaHaye and Ed Hindson, The Popular Encyclopedia of Bible Prophecy [Eugene, OR: Harvest House Publishers, 2004], pp. 309-16).

From the *position* believers have in Christ, Paul desires that there should come about *experiential* growth and inner peace, even though spiritual storms rage all about. This is why he calls God "the God of peace" (5:23). To "sanctify" (Greek, *hagiazo,* aorist active optative) means "to set apart, make holy, make unique." The word means "to consecrate, to separate" from things profane. Here, Paul desires that the Thessalonians grow progressively into sanctification. When he says he wants them to do this "entirely" *(Greek, holoteleis)*, he means "through and through," or completely.

When Paul writes that God "also will bring it to pass," there is a question about whether he is referring to the coming of Christ, the rapture, or to God fulfilling the sanctifying work in believers before that day arrives. Most scholars believe that the phrase has to do with the progressive sanctification God is working out in believers. The sovereign call of God is evidence of eternal grace that will be continually exercised toward believers. Believers will continue to grow spiritually until Christ comes and takes them home to be with Him. "The calling" is a participle, and with the pronoun "you," this could read "your Caller" (Nicoll, *Expositor's Greek New Testament,* 4:43). The believers shall "therefore be assuredly preserved [until] the consummation of the times" (Milligan, *Epistles to the Thessalonians,* p. 79).

Paul does not mean that the Thessalonians could arrive at complete sanctification this side of glory; that would be impossible. But his prayer is that his readers "would be preserved blameless (*amemptos,* that is, with no legitimate ground for accusation; cf. 2:10) in view of and until the appearing (*parousia*) of the Lord Jesus Christ for His saints" (Constable, "1 Thessalonians," *Bible Knowledge Commentary,* pp. 709-10).

2 THESSALONIANS

Many of the truths Paul stated in 1 Thessalonians are further developed in his second letter to the same church. Christ will someday come to judge the wicked (1:5-10). The righteous who are presently suffering will be vindicated (verses 5-12). The church at Thessalonica was heartened by Paul's assurance that they were not in the Tribulation and that that day would not arrive until the Antichrist was revealed (2:1-3). At the end of the Tribulation, Christ will come and defeat him—the "man of lawlessness" (verses 4-12). Meanwhile, Paul's prayer is that believers will have protection from "the evil one"—probably Satan (3:1-5).

THE COMING OF CHRIST TO JUDGE THE WICKED
2 Thessalonians 1:5-10

In the final chapter of earth's history, the Messiah will establish His earthly rule, "the kingdom of God" (verse 5). The suffering and persecution of the Thessalonians is working to show their perseverance and faith. God's judgment is right; He will punish all those who troubled and persecuted the children of God. The believers were suffering, and "after all it is only just for God to repay with affliction those who afflict you" (verse 6). When Christ returns to earth to reign He will come "in His glory, and all the angels with Him, then He will sit on His glorious throne" (Matthew 25:31). Paul calls the angels "His mighty angels [coming] in flaming fire" (2 Thessalonians 1:7).

Thomas Constable notes that this passage is

> not about the Rapture (1 Thess. 4:13-18; John 14:2-3), for no judgment accom-

panies the Rapture. Instead, it is the revelation of Jesus Christ in power and great glory (Psalm 2:1-9; Matt. 25:31), when He will set up His earthly kingdom (Rev. 19:11–20:4). At His return He will destroy the Armageddon armies gathered against Him (Rev. 16:12-16; 19:19-21) and will then judge living Jews (Ezek. 20:33-38) and living Gentiles (Matt. 24:31-46) ("2 Thessalonians," *Bible Knowledge Commentary,* p. 716).

Some argue that the Lord's return to establish the Davidic kingdom is far removed from the times of the Thessalonian church. But Paul seems to expand his thought about Christ coming for judgment. It will be a retribution for the sufferings of the Thessalonians as well as all those who have paid a price for their faith through all generations. Also, the punishment falls on all "those who do not know God and to those who do not obey the gospel of our Lord Jesus" (verse 8).

Vengeance is sure to come with eternal destruction, with unbelievers excluded from sharing in the glory of God. A day of wrath and judgment is certain (Romans 2:5; 1 Thessalonians 1:10; 2:16) just prior to the revelation of the Messiah to the world. To reject the gospel of Christ is to refuse what God has historically confirmed and testified with the first coming of His Son. When Christ returns to rule, He will judge the lost, who "will pay the penalty of eternal destruction, away from the presence of the Lord and from the glory of His power" (2 Thessalonians 1:9). As the life that God gives is called "eternal life," so is the condemnation the lost receive called "eternal punishment" (Matthew 25:46). The lost are expelled from the "presence" (Greek, *prosopon*) of the Lord. *Prosopon* is one of the most common Greek words for "face." This is the opposite of what will happen to the Thessalonians, who will be brought before the "presence" (in front of) God the Father and of Christ at the rapture (1 Thessalonians 2:19; 3:13).

What a joyous moment it will be when the Lord is glorified and marveled at among all who have believed. The Thessalonians will be there because they trusted in Christ and believed Paul's testimony of the truth (verse 10).

Paul's prayer is that the Thessalonians may be counted "worthy" of their calling (verse 12)—that their "work of faith with power" will come about and honor the Lord. The only thing that counts is that the name of the Lord will be glorified in their life, and that they will be glorified in their relationship "in Him." Only the grace of the Father and the Lord Jesus Christ can accomplish this (verse 12).

THE DAY OF THE LORD AND THE MAN OF LAWLESSNESS
2 Thessalonians 2:1-12

BECAUSE 2 THESSALONIANS WAS written shortly after 1 Thessalonians and touches on many of the issues addressed in the first letter, there must have been some interchange between Paul and the Thessalonians in between the letters. In reference to the doctrine of the rapture (verse 1), confusion had arisen, for some in the church body thought they were in the "day of the Lord" (verse 2). Yet the "gathering together to Him" referred to the rapture, which had not yet happened and about which Paul had recently written (1 Thessalonians 4). He writes that they should not be so "quickly shaken" or "disturbed" in thinking that the Day of the Lord had come. The verb "had come" (perfect active indicative of *enistemi),* in the Greek text, could be translated "has been installed, been put in place." Apparently some false apostles were opposing Paul's teaching and were going about saying that the church was in the Tribulation! These deceivers were disturbing the church through a false spirit, or attitude, and sending false messengers and letters.

The Greek word for "disturbed," *threo,* means "to be terrified, traumatized." It is used here, by the Lord Jesus in Matthew 24:6, and again by Jesus in the parallel reading in Mark 13:7. More than likely Paul was using the word because Christ had also. Christ warned some future generation of Jews not to be frightened or terrorized because one of the signs the Tribulation had arrived was that the nations would be thrown into a world conflagration—during which the Antichrist will desecrate the "holy place," the rebuilt temple (Matthew 24:6-15). The same applies here in 2 Thessalonians 2. The persecutions the Thessalonians were experiencing were not signs that the Tribulation had come, for no such conflagration had occurred.

One of the *key signs* that the Day of the Lord has come is that "the apostasy comes first" (verse 3). The Greek word *apostasia* means "to stand away from" in the sense of moving away from the truth. This apostasy will be a climatic revolt and an aggressive departure from God that will prepare the world for the appearance of the "man of lawlessness," the Antichrist. Since this apostasy comes *first,* before the revelation of the Antichrist, it must take place toward the end of the church age. Though the rebellion of the Antichrist is already at work in the world in seed form (1 John 4:1-3), a

The Second Coming
2 Thessalonians 2:1-12

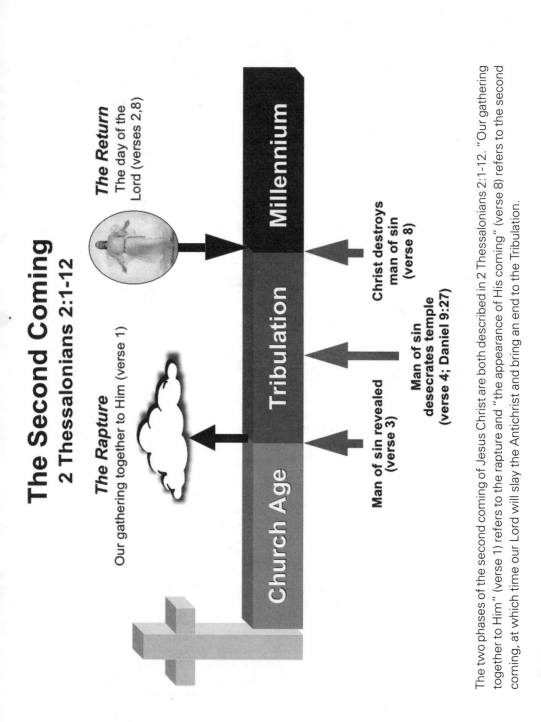

The Rapture
Our gathering together to Him (verse 1)

The Return
The day of the Lord (verses 2,8)

Church Age

Tribulation

Millennium

Man of sin revealed
(verse 3)

Man of sin
desecrates temple
(verse 4; Daniel 9:27)

Christ destroys
man of sin
(verse 8)

The two phases of the second coming of Jesus Christ are both described in 2 Thessalonians 2:1-12. "Our gathering together to Him" (verse 1) refers to the rapture and "the appearance of His coming" (verse 8) refers to the second coming, at which time our Lord will slay the Antichrist and bring an end to the Tribulation.

specific period of tribulation is yet to come. Paul twice made it clear that believers would be delivered from the Tribulation wrath (see 1 Thessalonians 1:10; 5:9).

The Antichrist has many names: 1) the Antichrist (1 John 2:18), 2) the prince (Daniel 9:26), 3) the "king" who speaks against God (11:36), 4) the man of lawlessness and 5) the son of destruction (2 Thessalonians 2:3), 6) the lawless one (verse 8), and 7) the beast (Revelation 13:1). He will oppose God and exalt himself above every deity ("every so-called god") or "object of worship," and he will take "his seat in the temple of God, displaying himself as being God" (2 Thessalonians 2:4). Verse 4 and Christ's words about the prophesied "abomination of desolation" (Matthew 24:15) spoken of in Daniel 9:27 prove there will be a rebuilt temple in Jerusalem during the Tribulation.

God will not allow the Antichrist to appear until the time of the Tribulation. The Antichrist is being restrained until "in his time he will be revealed" (2 Thessalonians 2:6). The word "restrain" (Greek, *katecho,* "to hold down") in both verses 6 and 7 is a present active participle, but in verse 6 it appears in the neuter gender ("what restrains") while in verse 7 it is in the masculine ("he who restrains, holds down"). Such usage also occurs in reference to the Spirit of God. The Greek word for "spirit," *pneuma,* is a neuter gender word, but the masculine pronoun is used when referring to the person of the Holy Spirit. The one doing the restraining, then, in all likelihood, is the Spirit of God. In church history some believed the restrainer was the Roman Empire or the witness of the church. But neither of these suggestions seems feasible. Constable says, "The Holy Spirit of God is the only Person with sufficient [supernatural] power to do this restraining....The removal of the Restrainer at the time of the Rapture must obviously precede the day of the Lord" ("2 Thessalonians," *Bible Knowledge Commentary,* p. 719).

Paul refers to "lawlessness" as "the mystery" (Greek, *musterion*) that is already at work (verse 7). This lawlessness is illusive and cannot be comprehended, though evidence for it can be seen. The Antichrist, the "lawless one," who will "be revealed" at the beginning of the Tribulation, will energize worldwide the manifestation of sin. His reign of terror will conclude at the end of the Tribulation when the Lord Jesus, coming as Israel's King and Messiah, will slay him "with the breath of His mouth...by the appearance of His coming" (verse 8). Though the Antichrist's physical body will be destroyed, his spirit, along with those who followed him, will be cast into the lake of fire and brimstone, and "the smoke of their torment [will go] up forever and ever" (Revelation 14:9-12; 19:20).

The Antichrist's coming will be "in accord with the activity of Satan, with all power and signs and false wonders" (2 Thessalonians 2:9). Through miraculous signs the Antichrist will deceive those who do not want to believe in Jesus as Savior—they will perish because they have no love of the truth (verse 10). Walvoord writes,

> It is quite illuminating that the Thessalonian church early in the Church Age experienced what today is called posttribulationism, the idea that the Rapture occurs after the Day of the Lord has begun. Posttribulationism usually makes the Rapture a phase of the second coming of Christ to set up His kingdom. It is clear that Paul denied this teaching and affirmed that the Day of the Lord, which includes the activities of the future world ruler, must follow rather than precede the Rapture of the church (*Prophecy Knowledge Handbook,* p. 494).

Those who deny the truth will be judged because they refused to trust Christ as Savior and instead "took pleasure in wickedness" (2 Thessalonians 2:12). "Took pleasure" is the Greek word *eudokeo,* which can be translated "to think good about"—that is, they have "good thoughts toward unrighteousness," or "they look at unrighteousness in a good light."

Paul wants the Thessalonians to live in the awareness that Christ could come at any time. He also wanted to give them confidence that the Antichrist would not appear until after the removal of the restrainer at the time of the rapture.

THE GLORIFICATION OF BELIEVERS
2 Thessalonians 2:14,16

The apostle Paul is grateful for the Thessalonian believers because of the Lord's sovereign work of bringing them to salvation. From the beginning God called them to salvation "through sanctification by the Spirit and faith in the truth" (verse 13). Both the work of the Spirit and the human response by faith are mentioned.

The calling came through the gospel given by Paul and his companions. The result of this call, and the goal, is that they "may gain the glory of our Lord Jesus Christ" (verse 14). "May gain the glory" is actually a prepositional phrase meaning "into the acquisition and possession of the glory of the Lord Jesus Christ." What the Lord determined in the past was carried out in history so that the future will grant them a share in the exaltation of Christ. Paul had earlier written of this divine act when he penned, "God...calls you into His own kingdom and glory" (1 Thessalonians 2:12).

Paul adds further thoughts about *salvation* when he writes, "Now may our Lord Jesus Christ Himself and God our Father, who has loved us and given us eternal comfort and good hope by grace, comfort and strengthen your hearts in every good work and word" (2 Thessalonians 2:16-17). Because of His love the Lord gave "eternal comfort" (Greek, *paraklasin aionian,* "comfort, consolation, encouragement") that has an eternal quality to it. Paul could mean a heavenly or spiritual comfort that touches the heart and soul, or he could mean a godly comfort that never ends. By the salvation granted through the love of God, the believer is refreshed by the *forever* nature of what God has done for him.

PROTECTION FROM THE EVIL ONE
2 Thessalonians 3:1-5

Paul now concludes with a request that the Thessalonians pray for him "that the word of the Lord may spread rapidly and be glorified, just as it did also with you" (3:1). He asks that they pray for his deliverance "from perverse and evil men" (verse 2). He then reminds the church that the Lord is faithful, and "He will strengthen and protect you from the evil one" (verse 3). His confidence is that the Lord will continue His work with them and that they will follow Paul's commands in their ministry.

It is not certain in the Greek text whether *tou ponērou* ("the evil one") is neuter or masculine. If neuter, it would read "from the evil thing" or simply "from the evil," but if masculine, it would read "from the evil one." The latter seems most likely because this is what Christ said in Matthew 13:38-39, where He is clearly speaking about the devil. The evil one is also mentioned in other passages (Matthew 13:19; Ephesians 6:16; John 17:15; 1 John 2:13). "When we also note that in 2:9 Satan is placed back of the apostasy and the Antichrist, it is not difficult to believe that here, too, Paul would put 'the wicked [evil] one' back of [working behind] 'the wicked [evil] men'" (Lenski, *I and II Thessalonians,* p. 449). As the Thessalonians labor for Christ, Paul's hope is that they will not be defeated by Satan. The unanimous opinion of Greek scholars takes "the evil one" as referring to Satan (Milligan, *Epistles to the Thessalonians,* p. 111). Satan will work against the church right up to the rapture, when believers are removed from the earth before the Tribulation begins.

1 TIMOTHY

As prophesied in the Old Testament, Christ came right at the appointed time (1 Timothy 2:4-6). And when He arrived, further revelation was given about His identity and His mission (3:16). Before the church age is over there will be a religious and moral apostasy on earth (4:1-3). Meanwhile, believers are to fight the good fight until Christ appears (6:14-16).

JESUS CHRIST CAME AT THE PROPER TIME
1 Timothy 2:4-6

God wants all men "to come to the knowledge of the truth" (verse 4). And that truth includes the fact that there is "one God, and one mediator also between God and men, the man Christ Jesus" (verse 5). He "gave Himself as a ransom for all" as predicted in the Scriptures, especially in Isaiah 53. There it was prophesied that the Messiah would take the penalty for the transgressions of God's people (verse 8), that He would render Himself "as a guilt offering" (verse 10), and that He would justify many and "bear their iniquities" (verse 11). This was fulfilled in the sacrifice of Christ on the cross, who came to live and die "at the proper time" (1 Timothy 2:6).

The last part of verse 6 reads that Christ's death was "the testimony given at the proper time." "The testimony" (Greek, *marturion*) can be translated "the witness" with the article. And that witness took place in "its own time" (Greek, *kairois idiois*), or at just the right time in God's providence. A better translation is "the witness of which was to be borne in its own times" (Ellicott, *Ellicott's Commentary on the Whole Bible,* 8:186). History is God's history; it is the unfolding of the plan of redemption.

When the Lord Jesus came to earth, He came to be the Savior. John the Baptist said that when He came, the time was right: "The time is fulfilled" (Mark 1:15). Paul adds, "When the fullness of the time came, God sent forth His Son, born of a woman, born under the Law" (Galatians 4:4). With regard to Christ's future coming, God "will bring [it] about at the proper time—He who is the blessed and only Sovereign, the King of kings and Lord of lords" (1 Timothy 6:15). Christ's first coming came about at the "proper time" (2:6), and His second coming will happen at the "proper time" (6:15).

THE MYSTERY OF GODLINESS
1 Timothy 3:16

In this one verse the apostle Paul sums up who Christ is and why He came to earth. Paul sets forth a "confession" that he labels "the mystery of godliness." By this mystery of godliness (Greek, *eusebeias*) he is referring to the incarnation of Christ and the significant doctrines that spring from this great miracle.

This mystery he calls the "common confession" (Greek, *homologoumenos*), the doctrinal belief that was held common in the early church.

This confession would include the fact that Christ was 1) seen in the flesh, 2) verified by the Spirit, 3) observed and seen by angels, 4) proclaimed among the nations, 5) believed on in the world, and 6) received up into glory. Each of these points is found in other passages of Scripture. As the Word of God, Christ "became flesh" (John 1:14), was confirmed by the Holy Spirit (Matthew 3:16-17), witnessed to by angels (Mark 16:5-7; Luke 2:13-14), proclaimed to the nations (Matthew 28:18-20), believed on wherever the gospel went (Acts 1:8; 1 Thessalonians 1:8), and taken up into heaven (Acts 1:9-11).

These six tremendous prophetic truths comprise the confession and were all fulfilled by Christ. This confession was probably a hymn sung by early congregations. It formed the core beliefs of the churches and was the substance they embraced and that we should continue to embrace today.

THE COMING APOSTASY
1 Timothy 4:1-3

THE APOSTLE PAUL ADDRESSES the issue of apostasy at the close of the church age and warns about what will come "in latter times" (verse 1). His words are not his own but are inspired by the Holy Spirit, who "explicitly" (Greek, *reetos*, "emphatically, expressly") says that some will "fall away from the faith." They will definitely depart! The verb "fall away" is the Greek word *aphistanai,* which is related to the word "apostasy" in 2 Thessalonians 2:3. Both words imply "to stand away from, depart." Because Paul uses the definite article "the" before the word "faith," he could be implying that these who will depart will move away from Christianity, though they are not believers in the Lord. Stott observes that some gullible people will listen to false teachers "and

in consequence abandon the apostolic faith" (*The Gospel and the End of Time,* p. 111).

The Greek word *aphistanai* is used by early church father Justin Martyr of deserting Jesus (*Apology* 50.12) and His words (*Trypho* 8.2) as well as the one God and the faith (*Trypho* 20.1). In the Septuagint the term is used to speak of putting distance between oneself and another, or between God and the religion of Israel (see the Septuagint's rendering of Deuteronomy 32:15).

These who *apostatize* pay "attention to deceitful spirits and doctrines of demons" (1 Timothy 4:1). When this apostasy arrives, these people will represent teaching that is counter to Christianity. They will be influenced by misleading spirits—the spirits that rule in the darkness of this world, and strive to keep it "in alienation from the life of God" (Fairbairn, *Commentary on the Pastoral Epistles,* p. 170). They will operate "by means of the hypocrisy of liars seared in their own conscience as with a branding iron" (verse 2). They will be "living in hypocrisy as their natural element, speaking lies as their proper vocation" (Fairbairn, pp. 170-71) .

Seeming to be religious, these people will "forbid marriage and advocate abstaining from foods which God has created to be gratefully shared in by those who believe and know the truth" (verse 3). As did ancient gnostics, they will lead ascetic lives, pretending to be spiritual by spurning marriage and certain foods (verses 4-5). The world will be impressed and think these people truly represent God because of the "sacrifices" they are making in their lives.

Paul repeats his warning about a coming apostasy in 2 Timothy 3:1-9. He writes "that in the last days difficult times will come" (verse 1). Some scholars do not believe the apostle is talking about the final days of the church age (Knight, *The Pastoral Epistles,* p. 189). However, it seems this is obvious by the setting in which he places these phenomena: "in later times" (1 Timothy 4:1) and "in the last days" (2 Timothy 3:1). Paul then summarizes what will take place in the apostasy of the church just before the rapture: "Evil men and impostors will proceed from bad to worse, deceiving and being deceived" (2 Timothy 3:13).

THE APPEARING OF THE LORD JESUS CHRIST
1 Timothy 6:14-16

Paul urges Timothy and those who are with him to flee from the love of money (6:10-11), and to "fight the good fight of faith; take hold of the eternal life to which you were called" (verse 12). He then gives Timothy the charge to keep himself "without stain or reproach until the appearing of our Lord Jesus Christ" (verses 13-14). Paul did not know when the Lord would come to rapture His own, and he is not writing here about Christ's second coming. Because the rapture could happen at any time, Timothy needed to be ready and to abstain from sins that would discredit him if the Lord suddenly snatched him up to the clouds. "At that time Timothy's exemplary life will be evaluated. The Christian life has its completion at the time of Christ's coming" at the rapture (Walvoord, *Prophecy Knowledge Handbook,* p. 495).

Christ will return "at the proper time" (verse 15; see 1 Timothy 2:4-6). He will arrive at just the right moment in God's prophetic plan. Though Christ is given the divine title "King of kings" in Revelation 17:14 and 19:16, here the subject is God the Father, who "possesses immortality and dwells in unapproachable light" (1 Timothy 6:16). The titles God of gods and Lord of lords come from Deuteronomy 10:17. Christ will be the final Judge as to how Timothy, and all believers, lived at the time of His appearing.

2 TIMOTHY

IN 2 TIMOTHY PAUL WRITES THAT HE CAN ENTRUST his life to the Lord until the day he stands before Him in glory (1:12). He repeats his prophecy from 1 Timothy 4:1-3 that an apostasy is coming that will sweep the world (3:1-9). Righteousness will not reign until Christ comes to establish His kingdom and judge the living and the dead (4:1-5). The faithful can look forward to a crown of righteousness (verse 8) and a final reward (verses 17-18).

THE REVELATION OF THE LORD JESUS CHRIST
2 Timothy 1:8-12

PAUL WAS IMPRISONED in a dungeon in Rome (4:10-12) for the sake of the gospel. He knew that his death was near (1:8,16; 4:6-8). He reminds Timothy that he is a prisoner suffering "for the gospel according to the power of God" (1:8). All believers have been called with a holy calling, "according to His own purpose and grace which was granted us in Christ Jesus from all eternity" (verse 9). Christ's purpose in coming to earth was to "abolish death" and bring "life and immortality to light through the gospel" (verse 10).

It was predicted in the Old Testament that Christ, at His first coming, would be victorious over death (Psalm 16:10; Isaiah 25:8; Hosea 13:14), bring light to the nations (Isaiah 42:6), and be a herald of good news (the gospel) (40:9; 61:1-3). In order to spread this good news, Paul was given three tasks: He was to be a preacher, an apostle, and a teacher (2 Timothy 1:11).

Though Paul is suffering in prison, he is not ashamed of his predicament. He knows whom he has believed and says, "I am convinced that [the Lord] is able to guard what I have entrusted to Him until that day" (verse 12). "Thus, even though Paul was suffering abuse and humiliation, he was confident of God's complete vindication in the end (cf. 1:18; 4:8)" (Lifton, "1-2 Timothy," in *Bible Knowledge Commentary*, p. 751). "That day" will be the day of the resurrection of the dead in Christ and the rapture of the church (1 Thessalonians 4:13-17). Then "we must all appear before the judgment seat of Christ, so that each one may be recompensed for his deeds in the body according to what he has done, whether good or bad" (2 Corinthians 5:10).

THE LAST DAYS
2 Timothy 3:1-9,12-13

THESE VERSES CONTINUE Paul's discussion that he introduced in 1 Timothy 4:1-5 concerning a coming apostasy. This apostasy starts "in the last days [when] difficult times will come" (2 Timothy 3:1). In 1 Timothy 4:1-5

Paul dealt with the "religious" departure, when false religions will abound, prompted by the doctrine of demons. Here in 2 Timothy 3 Paul mentions the social apostasy that will sweep the world, though he includes additional statements about religious departure.

In verses 2-3 Paul lists a number of sins that will affect culture and society. He writes about lovers of self and money, as well as those who are boasters and arrogant. Human kindnesses and personal relationships will be destroyed with children being "disobedient to parents, ungrateful, unholy, unloving, irreconcilable." People everywhere will be "without self-control, brutal, haters of good, treacherous, reckless, conceited, lovers of pleasure rather than lovers of God" (verse 4). They will have a form of godliness, "although they have denied its power" (verse 5). We are warned to "avoid such men as these."

Paul's description could describe a segment of humanity from any time in history, but his point is that such evils will multiply and worsen all over the world at a *specific time.* That time is the end of the church age. Walvoord observes,

> Apostasy, of course, was already present in the time that Paul lived, but with the progress of the present age, in spite of the dissemination of the truth and the availability of Scripture, the world undoubtedly will continue to follow the sinful description which the Apostle Paul gave here (*Prophecy Knowledge Handbook,* p. 495).

Paul then describes the apostasy of his present day in verses 6-9. He describes the sins of "weak women" who are led astray. He notes that people will be "always learning and never able to come to the knowledge of the truth" (verse 7). He uses as an example the rebellion of two personalities described (but not named) in the book of Exodus, "Jannes and Jambres" (2 Timothy 3:8; Exodus 7:11). With "depraved" minds, they opposed the truth and rejected the Word of God "as regards the faith." Such rebellion, arrogance, and folly

will someday come to an end (2 Timothy 3:9). However, before that end arrives, things will only grow worse: "Evil men and impostors will proceed from bad to worse, deceiving and being deceived" (verse 13).

Even Bible scholars who are not dispensationalists or premillennialists recognize that these verses are describing the final days of the church age. Fairbairn writes,

> It can scarcely be said to be beyond the bounds of probability that 'the last days' of the present dispensation are destined to witness in certain quarters a realization of the prophetic picture before us more appalling than has yet been exhibited in the history of the past (*Commentary on the Pastoral Epistles,* p. 366).

THE JUDGE OF THE LIVING AND THE DEAD
2 Timothy 4:1-5

ONLY WHEN CHRIST comes to earth and establishes His kingdom will righteousness reign on earth. He is the Judge of both "the living and the dead" (verse 1). Meanwhile, Paul urges Timothy and all ministers of the gospel to "preach the word" and be ready at all times, "in season and out of season," and to apply the truth in all situations, with "instruction" (verse 2). The day will come when the world "will not endure sound doctrine." People will desire to be entertained and to laugh, "wanting to have their ears tickled." They will want to hear teachers "in accordance to their own desires" (verse 3). As well, they "will turn away their ears from the truth, and will turn aside to myths" (verse 4). The Greek word for "myths," *muthos,* is not necessarily a reference to mythology or that which is mysterious, but rather, to any falsehood or lie. People will be gullible and follow after philosophies or religions that deceive rather than adhere to the truth of the gospel.

Meanwhile, Timothy is to "be sober in all things, endure hardship, do the work of an evangelist," and to fulfill his ministry (verse 5). "Thus Timothy is to be encouraged to perform his task by the fact that Christ will appear and that Timothy himself will receive the crown of righteousness at Christ's appearing and be safely brought into Christ's future" kingdom (Knight, *The Pastoral Epistles*, p. 453).

THE CROWN OF RIGHTEOUSNESS
2 Timothy 4:8

Paul reminds Timothy that in his ministry, "I have fought the good fight, I have finished the course, I have kept the faith" (2 Timothy 4:7). Because of this, "in the future there is laid up for me the crown of righteousness, which the Lord, the righteous Judge, will award to me on that day" (verse 8). Paul had lived a righteous Christian life, and he would be rewarded for that at the judgment seat of Christ. All who live as Paul did will be rewarded likewise and the motivation for serving in this way is a love and anticipation of Christ's soon appearing. This is another reference to the rapture as mentioned in verse 1.

What exactly is this *crown of righteousness?* The passage "can mean either that righteousness itself is the crown or reward, or that this crown is the reward *for* righteousness (cf. 2 Timothy 3:16). In favor of the first view is the fact that James 1:12 and Revelation 2:10 seem to say that the 'crown of life' means that life *is* the crown" (Lifton, "1-2 Timothy," *Bible Knowledge Commentary*, p. 758). On "that day"

Paul will be rewarded side by side with other believers who have longed for His appearing (cf. Philippians 3:20-21; Titus 2:13).

PAUL'S FINAL REWARD
2 Timothy 4:17-18

The apostle Paul knew that God had given him the task of reaching the Gentiles. His first defense, in which no one supported him (verse 16), took place either just before his present imprisonment, or in Rome some three to six years earlier. The "Lord stood with" him throughout his ordeal so that he might preach the gospel. Paul had been spared temporarily as if "out of the lion's mouth" (verse 17). He knew that God would deliver him "from every evil deed," bringing him safely home into His heavenly kingdom (verse 18). It is as if Paul is saying that through the Lord's providence he will dodge the spear until he has completed his earthly mission.

From the earthly perspective, Paul's death would seem a human tragedy. But Paul affirms here that if he is not raptured, God will deliver him even at death and transport him immediately into the "heavenly kingdom." Lifton writes, "[Paul] saw his death not as a victory for Rome but as a rescue of the Lord.... For this Paul, even in the face of his own death, could do nothing but praise God: To Him be glory forever and ever. Amen (cf. Eph. 3:21; 2 Peter 3:18)" ("1-2 Timothy," *Bible Knowledge Commentary*, p. 760).

TITUS

$P_{\text{AUL TELLS}}$ $T_{\text{ITUS THAT HIS TASK AS AN APOSTLE}}$ was to give the knowledge of the truth and the hope of eternal life (1:1-2). At the right moment the grace of God had appeared in order to bring salvation to all (2:11). Now believers can look for the rapture, the blessed hope and the appearing of the Savior (verse 13). God showed kindness to mankind by sending the Savior (3:4-5), who made it possible for believers to become heirs to eternal life, which they will enter into in the future (verse 7).

THE PROMISE OF ETERNAL LIFE
Titus 1:1-3

$P_{\text{AUL SAW HIMSELF}}$ as a "bond-servant of God" and an "apostle of Jesus Christ" who was to strengthen the faith of the "chosen of God" and impart "the knowledge of the truth which is according to godliness" (verse 1). He was a man with a mission from above! The truth he was imparting also had to do with a future "hope of eternal life" (verse 2). Presently the believer in Christ has life that is eternal, and this life will continue on into eternity at the rapture or at the time of death.

The Lord Himself has promised this eternal life "long ages ago" because "He cannot lie" (verse 2). "Long ages ago," in the Greek text, can be rendered "before eternal times." Fairbairn observes, "Though being connected with a promise, not with a purpose simply or decree, of God, it must be understood of eternity in the looser sense; that is, of a period indefinitely remote before the ordinary historical epochs of the world" (*Commentary on the Pastoral Epistles*, p. 258). Christ came into the world to give eternal life (Mark 4:19); whoever partakes

of Him will live forever (John 6:51) and never die (11:26).

The Lord Jesus came into the world at just the right time—"the proper time." Paul uses this expression also in 1 Timothy 2:6 and 6:15 to show that God had a plan that came to pass at just the right moment. Christ was born according to the Lord's decree. The "proclamation" of the gospel was then "entrusted" to Paul "according to the commandment of God our Savior" (Titus 1:3; 1 Timothy 1:1,11). Paul alone was given the full understanding of the gospel, and through him the message of the cross of Christ was systematized and placed into a doctrinal formula. The apostle seems to stress this by using the personal pronoun "I" (Greek, *egō*). "Entrusted" (aorist passive indicative of the Greek word *pisteuō*) could be translated "made faithful" or "seen as being trustworthy."

Couch writes,

> The apostle had a unique relationship to the gospel. His ministry was not a matter of his own choosing. He makes it clear that he was set apart from his mother's womb and was called through God's grace to reveal His Son (Galatians 1:15). He added "that I might

preach Him among the Gentiles, I did not immediately consult with flesh and blood" (verse 16).... Thus he was divinely commissioned to the gospel. This was a trust that he could not escape (*Pastor's Manual*, p. 158).

THE GLORIOUS APPEARING
Titus 2:11-15

AT THE RIGHT MOMENT in history "the grace of God" shone forth to "bring salvation to all men" (verse 11). Now this grace is "instructing" (Greek, *paidauō*) believers "to deny ungodliness and worldly desires." Grace is both *gracious* and *directive* as how to live the Christian life. It teaches the child of God "to live sensibly, righteously and godly in the present age" (verse 12). The word "present" (Greek, *nun*) means "the now age." Those who have the hope (confident expectation) of Christ's return still have a present life to live.

"Instructing" is a present participle, and so is "looking for" (verse 13). Christians are to mature and to anticipate the coming of the Lord to remove them from the Tribulation through the rapture. In 1 Thessalonians 1:9-10 we see similar words from Paul, where he commended the Thessalonian believers for the fact that they were *serving* a living and true God, and *waiting* for His Son from heaven.

The two statements are evidently parallel in Paul's mind since he uses present infinitives to get his point across. "Looking for" is a participle of the Greek term *prosdechomai* and speaks of expecting or waiting with great anticipation. The New Testament usage is "to take up, receive, welcome, wait for, expect." It means "to receive favorably, to admit to, receive hospitably." The idea of expectation is strong in the word. For example, Simeon was "waiting for" or "looking for" Israel's consolation (Luke 2:25).

The participles "instructing" in verse 12 and "looking for" in verse 13 could read, "The grace of God has appeared...instructing us [that we might live sensibly]...[as we are] looking for the blessed hope." According to Alford, this expectation is "an abiding state and posture" (*The Greek New Testament*, 3:419). The believers are to be looking for "the blessed hope and the appearing of the glory of our great God and Savior, Christ Jesus." Since the church is told to look in such anticipation, we can conclude that the rapture is in view here because it could happen at any time for those who were presently alive. This expectation is not for the second coming, when Christ will arrive to reign on earth as the son of David over His kingdom.

Some versions render the passage "glorious appearing," referring to Christ's present glorification now in heaven. Some scholars translate this, "His glory shall appear!" The Greek text has only one article and the full sentence should read "the blessed hope, the joyous anticipation, that is, the glorious appearing!" This implies that the reference is to *one event* viewed from two aspects. The One appearing is "our great God and Savior, Christ Jesus" (verse 13). God here does not refer to the heavenly Father, for He is Spirit and no one has seen Him. The article "the" is before "great God," but the article is omitted before "Savior."

Fairbairn writes, "The two expressions [are] as attributive of one and the same person.... The other consideration is, that nearly all the [church] Fathers—Greek, as well as Latin—who refer to this passage, understood it simply of Christ" (*Commentary on the Pastoral Epistles*, p. 283). It is the Lord Jesus Christ, the second person of the Godhead, who will be seen when He returns for those who are believers and who are looking (verse 13) for His coming.

And it is God the Son who "gave Himself for us to redeem us from every lawless deed, and to purify for Himself a people for His own possession, zealous for good deeds" (verse 14). This verse is one of the best descriptions of the work of salvation that Christ carried forth in order to save us.

THE KINDNESS OF GOD IN CHRIST
Titus 3:4-7

Along with the Lord Jesus Christ, God the Father is often called "our Savior" (verse 4). His kindness and love "for mankind" appeared, by which "He saved us, not on the basis of deeds which we have done in righteousness, but according to His mercy." God the Father designed the plan of redemption, and the Son became the substitute in order to save those who are lost. Salvation is applied "according to His mercy, by the washing of regeneration and renewing by the Holy Spirit" (verse 5). For those being saved, the Holy Spirit was "poured out upon us richly through Jesus Christ our Savior" (verse 6). The Spirit flooded the soul and took the old nature captive, making a new man out of those who were dead in their sins (Ephesians 2:1-5). Each person in the Godhead had a specific part in the plan of redemption.

Justification "by His grace" makes the believer an heir according "to the hope of eternal life" (verse 7). The word "heir" is the Greek term *klēronomos* and comes from two words: *klēros* ("share, portion") and *nomos* ("law"), together meaning "to legally declare." An heir is one who is rightfully and legally declared to receive an inheritance. Being made an heir is a common theme in Paul's letters. Paul writes of the guarantee or "pledge of our inheritance" (Ephesians 1:14) and of the "riches of the glory of His inheritance in the saints" (verse 18). This inheritance is an eternal promise (Hebrews 9:15), is incorruptible (1 Peter 1:4), and is a reward, not yet earned, but given as a gift from the Lord (Colossians 3:24). Those who are heirs have not yet enjoyed their inheritance; it has not yet been paid out to them. They can be absolutely certain of eternal life, yet they must wait until God opens the door of eternity. Final salvation is yet hidden, but it will be brought to pass in the future.

PHILEMON

Paul's letter to Philemon, like those written to Timothy and Titus, is addressed to an individual rather than a church. Unlike his other personal letters, this one is written to a layman and deals with the issue of slavery. Written during Paul's first imprisonment in Rome (A.D. 61), this letter was intimately connected to the letter to the Colossians, the hometown of Philemon and Onesimus, Philemon's runaway slave. While Paul acknowledges Hebrew fugitive law (cf. Deuteronomy 23:15), he urges forgiveness, reconciliation, and restoration of the runaway Onesimus—not as a slave, but as a brother (verse 16). While this book contains no specific prophecy, it does prefigure the Christian view of emancipation.

HEBREWS

Hebrews is the second-most prophetic book in the New Testament, after the book of Revelation. While Revelation looks into the future, Hebrews looks at past predictions now fulfilled in Christ. Though no one can say for sure who wrote Hebrews, the author was skilled in making connections between Old Testament passages and the coming of Christ. The writer addresses the predictions that lead up to the first coming of Christ, and mentions our Lord's deity and sovereignty as affirmed in prophetic sections of the Old Testament. He also goes into great detail about the work of redemption carried out by the promised Messiah.

THE SUPERIORITY OF THE SON OF GOD
Hebrews 1:1-4

Chapter 1 of Hebrews is an explosive declaration that the Lord Jesus is God. Verses 1-4 introduce Christ's glory and point to the fact that He was sent by providence to reveal God the Father. In the past God spoke to the ancient fathers of Israel "in the prophets in many portions and in many ways" (verse 1), but now, in these last days, He has spoken by His Son "whom He appointed heir of all things, through whom also He made the world" (verse 2). The relation of the Father to the Son is emphasized as well as the fact that Christ was the Creator, a work ascribed elsewhere to God (Psalm 8:3) and to the Spirit (Genesis 1:1-2). That God has a Son was already well established in the great messianic prophecy of Psalm 2. God's Son would be "begotten" and would later be given the nations for His inheritance and the very ends of the earth for His possession. And He shall "break them with a rod of iron...and shall shatter them like earthenware" (verses 7-9). His earthly messianic rule is certain!

Everything that can be said about the greatness of the Father can be said about Christ. "He is the radiance of His glory and the exact representation of His nature, and upholds all things by the word of His power." After His sacrifice for sins—"made purification of sins"—He fulfilled the prophecy of Psalm 110:1 by sitting "down at the right hand of the Majesty on high" (Hebrews 1:3). Psalm 110 is one of the most powerful messianic passages in the Old Testament. The fact that the Messiah is now seated by His Father on His throne to make intercession for His own is repeated often in the New Testament (Matthew 22:44; 26:64; Mark 14:62; Acts 2:33-34; 5:30; 7:55-56; Romans 8:34; Colossians 3:1; Hebrews 1:13; 8:1; 10:12; 12:2; 1 Peter 3:22).

Because of Christ's relationship to the Father, and because of His exalted position now, He is seen "as much better than the angels, as He has inherited a more excellent name than they" (Hebrews 1:4). This is a convincing argument for the orthodox Jews, who held the role of the holy angels in a superior position in their theology. The point of the author of Hebrews is that the Lord Jesus stands above even the glorious angels who serve the heavenly Father.

THE DEITY OF THE SON OF GOD
Hebrews 1:5-13

In the opening verses of Hebrews (1:1-4), the deity of Christ is established. Now, quoting a long list of Old Testament prophecies, the writer of Hebrews fires off a barrage of prophecies that substantiate the deity of the Lord Jesus. He is better than the angels because He is the Son of God (verse 5; Psalm 2:7); God is His Father and He is a Son to Him (Hebrews 1:5; 2 Samuel 7:14). Christ is the "firstborn" (Greek, *protokos*) or *preeminent-born One* who came into the world (Hebrews 1:6; Romans 8:29; Colossians 1:15), who is to be worshiped by the angels (Deuteronomy 32:43, Septuagint). Though the angels have power as the wind, and are God's ministers of "a flame of fire" (Hebrews 1:7; Psalm 104:4), the Son is deity, God Himself, whose throne exists "forever and ever" (Hebrews 1:8; Psalm 45:6) and stands for His righteous scepter, "the scepter of His kingdom." It is said of the Son that He loves righteousness and hates lawlessness (Hebrews 1:9); therefore, "God, Your God, has anointed You with the oil of gladness above Your companions" (verse 9; Isaiah 61:1,3). No Jew reading this portion of Hebrews could miss the fact of the deity of Christ.

To the Son it is said that He is the Lord who laid the foundation of the earth, with the heavens also being the work of His hands (Hebrews 1:10; Psalm 102:25). Though the universe will perish and become "old like a garment," He remains forever (Hebrews 1:11). In fact, the Son of God will roll up the universe "like a mantle" because it will wear out and not be used again. He is always the same, and His years will not come to an end (verse 12; Psalm 102:26-27).

Moreover, God never said to the angels that they would sit on His throne in glory. This is said only to the Son of God: "Sit at My right hand, until I make Your enemies a footstool for Your feet" (Hebrews 1:13; Psalm 110:1). This rule began at Christ's ascension, when He entered the throne room of the Father as prophesied by Daniel (7:13-14). Then when the time is right, He will come to earth to reign on the throne of David on Mount Zion in Jerusalem (Psalm 110:2). For now Christ presently makes intercession before God the Father for His saints (Romans 8:34; Hebrews 7:25; 1 John 2:1). While the angels are important in the providence of God, they now are but ministering spirits who render service for those for whom the Son of God died (Hebrews 1:14).

SALVATION PROCLAIMED
Hebrews 2:1-3

Because of what the author of Hebrews said in chapter 1, "for this reason" those reading this book must pay close attention and not drift away from what they have heard about Christ (2:1). If what is said by angels is "unalterable," and should be given careful attention as Scripture because it carries the weight of Scripture and has authority for those who are disobedient (verse 2), how "will we escape if we neglect so great a salvation" that comes about by the death of Christ (verse 3)?

This salvation was first spoken through Christ the Lord, and "it was confirmed to us by those who heard" (verse 3). The phrase "confirmed to us" indicates the author received the revelation about Christ by those who knew Him personally—most probably the apostles themselves. In fact, this seems to be the point when the author goes on to say, "God also testifying with them [the apostles] both by signs and wonders and by various miracles and by gifts of the Holy Spirit according to His own will" (verse 4).

THE SUPERIORITY OF THE SON OF MAN
Hebrews 2:5-10

HERE THE WRITER OF HEBREWS applies Psalm 8 directly to the coming of the Messiah. The author continues his discussion about Christ's superiority over the angels (verse 5). According to Psalm 8, all things have been made subject to "the Son of Man" (verse 4; Hebrews 2:6). There are two views about Psalm 8: 1) Some believe the central subject is about *humanity* and the fact that God assigned authority to the human race, but this authority was destroyed or nullified with the fall of Adam; and 2) others say Psalm 8 is really about *Christ*, "the Son of Man (or mankind)," with a messianic reference to the fact that the Son of God came to earth and became flesh.

The second view is worth studying because, regardless of what argument is given, the writer of Hebrews does indeed apply Psalm 8 almost in a direct sense to Christ. In Psalm 8:4, two subjects could be in view. The reference to "man" (Hebrew, *enosh*) seems to show how limited and weak the human race is, while the reference to "the son of man" (Hebrew, *ben-adam*) could be a change of subject and a first and direct reference to Christ, who was made "a little lower than God, and You crown him with glory and majesty" (verse 5). Was it ever said of Adam before the fall that he was "crowned with glory and majesty"? And in another sense, was he given rule over all the works of God's hands, with all things put under his feet (verse 6)?

In quoting Psalm 8:4-6, the writer of Hebrews makes a *direct prophetic connection to Christ* and adds, "In subjecting all things to him, He left nothing that is not subject to him. But now...we do see Him who was made for a little while lower than the angels, namely, Jesus, because of the suffering of death crowned with glory and honor, so that by the grace of God He might taste death for everyone" (Hebrews 2:8-9). The author of Hebrews is making either an indirect or a direct reference to Christ. Either way, Christ is seen as the supreme One who is more honored than the angels. Ellingworth argues, "that the Psalm originally referred to man is, though probable, 'hardly relevant.'" And he notes that because the Gospel writers so often use the expression "Son of God" concerning Christ, "that it may well have led the author of Hebrews to read Ps. 8 in a christological sense" (Ellingworth, *Commentary on Hebrews,* p. 150).

For certain, while all things now belong to Christ Jesus, He has not as yet subjected all things to Himself. This will begin with the inauguration of His kingdom reign.

THE SON AND THE SAVED
Hebrew 2:11-13

THOSE SAVED BY FAITH are now the "sanctified" and together with Christ "are all from one Father; for which reason He is not ashamed to call them brethren" (verse 11). In salvation, to be declared "sanctified" (Greek, *hagiazō*—"to be made special, unique") is to be united to Jesus Christ (1 Corinthians 1:2), and to be sanctified by the Holy Spirit (Romans 15:16) and the Father (John 10:36). Referring to the prophetic utterance in Psalm 22:22, the writer of Hebrews now shows how believers are made brothers with Christ: "I will proclaim Your name to My brethren, in the midst of the congregation I will sing Your praise" (Hebrews 2:12).

Quoting two other Old Testament verses (Isaiah 8:17-18), the writer says that "trust in Him" secures this relationship. Together believers are now "the children whom God has given" to Christ, who is their brother. Christ has this relationship with believers because He shared with humanity "in flesh and blood," even partaking in death, though death could not defeat Him (Hebrews 2:14). Christ, made like His earthly brothers yet without sin, can now be "a merciful and faithful high priest in things pertaining to God, to make propitiation for the sins of the people" (verse 17).

THE SUPERIORITY OF CHRIST TO MOSES
Hebrews 3:1-6

THE WRITER OF HEBREWS now urges his readers to especially consider "Jesus, the Apostle and High Priest of our confession" (verse 1). By "Apostle" he means "one sent with a message." Christ was the messenger from God who brought the good news of salvation from sin. He is also a high priest of the order of Melchizedek (5:5-10), not of the Levitical priesthood, since Christ is of the kingly tribe of Judah. Christ was faithful to His Father "who appointed Him, as Moses also was in all His house" (3:2), meaning that Moses was faithful with all the responsibilities given him to shepherd and manage the children of Israel who came out of Egypt.

But because Christ was faithful unto death, He is counted worthy to receive *more glory* than Moses (verse 3). Moses was faithful to his charge over the people of God's house "as a servant" (verse 5); however, Christ "was faithful as a Son over His house whose house we are, if we hold fast our confidence and the boast of our hope firm until the end" (verse 6). Believers can step out from under the authority and protection of Christ, though this does not imply loss of salvation but a breaking of fellowship. Fruchtenbaum writes,

> The closing statement shows the mark of a true believer: *if we hold fast our boldness and the glorying of our hope firm unto the end.* This does not mean that believers are saved only if they just hold on to the end. That would mean salvation is attained by works, not by faith. The point here is that the continuance in faith is the evidence that a person actually believed. Lack of continuance in faith does not mean the person is not saved; it only means that the person does not have the evidence that faith exists (*Messianic Epistles,* p. 41).

Moses predicted the coming of the Lord Jesus Christ, who would have higher rank than he. He wrote, "The Lord your God will raise up for you a prophet like me from among you, from your countrymen, you shall listen to him" (Deuteronomy 18:15). This allusion is clearly a prophecy about Christ (John 1:21,45; 6:14; Acts 3:22-23; 7:37).

THE ISSUE OF UNBELIEF
Hebrews 3:7-19

GIVEN THE ARGUMENT THAT Christ is now the faithful Son over His own house, the church (verse 6), it is high time to believe in Him and not harden the heart to provoke God, as the children of Israel did in the wilderness (verses 7-8). Interestingly, the writer of Hebrews quotes part of an Old Testament Sabbath hymn (Psalm 95:7-8) and ascribes its source to the Holy Spirit, who guided the human author in its composition. Three other verses are cited, Psalm 95:9-11, which relates how the Jews tested the Lord in the wilderness for 40 years (Hebrews 3:9). The Lord was angry with that generation (verse 10) and swore in His wrath, "They shall not enter My rest" (verse 11).

The writer then cautions against having an "evil, unbelieving heart that falls away from the living God" (verse 12). Because of the clear revelation about the sacrifice of Christ for sinners, each should be encouraged, "as long as it is called 'Today,'" to not "be hardened by the deceitfulness of sin" (verse 13). Partaking of Christ means holding fast "the beginning of our assurance firm until the end" (verse 14). Quoting Psalm 95:7, the writer urges that now is the time to accept Christ, for "today if you hear His voice, do not harden your hearts, as when they provoked Me" (Hebrews 3:15).

The author of Hebrews has in mind his Jewish brothers, who, in their stubbornness may be resisting the truth in the same way as the wayward generation that Moses led out of Egypt (verse 16). The Lord was angry with them for 40 years, and their bodies fell in the wilderness" (verse 17). For 40 years that disobedient generation did not enter into God's rest "because of unbelief" (verses 18-19). What happened to them was a kind of prophetic warning to the generation who knew Christ but refused to accept Him.

THE CONSEQUENCES OF UNBELIEF
Hebrews 4:1-10

As with the Israelites who came out of Egypt, God had given to a later generation of Jews a promise of entering into His spiritual rest (verse 1). The gospel, the good news, was preached to the generation alive at the time Hebrews was written, but it would not profit them unless they were "united by faith in those who heard" (verse 2). Those who are believers have entered into God's spiritual rest, but those who are not "shall not enter My rest" (Hebrews 4:3,5; Psalm 95:11). As the Lord rested on the seventh day from all His created works (verses 4,10; Genesis 2:2), so there is a rest for His own, that is, those who enter into it by faith (verse 6).

God has established a moment of reckoning for the generations signified by the word "Today" (verse 7), which hearkens to David's warning in Psalm 95:7-8, "Today…do not harden your hearts." For God's people there is a spiritual rest that cannot be spurned or rejected. Moses' successor, Joshua, could not lead all the Jewish people into the rest of the Promised Land because of their unbelief, and many perished before coming up to its borders. Likewise, there can be no rest without faith and trust (verse 8). The one who trusts Christ enters into the rest the Lord has provided; this spiritual rest becomes a true Sabbath rest "for the people of God" (verse 9). Some scholars believe that when the author here mentions the Sabbath, he is referring prophetically to the final and ultimate rest of heaven. "It must mean, therefore, *heaven*—the world of spiritual and eternal rest" (Barnes, *Notes on the New Testament,* 13:99).

CHRIST FULFILLS THE PRIESTHOOD OF MELCHIZEDEK
Hebrews 5:1-10

Here the author of Hebrews introduces the encounter Abraham had with the king-priest Melchizedek, which is documented in Genesis 14:17-24. Melchizedek "was a priest of God Most High" (verse 18), and his Hebrew name means "king of righteousness." He is certainly not of the priestly tribe of Levi, which would not be established for another 500 years. Though a king of Salem (which means "peace"), he represented God and probably made sacrifices to the Lord on behalf of others. He accepted a ten-percent gift from Abraham and was able to give to him in return a divine blessing (verse 19).

Since Melchizedek was *not of the Levitical line* of priests, he became a type (divinely ordained foreshadowing) of Christ, who is a King after the line of Judah who could offer Himself up as a sacrifice independent of the established priesthood. This issue is important in the theology of the sacrifice of Christ. It was prophesied in Psalm 110 that the Messiah would reign from Zion in Jerusalem (verse 2), and that He would be "a priest forever according to the order of Melchizedek" (verse 4). The Messiah would be both king and priest!

As was Aaron, the first priest of the tribe of Levi, all priests are called of God (Hebrews 5:4). So Christ did not *take* the priesthood to Himself for self-glory, but He *became* a high priest, as prophesied, and this priestly office is eternal (Hebrews 5:5-6). Before His crucifixion Christ offered up both prayers and supplications to God the Father (verse 7; Matthew 26:37-39). Though the Father heard Him for His "piety" (Greek, *eulabeias,* "good utterances," Hebrews 5:7), nevertheless, the cross was inevitable because He was an obedient Son (verse 8). For all those who obey Him in faith, He is "the source of eternal salvation" (verse 9) because He was "designated by God as a high priest according to the order of Melchizedek" (verse 10).

THE ORDER OF MELCHIZEDEK
Hebrews 7:1-22

IN THE HISTORICAL NARRATIVE in Genesis 14:18-20, the lineage of Melchizedek is not recorded, nor are his parents mentioned. He is presented with a continual and uninterrupted priesthood like that of "the Son of God, [who] remains a priest perpetually" (Hebrews 7:3). The Levitical priesthood had not yet begun when Abraham encountered Melchizedek, but in a genetic way, Levi was "still in the loins of his father" Abraham at the time Abraham was paying an offering to Melchizedek as a priestly representative of the Lord (verses 4-10). Thus the order of Melchizedek preceded the Levitical priesthood.

The writer of Hebrews then poses the question as to what was wrong with the Levitical priesthood (verses 11-18). For one thing, the priesthood operating under the Mosaic law had found it necessary for many priests to officiate through the ages because death kept them from continuing their work (verses 12-13,23). This Mosaic priesthood had to be set aside "because of its weakness and uselessness" (verse 18). The Levitical priesthood could never bring about "perfection" or maturity for those who lived under its yoke (verse 11).

To bring about permanent forgiveness of sins, "Jesus has become the guarantee of a better covenant" over the Mosaic Covenant and the laws of sacrifice that were part of that system (verse 22). This "better covenant" is the New Covenant, which the author of Hebrews will elaborate on from here through 8:13. The New Covenant was prophesied in Jeremiah 31:31-37 and promises something new in contrast to the Mosaic law (verse 32). Under this covenant, God's principles and laws will be written on the hearts of the Jewish people, (verse 33), and a deeper relationship between God and Israel will be established: "I will be their God, and they shall be My people." When the New Covenant is applied to Israel, all the people will know the Lord, and "[He] will forgive their iniquity, and their sin [He]

will remember no more"—they will know a permanent state of forgiveness (verse 34).

Christ inaugurated the New Covenant with the pouring out of His blood at the cross. At the Passover meal before His death, Christ told His disciples, "This cup which is poured out for you is the new covenant in My blood" (Luke 22:20). The Levitical priesthood was impotent, "obsolete and growing old [and] ready to disappear" (Hebrews 8:13). Christ, as a priest of the order of Melchizedek, would initiate the New Covenant, which would forever resolve humanity's problem with sin.

THE NEW COVENANT
Hebrews 7:23–8:13

AFTER INTRODUCING the "better covenant" (the New Covenant) (verse 22), the author of Hebrews explains how the priesthood under the Mosaic system was limited by the deaths of the priests (verse 23) and by the fact that when the priests offered sacrifices, they were also offering them for their own sins (verse 27). By contrast, Christ "continues forever, [and] holds His priesthood permanently" (verse 24), therefore He is "able also to save forever those who draw near to God through Him, since He always lives to make intercession for them" (verse 25). Only through Christ can eternal salvation become available. Christ, as a high priest, is "holy, innocent, undefiled, separated from sinners and exalted above the heavens" (verse 26). Because He is the holy Son of God, He was able to make an offering of Himself once for all for sinners (Hebrews 7:27). The law appointed priests who were human and weak, but Christ was appointed "a Son, made perfect forever" (verse 28). The Greek word for "perfect," *teleoo*, means "complete, mature, whole." In what sense was Christ "made perfect"? Nicoll explains, "He also, though a Son, became a man, and was exposed to human temptations, but by this experience was 'perfected' as our Priest" (*Expositor's Greek New Testament*, 4:319).

It was prophesied at Christ's ascension that

He would be seated as a high priest "at the right hand of the throne of the Majesty in the heavens, a minister in the sanctuary and in the true tabernacle, which the Lord pitched, not man" (Hebrews 8:1-2). The Mosaic sacrifices were but "a copy and shadow of the heavenly things," the heavenly tabernacle. The earthly tabernacle that God revealed to Moses was but a pattern of this heavenly one (Hebrews 8:5). This heavenly tabernacle comes about by the "better covenant, which has been enacted on better promises" than the Mosaic Covenant, which had human limitations (verse 6). The Mosaic Covenant was not faultless and made occasion for the covenant inaugurated by the blood of Christ (verse 7).

The author of Hebrews then cites the *prophecy of the new covenant* as recorded in Jeremiah 31:31-34 (Hebrews 8:8-12). It is clear that the New Covenant has replaced the Old Covenant, for the Mosaic law, with its animal sacrifices, could never make free from sin those who lived under it. When God said He would effect "a new covenant" (Jeremiah 31:31), it was clear that He would replace the old law that was "becoming obsolete" (Hebrews 8:13).

CHRIST AND THE EARTHLY PRIESTHOOD
Hebrews 9:1-26

THE WRITER OF HEBREWS continues his discussion of the New Covenant by comparing the Mosaic Covenant and the priesthood with Christ's New Covenant, which enables the believer to enter the heavenly holy place and know eternal life.

The Mosaic Covenant, "the first covenant," had to do with the earthly sanctuary (verse 1) that contained the lampstand and the table of the sacred bread—this sanctuary was "called the holy place" (verse 2). Then there was the Holy of Holies (verse 3) with the golden altar of incense and the ark of the covenant (which contained the jar of manna, Aaron's rod that budded, and the tables of the covenant, or the ten commandments) (verse 4). The cherubim

overshadowed the mercy seat in the Holy of Holies (verse 5), and it was here that the earthly high priest ministered, bringing in once a year blood offered for himself and for the sins of the people (verse 7). These offerings could never "make the worshiper perfect [complete] in conscience" (verse 9) because the tabernacle is only ceremonial, having to do with food and drink and various washings (verse 10).

But Christ came as a high priest with His *own blood* and entered the heavenly "more perfect tabernacle, not made with hands, that is to say, not of this creation," obtaining for the believer eternal redemption (verses 11-12). The sprinkling of the blood of goats and bulls could only "sanctify for the cleansing of the flesh" (verse 13), and "how much more will the blood of Christ, who through the eternal Spirit offered Himself without blemish to God, cleanse your conscience from dead works to serve the living God?" (verse 14). The earthly tabernacle was merely a type or a picture of what Christ would do in reality.

Therefore the Lord became the *mediator* of the New Covenant, and by His death, He provided redemption for the transgressions even of those who live under the Mosaic law, the first covenant (verse 15). The New Covenant was made by One who died (verses 16-17), for "without shedding of blood there is no forgiveness" (verse 22; Leviticus 17:11). The earthly tabernacle was indeed earthly because it held "copies of the things in the heavens to be cleansed with these, but the heavenly things themselves with better sacrifices than these" (Hebrews 9:23). Christ did not enter the "holy place made with hands, a mere copy of the true one, but into heaven itself, now to appear in the presence of God for us" (verse 24). He has no need to offer Himself every year with His blood (verse 25), for "once at the consummation of the ages He has been manifested to put away sin by the sacrifice of Himself" (verse 26).

The tabernacle and all of the priestly services were but prophetic shadows, types, pictures, and copies of what Christ would do as a high priest when He sacrificed Himself once for all sinners. His sacrifice would never need to be repeated again!

PROMISE OF THE SECOND COMING
Hebrews 9:27-28

IT IS AN IMPORTANT ISSUE that Christ exists eternally, giving believers eternal life for what He did at the cross. All of humanity faces a judgment, and the only escape is found in the blood of Christ. For "it is appointed for men to die once and after this comes judgment" (verse 27). God devised the plan of redemption; He was "in Christ reconciling the world to Himself" (2 Corinthians 5:19). For those who now trust in Christ for salvation, God will "not [count] their trespasses against them" (verse 19). That's because the righteousness of Christ is applied to the redeemed (verse 21).

Christ will never appear again to "bear the sins of many." However He "will appear a second time for salvation without reference to sin, to those who eagerly await Him" (Hebrews 9:28). While some believe this refers to the rapture of the church, it may also refer to the second coming. Since it says "a second time," this would be a return to *earth,* and in the rapture, believers are caught up to Christ *in the air.* Jesus came the first time to deal with our sin, and He will come again to reign, as foretold in dozens of prophecies throughout Scripture. This verse, more than any other single verse in the Bible, most clearly delineates the difference between the two comings—the first time to die for sinners, and the second time to reign on the throne of His earthly father David.

PROPHECY OF CHRIST'S SACRIFICE
Hebrews 10:1-18

NOW THE AUTHOR OF Hebrews focuses specifically on what Christ's sacrifice was all about. The Mosaic law was but a shadow, and the sacrifices were repeated yearly. The sacrifices made under this system of law could never "make perfect those who draw near" (verse 1).

These sacrifices were yearly reminders of sins (verse 3), "for it is impossible for the blood of bulls and goats to take away sins" (verse 4). To substantiate this, the author quotes Psalm 40:6-7, the great prophetic passage that spells out the sacrifice of the Messiah (Hebrews 10:5-7). In the words of the Messiah it is predicted that God would prepare a body for Him because the Lord does not desire "sacrifice and offering." God takes no pleasure in animal "burnt offerings and sacrifices," but instead, the Messiah will be sent "to do Your will, O God," meaning He will become a sacrifice Himself for the sins of His people.

By these prophecies from Psalm 40:6-7, God is taking away "the first" covenant "in order to establish the second" (Hebrews 10:9). Christ was sacrificed "once for all" (verse 10) in contrast to the earthly high priests who made offerings continually and ministered "time after time the same sacrifices, which can never take away sins" (verse 11). After Christ's sacrifice and His ascension to heaven "for all time, [He] sat down at the right hand of God, waiting from that time onward until His enemies be made a footstool for His feet" (verses 12-13; Psalm 110:1-2). By Christ's one offering He dealt with the issue of sin and "perfected for all time those who are sanctified" (Hebrews 10:14). As the Holy Spirit stated in Jeremiah 31:33 (verse 15), the New Covenant was to be established and written firmly in the hearts and minds of those who trust Christ (verse 16). "Their sins and their lawless deeds" would be remembered no more (verse 17; Jeremiah 31:34). "Now where there is forgiveness of these things, there is no longer any offering for sin" (verse 18).

WARNING TO ACCEPT CHRIST NOW
Hebrews 10:19-39

THE WRITER OF HEBREWS now elaborates on the fact that God is *forever* finished with the issue of sin. Christ's sacrifice was the ultimate and final offering—there will never be another one! The sacrifice made at the cross opens the way into "the holy place by the blood of Jesus" (verse 19). His sacrifice was not simply a ritualistic formality but "a new and living way," which He inaugurated "for us through the veil, that is, His flesh" (verse 20). He is now a great high priest "over the house of God" (verse 21), through which believers can "draw near with a sincere heart in full assurance of faith" (verse 22). Those who trust Him have a mutual faith (verse 23), an obligation to love one another (verse 24), and a responsibility to assemble together for encouragement (verse 25).

The appeal is that all stop sinning and receive the full knowledge of the truth, knowing that with Christ's sacrifice, "there no longer remains a sacrifice for sins" (verse 26). In fact, there is the terrible prophecy of impending judgment—"the fury of a fire which will consume the adversaries" (verse 27; see Numbers 15:30)—especially for those who deny Christ and who trample "under foot the Son of God" and see His blood as unclean, which is the blood of the promised New Covenant. To do this is to insult "the Spirit of grace" (Hebrews 10:29).

God has promised vengeance by which He will repay, judging His own people, the Jews, who refuse Christ (verse 30), and "it is a terrifying thing to fall into the hands of the living God" (verse 31). The Jews are further warned not to throw away their *messianic confidence,* "which has a great reward" (verse 35). By the gospel offered concerning Christ, the Jews will receive what was prophesied and promised by the Lord (verse 36). The promise of Christ's coming was certain, and would not be delayed (verse 37; Habakkuk 2:3). To come to Him is to come by faith and not by law. The one who does this is declared God's "righteous one [who] shall live by faith; and if he shrinks back, My soul has no pleasure in him" (Hebrews 10:38; see Habakkuk 2:4).

There were many Jews who thought they could be saved by law-keeping. But this is not true—one is saved only by faith! The Jews were warned not to "shrink back to destruction" from what they knew. Instead, they should be "those who have faith to the preserving of the soul" (Hebrews 10:39).

THE FAITHFUL AND THEIR HEAVENLY REWARD
Hebrews 11:1-40

WHILE THIS CHAPTER IS frequently called the great Hall of Faith, it can also be called the chapter of coming prophetic events. Here the writer of Hebrews lists the great saints of the Old Testament who believed God would fulfill His promises regarding the future. In fact, the point is that the saints of old lived for the completion of the plan that God had laid out before them. Their faith was "the assurance of things hoped for, the conviction of things not seen" (verse 1). In other words, these godly personalities "gained approval" with God by their trust in what He said, and this even included what He said about the creation of the worlds that are in outer space, made out of that which is invisible (verses 2-3).

Abel knew from His father, Adam, what was expected in regard to sacrifices. He followed suit with "a better sacrifice," an animal offering, through which God declared him as righteous (Hebrews 11:4). *Enoch* pleased God and did not see death but was "not found," having been taken up to heaven without dying (verse 5; Genesis 5:21-24). Only by faith can one come to God and please Him (Hebrews 11:6). "This text teaches a spiritual truth that touches the spiritual life of every believer.... In one beautifully constructed verse, the writer of Hebrews communicates the method of pleasing God, the necessity of believing his existence, and the certainty of answered prayer" (Kistemaker, *Hebrews,* p. 317).

Almost all the saints listed from verse 7 onward believed what God said was coming in the future. To begin, the Lord prophesied to *Noah* that a flood was coming. Noah believed this and prepared the ark, being declared righteous by his faith (verse 7). By faith, *Abraham* followed the voice of the Lord and received an inheritance to the land "not knowing where he was going" (verse 8). He lived by faith (verse 9) and realized there was more to come, "for he was looking for the city which has foundations, whose architect and builder is God" (verse 10).

Abraham's wife *Sarah* knew she was going to have a child because "she considered Him faithful who had promised," even though she and her husband were old (verse 11). Abraham, though impotent, had previously believed God when He promised Abraham so many children that to count them would be like trying to count all the stars of heaven (verse 12; Genesis 15:5; cf. 22:17; 32:12).

These Old Testament saints died without receiving all God's promises, yet they believed those promises would eventually come to pass. They were but "strangers and exiles on the earth" (Hebrews 11:13) who were looking ahead and not from where they had come. They were not ashamed to call God "their God; for He has prepared a city for them" (verse 16).

By faith Abraham, when tested by the Lord, offered up Isaac, his son, because he had received God's promises that "in Isaac your descendants shall be called" (verses 17-18; Genesis 21:12). He was so strong in his faith that he believed God would raise Isaac from the dead, if necessary (Hebrews 11:19). By faith *Isaac* blessed his sons Jacob and Esau "regarding things to come" (verse 20). By faith, when he was dying, *Jacob* blessed the sons of Joseph and worshiped the Lord (verse 21). By faith *Joseph,* when dying, gave orders that his bones be transported to the Promised Land because he knew that his children would end up there as God promised, though at the present time they were sojourning in Egypt (verse 22).

Moses listened to God and refused the pleasures of Egypt (verses 23-25), "considering the reproach of Christ greater riches than the treasures of Egypt; for he was looking to the reward" God had promised him (verse 26). (Here God commends the motivation of looking forward to eternal reward and denying the temptations of this world in the course

of one's service to Him [see 1 Corinthians 3:9-15].) This is not to say that Moses knew of Christ, but like Christ, he was willing to suffer the reproach and the repudiation of the king of Egypt. Leaving Egypt and not fearing the wrath of Pharaoh, Moses endured his troubles "as seeing Him who is unseen" (verse 27). Moses believed God in the crossing of the Red Sea (verse 29), and by faith, Joshua believed the walls of Jericho would fall down (verse 30). The harlot *Rahab* knew that the land of Canaan had been promised to the children of Israel, and by faith she hid the Israelite spies who came to her in the city of Jericho (verse 31). And there are others who belong to the Hall of Faith (verse 32), others who suffered terribly while trusting what God had said (verses 33-37), men "of whom the world was not worthy" (verse 38).

While these Old Testament saints did not receive all that was promised to them, they still "gained approval through their faith" (verse 39). God's promises were still to come, the "something better" that He would provide (verse 40). John MacArthur says,

> God has provided this "something better" for us, that is for those under the New Covenant, which is why apart from us they should not be made perfect. That is, not until our time, the time of Christianity, could their salvation be completed, made perfect. Until Jesus' atoning work on the cross was accomplished, no salvation was complete, no matter how great the faith a believer may have had.... Though their salvation was not completed in their lifetime, these were not second-rate believers. They were believers of the highest order (*Hebrews,* pp. 369-70).

LOOKING TO JESUS
Hebrews 12:1-2

ENCOURAGED BY ALL the believers who have gone before us (mentioned in Hebrews 11), who are a "great cloud of witnesses," we are to run the race of faith and not be encumbered with sin "which so easily entangles us" (Hebrews 12:1). We should look to Jesus, who "endured the cross, despising the shame, and has sat down at the right hand of the throne of God" (verse 2; Psalm 110:1). Christ is seated on the throne of His Father until He makes His "enemies a footstool for [His] feet." Then Christ will come to earth so that His Father will cause His strong scepter to be stretched forth "from Zion," or the capital city of David, the city of Jerusalem (verse 2). Entering the very throne room of God the Father, Christ had again the joy of being in His presence. From there He will rule over all of the nations of earth. The heavenly throne of the Father is not the millennial throne, as some have suggested. Revelation 3:21 makes it clear that although Christ is now on the throne of His Father, He will yet sit on His earthly throne, and that place of rule will be shared by the church saints as well.

When Stephen was being stoned to death, He saw a vision of Christ "standing at the right hand of God" (Acts 7:55-56). Christ may have been standing in honor of Stephen, who was the first martyr of the church.

With Christ at the right hand of the Father, believers now have the Lord Jesus as an advocate to plead our case and to intercede for us (1 John 2:1). He holds that office as a "propitiation" (Greek, *hilasmos*) or a satisfaction for sin before God (Romans 3:25; Hebrews 2:17).

THE PROPHECY OF FUTURE JUDGMENT
Hebrews 12:25-29

THE WRITER OF HEBREWS now warns any reader who has doubts about salvation in Christ. If the Old Testament Jews did not escape judgment when God "warned them on earth," how shall anyone escape today "who turn away from Him who warns from heaven" (verse 25). For the exodus generation the Lord "shook the earth then, but now He

has promised, saying, 'Yet once more I will shake not only the earth, but also the heaven'" (Hebrews 12:26). Quoting Haggai 2:6, the author of Hebrews sees another day of reckoning in this prophecy. More than likely he is referring not simply to a general judgment, but the pouring out of God's wrath during the seven-year Tribulation. This shaking will take place on earth, but its origin is heaven.

The phrase "yet once more" has to do with the removing of "created things," physical things, so that the things which cannot be shaken, or spiritual issues, "may remain" (Hebrews 12:27). The created world is polluted and is passing away (Romans 8:21-22; 2 Peter 3:10-13), and in its place there will come the millennial kingdom, "which cannot be shaken." This should call for gratitude, "by which we may offer to God an acceptable service with reverence and awe" (verse 28). For believers there is a blessing, and for those who refuse to trust there is judgment because "our God is a consuming fire" (verse 29).

THE IMMUTABILITY OF CHRIST
Hebrews 13:8

As IF IN THE MIDDLE OF a paragraph, the writer of Hebrews suddenly calls out, "Jesus Christ is the same yesterday and today and forever" (verse 8). The Lord Jesus now lives "that He might sanctify the people through His own blood" (verse 12). "He is the same" (Greek, *ho autos*), changeless and immutable, because He is God and not a mere man. As God, He is "the Alpha and the Omega" (Revelation 1:8; Isaiah 41:4), the start and the finish, the beginning and the end. This is the same attribute of eternality used to describe the nature of God the Father. "Forever" is "into the ages" (Greek, *eis tous aionas*) and means that Christ is the eternal Being, as is God. "Yesterday" goes to the days before the apostles walked with Christ. And presently, Christ exists continually day by day. He has always been and always will be! Flanigan writes, "Tomorrow, yea, and for ever, throughout the ages to come, He will be ours unchangeably, and we shall be with Him and like Him. Our earthly friends may come, and go. We appreciate them; we bid them farewell and we remember them. Jesus remains the same" (*Hebrews,* p. 283).

When God told Moses from the burning bush that He was the I AM (Exodus 3:14), He was describing His foreverness. Christ referred to this and said to the Jews, "Truly, truly, I say to you, before Abraham was born, I am" (John 8:58; cf. 5:17; 10:30). There is no doubt as to what Christ was saying!

THE CITY THAT IS TO COME
Hebrews 13:14-15

IN THE OLD TESTAMENT, under the law, Israel had to make continual sacrifices and offerings for sin. The blood of the sacrificed animals was brought into the holy place, but on the Day of Atonement, the animals were "burned outside the camp" (verse 11; cf. Leviticus 4:12,21; 9:11;

16:27). In like manner, Christ was crucified outside of the walls of Jerusalem, suffering "outside the gate," "bearing His reproach" (Hebrews 13:12-13). Likewise, for the present time, believers "do not have a lasting city, but we are seeking the city which is to come," meaning the millennial Jerusalem (verse 14). For now there is the continual "offer[ing] up a sacrifice of praise to God, that is, the fruit of lips that give thanks to His name" (verse 15). For now there is the doing of what is good and sharing with others, which are sacrifices that please God (verse 16).

In his classic commentary on Hebrews, Adolph Saphir writes,

> We must be separate from all that is against Christ, from all that beguiles men from the simplicity that is in Christ Jesus, and substitutes forms and outward legal observances for the body, the substance. In proportion as our worship, our affections, our aims are heavenly, as we seek the future and continuing city, we must expect to bear the reproach of Christ (*Epistle to the Hebrews,* p. 872).

JAMES

The book of James may be the oldest book in the New Testament. Written by the half-brother of Jesus, the book gets down to spiritual bedrock as it explains what the Christian life is all about. This little epistle pulls no punches. What the Christian says, he must live. "Faith without works is dead" (2:26).

While the book has few prophetic verses, many believe that one of the earliest appearances of the truth about the rapture of the church is given in 5:7-9. Believers need to be careful how they relate to each other in a negative way because "the coming of the Lord is at hand" (verse 8), and "the Judge is standing right at the door" (verse 9). Since these prophetic words are addressed to the church, they could not refer to the second coming of Christ to reign on the earth. Believers in the present church age are to be patient "until the coming of the Lord" in the same way that a farmer must wait for the early and late rains (verse 7).

THE FALLACY OF RICHES
James 1:10-11

The Jews considered the wealthy as especially favored by the Lord because of their riches. Those who were poor were believed to be cursed of God. The apostle James addresses this fallacious belief by pointing out the pride that most who were wealthy displayed. The rich man should be humble because his money cannot save him. He should instead glory "in his humiliation, because like flowering grass he will pass away" (verse 10). Just as flowers, in time, fade away, "so too the rich man in the midst of his pursuits will fade away" (verse 11). "Because men, including believers, have a natural tendency to trust in material things, James gives special attention to the dangers of wealth" (John MacArthur, *James,* p. 40).

This is a warning for those trusting in their accumulation of wealth. Their bank account will not save them, and to be humble is to trust in Christ and not in one's self. Jesus taught about the deception of riches, which can choke out the Word of God (Matthew 13:22) and are deceitful (6:19). They can give pleasure in this life (Luke 8:14) but have nothing to do with receiving the life to come. The Lord told the story of the wealthy man who had such an abundance of crops he had to build new barns (Luke 12:16-21). This man said to himself, "Soul, you have many goods laid up for many years to come; take your ease, eat, drink and be merry" (verse 19). But the night he said these words, the Lord said, "This very night your soul is required of you" (verse 20). The man entered eternity with no thought of his personal salvation.

THE CROWN OF LIFE
James 1:12

In contrast to the wealthy man who thinks of nothing but himself, James writes about the man who is approved of God because he loves Him. He lives his life for the Lord and not for the gathering of wealth. At the *bema* judgment (Romans 14:8-12; 1 Corinthians 3:10-15; 2 Corinthians 5:10-11), the Lord will reward him as promised with "the crown of life" (James 1:12). This crown reflects how the believer lived out his days. He ran the race placed before him to receive an imperishable wreath, a crown that indicates he served the Lord and not himself (1 Corinthians 9:24-27). This may be the ultimate crown because it is a reward for a life well lived for the cause of Christ.

THE POOR INHERIT THE KINGDOM
James 2:5

Often when the Bible speaks about the poor, it is speaking of those who lack wealth, but at times it is also speaking of the humility of spirit found in those who have little in this life. Though they may be poor materially, they are "rich in faith and heirs of the kingdom which He promised to those who love Him" (James 2:5). While some may interpret "the kingdom" here to mean a larger nondescript rule of life, it seems clear that James has in mind Christ's Sermon on the Mount, in which the kingdom is the prophesied messianic reign (Matthew 5–7). In that sermon the Lord said, "Blessed are the poor in spirit, for theirs is the kingdom of heaven" (5:3). The "kingdom of heaven" points to the millennial reign of Christ.

JUSTIFICATION BY FAITH
James 2:18-26

Some accuse the apostle James of teaching justification by works rather than faith. Nothing could be further from the truth. James' letter focuses on the external fruit of a Christian's faith. In other words, whatever is true about a person internally will show up externally. In this sense he argues that one is indeed "justified by works" before other people.

James argues that those who have a faith not accompanied by works are living out a dead faith because "it has no works...being by itself" (verse 17). The apostle says believers must show their faith by their works (verse 18), for even the demons have a form of belief in God, but this is not a saving faith (verse 19). Faith that does not produce good works is useless (verse 20). "If the man talks of faith, he certainly needs to go to the Scriptures to learn what God has to say about this subject.... James continues to reprove: 'Do you want evidence?'" (Kistemaker, *James and I–III John*, p. 95).

But what about Abraham? Was he not justified by works? On a human level, yes, but not before God! When Abraham offered up his only true son Isaac (Genesis 22:9-12), his trust in God's command regarding Isaac produced an action, a work that could be seen and tested. "As a result of the works [of Abraham], faith was perfected," or matured (James 2:22). Justification with God comes with faith, and justification with men comes with works. With regard to Abraham, "the Scripture was fulfilled which says, 'And Abraham believed God, and it was reckoned to him as righteousness'" (verse 23; Genesis 15:6). Abraham's faith set for all time the example as to how people are given a right relationship with the Lord.

UNCERTAINTY OF LIFE
James 4:13-16

Those who say they know what will happen to them today or tomorrow are wrong (verse 13). No one knows what his or her life will be like tomorrow, because we are "just a vapor that appears for a little while and then vanishes away" (verse 14). What we should say is, "If the Lord wills, we will live and also do this or that" (verse 15). To say anything else is

Though they predicted it, they still made "careful searches and inquiries, seeking to know what person or time the Spirit of Christ within them was indicating as He predicted the sufferings of Christ and the glories to follow" (verses 10-11). The Holy Spirit "of [from] Christ" was working *within* the ancient prophets even though they still groped forward to try to understand all that was prophesied. They understood that what was revealed to them was still to come in the future (verse 12).

The prophets of old received *two key messages:* 1) that Christ would suffer, and 2) that there would be "glories" to follow. In regard to the glories, more than likely the ancient seers were referring to the fact that the Messiah would reign on His glorious Davidic throne in Jerusalem. His coming to set up His kingdom would be "with power and great glory" (Matthew 24:30). "When the Son of Man comes in His glory, and all the angels with Him, then He will sit on His glorious throne" (25:31).

Those who were preaching the gospel in Peter's day were doing so by the revelation of the same Holy Spirit who was "sent from heaven." The truths regarding God's grace and the gospel were so great that even the angels longed to understand them (1 Peter 1:12).

cf. Isaiah 53; John 1:29). (For the requirement that sacrifices be pure, see also Exodus 29:1; Leviticus 22:17-25.)

Nowhere in the Old Testament were the Jews told they could find redemption through silver and gold. This may be referring to some Jews in Peter's day who thought they could buy their way to heaven. The Greek word for "futile," *mataios,* means "empty, vain, without substance." Only the blood of Christ saves, not riches.

The heavenly Father foreknew (Greek, *proginosko*) in a very intimate way His Son in eternity past—that is, "before the foundation of the world" (1 Peter 1:20). All of history, including salvation history, is God's age-old purpose. It includes His plans for believers, along with the passion and suffering of Christ (Kelly, *Epistles of Peter,* p. 76). But now Christ "has appeared in these last times for the sake of you" (verse 20). Through Christ, those who are lost become "believers in God, who raised [Christ] from the dead and gave Him glory, so that your faith and hope are in God" (verse 21). In these verses Peter scans the past, includes the present, and continues on into the future. God has completely supplied salvation in His Son; this is the "grace that would come to you" (verse 10).

WHILE IT IS TRUE THAT all things have been given into the hands of the Son of God (John 3:35), including all future judgment (5:22), there is still a sense in which the Father will be involved in the judgment of believers. Therefore Peter warns his readers, "Conduct yourselves in fear during the time of your stay upon earth" (1 Peter 1:17). Jewish believers should be especially made aware that their redemption was not by "perishable things like silver and gold from your futile way of life inherited from your forefathers," but "with precious blood, as of a lamb unblemished and spotless, the blood of Christ" (verses 18-19;

ALL WHO HAVE OBEYED the truth and trusted Christ as Savior manifest a "sincere love of the brethren" (verse 22). They have been "born again" from seed which is not "perishable but imperishable" (verse 23; cf. 1:3; John 3:3). The instrument used by the Holy Spirit in this new birth is the "living and abiding word of God." Since the Word of God "endures forever" (1 Peter 1:25), so will the believer. Peter in verses 24-25 quotes Isaiah 40:6-8, which talks about all flesh being like grass that is here today and gone tomorrow. James alludes to the same Old Testament passage

(James 1:10-11). Those who are born again by the Word of God now have "a living hope through the resurrection of Jesus Christ from the dead...an inheritance which is imperishable and undefiled and will not fade away, reserved in heaven" (1 Peter 1:3-4).

PROPHESIED REJECTION OF CHRIST
1 Peter 2:4-8

IN THESE VERSES PETER CALLS Christ the "living stone" (verse 4), the "corner stone" (verse 6), the "rejected" stone (verse 7), and the "stumbling" stone (verse 8). He is quoting Isaiah 28:16, Psalm 118:22, and Isaiah 8:14. That Christ was the "living stone" means He was more than simply a rock. He was essential as life itself, and He was not seen as an inanimate object. Though He was "rejected by men," he was "choice and precious in the sight of God." The cornerstone was the key stone by which a building was squared off and plumbed to have the right dimensions. Though Christ was the "corner stone" for Israel, He was still repudiated and rejected by the people. And as a "stone of stumbling," the Jewish people would, as it were, trip over Him, making Him a "rock of offense."

Those who accept Christ are like "living stones," built up "as a spiritual house for a holy priesthood, to offer up spiritual sacrifices acceptable to God through Jesus Christ" (1 Peter 2:5). Those who now are saved by His blood through faith become a "holy priesthood," in contrast to the Levitical priesthood, which has passed away. Christ becomes to believers "precious value" by their faith, in contrast to those who disbelieve and are doomed (verse 7).

ISRAEL, A CHOSEN RACE
1 Peter 2:9-10

THOUGH PETER IS WRITING to the Jewish believers in the church age, they still have an Old Testament heritage that is honorable. The Jews are a "chosen race" (see Deuteronomy 10:15; Isaiah 43:20), a "royal priesthood" (see Isaiah 61:6; 66:21), a "holy nation" (Exodus 19:6; Deuteronomy 7:6), and a "people for [God's] own possession" (Titus 2:14). God has called them "out of darkness into His marvelous light" (1 Peter 2:9). These Jews to whom Peter is writing are now fulfilling, in a spiritual way, all that God intended for the nation of Israel. However, they have not received the *land promises,* which they will receive when the Messiah comes. Peter tells them that "you once were not a people, but now you are the people of God; you had not received mercy, but now you have received mercy" (1 Peter 2:10; Hosea 1:10). "The practice of holiness, in which God's people serve as a holy and royal priesthood offering spiritual sacrifices and extolling His excellencies, is the proper response to the mercy (cf. 1 Pet. 1:3) they have received" (Raymer, "1 Peter," *Bible Knowledge Commentary,* p. 846). While these verses are addressed to the Jewish Christians to whom Peter is writing, in a broad sense they apply spiritually to Gentile believers as well.

THE DAY OF VISITATION
1 Peter 2:12

THE JEWISH BELIEVERS WERE to keep their "behavior excellent among the Gentiles" so that they could not be slandered as evildoers. Gentiles then would see their good deeds and "glorify God in the day of visitation" (verse 12). The word "visitation" is the Greek word *episkopee,* which is related to the word "bishop" or "overseer" (Greek, *episkopos*). The meaning then of "day of visitation" has to do with when they are examined or "looked over" at the *bema* judgment (Romans 14:10-12; 1 Corinthians 3:10-15; 2 Corinthians 5:10-11). There, "each one of us shall give account of himself to God." According to 1 Peter 2:13, believers in Christ will be called to account as to what the world sees in them as Christians. Will the world see evil, or godliness and holiness?

CHRIST'S SUFFERING FOR SIN
1 Peter 2:21-25

ISAIAH THE PROPHET PREDICTED that the Messiah would live a sinless life. He "committed no sin, nor was any deceit found in His mouth" (verse 22; Isaiah 53:7). He suffered not for His own sins but for the believer, "leaving you an example for you to follow in His steps" (1 Peter 2:21). When He was cursed and reviled "He uttered no threats, but kept entrusting Himself to Him who judges righteously" (verse 23). Isaiah again prophesied that by Christ's wounds believers would be healed (verse 24; Isaiah 53:5). As a substitute He would bear sins "in His body on the cross, that we might die to sin and live to righteousness." This is the doctrine of substitution: Christ would take the place of the sinner under the wrath of God (Isaiah 53:6,12; 2 Corinthians 5:21).

The "healing" by His wounds is not about physical healing being availed in the atonement. Peter applies Isaiah 53:5 to the issue of *spiritual* healing. The verse reads, "By His scourging we are healed." Peter repeats this in 1 Peter 2:24 but then adds in verse 25, "You were continually straying like sheep, but now you have returned to the Shepherd and Guardian of your souls." He refers to the healing as spiritual, not physical. "The reference is to salvation. Christ's suffering…and death accomplished 'healing,' the salvation of every individual who trusts Him as his Savior" (Raymer, "1 Peter," *Bible Knowledge Commentary,* p. 848).

CHRIST'S DEATH AND INTERCESSION
1 Peter 3:18-22

THIS IS A DIFFICULT PASSAGE that has engendered multiple interpretations. It starts with the fact that Christ came to bring the unjust to God (verse 18). This seems to be an allusion to Isaiah 53:12, where it is prophesied that the Messiah would bear the sin of many. Christ died to bring men to God, "having been put to death in the flesh, but made alive in the spirit" (1 Peter 3:18). Most translate "spirit" (Greek, *pneuma*) as referring to the Holy Spirit, who was the agent in the resurrection of Christ, though some believe it is a reference to Christ's own spirit in contrast with His human body (Raymer, "1 Peter," *Bible Knowledge Commentary,* p. 851). The Holy Spirit was active not only in the resurrection of Jesus, but also in His death. The author of Hebrews writes, "How much more will the blood of Christ, who through the eternal Spirit offered Himself without blemish to God, cleanse your conscience from dead works to serve the living God?" (Hebrews 9:14).

Following His death, Christ "went and made proclamation to the spirits now in prison, who once were disobedient, when the patience of God kept waiting in the days of Noah, during the construction of the ark, in which a few, that is, eight persons, were brought safely through the water" (1 Peter 3:19-20). The best understanding of this passage is expressed by Raymer, who writes,

> The preincarnate Christ was actually in Noah, ministering through him, by means of the Holy Spirit. Peter (1:11) referred to the "Spirit of Christ" in the Old Testament prophets. Later he described Noah as "a preacher of righteousness" (2 Pet. 2:5). The Spirit of Christ preached through Noah to the ungodly humans who, at the time of Peter's writing, were "spirits in prison" awaiting final judgment (Raymer, "1 Peter," *Bible Knowledge Commentary,* p. 851).

From the Greek text, 1 Peter 3:21 reads, "Which also you, a type, now baptism saves, not the flesh removal of dirt but an appeal to God for a good conscience—through the resurrection of Jesus Christ." In the NASB the word "type" is translated "And corresponding to that.…" The word "type" is the Greek term *antitupos* and refers to "a shadow, copy, representation." Peter is not saying that baptism saves, but that the sparing of Noah and his family by the fact that the ark was lifted up by water is a type of how baptism (not water baptism, which removes dirt, but spiritual baptism) saves by Christ's resurrection (see 1 Corinthians 12:12-14).

In a sense, the water of the flood became a prophecy of the "spiritual baptism" that indeed would bring salvation.

THE JUDGE OF THE LIVING AND THE DEAD
1 Peter 4:4-6

THOSE WHO DO NOT KNOW Christ "are surprised" that the believer does not run with them in their sin, their "excesses of dissipation" (verse 4). They malign the Christian and disparage his walk with Christ. "The point is that these Gentiles are now watching these Jewish believers. They think it very strange that the Jewish believers do not act in the same manner as Gentiles do; therefore, they begin to attack the believers by 'speaking evil of you'" (Fruchtenbaum, *Messianic Jewish Epistles,* p. 368). However, "they will give account to Him who is ready to judge the living and the dead" (verse 5). All generations of all ages will answer to the Lord. Believers will be justified not by their goodness but because their sins have been covered by the blood of Christ, "for by His wounds you were healed" (2:24).

The gospel was preached to those who have died and passed on. Those who have accepted Him as Savior will "live in the spirit according to the will of God" (verse 6). Better, this is the Holy Spirit, and they live "in regard to the Spirit." The believer has a future different from that facing the lost. For those who trust in Christ, the penalty for sins has been paid in full. "The death and resurrection of Jesus guarantees the final coming judgment for the unbeliever but, for the believer, it is an encouragement to live spiritually" (Fruchtenbaum, *Messianic Jewish Epistles,* p. 368).

GOD GLORIFIED THROUGH CHRIST
1 Peter 4:11

WHEN THE CHILD OF GOD SPEAKS, he should think of his words as if they were "utterances of God." Service rendered for the Lord should be done "by the strength which God supplies." Everything done in the Christian walk should be done in a way that brings glory to the Lord Jesus, for unto Him "belongs the glory and dominion forever and ever. Amen."

When Christ ascended to the heavenly Father, He was introduced as the "Son of Man," or the "Son related to humanity" (Daniel 7:13). He took flesh upon Himself, and He is now exalted in glory at the right hand of God the Father (Psalm 110:1). All dominion, glory, and a kingdom have been assigned to Him, though He presently is not occupying the rule on earth that has been assigned to Him. The writer of Hebrews observes, "In subjecting all things to him, He left nothing that is not subject to him. But now we do not yet see all things subject to him," though He has been crowned with glory and honor (Hebrews 2:7-8; cf. Psalm 8:5-6).

Peter is ascribing to Christ "even that which he ascribes to the Father, namely, divine glory and dominion, which he has from everlasting to everlasting. This Peter would not have done were Christ not truly God. Otherwise, it would have been called robbing God of his glory" (Luther, *Commentary on Peter & Jude,* p. 191). And God will share His glory with no one (Isaiah 42:8).

JUDGMENT ON THE HOUSEHOLD OF GOD
1 Peter 4:17-18

SINCE THE "SPIRIT OF GLORY and of God rests on" believers, they are blessed when they are reviled and cursed for the name of Christ (verse 14). It is one thing for believers to suffer for committing sin (verse 15), but something else to suffer as Christians. If this happens, believers should not feel ashamed, but instead, they should glorify God (verse 16). Judgment for what is done in this life begins with "the household of God." And "if it begins with us first, what will be the outcome for those who do not obey the gospel of God?" (verse 17). The eternal *position* of believers as children of

God is a settled issue (Romans 8:1), but the temporal *experience* of believers—their walk here on earth—will be judged or rewarded at the *bema* judgment (Romans 14:10-12; 1 Corinthians 3:10-15; 2 Corinthians 5:10-11).

The lost will face judgment at the Great White Throne Judgment where their destiny will be based on what they did in this life (Revelation 20:11-15). Since they did not trust Christ as Savior, the Lord has no other recourse but to judge them on their life merit. No one, however, can be saved by his or her "good" works. Whatever sins they committed during life on earth will only bring about condemnation! Here, Peter quotes Proverbs 11:31, which makes it clear that if it is difficult "that the righteous is saved, what will become of the godless man and the sinner?" (1 Peter 4:18). And finally, when believers suffer according to the will of God, they must "entrust their souls to a faithful Creator in doing what is right" (verse 19).

GLORY TO BE REVEALED!
1 Peter 5:1,4

Peter continually reminds his readers that he was a "witness of the sufferings of Christ, and a partaker also of the glory that is to be revealed" (verse 1; Matthew 17:1-6; cf. 2 Peter 1:16-18). Peter, James, and John witnessed the transfiguration of Christ, which was a preview of His coming kingly glory when He reigns in Jerusalem. Presently, Jesus is the Shepherd and Guardian of the souls of believers (1 Peter 2:25). When He returns, the leaders and elders of the church will receive "the unfading crown of glory" for their testimony (5:4). William Baker comments,

> Peter had been dealing with elders, who are shepherds of souls, and such "shepherds" are accountable to the "Chief Shepherd." Both Peter and Paul make reference to "crowns" as symbols of

rewards. The "crown" was probably a garland or wreath made of leaves or gold in ancient athletic competitions. Such rewards are not payment for human accomplishment but tokens of faithfulness (*James & First and Second Peter,* pp. 169-70).

DEALING WITH THE DEVIL
1 Peter 5:8-11

Believers are to live out the Christian life soberly because "your adversary, the devil, prowls about like a roaring lion, seeking someone to devour" (verse 8). They are to "resist him" because they know "that the same experiences of suffering are being accomplished by your brethren who are in the world" (verse 9). This is a reminder that Satan is behind all attacks against believers and that he is alive and well on planet earth—contrary to those who assert that he is already "bound" today.

After you have suffered, "the God of all grace, who called you to His eternal glory in Christ, will Himself perfect, confirm, strengthen and establish you" (verse 10). This is Peter's way of describing the maturing work that God does in the life of the Christian. God's calling has to do with divine election, and its destiny is the "eternal glory" of God because believers are *in* Christ (cf. 2 Corinthians 4:17). Paul says this as well in 2 Timothy 2:10: Believers are "chosen, so that they also may obtain the salvation which is in Christ Jesus and with it eternal glory."

Peter then closes with a doxology and an anthem that alludes to Daniel 7:14-27: "To Him be dominion forever and ever. Amen" (1 Peter 5:11). This "is a statement of the ultimate goal of God in the universe. That goal is 'dominion,' His acknowledged supremacy. It exists now, but complete human recognition of it is future, as God allows history to play itself out" (Baker, *James & First and Second Peter,* p. 174).

PETER REMINDS HIS READERS THAT HE WAS AN EYEWITNESS of the glorious transformation of Christ on the Mount of Transfiguration (1:16-18; Matthew 17:1-8). Jesus was miraculously presented as Israel's king with a preview of all the splendor that will someday be revealed to the world in the messianic kingdom. The prophecy of Scripture did not come about by the personal thoughts of the prophets of old. Rather, "men moved by the Holy Spirit spoke from God" (2 Peter 1:21). This verse is a potent reminder of how we got our Bible.

With prophetic fervor Peter reminds his readers that false prophets will surely come to deceive true believers (2:1-3). Believers are not to be caught off guard or be surprised when this happens. Believers are to be diligent (3:14), for there is coming a time of cataclysmic judgment upon the earth (3:1-9). And finally, "the day of the Lord" is coming, a day in which the earth and all its works will be burned up (verse 10). Yet for the child of God, there is no fear of the future. God will have the final say! "According to His promise we are looking for new heavens and a new earth, in which righteousness dwells" (verse 13).

MAKING CERTAIN OF THE CALLING
2 Peter 1:10-11

REFERRING BACK TO 1 PETER 5:10, the apostle continues his thought about God's "calling and choosing" of the believer (2 Peter 1:10). The Christian life should exemplify that sovereign spiritual work of God, and the believer should also be "more diligent to make certain about His calling." This does not imply that the believer is working to keep his salvation. Rather, he is to live in such a way that his position in Christ brings glory to God. By living morally and spiritually pure, he "will never stumble," or "fall as into ruin" (Greek, *ptaio*) in the Christian walk. Living out the spiritual life this way, the "entrance into the eternal kingdom of our Lord and Savior Jesus Christ will be abundantly supplied to you" (verse 11).

"Abundantly supplied" (Greek, *plousios ephchoregein*) is better translated "richly provided." The idea here is one of providing lavishly without cost to the beneficiary. God's divine grace and generosity are highlighted (Kelly, *Epistles of Peter*, pp. 309-10). The "eternal kingdom" into which the believer enters here may not be the messianic kingdom, but rather, the present spiritual kingdom by which the Lord is carrying out His plans and purposes.

PETER'S DEPARTURE TO HEAVEN
2 Peter 1:13-15

THE APOSTLE PETER KNEW that his days were numbered. However, as long as he lived "in this earthly dwelling," he felt he had an obligation to keep speaking to believers of spiritual priorities, "to stir you up by way of reminder" (verse 13). The Lord Jesus Christ had made clear to him that he would be laying aside his life (verse 14), and He had predicted this before His ascension (John 21:18). While alive, Peter wanted to keep pressing believers as to how they should live. He wanted them to draw on his words long after he was gone. "I will also be diligent that at any time after my departure you will be able to call these things to mind" (2 Peter 1:15).

Church tradition says that Peter was martyred in Rome sometime in the 60s. During most of his ministry he knew that both the Jews and the Romans wanted to silence his preaching about the risen Christ. Kistemaker remarks, "If Peter suffered a martyr's death in the last few years of Nero's reign, according to tradition, we aver that Peter died in the mid-sixties. Nero committed suicide on the ninth of June A.D. 68" (*Peter and Jude,* p. 261).

EYEWITNESS OF CHRIST'S TRANSFIGURATION
2 Peter 1:16-19

PETER, JAMES, AND JOHN WERE the only disciples to be given a preview of the Lord's kingdom glory. They were the ones Jesus spoke of when He said, "Truly I say to you, there are some of those who are standing here who shall not taste death until they see the Son of Man coming in His kingdom" (Matthew 16:28). Peter says he was not teaching tales of deception, but in fact he himself had witnessed "the power and coming of our Lord Jesus Christ" and of His majesty (2 Peter 1:16). The Lord's transfiguration, in which the three apostles saw His full glory, took place on a high mountain and is recorded in Matthew 17:1-8. In that event, the heavenly Father bestowed honor and glory upon Christ, and Peter heard Him say, "This is My beloved Son with whom I am well-pleased" (2 Peter 1:17; Matthew 17:5). The Father then added, "Listen to Him!" (Matthew 17:5).

Peter was deeply moved by the transfiguration and said to Jesus, "Lord, it is good for us to be here; if You wish, I will make three tabernacles [tents] here, one for You, and one for Moses, and one for Elijah" (verse 4). The two great Old Testament prophets who were speaking with Christ (verse 3) may well be the two witnesses in Revelation 11. Moses was the great lawgiver, and Elijah the prophet was the herald who would announce the coming Davidic king (Malachi 4:5-6). In this encounter, Christ's "face shone like the sun, and His garments became as white as light" (Matthew 17:2). Peter confirms the fact of this dramatic event by saying, "We ourselves heard this utterance made from heaven when we were with Him on the holy mountain" (2 Peter 1:18).

A SURE PROPHECY
2 Peter 1:20-21

PETER'S TESTIMONY ABOUT the transfiguration (Matthew 17:1-8) made sure "the prophetic word" to which believers should "pay attention as to a lamp shining in a dark place" (2 Peter 1:19). They should continue to do this until Christ's coming, which will be when "the day dawns and the morning star arises in your hearts." Arnold Fruchtenbaum writes,

> Believers walk in the midst of a dark world, and the believer's only light is the light of the Word of God. Now, Peter promises, the day is coming when the full light of God's revelation will shine in your hearts; when believers will see Him as He is; and when the day-star will arise. The *day-star* is Jesus Himself according to Revelation 22:16. The Greek word for *day-star* means "morning star." The timing of this fullness of light is at the Second Coming (*Messianic Jewish Epistles,* pp. 399-400).

Since Peter has been dealing with prophecy, he reminds his readers, "Know this first of all, that no prophecy of Scripture is a matter of one's own interpretation, for no prophecy was ever made by an act of human will, but men moved by the Holy Spirit spoke from God" (2 Peter 1:20-21). The third person of the Trinity, the Holy Spirit, is doing the will of God the Father when the divine revelation is given to the human prophets. Paul adds to this and writes that "all Scripture is inspired by God," or *God-breathed* (2 Timothy 3:16). Though the Holy Spirit uses the experiences and the personalities of the prophets as they consciously write, they record only the message He wants to convey as the authoritative Word from the Lord. The word "moved" (Greek, *phero*) means "to carry along." The prophets were picked up and carried along by the Spirit, and they conveyed only what He gave to them.

THE JUDGMENT OF FALSE PROPHETS
2 Peter 2:1-3

Just as false prophets arose among the children of Israel (Deuteronomy 13), so they will arise in the church (2 Peter 2:1). The Lord told the Jews, "You shall not listen to the words of that prophet or that dreamer of dreams.…you shall follow the Lord your God and fear Him" (Deuteronomy 13:3-4). False teachers will come to the churches and "secretly introduce destructive heresies, even denying the Master who bought them, bringing swift destruction upon themselves" (2 Peter 2:1). "Secretly" is better translated as "smuggle" (Greek, *pareisagein*) as though "unnoticed" (Jude 4). "Heresies" (Greek, *hairesis*) refers to that which is different, and is not orthodox or correct. God will deal with false teachers quickly with "swift destruction," and they will also face the final judgment of the lost (Revelation 20:11-15). In their sins, these false teachers are even denying Christ the Master, who gave His life for them!

Those who follow false teachers often fall into "sensuality" (Greek, *aselgeia,* "excessive licentiousness"), and "because of them the way of the truth will be maligned" (2 Peter 2:2). Their sinfulness destroys the witness of the blessed gospel. False teachers are also motivated by greed and "exploit you with false words." For them, judgment is certain and it has been established long ago, "and their destruction is not asleep" (verse 3). Kelly says, "The verdict has already been pronounced on them, and the doom which will surely overtake them has been set in motion from of old (*ekpalai*)" (*Epistles of Peter,* p. 329).

THE LORD KNOWS HOW TO RESCUE THE GODLY
2 Peter 2:9

God was able to deliver righteous Lot from the evil of Sodom and Gomorrah (verse 7; Genesis 19:15-29). Though Lot had placed himself and his family in harm's way of the terrible sins of that area (2 Peter 2:8), possibly for material gain (Genesis 13:10-11), God still heard him. Lot's "righteous soul [was] tormented day after day with their lawless deeds." For "the Lord knows how to rescue the godly from temptation, and to keep the unrighteous under punishment for the day of judgment" (2 Peter 2:9). The story of Lot shows that there are consequences to bear when the righteous place their lives in the midst of moral decay. The unrighteous may receive swift and immediate condemnation here on earth, but a final and eternal punishment ("the day of judgment") is definitely certain in the future (Revelation 19:11-15).

THE COMING DAY OF GOD
2 Peter 3:1-14

Here, Peter tells believers he wants to stir up their "sincere mind by way of reminder"

A New World Coming
2 Peter 3:1-14

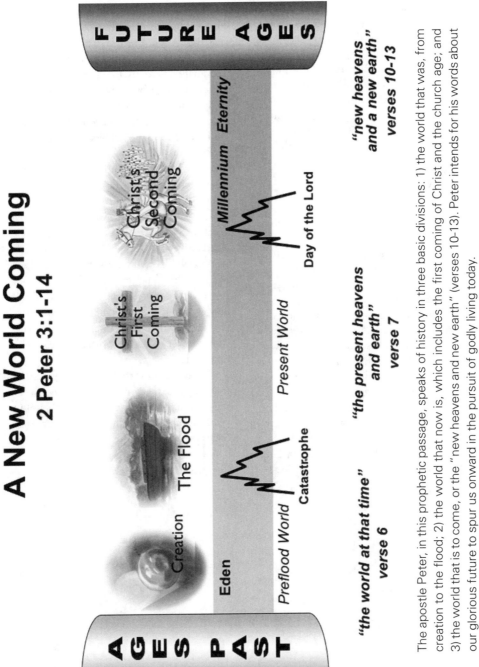

AGES PAST

Creation — The Flood — Christ's First Coming — Christ's Second Coming

Prefaged World — *Present World* — *Millennium* — *Eternity*

Eden — Catastrophe — Day of the Lord

FUTURE AGES

"the world at that time"
verse 6

"the present heavens and earth"
verse 7

"new heavens and a new earth"
verses 10-13

The apostle Peter, in this prophetic passage, speaks of history in three basic divisions: 1) the world that was, from creation to the flood; 2) the world that now is, which includes the first coming of Christ and the church age; and 3) the world that is to come, or the "new heavens and new earth" (verses 10-13). Peter intends for his words about our glorious future to spur us onward in the pursuit of godly living today.

(verse 1). He wants them to "remember the words spoken beforehand by the holy prophets and the commandment of the Lord and Savior spoken by your apostles" (verse 2), and remember that there would be mockers who would be "following after their own lusts" (verse 3), asking, "Where is the promise of His coming?" (verse 4). These unbelievers will doubt the Lord's return and point out that all things seem to going on as usual since the "fathers fell asleep." The doubters forget that God made the heavens and the earth by His word, formed the earth "out of water and by water" (verse 5), and brought on the terrible flood that destroyed the world by water (verse 6). It is this same God who has "reserved for fire" the world and ungodly men "for the day of judgment" (verse 7).

The lost think the world will simply continue as it is. They fail to realize that time is no object with God. With Him "one day is as a thousand years, and a thousand years as one day" (verse 8), meaning He counts time differently than people do. What He has planned will unfold as He wishes. But He is not slow as to His promise, "as some count slowness." He is patient with the world, "not wishing for any to perish but for all to come to repentance" (verse 9). God's desire is for all to be saved, though the Bible makes it clear this will not happen. Nevertheless, God is patient toward the lost.

The "day of the Lord" will come upon men like a thief, "in which the heavens will pass away with a roar and the elements will be destroyed with intense heat and the earth and its works will be burned up" (verse 10). In this context, the Day of the Lord is not the seven-year tribulation, but the final conflagration that ends this present system of the universe. The smallest particles, the elements, will cease to be. Because of this the human race must realize that an end is coming. Believers need to examine their priorities and look at the issue of "holy conduct and godliness" (verse 11).

Believers are to be joyously looking for "the coming of the day of God" (verse 12). By this Peter is referring to that day of destruction that ushers in the "new heavens and a new earth, in which righteousness dwells" (verse 13; see Isaiah 66:17-22; Revelation 21:1). In this renovated universe, "the holy city, new Jerusalem" (verse 2) will descend from heaven, and there will never again be any crying, death, or pain (verse 4). The new Jerusalem is a beautiful city in which the redeemed of the nations will walk (verse 24), with nothing unclean within, with "those whose names are written in the Lamb's book of life" (verse 27).

Again, because these things are certain to take place, the believers should watch for them, being "diligent to be found by Him in peace, spotless and blameless" (2 Peter 3:14). Such awesome promises should excite every believer to walk in purity and in spiritual integrity in this life!

1 JOHN

JOHN WROTE HIS FIRST EPISTLE AROUND A.D. 90–95, and it is one of the last New Testament documents completed. Its compelling theme is the believer's present and continual fellowship with the Lord; those who walk in darkness are not practicing the truth (1:6).

John reminds his readers that he walked with Christ, touched Him, and bore witness to the fact that He is the Savior who imparts eternal life (verses 1-3). John also confirms that Christ is an advocate who helps believers in the Christian experience (2:1).

Two key prophetic passages in the book include 3:2-3 and 4:3. In connection with the rapture John writes, "When He appears, we shall be like Him, because we shall see Him just as He is" (3:2). This hope purifies the believer in his daily walk with Christ (verse 3). John then reminds his readers that there is an Antichrist coming into the world, though his influence is present even now (4:3).

THE WORLD IS PASSING AWAY
1 John 2:16-17

THE WORLD IS DRIVEN BY "the lust of the flesh and the lust of the eyes and the boastful pride of life" (verse 16). "'Flesh' is probably used in the wide, Jewish sense which it bears so commonly in the writings of Paul (such as in Romans 8:3-ff; Galatians 5:19): it signifies all the sinful tendencies of man" (Houlden, *The Johannine Epistles*, p. 74). This way of life is not from the heavenly Father, "but is from the world." This world will not last. It "is passing away" along with its lusts. "But the one who does the will of God lives forever" (verse 17). The Greek word for "does" is the present participle of the verb *poieo*. This is the same Greek word and verb form that appears in verse 29, though translated there as "practice." To do the will of God and to "practice righteousness" (verse 29) is to be born of Him, or "born again" (John 3:7). John is not arguing that doing the will of God is a form of works salvation. Instead, it is a sign of salvation. The lost cannot do God's will, nor can they "practice righteousness." "Doing the will of God expresses the normal conditions and activity of the believer. The will of God is set in contrast to all that is in the world, for the world lies in the Evil One. Again, doing the will of God is set in contrast to the love of the world; there is a double antithesis" (Vine, *The Collective Writings of W.E. Vine*, 3:354).

THE COMING OF THE ANTICHRIST
1 John 2:18

THE BIBLE PREDICTS THAT during the Tribulation, the Antichrist will appear, the one who is "against Christ." He will be the *great pretender* to the messianic throne. There were in John's day many such false antichrists, yet there is still one distinct person who will bear this title in the future (verse 18). The other false messiahs came in the "spirit of the antichrist," and they denied that Jesus comes from God the Father (4:3). Some of these false christs (or supposed "anointed ones") went out from among those in the churches, and they proved that "they all are not of us" (2:19).

The Antichrist has many names and designations. He is called "the prince" (Daniel 9:26), the "one who makes desolate" (verse 27), "the king" who does as he pleases (11:36), "the lawless one" (see 2 Thessalonians 2:3), "the son of destruction" (verse 3), "the deceiver" (2 John 7), and "the beast" (Revelation 13:1). His end is certain. He will be cast into "the lake of fire which burns with brimstone" along with the false prophet and Satan (19:20–20:3,10).

APPEARING LIKE CHRIST AT THE RAPTURE
1 John 2:28–3:3

By ABIDING WITH CHRIST in the Christian walk, the believer will have spiritual and moral confidence "and not shrink away from Him in shame at His coming" (verse 28). John's point is that the child of God will be doing what is right, and not be sinning, when the rapture trumpet sounds (1 Thessalonians 4:16-18). Those who are born again must be practicing righteousness (1 John 2:29). God has bestowed His love on those who are His, and they can be "called children of God" (3:1). When He comes to resurrect the believer, and take up the ones who are still alive, then "we will be like Him, because we will see Him just as He is" (verse 2). The believer will have an eternal new body like Christ's! This "hope" (Greek, *elpis*) has a purifying effect on the child of God. It "purifies" the believer, "just as He is pure" (verse 3). Vine observes that this is not about only a few "who are characterized in this

way in distinction from other believers, it lays down what is a normal characteristic, common to all the children of God.... It is a hope set on Christ, a hope that rests upon Him"(*The Collective Writings of W.E. Vine*, 3:364).

CHRIST, THE PROPITIATION FOR SIN
1 John 4:9-10

BECAUSE GOD LOVES THOSE who would be saved, He sent Christ "to be the propitiation for our sins" (verse 10; 2:2). The Greek word for "propitiation" is *hilasmos.* The idea is that God would be merciful. The word can also describe the mercy seat that was in the inner sanctum of the temple (Hebrews 9:5). The believer has salvation in Christ, who is "a propitiation in His blood through faith" (Romans 3:25). The tax gatherer used the word when he cried, "God be *merciful* to me a sinner" (Luke 18:13). In Hebrews 2:17 the word is translated "reconciliation." The idea of God being merciful to sinners is seen throughout the great chapter on the Suffering Servant, Isaiah 53. The Messiah would bear the iniquities of the sinners and "intercede for the transgressors" (verses 11-12). Lightner says, "*Propitiation* carries the meaning of satisfaction. The work of the Lord Jesus Christ on the cross is a complete satisfaction of the offended righteousness of God. God the Father is satisfied with the finished work of His Son. He paid it all (cf. 2:2)" (*John and Jude*, p. 63).

CONFIDENCE AT THE DAY OF JUDGMENT
1 John 4:17

THE "DAY OF JUDGMENT" mentioned here is the *bema* judgment for Christians, at which their service for the Lord will be evaluated. John wants the love of God "perfected"

(Greek, *teleioo*, perfect passive indicative), which better reads "having been completed, matured, brought to fulfillment." God's love will give confidence when the believer is called to account not in regard to salvation, but in regard to rewards (Romans 14:10-12; 1 Corinthians 3:10-15; 2 Corinthians 5:10-11). This "perfected" love also has a temporal purpose because it casts out fear from the life of the believer (1 John 4:18). Candlish adds,

> What is perfected is love...love which is God's nature, and which comes out in the saving gift of his Son. It is to be perfected as "love with us."...It is God's love so shared by him with us as to constitute a love relationship, a fellowship, between him and us (*1 John*, p. 324).

ASSURANCE OF ETERNAL LIFE
1 John 5:13

THE EPISTLE OF 1 JOHN WAS written to the believer "so that you may know that you have eternal life" (5:13). John wrote to give assurance to the child of God. The Greek text actually reads "because life you are having eternal." John makes sure the believer knows he possesses "life" that will go on forever. The allusion to "life" is reminiscent of the verse in John's Gospel that reads, "In Him was life, and the life was the Light of men" (1:4). And whosoever believes in Him "shall not perish, but have eternal life" (3:16). John clearly understood Jesus' evangelistic mission and the assurance of eternal salvation.

2 JOHN

IN THIS EXTREMELY SHORT EPISTLE (13 VERSES), the apostle John reminds his readers, as he did in 1 John, that the ultimate deceiver is the Antichrist (2 John 7). The ultimate deception is to cast doubt that Christ ever came in the flesh. John raises these warnings to the churches because of the growing influence of gnosticism. Gnosticism said that flesh—human physical skin—was sinful in itself; therefore, Christ did not come to earth in flesh. He was but an apparition, a phantom or ghostlike being. John refuted that false teaching in 1 John 1:1-3.

THE LIES OF THE ANTICHRIST
2 John 7-8

THE ANTICHRIST WILL COME at the start of the seven-year Tribulation. But many "deceivers" (Greek, *planos*) had already begun their activity against Christ in the world in John's day (verse 7; 1 John 2:26). The Greek word *planos* means "to promote error, delude, mislead, lead astray." The word is used to describe seducing spirits who in this present dispensation promote false doctrine (1 Timothy 4:1). One sign of a deceiver is that he does not acknowledge Jesus Christ as having come in flesh. This is true of the gnostic cults that said that Jesus was just an apparition, a ghost, a mystical spiritual being. This deception and all lies originate with the Antichrist.

John instructs believers to "watch yourselves, that you do not lose what we have accomplished" (2 John 8). John is speaking about the "full reward" given to those who hold the line and do not waver when tempted. He is not speaking of the believer losing salvation; many Christians can be fooled and go "too far" and not remain steadfast in the teaching of Christ (verse 9).

3 JOHN

JOHN'S THIRD LETTER IS VERY PERSONAL IN NATURE. It focuses on these people: Gaius, Diotrephes, and Demetrius. While it contains no prophetic or eschatological material, it reveals much about the life of the early church and the experiences of the first generation of Christians. John writes to Gaius, criticizes Diotrephes, and commends Demetrius. As in all John's letters, there is a strong emphasis on knowing, believing, and living the truth. He writes as an elder statesman in the faith as he commends us all to "work in the truth" (verse 3).

JUDE

MOST BELIEVE THAT, LIKE THE AUTHOR JAMES, Jude was a half-brother of Christ. His epistle was written late—between A.D. 70 and 80. Jude was at war with false prophets in the church. He urged his readers to "contend earnestly for the faith which was once for all delivered to the saints" (verse 3). He prophesied the doom of lying prophets and predicted that God will reserve His holy angels to "execute judgment upon all" ungodly sinners (verse 15). With the language of Daniel 7:14, Jude looks forward to the coming glory of Christ: "To the only God and Savior, through Jesus our Lord, be glory, majesty, dominion and authority, before all time and now and forever" (verse 25).

COMING APOSTASY
Jude 4

IN THE EARLY CHURCH ERA, deceivers were infiltrating the churches and promoting immorality and doctrinal heresy. Generally they came in with stealth and "crept in unnoticed." These deceivers were never saved and "were long beforehand marked out for this condemnation." They were ungodly "persons who turn the grace of our God into licentiousness and deny our only Master and Lord, Jesus Christ" (Jude 4). They were bought by Christ and yet they denied Him (2 Peter 2:1). Because of them "the truth will be maligned" (verse 2). Their judgment is certain and they will stand before the Great White Throne Judgment and then be "thrown into the lake of fire" (Revelation 20:11-15). Kelly states it is more than likely that "these people had gnostic leanings, for with its distinction between the Supreme God and the Demiurge, or creator-God, and its

disparagement of [physical] matter Gnosticism offered a standing threat to strict monotheism and the reality of the incarnation" of Christ (*Epistles of Peter and of Jude*, p. 253).

THE FUTURE JUDGMENT OF THE FALLEN ANGELS
Jude 6-7

MANY OF THE ANGELS "who did not keep their own domain, but abandoned their proper abode" God has now confined "in eternal bonds under darkness for the judgment of the great day" (verse 6). Many believe the angels who fell with Satan were the "stars of God" over which he wished to rule (Isaiah 14:13). Christ sent His disciples out to spread the gospel. They reported to Him that "even the demons are subject to us in Your name" (Luke 10:17). Jesus seems to respond to their comment when He said, "I was watching Satan fall from heaven like lightning" (verse 18). As the eternal second person of the Godhead, Jesus would have witnessed the casting of Satan and the evil angels from the presence of God in glory.

When will judgment day take place for the fallen angels? More than likely it will occur when Satan is cast into the lake of fire (Revelation 20:10). The fallen angels, the demons, know this day is coming. On one occasion they told Jesus, "What business do we have with each other, Son of God? Have You come here to torment us before the time?" (Matthew 8:29). Manton believes the saints of the Lord will witness the judgment of the fallen angels. Manton writes,

> There is a time coming when the wrath of God shall be increased upon [the demons], and this time is the day of judgment, the great day of the Lord, when they shall be brought forth before the tribunal of Christ and his saints…. This is a day that will work upon their envy, thwart their pride, to see the glory of Christ, and of the good angels and the saints (*Jude,* pp. 217-18).

THE FUTURE JUDGMENT OF THE LOST
Jude 11-15

FALSE TEACHERS, LYING PROPHETS, and those who preach heresy are "doubly dead, uprooted" (verses 11-12). They are like "wandering stars, for whom the black darkness has been reserved forever" (verse 13). Christ often spoke of the lost as cast into "outer darkness" (Matthew 8:12; 22:13; 25:30). At the end of the terrible seven-year Tribulation the Lord will come (Jude 14) "to execute judgment upon all, and to convict all the ungodly of all their ungodly deeds which they have done in an ungodly way, and of all the harsh things which ungodly sinners have spoke against

Him" (verse 15). A final judgment is certain (Revelation 20:11-15).

In verses 9-10, Jude quotes the apocryphal books of 1 Enoch and the Testament of Moses, and possibly the writing called the Assumption of Moses. Does Jude consider these works as inspired prophecies on the same level as Scripture? It is highly doubtful, though the quotes themselves (and not the whole books) may certainly reflect ancient traditions or thoughts that are accurate. By the same token, Paul quotes pagan poets to prove his points in Acts 17:28 and 1 Corinthians 15:33.

APOSTASY IN THE LAST TIME
Jude 17-19,22-23

AT THE END OF THE CHURCH AGE, in the "last time," there "will be mockers, following after their own ungodly lusts" (verse 18). They are the lost, the "worldly-minded, devoid of the Spirit" (verse 19). They will enter among believers and will speak and teach lies (verse 18). Believers should be aware of this and build themselves up in their "most holy faith, praying in the Holy Spirit" (verse 20).

Even though bad things will come upon the church in the last days, believers are to be "waiting anxiously for the mercy of our Lord Jesus Christ to eternal life" (verse 21). While waiting for deliverance, the rapture of the church, believers are to have mercy "on some, who are doubting" (verse 22), and work to "save others, snatching them out of the fire" (verse 23). Believers are to share the gospel with all who will listen.

PRESENTATION OF THE SAVED BEFORE THE LORD IN GLORY
Jude 24-25

SOME BELIEVE THESE VERSES are about Christians standing in the presence of Christ at death, or seeing Christ at the time of the rapture of the church. But another possibility is that all believers will join the Lord when He comes to reign on earth in the millennial kingdom. Christ will preserve all those who belong to Him, keep them from stumbling, and welcome them into "the presence of His glory blameless with great joy" (verse 24).

That these verses refer to Christ's *earthly* Davidic reign seems clear from Jude's anthem in verse 25. To "Jesus Christ our Lord, be glory, majesty, dominion and authority, before all time and now and forever." Part of this language comes from the great messianic language in Daniel 7. The Messiah is given from "the Ancient of Days" (the God of heaven), "dominion, glory and a kingdom, that all the peoples, nations and men of every language might serve Him. His dominion is an everlasting dominion which will not pass away; and His kingdom is one which will not be destroyed" (7:13-14). While Christ has been granted all rule and authority from His Father in heaven, He is not yet exercising all sovereignty. That will take place when He returns to earth to reign (see Hebrews 2:6-10).

THE
REVELATION

REVELATION

The book of Revelation is fascinating—it captivates our attention, stirs our imagination, and points to our glorious future destiny. In this dynamic vision of the end of the world we are swept up into the unveiling of the panorama of the future, which the apostle John unfolds for us. This final book of the biblical record is the capstone of divine revelation: In a series of seven visions and numerous symbolic word pictures, the climax of human history is foretold in lucid detail.

The word "Revelation" (1:1) translates the Greek word *apokalypsis,* which means "to reveal" or "unveil." This is not the first time it appears in the New Testament, for it occurs 18 times, and appears, for example, in Luke 2:32, Galatians 1:12, 2 Thessalonians 1:7, and 1 Peter 1:7. The word means "to show" or "expose to view" as one would unveil a painting. While much of the book is written in symbolic language, we must remember that these are symbols of realities that cannot be spiritualized and dismissed as nonliteral events.

Much of the debate over Revelation has to do with how to interpret the book. Many scholars want to deny the wrath and terror described so vividly in a literal, future Tribulation. One school of thought places Revelation in the genre of apocalyptic literature, meaning that it is symbolic prophecy that is mysterious and beyond full comprehension. Apocalyptic literature has been often defined as highly figurative, allegorical literary drama and apocalyptic hyperbole.

Looking more carefully at Revelation through the lens of normal interpretation, the book can be seen as describing literal and historical events, many of which were predicted in the Old Testament. The illustrations and vivid descriptions in the book do not take away from its literalness. In fact, it seems clear that in his visions John the apostle saw many literal things he could not describe. He had been transported to heaven in his visions and led by the Holy Spirit into the distant future day when the events of the book will come to pass. Throughout the book, John uses two Greek particles (*hos* and *homoios*) a total of about 100 times. They are synonyms in meaning and are translated "it seems to be, as, like as, like" or "something like." These are words of comparison that show John was struggling to describe the indescribable things he had never seen before.

New Testament scholar Bruce Metzger reminds us, "In order to become oriented to the book of Revelation one must take seriously what the author says happened. John tells us that he had a series of visions. He says that he 'heard' certain words and 'saw' certain visions.... Such accounts combine cognitive insight with emotional response. They invite the reader or listener to enter into the experience being recounted and to participate in it, triggering mental images of that which is described" (*Breaking the Code,* pp. 12-13).

This exciting sense of personal participation raises one of the major challenges encountered in studying the Apocalypse: There is always a great temptation to read about the future through the eyes of the present. Students of Revelation have often speculated on how its predictions will be fulfilled as though the end would come in their lifetime. Therefore, caution must be exercised that we let the book speak for itself, and that we not attempt to interpret it through the lens of today's events.

We must also remember that these are prophecies of real events. Reading the Apocalypse is like watching a movie of future events. Therefore, many elements in the book can be understood only by *literal interpretation.* John was really on the island of Patmos when he had this vision. The risen Christ literally appeared to him. The seven churches actually existed in Asia Minor. The predicted future judgments are real and involve real armies, weapons, and mass destruction. Earthquakes are earthquakes. Nations are nations. Jews are Jews. Gentiles are Gentiles. Heaven is real. So is the lake of fire!

Futurists believe the events described in Revelation will be fulfilled literally at some future time. The majority of the prophecies in the book describe what is known as the Tribulation period, or Daniel's seventieth week (a seven-year period of future judgment—Daniel 9:24-27). Only the futurist view provides any reasonable coherence with what is described in the book and the fulfillment of its prophetic message. After Revelation 3, the book describes future events involving worldwide catastrophes, the rise of a dominant world ruler, and the literal return of Christ to establish a kingdom on earth.

It is a compelling fact that the word *church* is not mentioned beyond chapter 3. There is nothing that would describe a congregation or Christian assembly in chapters 4–18. There is no description of the body of Christ, nor do we read phrases such as "in Christ," "in Jesus," and so on. The only conclusion that makes sense about the church's absence in chapters 4–18 is that it has been transported heavenward by the rapture (1 Thessalonians 4:13-18). The prominent peoples remaining on earth during this time are the unsaved Gentiles and the 144,000 witnessing Jews. While many thousands will turn to Christ during this period, many will also be martyred. Those who are saved and survive will be terribly persecuted until Christ returns.

As the events of the Tribulation mentioned in the book of Revelation draw closer, we will understand better what is being described in these prophetic chapters. Custer remarks,

The Book of Revelation is the capstone of the Word of God. It gathers up the truths of all the rest of Scripture and organizes them into the plan of God for the ages. It shows us the divine purpose in permitting good and evil to wage war against one another. God is the holy and righteous King, who will defeat all His foes and will bring His redeemed people into His eternal kingdom of peace and glory.... When He has finished His mighty work, all the universe will know that He has done all things well (*Patmos to Paradise,* p. ix).

THE BOOK OF REVELATION AS PROPHECY
Revelation 1:3

The book of Revelation is not only the closing portion of Scripture, but its message is a summary of the entire Word of God. Because of this, "blessed" (Greek, *makarios*) is the person who reads or hears these words and takes heed to live by them. Prophecy should act as a cleansing element in the life of the believer. John writes this in relation to the rapture of the church: "We know that, when He appears, we will be like Him, because we will see Him just as He is. And everyone who has this hope fixed on Him purifies himself, just as He is pure" (1 John 3:2-3).

When John says "the time is near" (Revelation 1:3), he is identifying what is described in the book as the last great epochs of history that have been prophesied by the Lord. "Time" (Greek, *kairos*) is not simply about chronology but about the "seasons, epochs, significant periods" of events that mark earth's history. Henry Morris states:

> The exhortation to recognize the *imminence* of the "time" is explicitly repeated at the end of the book (22:10). If it was urgent for Christians in John's time to study this book of prophecy, how much more urgent it is for those of us who are 1900 years closer to the time when

it will all be actually taking place (*The Revelation Record,* p. 36).

The heart of the book of Revelation describes the Tribulation period on earth. "Is near" (Greek, *engys*) is related to the Greek word *egnos,* which can be translated "it is certain, guaranteed, sure to take place." These things are going to happen! The believer who lives by God's divine time line is blessed and understands that what we now know is not all there is. There is coming an end to the sinful story of the human race. And that story is described in Revelation, which concludes with the advent of a new heaven and a new earth. Sin will be eradicated and eternal blessings will follow for those who are saved in Christ.

JESUS CHRIST: RULER OF THE KINGS OF THE EARTH
Revelation 1:5,7

These two verses testify to the first and the second comings of the Lord Jesus. He is the "faithful witness" of God's plan of redemption (verse 5). Scott points out that "the whole life of our Lord from the manger to the Cross is embraced in this comprehensive title. The epithet 'the faithful' is in marked contrast to all preceding witnesses for God" (*Exposition of the Revelation,* p. 25). The expression "the ruler of the kings of the earth" is an allusion to Psalm 89:35-37, which speaks of the establishment of the throne of David in terms of the moon, which is a faithful witness in the sky. It is to this end that the book of Revelation is headed.

The Lord Jesus will someday reign and rule in Jerusalem over the people of Israel and worldwide over the nations of earth. Christ also guarantees resurrection from the dead and new life for those who trust Him. He is the "firstborn" (Greek, *prototokos*), the preeminent one who makes possible the resurrected eternal life. Christ is the promised seed who will sit on David's throne as "the firstborn from the dead [ones]" (Revelation 1:5; cf. Acts 2:29-32). Though He is presently the promised King, He is *not yet* reigning in the earthly historical sense over "the kings of the earth." Someday He will be "the ruler" before whom all sovereigns and peoples will bow (see Revelation 19:11-16). He is also the One who "loves us" and releases us from our sins "by His blood."

Christ's second coming is brought into focus in 1:7. His coming "with the clouds" will be seen by every eye and is a dominant picture in Scripture. This prophecy is first mentioned to the Jews in Zechariah 12:10-14. The Scriptures point out that they are those "who pierced Him." The Lord repeats this prophecy of His coming in the clouds before His disciples (Matthew 24:30) and at His trial before Caiaphas and the Jewish Sanhedrin (26:64). Both the Jews and "all the tribes of the earth will mourn over Him" when He returns (Revelation 1:7). This glorious but tragic scene is mentioned again in Luke 23:28 and John 19:37.

Because Christ's prophesied return is such an important doctrine in Scripture, particularly in the book of Revelation, John closes Revelation 1:7 with the benediction, "So it is to be. Amen" (NKJV).

INTRODUCTION TO THE SEVEN CHURCHES
Revelation 1:9-20

JOHN IDENTIFIES HIMSELF AS a fellow partaker of the suffering being experienced by all believers for the sake of the kingdom. He had been exiled to the island of Patmos by the Roman emperor Domitian (A.D. 81–96) "because of the word of God and the testimony of Jesus" (verse 9). John's exile can be clearly dated to the closing years of Domitian's reign (see Hitchcock, *Date of Revelation*). Patmos sits in the Aegean Sea, about 40 miles from Ephesus. John was given this last great prophetic vision while "in the Spirit on the Lord's day" (verse 10). The "Lord's day" refers to Sunday (the resurrection day). It could also be translated "a lordy kind of a day," meaning a day centered on the Lord, when the Spirit would give John a special message, the Lord's message to him.

The apostle is told to write "what you see" and send it to the *seven churches* that were in the province of Asia—fairly close to the Aegean coast and near Patmos (verse 11). The vision is audible in that John hears "a loud voice" (verse 10). Later we read of a voice that says, "Come up here, and I will show you what must take place after these things" (4:1), or the things that follow the age of the churches. So this vision was not only heard, but seen.

John then sees "seven golden lampstands" (1:12) with one in the middle like "a son of man" clothed in royal garments (see verse 13), a reference to Christ as seen in Daniel 7:13-14. John is given a dramatic presentation of Christ in glory reflecting the splendid attributes of authority and divinity (verses 14-16). The exalted Lord Jesus speaks to him: "I am the first and the last, and the living One; and I was dead, and behold, I am alive forevermore, and I have the keys of death and of Hades" (verses 17-18).

The command is then given for John to record "the things which you have seen, and the things which are, and the things which will take place after these things" (verse 19). The "things which you have seen" refer to the glorified Lord Jesus in heaven (verses 12-18); "the things which are" have to do with the seven churches in chapters 2–3; and "after these things" refers to the future, or Revelation chapters 4–22.

The "seven golden lampstands" (1:12) are the seven churches to which John will write, and the "seven stars" (1:16) are the angels (or messengers) of these churches. Before John can write about the future, he must address the current problems within the seven churches.

There is some difference of opinion as to the identity of the "overcomers" (Greek, *nikao,* "to be victorious") mentioned at the end of the letters to the seven churches. Some assume they are Christians who have triumphed over sin. But it is possible John is addressing members of the congregations who need to become victorious over the tug of the world and remain faithful to Christ the Savior. This fits with what the apostle says in 1 John 5:4-5: "For whatever is born of God overcomes the world; and this is the victory that has overcome the world—our faith. Who is the one who overcomes the world, but he who believes that Jesus is the Son of God?"

MESSAGE TO EPHESUS
Revelation 2:1-7

Though John the apostle is the human author of these short letters, they are really from Christ Himself, inspired by the Holy Spirit. They are addressed to "the angel" of each church. Some believe this means each church had a specific guardian angel, but more likely the reference is to the messenger or "reader" in each congregation. The reader was probably the courier, the deliverer of this book from John, and the "explainer" of what was written.

Ephesus was a large city on the west coast of Asia Minor with a population of 250,000. It was the center of worship for the goddess Artemis (or Diana) with a temple that had 127 columns. The local coins were inscribed "Diana of Ephesus." Paul faced opposition from the worshippers of this goddess in Acts 19:21-41. Despite nearly losing their lives here, Paul's team planted the church at Ephesus in about A.D. 52. Tradition says that John lived in

the city toward the end of his life and had even been the pastor of the congregation.

Besides enduring the raw paganism of the city, "the Ephesian Christians had to confront itinerant missionaries who entered the church and brazenly called themselves apostles. But the followers of Christ tested them and found them to be counterfeit" (Kistemaker, *Revelation,* p. 113). Along with such evil and insidious attacks, the Christians suffered persecution and other problems within their church fellowship.

While this congregation had endured persecution for Christ's sake (2:3), they had become cold to Him, having "left [their] first love" (verse 4). Christ also hated the deeds of the Nicolaitans (verse 6). This was probably a lawless and licentious religious cult, an early pagan form of gnosticism that disappeared in a very short time. If the Ephesian Christians did not repent, Christ would come and remove their lampstand, or the light of their witness in a dark and evil culture. It is possible that the church did repent to some degree, for Ephesus continued to play a prominent role in the history of the early church. A long line of bishops in the Eastern church served there. In A.D. 431 the Council of Ephesus officially condemned the Nestorian heresy, which taught that Jesus Christ existed as two separate persons, one divine and one human.

The Spirit of God says those who overcome the sins they are tempted by will be granted "to eat of the tree of life which is in the Paradise of God" (verse 7). The postscript here is addressed to all the churches, which means the messages were applicable to all the churches, not just the one the letter was directed to.

MESSAGE TO SMYRNA
Revelation 2:8-11

The church at Smyrna had a great natural harbor in western Asia Minor. The city was given the privilege of building a temple dedicated to Emperor Tiberias in 23 B.C. because of

Smyrna's years of faithfulness to Rome. Thus the city was a center for the cult of emperor worship. The assembly of Christians in this city suffered from persecution and poverty, and yet they were spiritually rich (2:9). The Jews were so hateful toward the Christians that their synagogue was called "a synagogue of Satan." More persecution would follow, with some Christians being cast into prison and tested. In A.D. 156, John's disciple, Polycarp, was burned at the stake in Smyrna for refusing to worship the emperor. By being faithful unto death, these Christians were promised "the crown of life" for their fortitude (verse 10), and they would not be harmed by the second death (verse 11). Peter wrote, "When the Chief Shepherd appears, you will receive the unfading crown of glory" (1 Peter 5:4). Some believe this is the same as the crown of life. These crowns could be given for service to the Lord done in this lifetime, or they could represent the actual giving of eternal life (on the crown of life, see also Revelation 3:11).

MESSAGE TO PERGAMUM
Revelation 2:12-17

This city was the chief city of Mysia near the Caicus River in northwest Asia Minor. The city became a head of the region after Attalus I (241–197 B.C.) defeated the Gauls (Galatians), and it stood as a symbol of Greek superiority over the barbarians. The city had a massive library of 200,000 volumes. The Christians abhorred the local cult of Aesculapius (Asclepius), whose symbol was the serpent, which was called the god of Pergamum. This may be why the Lord called the city "Satan's throne" (verse 13). It was also the headquarters of the Roman military presence in Asia Minor.

Some in the church held to the "teaching of Balaam" (verse 14). The allusion goes back to Numbers 22–24, where the king of Moab, Balak, tried to get the false prophet Balaam to curse Israel. The people of Israel had been tempted to commit sexual immorality, inter-

marry with the heathen, and compromise in the matter of idolatrous worship, and the same temptations were seducing the church in Pergamum. The people of Pergamum were being attracted also to the gnostic cult of the Nicolaitans (Revelation 2:15).

Unless the people repented, Christ would come and make war against this church (verse 16). The overcomers were promised they would receive "the hidden manna" and "a white stone, and a new name written on the stone" (verse 17). When Israel was in the wilderness, manna was a miracle food the people gathered each morning during their desert travels (Exodus 16:33-34). The manna here in Revelation would be the spiritual feeding of the believers in Pergamum in contrast to the pagan banquet meals of the general population. There is much debate about the "white stone." It probably refers to the Urim on the high priest's vestment in Exodus 28:30. It could also refer to a ticket of admission, and in this case, an admission to the future heavenly feast. Another view relates it to elections in which white stones were used as ballots. The white stone is clearly meant to signal a blessing for spiritual endurance and fortitude.

MESSAGE TO THYATIRA
Revelation 2:18-29

The city of Thyatira was a province of Lydia in western Asia Minor on the road from Pergamum to Sardis. Though never a large city, Thyatira was a busy manufacturing and commercial center during New Testament times. Many unions and guilds thrived here. Membership meant practicing superstitious worship, feasts in which union members ate food sacrificed to pagan gods, and sexual immorality.

The woman "Jezebel" beguiled many Christians at Thyatira to conform to the paganism and sexual immorality that were rampant all around them (1:11; 2:18-29). Jezebel may have been an actual woman serving as a pagan witch. More likely the name is a comparative reference used by John to speak of someone with the kind of evil influence King Ahab's wife Jezebel exhibited in 1 Kings 18–21. She led Israel into harlotries and evil practices and eventually was trampled by horses (2 Kings 9:33) and eaten by scavenger dogs (1 Kings 21:23). Here in Revelation, "Jezebel" represents a false prophetess of some kind.

Verse 19 is important because the Lord compliments the church for its "love and faith and service and perseverance." Unlike Ephesus, Thyatira "had not grown slack in love. Love had remained active and diligent so that the last works were not, indeed, lesser but more numerous than the first. The Lord here bestows high praise and full credit for all that he with his all-seeing eyes beheld in the church of Thyatira" (Lenski, *Revelation*, p. 114).

The Lord then prophesies that this "Jezebel" would be cast on a bed of sickness (Revelation 2:22) and that her children, meaning those who followed her, would be slain with pestilence so that the congregation will know that God "searches the minds and hearts" and will recompense the people for their deeds (verse 23). Christ tells this church to hold fast to the truth "until I come" (verse 25). The promise is that they will reign with Him in the kingdom and carry out His "authority over the nations" (verse 26). Verse 26 tells the church that it will join Christ in carrying out His work in the millennial reign. The faithful believer will also be given "the morning star" (verse 28). The morning star shines the brightest in the early dawn, and Peter used this expression to assure that God's promises about the future *will* come to pass. "So we have the prophetic word made more sure, to which you do well to pay attention as to a lamp shining in a dark place, until the day dawns and the morning star arises in your hearts" (2 Peter 1:19). In Revelation 2:28 the morning star is Jesus Christ Himself. Possibly the idea is that He will grant assurance to believers that all is well and that the end of pain and sin is near.

MESSAGE TO SARDIS
Revelation 3:1-6

SARDIS WAS THE CAPITAL CITY of Lydia, an Asian province in western Asia Minor situated on the east bank of the Pactolus River about 50 miles east of Smyrna. It had once been the capital of the ancient Lydian Empire, but it was passed successively to the Persians, the Greeks, and finally the Romans. It became an important Christian city, but in time the church was evidently affected by the complacency of the city itself and its reliance on its past glory. By the end of the first century A.D., Sardis was already viewed as a dying city with a dying church.

John wrote to the assembly that "you have a name that you are alive, but you are dead" (3:1). The church was like "whitewashed tombs which on the outside appear beautiful, but inside they are full of dead men's bones" (Matthew 23:27). The apostle urges the people to wake up "and strengthen the things that remain, which were about to die" (Revelation 3:2). They were to repent or Christ "will come like a thief, and you will not know at what hour I will come upon you" (verse 3). Some in the congregation had not "soiled their garments" and will be rewarded to walk with Christ "in white, for they are worthy" (verse 4).

Because some had not dirtied themselves with sin, they were "worthy" (Greek, *axios*) and had shown themselves to be spiritually responsible in their walk as followers of the Lamb; or, they possessed character that was fitting for heaven. There may have been many "professors" among the congregation who were not "possessors" of Christ as their Savior. Jesus then promises that the overcomers will be clothed in white garments (not soiled clothes) and their names will not be erased from the book of life. They will be confessed someday in glory before God the Father (verse 5). To "not erase" is understood as the literary figure of speech called *litotes,* in which an affirmative is expressed by the negative of a contrary statement. Coming by way of a denial of the opposite, "this is an understatement to express emphatically the assurance that the overcomer's name will be retained in the book of life" (Thomas, *Revelation 1–7*, p. 261).

MESSAGE TO PHILADELPHIA
Revelation 3:7-13

LIKE SARDIS, PHILADELPHIA (meaning "brotherly love") was a city and province of Lydia. It was about 28 miles southeast of Sardis. It was founded by Attalus II (Philadelphus), who reigned as king of Pergamum from 159 to 138 B.C. The city was a center for the wine industry, and its chief deity was Dionysus, who in Greek mythology is the god of wine (the Roman Bacchus). The church here is described as a faithful church that stood at the gateway of a great opportunity (3:7-13). The "open door" meant access to God and service to Him (3:8). Thus, Philadelphia, the ideal church, is often described as the "church of the open door," in contrast to the "closed door" at Laodicea. Satan was working through the Jewish synagogue in the city to fight against the truth, but someday the Jews would bow before the believers (verse 9). It is not certain if that prophecy happened within the time of the ancient church, or if this is a broad description of when the Jews in the future will acknowledge the truth about their Lord, Jesus Christ.

Because this church "kept the word of My perseverance," Christ will keep them from the hour of testing that will fall on the "whole world, to test those who dwell on the earth" (verse 10). When John says the testing "is about to come" he uses the Greek word *mello,* which carries the thought "it is inevitable, with certainty." It serves to express in general a settled futurity that will absolutely come about. Some scholars believe this is referring to the period of Roman persecution against the church that would begin about this time and continue for hundreds of years. But because these short letters are addressed to all the churches, the messages could be applicable even to the end

of the church age. Thus the "test" could be a reference to the far-distant Tribulation, or the Day of the Lord (1 Thessalonians 5:1-5; 2 Thessalonians 2:1-12), at which time believers will be kept from (Greek, *ek,* "out from" as in "exit") this event through the rapture (1 Thessalonians 4:13-18).

Christ promises to come "quickly" (Greek, *tachu*), meaning that when He comes, He will do so with swiftness, all at once, with rapidity, at a rapid rate, and without a warning (at any moment). He will give a reward, a crown to those who "hold fast" in their conviction and their walk (Revelation 3:11). This speedy arrival will include the rapture of the church, which happens in the blink of an eye (1 Corinthians 15:52) and with a shout and the voice of the archangel (1 Thessalonians 4:16).

The overcomer will also reign with Christ in the millennial kingdom. The Lord Jesus says the overcomer will be called (metaphorically) "a pillar in the temple of My God" (Revelation 3:12). He will have a special name written upon him, "the name of My God, and the name of the city of My God, the new Jerusalem," which in the future will "come down out of heaven from My God" (verse 12). These believers will be especially honored both in the kingdom reign of Christ and in the eternal new Jerusalem. They will be forever marked for their faithfulness under great earthly persecution and stress. "Further, the promise is given, 'He shall go no more out.' This seems to mean that they will no longer be exposed to the temptations and trials of this present life and will have their permanent residence in the very presence of God" (Walvoord, *Revelation,* p. 89).

MESSAGE TO LAODICEA
Revelation 3:14-22

LAODICEA WAS A CITY IN the fertile Lycus Valley in the province of Phrygia. It was about 40 miles east of Ephesus and some ten miles west of Colossae. It was a prosperous city founded by the Grecian Seleucid family around 261–247 B.C. The city was completely destroyed by an earthquake in A.D. 65, and was later rebuilt and served as a prosperous retirement center for wealthy Romans.

Christ presents Himself to this congregation as "the Amen, the faithful and true Witness, the Beginning of the creation of God" (verse 14). The word "amen" means "truly," or the fact that something is firmly established and certain. Jesus is the witness for God and His truth. He is the "beginning" (Greek, *arche*), a higher order than anything God has created. This does not mean that the Son of God was created, for He has always existed. Rather, it means that as the God-Man come in human flesh, He is the ultimate Being of all creation.

The Laodicean church was lukewarm, neither hot nor cold (verse 15). Therefore, it was useless for the Lord's service. The "mild" testimony the church had for the truth would be rejected by Christ (verse 16). In relation to the wealth of the city, the people also considered themselves as wealthy, though they were poor spiritually (verse 17). Christ urged them to draw from Him true spiritual riches and to clothe themselves in "white garments" that reflected true righteousness and repentance (verses 18-19).

Verse 20 records the well-known words of Christ, "Behold, I stand at the door and knock; if anyone hears My voice and opens the door, I will come in to him, and will dine with him, and he with Me." Is this an invitation for those who are lost to turn to Christ for salvation, or is this an appeal for wayward believers to restore their relationship with Christ? Either way, Christ is pictured as being locked outside and knocking on the door of the church to seek admission. The words seem to be potentially applicable to either situation. If Jesus was referring to redemption, the words form "the simplest explanation of the plan of salvation encompassed in so brief a statement within the [confines] of God's Word" (Tim LaHaye, *Revelation Unveiled*, p. 65). The Lord Jesus does not force Himself upon believers. He does not "employ force to find admission to the heart.

If admitted, he comes and dwells with us; if rejected, he turns quietly away—perhaps to return and knock again, perhaps never to come back" (Barnes, *Revelation*, p. 103).

The Lord promises fellowship to those who open the door. And to the overcomer, He promises the right to sit with Him on His millennial throne, just as He "sat down with My Father on His throne" (verse 21). At His ascension Christ entered the heavenly throne room and was told by God the Father, "Sit at My right hand, until I make Your enemies a footstool for Your feet" (Psalm 110:1). The Lord will someday cause the scepter of His Son, the Messiah, to go forth from Zion, by which He will "rule in the midst of [His] enemies" (verse 2). The promise to believers here is that they will join Him in the administration of that glorious kingdom rule.

THINGS THAT MUST TAKE PLACE
Revelation 4:1-3

THESE THREE VERSES FORM the introduction to the rest of the book of Revelation. They come at the end of "the things which are" (1:19)—that is, the dramatic events, both blessed and destructive, taking place in the seven churches in Asia Minor. Again, it must be remembered that what is said to these churches is applicable "to the churches" everywhere in a general sense. All congregations have many of the spiritual blessings and foibles described in these letters, which is confirmed by the fact each individual letter is addressed to the "churches" collectively.

Now the spotlight is focused on "a door standing open in heaven" (4:1), where a commanding voice like a trumpet declares to John, "Come up here, and I will show you what must take place after these things." The language implies that what John sees and hears next takes place after the dispensation of the church has ended. There are no references to the church, or the "saints in Christ," from this point onward, implying that the church has been lifted from the earth. Only a pretribulational rapture seems to explain the *absence* of any reference to the church.

John "was in the Spirit" when he saw "a throne standing in heaven, and One sitting on the throne" (verse 2). Before Christ returns to earth to reign in the millennial kingdom, He sits with His Father on the heavenly throne (3:21; Psalm 110:1-2). Here in chapter 4 the emphasis seems to be that the heavenly Father is in view because Christ will appear separately as the Lamb of God. The splendor of the one reigning (Revelation 4:3) seems to clearly refer to God the Father as presented in the Old Testament (1 Kings 22:19; Isaiah 6:1; Ezekiel 1:26; Daniel 7:9).

PROPHECY OF THE CHURCH IN HEAVEN
Revelation 4:4-11

THE GLORIOUS VISION in these verses gives a sense of the majesty and holiness of the heavenly court. The 24 seated elders who are arrayed in white garments and wear golden crowns (verse 4) represent the raptured church, the body of Christ in heaven. Two other views have been suggested. Some say the elders represent the saints of all ages, and others say they are priestly heavenly judges—the "court that sat" before the Ancient of Days in glory (cf. 1 Chronicles 24:7-19; Daniel 7:10,26). The word "court" in Aramaic is *de'nah,* referring to those who adjudicate or pass judgment. This heavenly body gives witness to the actions of God in His providential decisions, and some have suggested the elders here in Revelation are the same body.

From the throne come awesome displays of lightning and thunder (Revelation 4:5). Judgment is about to be passed on events taking place on earth. And there are seven lamps "before the throne, which are the seven Spirits of God" (cf. 1:4). The Spirit is represented by *seven manifestations,* as seen when it was prophesied that He would come upon the "branch,"

Israel's Messiah (Isaiah 11:1-2). In Isaiah 11, the Spirit is said to manifest the Lord, and also wisdom, understanding, counsel, strength, knowledge, and the fear of the Lord.

Before the throne of God there is pristine purity, which is illustrated by the "sea of glass like crystal." Around the throne are four angelic *living* creatures who are extremely intelligent, with "eyes in front and behind" (Revelation 4:6). The four creatures are "like" (in comparison) a lion, a calf, a flying eagle, and one with a face like that of a man (verse 7). The lion pictures power and majesty, the calf illustrates docility, the creature with the face of a man represents intelligence, and the eagle shows swiftness and decision. To some scholars these qualities are representative of the characteristics of God and Christ. Walvoord writes,

> Taken in general, the four living creatures are representative of God; they are, as in the case of the seven lamps, a physical embodiment of that which would be otherwise invisible to the natural eye. To John the scene was unmistakably one of majestic revelation. An alternative explanation is that the four living creatures are angels whose function it is to bring honor and glory to God.

These living creatures move swiftly, "having six wings," and show supernatural intelligence, being full of eyes "around and within." "Day and night" they do not cease to praise God, saying, "Holy, holy, holy, is the Lord God, the Almighty, who was and who is and who is to come" (verse 8). The prophet Isaiah (6:3) refers to these angelic creatures as seraphim ("burning ones"). They appear to be *angelic incendiaries* ablaze with the glory of God. God is the most holy One who exists, and He is eternal in that He existed continually in the past, He exists ever in the present, and He will continually exist forever into the future.

The scene here in Revelation 4 is one of unending worship from the living creatures and the 24 elders, who cast their crowns before God's throne (Revelation 4:9-10) and say that the Lord "our God" alone is worthy "to receive glory and honor and power" because He is the Creator of "all things" and because He willed the existence of all things and they "were created" (verse 11).

While there is little doubt that such accolades and honor have been showered upon the Lord from all eternity past, this scene receives particular emphasis in Revelation because of all that is prophesied to happen in the rest of the book. God is in charge of His creation, and He is the Master of the events about to take place. Though His wrath will be terrible, He is still the holy and glorified One who forever receives honor. One of the aims of the book of Revelation is to bring universal recognition to God, the creator of all.

THE SEVEN-SEALED SCROLL
Revelation 5:1-10

THE STAGE IS SET IN this chapter for the seven-year Tribulation, which will be activated by the commands found in the document described in these verses. A book (scroll) is seen in the right hand of the Lord, who is seated on His throne. What is written is lengthy and detailed, for the scroll is inscribed "inside and on the back." The scroll is an official document "sealed up with seven seals" (verse 1). A strong and powerful angel asks who is worthy to open the scroll and to break its seals (verse 2). No one in the entire universe is worthy to open it (verse 3) except for the Son of God, who gave Himself on the cross for humanity. He alone is worthy to carry out the future plan for the world (verse 8).

John begins to "weep greatly" (literally, "sob uncontrollably") since no one was found to open the scroll (verse 4). John wept because he knew this scroll represented the title deed to the earth and that as long as the scroll was left sealed, Satan would remain in power over the earth (LaHaye, *Revelation Unveiled,* p. 86). One of the 24 elders responded to John and urged him to "stop weeping" (verse 5). The

Lord Jesus is the Lion of the tribe of Judah (Genesis 49:8-10), the messianic king, the "root" of the first king, David (Isaiah 11:1,10; 53:12; 63:1-3).

Symbolically, Christ is featured as the *Lamb* who was slain (Isaiah 53; John 1:29). Revelation pictures Christ as the Lamb 28 times. He is pictorially described as having seven horns (power) and seven eyes (intelligence), which show forth the seven manifestations of the Holy Spirit (Isaiah 11:1-2; Revelation 1:4; 3:1; 4:5). In preparation for what is about to come, the seven manifestations of the Holy Spirit are sent forth into the earth. Thomas observes, "The Holy Spirit proceeds from the Son just as He does from the Father (cf. John 15:26). He is Christ's agent for keeping in touch with the affairs of the world" (Thomas, *Revelation 1–7,* p. 393).

The fact that God gave the Lamb the authority to open the seven seals should not be understated. Jesus told His disciples that He had been given authority over all things under heaven by God His Father (Matthew 28:18). That is, He has the authority to exercise justice. Without hesitation, the Lamb steps forward and takes the scroll from the right hand of God the Father (Revelation 5:7). When this happens the four living creatures and the 24 elders fall before Christ the Lamb. Each played a harp and had bowls of incense, "which are the prayers of the saints" (verse 8). The bowl-like dishes of incense were used in the Old Testament as tribute to God in the dedication of the tabernacle (Numbers 7), and the harp indicates worship and is associated with joy and gladness (cf. 1 Chronicles 25:1,6; 2 Chronicles 29:25; Psalm 71:22).

A *new song* is sung in this heavenly chorus (Revelation 5:9), more than likely referring to the fact that this redeemed company described in verses 9-10 has experienced spiritually what no other portion of humanity has. Their song praises Christ, who is worthy to take the scroll, break open the seals, and send upon the earth the wrath of God. For those who rejected the offer of salvation in Him, there is no other alternative but judgment. It only makes sense that this great company is the church saints who were purchased for God by Christ's blood, human beings from "every tribe and tongue and people and nation" (verse 9). They are the church saints who had been resurrected and raptured, and who would from that moment "always be with the Lord" (1 Thessalonians 4:17).

These believers had already been made a kingdom and priests to God, and someday they will reign (future tense) "upon the earth" (Revelation 5:10; cf. 1:6). According to Revelation 5, then, the church saints are a kingdom of people and act as priests representing the Lord before others on earth. This does not mean that the church, the spiritual kingdom described here, is the messianic earthly kingdom. The 1000-year messianic kingdom is distinct (20:4-6) from the church. It will not become a reality on earth until after the Tribulation.

The angels in heaven continue this great chorus of worship (5:11-12) along with "every created thing" (verses 13-14). The blessings and honor are applied to both God the Father on His throne and to the Lamb of God, the Lord Jesus Christ.

THE OPENING OF THE SEVEN SEALS
Revelation 6:1-17; 8:1

THE TRIBULATION BEGINS with this chapter. The unleashing of the Lord's judgments upon the earth is precipitated by the opening of the seven seals. Terrible catastrophic events come down from the "wrath of the Lamb." With each successive opening of a seal, the world falls further into ultimate disaster. When the final seal is opened (8:1), the sounding of seven trumpets begins a course of even greater judgments that destroy even more people on earth. Ed Hindson observes, "With the sixth chapter, the main events of the book may be said to properly begin" (*Revelation*, p. 75).

The first seal broken (6:1-2). When John sees the Lamb break the first of the seven seals, he hears the four living creatures with a voice of thunder say, "Come" in order to see what is about to take place (verse 1). The one on the white horse with a bow and a crown goes forth "conquering, and to conquer" (verse 2). The *white horse* represents the coming of the Antichrist, who carries a destructive bow to begin the carnage on earth. He is the beast (13:1-18), the man of lawlessness (2 Thessalonians 2:3), the son of perdition (John 17:12), and the Antichrist (1 John 4:3). He is given authority, as represented by the crown (Greek, *stephanos*), to wreak havoc on a global scale. The rider on the white horse is not Christ, despite the fact Christ rides a white horse in chapter 19. Jesus wears the *diadem* crown, not the *stephanos,* and He comes with a sword, not a bow. Besides, He is the One who unleashes judgment on the earth by opening the first seal.

The second seal broken (6:3-4). The rider on the *red horse* is involved with war and the removing of peace from the earth. Red pictures violence and bloodshed, and this rider causes people to turn against each other and kill one another. He is given a "great sword" to carry out his own destructive purposes (verse 4). Some think the Antichrist will come to earth peacefully during the chaos that follows the rapture of the church. If this is the case, then violence erupts quickly in the beginning stages of the Tribulation. We must remember that the Antichrist ("the prince") of Daniel early breaks the covenant he has made with Israel (Daniel 9:26-27).

The third seal broken (6:5-6). The rider on the *black horse* holds a pair of scales—the kind for measuring out food—and represents the scarcity of this food (verse 5). This horse represents death and famine. The quart of wheat, about one liter, and a "denarius" (about a day's wage, Matthew 20:2) represent famine and near-starvation prices. The same is true about three quarts of barley for a denarius. People will barely be able to get enough food to survive, and the world situation will continue to get worse. Basic foodstuffs will such as oil and wine will be spared, but survival, especially for the poor, will be tenuous.

Major Events of the Tribulation

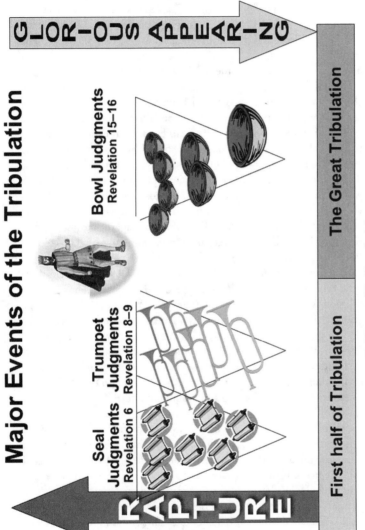

Seal Judgments
Revelation 6

Trumpet Judgments
Revelation 8–9

Bowl Judgments
Revelation 15–16

RAPTURE

GLORIOUS APPEARING

First half of Tribulation

The Great Tribulation

7-Year Tribulation

The significance of the seven-year Tribulation is seen in that much space is given to it in the Bible. It is mentioned some 49 times by the Hebrew prophets, by most of the apostles, and takes up all of Revelation chapters 6 through 19. Revelation tells us the Tribulation will consist of two periods of 42 months, or 1260 days, or 3½ years ("a time and times and half a time"—Revelation 12:14). These two periods of time, brought together, total seven years. The seal and trumpet judgments will occur during the first half of the Tribulation, and the bowl judgments during the second half, or the Great Tribulation.

The fourth seal broken (6:7-8). The *pale horse* is next, and it represents death. "Pale" or "ashen" (Greek, *cloros,* from which we derive the word *chlorine*) symbolizes the pasty color of death. The other riders, carrying a bow, sword, and balance, are now followed by the grim reaper, death (Greek, *thanatos*). "Hades" follows after, which is the grave where the dead are consigned. This rider also bears a sword and adds famine, pestilence, and "the wild beasts of the earth" to his arsenal of death (verse 8).

The verses describing the fair horses and their riders picture the chaos and lack of order that will overwhelm the entire world population. The interconnection of description makes it obvious that all four seals and riders are related. Thus, they are often called the four horsemen of the Apocalypse. The expressions "was given" (verse 2), "was granted" (verse 4), and "authority was given" (verse 8) are in the passive voice, meaning that an outside force or power allowed or gave permission for these things to take place. Since the scroll comes from the throne room of God the Father, and since the Lord Jesus is the One who breaks open the seals, the conclusion is that divine sovereignty is allowing these terrible events to come about on the earth.

The fifth seal broken (6:9-11). The scene now shifts to a heavenly vision. John sees the *souls of the righteous* "underneath the altar" who were slain on earth for their testimony (verse 9). These are the *martyrs* who were killed on earth when the first four seals were broken. They are not the church saints who had earlier been raptured to glory (1 Thessalonians 4:13-18). These are those who had accepted Christ as their Savior at the beginning of the Tribulation. They are not technically church-age believers, but believers who were slaughtered during the Tribulation. They plead for God not to "refrain from judging and avenging our blood on those who dwell on the earth." Their life and their death had been so terrible they are here begging for retribution.

These martyred saints are given white robes as emblems of their righteous suffering for the sake of the Lord. They are told to rest and wait for a little while until "their fellow servants and their brethren" who were to be killed are brought home to glory (Revelation 6:11). During the Tribulation, God will have Gentile witnesses on the earth who serve as lights of the truth. They will die for their testimony. There will also be 144,000 Jewish witnesses—12,000 from each of the 12 tribes—who will be sealed as Tribulation evangelists (7:4-8). They will be sealed and protected for a period of time in order to share their faith with unbelievers.

The sixth seal broken (6:12-17). When the sixth seal is broken, a *great earthquake* will shake the globe. This will be followed by the sun being darkened and the moon appearing as blood, or shaded by massive atmospheric pollution that dims these heavenly lights (verse 12). The stars (perhaps asteroids—Greek, *asteres*) will fall to the earth like figs shaken from a fig tree by a great wind (verse 13). The sky will then be "split apart" like a scroll, and "every mountain and island [will be] moved out of their places" (verse 14).

Christ told His disciples that when these things happen, people will be "fainting from fear and the expectation of the things which are coming upon the world; for the powers of the heavens shall be shaken" (Luke 21:26). Those on earth will panic in fear and hide underground "in the caves and among the rocks of the mountains" (Revelation 6:15). They will beg the mountains and the rocks to fall and hide them "from the presence of Him who sits on the throne, and from the wrath of the Lamb" (verse 16). They will understand that the period called "the great day of [Christ's] wrath has come"—a day in which no one "is able to stand" (verse 17).

Unbelievers will try to escape the wrath of God and Jesus Christ, and they will correctly understand that these events are pouring forth from heaven. Some teachers suggest the events in the early part of the Tribulation are from nature, man, and/or Satan, and not from God. They suggest that God's wrath does not begin until about Revelation 14:9-10,19. However, 6:16-17 indicates that these early years or months of the Tribulation are part of

God's wrath. And because the Bible promises that the church saints will not be subject to God's wrath (1 Thessalonians 1:10; 5:9), the rapture of the church *must* occur before the Tribulation begins. This is a strong argument for the pretribulational rapture.

The seventh seal broken (8:1). Chapter 7 is a parenthesis that describes certain events taking place on earth and in heaven. The final seal is opened in 8:1. When it is broken, "there [will be] silence in heaven for about an hour." It appears this silence is because the heavenly court and its citizens are waiting breathlessly for what comes next. With this final seal broken, the sounding of seven trumpets begins. These trumpets herald even more intense and destructive judgments that will fall upon the earth (8:2–9:21; 11:15-19). In every sense, these judgments are more violent than the ones that accompanied the opening of the earlier seals (see chapters 8–9).

SALVATION DURING THE TRIBULATION
Revelation 7:1-17

JOHN NOW RECEIVES A VISION of four angels who are placed around the earth at its "four corners" (verse 1). The phrase "four corners" is hyperbolic and means that these angelic ministers of the Lord were placed strategically on the earth to hold back "the four winds" so that they should not blow on the land, the sea, or "on any tree." Another angel appears, "having the seal of the living God," and commanding that the earth be not harmed (verse 2) until "we have sealed the bond-servants of our God on their foreheads" (verse 3). This seal, like that stamped on a scroll, indicates that the object that is sealed comes from the sovereign king and the instructions protected by the seal must be carried out and obeyed. The bond-servants, the 144,000 *Jewish witnesses* of the Lord as well as Gentile believers of the Tribulation, will be protected by the Lord for a distinct purpose and for a period of time.

Unfortunately, some Bible teachers have taught that the 12 tribes and the 144,000 witnesses listed here (verses 4-8) represent the church. They suggest there will not be exactly 12,000 representatives from each of the 12 tribes of Jewish people as so clearly stated in the verses. But when the Bible takes such great pains to describe actual Jewish tribes and numbers, doesn't it make more sense to interpret this in a normal, literal sense than a symbolic one?

These 144,000 Jewish evangelists in verses 4-8 are permitted to bear a strong witness for the Lord until about halfway into the Tribulation. In Revelation 14:1 they are seen in glory, "standing on Mount Zion" in heaven with the Lamb with the name of His Father "written on their foreheads." Because of what they have been through they sing a new song, and after their martyrdom, they "had been purchased from the earth" (verse 3).

Next John sees a great crowd from all the peoples of the earth, "clothed in white robes, and palm branches were in their hands" (7:9). These are *Gentiles* who are coming out of the Tribulation shouting, "Salvation to our God who sits on the throne, and to the Lamb" (verse 10). The 24 elders and the four living creatures are there to join in on the praise (verse 11; cf. 4:4,6). More accolades and honor are given to the Lord for His great redemption of all those believers who suffered during the Tribulation (verse 12). Twice in this verse they shout, "Amen."

It is interesting to note the question about who these witnesses are and where they came from (verse 13). The answer given is that "these are the ones who come out of the great tribulation, and they have washed their robes and made them white in the blood of the Lamb" (verse 14). Because of the suffering these people endured on earth, they appear to be given a special place in glory before God's throne, where "they serve Him day and night in His temple" (verse 15). Never again will they go through what they did on earth: hunger, thirst, and exposure to the elements (verse 16). Christ will act as their heavenly Shepherd and "will guide them to springs of the water of life; and God will wipe every tear from their eyes" (verse 17). One could not ask for more comforting words in light of all the suffering experienced by these Tribulation martyrs. Hindson says, "This chapter ends with all of heaven on its face before God. His sovereignty is extolled in His redemption of Israel and the Gentiles alike…. What a powerful and beautiful picture! God is the One who saves people" (*Revelation*, p. 94).

THE SEVEN TRUMPETS
Revelation 8:2–9:21; 11:15-19

THE SEVEN TRUMPETS come out of the breaking of the seventh seal. Seven angels will sound forth the events that are to come with each trumpet. Verses 3-6 act as the prelude to the trumpet judgments, and these verses give to the reader another vision of what is taking place in heaven. "Another" angel, distinct from the seven (verse 3), stands before the heavenly altar, holding a golden censer. More incense is added, which represents the additional prayers of all the Tribulation saints (5:8). The prayers are symbolically placed "on the golden altar which was before the throne" of God (8:3). These prayers are like sweet incense that goes "up before God out of the angel's hand" (verse 4).

The Lord then commands that the fire on the altar be thrown to the earth in judgment. This is graphically illustrated with the "peals of thunder and sounds and flashes of lightning and an earthquake" (verse 5). The Lord is furious with the death of His saints, who are tormented and tortured to death by the cruel acts of persecution taking place all over the earth. All of this precedes the sounding of the trumpets from the seven angels (verse 6). These trumpet judgments will bring even greater cataclysmic events upon the earth.

The first trumpet sounded (8:7). Atmospheric phenomena will cascade down upon the world, described as "hail and fire, mixed with blood…thrown to the earth." This could be the result of massive volcanic explosions or asteroids showering the land and sea. One-third of the earth's surface will burn up, and one-third of the trees and the green grass will be consumed.

The second trumpet sounded (8:8-9). Explanations of the "great mountain burning with fire" (verse 8) include much speculation. Some have suggested it is an atomic mushroom cloud that emits fallout into the ocean with the result that one-third of the sea becomes blood. Blood is a great incubator of disease and is used in Scripture to portray pollution and uncleanness. The comparative word "like" (Greek, *hos*) indicates that John, in his vision, is seeing something he has never witnessed before. He struggles to describe this awesome event. The figure "a third" can certainly be taken literally, as in verse 7. As is often the case in these judgments, John is attempting to describe future phenomenon using first-century terminology. Whatever the burning mountain is, it kills a third of the ocean life and destroys a third of the sea vessels. There has never been such a singular catastrophic event recorded of this magnitude in the history of humanity!

The third trumpet sounded (8:10-11). Another stellar phenomenon—a great *aster* ("asteroid") falls from heaven "burning like a torch" and pollutes a third of the rivers and even the springs of water (verse 10). The "star is called Wormwood" and pollutes the earth's waters, making them bitter and poisonous so that those who drink this water die (verse 11). Wormwood is a terribly bitter and caustic plant of the Middle East that renders water completely undrinkable. It is difficult to imagine the horror, confusion, and panic of the world's population as these plagues strike with explosive force upon the earth in rapid succession.

The fourth trumpet sounded (8:12-13). With the sounding of the fourth trumpet, the lights of the heavens appear to be smitten. The rays of the heavenly bodies are dimmed, causing the night sky to turn even darker (verse12). Some have suggested this may be thick atmospheric dust and pollution that darken the lights in heaven and shroud the blue sky. As if listening to the screech of an "eagle" (better, "vulture") high in "midheaven," John hears it say, "Woe, woe, woe" (Greek, *ouai*) to all those on earth. There are three more trumpet blasts to be sounded (verse 13). "Woe" is an intense, painful exclamatory term of despair and resignation that speaks of no hope of survival for those still left on the earth. There will be three series of woes to follow, and they are mentioned in Revelation 9:12, 11:14, and 12:12.

The fifth trumpet sounded (9:1-12). Chapter 9 seems to present two phases of demonic activity. The chapter is full of pictorial language that vividly describes demons released from the bottomless pit to bring torment upon people during the Tribulation.

The "star from heaven" appears to be an angelic being who brings a key to unlock "the bottomless pit" and release a swarm of evil creatures (verse 1). In the original Greek text, "the bottomless pit" translates to "the shaft of the abyss." Coming from heaven, this angel would be one of the servants of the Lord and not an evil agent of Satan. When the pit is opened, smoke "like that of a great furnace" billows out (verse 2), from which locust-like creatures emerge "upon the earth" with the power to torment people as a scorpion does (verse 3). The pit is a temporary place of confinement and punishment for fallen angels.

At this stage, the creatures are not allowed to hurt the greenery of earth but "only the men who do not have the seal of God on their foreheads" (9:4). This clearly indicates that the "locusts" are symbolic of a horde of demons. The "seal" on people's foreheads is a sign of God's ownership and protection. The lost will not be protected from this demonic attack! This seal, however it appears, must carry some meaning to those who can see it.

The demonic creatures are not allowed to kill anyone, but their sting can "torment for five months" (verses 5,10). The phrase "five months" is expressed in an accusative of duration, though it is difficult to determine the exact purpose for this specific length of time. Some see the five months as having a nonliteral meaning. The torment caused by

these creatures is so great that people will want to die, but death will elude them (verse 6). The comparative words "like" and "as" are used nine times in verses 1-12, which indicates the creatures John is trying to describe defy explanation and description. One has to conjecture what the descriptions might mean.

The locust-demons are seen as something "like horses" with crowns on their heads and faces like men (verse 7), which may be symbolic of strength, authority, and intelligence. The hair "like the hair of women" may depict the flowing locks of a seductress who tempts and then destroys her victims. The teeth "like the teeth of lions" may support that idea (verse 8). The "breastplates" like that of "iron" could refer to invincibility or the fact these creatures cannot be destroyed by natural means. The "sound of their wings" was like that of "chariots, of many horses rushing to battle," which reinforces the warlike purpose of the demons (verse 9). In ancient times, infantry troops were no match for rushing chariots, and these creatures will likewise prove overwhelming in power. The demons have no peaceful intentions, and their task is to do the bidding of their master, Satan.

The "king" over this evil horde is "the angel of the abyss." His Hebrew name is *Abaddon,* and his Greek name is *Apollyon* (verse 11). The names are similar—*Abaddon* means "destruction," and *Apollyon* means "destroyer." *Abaddon* is mentioned in Job 26:6, 28:22, and 31:12 as well as Proverbs 15:11 as a synonym of death. Most believe this is a fallen archangel who serves Satan, but some think this could be Satan himself. Whatever the case, he is never connected directly with the abyss until he is finally cast into it at the very end of human history (Revelation 20:1-3). He is featured prominently in Revelation 12, and has many followers and leaders under his command (Ephesians 6:12), of which Apollyon may well be one.

The sixth trumpet sounded (9:13-21). From the golden altar in heaven (verse 13) goes the command, "Release the four angels who are bound at the great river Euphrates" (verse 14). Holy angels are not bound or confined. These are *diabolical creatures* who have a specific role to play in relationship to the historic river Euphrates (verse 15). This great company of wicked and supernatural beings is 200 million strong and will kill a third of mankind (verses 15-16). This is in strong contrast to the demonic beings in verses 1-12, who were not allowed to destroy human beings.

The river Euphrates runs through Babylon, which is the ancient birthplace of evil, idolatry, and false religion. Babylon's influence is graphically portrayed in connection with the great harlot in chapters 17–18. The river served as a military barrier between Babylon and Assyria, a divide between east and west, and it separated Israel from her enemies to the east.

The demons who are released are colorfully described as riders on war horses (9:17). They have protective breastplates, and the heads of the horses are "like the heads of lions" with "fire and smoke and brimstone" coming from their mouths. A third of mankind will be killed by the plagues, fire, smoke, and brimstone that proceeds "out of their mouths" (verse 18). That these things are coming from their mouths is probably hyperbole, but clearly they have the power to speak and bombard the world with terrible natural catastrophes. The horses also have tails "like serpents" by which "they do harm" (verse 19).

In spite of all the judgments and warnings from God, we read that those who have somehow survived up to this point still did not "repent of the works of their hands, so as not to worship demons, and the idols of gold and of silver and of brass and of stone and of wood, which can neither see nor hear nor walk" (verse 20), nor did they repent of their murders nor of their sorceries nor of their immorality nor of their thefts (verse 21). This could be the crowning moment of human rebellion, when even the strongest of warnings from God will not reach the human heart and bring about repentance!

The seventh trumpet sounded (11:15-19). Revelation 10:1–11:14 is another parenthesis or interlude in the chronology of the Tribulation. The seventh trumpet is really a *preview of things*

to come. It announces the future establishment of the promised earthly kingdom of Christ, who will "reign forever and ever" (Revelation 11:15). His kingdom will replace the "kingdom of the world," and He will be Lord over all (Daniel 7:9-14,26-28). The heavenly court of elders, in response, "fell on their faces and worshiped God" (Revelation 11:16; cf. 4:4; Daniel 7:26). They gave glory to God and acknowledged that He had "begun to reign" (Revelation 11:17). The phrase "had begun," which is in the aorist tense, speaks of the certainty of this future event by referring to it as though it is already past. Thomas writes,

> The seventh trumpet triggers an anticipation of the final triumph when the future visible kingdom of God on earth will become a reality, when a transference of powers from the heathen nations to God, as described in Psalm 2, will come. The change has not yet happened, but the time has come for it to happen (*Revelation 8–22,* p. 106).

Like a disturbed hive of wasps, the nations "were enraged" because God's wrath came. "The time came" for the dead to be judged and for rewards to be distributed to "Your bond-servants the prophets and the saints and those who fear Your name" (Revelation 11:18). Rewards will be given to those who have been faithful, and judgment will come upon "those who destroy the earth." John then sees the temple in heaven opened, and the spiritual ark of the covenant appears. More judgment is forecast with "flashes of lightning and sounds and peals of thunder and an earthquake and a great hailstorm" (verse 19). The judgment will be of the lost at the Great White Throne (20:11-15).

NO MORE DELAY
Revelation 10:1-7

THIS IS PART OF THE *parenthesis* between the sixth and the seventh trumpets in the seven trumpet judgments. It is a heavenly vision in which a special angel pronounces that more wrath is coming and that the end is near. This angel is described as a "strong" angel as well as "another" (Greek, *allon*, "the one similar to" or "one of the same type") in contrast to the strong angel in 5:2. Some have suggested this is Christ, but this is unlikely in light of 10:5-6, where he speaks of the Creator as someone else and not himself. While Christ is referred to as the "Angel of Yahweh" in the Old Testament, nowhere in the New Testament is He referred to merely as "an angel." That this angel is part of the heavenly court and one who is near the Lord is seen by the fact that he is "clothed with a cloud; and the rainbow was upon his head" (verse 1). His face is radiant like the sun (similar to Christ's face in 1:16), and his feet are sturdy and strong, "like pillars of fire."

This angel has in his hand "a little book [scroll]" and his authority encompasses both the sea and the land (10:2). When this angel cries out, "seven peals of thunder" are heard (verse 3). In the Bible, the number seven is symbolic of completion, and the "peals of thunder" herald more trouble to come on earth. Interestingly, John is told to not write what the thunder peals "had spoken" (verse 4). He is ordered instead to seal up or hide away what was "spoken" by the thunder. Some have suggested that the hiding away of this message could have been a way of shortening the Tribulation for the sake of the Christians alive during the Tribulation (Mark 13:20). More likely, it could have been that the message was so terrible it had to be contained. God tells us only what we need to know about the future and no more.

The angel gives an oath (Revelation 10:4) and swears to the eternal Lord "who created heaven and the things in it, and the earth and the things in it, and the sea and the things in it, that there will be delay no longer" (verses 5-6). The message of God's wrath is emboldened by chapter 10, and here it is predicted that the seventh angel "is about to sound" his trumpet (verse 7). With this, "the mystery of God" will be finished. The "mystery" (Greek, *musterion*) denotes a secret revealed by the Lord (Ephesians 3:1-10). In this passage it speaks of the great and final purpose

of God in the flow of human history (Thomas, *Revelation 8–22,* p. 70). That message had been "preached to His servants the prophets," who revealed God's plan over time, and the final part of God's plan was about to be unveiled.

JOHN TO CONTINUE PROPHESYING
Revelation 10:8-11

THE ANGEL MENTIONED EARLIER in verse 1 now tells John in verse 8 to take the scroll from the angel standing "on the sea and on the land" (verse 5). John is instructed to take the scroll and eat it. The scroll will make his stomach bitter, but it will taste sweet as honey in his mouth (verse 9). Upon eating the scroll the angels together tell him, "You must prophesy again concerning many peoples and nations and tongues and kings" (verse 11). This was the way the church was described in heaven in 5:8-10, but here in chapter 10, the setting is earth and not heaven. Apparently God's plan and outline for the last half of the Tribulation is in the little scroll, and John is commanded that he "must prophesy" about what is on the horizon. The horrors of God's coming wrath give John heartburn and indigestion, but it also tastes good as honey because the final stages of God's plan include the coming of the Son of God to bring peace on earth (19:11-21).

PROPHECY OF THE TWO WITNESSES
Revelation 11:1-14

CHAPTER 11 PRESENTS TO US the halfway point in the seven-year Tribulation. John is instructed to measure the temple and the altar (of incense), including the area where the people worship (verse 1). In his measuring of the temple, John is told to leave the outer court out of his calculations. Normally Gentiles could enter the outer court, but according to John's vision, it will become wrongly dominated and desecrated by the nations, or unbelievers (verse 2). The temple mentioned here is not the one that stood in Jerusalem during the time of Christ and the apostles, called the Herodian or Second Temple, which was destroyed in A.D. 70. That temple was already gone by the time John wrote those words around A.D. 90–95. Nor is this the spiritual temple in heaven. It is the temple that will be standing in Jerusalem during the Tribulation, which means we can expect the temple to be rebuilt for the end times. The halfway point of the Tribulation is three and a half years, or "forty-two months" (verse 2). At this point the temple described here, along with the city of Jerusalem ("the holy city"), will be "tread under foot" by the nations.

The *chronology* of this period runs as follows: At some point following 1) the rapture of the church, 2) the "prince" of Daniel 9:26-27 will make a peace pact, "a firm covenant" for one week, or one *heptad* (Hebrew), a seven-year agreement. 3) In the middle of this week, or seven-year period (42 months), this "prince" (the Antichrist) will enter the temple and proclaim himself as God, exalting himself "above every so-called god or object of worship" (2 Thessalonians 2:3-4). In this rebuilt temple the Jews will have revived their sacrificial system, but the Antichrist will bring a stop to it. From this point onward, 4) the Tribulation will intensify and the destruction that comes upon the earth will become greater (Daniel 9:27). The temple will be desecrated by the Antichrist, who proclaims himself to be God, and the destruction that follows will be astounding.

During the first three and a half years of the Tribulation, the Lord will place *two witnesses in Jerusalem* (Revelation 11:3) to perform miracles (verses 5-6) and to proclaim the gospel message of salvation in Christ (verse 7). These witnesses will be like "two olive trees" and two lampstands that give the light of the truth during the Tribulation (verse 4). The olive tree symbolism goes back to Zechariah 4:3 and the "two anointed ones," Zerubbabel (a governor) and Joshua (a high priest). That they were lampstands symbolizes they were empowered

by the Holy Spirit to witness for God. The description of their ministries parallels those of Moses and Elijah, who appeared as two witnesses with Christ at the transfiguration (Matthew 17:1-13).

The two witnesses of Revelation 11 will have extraordinary ability to destroy those who come against them and their message (verse 5). God will also impart to them authority over nature. In "the days of their prophesying," they will have the power to stop the rain, turn the waters to blood, and "strike the earth with every plague" whenever they wish (verse 6). When their testimony is finished, the beast will "make war with them, and overcome them and kill them" (verse 7).

The death of the two witnesses will seem to finally silence their message. Their bodies will lie in the streets of Jerusalem (where "the Lord was crucified"). Jerusalem is referred to "mystically [as] Sodom and Egypt" (verse 8). The word "mystically" is literally "spiritually" (Greek, *pneumatikos*). In a spiritual sense, Sodom and Egypt both depict the degradation of the people of Jerusalem. Egypt was the land that first enslaved God's people, and it was a center of paganism and idolatry. During Moses' encounter with Pharaoh, Egypt became a battleground between the gods of that land and the God of Israel. Later the prophet Ezekiel said that harlotries originated in Egypt (Ezekiel 23:3-4,8,19). In these ways Jerusalem is metaphorically likened to Sodom and Egypt.

As for the two witnesses, the entire population of the world will see their "dead bodies for three and a half days, and will not permit their dead bodies to be laid in a tomb" (Revelation 11:9). The people of earth will "celebrate" and send gifts to each other in response to the deaths of these two prophets, who "tormented those who dwell on the earth" (verse 10). Some have suggested the only way the people of earth could all see the two witnesses is by satellite television, which could easily be fulfilled literally.

The *resurrection and rapture* of the witnesses will verify that the earlier disappearance of believers was indeed the rapture of the church! After three and a half days "the breath of life from God" will raise the two prophets, and fear will strike those who see this happen (verse 11). The two will be transported heavenward with their enemies looking on (verse 12). The witness and testimony of these two will be a "last chance" at this stage of the Tribulation for people to come to Christ for salvation. After the two are gone, "in that hour" God will send a great earthquake that destroys a tenth of the city of Jerusalem and kills 7000 people. Those still left alive will give glory "to the God of heaven" (verse 13). Some question whether this means the people of Jerusalem will become converted. Walvoord states, "Even though they recognize the power of the God of heaven, it does not seem to indicate that they have come to the point of true faith in Christ" (*Revelation,* p. 183).

ISRAEL IN GOD'S PROPHETIC PLAN
Revelation 12:1-17

TO SOME DEGREE, this chapter is like a *parenthesis* in the drama taking place in Revelation. Here we have a prophetic lineup of the key individuals in the great end-times drama. There are *seven major figures* mentioned: 1) the woman who represents Israel; 2) the dragon who is Satan; 3) the man-child, or Christ; 4) Michael the archangel, who represents the elect angels; 5) Israel, the remnant of the seed of the woman; 6) the beast out of the sea, the Antichrist; and finally, 7) the false prophet and religious leader, or the beast out of the earth.

The great "sign" (Greek, *sēmeion*) in heaven means that the vision John is about to record is extremely important. Six other signs are described in Revelation (12:3; 13:13-14; 15:1; 16:14; 19:20). The description of the *woman* contains parallels to Joseph's dream about his brothers (Genesis 37:9), so the nation of Israel is clearly in view. The 12 stars, then, would be the 12 tribes of Israel (Revelation 12:1), and

the child is the Lord Jesus Christ, who came from the nation of Israel (verse 2). The woman cannot represent the church, as some suggest. The church is the *bride* of Christ, whereas this woman is the *mother* of Christ! There was much labor and political intrigue when Christ was born, which is vividly confirmed in the drama recorded by Matthew (Matthew 1:18–2:18). King Herod had ordered the mass murder of male children in Bethlehem in the hopes of eliminating the One who was to become Israel's ruler (2:16).

Satan, the *great red dragon* (Revelation 12:3), comes on the scene upholding the powers of the final world empire, the revived Roman Empire. The description given of this empire is similar to what is recorded in Daniel 7:7-8,24 and Revelation 13:1, both of which describe Satan's control over world empires. Satan is seen as supporting seven heads (rulers) and ten horns (nations) with authority to dictate and rule, as portrayed by the seven crowns, or "seven diadems." The red dragon's tail sweeps "a third of the stars of heaven, and threw them to the earth" (12:4). Most commentators say this verse describes part of what occurs during the Tribulation, but it may be preferable to say that this looks back at what happened when Satan fell long ago, which Jesus described when He said, "I was watching Satan fall from heaven like lightning" (Luke 10:18). Ezekiel, too, spoke of this fall: "I have cast you [the anointed cherub] as profane from the mountain of God" (Ezekiel 28:16). Whatever the case, at the birth of Christ, Satan "stood before the woman" (Israel) ready to devour the child (Revelation 12:4).

The *male child* (Christ) born from the woman (Israel) will "rule all the nations with a rod of iron" (verse 5). Before this happens, He is taken "up to God and to His throne." He is presently seated at the right hand of the Father until He subdues all His enemies and reigns from Jerusalem, the holy mountain of Zion (Psalm 110:1-3).

The drama now returns to the future, to the last half of the Tribulation, during which the nation of Israel will be pursued by Satan. The surviving *Jewish remnant* of that time will go into "the wilderness where she [has] a place prepared by God, so that there she would be nourished for one thousand two hundred and sixty days" (Revelation 12:6). This "remnant of Israel" will hide out in the ancient city of Bozrah, located in the region of Mount Seir in the wilderness portion of Edom (Micah 2:12; see also Revelation 12:6). There is strong indication that Isaiah 33 is about both Israel's purging and protection during this time. The sinners in Zion will be terrified (verse 14), and the Jews hiding in the mountains will have refuge in the "impregnable rock" and will miraculously receive bread and water (verse 16). Many commentators suggest these Jews will flee to the ancient mountain fortress of Petra which is in the wilderness of Jordan.

In heaven, *Michael and his angels* will wage combat against Satan and his angels (Revelation 12:7). Though Satan and his forces were earlier cast from heaven, Satan can still communicate with God (cf. Job 1:6-12; 2:1-7). The final expulsion will take place in the future, and Satan will then intensify his deceptive attacks on the population of earth (Revelation 12:9). While Satan is increasing his persecution against the righteous on earth, a voice in heaven will announce that "the power, and the kingdom of our God and the authority of His Christ have come" (verse 10). Despite the fact that many will die from Satan's attacks, the Tribulation saints will know spiritual victory "because of the blood of the Lamb and because of the word of their testimony." They will not be afraid to die for their faith (verse 11). Those in heaven will rejoice, yet there will be another woe on the earth because "the devil has come down to you, having great wrath, knowing that he has only a short time" to persecute and torment the population (verse 12). The fact that Satan's time is short indicates that this judgment is limited to the Tribulation period. This cannot logically refer to the thousands of years that have transpired since Satan's fall at the dawn of creation.

The woman will be persecuted by "the dragon" (verse 13), and will be given "two wings of the great eagle" so that she can be taken away into the wilderness to be protected (verse 14). As already mentioned, this protection will last three and a half years (verse 6). Satan will attempt to cause the woman (Israel) to be "swept away" (verse 15), but she will be protected by the earth (verse 16). Whether by natural or supernatural means, a godly remnant will be preserved by God, though according to Zechariah 13:8, two-thirds of the nation of Israel will perish. While it is said that Satan will pour water "like a river out of his mouth after the woman," this probably isn't to be taken literally, but may refer to a flood-like catastrophe initiated by Satan. Satan's final "war" against Israel will fall upon the believing Jews, the "rest of her children, who keep the commandments of God and hold to the testimony of Jesus" (Revelation 12:17). The Jewish people are God's chosen people, and their existence and survival are signs of the faithfulness of the Lord and the truthfulness of the fulfillment of His prophetic Word.

THE RISE AND REIGN OF THE BEAST
Revelation 13:1-10

REVELATION 13:1-10 SUMMARIZES the activity of the beast who was first mentioned in 11:7. He has many names: 1) the wicked one (Psalm 10:2-4), 2) the little horn (Daniel 7:8), 3) the prince (9:26), 4) the despicable person (11:21), 5) the king [who] will do as he pleases (11:36), 6) the man of lawlessness (2 Thessalonians 2:3), 7) the son of destruction (verse 3), 8) the lawless one (verse 8), 9) the Antichrist (1 John 2:18), and 10) the beast (Revelation 13:1).

The *beast* comes "out of the sea," or out of the nations, meaning that more than likely he is a Gentile and not a Jew. He will be "like a leopard, and his feet [are] like those of a bear, and his mouth like the mouth of a lion," and he will be given his power by Satan, the dragon. He will have a throne "and great authority" (verse 2). This animal symbolism is drawn from Daniel 7:4-8, where the lion refers to Babylon, the bear to Medo-Persia, and the leopard to Greece, the empire of Alexander the Great. They are symbols of the empires that preceded the Roman Empire, the composite beast of verse 7. The lion represents regal power, the bear ferociousness, and the leopard great speed. The beast will move forcefully and quickly to establish his worldwide domination.

One of the beast's heads, and not necessarily the beast himself, will receive a "fatal wound" (Revelation 13:3). It is not stated definitely that the beast will die. It is questionable whether Satan has the power to restore to life one who is killed, even though his power is great. However, the whole earth will be "amazed" and will follow after the beast because they will think a resurrection has taken place. Because of this seeming miracle, the entire world will worship the dragon, who "gave his authority to the beast" (verse 4). Satan wants such worship, for that is what he wanted long ago when God cast him out of heaven. In Isaiah 14:14 Satan said, "I will ascend above the heights of the clouds; I will make myself like the Most High."

The beast will speak arrogantly and hold authority for 42 months, or three and a half years (Revelation 13:5). He will also blaspheme God, "His name and His tabernacle, that is, those who dwell in heaven" (verse 6). The beast's rebellion against God will occur when he enters the restored temple in Jerusalem and displays "himself as being God" (2 Thessalonians 2:4). Apparently God will allow the beast to gain worldwide authority and to gain power "to make war with the saints and to overcome them" (Revelation 13:7). The righteous will be martyred, and unbelievers will be blinded to the truth. "For this reason God will send upon them a deluding influence so that they might believe what is false, in order that they all may be judged who did not believe the truth, but took pleasure in wickedness" (2 Thessalonians 2:11-12). Except for the righteous, "all who dwell on the earth will worship [the dragon], everyone whose name has not been written from the foundation of the world in the book of life of the Lamb who has been slain" (Revelation 13:8).

Some believe "the book of life" here seems to indicate that there is a book that includes the names of all who have been born into this world. Those who do not become believers are then blotted out of the book, leaving only those who are saved (cf. 3:8; 22:19). "The simplest explanation here seems the best, namely, that their names were written in the book of life from eternity past" (Walvoord, *Revelation*, p. 203). There is a fair warning to unsaved people who read Revelation: "If anyone has an ear, let him hear" (13:9).

This passage ends on a sober note: Whatever will be, will be! Those destined for captivity will be made captive; and those destined to die "must be killed" (verse 10). This verse has allusions that go back to Jeremiah 15:2; 43:11 and Zechariah 11:9. All the Tribulation saints can do is be patient (persevere, endure) and be faithful! And they can have full confidence that Christ *will* return and that the wrongs of the earth will be finally righted (Couch, *Revelation*, p. 265).

THE RISE OF THE FALSE PROPHET
Revelation 13:11-18

THE BEAST HAS A COHORT who is said to come "up out of the earth" (verse 11). This false prophet has power, represented by his two horns "like a lamb," though he speaks like a dragon. The portrayal as a lamb would show a certain docility that elicits a reminder of the nonresistance of Christ as "the Lamb of God." But this beast will speak with frightening authority like a hissing dragon! He will have equal authority as the first beast and will cause the whole population of earth to worship him (verse 12). He will have the power to make fire come down upon the earth (verse 13), and he will deceive "those who dwell on the earth because of all the signs...given him to perform" (verse 14). He will also inspire the whole earth to make an image of the first beast, "who had the wound of the sword and has come to life" (verse 14).

The fact that this second beast causes the

world to worship the first beast is the reason the second one is called the religious beast or the false prophet (16:13). His end is recorded in 19:20, where he is thrown into the lake of fire along with the first beast. There, he will be tormented "day and night forever and ever" (20:10).

This second beast will give breath to "the image of the [first] beast" and even cause it to speak. Those who do not worship the image will be killed (13:15). The second beast will cause all men of all social stations in life to have a "mark on their right hand or on their forehead" (verse 16). This technology is already available today, and by this mark the second beast will control the population of the world. No one will be able to survive economically without this mark (verse 17). The "mark" (Greek, *charagma,* "tattoo") must show either the name of the first beast "or the number of his name" (verse 17), which is "six hundred and sixty-six" (verse 18). The reference to "wisdom" in verse 18 means the Tribulation saints will understand what is happening when they see this mark and its number required of all peoples on the earth.

Some have attempted to tie the number 666 to some Roman emperor or political figure in the past. The church father Irenaeus said the number represented the "Latin Empire" of Rome. Others have calculated that the number points to the Roman emperor Nero, and modern candidates have been Kaiser Wilhelm, Benito Mussolini, Adolph Hitler, Joseph Stalin, Mikhail Gorbachev, and Saddam Hussein. Even some American presidents and diplomats have been added to the list! Such interpretations frequently ignore the context of Revelation 13 and allegorize what the apostle John wrote to describe the literal, historical, and future events of the Tribulation.

THE 144,000 IN GLORY
Revelation 14:1-5

In Revelation 14 we have *another pause* in the progression of the narrative in the book.

The 144,000 Jewish witnesses who were "sealed" and protected by the Lord (7:4) are now with the Lamb, the Lord Jesus Christ, on Mount Zion. This is not the earthly Mount Zion but the heavenly (14:3). In contrast to the lost on earth, who have the name of the Antichrist on their foreheads or right hand (13:16-17), the 144,000 sealed Jews have the name of Christ and His Father "written on their foreheads" (14:1). They are singing "a new song" in heaven, along with a heavenly chorus, before the throne of God (verse 3). And because of their experiences as the Lord's witnesses, "no one could learn the song." Evidently there will be a point at which the Lord will remove His seal on them, making it possible for them to be martyred. These Jews will live undefiled lives, keeping themselves chaste with women and refraining from lying (verse 5). They will follow "the Lamb wherever He goes," meaning they will let Him lead them through their witnessing endeavors here on earth (verse 4). John writes that they will be "purchased from the earth" (verse 3) and "purchased from among men" (verse 4), implying more than likely their martyrdom.

At the end of the Tribulation these 144,000 Jews will be resurrected "to everlasting life" (Daniel 12:2), and will be among those "who have insight [who] will shine brightly like the brightness of the expanse of heaven, and...who lead the many to righteousness, like the stars forever and ever" (verse 3).

THE GOSPEL PREACHED TO THE NATIONS
Revelation 14:6-7

John the apostle here sees "flying in mid-heaven" another angel preaching "an eternal gospel" to all who live on the earth (verse 6). The "gospel" (Greek, *euangelion,* "good news") of the death, burial, and resurrection of the Lord Jesus (1 Corinthians 15:1-8) may certainly be in view here, but there may be more meaning to the word in this context. Walvoord writes,

Some expositors use the term "gospel" to include all the revelations God has given in Christ and hence conclude that there is only one gospel with various phases of truth belonging to the gospel....The everlasting gospel seems to be neither the gospel of grace nor the gospel of the kingdom, but rather the good news that God at last is about to deal with the world in righteousness and establish His sovereignty over the world. This is an ageless gospel in the sense that God's righteousness is ageless (*Revelation*, p. 217).

For certain, the gospel here would have to include the great truth of Christ as the only Savior. And because the angel carries the message "to every nation and tribe and tongue and people," no one living in this terrible time can offer an excuse for rejecting God's gift of salvation through Christ. How the angel delivers the gospel is not explained.

The angel will also proclaim, "Fear God, and give Him glory, because the hour of His judgment has come" (Revelation 14:7). The word "hour" is used here to describe the fact that God's judgment has come near and He will soon try the nations before His bar of justice. The command to the earth is to "worship Him" who made the heaven and the earth "and sea and springs of waters." More than likely, at this stage in the Tribulation, drinkable water will be scarce because of the disasters that will pollute the earth's waters (see 8:10-11).

BABYLON'S FALL
Revelation 14:8

ANOTHER ANGEL WILL FOLLOW the one mentioned in Revelation 14:6-7 and cry out, "Fallen, fallen is Babylon the great, she who has made all the nations drink of the wine of the passion of her immorality" (verse 8). The words "fallen" (Greek, *pimpō*) are both in the Greek aorist tense, indicating a certainty of

what is to come. The fall of Babylon is yet future in Revelation (chapters 17-18).

Ancient Babylon cast a long and dark shadow over the Middle East, and it also greatly influenced the affairs of the Jewish people. The story of Babylon began with the waters that nourished the Garden of Eden. Four rivers flowed out of the garden including the Tigris and the Euphrates (Genesis 2:10-14). This was the area where, in later years, Nimrod first settled "his kingdom Babel" (10:10). "Babel" is an early name for Babylon, and the Hebrew root word *balal* means "confusion." In this area in the plain of Shinar the great tower of Babel ("gate of God") was constructed to "reach into heaven" (11:4). And from there God scattered humanity "over the face of the whole earth" (verse 9). From this region polytheism quickly began to flourish and mature. People began to worship the stars of heaven, and soon an entire religious system was developed with a pantheon of gods. During the Tribulation, Babylon and her religious influence will be revived to further lead the world astray, but her rise to prominence won't last long, for her doom is certain (see Revelation 17-18).

THE DOOM OF THE WORSHIPPERS OF THE BEAST
Revelation 14:9-12

AT THIS POINT A THIRD ANGEL comes forth, saying with a loud voice, "If anyone worships the beast and his image, and receives a mark on his forehead or upon his hand, he also will drink of the wine of the wrath of God" (verses 9-10). As the Tribulation progresses in the book of Revelation, people are pushed against the wall spiritually to make a decision as to whom they will serve. To follow and worship the beast brings on even heavier judgment from God. But to serve the Lord will likely mean martyrdom and death. There is no middle ground! The severity and quickness of God's promised judgment seems to indicate that the people of the world will fully understand the issues and the decisions they must make. They will not be ignorant of the spiritual struggle taking place between God and the powers of darkness.

God's wrath will fall heavily on those who worship the beast. It will fall "mixed in full strength in the cup of His anger; and [these people] will be tormented with fire and brimstone in the presence of the holy angels and in the presence of the Lamb" (verse 10). The scene is made more terrible by the fact that the witnesses to this outpouring of judgment will be the holy angels of heaven and the Lamb, the Lord Jesus Christ! The fires of punishment, with the smoke ascending upward, will continue "forever and ever" with no rest for the tormented who aligned themselves with the beast by taking his mark, an oath of loyalty (verse 11; cf. 13:16-18). The Tribulation saints, by contrast, will persevere and will obey God's commandments and hold fast "their faith in Jesus" (14:12).

BLESSINGS ON THE MARTYRED BELIEVERS
Revelation 14:13

THOSE SAINTS WHO PERISH during the Tribulation and who "die in the Lord from now on" are given a pronouncement of a special blessing for their martyrdom (verse 13). They are especially blessed in light of this added acclamation: "'Yes,' says the Spirit, 'so that they may rest from their labors, for their deeds follow with them.'" While in all ages of Christianity there have been martyrs for the faith, these believers will suffer some of the worst torments for the sake of Christ. Some Bible commentators have attempted to interpret these words to extend to all martyrs through the ages, but the context of these words limits their application to those who die under the persecution of the beast. That is evident in the phrase "from now on." Hindson observes that these believers "can face death because what awaits them in heaven is far better than anything on earth" (*Revelation*, p. 158).

A PREVIEW OF THE HARVEST OF THE EARTH
Revelation 14:14-20

IN REVELATION 14:14, John sees the Lord Jesus in His future messianic glory as "the son of man" (verse 14). This messianic title was first given in Daniel 7:13 and means "the Son related to mankind." Christ is also the Son of God, or "the Son related to God," as indicated by Psalm 2:7. The white cloud John sees here is an allusion to Daniel 7:13-14, Matthew 16:27-28; 25:30-31; 26:64, and Acts 1:9,11. In Scripture, clouds sometimes represent a great company of angels who attend the Messiah when He comes to "sit on His glorious throne" on earth (Matthew 25:31). His "golden crown" (Greek, *diadem*) identifies His royalty and His right to reign (Revelation 14:14).

One of the first things Christ will do is bring judgment to the world with a "sharp sickle," because "the hour to reap has come, because the harvest of the earth is ripe" (verse 15). This harvest will be urged on by an angel who comes "out of the temple" in heaven crying with a loud voice. Hindson notes that the imagery of the harvest and vintage is taken from Joel 3:3 (*Revelation*, p. 158). Another angel who has power over fire (16:8) will come from the heavenly altar and call for the sharp sickle that will cut "and gather the clusters from the vine of the earth, because her grapes are ripe" (14:18).

The harvested grapes refer to the evil people of the earth, who will be gleaned and then thrown "into the great wine press of the wrath of God" (verse 19). This terrible scene of judgment occurs "outside the city" of Jerusalem. The blood of those who came against the city of David comes "up to the horses' bridles, for a distance of two hundred miles" (verse 20). This carnage is described in detail in 19:17-19; it is the battle of Armageddon ("the hill of Megiddo"). The Old Testament predicts this final battle will take place near the Valley of Jehoshaphat, which is near the Kidron Valley (cf. Joel 3:12-14; Zechariah 14:4). While the hill of Megiddo is somewhat of a distance north of Jerusalem, the problem of distance, as seen by some, is not insuperable. This final battle will spread from Megiddo southward and virtually throughout the Holy Land. We must also remember that the Valley of Megiddo is a broad plain that runs one to two hundred miles north and south. Here the military forces of most of the nations of the world will gather to destroy the Jewish people. It is at this time that Christ will make His dramatic return to earth as Judge! That the blood will come "up to the horses' bridles" indicates the enormity of the casualties in this battle.

In regard to this chapter, we must remember that the prediction that Christ will judge the earth comes after three angelic warnings: 1) the preaching of the everlasting gospel; 2) the warning that Babylon and her religious influence will be destroyed; and 3) the assurance that the worshippers of Antichrist will be destroyed. That many will *still* reject Christ even after receiving these warnings is strong confirmation of the depravity of the human heart.

PRELUDE TO THE SEVEN BOWL JUDGMENTS
Revelation 15:1-8

CHAPTER 15 INTRODUCES the final series of plagues to come upon the earth (verse 1). With these plagues "the wrath of God is finished." These eight verses are a prelude to God's most severe judgments, or the seven bowls of wrath (chapter 16). This wrath will be like hot, scalding liquid poured out on the earth from heaven.

The apostle is given a vision of heaven and the Tribulation martyrs who had victory over the beast by refusing to pay homage to him and take his mark of loyalty (15:2). These saints are standing in heaven on "a sea of glass mixed with fire." The original Greek text reads a "glassy, crystal" sea, as stated in 4:6. This is a pavement of glass that resembles an expanse of water that is crystal-clear. The four living

creatures, or angels, seen earlier (15:7) are also here. While there is a certain tranquility about the scene, fire is also mentioned, which generally represents God's righteous judgment. The martyrs are playing the "harps of God" in gratitude and honor to the Lord for their salvation. The only other musical instrument that appears in Revelation is the trumpet, which is used to sound judgment.

The martyrs are singing the song of Moses and the song of the Lamb (verse 3). The song of Moses is identified with the song recorded in Exodus 15, although some have suggested that Moses' song is recorded in Deuteronomy 32. Walvoord writes that "both passages however ascribe praise to God and are similar in many ways to the hymn here recorded" (*Revelation*, p. 228). God will receive the glory for the final salvation that is yet to come. The works of the "Almighty" are praised, and He is titled "King of the nations" (Revelation 15:3). The futuristic context of this passage is indicated by the question in verse 4: "Who will not fear, O Lord, and glorify Your name?" Only He is holy, and all the nations will come "and worship before Thee." The world will have to honor Him because His "righteous acts have been revealed" (verse 4). At the end of the Tribulation and the beginning of the kingdom, there will be no question that God was just and even gracious in His dealings with the sinful, rebellious peoples of the earth. That all the nations will worship the Lord is a familiar theme of the Old Testament prophets (cf. Psalm 2:8-9; 24:1-10; 66:1-4; 72:8-11; Isaiah 2:2-4; Zephaniah 2:11; Zechariah 14:9).

As John continues to watch, he sees the temple "of the tabernacle of testimony in heaven" opened (Revelation 15:5). The "temple" (Greek, *naos*) describes the inner holy place of the tabernacle (the tent-like structure) that held the tablets of stone containing the Ten Commandments (Exodus 32:15; Acts 7:44), and is often mentioned in relation to the ark of the testimony in the Holy of Holies in the Old Testament (Exodus 38:21; Numbers 1:50,53; 10:11; 17:7-8; 18:2). Out of the temple, where the law of God resides, will come seven angels bearing the seven plagues of judgment that will be poured out on the earth (Revelation 15:6). Because God's laws have been violated, judgment is certain. While all God's angels are holy, these angels are particularly notable because they are robed in "linen, clean and bright, and girded around their chests with golden sashes" (verse 6). These angels apparently worked closely with God, and their dress seems to reflect their position.

The four special angels ("the four living creatures" in Revelation 4:6) hand a golden bowl of wrath to each of the seven angels (15:7). The heavenly temple is "filled with smoke from the glory of God and from His power" (verse 8). The smoke is from the heavenly incense that continually burns in honor of the Lord (Exodus 19:18; 40:34-35). No one can enter the temple in heaven until this ordeal of judgment is finished and all seven plagues, the seven bowls of wrath, have been poured out on the earth. With these judgments the Tribulation will be concluded and the millennium and the earthly reign of Christ will begin.

THE SEVEN BOWLS OF WRATH
Revelation 16:1-21

THE SEVEN PLAGUES, or seven bowls of wrath, descend upon the earth in rapid succession. Each bowl is poured out by a specific angel (15:6) who is commanded by "a loud voice from the temple" to pour out the "wrath of God" on the earth (16:1).

The first bowl of wrath (16:1-2). The "loud voice" is not of an angel but appears to be the voice of God, as shown in 15:8, since no one—and that would include angels at this point—can enter the temple of the Lord. This is the same voice heard in 16:17. When the first bowl of wrath is poured out on the earth, "a loathsome and malignant sore" comes upon all those who have aligned themselves with the beast by taking his mark and worshiping his image (verse 2). The sores are ulcers, cancerous lesions, or suppurated wounds that

infect everyone on earth except the righteous. Such running, puss-like ailments seem similar to other sores described in Scripture (Exodus 9:9-11; Leviticus 13:18-27). The descriptions imply painful or agonizing ulcers that resist healing.

The second bowl of wrath (16:3). The second bowl is poured "into the sea," causing the water to become like the blood of a dead man—probably through pollutants of some kind. The waters will become foul, odorous, and loathsome, and all sea life will die from this worldwide ecological disaster. This is reminiscent of the first Egyptian plague (Exodus 7:17-21) and the other blood-like plagues in Revelation (8:8-9; 11:6).

The third bowl of wrath (16:4-7). Next the inland waters, such as rivers and springs of water, will become polluted (verse 4). The angel who pours out this bowl of judgment calls out, "Righteous are You, who are and who were, O Holy One, because You judged these things" (verse 5). The God who exists now and existed in the past is the holy God who has a right to judge His creatures. The expression of His eternality and His righteousness is similar to what has been said of Him before (cf. 1:4,8; 4:8; 11:17; 15:3; 19:2), and it is also a reminder of His everlasting nature as revealed to Moses in Exodus 3:14. The judgments of the eternal and righteous God cannot be questioned.

The fourth bowl of wrath (16:8-9). The plague poured out of the fourth bowl seems to cause what would be called today a solar flare that bombards the earth with intense radiation. The heat of the sun increases "to scorch men with fire" (verse 8) and with "fierce heat," which causes them to blaspheme and curse the name of God, "who has the power over these plagues" (verse 9). The implication is that the Lord would remove this plague if people repented, but "they did not repent, so as to give Him glory." The judgment of God was right, yet sadly, judgment rarely brings people to repent and call out to the Lord. Thomas observes, "The human response is blasphemy against the God who is directly responsible for all this human misery" (*Revelation*, 8–22, p. 257).

The fifth bowl of wrath (16:10-11). When the fifth angel pours out his bowl, the worldwide kingdom of the beast will become "darkened," and people will "[gnaw] their tongues because of pain" (verse 10). If this darkness is physical and atmospheric, there will have to be a sudden reversal of the intense heat and light caused by the fourth bowl of wrath—in other words, a rapid loss of sunlight. This is certainly not impossible because these plagues are from God and they are miraculous. However, the darkness here could also be spiritual and even emotional and oppressive darkness. Again, the people of earth blaspheme "the God of heaven because of their pains and their sores; and they [do] not repent of their deeds" (verse 11).

The sixth bowl of wrath (16:12-16). The Euphrates River dries up in preparation for the final invasion of the "kings of the east." Some take verses 13-16 as a parenthetical pause in the narrative of the seven bowl judgments. But more than likely these verses describe events connected to the sixth bowl, which is introduced in verse 12. The reason some say verses 13-16 are parenthetical is because they mention activities carried out by Satan (the dragon), the beast, and the false prophet. However, as Hindson observes, "Up until this bowl, the previous bowls have involved a direct outpouring of divine wrath. There is no mention of any specific human instrumentality. These judgments may well be the aftermath of the previous ones (seals and trumpets)" (*Revelation*, p. 170).

From the dragon, the beast, and the false prophet will come forth, as if from their mouths, increased demonic activity described as "unclean spirits like frogs" (verse 13). The word "frogs" speaks of something revulsive. These demons will perform signs and "go out to the kings of the whole world, to gather them together for the war of the great day of God, the Almighty" (verse 14). This war is Armageddon, which will be the last great battle before the coming of the Lord Jesus to reign on earth (see 14:14-20; 19:11-21).

Some scholars believe "Armageddon" ("hill of Megiddo") is used here in a figurative sense and not a literal one. Some think the term is illustrative of all the hills that surround Israel. For example, Ezekiel prophesied about the "mountains of Israel" that will figure prominently in the final wars of the last days (Ezekiel 30:1-9; 38:8-21; 39:1-4). However, Scripture gives a specific location for this battle. The Megiddo plain is where the final conflict will take place, or it will serve as the staging area for the invasion that will come against Jerusalem. The Lord will gather the nations to this place (Revelation 16:16), and the inhabitants of the entire earth will be involved.

Christ then gives a warning and an invitation to those who will be reading this book when these events take place: "Behold, I am coming like a thief. Blessed is the one who stays awake and keeps his clothes, so that he will not walk about naked and men will not see his shame" (verse 15). When judgment is imminent, God often expresses mercy and grace to those who will listen to His warnings.

The seventh bowl of wrath (16:17-21). When the seventh bowl is poured out into the air, the Lord will shout with a loud voice, "It is done" (verse 17), meaning the final outpourings of wrath are finished. Great atmospheric storms and a powerful earthquake will herald the end. The shaking of the earth will be "such as there had not been since man came to be upon the earth, so great an earthquake was it, and so mighty" (verse 18). While it's tempting to say that the "great city" that is split apart in verse 19 is Babylon, Revelation 11:8 has already identified the "great city" as apostate Jerusalem, and 11:13 tells of a previous earthquake that causes a tenth of the city to fall and 7000 people to die. Here in chapter 16 the city will be split "into three parts" (verse 19), and "the cities of the nations" will also fall. With this earthquake God will give "Babylon the great...the cup of the wine of His fierce wrath" (verse 19).

As a result of the earthquakes and storms, every island (or coast line) will flee away and the mountains will "not [be] found" (verse 20). Monstrous hailstones (about 100 pounds each) will pummel the earth, and yet again, people will blaspheme God "because of the plague of the hail, because its plague was extremely severe" (verse 21). The mention of Babylon (verse 19) in the narrative establishes a parenthetical pause (chapters 17–18) in which we read about what will happen toward the end of the tribulation to "Babylon the great, the mother of harlots" (17:5).

BABYLON: THE GREAT HARLOT
Revelation 17

SOME SCHOLARS BELIEVE chapters 17 and 18 talk about two different aspects of Babylon. Chapter 17 has to do with *spiritual* Babylon, and chapter 18 describes the fall of *economic* Babylon. Others say there is no relation between the two. Though interpreting these chapters is difficult, it appears best to say that there is but one Babylon, with the ecclesiastical or spiritual entity featured in chapter 17 and a political and economic entity described in chapter 18.

The rapid rise of Babylon is seen in chapter 17 and could well have occurred at the beginning of the Tribulation. Chapter 18 tells of the downfall of Babylon, who is the "great harlot [Greek *porne*] who sits on many waters" (17:1). In Scripture, "waters" often describe the vastness of the nations of the earth (cf. verse 15). Babylon is then ruling or spiritually influencing the nations by her evil nature, causing "those who dwell on the earth [to be] made drunk with the wine of her immorality" (verse 2). The religious harlotry of Israel is well documented in Ezekiel 16 and 23, and in similar manner, the world will wallow in spiritual and moral darkness under Babylon's influence.

John the apostle is then carried away by the Holy Spirit into "a wilderness" to see the evil workings of the harlot (Revelation 17:3). He sees her riding the beast introduced in 13:1. The beast's scarlet color represents the bloodthirsty nature of his royalty, and the woman is clothed

in a similar fashion (17:4). The "seven heads and ten horns" are also mentioned in 13:1. Daniel 7:24 explains that the ten horns represent a confederation of ten Gentile powers who form a revived Roman Empire. The seven heads represent the committee of leaders and rulers who govern this conglomerate of nations now acting as one under the sway of the beast.

The harlot is clothed in the most ostentatious of finery (Revelation 17:4), yet the gold cup in her hand is full of filth, abominations, and "unclean things of her immorality." The picture painted here is one of a seductive prostitute who looks regal but is disease-ridden and able to infect her suitors. Babylon will seduce and charm the world with her evil, but only for a while. Prominent on her forehead is a name that is a "mystery" (Greek, *musterion*), "Babylon the great, the mother of harlots and of the abominations of the earth" (verse 5). There is something about her name that will not be known until then. Possibly it is the fact that no one could imagine that Babylon would be the source of all false religion and that this falsehood would spread so rapidly and take root in all the nations of the world. Or it could be the fact people would not have expected religion to play such a major role in the end times.

Corporate human rebellion first began at Babel (Genesis 10:9-10), where the city of Babylon was built. It was here that false religion and polytheism originated (11:1-9). While there is a historical connection between false religion and Babylon, the expression "mystery" in Revelation 17:5 suggests that what is about to take place is not literal but deeply figurative in nature. Many prophecy scholars are expecting a literal revival of geographical and political Babylon, which is centered in present-day Iraq. Others believe the "Babylon" described in Revelation 17–18 is a code name for Rome (and thus, the revived Roman Empire of the future).

The charge against Babylon is that through the corridors of history, she has been sated with the "blood of the saints, and with the blood of the witnesses of Jesus" (Revelation 17:6). She is described as being drunk with the murder of the saints. As John looks at her, he wonders greatly at this "mystery" Babylon, who is far more evil than he could have imagined!

Part of the *mystery* also has to do with the relationship between the harlot and the beast (verse 7). The beast who "was and is not, and is about to come up out of the abyss and go to destruction" (17:8) is now closely related to the beast who had suffered a deadly wound and was healed (13:3,12,14). The people on earth will be shocked and amazed and "will wonder" at what is happening (17:8). In a twist of thought, this is the same as "his reappearance as an eighth king in 17:11. His departure to perdition...is his future assignment to the lake of fire (19:20)" (Thomas, *Revelation 8–22*, pp. 292-93). This passage is difficult to follow, but Thomas explains it this way:

> [17:8] is a part of the chapter that is purely prophetic, but verses 9-11 are an injected explanation to help in understanding the prophecy. All these considerations lead to the conclusion that the perspective of this description of the beast is entirely future, at a point just before the beast from the sea begins his three-and-a-half-year reign (*Revelation 8–22*, p. 293).

For future readers of the book of Revelation, verse 9 is a reminder to observe what is taking place. They are told, "Here is the mind which has wisdom" (cf. 13:18). The seven heads of the beast (17:9) are seven kings: "five have fallen, one is, the other has not yet come, and when he comes, he must remain a little while" (verse 10).

To understand verse 11, we need to recall from chapter 13 the interchange between the beast and its wounded head (verses 3,12,14). It seems that sometimes the beast is the same as its heads, and yet the beast may also be distinct from them. In 17:11, we read that the seventh head becomes the eighth. The beast would be one of the seven kings in his kingdom, but then the eighth king is seen to be the ruler who receives the deadly wound

and then comes up from the abyss (verse 8). When this takes place, he becomes the eighth king (verse 11). This eighth king will be a world dictator who receives supernatural power when he is "revived" by Satan. Making the eighth king identical to the beast out of the abyss seems to be the only interpretation that makes sense.

For a short period (one hour), the ten horns (or powers, verse 7) are ten kings who receive a kingdom, but their authority is tied to the beast (verse 12). That their authority lasts for only "one hour" means they were in power but a short time. They then unite with "one purpose," and "give their power and authority to the beast" (verse 13). Though not stated, it could be argued that the reason these world leaders sign their authority over to the beast is because the world is getting much worse, and out of desperation they allow the beast to act unilaterally and bring about order by force.

Verse 14 could mean that throughout the Tribulation these kings, along with the beast, are continually waging war with Christ the Lamb. But it could also refer specifically to the battle of Armageddon, which will take place soon (19:11-21). Christ will be victorious because "He is King of kings and Lord of lords," (cf. 19:16; 1 Timothy 6:15).

Before the battle of Armageddon, the ten powers ("horns") and the beast will turn against the harlot and "make her desolate and naked, and will eat her flesh and will burn her up with fire" (Revelation 17:16). We are then told that it is God who will put into the hearts of these rulers the compulsion to give their kingdom to the beast (verse 17). Now we see this period of terrible wrath from God coming to a climax, and the beast will rule this kingdom "until the words of God will be fulfilled" (17:17). John then reminds us that the harlot, the woman, is not simply a revived nation, such as ancient Babylon, but a city "which reigns over the kings of the earth" (verse 18).

Many prophecy scholars believe that verse 18 is a reference to the Roman Catholic Church exercising spiritual power worldwide. If this is the case, the city in view would be Rome, and it is the Roman Church that would team up with the beast to control the nations. The leaders of that religious system would even control the beast for a time.

That the false religion of the last days is represented by a woman hearkens back to ancient Babylonian religion, which spawned mother goddess worship, astrology, black magic, and occult practices (Hindson, *Revelation,* p. 177). Despite what some may think, it is no small matter that the harlot occupies two long chapters toward the end of the book of Revelation. Walvoord says, "The picture of the woman as utterly evil signifies spiritual adultery, portraying those who outwardly and religiously seem to be joined to the true God, but who are untrue to this relationship" (*Revelation,* p. 244).

BABYLON DESTROYED
Revelation 18:1-19

THERE ARE THREE MAIN observations about Babylon in this chapter: 1) It is spiritually evil; 2) it is described as a city; and 3) the nations of the world will trade sumptuously with her. "Another" angel now takes over the narrative and announces Babylon's impending destruction (verse 1). This angel is one of the most powerful in the heavenly court. He comes down from heaven "having great authority, and the earth was illumined with his glory" (verse 1), and he cries out, "Fallen, fallen is Babylon the great!" (verse 2). The most perverse of demonic personalities will inhabit Babylon, which is said to be "a dwelling place of demons and a prison of every unclean spirit, and a prison of every unclean and hateful bird" (verse 2). From Babylon these demonic creatures will influence the world spiritually and tempt humans to give their loyalty to the beast. The demons are "spirit" (Greek, *pneuma*) beings, described as "unclean" (Greek, *akathartos*) or "dirty, filthy, impure." This is a reference to their moral state and the fact they tempt people to engage in the most evil of practices.

All the nations of the earth will have partaken of Babylon's immorality, and the merchants will "have become rich by the wealth of her sensuality" (verse 3). "Immorality" (Greek, *porneia*) can be translated "fornication" or "lasciviousness" and refers to various forms of sexual sins. In some way not explained, the nations relish in Babylon's "sensuality," which may indicate the fleshly luxury and self-indulgence she promotes. "Babylon traded in both sin and 'all things that were luxurious and splendid' (verse 14), including numerous kinds of expensive goods (verses 12-16), and even the trade of 'slaves and human lives' (verse 13)" (Couch, *Revelation,* p. 284).

All the Tribulation saints will be called out of Babylon and commanded to not participate in her sins so as not to "receive of her plagues" (verse 4). John says that Babylon's sins have piled up as high as heaven, "and God has remembered her iniquities" (verse 5). As if making a request to the Lord, John urges Him to "pay her back even as she has paid" in regard to the evil she brought upon the world. The cup of wrath has been mixed "twice as much for her" (verse 6), and she will be given "torment and mourning" because she says in her heart, "I sit as a Queen and I am not a widow, and will never see mourning" (verse 7). Here John is paraphrasing and quoting the words of evil Babylon, the "daughter of the Chaldeans" (Babylonians), as cited in Isaiah 47:7-8. Isaiah 47 is most descriptive of Babylon's sins and her fall. Isaiah said, "Evil will come on you which you will not know how to charm away; and disaster will fall on you for which you cannot atone; and destruction about which you do not know will come on you suddenly" (verse 11).

Though Isaiah's words were about ancient Babylon, they also preview what will happen to Babylon in Revelation 18. In verse 8 it is written that "in one day her plagues will come" accompanied with pestilence and mourning and famine, and Babylon will be consumed by fire, "for the Lord God who judges her is strong."

The rulers of the earth who cavorted with Babylon will "lament over her when they see the smoke of her burning" (verse 9). Ships carrying cargo to her will stand at a distance as torment falls upon her, and people will cry, "Woe, woe, the great city, Babylon, the strong city! For in one hour your judgment has come" (verse 10). The lavish trade with her will cease, as will the slave trade of "human lives" (verses 11-13). The luxurious and splendid things will pass away and will no longer be found (see verse 14). The merchants who became wealthy off Babylon "will stand at a distance because of the fear of her torment, weeping and mourning" (verse 15), and they will cry, "Woe, woe" (verse 16).

Verse 17 restates the fact that the city is destroyed in one hour (cf. verse 10). Those who ply the sea will view the destruction from afar and weep, saying "What city is like the great city?" (verse 18). Again people will cry, "Woe, woe...for in one hour she has been laid waste!" (verse 19). God will not forget to carry out the judgment due to Babylon. Though she will seem invincible, she will fall.

HEAVENLY REJOICING
Revelation 18:20-24

THE DESTRUCTION OF THE EVIL CITY of Babylon will cause all of heaven, the "saints and apostles and prophets," to rejoice (verse 20). Some scholars have surmised that the "saints" represent the saints of all dispensations in both the Old and the New Testaments. This would make sense because Babylon's evil history goes back far in biblical history. But a good argument could also be made that these are the Tribulation saints who had suffered terribly during this time. LaHaye writes that these "could be tribulation saints, people who were not Christians at the time of the Rapture of the Church but who, during the Tribulation, received Christ as Savior and Lord" (*Revelation Illustrated and Made Plain*, p. 244).

The "apostles" and "prophets" mentioned in verse 20 could be the spiritual leaders of the early church, though some see the prophets as those of the Old Testament. Thomas (*Revelation 8–22*, p. 342) believes John the apostle had in mind his fellow apostles who were martyred, including his brother James, in early church history (Acts 12:1-2).

Babylon, "the great city," will be drowned in the sea as with a great millstone (Revelation 18:21). Her demise will come with violence, and she "will not be found any longer." No longer will people hear the sound of pagan reveling in the city with harps, flutes, trumpets, nor will the skill of craftsmen be seen, nor the sound of the mill at work (verse 22). No longer will the light shine in the city, nor will be heard the sound of young people marrying (verse 23). The merchants of the world will no longer prosper from her. Babylon's judgment will be severe because "all the nations were deceived by [her] sorcery" (Greek, *pharmakeia*). *Pharmakeia* could refer to the use of hallucinogen substances in pagan religious rituals, or it could refer to the fact that the people of that future era will be known for the use of mind-numbing drugs for psychological escape.

Verse 24 tells us that in Babylon "was found the blood" of the saints and prophets of old. The Old Testament confirms that ancient Babylon was a city of bloodshed (Jeremiah 51:35), and we see in Revelation 18 that during the Tribulation she will persecute the saints of the Lord with a vengeance.

PRELUDE TO THE FINAL VICTORY
Revelation 19:1-6

ENTERING INTO REVELATION chapter 19, the heavenly rejoicing over the demise of Babylon continues. Four *hallelujahs* are sounded. "Hallelujah! Salvation and glory and power belong to our God" (verse 1). The Hebrew word *hallelujah* is a compound term that means "praise the ever-existing One!" This same exclamation is used at the end of some of the Psalms. The early church congregations picked up the word as used in the Jewish synagogues.

Three more hallelujahs are offered in the

next few verses (verses 3,4,6) because God's judgment upon the "great harlot" has now been completed (verse 2). The end of Babylon is predicted in Jeremiah 51:48-49, where we read, " 'Then heaven and earth and all that is in them will shout for joy over Babylon, for the destroyers will come to her from the north,' declares the Lord. Indeed Babylon is to fall for the slain of Israel, as also for Babylon the slain of all the earth have fallen." The heavenly multitude continues to give God glory because He has "avenged the blood of His bond-servants on her" (Revelation 19:2). Those words are a direct quote from the Song of Moses in Deuteronomy 32:43. The multitude also quotes Isaiah 34:10, which also predicts Babylon's fall: "Her smoke rises up forever and ever" (Revelation 19:3).

The heavenly court, the 24 elders (4:4,10), and the four "living creatures" or special angels (verse 6) will also join in on the worship and fall down before God on His throne, saying, "Amen. Hallelujah!" (19:4). A voice from the throne then gives a summons for God's bond-servants to give praise to Him (verse 5). The call seems to be for all of the saints in glory from all dispensations, and together they proclaim, "Hallelujah! For the Lord our God, the Almighty, reigns" (verse 6).

This exuberant joy in heaven is not simply an account of the slaying of Babylon, but it is also in anticipation of the Lord Jesus descending from glory to begin His messianic reign on earth. All the heavenly host now know that sin's prevalence over the earth is about to end.

THE MARRIAGE OF THE LAMB
Revelation 19:7-10

To UNDERSTAND Revelation 19:7-10, we must first look at some promises made to the church. Christ said He was going to prepare a place in heaven for His disciples, and that He would come back to take them there (John 14:3). This promise was not only for the apostles, but also includes all future generations of Christians. Added to this is the promise that someday believers will be changed, by the resurrection or the rapture, and be taken to glory "in a moment, in the twinkling of an eye, at the last trumpet" (1 Corinthians 15:51-52). Paul explains this great hope further in 1 Thessalonians 4:14-17. Those who have died in Jesus will go first when the trumpet of God is sounded, and then "we who are alive and remain will be caught up together with them in the clouds to meet the Lord in the air" (verse 17).

When will this resurrection/rapture of the church happen? Since the church is never mentioned or seen on earth after Revelation 3, the only possible answer is that the church will be taken away before the terrible events of the Tribulation take place. The great heavenly company from every tribe, tongue, people, and nation (Revelation 5:9) must be the church taken to glory before the Tribulation begins in chapter 6. The rapture is the event by which Jesus will deliver the church "from the wrath to come" (1 Thessalonians 1:10). Paul states the reason: "For God has not destined us for wrath, but for obtaining salvation through our Lord Jesus Christ" (5:9).

In Revelation 19:7 we see the *heavenly marriage* of the Lamb and the bride, the church. The bride is clothed in "fine linen, bright and clean," which represents "the righteous acts of the saints" (verse 8). Christ, by His death on the cross, made it possible for believers to be sanctified and cleansed so that "He might present to Himself the church in all her glory, having no spot or wrinkle or any such thing; but that she would be holy and blameless" (Ephesians 5:26-27). Positionally, then, believers are saved by Christ's cleansing work. But the fine linen in Revelation 19:8 is said to be the righteous acts of the saints. Walvoord explains:

> Though even this righteousness is a product of the grace of God, it is distinguished as being related to human works, an experience, rather than to a divine fiat. The fine linen may, in some sense, be a part of the reward given at

the judgment seat of Christ to those who have served the Lord, here seen collectively in the wife of the Lamb (*Revelation*, p. 272).

John is urged to invite others to this "marriage supper of the Lamb," and there will be a blessing of salvation for those who come (verse 9). This *invitation* seems to be intertwined with the running narration of this book, and it is among other invitations given so that readers of Revelation can come to Christ while pondering its words. John then suddenly falls before the feet of the angel delivering this message, and the angel rebukes him, saying, "[I am] a fellow servant of yours and your brethren who hold the testimony of Jesus" (verse 10). The angel then tells John to "worship God."

This passage closes with the statement that "the testimony of Jesus is the spirit of prophecy" (verse 10). In other words, the testimony given by Christ is the total substance of what the Holy Spirit inspired Christian apostles and prophets to say. John and other writers of Scripture were gifted as prophets and received the inspired messages of this testimony so that it may be known to all future generations.

THE SECOND COMING OF CHRIST
Revelation 19:11-16

HERE WE COME TO the most dramatic passage in all the Bible: the description of Jesus Christ's triumphal return to earth on a white horse. In verses 11-16 we are swept into the triumphal entourage of the redeemed saints as they follow Christ riding forth from heaven. The Lord Jesus, the One who is "called Faithful and True" (see Revelation 3:7,14), will come to earth to make war "in righteousness." As the apostle Paul predicted, He will come "in flaming fire, dealing out retribution to those who do not know God" (2 Thessalonians 1:7). The "flame of fire" in Jesus' eyes represents His perfect discernment for judgment, and

the "many diadems" on His head represent His authority and His right to rule. He has a "name written upon Him which no one knows except Himself." No one has ever seen Christ in this light before—He now comes as the King of kings, the absolute monarch who brings forth judgment.

This scene in Revelation 19 is a fulfillment of Isaiah 63:1-6, a messianic passage that shows the King coming with wrath and vengeance, His clothes sprinkled with the blood of His enemies (verse 3). He will arrive on earth to "speak in righteousness" (verse 1), which will take place during His year of redemption (verse 4). He will utter the words, "I trod down the peoples in My anger...and I poured out their lifeblood on the earth" (verse 6).

In Revelation 19:13 we read that Christ is also called "the Word of God," which is a reference to John 1:1 and 1 John 1:1 and an expression of His full deity. He is the complete revelation of God to humanity. With Jesus are "the armies" from heaven, clothed in fine linen and riding white horses (verse 14). These armies are the saints in glory who will return with Jesus to earth to enjoy His rule. These armies may also include holy angels who come to carry out the Lord's authority on earth, as mentioned in Matthew 25:31. But the major emphasis here is the church, the bride of Christ, who will ride out of heaven with Jesus in triumph (19:14). They are no longer the church rejected, persecuted, and martyred. Now they are the church triumphant!

From the mouth of Christ will come judgment upon the rebellious nations like "a sharp sword." He will "smite the nations; and He will rule them with a rod of iron" (verse 15). God the Father had promised the Son, "Ask of Me, and I will surely give the nations as Your inheritance, and the very ends of the earth as Your possession. You shall break them with a rod of iron, You shall shatter them like earthenware" (Psalm 2:8-9). The overcomers in the dispensation of the church will also share in that rule. The one who "keeps" the deeds of God the Son will co-rule with Him under His authority (Revelation 2:26-27). Christ's judgment will be thorough, for He will tread "the wine press of the fierce wrath of God, the Almighty" (19:15).

On His robe and clothing Christ "has a name written, King of kings, and Lord of lords" (Revelation 19:16; cf. 17:14; 1 Timothy 6:15). This title given to Christ is similar to what is said of the Lord through Moses: "For the Lord your God is the God of gods and the Lord of lords, the great, the mighty, and the awesome God" (Deuteronomy 10:17). This connection is no accident, and it adds further evidence of the deity of Christ.

THE BATTLE OF ARMAGEDDON
Revelation 19:17-21

WE NOW COME TO the final confrontation between God and the forces of evil in the seven-year Tribulation. An angel standing in the brightness of the sun announces that a new day has come (verse 17). With a loud voice a call goes out to "all the birds which fly in mid-heaven, 'Come, assemble for the great supper of God'" (verse 17). An awful carnage is about to take place here—this is the battle of Armageddon (previewed in Revelation 16:16), in which the beast and the kings of the world take out their violent anger against the Jews, God's people, in Jerusalem. However, these forces, gathered apparently from around the world, will be stopped at the plain of Megiddo.

The slaughter will be so great that birds are called upon to eat the flesh of this massive army, which includes kings, commanders, mighty men, both free men and slaves, both small men and great (19:18). These forces will be defeated by the Lord (verses 11,19,21), along with the beast and his allies, who have "assembled to make war against Him who sat on the horse and against His army" (verse 19). The hatred of the nations is directed not only at the Jewish people, but also at the Lord God and His Son. This was clearly predicted in Psalm 2:1-3:

Why are the nations in an uproar and the peoples devising a vain thing? The kings of the earth take their stand and the rulers take counsel together against the LORD and against His Anointed [the Messiah] saying, "Let us tear their fetters apart and cast away their cords from us!"

In this battle, both the beast and the false prophet will be seized by the Lord (Revelation 19:20). Together they will be "thrown alive into the lake of fire which burns with brimstone," and the armies that gave their allegiance to the beast and the false prophet will be "killed with the sword...from the mouth of Him who sat upon the horse" (verse 20-21). Indeed, Christ's second coming will be a dramatic and literal intervention into the final stages of world history. As Revelation 19 indicates, God's judgment against His adversaries will fall quickly and without hesitation.

SATAN BOUND DURING THE KINGDOM
Revelation 20:1-3

FOLLOWING ARMAGEDDON, an angel will come from heaven with "the key of the abyss and a great chain" (verse 1) and bind Satan "for a thousand years" (verse 2). The angel will throw Satan into the abyss "and shut it and sealed it over him, so that he should not deceive the nations any longer, until the thousand years were completed" (verse 3). Afterward, Satan "must be released for a short time."

Those who reject a literal earthly millennium, or 1000-year kingdom of Christ on earth, try to interpret the Greek word *chilia* ("thousand") in an allegorical or spiritual manner. They say *chilia* refers to an indefinite age or a longer period of time. And they generally apply this kingdom to the church age, which means Satan is bound during the church age. But that can hardly be true in light of Peter's admonition that "your adversary, the devil, prowls around like a roaring lion, seeking someone to devour" (1 Peter 5:8). In other words, Satan is very much on the loose during the church age.

The idea of a *literal* kingdom of God on earth is central to all biblical teaching. The prophets predicted it. Jesus announced it. And the apostles foretold it again. The kingdom of God has always existed and will always exist from eternity past to eternity future. LaSor states,

> The messianic kingdom on earth is a vindication of God's creative activity... The triumph of God over the Satanic dominion of this planet is necessary for the glory of God. If there were no messianic age, if God simply picked up the redeemed remnant and took them off to heaven, then we would have to conclude that God was unable to complete what He began (LaSor, *The Truth About Armageddon*, pp. 160-61).

When we look at all that is said about this 1000-year period at the beginning of Revelation 20, we cannot help but realize that only a literal interpretation of the text makes sense. The words of the Bible are meant to be taken literally unless there is a compelling reason not to do so. And generally when a nonliteral meaning is in view, there is a marker or interpretive point that leads the reader to see a passage in a nonliteral way. But notice that Revelation 20 gives the millennium a completion point: "until the thousand years were completed" (verse 5). It assigns a specific length: They "will reign with Him [Christ] for a thousand years" (verse 6). And it has a specified ending: "When the thousand years are completed" (verse 7). So this is not an unspecified time, and there is no reason to interpret it allegorically. One cannot place another interpretation upon this word; it is self explanatory!

Why is Satan released for a short time following the 1000-year reign of Christ (verse 3)? We must remember that at the end of the Tribulation, all the surviving Tribulation saints will enter the kingdom in their natural bodies and produce "kingdom" children. These people will not have glorified bodies, which means they are still capable of sinning. As these children grow up, they will need to make a personal choice to trust Christ as their Savior, just as people in the church age had to. But not everyone will choose Christ, and their true allegiance will be revealed when Satan is released at the end of the 1000 years. There will be a large number of people who rebel against Christ at that time, and Satan will "deceive the nations" and gather many people to bring about a final and ultimate rebellion (verse 8). However, the insurrection will end quickly (verse 9).

Those who hold to a view of the end times that insists Satan is already bound today are at a loss to explain when and how he will be released in the future. The view that the 1000-year kingdom is literal and still future is the only one that makes any legitimate sense of the context. There is nothing in the text itself to indicate that this 1000-year period should not be taken literally. Otherwise, all the other time indicators in the Revelation would be meaningless. Harold Hoehner says, "The denial of a literal one thousand years is not because of the exegesis of the text but a predisposition brought to the text" (pp. 249-50).

THE FIRST RESURRECTION FOR THE KINGDOM
Revelation 20:4-6

THERE IS MORE THAN ONE resurrection mentioned in the Bible, though some people attempt to place the different resurrections into one event that includes the church saints, Old Testament saints, and Tribulation saints all rising from the grave together. The first resurrection, which will take place at the time of the rapture, is for the church, or those who "have fallen asleep in Jesus" (1 Thessalonians 4:14). Old Testament saints are promised a resurrection to everlasting life. This will occur when Israel's Messiah comes to rule over the kingdom of His father David. Daniel was promised that he would see that day: "As for you [Daniel], go your way to the end; then you will enter into rest and rise again for your allotted portion at the end of the age" (Daniel 12:13). LaHaye points out three phases to this resurrection: 1) church age saints, 2) Old Testament saints, and 3) Tribulation saints (*Revelation Illustrated and Made Plain,* p. 281).

When the kingdom of Christ is established on earth, there will be thrones set up for judgment. The martyred Tribulation saints who "had been beheaded because of the testimony of Jesus and because of the word of God" will rise up to "reign with Christ for a thousand years" (Revelation 20:4). These resurrected Tribulation martyrs will judge their tormentors, who now stand before Christ! The martyrs will take part in the "first resurrection" and will enter into the millennial kingdom (verse 5). The "rest of the dead" are the lost, including the wicked who perished during the Tribulation. All the lost people of all generations will later be resurrected for judgment at the Great White Throne Judgment, which takes place at the end of the millennial kingdom (Revelation 20:11-15). In Luke 14:14, Christ spoke of the resurrection of the just in an Old Testament context without reference to the resurrection of the church saints.

Those who take part in this first resurrection are called "blessed and holy" (Revelation 20:6). The first death human beings experience is physical, and the second death, which is spiritual, will not affect believers. And "they will be priests of God and of Christ and will reign with Him for a thousand years" (verse 6). The "second death," or spiritual death, is also mentioned in 2:11; 20:14; 21:8.

THE FINAL REBELLION AND VICTORY
Revelation 20:7-10

FOLLOWING THE 1000-YEAR REIGN of Christ, Satan will be "released from his prison" (verse 7). He will go out to deceive the nations to turn against Christ and "the camp of the saints and the beloved city," which would be Jerusalem (verse 9).

John says the number of this great company "is like the sand of the seashore" (verse 8). John also uses the terms "Gog" and "Magog" without much explanation. Gog (the rulers) and Magog (the people) from the far north are mentioned as coming against the restored Jewish nation in Ezekiel 38–39. They will come with a multinational army (38:5-9) against Israel, which is "living securely" (38:14) in the "last days" (38:16). The Lord will stop the invading force and send fire "upon Magog and those who inhabit the coastlands in safety" (39:6). The carnage will be so great it will take seven months to cleanse the land from this battle (39:12).

While at first glance this conflict seems to be the same event as that described in Revelation 20:7-9, there are *differences* that may indicate they are not the same war. Though some of the participants are the same (Gog and Magog), the time frame is not. The invasion of Israel mentioned in Ezekiel 38–39 seems to come at the *beginning* of the Tribulation. There, for a short time, the Jews appear to be victorious, and the world is stunned by the defeat of the great northern power and its alliance. By contrast, the battle in Revelation 20:7-9 comes at the end of the kingdom period.

The conclusion of the invasion in Revelation 20:7-9 is quick and to the point. God will send fire "down from heaven," and the people will be "devoured" (verse 9). The devil, who was released for the rebellion, will be thrown "into the lake of fire and brimstone, where the beast and the false prophet are also; and they will be tormented day and night forever and ever" (verse 10). By this time, the beast and the false prophet will have already spent 1000 years in the lake of fire. "Their condition emphasizes the seriousness of the eternal punishment of the damned. They are condemned forever with no hope of escape or release. That is why consignment there is called the 'second death'" (Hindson, *Revelation,* p. 205).

It is here that Satan, the perpetrator and

promoter of all evils in the universe, is finally and forever removed from his place of influence.

GREAT WHITE THRONE JUDGMENT
Revelation 20:11-15

THE VERY DESCRIPTION OF the Great White Throne Judgment gives the impression of a judgment that is pure, righteous, and fair in the verdicts handed down to sinners. This is not a judgment for believers because the matter of the *positional* judgment of God is a settled issue for all those who have trusted in Christ for salvation. LaHaye emphasizes, "This judgment of the Great White Throne is for unbelievers only" (*Revelation Illustrated and Made Plain*, p. 300). Paul writes, "There is therefore now no condemnation for those who are in Christ Jesus" (Romans 8:1).

Believers will be judged at the *bema* judgment for the godly things done in their Christian walk (Romans 14:10-12; 1 Corinthians 3:12-15; 2 Corinthians 5:10). There is some debate as to who sits on the Great White Throne. It may be the Lord Jesus Christ because God the Father "has given all judgment to the Son" (John 5:22). Hindson believes "God the Father is the Judge on this occasion. Christ has judged the believers [for their works]; now the Father judges the unbelievers" for their final destiny (*Revelation*, p. 205).

When the Judge is seated heaven and earth will flee away, and no place will be "found for them," or for those who will be judged (Revelation 20:11). No one will be able to hide; all the wicked will find themselves brought before the bar of justice. Even the sea and Hades will give up their dead to ensure that all are judged. A set of books (scrolls) will be opened, with one book called "the book of life" (verse 12). Since those who stand before this throne will not have accepted Christ as their Savior, the only other criteria left for judgment will be their works (deeds) as recorded in the books. The Old Testament Hebrew word *Sheol*

and the New Testament Greek word *Hades* usually refer to the intermediate state, or as some hold, to the grave. *Gehenna* is the New Testament term generally used to describe the final place of eternal punishment (Matthew 5:22,30; 10:28; 23:33). *Gehenna* refers to the Valley of Hinnom, just outside of the city of Jerusalem, where the city's garbage was dumped and fires continually burned. Those whose names are not in the book of life will be "thrown into the lake of fire. This is the second death, the lake of fire" (Revelation 20:14). There is no escape from this eternal verdict! The question is often asked: If the unsaved have no hope of redemption, why must their works be judged, as if they stand a chance? God does all things in a righteous manner and allows the lost their day in court. They are given an opportunity to answer for their sins. However, no excuse will be accepted, for a holy God cannot permit even a speck of sin in His presence. And the lost will have no second chance. The only way to make it into heaven is for your name to be found "written in the Lamb's book of life" (Revelation 21:27).

NEW HEAVEN AND NEW EARTH
Revelation 21:1-8

FOLLOWING THE FINAL JUDGMENT, the history of the world as we know it will come to an end. Some have said that God will renovate the entire universe, creating a "new heaven and a new earth" (verse 1). Whether this is a renovation or a brand-new creation has been debated by many. Isaiah 65:17, which speaks of this event, uses the Hebrew word *bara*, (which means to create *ex nihilo*), implying a brand-new heaven and earth. "For behold, I create [*bara*] new heavens and a new earth; and the former things will not be remembered or come to mind." This new creation "will endure" forever before the Lord (66:22). With this new creation the old heavens "will pass away with a roar and the elements will be destroyed with intense heat, and the earth and its works will be burned up" (2 Peter 3:10-12). According to God's promise, believers will one day live in this new system "in which righteousness dwells" (verse 13).

Then a new Jerusalem will descend from heaven "from God, made ready as a bride adorned for her husband" (Revelation 21:2). In this new Jerusalem, "the tabernacle of God is among men, and He will dwell among them, and they shall be His people, and God Himself will be among them" (verse 3). Believers from all generations will enjoy the presence of the Lord together, and He will eliminate all tears, mourning, pain, and death because "the first things have passed away" (verse 4). In other words, all the sorrows and sufferings that are a part of life today will be no more. Paul writes that we all, along with all of creation, "groan within ourselves, waiting eagerly for our adoption as sons, the redemption of our body," and that "we wait eagerly for it" (Romans 8:22-25).

The apostle John records God as saying, "Behold, I am making all things new.... Write, for these words are faithful and true" (Revelation 21:5). With regard to the new creation, God will say, "It is done" (verse 6). The One who exists forever—"the Alpha and the Omega, the beginning and the end"—has declared this (verse 6; cf. 1:8; 22:13; Isaiah 43:13; 44:6; 48:12). With this, God urges all who are reading these words, and who are spiritually thirsty, to come to the spring of the water "of life without cost" (Revelation 21:6).

God says that the one who turns from his sin and accepts Christ "will inherit these things, and I will be his God and he will be My son" (verse 7). But those who are unbelievers and who remain in their sins "will be in the lake that burns with fire and brimstone, which is the second death" (verse 8; cf. 2:11).

THE NEW JERUSALEM
Revelation 21:9-27

AFTER GOD ANNOUNCES that He will make all things new, one of the angels who had the seven bowls of judgment comes to John and says, "Come here, I will show you the bride, the wife of the Lamb" (verse 9). John is then transported to a high mountain, where he can obtain a panoramic view of "the holy city, Jerusalem" (Revelation 21:10), which will come down out of heaven from God Himself.

The city itself reflects the *glory of God* with a brilliance like that of a costly stone (verse 11). The city has high walls with 12 angels attending the 12 gates (verse 12). They are not stationed at the gate entrances to serve as guards, but as greeters who welcome the righteous into the city. The gates, three on each side (verse 13), honor and recognize the 12 tribes of Israel. The wall encompassing the city has 12 foundation stones, recognizing and honoring the "twelve apostles of the Lamb" (verse 14). With both Israel and the church represented in the city, God's intention is to show that citizens from every dispensation will be represented, including the redeemed of the Tribulation period. Walvoord states,

> As far as this scripture is concerned, there is only one eternal resting place for the saints, and that is the new Jerusalem. All saints, therefore, must necessarily participate in the city, just as many of them did also in the millennial scene without destroying the distinction between different companies of saints (*Revelation*, pp. 322-23).

The city is measured with a measuring rod (about 18 feet in length) (verse 15), and found to be laid out "as a square," to a dimension of "fifteen hundred miles," and its "length and width and height are equal" (verse 16). There is little doubt that all the redeemed of all generations could easily fit in this city and reside here as eternal guests of the Lord Himself. Then the wall is measured and found to reach up 72 yards, or about 216 feet. Whether measured by human beings or angels, the measurement is the same (verse 17). The walls, foundation stones, and 12 gates are all adorned with the most precious and costly of gems and stones of great of brilliance and color (verses 18-21).

This includes sapphires, jasper, chalcedony, emeralds, and chrysolites. The street of the city is "pure gold, like transparent glass" (verse 21). Though we do not know with certainty the colors of some of the stones, there is no question that the city will reflect the glory of God in a shining display of magnificent beauty.

"The Lord God the Almighty and the Lamb" are the temple in this city—that is, the Father and the Son together constitute the temple in the new Jerusalem (verse 22). And "the glory of God" will illumine it, and "its lamp is the Lamb" (verse 23). The throne also is said to be "the throne of God and of the Lamb" (22:1,3). The Father and the Son *are together* the temple, the light, and the throne!

These words shout to us of the deity of Christ, who is coequal with the Father. The saved of the nations will walk in the city's glory, and the great rulers and kings of history who received Christ as their Savior will also be there (21:24). Their prestige and glory will be displayed in the city, along with the glory and honor of all the nations (verses 24,26). By this, the Lord will be honoring the righteous acts of the redeemed. There will be no nighttime, and the city gates will never close because there will no longer be any fear, for all sin will have been purged from the universe (verse 25). There will be nothing unclean in the city, nor anyone who practices "abomination and lying" (verse 26). The citizens will be only those "whose names are written in the Lamb's book of life" (verse 27; see also 3:5; 13:8; 17:8; 20:12; 22:19).

THE THRONE OF GOD AND THE LAMB
Revelation 22:1-5

APPARENTLY THE ONLY SOURCE of water ("a river of water of life") in the eternal state is that which comes "from the throne of God and of the Lamb" (verse 1). In the old creation, water is a symbol of sustenance because it's so crucial to keeping us alive. In the eternal state, however, water will symbolize new life.

This water will come from the throne that is occupied by both God the Father and Christ the Lamb. Christ is described as the substitutionary Lamb of God (Isaiah 53:6-7; cf. John 1:29,36) twenty-eight times in Revelation, and that includes nine times in the final chapters of the book (chapters 19–22). Throughout eternity believers will be reminded that their salvation was made possible by Jesus' death on the cross, in which He died as a sacrificial lamb for our sins.

The water coming from the throne of God will flow through the street of the new Jerusalem, with the tree of life on either side of the river bearing 12 kinds of fruit. The trees will yield fruit every month, and "the leaves of the tree [are] for the healing of the nations" (Revelation 22:2). What is the significance of leaves "for the healing of the nations"? Some have surmised these leaves may be intended for those who enter the kingdom in unglorified bodies—and those born to these unglorified individuals. Because they do not have new, transformed bodies, they will need the leaves of the tree of life to help to sustain their existence in the new Jerusalem. Whatever the case, the context seems to imply that the tree and its leaves are seen as a source of life and health in the eternal state.

In the old creation trees bear fruit annually. But in the new creation, they will bear monthly. The monthly yield of fruit described here is identical to what Ezekiel 47:12 says about the eternal kingdom. Thomas says:

> Though eating the fruit of the Tree of Life is unmentioned here, the implication is that this is what brings immortality, the same as was true for Adam and Eve originally (Gen. 3:22). Conditions of future bliss will mean a return to the original glories and privileges of God's presence with man, before sin raised a barrier that prevented that direct contact (*Revelation, 8–22*, p. 484).

In the new creation, "there will no longer be any curse." Christ's "bond-servants will serve Him" (Revelation 22:3), and "His name will be on their foreheads" to show that they belong to Him (verse 4). The redeemed bear the name of the Lord on their foreheads as a mark of their proven fidelity. Hengstenberg suggests that the name is written as a sign of a reward—"a pledge of their right to participate in all the benefits of the kingdom of glory" in eternity (*Revelation*, vol. 2, p. 360). There will no longer be any night, and there will be no need for the light of the sun, for "the Lord God will illumine them; and they will reign forever and ever" (verse 5).

THE FINAL MESSAGE OF SCRIPTURE
Revelation 22:6-15

THE ANGEL WHO HAS accompanied John since Revelation 21:9 now gives his final message and appeal. He assures John that what the apostle has heard is accurate: "These words are faithful and true" (verse 6). The Lord, the God who has spoken to "the spirits of the prophets," sent His angel to John to show "to His bond-servants the things which must shortly take place." Two related Greek words play an important role in helping us to get a clear understanding of the phrase "shortly take place." *Tachos,* here in verse 6 and in 1:1, carries the meaning of "speedily," "in swift succession," or with rapidity of action. When the Tribulation events begin to take place, they will happen "quickly" with speed and certainty. The Greek adverb *tachu* (verses 7,12,20) can have a similar meaning. Christ, speaking of the rapture of the church, says that He is coming quickly (verse 7)—therefore the appeal, "Blessed is he who heeds the words of the prophecy of this book." LaHaye and Ice observe,

> The book of Revelation ends with the same thought [of certainty and urgency]. When the terrible events described in the book begin, they will come about with rapidity. John goes on and uses from the *tachos* family the

adverb *tachu* and closes the book of Revelation by writing, "Behold, I am coming *quickly*" (22:7,12), and finally at the very end of the book, "Yes, I am coming *quickly*" (verse 20) (*Charting the End Times,* p. 296).

John now testifies that when he heard and saw these things, he fell down to worship at the feet of the angel (verse 8). But the angel reminded John that he is only a "fellow servant" of John and of all his "brethren the prophets" and of all who heed the words of this book, and he directs John to worship God alone (verse 9). The angel then tells John "do not seal up the words of the prophecy of this book" because the "time" (Greek, *kairos*) or season "is near" (Greek, *engus*) or certain to take place (verse 10). The events described in Revelation could begin at any moment, starting first with the sounding of the trumpet and the rapture of the church (1 Thessalonians 4:13-18). Those who do evil will continue to do so, but "let the one who is righteous still practice righteousness; and let the one who is holy, still keep himself holy" (Revelation 22:11). This is an appeal to perseverance and patience. The believer is not to become discouraged but is to continue on and live a godly life no matter what comes.

Christ has stated before the fact that He is coming quickly, but this time He adds, "My reward is with Me, to render to every man according to what he has done" (verse 12). Since this has to do with the rapture of the church to glory, the reward has to do with recognizing what the saints have done in His name during their time on earth (Romans 14:10-11; 1 Corinthians 3:12-15; 2 Corinthians 5:10). Jesus then reminds the reader that He is "the Alpha and the Omega, the first and the last," and the beginning and end of everything (Revelation 22:13; cf. 1:8,17; 2:8). The robes of the redeemed are washed by means of the blood of Christ (22:14), and it is through Him that believers have access to the tree of life (verse 2) and entrance into the holy city of Jerusalem (21:25). The washing of the robes is an allusion to the multitude in glory who washed their robes and made them white by the blood of Christ, the Lamb of God (7:14).

Some have mistaken 22:15 as saying that there will be dogs, sorcerers, and sinners living outside the walls of the new Jerusalem. "The dogs" is a metaphor for the most vile of sinners. In Scripture the term is used to speak of male prostitutes (Deuteronomy 23:18) or impure Gentiles (Matthew 15:26), among other things (2 Kings 8:13). The lost, those whose names will not be found in the Lamb's book of life, will have already been thrown into the lake of fire (Revelation 20:14-15), and therefore there is no chance that they could possibly live just outside the city gates. Revelation 22:15 is God's assurance that the unsaved will never gain access into the celestial city.

THE FINAL INVITATION OF SCRIPTURE
Revelation 22:16-19

IN REVELATION 22:16, Christ assures the reader that He sent His angel to testify to John of the aforementioned truths "for the churches." Jesus' final appeal makes it clear that He intends for the book of Revelation to be read and taught in the churches. And He is not only the Savior of the church, He is also Israel's Messiah, "the root and the descendant of David, the bright morning star." Christ is the descendant of king David (5:5; cf. 2 Samuel 7:12-16; Psalm 132:11; Isaiah 11:1,10; Jeremiah 23:5; 33:15-16). He is the one who has the right to rule on the throne of David in the millennial kingdom (Luke 1:31-33) and on the throne of God in the eternal city. He is also "the bright morning star"—the last star seen in the heavens as the new day dawns (cf. Revelation 2:28).

Both the Holy Spirit and the bride (the church) say, "Come" (Revelation 22:17). The bride, the redeemed people of God, join here with one voice to appeal to the reader to accept the invitation of Christ now. For the one who hears and who responds is the one who is spiritually thirsty, "who wishes [to] take the water of life without cost." Salvation cost Christ everything, but to those who accept Him salvation costs nothing! The reason is that it is impossible to purchase redemption and to satisfy a holy, righteous God. "For all of us have become like one who is unclean, and all our righteous deeds are like a filthy garment; and all of us wither like a leaf" (Isaiah 64:6). Throughout Scripture, it is very clear that salvation is a gift offered by the grace of God to all who will receive it by faith.

Revelation 22:18-19 is addressed to the lost or the deceiver who attempts to add to the Word of God, or remove what is written in this prophecy. The allusion is to Deuteronomy 4:2, which reads, "You shall not add to the word which I am commanding you, nor take away from it" (cf. Proverbs 30:5-6; Jeremiah 26:2). The one who does this must face the plagues mentioned in Revelation. The point of this warning is that we must accept God's entire prophecy as it stands. We cannot arbitrarily add to it or take away from it.

In the original Greek text, the expression that God "shall take away his part from the tree of life and from the holy city" is a word play emphasizing that the one who tampers with God's Word will never partake of the tree of life. Couch observes,

> The warning is probably aimed at false prophets, who are "religious" and certainly not born again. They act with great boldness in claiming divine revelation, but if they were God's own children, they would humble themselves before God in light of what He has already written (*Revelation*, p. 309).

THE FINAL PREDICTION
Revelation 22:20-21

IT IS THE LORD JESUS HIMSELF who "testifies" (Greek, *marturon*) to the book of Revelation and the writings of the apostle John (verse 20). Christ then says, "Yes, I am coming quickly."

John the apostle concurs and writes, "Amen. Come, Lord Jesus." The expression "I am coming quickly" is used four times in Revelation (3:11; 22:7,12,20). The word "quickly" is the Greek particle *tachu,* which has to do with coming suddenly. So when Christ comes back, the events of the last days will take place at a rapid rate—things will fall into place in rapid order. Couch observes, "This idea is reinforced by the Lord's statements in 3:3 ('I will come like a thief, and you will not know at what hour I will come to you') and 16:15 ('I am coming like a thief. Blessed is the one who stays awake and keeps his clothes, so that he will not walk about naked')" (*Revelation,* p. 306). This sudden and instantaneous return Christ speaks of would have to be the rapture of the church. This is why we are to keep watching—the apostle Paul writes that believers should be "looking for the blessed hope and the appearing of the glory of our great God and Savior, Christ Jesus" (Titus 2:13).

The word "amen" in Revelation 22:20 means, "verily, truly, certainly." The apostle John is giving a hearty confirmation that Christ may come back immediately! And in a warm closing, the apostle adds this postscript: "The grace of the Lord Jesus be with all. Amen" (verse 21). Henry Morris writes,

In closing, John adds his personal greeting and prayer for his own friends in the seven churches, who will soon be reading and hearing his amazing record of things to come. The Holy Spirit, however, is also sending this same message to all churches everywhere, and He would convey the same greeting and exhortation to them, for there is no more fitting way to close the Book of Revelation, and the entire written Word of God, than this" (*Revelation Record,* p. 489).

The Revelation begins with Christ appearing to John on Patmos, and it ends with Christ's promise to return again. It begins with grace (1:4) and it ends with grace (22:21). Even John's final benediction is a prophecy of all the redeemed people of God who will experience the riches of His grace in the ages to come.

The way to eternal happiness is to receive Christ as Savior and Lord. This will entitle you to enter into the glorious holy city and partake of the tree of life and all the marvelous blessings of God. All this and much more is available to us…all because of His amazing grace.

BIBLIOGRAPHY

Alexander, J.A. *Commentary on the Acts of the Apostles.* Grand Rapids: Zondervan, 1956.

———. *Commentary on the Gospel of Mark.* Minneapolis: Klock & Klock, 1980.

———. *Commentary on the Prophecies of Isaiah.* Grand Rapids: Zondervan, 1970.

Alford, Henry. *The Greek New Testament,* 4 vols. Chicago: Moody Press, 1958.

Allen, Leslie C. "1 and 2 Chronicles" in *The New Interpreter's Bible,* vol. 3. Nashville: Abingdon, 1999.

———. *Ezekiel 20–48. Word Biblical Commentary,* vol. 29. Edited by John D.W. Watts. Dallas, TX: Word Books, 1990.

Allen, Ronald B. "Numbers," *The Expositor's Bible Commentary,* vol. 2, Frank E. Gabelein, gen. ed. Grand Rapids: Zondervan, 1990.

Anderson, A.A. *Psalms 1–72.* The New Century Bible Commentary. Grand Rapids: Eerdmans, 1972.

Anderson, Francis I., *Job.* Tyndale Old Testament Commentaries. D.J. Wiseman, gen. ed. Downers Grove, IL: InterVarsity, 1982.

Anderson, Sir Robert. *The Coming Prince.* Grand Rapids: Kregel, 1976.

Archer, Gleason L. *A Survey of Old Testament Introduction.* Chicago: Moody Press, 1964.

Arndt, W.F., and F.W. Gingrich, *A Greek-English Lexicon of the New Testament.* Chicago: University of Chicago Press, 1975.

Baker, William. *James & First and Second Peter.* Chattanooga, TN: AMG Publications, 2004.

Baldwin, Joyce G. *1 and 2 Samuel.* Tyndale Old Testament Commentaries. Downers Grove, IL: InterVarsity, 1982.

Barbieri, Louis. *Mark.* Chicago: Moody, 1995.

Barnes, Albert. *Barnes' Notes on the New Testament.* 14 vols. Grand Rapids: Baker, 1983.

Barrett, C.K. *First Epistle to the Corinthians.* New York: Harper & Row, 1968.

———. *The Second Epistle to the Corinthians.* Peabody, MS: Hendrickson, 1997.

Beasley-Murray, G.R. *The Book of Revelation* New Century Bible Commentary. London: Marshall, Morgan & Scott, 1978.

Bergin, Robert D. *1, 2 Samuel.* New American Commentary. Nashville: Broadman and Holman, 1996.

Billington, Clyde. "The Rosh People in History and Prophecy" (Parts 1-3), *Michigan Theological Journal* 3:1-2 (1992), pp. 54-64, 142-74; 4:1 (1993), pp. 38-62.

Block, Daniel I. *The Book of Ezekiel: Chapters 25–48.* The New International Commentary on the Old Testament. Grand Rapids: Eerdmans, 1998.

———. *Judges, Ruth.* New American Commentary. Nashville: Broadman and Holman, 1999.

Boutflower, Charles. *In and Around the Book of Daniel.* Grand Rapids: Zondervan Publishing, Co., 1973.

Breuer, Joseph. *The Book of Yechezkel: Translation and Commentary.* New York, Jerusalem: Philipp Feldheim, Inc., 1993.

Bruce, F.F. *The Book of the Acts.* Grand Rapids: Eerdmans, 1988.

———. *The Epistle to the Galatians.* New International Greek Testament Commentary. Grand Rapids: Eerdmans, 1982.

Brueggemann, Walter. *First and Second Samuel.* Louisville, KY: John Knox, 1990.

———. *The Message of the Psalms.* Minneapolis: Augsburg, 1984.

Buzzell, Sid S. "Proverbs," *The Bible Knowledge Commentary,* vol. 1. John F. Walvoord and Roy B. Zuck, eds. Wheaton, IL: Victor, 1985.

Campbell, Donald K. *Daniel: Decoder of Dreams.* Wheaton, IL: SP Publications, Victor, Books, 1977.

———. "Joshua," *The Bible Knowledge Commentary,* vol. 1. John F. Walvoord and Roy B. Zuck, eds. Wheaton, IL: Victor, 1985.

Candlish, Robert S. *Commentary on 1 John.* Grand Rapids: Kregel, 1992.

Chisholm, Jr., Robert B. "Evidence from Genesis," in Donald K. Campbell and Jeffrey L. Townsend, eds., *A Case for Premillennialism.* Chicago: Moody, 1992.

Clowney, Edmund P. "The Final Temple," in C.F.H. Henry, ed. *Prophecy in the Making.* Carol Stream, IL: Creation House, 1971.

Cogan, Mordechai. *I Kings.* The Anchor Bible, vol. 10. New York: Doubleday, 2000.

Cogan, Mordechai and Hayim Tadmore. *II Kings.* Anchor Bible Commentary, New York: Doubleday, 1988.

Cohen, Gary. *Understanding Revelation.* Chicago: Moody, 1968.

Cole, R. Alan. *Exodus: An Introduction and Commentary.* Tyndale Old Testament Commentaries. Downers Grove, IL: InterVarsity, 1973.

Cole, R. Dennis. *Numbers.* The New International

American Commentary. Nashville: Broadman and Holman, 2000.

Coleman, Robert. *Songs of Heaven*. Old Tappan, NJ: Fleming H. Revell, 1980.

Constable, Thomas L. "1 Kings" and "2 Kings," *The Bible Knowledge Commentary*, vol. 1. John F. Walvoord and Roy B. Zuck, eds. Wheaton, IL: Victor, 1985.

———. "1–2 Thessalonians," *The Bible Knowledge Commentary*, vol. 2. John F. Walvoord and Roy B. Zuck, eds. Wheaton: Victor, 1985.

Cooper, Lamar. *Ezekiel*. The New American Commentary. Nashville: Broadman & Holman, 1996.

Couch, Mal, gen. ed. *A Bible Handbook to the Acts of the Apostles*. Grand Rapids: Kregel, 1999.

———. *A Biblical Theology of the Church*. Grand Rapids: Kregal, 1999.

———. *A Bible Handbook to Revelation*. Grand Rapids: Kregel, 2001.

———. *Dictionary of Premillennial Theology*. Grand Rapids: Kregel, 1999.

———. gen. ed. *God Has Spoken*. Chattanooga, TN: AMG Publishers, 2003.

———. *Hope of Christ's Return*. Grand Rapids: Kregel, 2001.

———. *An Introduction to Classical Evangelical Hermeneutics*. Grand Rapids: Kregel, 2000.

———. *A Pastor's Manual on Doing Church*. Springfield, MO: 21st Century Press, 2004.

Crawford, Sidnie White. "Esther," *The New Interpreter's Bible,* vol. 3. Nashville: Abingdon, 1999.

Culver, Robert Duncan. *Daniel and the Latter Days,* rev. ed. Chicago: Moody, 1977.

Cundall, Arthur E., and Leon Morris. *Judges and Ruth.* Tyndale Old Testament Commentaries. Downers Grove, IL: InterVarsity, 1968.

Custer, Stewart. *From Patmos to Paradise.* Greenville, SC: BJU Press, 2004.

Deere, Jack S. "Deuteronomy," *The Bible Knowledge Commentary,* vol. 1. John F. Walvoord and Roy B. Zuck, eds. Wheaton, IL: Victor, 1985.

Doukan, J.B. *Daniel: The Vision of the End.* Berrien Springs, MI: Andrews University Press, 1989.

Driver, S.R. *The Book of Daniel.* Cambridge: University Press, 1922.

———. *An Introduction to the Literature of the Old Testament.* Edinburgh: T&T Clark, 1898.

Durham, John I. *Exodus.* Word Biblical Commentary, vol. 3. Waco, TX: Word, 1987.

Dyer, Charles. "Daniel." *The Bible Knowledge Commentary,* vol. 1. John F. Walvoord and Roy B. Zuck, eds. Wheaton, IL: Victor, 1985.

Eadie, John. *Commentary on the Epistle to the Colossians.* Grand Rapids: Zondervan, 1957.

———. *Commentary on the Epistle to the Galatians.* Grand Rapids: Zondervan, 1955.

Edersheim, Alfred. *The Life and Times of Jesus the Messiah.* Bellingham: Logos Research Systems, Inc., 1896, 2003.

Edwards, Thomas. *A Commentary on the First Epistle to the Corinthians.* Minneapolis: Klock & Klock, 1979.

Eisenmann, Rabbi Moshe. "The Book of Ezekiel: A New Translation with a Commentary Anthologized from Talmudic, Midrashic, and Rabbinic Sources." *The Artscroll Tanach Series.* Brooklyn, NY: Mesorah Publications, Ltd., 1979.

Ellicott, Charles John. *Ellicott's Commentary on the Whole Bible.* 6 vols. Grand Rapids: Zondervan, 1959.

Ellingworth, Paul. *Commentary on Hebrews.* Grand Rapids: Eerdmans, 1993.

Enns, Paul. *The Moody Handbook of Theology.* Chicago: Moody, 1989.

Evans, Craig A., "Messianism," in Craig A. Evans and Stanley E. Porter, eds., *Dictionary of New Testament Background: A Compendium of Contemporary Biblical Scholarship,* electronic edition. Downers Grove, IL: InterVarsity, 2000.

Fairbairn, Patrick. *Commentary on the Pastoral Epistles.* Grand Rapids: Zondervan, 1956.

Feinberg, Charles Lee. *A Commentary on Daniel: The Kingdom of the Lord.* Winona Lake, IN: BMH Books, 1981.

———. *Jeremiah: A Commentary.* Grand Rapids: Zondervan, 1982.

———. *The Prophecy of Ezekiel: The Glory of the Lord.* Chicago: Moody, 1969.

Fensham, F. Charles. *The Books of Ezra and Nehemiah.* The New International Commentary on the Old Testament. Grand Rapids: Eerdmans, 1991.

Flanigan, J.M. *Hebrews.* Kilmarnock, Scotland: John Ritchie, 1997.

Foos, Harold. "Jerusalem in Prophecy." Th.D. dissertation: Dallas Theological Seminary, 1965.

Ford, Desmond. *Daniel.* Nashville: Southern Publishing Association, 1975.

Friedman, David. "Israel from the Eyes of a Messianic Jew Living in the Land." *Kesher* 13, Summer 2001.

Fruchtenbaum, Arnold G. *Deuteronomy,* cassette tape lectures. Tustin, CA: Ariel Ministries.

———. *Exodus,* cassette tape lectures. Tustin, CA: Ariel Ministries.

———. *The Footsteps of the Messiah.* Tustin, CA: Ariel Ministries, 2004.

———. *Hebrews—James, 1 & II Peter—Jude.* Tustin, CA: Ariel Ministries, 2005.

———. *Leviticus,* cassette tape lectures. Tustin, CA: Ariel Ministries.

———. *Messianic Christology.* Tustin, CA: Ariel Ministries, 1998.

Geisler, Norman. "Colossians," *Bible Knowledge Commentary,* vol. 2. John F. Walvoord and Roy B. Zuck, eds. Wheaton, IL: Victor, 1983.

Ger, Stephen. *The Book of Acts.* Chattanooga, TN: AMG Publishers, 2004.

Gesenius, Wihelm. Thesaurus Linguae Hebraeae et Chaldaeae Veteris Testamenti, 13th edition (Boston: Houghton, Mifflin, 1854), p. 955.

Getz, Gene A. "Nehemiah," *The Bible Knowledge Commentary*, vol. 1. John F. Walvoord and Roy B. Zuck, eds. Wheaton, IL: Victor, 1985.

Gill, John. *Gill's Commentary*, 6 vols. Grand Rapids: Baker, 1980.

Glickman, S. Craig, *A Song for Lovers*. Downers Grove, IL: InterVarsity, 1976.

Goldwurm, Hersh. "Daniel." *The Artscroll Tanach Series*. Brooklyn, NY: Mesorah Publications, Ltd., 1989.

Greenberg, Moshe. *Ezekiel 21–37*. Anchor Bible Commentary, vol. 23. New York: Doubleday, 1997.

Gromacki, Robert. *The Books of Philippians and Colossians*. Chattanooga, TN: AMG Publishers, 2003.

———. *The Virgin Birth: Doctrine of Deity*. Nashville: Word, 2000.

Hackett, Horatio B. *Commentary on Acts*. Grand Rapids: Kregel, 1992.

Haldane, Robert. *Commentary on Romans*. Grand Rapids: Kregel, 1996.

Hannah, John D. "Exodus," *The Bible Knowledge Commentary*, vol. 1. John F. Walvoord and Roy B. Zuck, eds. Wheaton, IL: Victor, 1985.

Harris, R. Laird. "Leviticus," *The Expositor's Bible Commentary*, vol. 2, Frank E. Gabelein, gen. ed. Grand Rapids: Zondervan, 1990.

Harrison, R.K. *Leviticus*. Tyndale Old Testament Commentaries. Downers Grove, IL: InterVarsity, 1980.

Hendriksen, William. *Galatians, Ephesians, Philippians, Colossians and Philemon*. Grand Rapids: Baker, 1995.

———. *The Gospel of Luke*. Grand Rapids: Baker, 1981.

———. *The Gospel of Mark*. Grand Rapids: Baker, 1990.

Hengstenberg, E.W. *The Revelation of St. John,* 2 vols. Edinburgh: T. & T. Clark, 1852.

Hess, Richard S. *Joshua*. Tyndale Old Testament Commentaries. Downers Grove, IL: InterVarsity, 1996.

Hindson, Edward E. *Final Signs*. Eugene, OR: Harvest House, 1996.

———. *Isaiah's Immanuel*. Philadelphia: Presbyterian & Reformed, 1979.

———. "Isaiah," in Edward Hindson and Woodrow Kroll, eds. *King James Bible Commentary*. Nashville: Thomas Nelson, 1999.

———. *The Book of Matthew*. Chattanooga, TN: AMG Publishers, 2006.

———. *The Book of Revelation*. Chattanooga, TN: AMG Publishers, 2002.

Hocking, David. *Comfort My People: Studies in Isaiah*. Tustin, CA: HFT Publications, 2004.

———. *The Coming World Leader*. Portland, OR: Multnomah, 1988.

Hodge, Charles. *A Commentary on the Epistle to the Ephesians*. London: Banner of Truth, 1964.

———. *Commentary on the Epistle to the Romans*. Grand Rapids: Eerdmans, 1970.

———. *An Exposition of the First Epistle to the Corinthians*. Grand Rapids: Eerdmans, 1956.

———. *An Exposition of the Second Epistle to the Corinthians*. Grand Rapids: Eerdmans, n.d.

Hoehner, Harold. "Ephesians," *The Bible Knowledge Commentary*, vol. 2. Wheaton, IL: Victor, 1983.

Hort, F.J.A. *Expository and Exegetical Studies*. Minneapolis: Klock & Klock, 1980.

Houlden, J.L. *The Johannine Epistles*. London: A & C Black, 1994.

Huckel, Tom. "Leviticus," *The Rabbinic Messiah*, electronic ed. Philadelphia: Hananeel House, 1998.

———. "Numbers," *The Rabbinic Messiah*, electronic ed. Philadelphia: Hananeel House, 1998.

———. "Psalms," *The Rabbinic Messiah*, electronic ed. Philadelphia: Hananeel House, 1998.

———. "Ruth," *The Rabbinic Messiah*, electronic ed. Philadelphia: Hananeel House, 1998.

Ironside, H.A. *The Great Parenthesis*. Grand Rapids: Zondervan, 1940.

Jenkins, Erwin. "The Authorship of Daniel." Th.M. thesis: Talbot Theological Seminary, 1955.

Jeremiah, David. *Escape the Coming Night*. Dallas: Word, 1990.

Johnson, Luke Timothy. *The Acts of the Apostles*. Collegeville, MN: The Liturgical Press, 1992.

Jones, Floyd Nolen. *The Chronology of the Old Testament*. Green Forest, AK: Master Books, 2004.

Josephus, Flavius, and William Whiston. *The Works of Josephus: Complete and Unabridged*. Peabody, MA: Hendrickson, 1996, 1987.

Kac, Arthur W. *The Messianic Hope*. Ann Arbor, MI: Baker, 1975.

Kaiser, Jr., Walter C. *Ecclesiastes: Total Life*. Chicago: Moody, 1979.

———. "Exodus," *The Expositor's Bible Commentary*, vol. 2. Frank E. Gaebelein, gen. ed. Grand Rapids: Zondervan, 1990.

Kalafian, Michael. *The Prophecy of the Seventy Weeks of the Book of Daniel*. Lanham, MD: University Press of America, 1991.

Keil, C.F., and Franz Delitzsch. *Ezekiel*, vol. 2. Translated by James Martin. Grand Rapids: Eerdmans, 1966.

———. *Daniel*. Grand Rapids: Baker, 1976.

———. *Proverbs, Ecclesiastes, Song of Solomon*. Grand Rapids: Eerdmans, 1986.

Kelly, J.N.D. *The Epistles of Peter and of Jude*. London: A & C Clark, 1990.

Kidner, Derek. *Ezra and Nehemiah*. Tyndale Old Testament Commentaries. Downers Grove, IL: InterVarsity, 1979.

———. *Genesis*. Tyndale Old Testament Commentaries. Downers Grove, IL: InterVarsity, 1967.

———. *Psalms 1–72*. Tyndale Old Testament Commentaries. Downers Grove, IL: InterVarsity, 1973.

Kistemaker, Simon J. *Acts*. Grand Rapids: Baker, 1995.

———. *Hebrews*. Grand Rapids: Baker, 1995.

———. *James and I–III John*. Grand Rapids: Baker, 1992.

———. *Peter and Jude*. Grand Rapids: Baker, 1993.

———. *Psalms 73–150*. Tyndale Old Testament Commentaries. Downers Grove, IL: InterVarsity, 1981.

———. *Revelation*. Grand Rapids: Baker, 2001.

Kitchen, K.A. "The Aramaic of Daniel," in D.J. Wiseman, ed. *Notes on Some Problems in the Book of Daniel*. London: Tyndale Press, 1965.

———. *On the Reliability of the Old Testament*. Grand Rapids: Eerdmans, 2003.

Knight III, George W. *The Pastoral Epistles*. New International Greek Testament Commentary. Grand Rapids: Eerdmans, 1996.

Kroll, Woodrow. *The Book of Romans*. Chattanooga, TN: AMG Publishers, 2002.

LaHaye, Tim and Ed Hindson, eds. *Popular Encyclopedia of Bible Prophecy*. Eugene, OR: Harvest House, 2004.

———. *Popular Bible Prophecy Workbook*. Eugene, OR: Harvest House, 2005.

LaHaye, Tim. *Revelation Illustrated and Made Plain*. Grand Rapids: Zondervan, 1975.

Lang, G.H. *The Histories and Prophecies of Daniel*. Grand Rapids: Kregel, 1973.

LaSor, William S. *The Truth About Armageddon*. Grand Rapids: Baker, 1982.

Leighton, Robert. *Commentary on First Peter*. Grand Rapids: Kregel, 1972.

Lenski, R.C.H. *The Interpretation of I and II Corinthians*. Minneapolis: Augsburg, 1965.

———. *The Interpretation of I and II Epistles of Peter, the Three Epistles of John, and the Epistle of Jude*. Minneapolis: Augsburg, 1966.

———. *The Interpretation of I and II Thessalonians*. Minneapolis: Augsburg Press, 1961.

———. *The Interpretation of the Acts of the Apostles*. Minneapolis: Augsburg, 1961.

———. *The Interpretation of Colossians*. Minneapolis: Augsburg, 1960.

———. *The Interpretation of St. John's Revelation*. Minneapolis: Augsburg, 1960.

———. *The Interpretation of St. Mark's Gospel*. Minneapolis: Augsburg, 1964.

———. *The Interpretation of St. Paul's Epistles to the Galatians, Ephesians and Philippians*. Minneapolis: Augsburg, 1969.

Levenson, Jon. *Theology of the Program of Restoration of Ezekiel 40–48*. Missoula, MT: Scholars Press, 1976.

Lifton, Duane. "1-2 Timothy," *The Bible Knowledge Commentary*, vol. 2. John F. Walvoord and Roy B. Zuck, eds. Wheaton, IL: Victor, 1983.

Lightfoot, J.B. *St. Paul's Epistles to the Colossians and to Philemon*. Grand Rapids: Eerdmans, 1979.

Lightner, Robert. *The Epistles of John and Jude*. Chattanooga, TN: AMG Publishers, 2003.

Lindsey, F. Duane. "Judges," *The Bible Knowledge Commentary*, vol. 1. John F. Walvoord and Roy B. Zuck, eds. Wheaton, IL: Victor, 1985.

———. "Leviticus," *The Bible Knowledge Commentary*, vol. 1. John F. Walvoord and Roy B. Zuck, eds. Wheaton, IL: Victor, 1985.

Lowery, David. "1 Corinthians," *The Bible Knowledge Commentary*, vol. 2. John F. Walvoord and Roy B. Zuck, eds. Wheaton, IL: Victor Books, 1983.

Luther, Martin. *Commentary on Galatians*. Grand Rapids: Zondervan, n.d.

———. *Commentary on Peter & Jude*. Grand Rapids: Kregel, 1990.

MacArthur, John. *Acts 1–12*. Chicago: Moody, 1994.

———. *Acts 13–28*. Chicago: Moody, 1996.

———. *Hebrews*. Chicago: Moody, 1983.

———. *James*. Chicago: Moody, 1998.

———. *Matthew 1–7*. Chicago: Moody, 1985.

———. *Matthew 8–15*. Chicago: Moody, 1987.

———. *Matthew 16–23*. Chicago: Moody, 1988.

———. *Matthew 24–28*. Chicago: Moody, 1989.

Machen, J. Gresham. *The Virgin Birth of Christ*. Grand Rapids: Eerdmans, 1965.

MacRae, Allan A. *The Prophecies of Daniel*. Singapore: Christian Life Publishers, 1991.

Madvig, Donald H., "Joshua," *The Expositor's Bible Commentary*, vol. 1. John F. Walvoord and Roy B. Zuck, eds. Wheaton, IL: Victor, 1985.

Maimonides, *Mishnah Torah*, Hilkhot Melakhim Umilchamoteihem (Laws of Kings), chp. 11.

Manton, Thomas. *Commentary on Jude*. Grand Rapids: Kregel, 1988.

Martin, John A. "Esther," *The Bible Knowledge Commentary*, vol. 1. John F. Walvoord and Roy B. Zuck, eds. 1. Wheaton, IL: Victor, 1985.

———. "Ezra," *The Bible Knowledge Commentary*, vol. 1. John F. Walvoord and Roy B. Zuck, eds. Wheaton, IL: Victor, 1985.

Mathews, Kenneth A. *Genesis 1–11:26*. The New International American Commentary. Nashville: Broadman and Holman, 1996.

Matthews, V.H., M.W. Chavalas and J.H. Walton. "Job," *The IVP Bible Background Commentary: Old Testament*, electronic ed. Downers Grove, IL: InterVarsity, 2000.

Mayhue, Richard. *First and Second Thessalonians*. Rosshire, Scotland: Christian Focus, 1999.

Mayor, Joseph B. *The Epistle of James*. Grand Rapids: Kregel, 1990.

McCarter, Jr., P. Kyle, *I Samuel*. The Anchor Bible, vol. 8. New York: Doubleday, 1980.

McCarter, Jr., P. Kyle, *II Samuel*. The Anchor Bible, vol. 9. New York: Doubleday, 1984.

McClain, Alva J. *Daniel's Prophecy of the Seventy Weeks*. Grand Rapids: Zondervan, 1960.

McDowell, Josh. *Daniel in the Critic's Den*. San Bernardino, CA: Here's Life, 1979.

McFall, L., "Serpent," in T. Desmond Alexander and Brian S. Rosner, eds., *New Dictionary of Biblical*

Theology, electronic ed. Downers Grove, IL: Inter-Varsity, 2001.

McLean, John A. "The Seventieth Week of Daniel 9:27 as a Literary Key for Understanding the Structure of the Apocalypse of John." Ph.D. dissertation: The University of Michigan, 1990.

Merrill, Eugene H. "1 Chronicles," *The Bible Knowledge Commentary,* vol. 1. John F. Walvoord and Roy B. Zuck, eds. Wheaton, IL: Victor, 1985.

————. "2 Chronicles," *The Bible Knowledge Commentary,* vol. 1. John F. Walvoord and Roy B. Zuck, eds. Wheaton, IL: Victor, 1985.

————. *Deuteronomy.* New American Commentary. Broadman and Holman, 1994.

————. "Numbers," *The Bible Knowledge Commentary,* vol. 1. John F. Walvoord and Roy B. Zuck, eds. Wheaton, IL: Victor, 1985.

————. "1 Samuel." *The Bible Knowledge Commentary,* vol. 1. John F. Walvoord and Roy B. Zuck, eds. Wheaton, IL: Victor, 1985.

————. "2 Samuel." *The Bible Knowledge Commentary,* vol. 1. John F. Walvoord and Roy B. Zuck, eds. Wheaton, IL: Victor, 1985.

Metzger, Bruce. *Breaking the Code: Understanding the Book of Revelation.* Nashville: Abingdon, 1993.

Michaels, J. Ramsey. *Interpreting the Book of Revelation.* Grand Rapids: Baker, 1992.

Miller, Stephan R. *Daniel.* New American Commentary. Nashville: Broadman & Holman, 1994.

Milligan, George. *St. Paul's Epistles to the Thessalonians.* Minneapolis: Klock & Klock, 1980.

Mitchell, Daniel. *Book of 1 Corinthians.* Chattanooga, TN: AMG Publishers, 2004.

Moo, Douglas. *Romans 1–8.* New International Commentary on the Bible. Chicago: Moody, 1991.

Morris, Henry. *The Revelation Record.* Wheaton, IL: Tyndale, 1983.

Morris, Leon, *The Revelation of St. John.* Tyndale New Testament Commentaries. Grand Rapids: Eerdmans, 1969.

Morris, Leon, and Arthur E. Cundall. *Judges and Ruth.* Tyndale Old Testament Commentaries, Downers Grove, IL: InterVarsity, 1968.

Mounce, Robert. *The Book of Revelation.* Grand Rapids: Eerdmans, 1977.

Neusner, Jacob. *The Mishnah : A New Translation.* New Haven: Yale University Press, 1996, 1988.

Nicoll, W. Robertson. "Romans," *The Expositor's Greek New Testament,* vol. 5. Grand Rapids: Eerdmans, 1988.

O'Brien, Peter T. *Commentary on Philippians.* Grand Rapids: Eerdmans, 1991.

————. *Letter to the Ephesians.* Grand Rapids: Eerdmans, 1992.

Pentecost, J. Dwight. *Things to Come.* Grand Rapids: Zondervan, 1958.

————. *Thy Kingdom Come.* Wheaton: Victor, 1990.

Pfandl, Gerhard. *The Time of the End in the Book of Daniel.* Berrien Springs, MI: Andrews University Press, 1992.

Phillips, John, and Jerry Vines. *Exploring the Book of Daniel.* Neptune, NJ: Loizeaux Brothers, 1990.

Philo. *The Works of Philo: Complete and Unabridged.* Peabody, MA: Hendrickson, 1996.

Plumer, William S. *Commentary on Romans.* Grand Rapids: Kregel, 1993.

Polhill, John B. *Acts.* New American Commentary. Nashville: Broadman & Holman, 1992.

Pope, Marvin H. *Job.* The Anchor Bible Commentary. Garden City: Doubleday, 1986.

Price, James D. "Rosh: An Ancient Land Known to Ezekiel," *Grace Theological Journal,* 6:1 (Spring 1985), pp. 67-89.

Price, Randall. *The Desecration and Restoration of the Temple as an Eschatological Motif.* Ann Arbor, MI: University Microfilms, 1984.

————. *An Exegetical and Theological Study of Ezekiel 36:16-38.* Th.M. Thesis: Dallas Theological Seminary, 1981.

————. *Jerusalem in Prophecy.* Eugene, OR: Harvest House, 2005.

————. "Prophetic Postponement in Daniel 9:24-27," *Progressive Dispensationalism: An Analysis of the Movement and Defense of Traditional Dispensationalism.* Ron J. Bigalke, ed. Lanham, MD: University Press of America, 2005.

————. *The Temple in Bible Prophecy.* Eugene, OR: Harvest House, 2005.

Price, Walter K. *In the Final Days.* Chicago: Moody, 1977.

Propp, William H.C. *Exodus 1–18.* The Anchor Bible Commentary. New York: Doubleday, 1998.

Rooker, Mark. "Evidence from Ezekiel," *A Case for Premillennialism.* Donald K. Campbell and Jeffrey L. Townsend, eds. Chicago: Moody, 1992.

————. *Leviticus.* The New International American Commentary. Nashville: Broadman & Holman, 2000.

Rosenthal, Franz. *Die Aramaistiche Forschung.* Leiden: E.J. Brill, 1939).

Ross, Allen P. *Creation and Blessing: A Guide to the Study and Exposition of the Book of Leviticus.* Grand Rapids: Baker, 1988.

————. "Genesis," *The Bible Knowledge Commentary,* vol. 1. John F. Walvoord and Roy B. Zuck, eds. Wheaton, IL: Victor, 1985.

————. *Holiness to the Lord: A Guide to the Exposition of the Book of Leviticus.* Grand Rapids: Baker Academic, 2002.

————. "Proverbs," *The Expositor's Bible Commentary.* Frank E. Gaebelein, gen. ed. Grand Rapids: Zondervan, 1991.

————. "Psalms," *The Bible Knowledge Commentary,* vol. 1. John F. Walvoord and Roy B. Zuck, eds. Wheaton, IL: Victor, 1985.

Sailhamer, John H. "Genesis," *The Expositor's Bible Commentary.* Frank E. Gaebelein, gen. ed. Grand Rapids: Zondervan, 1990.

Santala, Risto. *The Messiah in the Old Testament in Light of Rabbinical Writing.* Translated by William Kinnaird. Jerusalem: Keren Ahvah Meshihit, 1992.

Schmitt, John, and Carl Laney. *Messiah's Coming Temple: Ezekiel's Prophetic Vision of the Future Temple.* Grand Rapids: Kregel, 1997.

Scott, Walter. *Exposition of the Revelation of Jesus Christ.* Grand Rapids: Kregel, 1982. Reprint of 1920 edition.

Seiss, Joseph. *The Apocalypse.* Grand Rapids: Zondervan, 1957.

Selman, Martin J. *1 Chronicles.* Tyndale Old Testament Commentaries. Downers Grove, IL: InterVarsity, 1994.

———. *2 Chronicles.* Tyndale Old Testament Commentaries. Downers Grove, IL: InterVarsity, 1994.

Seow, Choon-Leong. "1 and 2 Kings," *The New Interpreter's Bible.* Nashville: Abingdon, 1999.

Showers, Renald E. *The Most High God: A Commentary on the Book of Daniel.* Bellmawr, NJ: Friend of Israel, 1994.

Spurgeon, C.H. *The Treasury of David,* vol. 1. Grand Rapids: Zondervan, 1970.

Stallard, Michael. "Hermeneutics and Matthew 13, Part II." *The Conservative Theological Journal,* vol. 5, no. 16. December 2001.

Stanley, Arthur P. *The First Epistle of St. Paul to the Corinthians.* Minneapolis: Klock & Klock, 1979.

Stott, John. *The Gospel and the End of Time.* Downers Grove, IL: InterVarsity, 1991.

———. *What Christ Thinks of the Church.* London: Harold Shaw, 1990.

Tatford, Frederick A. *Paul's Letters to the Thessalonians.* Neptune, NJ: Loizeaux Brothers, 1991.

Taylor, John B. *Ezekiel.* Tyndale Old Testament Commentaries. Downers Grove, IL: InterVarsity, 1969.

Tenney, Merrill. *Interpreting Revelation.* Grand Rapids: Eerdmans, 1957.

Thomas, Robert L. *Revelation 1–7.* Chicago: Moody, 1992.

———. *Revelation 8–22.* Chicago: Moody, 1995.

Thompson, J.A. *Deuteronomy.* Tyndale Old Testament Commentaries. Downers Grove, IL: InterVarsity, 1974.

Toussaint, Stanley D. *Behold the King.* Grand Rapids: Kregel, 1980.

Towns, Elmer. *The Gospel of John.* Chattanooga, TN: AMG Publishers, 2002.

Unger, Merrill F. *Unger's Commentary on the Old Testament.* Chattanooga, TN: AMG Publishers, 2002.

VanGemeren, Willem. "Psalms," *The Expositor's Bible Commentary.* Frank E. Gaebelein, gen. ed. Grand Rapids: Zondervan, 1991.

Vine, W.E. *The Collective Writings of W.E. Vine,* 5 vols. Nashville: Thomas Nelson, 1996.

Waltke, Bruce K. "The Date of the Book of Daniel," *Bibliotheca Sacra* 133:532. October-December, 1976, pp. 319-29.

Walvoord, John F. *Daniel: The Key to Prophetic Revelation.* Chicago: Moody, 1971.

———. *The Prophecy Knowledge Handbook.* Wheaton, IL: Victor, 1990.

———. *The Revelation of Jesus Christ.* Chicago: Moody, 1966.

Walvoord, John F., and Roy Zuck, gen. eds. *The Bible Knowledge Commentary,* 2 vols. Wheaton, IL: Victor, 1983.

Wenham, Gordon J. *The Book of Leviticus.* The New International Commentary on the Old Testament. Grand Rapids: Eerdmans, 1979.

———. *Numbers.* Tyndale Old Testament Commentaries. Downers Grove, IL: InterVarsity, 1981.

Whitcomb, John C. *The Book of Daniel.* Everyman's Bible Commentary. Chicago: Moody, 1985, p. 9.

Williamson, H.G.M. *1 and 2 Chronicles.* The New Century Bible Commentary. Grand Rapids: Eerdmans, 1982.

Wilson, Robert Dick. *Studies in the Book of Daniel.* Grand Rapids: Baker, 1979.

Wiseman, Donald J. *1 and 2 Kings.* Tyndale Old Testament Commentaries. Downers Grove, IL: InterVarsity, 1993.

Witmer, John A. "Romans," *The Bible Knowledge Commentary,* vol. 2. John F. Walvoord and Roy B. Zuck, gen. eds. Wheaton, IL: Victor, 1983.

Wood, Leon. *A Commentary on Daniel.* Grand Rapids: Zondervan, 1978.

Woudstra, M.H. *The Book of Joshua.* The New International Commentary on the Old Testament. Grand Rapids: Eerdmans, 1991.

Wright, J. Stafford, "Ecclesiastes," *The Expositor's Bible Commentary.* Frank E. Gaebelein, gen. ed. Grand Rapids: Zondervan, 1991.

Yamauchi, Edwin. *Persia and the Bible.* Grand Rapids: Baker, 1990.

Young, Edward J. *The Book of Isaiah,* 3 vols. Grand Rapids: Eerdmans, 1969.

———. *Studies in Isaiah.* Grand Rapids: Eerdmans, 1954.

Youngblood, Ronald F., "1 Samuel," *The Expositor's Bible Commentary.* Frank E. Gaebelein, gen. ed. Grand Rapids: Zondervan, 1992.

———. "2 Samuel," *The Expositor's Bible Commentary.* Frank E. Gaebelein, gen. ed. Grand Rapids: Zondervan, 1992.

Zimmerli, Walther. "A Commentary on the Book of the Prophet Ezekiel Chapters 25–48," *Hermenia.* Translated by James D. Martin. Philadelphia: Fortress, 1983.

Zuck, Roy B. "Job," *The Bible Knowledge Commentary,* vol. 1. John F. Walvoord and Roy B. Zuck, eds. Wheaton, IL: Victor, 1985.

CHART INDEX

TOPICAL INDEX

TOPIC	REFERENCE
Abomination of desolation.........	Daniel 9; Matthew 24
Abrahamic Covenant............	Genesis 12, 13, 15, 17, 22
Antichrist...................	Daniel 9; 2 Thessalonians 2; 1 John 2, 4; 2 John 7; Revelation 13
Apostasy....................	2 Thessalonians 2; 2 Timothy 3; 2 Peter 2; Jude
Armageddon	Daniel 11; Joel 3; Zechariah 14; Revelation 16, 19
Babylon	Genesis 11; Isaiah 13–14; Jeremiah 50–51; Daniel 1–12; Zechariah 5; Revelation 17–18
Beast	Revelation 13, 17–19
Blessed hope.................	1 Thessalonians 4; Titus 2
Book of Life.................	Philippians 4; Revelation 3, 13, 17, 20–22
Bowl judgments...............	Revelation 15–16
Church.....................	Matthew 16; John 14; Acts 2–28; Romans 16; 1 Thessalonians 4; Ephesians 3; 1 Timothy 4; 2 Timothy 3; James 5; 2 Peter 2; Revelation 2–3, 19
Davidic Covenant	1 Samuel 16, 24; 2 Samuel 7; Psalm 89; Ezekiel 34
Day of the Lord	Isaiah 2; Obadiah; Joel 2; Amos 5; Zephaniah 1; Zechariah 14; Malachi 4; 1 Thessalonians 5; 2 Thessalonians 2; 2 Peter 3
Deception	Matthew 24; Mark 13; Luke 21; 2 Thessalonians 2; 2 Timothy 3; 2 Peter 2; 1 John 2; Jude
Eternity	John 3, 5, 11; Romans 8; 1 Corinthians 15; 2 Corinthians 5; Philippians 3

TOPIC	REFERENCE
Last days	Deuteronomy 4; Isaiah 2; Jeremiah 23, 30; Ezekiel 38–39; Daniel 8–12; John 6, 11–12; 1 Timothy 4; 2 Timothy 3; Hebrews 1; 1 Peter 1; 2 Peter 3; 1 John 2; Jude; Revelation 3–20
Lawless one	2 Thessalonians 2
Mark of the Beast	Revelation 13–14, 16, 19–20
Marriage of the Lamb	Matthew 22; Luke 12, 14; John 3; 2 Corinthians 11; Ephesians 1, 5; 1 Peter 1; Revelation 19
Messianic psalms	Psalm 2, 8, 16, 22, 31, 34–35, 40–41, 68–69, 78, 102, 110, 118
Millennial temple	Ezekiel 40–48
Millennium	Revelation 20
New Jerusalem	Revelation 21–22
Olivet Discourse	Matthew 24–25
Pentecost	Acts 2
Rapture	John 14; 1 Corinthians 15; 1 Thessalonians 4; Titus 2
Restrainer	2 Thessalonians 2
Resurrection	Daniel 12; Matthew 12; Acts 2; Romans 6; 1 Corinthians 15; Hebrews 9; Revelation 1, 11, 20
Rewards	Matthew 25; 1 Corinthians 9; 2 Corinthians 5; Galatians 5; Philippians 4; 1 Thessalonians 2; 2 Timothy 2; James 1; 1 Peter 5; 1 John 2; Revelation 2
Satan	Genesis 3; Job 1–2; Isaiah 14; Ezekiel 28; Matthew 4; John 12; 2 Corinthians 4, 6–7; Ephesians 2; 2 Thessalonians 3; 1 Peter 5; 1 John 2; Revelation 12, 19–20
Seal judgments	Revelation 6–8
Second coming	Matthew 24–25; Mark 13; Luke 21; John 14; 1 Thessalonians 1–5; 2 Thessalonians 1–3; Jude; Revelation 4–22
Seven churches	Revelation 2–3

The Rapture
Tim LaHaye

When friends and colleagues began wavering in their beliefs about the end times, LaHaye began a vast research project resulting in this complete defense of the pretribulation theory. Straightforward, understandable, in a beautiful hardcover edition.

Understanding Bible Prophecy for Yourself
Tim LaHaye

Tim LaHaye's bestselling book, redesigned and updated! This easy-to-follow guide offers the tools believers need to accurately interpret biblical prophecy. Includes charts, tips for interpreting difficult passages, and summaries of Bible history, customs, and beliefs.

ALSO RECOMMENDED...

Tim LaHaye Prophecy Study Bible
Available in King James Version and New King James Version

A study Bible that is faithful to the pretribulational view of Bible prophecy, with a large number of articles from prophecy experts and 84 charts and tables that help to make clear God's prophetic plan.

ABOUT THE PRE-TRIB RESEARCH CENTER

In 1991, Dr. Tim LaHaye became concerned about the growing number of Bible teachers and Christians who were attacking the pretribulational view of the rapture as well as the literal interpretation of Bible prophecy. In response, he wrote *No Fear of the Storm* (Multnomah Publishers, 1992; now titled *The Rapture*). In the process of writing this book, Tim was impressed by the Christian leaders who, in Great Britain during the 1820s and 1830s, set up conferences for the purpose of discussing Bible prophecy. In 1992, Tim contacted Thomas Ice about the possibility of setting up similar meetings, which led to the first gathering of what is now known as the Pre-Trib Study Group in December 1992.

In 1993, Dr. LaHaye and Dr. Ice founded the Pre-Trib Research Center (PTRC) for the purpose of encouraging the research, teaching, propagation, and defense of the pretribulational rapture and related Bible prophecy doctrines. It is the PTRC that has sponsored the annual study group meetings since that time, and there are now over 200 members comprised of top prophecy scholars, authors, Bible teachers, and prophecy students.

LaHaye and Ice, along with other members of the PTRC, have since produced an impressive array of literature in support of the pretribulational view of the rapture as well as the literal interpretation of Bible prophecy. Some of these members are among the contributors to this encyclopedia. Members of the PTRC are available to speak at prophecy conferences and churches. The organization has a monthly publication titled Pre-Trib Perspectives.

To find out more about the PTRC and its publications, write to:

Pre-Trib Research Center
Liberty University
1971 University Blvd.
Lynchburg, VA 24502

You can also get information through the Web site:
www.pre-trib.org